Complex Organizations:
Critical Perspectives

Mary Zey-Ferrell
Illinois State University

Michael Aiken
University of Wisconsin, Madison

Scott, Foresman and Company   Glenview, Illinois

Dallas, Tex.   Oakland, N.J.   Palo Alto, Cal.   Tucker, Ga.   London, England

1 2 3 4 5 6-VHS-85 84 83 82 81 80

Library of Congress Cataloging in Publication Data.
Main entry under title: Complex organizations.
    Includes bibliographies.
    1. Organization — Addresses, essays, lectures. 2. Bureaucracy — Addresses, essays,
lectures. 3. Social structure — Addresses, essays, lectures. 4. Structuralism — Addresses,
essays, lectures. I. Zey-Ferrell, Mary. II. Aiken, Michael T., 1932-
HM131.C74294   302.3'5   80-39713
ISBN 0-673-15269-3

Front and back cover photo by Ray K. Metzker

CONTRIBUTORS

We would like to express our sincere gratitude to the authors for permission to include their excellent selections in our anthology. The authors and their affiliations in alphabetical order include:

Graham T. Allison, Dean, J.F.K. School of Government, Harvard University, Cambridge;

J. Kenneth Benson, Professor of Sociology, University of Missouri, Columbia;

Alfred Chandler, Jr., Straus Professor of Business History, Graduate School of Business Administration, Harvard University, Cambridge;

David Cray, Assistant Professor, University of Wisconsin, Madison;

Richard Colignon, University of Wisconsin, Madison;

Richard C. Edwards, Associate Professor of Economics, University of Massachusetts, Amherst;

Andrew L. Friedman, Lecturer in Economics, University of Bristol, Bristol, England;

Petro Georgiou, Senior Adviser to the Prime Minister of Australia, Canberra, Australia;

Paul Goldman, Assistant Professor of Sociology, University of Oregon, Eugene;

Duncan Gallie, Reader in Sociology, University of Warwick, Essex, England;

Stephen Hymer, deceased;

Lucien Karpik, Centre de Sociologie de L'Innovation, Ecole Nationale Supérieure des Mines, Paris, France;

Kenneth McNeil, University of Wisconsin, Madison;

John W. Meyer, Professor of Sociology, Stanford University, Stanford;

Brian Rowan, Assistant Professor of Sociology, Stanford University, Stanford;

Graeme Salaman, Senior Lecturer, Faculty of the Social Sciences, The Open University, Milton Keynes, England;

Katherine Stone, Attorney at Law, Cohen, Weiss, and Simon, Counselors at Law;

Anselm Strauss, Professor of Social and Behavorial Sciences, University of California, San Francisco;

Donald R. Van Houten, Associate Professor of Sociology, University of Oregon, Eugene;

Karl E. Weick, Nicholas H. Noyes Professor of Organizational Behavior and Professor of Psychology, Cornell University, Ithaca;

Joseph W. Weiss, Department of Health and Social Services, State of Wisconsin, Madison;

Mayer N. Zald, Professor of Sociology and Social Work, University of Michigan, Ann Arbor.

Preface

This anthology was conceived in the spring of 1978 while Professor Zey-Ferrell was visiting the Department of Sociology at the University of Wisconsin in Madison. Both of us had worked in the field of organizational analysis for several years, using what we call here a comparative structural perspective. Both of us had become keenly aware of the limitations of this and other currently dominant perspectives; yet these popular conceptions of organizations so dominated the thinking of most organizational researchers that we deemed it necessary to go outside what is traditionally defined as organization analysis to find fresh, insightful approaches.

Our major purpose in editing this anthology is to present some of the more important criticisms and available alternatives to the quantitative comparative structural and structural contingency approaches. As we began a wide search for relevant and important selections, we were surprised to find numerous, extensive critiques of these dominant perspectives, all the more powerful once they were pulled together and synthesized, as we have attempted to do in the introduction to Part I. We were discouraged, however, by the limited number of well-developed, thoughtful alternative approaches. As in any field, critiquing existing work is easier than developing well-conceived, fresh exciting alternatives. Our search led us into literature that for the most part does not conform to the logic of what is currently considered to be organizational analysis but rather is derived from societal questions about social control, power in society, and the like. Yet our doubts as to the relevance of this literature to organizational analysis subsided as we discovered increasing implications of these new approaches.

Our selections were chosen to both define and demonstrate the underlying assumptions, theoretical propositions, and methods of analysis of these alternative perspectives. Our objectives are to broaden our own and our colleagues' perspectives and to facilitate the growing movement in our discipline toward considering these alternatives. We believe this will enhance our understanding of organizations since it entails integrating the analysis of organizations with analysis of the individual, group, and society and links the field of organizational studies both to the more micro concerns of social psychology as well as to the more macro concerns — historical, economic, and political — of society.

The interdisciplinary nature of the selections in this book should appeal to psychologists, sociologists, political scientists, and others concerned with understanding organizations. Also, since many different types of organizations are covered, professionals in both the public and private sectors, in production organizations, educational organizations, and related fields of work may all find these selections of interest.

Finally, many scholars have contributed to the ideas included in this anthology. We wish we could acknowledge all of them. We especially thank those listed on the contributors' page, and, in addition, we thank our families for providing us with a supportive milieu that has allowed us to grow intellectually.

Mary Zey-Ferrell

Michael Aiken

Contents

I

Introduction To Critiques Of Dominant Perspectives[1]

This introduction synthesizes critiques of the contemporary perspectives on organizations that have dominated sociology for the past two decades. Selections 1-5, included in Part I, do not all critique the same writers or make the same points; but they do, for the most part, critique the quantitative, comparative structural and the structural contingency approaches to the study of organizations. There is no attempt here to develop a history of these or other perspectives, although the major authors are identified in order to give the reader an understanding of the views toward which most of these critiques are directed. Rather, this essay is a systematic review of the criticisms and limitations of the ideology, assumptions, theory, logic, and methodology that have been generated, mostly in the last decade, from the multiple critical perspectives that are represented in this anthology.

Although sociologists who write from the institutional approach (Selznick, 1949; Gouldner, 1954) were concerned with irrationality within organizations and its cultural and institutional origins (for an analysis see Perrow, 1979), by the early 1960s this concern has become dominated by the quantitative, comparative structural approach, which eliminated the cultural and social psychological influences in an attempt to be more "sociological" (meaning structural). Thus the analysis of motivations, incentives, and of the desire to dominate and control was relegated to the social psychological domain, and characteristics of the organization as a whole system became *the domain* of the sociology of organizations. The comparative structural study of organizations was initiated by Udy (1959) and Stinchcombe (1959). While Emile Durkheim is seldom referenced as the inspiration for such an approach to the study of organizations, primarily because he never studied organizations per se, the influence of his intellectual approach on the dominant approaches to the study of organizations is evident.

The proper role of sociologist came to be defined as the study of properties of aggregates, not individuals, and those analysts who studied organizations from the comparative structural and structural contingency approaches followed this dictate with a vengeance. Blau (1970) concentrated on the characteristics of size, differentiation, and the administrative ratio; Hage and Aiken (1967a, 1967b) and Hall (1963) analyzed the interrelationships among such characteristics as complexity, centralization, and formalization; Pugh and associates (1968) examined a wide range

1

of contextual, structural, and performance characteristics and their interrelationships; and Hinings (1971) and Child (1973) developed and extended the Aston Group's taxonomy. By the end of two decades of intense quantitative research, these major works were being summarized in anthologies such as Heydebrand's *Comparative Organizations* (1973) and Zey-Ferrell's *Readings on Dimensions of Organizations* (1979).

The inability of the comparative structural approach to deal with the effects of technology and environment led to the development of structural contingency models. Prime exponents of the technological model include Burns and Stalker (1968), Woodward (1965), and Perrow (1967). Likewise, Lawrence and Lorsch (1967) took the lead in developing the environment as an explanatory variable. A major contribution to the contingency perspective was James D. Thompson's *Organizations in Action* (1967), which treated organizations as open systems subject to uncertainty arising from both environment and technology. But the limitations of the structural contingency approach soon became apparent.

In cataloging the various criticisms of the dominant approaches, it becomes evident that the critics did not review all the works of a given perspective, or even all of a single author's works, but have simply chosen to critique certain points. Moreover, the dominant approaches are variously labeled "rational paradigm" (Benson, 1977, and Colignon and Cray, original article for this volume, Selection 5), "rational selection model" (Benson, 1971), "bourgeois sociology of organizations" (Goldman and Van Houten, 1977, Selection 4), "prevailing rational and functional theories" (Meyer and Rowan, 1977, Selection 16), "goal paradigm" (Georgiou, 1973, Selection 3), "tool view" (Perrow, 1972), "conventional organizational analysis" Salaman, 1978, Selection 1), and "comparative structuralism" (McNeil, 1978, Selection 2).

From these various critiques, twelve key criticisms have been culled and are presented below. Some are obviously related to others, and some contain more than one point. For example, the methodological criticisms that stem from theoretical assumptions and formulations are included in the section with the underlying theoretical issue. Generally, however, the criticisms of the comparative structural and structural contingency approaches are that analysts who have used these approaches:

1. endorse asociological views of organizations;
2. conduct ahistorical analyses of organizations;
3. generate ideologically conservative assumptions and methods of analysis;
4. construct theory which reifies organizational goals;
5. hold to an overly rational image of the functioning of organizations;
6. view organizational systems as integrated through the value consensus of its employees/members;
7. hold images of humans as non-volitional;
8. view organizations as overly constrained;
9. emphasize only the static structural aspects of organizations;
10. view organizations as the exclusive unit of analysis;
11. construct universal generalizations about the structure and functioning of organizations;
12. give inadequate attention to the analysis of power relationships in organizational studies.

This list contains serious indictments of much of the contemporary work in organizational analysis. In many instances these critiques represent insights from a variety of different theoretical perspectives, each with its own individual alternative position on the above points. For example, authors using both the negotiated order and Marxian perspectives feel that the organization as the sole unit of analysis is too limited an approach, but the negotiated-order theorist is more likely to move down to the group and interpersonal level, while the Marxian perspective advocates focusing on the societal level. Let us not forget that it is a tribute to the "dominant paradigm," and we use this term loosely, that it has been challenged by all those perspectives that are contenders and has emerged as *the* dominant paradigm.

ASOCIOLOGICAL VIEW OF ORGANIZATIONS

The bases on which the last two decades of research and theory have been called into question are numerous; perhaps the broadest is that these dominant perspectives are "not sociological" (for an insightful explanation of this criticism, see Salaman, 1978, Selection 1). In what way are these dominant perspectives not sociological? What questions are asked and answered that cause critics to label these perspectives "asociological"? Unfortunately these questions have been the same as those asked by practical and academic business managers, hospital and educational administrators, and political scientists — questions of organizational and managerial performance as measured by industrial efficiency and productivity (Mouzelis, 1968). Even our large industrial (Gouldner, 1954) and governmental (Blau and Scott, 1963; Blau and Schoenherr, 1971) agencies have been analyzed in search of the answer to management questions of how to make their functioning more effective and efficient, with major emphasis on discovering generalizations that would apply to all types of organizations — business, profit and non-profit; educational, private and public; health care, hospitals and welfare; governmental, local and national. Needless to say, the degree to which sociologists, as well as other disciplines in the field, have been successful in discovering rational laws of organizational behavior is now in question along with the validity of such a pursuit.

If comparative structural and structural contingency approaches are not sociological, what is a sociology of organizations? Salaman's (1978:519) answer to this question is that a sociological approach "addresses the question of the relationship between the design of work and control within employing organizations and the nature of the society within which they occur." In addition, he asserts that a sociology of organizations "focuses on the nature and functions of ideologies which buttress, disguise, or justify organizational inequalities and hierarchy." In short, it takes as the topic to be investigated exactly that which is assumed and glossed over by conventional organizational analysis: *"the relationship between internal organizational structures, processes and ideologies and the society within which they exist."* The selections in Parts II and III of this anthology present some research strategies and questions that are alternatives to those of the comparative structural and structural contingency approaches.

AHISTORICAL ANALYSIS OF ORGANIZATIONS

One overriding characteristic of these various approaches to the study of organizations such as the comparative structural, structural contingency, and even human relations approaches is their pronounced ahistoricism. In the work of most researchers, the historical development of the organization(s) is either disregarded or assumed to have little or no effect on the variables being examined. There is no investigation of the historical process by which the present management gained its power and no acknowledgement of its significance for present and future organizational relationships. (Among the notable exceptions are the works of Alfred Chandler, 1962, Selection 17, and 1977; Katherine Stone, 1974, Selection 18; Lucien Karpik, 1978, Selection 20).

Historical concerns, when they have been included, have been grouped with contextual dimensions (Pugh and associates) and are seldom satisfactorily operationalized, hence they usually explain little variance and therefore are relegated to a position of little consequence in comparison to such variables as organizational size and technology. Thus organizational change is not considered a historical issue, but a result of growth in size or some form of technologically determined mechanism.

These types of analyses that are lodged firmly in the present, analyzing the functioning of the organization and concentrating on the internal characteristics of the organization (intraorganizational structure), are not only ahistorical but tend to reify the *status quo* by failing to deal with the major ways in which organizational changes have occurred. Further, they are able to explain only minor evolutionary adjustments within the organization. Power distributions within the organization are not questioned by these analyses, much less the power of the organization in relation to other organizations and societal entities. For example, the selections of Goldman and Van Houten (Selections 4 and 10), Edwards (Selection 8), Friedman (Selection 9), and Stone (Selection 18) demonstrate that without a historical approach we cannot understand the development of management's methods of controlling the worker. They demonstrate that bureaucratic control techniques of hierarchy and division of labor result as much from the need to impose labor discipline as from abstract notions of rational work efficiency, technology, or environmental determinism. Likewise, Marglin (1974) has shown that nineteenth century British entrepreneurs established hierarchy in manufacturing organizations primarily to guarantee themselves a central role in the production process, which could have operated at least as efficiently without them.

The methodological implications of the historical approach are readily apparent. Tracing the development of the history of an organization or a network of organizations usually necessitates a case study, the aim of which is not to produce a general abstract theory of organizational functioning, but rather to arrive at a more detailed understanding of the historical (cultural, social, and economic) process through which organizational phenomena originate and persist. Mayntz (1964:113) links this ahistorical criticism to the specificity criticism developed later in this section when she writes:

> Once we get down to the question *which* of its features or properties a particular organization can or should keep invariant against *which* external influences, and *what kinds* of regulating mechanisms can serve this purpose, we must obviously leave the level of general propositions for all organizations and are forced to take historically specific conditions into account.

Thus by ignoring the historical context in which relationships develop, the currently dominant approaches have generated increasingly abstract and trivial generalizations that apply to a wide range of types of organizations but that explain only a limited range of general phenomena and very little about any one type of organization. Organizational functioning is explained in terms of other characteristics, properties, or dimensions of organizations, not through the historical conditions associated with their development.

IDEOLOGICALLY CONSERVATIVE IMAGE
OF ORGANIZATION

A third major criticism leveled against the comparative structural and structural contingency approaches is that they are ideologically "conservative," "status quo," "elite," and "bourgeois" (Blackburn, 1972:42; Benson, 1977a:1; Goldman and Van Houten, 1977:111, Selection 4). Albrow (1973) points out that the field of organizational study is dominated by administrative and technological concerns of organizational efficiency, and that consequently research questions have been posed from the same standpoint, that of the administration — the most powerful organizational members. The usual problem is to discover which combination of organizational characteristics is functionally compatible with the achievement of organizational goals (efficiency and/or effectiveness). The status quo is reinforced by obtaining data primarily from administrators on the assumption that they are the ones who really count, or that they *are* the organization. Researchers seldom question the validity of choosing elite respondents. Often they justify the decision with a rationale like the following:

> Inasmuch as experts judge issues in terms of universal criteria of rationality and efficiency, they cannot be blamed for the conclusions they reach, even though these conclusions may lead to actions of powerful organizations that are contrary to the interest of most people (Blau and Schoenherr, 1971:355).

In labeling the ideological conservatism of the dominant perspectives as "elitism," Goldman and Van Houten (1977, Selection 4, and 1979, Selection 10) correctly observe that managerial work is defined as being highly complex, necessitating more sophisticated intellectual skills and entailing the responsibility for coordination of work. Therefore managers, not workers, are defined as "organizational resources." Subsequently, management has been able to deskill the labor force and at the same time create a hierarchy of control that is reinforced by their control of work-related knowledge (see Goldman and Van Houten, 1979, Selection 10 for a more complete explanation).

In addition, administrative status quo interests may actually be built into an explanation of the functioning of the organization in the form of assumptions that observed patterns or structures result from a rational selection process in the environment (see Aldrich and Pfeffer, 1976, for a discussion of the natural selection model) or as a result of technological development (Blackburn, 1972) and are thus unavoidably the "best fit" and beyond the control of administrators and workers.

Researchers perpetuate the "status quo." The frequent dual roles of consultant and researcher often bias the perceptions, observations, and reporting of research. Such a researcher must be committed to the employing organization's efforts to preserve or improve the leader's objectives, and hence the status quo, or be willing to be fired for not being so committed. Consequently, Robert Merton (1968:625) has noted that industrial research is for the most part "oriented towards the needs of management."

Organizational research is only infrequently commissioned by workers. This is not a trivial point because those who commission the research also control which questions are asked and often decide what is acceptable for communication to others. Even more important than who commissions the research is why they are able to commission it. As Goldman and Van Houten (1977, Selection 4) point out, managers, not workers, have the control over organizational financial resources that is necessary to commission organizational research. These managers also have control over the findings. If the status quo is not enhanced by the findings of researchers, managers do not have to act on them. Often findings are reported as recommendations or directives for the future actions of administrators, and these recommendations often define methods of control of the work force.

The questions that are pursued in research are determined by many factors in addition to those of management control, not the least of which are the theoretical orientation and methodological training of the researcher. What the researcher defines as important is based on a wide range of what Gouldner has labeled "domain assumptions" (1970) concerning the nature of organizational phenomena: its rationality, boundaries, the unit of analysis, the nature of change, etc. The researcher's assumptions about these issues determine which types of questions will be deemed most important, those pertaining to: structure or process, differences within or between organizations, and evolutionary or radical change. The selection of questions is also determined by the demands of certain audiences: those who sponsor and fund research, the academicians who read the journals and who accept or reject publications for these journals, and finally those organizations in which the problems are being investigated. All of these factors tend to perpetuate the status quo of the dominant ideology and, Goldman and Van Houten (1979, Selection 10) charge, restrict the sociologist from a full exercise of sociological imagination. Goldman and Van Houten view the dominant approaches as closely tied to sustaining the capitalist system and the inequalities associated with it in that they never challenge managerial control, knowledge, or expertise.

REIFICATION OF ORGANIZATIONAL GOALS

The fourth criticism of the dominant perspective centers around the questions: Do organizations have goals or do individuals have goals? If goals are defined as "organizational goals," are they really the goals of dominant coalitions or management?

The dominant perspectives assume that much of what occurs within organizations can be understood as a result of the organization's pursuit of goals and/or need fulfillment. The organization is seen as an instrument designed for the purpose of goal attainment, with its structures and processes functioning in such a way as to enhance this attainment process (Parsons, 1960; for elaboration of this point see Benson, 1971; Georgiou, 1973, Selection 3; and Perrow, 1972). This functioning includes designing motivational strategies and incentives that will result in the control of members' behavior in order to support these goals. Thus the internal structure of the organization is defined as a rational, functional operation that results from the goal-seeking tendency of organizations. The question becomes not whether or not organizations are goal-seeking collectives (this is an assumption), but rather, what are the goals and how effective and efficient are organizations in attaining these goals?

This type of perspective has several theoretical limitations that have been observed from other perspectives. One is the personification of organizations. People, not organizations, have motivations and goals (see Etzioni, 1975; Clark and Wilson, 1961; Georgiou, 1973, Selection 3). The dominant coalition within the organization and/or the managers of the organization can only offer incentives that they think will motivate the employee to conform to the goals they feel are paramount. Second, the goals assumption has led to a conceptualization of organizations as *boundary maintaining* systems, closed and changeless (Pettigrew, 1973:1); only those persons who contribute to the achievement of organizational goals are considered to be part of the organization. Third, by defining the boundaries in terms of the existing goals, analysts are able to demonstrate that organizations actually exist as entities and units of analysis, thus this assumption of goals can be criticized for facilitating the *reification* of organizations and goals (Silverman, 1970; Crozier and Friedberg, 1977). Fourth, the goals premise assumes that organizations are *rational,* that through the implementation of certain means the organization can achieve corresponding goals. This assumption of rationality has in itself generated a multitude of criticisms, discussed in the next section. Perhaps the strongest criticism is that humans within organizations are not totally rational; their perceptions are limited and their information is limited and often inaccurate (Schelling, 1960). Even if humans were rational, administrators in organizations could never hope to eliminate the nonrational aspects of the functioning of organizations, the spontaneous patterns that arise and could not have been predicted. Fifth, the assumption that organizational members have developed some *consensus* about goals has been rejected since it is clear that not all organizational members have decided what "the goals" of the organization are, and those who have, do not always agree. Moreover, not all of the goals envisioned are attainable. Finally, whatever goals are set are shaped by "the administration," "management," or the "dominant coalition," not by the entire membership, and thus reflect the priorities of those selected people. These priorities issue from their positions in the organization and their training, careers, competencies, etc. (Perrow, 1961:856-857). Thus organizational goals are the means some members of the organization use to control and manipulate other members in order to attain their personal or group goals.

But there is not unanimity of opinion among the critics on this point. For example, Georgiou (1973:297-298, Selection 3) argues that one group cannot completely determine organizational goals or the operation of the organization, whereas the Marxian theorists argue that under capitalism the bourgeois class has been fairly successful in doing so. The negotiated order perspective views organizational goals as the "outcome of the process of negotiation" (Strauss, et al., 1963; Bucher and Stelling, 1969). Allison, on the other hand, maintains that decision-making related to goals is the "resultant" of actions not determined by the goals of any *one* group but rather determined by the pulling and hauling that is politics (1971:144, Selection 7). More recently, therefore, organizational goals have been seen as either the result of the social construction of reality (Berger and Luckmann, 1967) or of the imposed reality of the capitalist (Friedman, 1977, Selection 9; Edwards, 1978, Selection 8). These two conceptions differ significantly from the comparative structural and structural contingency approaches in which goals are viewed as resulting from structure or from contingent environments and technologies.

OVERLY RATIONAL IMAGE OF ORGANIZATIONAL FUNCTIONING

Here we discuss two very closely related but separate assumptions of the dominant perspectives. First is that people are viewed as rational by the dominant perspectives; the second is that organizations are viewed as rational. The mixing of these assumptions has occurred by erroneously labeling as the rational model of organizations what is, in fact, a rational model of administrative behavior. In actuality this is an attempt by administrators and managers to map out the necessary conditions for the most effective and efficient (rational) methods of administration. (See Albrow, 1970, for an explanation of the misunderstanding of the equation of "rational" with "efficient'' behavior.) Such models are adapted by sociologists in the name of Max Weber (1968) as a result of either very shallow reading or limited understanding of his sociological approach and of the relationships between the process of rationalization and capitalism and the accompanying development of bureaucratic organizations.

A major reason that organizations are not totally rational instruments in their pursuit of goals is, as mentioned earlier, that people are not rational: they often do not have a consistent ordering of their goals; they do not always systematically pursue the goals that they do hold; in many instances, they do not have complete information; they seldom have a complete listing of alternatives; they often cannot conduct an exhaustive search of alternatives; and they may not know the relationship between organizational means and ends. If this is the case, then how do organizations function? As Weick (1976) tells us, we must start with a different set of assumptions and beliefs; if we don't believe things when we see them, we must be operating on the basis that we see things only when we already believe them. The essence of bureaucracy is not rationality but rather what we believe is real. So we must begin with the assumption that people are not totally rational. When we believe that structure causes technology, that behavior and condition cause attitudes, or as Allison puts it, where we stand depends on where we sit in the organization, then this will lead us to the demystification of our assumptions of rationality.

Another reason that organizations are not totally rational is that the rational model avoids the question of just whose rationality is dominant, because there is only one organizational rationality — that of the dominant coalition. This in turn renders the model unable to explain differences in interest, conflicts, domination, and subjugation within the organization. Because there is only one rationality, that of the dominant-administrative segment of the organization, there is no questioning of the status quo, the existing distribution of rewards, and the present power arrangements. Rather there is only the questioning of how well the organization functions, given the goals and objectives of that dominant coalition. Of course, there is a multiplicity of rationalities originating from various actors and groups within all organizations. Not only do white-collar and blue-collar crime, cheating, stealing, and coercion make the organization irrational from the dominant coalition's point of view, but ineptitudes, inactions, negligence, and human error (sins of omission) also make these organizations nonrational from this point of view.

By the late 1960s the equation of rationality with the goal of efficiency and the questioning of the assumption of efficiency as the only measure of organizational performance had brought to prominence the structural contingency models. In these models, structure varies depending on what the goal of the organization is. For example, an organization that is designed to maximize innovation will be more complex, decentralized, and have greater communication than one that is designed to maximize efficiency (Hage and Aiken, 1970). Likewise, structure that is contingent upon a nonroutine technology will be decentralized and more complex than one that is contingent upon routine technology (Thompson, 1967; Perrow, 1972; and Hage and Aiken, 1970). Environmental change, complexity, and the uncertainty of decision-makers in dealing with such environments also are associated with less rational or bureaucratic structures (Lawrence and Lorsch, 1967). Thus the rational (bureaucratic) structure has come to mean a certain set of structural characteristics that exist (fit) only under conditions of efficiency goals, routine technology, and relatively static and certain environments. Other types of structures ''fit'' organizations with goals of innovation, nonroutine technologies, and highly complex and uncertain environments.

Consequently, for much of the past two decades analysts have assumed that organizational means and ends are connected and, more recently, that certain environments, technologies, and other parameter variables are related to certain internal structures. Even more recently these assumptions have come into question. For example, Meyer and Rowan (1977:342, Selection 15) write:

> Structural elements are often loosely linked to each other and to activities, rules are often violated, decisions are often unimplemented, or if implemented have uncertain consequences, technologies are of problematic efficiency, and evaluation systems are subverted or rendered so vague as to provide little coordination.

As a result, the term "loose coupling" (March and Simon, 1958; Weick, 1976, Selection 11) has been coined to denote that the fit between such dimensions is not as tight as has been assumed in many earlier studies. The relationship between these organizational characteristics is often assumed rather than proven, and Weick (1976) characterizes these rational assumptions as "post hoc dissonance reduction" on the part of organizational theorists. Similarly, Cohen, March, and Olsen (1972) demonstrate the lack of rationality in the decision-making processes in organizations while developing what they have labeled the "garbage can" model of organizational decision-making (also see March and Olsen, 1976). Certainly we are not advocating that organizations and individuals operate in totally nonrational fashions. Weick (1976, Selection 11) and Meyer and Rowan (1977, Selection 15), as well as most of the authors in Part III, explain the importance of nonrational human, institutional, and societal elements that are little accounted for by the comparative structural and structural contingency approaches.

These selections raise the question: If rational, efficiency-seeking organizational structures do not explain the functioning of organizations, then what does? Perhaps the preferences, motivations, and values of people within these organizations and the institutional and societal environments outside do. Individuals' preferences and incentives give rise to organizational politics and power relationships within organizations (Clark and Wilson, 1961; Georgiou, 1973, Selection 3). Likewise, societal elements may create institutionalized nonrationalities as is reported by Meyer and Rowan (1977, Selection 15).

Research on societal and class preferences is infrequent in organizational analysis today. What does exist is more likely to be reported in case studies and historical approaches of the French and Marxian sociologists (see Parts II and III below). Therefore, the analyses presented in this volume do not concentrate on the authority that develops in modern work organizations. This pursuit of technical production goals in a rational manner by organizational decision-makers is what the dominant perspectives label rationality and what the Marxian theorists see as the power to exploit the worker. Marxian theorists also realize that this power-and-reward distribution inside the organization is determined by the larger societal class structure (see Hymer, 1972, Selection 14). Similarly, Meyer and Rowan (1977, Selection 15) argue that organizations in post-industrial society are adapting to the rationalities of their larger societal and institutional contexts. They point out that the rationality around which the organization is developed has little to do with the efficient production of products and services but is the rationality of the *sovereign,* little impeded by technical constraints.

The alternative perspectives presented in Parts II and III advocate our bringing these peripheral assumptions, ideologies, theories, and methodologies from the edges to the center of our concerns in organizational analysis. In other words, these perspectives advise that we should not merely acknowledge the nonrational and irrational aspects of organizations and then rush to analyze the rational aspects but that our analysis should center on these nonrational and irrational aspects, because these are the ways organizations operate in the real world.

VALUE CONSENSUS IN ORGANIZATIONS

The sixth criticism centers around the question of the validity of the unitary assumption: that all members of an organization share common values and attitudes and thus act in consensus. Is it legitimate to assume that although individuals may exhibit different ambitions and aspirations based on different motives, these exist within the common values and contribute to the general organizational consensus? Under these assumptions workers engaged in conflict are held to be acting irrationally, or not in their own self-interest, since their self-interest would be served by action that is in the interest of the organization. The consequences of this assumption are that workers' interests are defined as synonymous with those of management, because management defines the ends of the organization. Thus management, through the exercise of authority, is justified in exercising coercive control over those who oppose organizational values, because they are acting irrationally, "not in their own interest."

The alternative pluralistic assumption is that organizations are composed of actors and coalitions of actors, each with their own goals, divergent interests, aspirations, and perceptions (Pettigrew, 1973; Allison, 1971, Selection 7; Cyert and March, 1963; Child, 1972; and Crozier and Friedberg, 1977:135). Organizational elites (top management) occupy critical positions in organizations and often make decisions with far-reaching consequences for members of organizations and societies. However, the pluralistic view of organizations holds that the aspirations, perceptions, and actions of lower-level organizational participants are as important and deserving of study as those of management (Goldman and Van Houten, 1977, Selection 4; Heydebrand, 1977; Stone, 1974, Selection 18; Gallie, 1978, Selection 16; and Mechanic, 1962).

In *Power and Discontent,* Gamson (1968) examines the "authoritative actors" and "partisans" that are the actors in our dual perspectives of organizations. The authoritative actor is a "top down" view of organizations, emphasizing the problems of managers in coordinating organizational functions and controlling workers. The partisan view is a "bottom up" view of organizations that emphasizes the problems of lower-level organizational workers and their actions in surviving in their often powerless roles in organizations. Perhaps Allison (1971:144, Selection 7) best states the pluralistic assumption when he writes that, in contrast to other models, the political model sees no unitary actor or leader who sits at the top of the organization and "no monolithic group" but rather "many actors as players — players who focus not on a single static issue but on many diverse intra-national problems as well; players who act in terms of no consistent set of strategic objectives but rather according to various conceptions of national, organizational, and personal goals."

IMAGE OF HUMANS AS NONVOLITIONAL

Many of the criticisms elaborated under this heading are related to the theorist's assumptions in the dominant perspectives about the nature of humans in organizations. The seventh criticism is that the dominant perspectives implicitly view humans as nonvolitional, sponge-like, malleable organisms that absorb and adapt to their environments rather than as volitional actors pursuing their own self-interests. This view of human behavior by definition eliminates the possibility of humans changing the social organizations in which they exist. As a result of these "objective realities" (Berger and Luckman, 1967), humans are further implicitly viewed as relatively powerless, determined and controlled by the organizations in which they work. On the other hand, Blumer defines human behavior from a different perspective (1953:199): "capable of self-interaction," forging action "out of process of definition involving choice, appraisal, and decision . . . Cultural, status positions, and role relationships are only frameworks inside of which that process of formative transition goes on." Humans shape and mold their destinies as well as the social structures in which they exist.

If human actions are not determined by external constraints, then what are the bases of action? The answer is that actions are based on the meanings that are developed in interaction processes. Perhaps the argument of Argyris (1972) best epitomizes this criticism of the comparative structural approach. His most far-reaching challenge is that the comparative structural approach cannot develop a theory of organizational behavior without incorporating a theory of human nature and assumptions and principles of the psychology of individual participants, specifically an analysis of the meanings of actions. The symbolic interactionists have extended this to an even more basic criticism emphasizing the meaning of organizational relationships for the organizational participants. This "verstehen" approach is also advocated by Manning (1977) when he insists that organizational analysis necessitates an understanding of the interests and meanings that actors bring into interaction within organizational settings.

The assumption is that actions arise out of meanings that are the bases of social realities. These meanings are generated out of individual definitions of reality. Thus while society defines humans, humans in turn define society. People create institutions, modify organizations, and transform societies. Therefore, "the positivistic explanations, which assert that action is determined by external and constraining social or non-social forces, are inadmissible" (Silverman, 1970:127). (For additional perspectives of the *action frame of reference* see Schutz, 1962; Berger and Luckmann, 1967; Goffman, 1959; and, included in this anthology, Selection 6, Strauss' action framework, which he labels the negotiated order perspective.) These assumptions are the essence of the action perspective, which holds that we cannot hope to understand organizations unless we study the social actions that occur in organizations and the meanings behind these actions by analyzing the attitudes, beliefs, and values of those who participate in these organizations. This form of analysis constitutes the underpinnings of many of the selections included in this anthology such as Strauss's (1978a, Selection 6) negotiated order perspective and the political perspectives of Allison (1971, Selection 7). Also, the social action system is explicitly defined and elaborated in the works of Touraine (1971), Gallie (1978, Selection 16), Crozier and Friedberg (1977), and Goldthorpe, et al. (1969).

Thus the structural and action perspectives arise out of quite different assumptions and also proceed in quite different manners. The goals and structural approaches locate actors in positions within the organization and work deductively, while the action approach begins with the social act and attempts to construct propositions through the accumulation of meaning-based actions in an inductive manner (see Silverman, 1970).

The criticisms leveled against the comparative structural and structural contingency theorists emanate from the distinction between action based on the meanings of individuals and action occurring as a goal-oriented reaction. The action perspective assumes that people have the ability to determine their own realities. The researcher must therefore focus on the production and the reproduction of these organizational realities as they affect the actions of others. No longer can the researcher assume that there is only one organizational reality, that of the administration, and then proceed by treating that reality as objectively defined. Finally, the logic of the action perspective limits the degree to which analysts can run correlations between measured organizational characteristics and the extent to which they can assume that there are connections between these characteristics in the minds of the employee. The action perspective also refrains from assuming that all employees who act in the same manner are acting rationally as the researcher has defined rationality, or that all these employees have the same meanings for their actions.

In sum, the omission of the grounding and production of reality from the dominant perspectives has been a central critical issue for at least a decade, and criticisms have originated from many alternative perspectives, including Marxism (Giddens, 1976), phenomenology (Silverman, 1970), and negotiated order (Strauss, 1978a).

IMAGE OF OVERLY CONSTRAINED ORGANIZATIONS

The eighth criticism is that the dominant perspectives contain overly constrained views of organizations. This view originates from models that see (1) environment, (2) technology, and (3) size as determinants of organizational structure and performance. Certain combinations of these factors are even considered to be functional imperatives for good organizational structure and performance.

Structure that is contingent on its environment is well documented in open systems analysis. As elaborated by Sadler and Barry (1970:58): "An organization cannot evolve or develop in ways which merely reflect the goals, motives or needs of its members or of its leadership, since it must always bow to the *constraints* imposed on it by the nature of its relationship with the environment" (emphasis added). Various dimensions of the organizational environment have been demonstrated to affect the structure, functioning, and performance of organizations. These dimensions are environmental change (Stinchcombe, 1959; Burns and Stalker, 1968; and Lawrence and Lorsch, 1967), environmental complexity (Lawrence and Lorsch, 1967; Emery and Trist, 1965), and environmental uncertainty, which is the decision-makers' ability to predict the preceding environmental dimensions plus other threats that might impair goal achievement (Khandalla, 1970). Likewise, the several different definitions and dimensions of technology have resulted in the same types of propositions proposed by Hickson, et al. (1969), Woodward (1965), and Perrow (1967, 1979), all of whom argue that the nature of technology presents important implications for the design of effective organizations. Finally, Pugh and associates (1969) and Blau (1970) are the major exponents of size as the most powerful predictor of the internal structure of the organization. Thus all three of these approaches explain observable patterns of organizational structure as results of environmental and contextual constraints.

Crozier and Friedberg (1977) criticize the perspectives of Burns and Stalker (1968) and Lawrence and Lorsch (1967) for their development of open systems models in which the environment is imposed automatically on the organization. This one-way process does not allow for the organization's ability to affect the environment. Furthermore, Crozier and Friedberg criticize the structural contingency model for assuming that the entire organizational environment can be characterized as complex or change-oriented. They argue that the environment is not a homogeneous entity but a multiplicity of characteristics, with unlimited diversity. We counter this argument with our observation that organizations are not shaped by their environ-ments to any greater extent than environments are shaped by organizations. Further-more, the environment of organizations is almost always other organizations, so organizations are shaped by other organizations.

Still another related argument is that these structural contingency models are inadequate because they do not take into consideration choices of those who are in power. These choices have been labeled "strategic choice" by Crozier (1964), Child (1972), and Chandler (1962, Selection 17).

In selection 17, Chandler summarizes his historical analysis of American indus-trial enterprises. In this analysis (1962:13) he defines the concept of strategy as "the determination of the basic long-term goals and objectives of an enterprise, and the adoption of courses of action and the allocation of resources necessary for carrying out these goals. Decisions to expand the volume of activities, to set up distant plants and offices, to move into economic functions, or become diversified along lines of business involve the defining of new basic goals." These are the strategic choices of the dominant coalition, and the direction of these choices is a major source of organizational variation. Thus the political system within organizations determines contextual dimensions through its choices of technologies, its expansion, and the dominant coalition's definitions of the environment.

The contention of the authors of the selections in Parts II and III is that organiza-tions cannot be understood as a result of structural constraints or functional impera-tives alone, but rather as a result of political actions and processes of those in power. The concept of "dominant coalition" formulated by Cyert and March (1963) and extended by Thompson (1967) forms the basis of the strategic choice alternative. The dominant coalition does not necessarily, but could, consist of those who hold authoritative positions in the organizations; rather it refers to those who collectively hold the most power in the organization. These are not the only members of the organizations who have power; others have the ability to modify decisions, control information, and so forth. This concept of dominant coalition facilitates a view of organizational structure as a political resultant of the distribution of power and the process of strategic decision-making in the organization.

The comparative structural and the structural contingency approaches do not incorporate an analysis of the strategic decisions of the dominant coalition. They deal with constraints on these choices, which are a necessary phase of the analysis, but they omit the heart of the political process itself. On the other hand, many of the perspectives represented here view organizations as both reacting to and attempting to dominate and influence their environments. Thus organizations are defined as pow-erful social entities that can influence and determine not only their destinies but also the destinies of other social entities. For example, both Chandler (1962, Selection 17) and the authors of the Marxian selections (Edwards, 1978, Selection 8, and Fried-man, 1977, Selection 9) attest to the power of industrial organizations in influencing institutional structures; Hymer (1972, Selection 14) demonstrates the impact of multinational cooperation on the world system, and all present an image of organiza-tions as powerful influences on society. Hence organizations have enormous power and are able to dominate and subordinate other organizations as well as social and economic institutions of society.

STATIC IMAGE OF ORGANIZATIONS

The ninth criticism is that the comparative structural and structural contingency approaches are, through their emphases on structure, unavoidably static. The central concern here is whether organizational analysts should use more static structural images of organizations or more dynamic fluxional process images. The distinction between social structure and process is fairly common in most sociological analyses. The two are unavoidably connected; by defining the patterns of process, the researcher can describe in a fairly stable and static form the nature of structure, but this often leads to a neglect of the more dynamic aspects of organization. As Benson (1977:11) writes:

> A process-oriented analysis would deal with changes in the underpinnings, in the infrastructure upon which the organization is built. This would involve attending to the micro-processes continuously occurring within the organization and its environment within a particular period of time, that is, the ongoing interactions that continuously reproduce the organization and/or alter it. It would also involve examining the transformations of context involved in major historical breaks.

Perhaps Crozier and Friedberg (1977:125-126) level the most devastating criticisms against the static view of the structural contingency approaches, charging that statistical correlations teach us nothing about why organizational phenomena occur, under what circumstances, or through which mediating mechanisms. Furthermore, this type of structural analysis does not tell us the rules of the game governing interaction. Finally, Crozier and Friedberg assert that the structural contingency model poses a deterministic view of organizational change.

The dividing line between structure and process is not always clear. Both structural and process images focus on the same social behavior, but one emphasizes the more static aspects of that behavior while the other emphasizes the more dynamic aspects. The structuralists have clearly emphasized, perhaps overemphasized, the more static aspects of human behavior, and their images and concepts have not been sufficiently sensitive to the view that humans in organizations are continually negotiating and renegotiating their roles, positions, and rewards. This alternative perspective maintains that organizations are continually changing (Strauss, 1978, Selection 6) and that therefore we need theories that allow for these changing aspects of organizations.

The essential question here is not whether or not structure and process are in conflict, but rather which is the cause and which the effect — what is the causal priority of these two elements? Does the organizational structure largely determine the outcome of the processes involved, or is the structure constantly undergoing change as a result of the fluxional process of the organization? The selections in Part II by Strauss (1978, Selection 6) and Allison (1971, Selection 7) demonstrate how an analysis of processes provides satisfactory explanations of the causes of specific events and changes, explanations which structural analysis cannot provide. Chandler (1962, Selection 17), through historical analysis of the American industrial enterprises further demonstrates that the structure of business organizations is a result of the implementation of strategies — political processes within these firms. Thus the selections in this anthology concentrate on process as opposed to structural analyses of organizations.

ORGANIZATION AS THE EXCLUSIVE UNIT
OF ANALYSIS

The tenth criticism centers around the proper unit of organizational analysis and the question of whether a perspective that focuses on organizations should be limited only to the general characteristics of the organization, excluding analysis of the more micro social-psychological concerns and the more macro economic, political, historical, and societal interrelationships with the organization.

The organization as the unit of analysis is justified by the assumption that it is a separate goal-seeking, boundary-maintaining system. This assumption is reinforced by the analysis of interrelated internal structural characteristics, assuming that the system (bounded organization) is able to accept some structural arrangement, technologies, etc., and reject others depending on organizational goals. It is important to note that the organization is defined as dealing with, being mediator of, and responding to its environment, which consists of other organizations, multinational systems, and institutional complexes — a natural selection perspective. Too infrequently is the organization defined as controlling, manipulating, changing, and dominating this environment, although such images of organizations are becoming more frequent (for example, see Selection 18 by Stone; also see Aldrich and Pfeffer, 1976, for a discussion of the essential differences in the natural selection and resource dependency models).

These assumptions about the nature of organizations, combined with the concern of organizational sociologists over delimiting a unit of analysis that, strictly defined, would legitimize their professional involvement and differentiate them from other sociological fields, have resulted in the isolated analysis of organizations. This preoccupation with organizations as the unit of analysis has been criticized for its neglect of the society within which the organization exists (Salaman, 1978:524, Selection 1), its reification of systems and goals (Glaser and Strauss, 1967), its abandonment of concern about organizational domination in exchange for an over-concern about the system's adaption to external forces, its neglect of the power dynamics through which organizations gain control over their environments (McNeil, 1978:78, Selection 2), and its isolation from issues of social class, social stratification, and social conflict (Goldman and Van Houten, 1977:108-125, Selection 4). This results in approaches in which organizations are viewed as actors rather than as individuals acting in their own interests (Clark and Wilson, 1961) or as individuals in social classes acting in defense of their class interest. Thus Goldman and Van Houten (1977:111-112, Selection 4) assert that this emphasis on microanalysis of single organizations has revealed little of how the economy, the political context, or the community affects day-to-day organizational life. Consequently, Hirsch (1975:9) recommends that organizational analysis move beyond the technical and managerial levels of single firms to institutional and societal environments.

The separation of organizations from more micro social-psychological analyses and from macro-social analyses in order to justify a separate field of study has been a major theoretical limitation of these structural approaches. Since organizational processes are not linked to macro- and micro-processes in any systematic fashion, one notes a discontinuity as one moves through the social-psychological, structural, and societal literature as it relates to the study of organizations.

UNIVERSAL GENERALIZATIONS ABOUT ORGANIZATIONS

Underpinning the eleventh criticism is the assumption of some comparative structural and structural contingency theorists that there are universal laws of organizational structure and functioning and that through empirical research these generalizations can be discovered. Blau's formal theory of differentiation (1970) and Hage's axiomatic theory (1965) are two such attempts in organizational theory; but this assumption dates back to the founders of sociology and their attempts to discover and codify the positivistic laws of social order. This logic follows that of the natural sciences in that it is assumed that natural laws of social behavior need only be discovered through the search process of positivistic methodology and that once revealed, these laws can be applied to all organizations. This assumption is easily integrated into the systems perspective in an attempt to develop a general theory of organizations, although attempts have centered almost totally on the interrelationship of internal characteristics of organizations (see Hall, 1978). At the basis of these sets of principles or causal relationships is the assumption that there is one best way for the structure and functioning of all organizations and that, consequently, any changes or conflict in the organization must be due to the lack of integration or fit between organizational characteristics.

An alternative view, which we call the specificity or particularistic approach, holds that different types of organizations have different processes, structures, environments, customers, clients, employee aspirations, and contingencies. Under this assumption, it is considered more fruitful to try to understand organizations in terms of those elements that are unique or specific to them rather than in terms of those things that are general to all organizations (Colignon and Cray, 1979). The particularistic strategy holds that not until there have been a sufficient number of studies of different types of organizations using various types of organizational models can we begin to synthesize our knowledge about organizations. The universalistic and particularistic assumptions lead to different strategies of organizational analysis. The particularist holds that it is premature, if not impossible, to develop universal generalizations about a given type of organization.

INADEQUATE ATTENTION TO POWER RELATIONS
IN ORGANIZATIONAL ANALYSIS

The twelfth criticism is that neither the comparative structural nor the structural contingency approach places power at the center of its analysis. Power is seldom presented as the major explanatory variable, nor are power relationships viewed as the essential ones to be explained. If power is analyzed at all, it is in terms of influence or authority, the legitimized position-based power of management or organizational elites. Almost never are domination, subjugation, coercion, manipulation, or extortion of one group or class of organizational member by a more powerful group or class analyzed. This type of question is not within the definition of authority and therefore is not relevant to analysis of bureaucracies. But these are very real aspects of power. Certainly domination can be achieved through the bureaucratic authority of rules and regulation, hierarchy of authority, division of labor, and monopoly of knowledge (see Edwards, 1978, Selection 8; Friedman, 1977, Selection 9; Goldman and Van Houten, 1979, Selection 10). But domination can also be achieved by blackmail, manipulation, threats, and other more coercive methods. Strauss's negotiated order perspective (Selection 6), the Marxian perspectives mentioned previously, and the political approaches of Pettigrew (1973) and Allison (1971, Selection 7) are among the perspectives that place power at the very center of organizational analysis.

Placing power at the center of organizational analysis has pervasive consequences for the strategy of analysis. Power becomes an overriding concern of the organizational analysis, and it is no longer just one dimension among the many, such as division of labor, formalization, communication, etc. An analysis of power has to include some of the following questions concerning the existing distribution of power: How did the existing relationship originate? Which classes and groups are benefited by the existing relationship? How does the dominant coalition maintain and perpetuate its control? What are the consequences of the present distribution of power in the organization for present society and for future generations?

This introduction has presented the problems and criticisms of the comparative structural and structural contingency approaches in the form of a debate over the choices of assumptions, ideologies, contents, and methods, not unlike those debates posed by Aldrich's (1979:137) dichotomy of "choice versus constraints", Pfeffer and Salanick's (1978:81) dichotomy of "structure versus flexibility", Crozier's (1977) dichotomy of "system versus action," and Touraine's (1976:246) dichotomy of "system versus unit of action." The criticisms outlined suggest the need for the alternative approaches presented in Parts II and III.

As the reader has progressed through the various criticisms of the comparative structural and structural contingency approaches, it has no doubt become clear that these criticisms have been made from diverse theoretical perspectives. There is no unified perspective that incorporates all the alternative assumptions, methods, substantive theory, and ideologies that have been outlined. Thus in this anthology we have purposely attempted to incorporate a wide range of alternatives to aid the student of organizations in making informed decisions as to the most appropriate perspective for his or her analysis.

BIBLIOGRAPHY

Albrow, Martin
1970   *Bureaucracy.* London: Macmillian.
1973   "The study of organizations—objectivity or bias." Pages 396–413 in Graeme Salaman and Kenneth Thompson (eds.) *People and Organizations.* London: Longman for Open University Press.

Aldrich, Howard E.
1971   "Organizational boundaries in interorganizational conflict," *Human Relations* 24:279–287.
1979   *Organizations and Environments.* Englewood Cliffs, New Jersey: Prentice-Hall.

Aldrich, Howard E., and Jeffrey Pfeffer
1976   "Environments of organizations," *Annual Review of Sociology* II: 79–105.

Allison, Graham T.
1971   "Model III: governmental politics." Chapter 5 in *Essence of Decision: Explaining the Cuban Missile Crisis.* Boston: Little, Brown and Company.

Argyris, Chris
1972   *The Applicability of Organizational Sociology.* London: Cambridge University Press.

Benson, J. Kenneth
1971   "Models of structure selection in organizations: On the limitations of rational perspectives." Paper presented at Annual Meetings of the American Sociological Association, Denver, Colorado, August.
1976   "The interorganizational network as political economy," *Administrative*

Science Quarterly 20:229–249.

1977a "Organizations: A dialectical view," *Administrative Science Quarterly* 22:1–21.

1977b "Innovation and crisis in organizational analysis," *Sociological Quarterly* 18 (Winter): 3–16.

Berger, Peter, and T. Luckmann
1967   *The Social Construction of Reality*. Allen Lane.

Blackburn, R.
1972   "A brief guide to bourgeois ideology." In R.C. Edwards, M. Reich, and E. Weisskopf (eds.) *The Capitalist System*. New Jersey: Prentice-Hall.

Blau, Peter M.
1970   "A formal theory of differentiation in organizations," *American Sociological Review* 35:201–218.

Blau, Peter M., and Richard A. Schoenherr
1971   *The Structure of Organizations*. New York: Basic Books.

Blau, Peter M., and William Scott
1963   *Formal Organizations*. Routledge and Kegan Paul.

Blumer, Herbert
1953   "Psychological importance of the human group." Pages 199–207 in M. Scherif and M.O. Wilson (eds.) *Group Relations at the Crossroads*. New York: Harper and Row.

Braverman, Harry
1974   *Labor and Monopoly Capital*. New York: Monthly Review.

Bucher, R., and J. Stelling
1969   "Characteristics of professional organizations," *Journal of Health and Social Behavior* 10:3–15.

Burns, T., and G.M. Stalker
1968   *The Management of Innovation* (second edition). Tavistock.

Callon, Michel, and Jean-Pierre Vignolle
1977   "Breading down the organization: Local conflicts and societal systems of action," *Social Science Information* 16:147–167.

Chandler, Alfred D., Jr.
1962   "Conclusion—chapters in the history of the great industrial enterprise." Pages 383–396 in *Strategy and Structure: Chapters in the History of the American Industrial Enterprise*. Cambridge, Massachusetts: The M.I.T. Press.

1977   *The Visible Hand: The Managerial Revolution in American Business*. Cam-

bridge, Massachusetts: The Belknap Press of Harvard University Press.

Child, John
1972   "Organization structure, environment and performance—the role of strategic choice," *Sociology* 6 (January): 1–22.

1973a "Organization: A choice for man." Pages 234–255 in John Child (editor) *Man and Organization*. Allen & Unwin.

1973b "Predicting and understanding organization structure," *Administrative Science Quarterly* 18:168–185.

Clark, Peter B., and James Q. Wilson
1961   "Incentive systems: A theory of organizations," *Administrative Science Quarterly* 6:129–166.

Cohen, Michael D., James C. March and Johan P. Olsen
1972   "A garbage can model of organizational choice," *Administrative Science Quarterly* 17: 1–25.

Colignon, Richard, and David Cray
1979   "Critical organizations." Unpublished revision of 1978 American Sociological Association Meetings paper.

Crozier, Michel
1964   *The Bureaucratic Phenomenon*. Chicago: University of Chicago Press.

1973   *The Stalled Society*. New York: Viking.

Crozier, Michel, and Erhard Friedberg
1977   *L'Acteur et le Systeme: Les Contraintes de l'Action Collective*. Paris: Editions du Seuil.

Cyert, R.M., and J.G. March
1963   *A Behavioral Theory of the Firm*. Englewood Cliffs: Prentice-Hall.

Edwards, Richard C.
1978   "The social relations of production at the point of production," *The Insurgent Sociologist* 8:109–125.

Emery, F.E., and E.L. Trist
1965   "The causal texture of organizational environments," *Human Relations* 18:21–32.

Etzioni, Amitai
1975   *A Comparative Analysis of Complex Organizations* (revised edition). New York: The Free Press.

Friedman, Andrew
1977   "Management—preliminary argument." Pages 77–85 in *Industry and Labor: Class Struggle at Work and Monopoly Capitalism*. London: The Macmillan Press.

Friedrichs, Robert W.
1970   *A Sociology of Sociology*. New York: The Free Press.

Gallie, Duncan
1978   "Managerial strategies, the unions and the social integration of the work force." Pages 295–318 in *In Search of the New Working Class*. London: Cambridge University Press.

Gamson, William
1968   *Power and Discontent*. Homewood, Ill.: Dorsey Press.

Georgiou, Petro
1973   "The goal paradigm and notes towards a counter paradigm," *Administrative Science Quarterly* 18:291–310.

Giddens, Anthony
1976   *New Rules of Sociological Method, A Positive Critique of Interpretive Sociologies*. New York: Basic Books, Inc.

Glaser, Barney G., and Anselm L. Strauss
1967   *The Discovery of Grounded Theory: Strategies of Qualitative Research*. Chicago: Aldine Publishing Company.

Goffman, E.
1959   *The Presentation of Self in Everyday Life*. New York: Doubleday.

Goldman, Paul, and Donald R. Van Houten
1977   "Managerial strategies and the worker: A Marxist analysis of bureaucracy," *Sociological Quarterly* 18 (Winter): 108–125.

1979   "Bureaucracy and domination." Chapter 5, pages 108–141 in *The International Yearbook of Organization Studies*. London: Routledge and Kegan Paul.

Goldthorpe, John H., David Lockwood, Frank Bechnofer, and Jennifer Platt
1969   *The Affluent Worker in the Class Structure*. Cambridge: Cambridge University Press.

Gouldner, Alvin W.
1954   *Patterns of Industrial Bureaucracy*. New York: Free Press of Glencoe.
1970   *The Coming Crisis of Western Sociology*. New York: Basic Books, Inc.

Hage, Jerald
1965   "An axiomatic theory of organizations," *Administrative Science Quarterly* 10:289–320.

Hage, Jerald, and Michael Aiken
1967a   "Program change and organizational properties: A comparative analysis," *American Journal of Sociology* 72:503–519.

1967b   "Relationship of centralization to other structural properties," *Administrative Science Quarterly* 12:72–91.

1969   "Routine technology, social structure and organizational goals," *Administrative Science Quarterly* 14:366–377.

1970   *Social Change in Complex Organizations*. New York: Random House.

Hall, Peter M.
1972   "A symbolic interactionist analysis of politics." Pages 35–75 in Andrew Effrat (editor) *Perspectives in Political Sociology*. Indianapolis and New York: Bobbs-Merrill.

Hall, Richard
1963   "The concept of bureaucracy: An empirical assessment," *American Journal of Sociology* 69:32–40.
1978   *Organizations, Structure and Process* (second edition). Englewood Cliffs, New Jersey: Prentice-Hall.

Heydebrand, Wolf (editor)
1973   *Comparative Organizations: The Results of Empirical Research*. Englewood Cliffs, New Jersey: Prentice-Hall.

1977   "Organizational contradictions in public bureaucracies: Toward a Marxian theory of organizations," *Sociological Quarterly* 18 (Winter): 83–107.

Hickson, David J., C.R. Hinings, C.A. Lee, R.E. Schneck, and J.M. Pennings
1971   "A strategic contingencies theory of intraorganizational power," *Administrative Science Quarterly* 16 (June): 216–229.

Hinings, C.R., and G.L. Lee
1971   "Dimensions of organization structure and their context: A replication," *Sociology* 5: 83–93.

Hirsch, Paul M.
1975   "Organizational analysis and industrial sociology: An instance of cultural lag," *American Sociologist* 10 (February): 3–12.

Hymer, Stephen
1972   "The multinational corporation and the law of uneven development." Pages 113–140 in J. Bahagwati (editor) *Economic and World Order from the 1970's to the 1990's*. New York: Collier-Macmillan. Reprinted in Hugo Radice (editor) *International Firms and*

Modern Imperials. London: Penguin Books, pages 37–62.

Karpik, Lucien
1978   *Organization and Environment*. Beverley Hills: Sage.

Khandwalla, P.N.
1970   *Environment and the Organization Structure of Firms*. McGill University Faculty of Management Working Paper.

Kuhn, Thomas S.
1970   *The Structure of Scientific Revolution* (second edition). Chicago: University of Chicago Press.

Lawrence, Paul R., and Jay W. Lorsch
1967   *Organization and Environment*. Cambridge, Massachusetts: Harvard University Press.

Likert, Rensis
1967   *The Human Organization*. New York: McGraw-Hill.

Manning, Peter K.
1977   "Rules in organizational context: Narcotics law enforcement in two settings," *Sociological Quarterly* 18 (Winter): 44–61.

March, James G., and Johan P. Olsen
1976   *Ambiguity and Choice in Organizations*. Bergen: Universitelsforlaget.

Marglin, Stephen
1974   "What the bosses do: The origins and functions of hierarchy in capitalist production," *Review of Radical Political Economics* 6 (Summer): 60–112.

Mayntz, Renate
1964   "The study of organizations," *Current Sociology* 13: 94–157.

McNeil, Kenneth
1978   "Understanding organizational power: Building on the Weberian legacy," *Administrative Science Quarterly* 23 (March): 65–90.

Mechanic, David
1962   "Sources of power of lower participants in complex organizations," *Administrative Science Quarterly* 7:349–364.

Merton, Robert K.
1968   *Social Theory and Social Structure*. New York: The Free Press.

Meyer, John, and Brian Rowan
1977   "Institutionalized organizations: Formal structure as myth and ceremony," *American Journal of Sociology* 83:440–463.

Mouzelis, Nicos P.
1968   *Organization and Bureaucracy*. Chicago: Aldine.

Parsons, Talcott
1956   "Suggestions for a sociological approach to the theory of organization — I and II," *Administrative Science Quarterly* 1:63–85.
1960   *Structure and Process in Modern Society*. New York: Free Press of Glencoe.

Perrow, Charles
1961   "Goals in complex organizations," *American Sociological Review* 26 (December): 854-865.
1967   "A framework for the comparative analysis of organizations," *American Sociological Review* 32: 194–208.
1979   *Complex Organizations: A Critical Essay* (second edition). Glenview, Illinois: Scott, Foresman and Company.

Pettigrew, Andrew
1973   "Conceptual orientation" and "Decision making as a political process," Pages 1–31 in *Politics of Organizational Decision Making*. London: Tavistock.

Pfeffer, Jeffrey, and Gerald R. Salanik
1974   "Organizational decision making as a political process: the case of a university budget," *Administrative Science Quarterly* 19:135–151.
1978   *The External Control of Organizations*. New York: Harper and Row. Pugh, D.S. (editor)
1971   *Organizational Theory*. Harmondsworth, Middlesex, England: Penguin Books.

Pugh, D.S., D.J. Hickson, C.R. Hinings, and C. Turner
1968   "Dimensions of organizational structure," *Administrative Science Quarterly* 13 (June):65–104.
1969   "The context of organization structures," *Administrative Science Quarterly* 14:91–114.

Sadler, P.J., and B.A. Barry
1970   *Organizational Development*. Longman.

Salaman, Graeme
1978   "Toward a sociology of organizational structure," *The Sociological Review* 26:519–554.

Schelling, T.C.
1960   *The Strategy of Conflict*. Cambridge,

Massachusetts: The Harvard University Press.

Schutz, Alfred
1962   *Collected Papers* (volume I). The Hague, Nijhoff.

Selznick, Philip
1949   *TVA and the Grass Roots*. Berkeley: University of California.

Silverman, David
1968   "Formal organizations or industrial sociology: Toward a social action analysis of organizations," *Sociology* 2:221–238.
1970   *The Theory of Organizations*. New York: Basic Books, Inc.

Stinchcombe, Arthur L.
1959   "Bureaucratic and craft administration of production: A comparative study," *Administrative Science Quarterly* 4:168–187.

Stone, Katherine
1974   "The origins of job structures in the steel industry," *The Review of Radical Political Economics* 6:61–97.

Strauss, Anselm
1978a "Summary, implications and debate." Pages 234–247 in *Negotiations: Varieties, Process and Social Order*. San Francisco: Jossey-Bass, Inc.
1978b "The psychiatric hospital case." Pages 107–122 in *Negotiations: Varieties, Process and Social Order*. San Francisco: Jossey-Bass, Inc.

Strauss, Anselm, Leonard Schatzman, Danuta Ehrlich, Rue Bucher, and Melvin Sabshin.
1963   "The hospital and its negotiated order." Pages 147–169 in E. Freidson (editor) *The Hospital in Modern Society*. New York: Free Press.

Thompson, James
1967   *Organizations in Action*. New York: McGraw-Hill.

Touraine, Alain
1971a "The firm: Power, institutions and organization." Pages 139–192 in *The Post-Industrial Society*. New York: Random House.
1971b *The Post-Industrial Society*. New York:

Random House.
1976   *The Self-Production of Society*. Chicago: University Press.

Turner, Jonathan, and Alexandra Maryanski
1979   *Functionalism*. Menlo Park, California: The Benjamin/Cummings Publishing Co.

Udy, Stanley, H.
1959   " 'Bureaucracy' and 'rationality' in Weber's organizational theory," *American Sociological Review* 24:791–795.

Wamsley, Gary, and Mayer N. Zald
1973   *The Political Economy of Public Organizations*. Lexington, Massachusetts: Lexington Books, D.C. Heath.

Weber, Max
1968   *Economy and Society* (Volumes I–III) New York: Bedminster Press.

Weick, Karl E.
1967   "A system resource approach to organizational effectiveness," *Administrative Science Quarterly* 21:1–19.
1976   "Educational organizations as loosely coupled systems," *Administrative Science Quarterly* 12:1–11.

Woodward, Joan
1965   *Industrial Organization: Theory and Practice*. Oxford, England: Oxford University Press.
1970   "Industrial Organizations: Behavior and Control*. Oxford, England: Oxford University Press.

Zald, Mayer N.
1970   "Political economy: A framework for comparative analysis." Pages 221–261 in *Power in Organizations*. Nashville, Tennessee: Vanderbilt University Press.

Zey-Ferrell, Mary
1979   *Readings on Dimensions of Organizations*. Santa Monica, California: Goodyear Publishing Company.

Zwerman, William L.
1970   *New Perspectives on Organization Theory: An Empirical Reconsideration of Marxian and Classical Approaches*. Westport, Connecticut: Greenwood.

¹ Portions of this partheading were adapted from "Criticisms of the Dominant Perspectives on Organizations" by Mary Zey-Ferrell, published in *Sociological Quarterly*, 1981, vol. 22, no. 2.

1. Towards A Sociology Of Organisational Structure*

Graeme Salaman

This article is concerned to describe and advocate a genuine sociology of organisational structure, to trace its major elements in the work of Weber and Marx and its re-emergence in some recent publications. Despite the plethora of writing and research on organisations, there exists relatively little work of a truly sociological nature. The reasons for this are described.

A sociological approach to organisations addresses the question of the relationship between the design of work and control within employing organisations and the nature of the society within which they occur. It maintains that organisational power and control must be seen in terms of the nature and priorities of the 'host' society rather than as consequences of particular forms of work process or technology. It insists on a critical consideration of the widely prevalent notions of 'efficiency' and 'rationality' which conceptualise the hierarchic and inegalitarian nature of organisational structure and the distribution of rewards and deprivations associated with them, as inevitable and inexorable consequences of the application of the criterion of efficiency to the achievement of generally beneficial societal tasks. It considers the sectional advantages and functions of ostensibly neutral organisational elements such as mechanisation, automation, technology and science. And it focuses on the nature and functions of ideologies which buttress, disguise, or justify organisational inequalities and hierarchy. In short, it takes as the topic to be investigated exactly that which is assumed and glossed over by conventional organisational analysis: the relationship between internal organisational structures, processes and ideologies and the society within which they exist.

The conception of organisational structure and work design advocated in this article differs from that of conventional organisational analyses, which fail to separate organisational accounts of organisational structure and functioning from *sociological* analyses.[1] They accept the ready emphasis that senior members of organisations place on the rôle of efficiency as a determinant of organisational structure and process, failing to question the purposes and values that lie behind the notion of efficiency in capitalist society; their analyses being vulnerable to such failures by virtue of their initial definition of organisations in terms of goals, objectives, etc. Thus in much conventional analysis of organisations the major elements of organisational structure — hierarchy, extreme division of labour, etc. — are presented as functional consequences of the imperatives of efficiency, of industrialisation and industrial technology. All that remains to explain is small-scale variation *between* organisations. Blackburn has noted the deficences of such analyses:

> This way of thinking . . . contains a large dose of technological determinism since it suggests that the industrial nature of technology dominates social organisation as a whole

* "Towards a Sociology of Organisational Structure" by Graeme Salaman from *The Sociological Review*, Vol. 26, No. 3, 1978, pp. 519-554. Copyright © 1978 by *The Sociological Review*. Reprinted by permission.

. . . Thus the unavoidable concomitant of modern industry will be bureaucratic organisation . . . By deducing social organisation from industrial technology bourgeois sociology
can portray capitalist society as void of contradictions.[2]

A great deal of conventional organisational analysis accepts the 'rationality' of
modern organisations. While being prepared to bemoan the 'human consequences' of
such forms of organisation, they are seen as embodying inexorable and unavoidable
constraints deriving from the basic processes of industrialisation — the application of
rationality to work and organisation. Blau and Schoenherr have noted the ideological
advantages — in terms of mystification and justification — of this sort of analysis:

> In as much as experts judge issues in terms of universal criteria of rationality and
> efficiency, they cannot be blamed for the conclusions they reach, even though these
> conclusions may lead to actions of powerful organisations that are contrary to the interests
> of most people.[3]

In much the same way, conventional organisation theory, by 'discovering' causal
relationships which reveal the inevitability of current organisational forms, becomes
so embedded within, and celebratory of, these forms as to be unable to envisage
alternative structures.

Writers who hold such views ignore the political, sectional, nature of apparently
neutral procedures and technology. Like Mannheim's functionary they transform
problems of politics into problems of administration, and fail to see that '. . . behind
every law that there has ever been there lie the socially fashioned interests and
Weltanschaungen of a specific group'.[4]

Conventional organisational analysis accepts organisational definitions of organisational rationality (while conceding the possibility of some degree of irrationality
due to informal organisation, or 'human factors'). In this way the assumptions lying
behind such rationality are overlooked, as is the relationship between these rational
criteria and sectional or class advantage — or disadvantage. Furthermore the emphasis on organisational rationality as the main determinant of organisational structure and process — operating to ensure that for a given size, technology, market,
product, 'environment', etc., an organisation *must* adopt particular characteristics —
removes organisational structure and function from the world of class interests or
politics. The problems of organisational analysis — like the problems for organisations themselves — become technical ones. And, 'In so far as more spheres of
decision-making are construed as ''technical problems'' requiring information and
instrumental strategies produced by technical experts, they are removed from political debate'. The result? '. . . an infinitely flexible ideology which can be interpreted
in ways that legitimate public or private policy adopted by established power and
privilege groups'.[5]

However, a more genuinely sociological approach to organisation is possible.
This approach replaces an emphasis on efficiency and the constraints of industrialism
with a '. . . study of the changing forms and consequences of socio-economic
exploitation in the production of all goods and services, especially of those consequences which generate challenges to the principle of exploitation itself'.[6] And seeks
to widen '. . . the scope of organisation theory in order to account for social, political,
economic and historical influences within society in their impact on organisations'.[7]
It will be seen that this sociology of organisations proceeds from different assumptions and asks different questions to those of conventional organisational analysis.
Specifically this approach contains a number of elements.

First, a concern to isolate and describe the main features of organisational structure and the design of work and control and the principles, philosophies, interests and purposes that lie behind them. Secondly, to relate the structure of organisations to the society within which they occur, paying particular attention to the ways in which values prevalent in that society are reflected in organisations, or to the relationship between sectional or class memberships, cultures and interests and organisational structures and processes. Thirdly, to analyse the rôle of ideas and values, including sociological theories of organisations[8] in buttressing and legitimating (or disguising) the nature, function and origins of organisational structures.

This approach to the design of work and the structure of control (the two major elements of organisational structure) within organisations is not entirely new with organisational analysis, having been revealed in the work of Gouldner, Crozier and, more recently, Elger, Collins, Clegg and Dunkerley, and Benson.[9] However such works constitute the exception: conventional organisational theory, possibly because of its location within business schools, its close links with management consultancy,[10] the nature of the audience it serves, or the groups and corporations that fund research,[11] has shown a marked indifference to a genuinely critical sociological approach to organisation, failing, as Benson notes, '. . . to deal with the production of organisational arrangements or to analyse the entanglement of theory in those arrangements'.[12]

It is, of course, true that the systems approach to organisations considers one of the features mentioned above: the relationship between the structure and activities of organisations and the society within which they occur. But within systems analysis this relationship is asserted rather than explored, an assertion which is based on the systems conceptualisation of the relationship between 'environment' and organisation in terms of 'inputs' and 'outputs' between the social system and the goal-oriented organisational system.

This approach is exemplified in the ambitious theory of organisations of Talcott Parsons. For Parsons, organisations must be seen in terms of their relationship with the larger society, for which they produce socially necessary and desirable goods, services or functions. Organisations, he claims, can be classified in terms of the sort of goals which they achieve for the society. Organisational goals are societal functions. Parsons claims that he wishes to '. . . define an organisation by locating it systematically in the structure of society in relation to other categories of social structure'.[13] But his insistence on restricting his analysis to classifying organisational 'outputs' in terms of postulated and tautological societal 'needs' leads him to ignore, as many other organisational writers have done, the relationship between organisational structure and function and the patterns of interests and domination within the surrounding 'social system'. An omission which is a systematic product of his employment of the systems approach. It is better to remember, as Perrow remarks, that organisations reflect and reveal societal resources and interests. Organisations, Perrow remarks, are tools that some few people use to impose their '. . . definition of the proper affairs of men upon other men. The man who controls an organisation has power that goes far beyond that of those who do not have such control. The power of the rich lies not in their ability to buy goods and services, but in their capacity to control the ends towards which the vast resources of large organisations are directed'.[14]

Perrow's view is exceptional, however. A genuinely sociological approach to organisations which investigates the relationship between societal forms and their attendant structures of interests, domination and values and the design of work and control systems within large scale employing organisations, has found little appeal within established organisation theory, for three main reasons.

Firstly, the popularity and pervasiveness of systems thinking — of various sorts — has resulted in a form of organisation theory, with its related concepts, which is at least indifferent, if not antithetical, to the approach under discussion. The deficiencies of the systems approach have been well rehearsed by Silverman.[15] The confusion of the prescriptive and the descriptive is particularly important in this connection, since the prescriptive ingredient, coming as it is likely to from those who own or run the organisation, will minimise the approach discussed here and exaggerate the rôle of societally necessary organisational goals in determining the internal structure and process of organisations. As Benson remarks: '. . . the participants' explanations for the structure of the organisation have been formalised as scientific theories'.[16] The problems with the 'goal-oriented' approach have been reviewed elsewhere.[17] Similarly, while it is true that the systems approach is not entirely blind to the existence of conflict within organisations, it exaggerates the degree of consensus, and conceptualises the origins of intra-organisational struggle in excessively parochial, i.e. internal, organisational, terms.

Secondly, and relatedly, much thinking on organisations has employed not only as a desirable end-state but as an explanatory variable, the concept of *efficiency*. Clearly this concept is particularly appropriate within a systems setting. Frequently, typologies of organisations employ, explicitly or implicitly, the concept efficiency as a necessary causal link between a certain state of the postulated independent variable and the related organisational type. It is because certain organisational forms are more *efficient* under the conditions in question, so the argument goes, that the observed or claimed variation in organisational structures occurs. The importance of efficiency in analyses of organisations has a number of drawbacks. Firstly, the concept of efficiency is insufficiently explained and defined (efficient for whom or for what?). Secondly, it demonstrates a preoccupation with managerial issues and problems. As Benson notes,

> According to this problematic, much of what occurs in the organisation is understood as a result of goal pursuit and/or need fulfilment. This view has been coupled with a methodological stance which accepts the conventionally understood components of the organisation as scientific categories. The combination has uncritically accepted existing organisational arrangements and adapted itself to the interests of administrative elites. As a consequence organisational analysis has been dominated by issues of administrative concern.[18]

Thirdly, it reduces curiosity about the determinants of organisational structure, by assuming precisely what needs to be explained — the relationship between organisational forms and dependent variables — and by regarding as causal a connection which may merely be correlation. Rather than assuming such relationships as causal, the sociologist should analyse the nature and origins of such correlations.

The numerous classifications of organisations which demonstrate this reliance on the unexplored notion of organisational efficiency also demonstrate another obstacle to the development of a truly critical, sociological approach to organisations: their constant search for, and measurement of, organisational *variations*, distracts attention from the equally, if not more, important similarities between large scale employing organisations. No doubt it is true that organisations whose prime beneficiaries are their owners and managers differ from organisations that exist to serve the public rather than to make a profit,[19] or that organisations with a technology for processing oil differ from those making precision instruments. But how important are these differences? And what is gained (whose interests are served) by establishing and measuring these variations? It is not to be lost sight of that much as they may differ in detail, there are broad similarities between employing organisations within capitalism. Similarities which can be related to their location within a capitalist economic system.

Thirdly, conventional organisational theory has been resistant to the sort of sociological analysis described here because, paradoxically, of a preoccupation with organisations themselves. The society within which these organisations occur, and its relationship with these organisations, has been studied very little. To the extent that the outside world does impinge on the structure and functioning of organisations, it is conceptualised not as a source of interests, values, class loyalties, ideologies, market developments, etc., but as the organisation's 'environment'. Environment is defined in terms of *senior members'* conceptions of their organisational environment. Environment '. . . is to be considered only in as much as it affects the problems of the organisations, which is to say the problems of those with authority'.[20] Silverman argues for an approach more compatible with a sociological approach to organisational structure: '. . . it would be more fruitful to analyse organisations in terms of the different ends of their members and of their capacity to impose these ends on others — it suggests an analysis in terms of power and authority'.[21] But conventional treatments of organisational environments, far from investigating the significance of class memberships, resources and interests in structuring organisational work and control systems — or resistance to them — prefers to restrict attention, at best, to the rôle of market demands, the behaviour of clients, customers, competitors. Again as Benson has remarked, the significance of extraorganisational structure and functioning has been largely overlooked by most conventional organisational analysis. Certainly some writers have noted that organisations are tools, that they must be analysed in terms of their prime beneficiary, etc., but what is lacking is any serious effort to explain internal organisational structure and process in extra organisational terms. Instead,

> . . . the organisation is assumed to be an instrument designed for a purpose, and research focuses on the structural consequences flowing from that and on the technical adjustments necessary to enhance goal pursuit. The power base of the leadership is not examined; alternative systems based on different power bases are not considered . . . An examination of the power bases of authority figures would generally extend beyond the boundaries of the organisation itself and this is perhaps why most organisation theorists have avoided the problem.[22]

Furthermore, a genuine sociology of organisations is not assisted by the efforts of some organisation analysts to develop hypotheses about organisations *in general,* lumping together such diverse examples as voluntary organisations, charities, political parties and employing organisations.[23] Such an ambition results in generalisations of an extremely high level of abstraction. It also obstructs the analysis of those structural elements which are dramatically revealed in employing organisations (see above) but not necessarily in all forms of organisation. The search for general organisational laws reflects in its findings, the bland assumptions from which it proceeds; that it is in the facts and problems of organisation *per se* (regardless of context or location) that the structural and processual elements of organisations are based.

Allen has remarked on the extent to which models of organisations are underpinned by a 'static' version of reality. He writes: 'The aspect of reality in question, namely organisation activity, can in consequence, be analysed without reference to any factor external to it'.[24] Despite recent theoretical developments, Allen argues, the feature of organisational theory mentioned above persists: organisations are analysed independently of external environmental factors. The emphasis on efficiency as a causal link is an important part of this parochialism. But the conceptualisation of the 'environment' is also crucial.[25] Other recent writers have noted the close links between much organisation theory, its concepts, interests, assumptions — and the interests and 'problems' of senior organisational members.[26]

There are important exceptions to these remarks: some writers on organisations (particularly industrial sociologists) have shown an awareness of the significance of capitalist priorities and values in determining organisational structure and functioning[27] and some writers have distinguished themselves by recognising that 'lower level participants' in organisations are the same people who are known in other sociological specialities as employees or workers;[28] just as occasionally, senior members of organisations, who play such a large part in structuring sociological interest in organisations, as well as the organisations themselves, are seen as the same people who are known elsewhere as members of the ruling class, or their agents.[29] Of particular importance in reflecting a more conscious approach to organisations are two recent publications, both of which have influenced this work.[30]

Nevertheless, the main point remains: on the whole, conventional organisational analysis and theory has ignored the sorts of interests described earlier as constituting a genuinely sociological approach to the design of work and control in large scale employing organisations, despite the useful and important contributions of the early theorists.

WEBER AND MARX AND THE SOCIOLOGY OF ORGANISATIONS

Weber's work on the nature and basis of bureaucracy constitutes an important attempt to categorise the principles which find expression in bureaucracy and their relationship with external, societal, beliefs and principles. Weber's work on bureaucracy is enormously important for the influence it has exerted and the argument it has stimulated, yet certain highly significant features of his work on bureaucracy have tended to be overlooked in the eagerness to discover ambiguities or contradictions in the model, or to assess its empirical validity.

Weber's writings on a particular type of organisation-bureaucracy establish and articulate many of the elements of a genuine sociology of organisations. Firstly, he was concerned not with detailed empirical variations between organisations, but with the overall tendencies and principles which he could discern as being expressed in the ideal-typical bureaucracy. He was prepared to risk empirical inaccuracy in order to attempt a categorisation of dominant features of the phenomenon. This approach has the advantage not only that it facilitates a more ambitious level of theorising about the nature, consequences and functions of bureaucracy in general but also has the merit that it opens up and permits an exploration of the relationship between these general, ideal-typical organisational forms and the society within which they occur.

This is the second sociological element of Weber's approach: it relates the major features of the form of organisation under discussion to developments in society. His analysis of bureaucracy is an integral part of, and cannot be understood except in terms of, his analysis of large scale social developments, especially the process of rationalisation, '. . . the growing precision and explicitness in the principles governing social organisation'.[31]

In relating a specific pattern of control and legitimation within organisations to features of the society within which these bureaucratic organisations occur, Weber develops a level of sociological theorising which is significantly different from the more detailed analyses of intraorganisational variation which have so pre-occupied more recent writers. A surprising number of recent accounts of organisational structure, or classifications of organisational types, pay little, if any, attention to the societal context within which they occur. There is rarely, if ever, any suggestion that large scale organisations might reflect values, priorities or principles from the host society, or that the activity and structure of the organisation can be explained in anything other than neutral, context-free terms — i.e. in terms of the requirements and imperatives of the task and the 'need' to perform it efficiently.

Weber's approach differed radically from such analyses. For Weber, bureaucracy was a form of organisation characterised by particular structures and legitimations of control, a form where rationality was represented in its purest form. He remarks, for example, that the purely bureaucratic form of administrative organisation is formally the most rational known means of carrying out imperative control over human beings.[32] Some have argued that Weber regarded this rationality as synonymous with efficiency, a charge which, if well-founded, would seriously weaken the claim that Weber was one early originator of a genuinely sociological approach to organisations which sees organisational structure not as the outcome of the search for efficiency but in terms of priorities, problems and interests based in the society outside the organisation.

But, as Albrow has remarked[33] the notion that Weber regarded rationality and efficiency as synonymous is highly questionable. Albrow points to the complexity and subtlety of Weber's writings on rationality and demonstrates that Weber defined rationality not in terms of the appropriateness of means to ends but in the application of certain formal principles of administration.[34] To this extent Weber was not concerned to describe efficient organisational structures, but to demonstrate the organisational expression of certain values and ways of thinking current within society. He describes the mutually inter-dependent ideas upon which bureaucratic forms of control and authority depend, as well as specifying the organisational forms taken by a system of thought which was prevalent in the society at large: 'Bureaucracy offers the attitudes demanded by the external apparatus of modern culture in the most favourable combination'.[35]

It is, of course, true that while Weber regards bureaucratic forms of control and organisation as reflections of aspects of modern culture he is clear that such developments are not specific to capitalism, but are part of the process of modernisation. Despite the historical links between capitalism and bureaucracy, Weber saw socialism as even more dependent on bureaucratic forms.[36] Nevertheless, in explaining broad organisational patterns in terms of societal values and priorities rather than in the neutral rhetoric of the organisations themselves, Weber made an important contribution to a genuine sociology of organisations.

However, if Weber established the broad parameters for a sociology of organisations, it is Marx who supplied the ingredients for a critical sociology of organisations. Marx's contribution stems from two somewhat disparate sources: his work on state bureaucracy and his analysis of the relationship between capitalism and the design of work.

The first of these discussions has been accorded considerable attention because of its theoretical and political significance. The analysis of the nature and function of bureaucracy constitutes a central controversy within Marxist thought and one which divided the early Marxist writers and politicians.[37] Marx's major interest in bureaucracy was limited to state administrative bureaucracies. For him these structures were, under capitalism, instruments of class rule and oppression: the administrative apparatus is a part of the State, and the State is class-based, an expression of class interests. What then, of bureaucracy under socialism? Marx asserts the necessity for the proletariat to 'smash' the established 'state edifice', not simply perfect it, but does not present a single unambiguous statement of the role and nature of bureaucracy under socialism.[38] As Eldridge and Crombie put it: Marx does not supply a clear answer to the question '. . . how in organisational terms is the proletariat to proceed?'[39] These authors suggest that Marx saw a number of options, depending on local circumstances, and they note that the important debate within Marxism concerning the nature and organisation of the Party and its relation to working class consciousness constitutes an expression of Marx's discussion of the nature of political organisations and bureaucracies.[40] The two major axes of the debate are represented by Luxembourg's emphasis on the spontaneous *emergence* of the Party from the experiences and struggles of the working class on the one hand and Lenin's insistence on the need for a limited organisation of professional revolutionaries, the revolutionary vanguard, on the other.

Lenin's views on the nature and origins of hierarchy, and control within organisations in general are developed in *The State and Revolution*. In this work his remarks are not restricted to party or state bureaucracies, but refer to general issues of organisation — the inevitability of hierarchy, the possibility of democracy within organisations, etc. In this work Lenin argues for the necessity for destroying previous, capitalist, state bureaucratic machinery, but asserts the need for the workers to administer the state themselves:

> 'From the moment all members of society, or even only the vast majority, have learned to administer the state *themselves,* they have taken this work into their own hands, . . . from this moment the need for governments of any kind begins to disappear . . . The more democratic the ''state'' which consists of the armed workers, and which is ''no longer a state in the proper sense of the word'', the more rapidly does every form of state begin to wither away'.[41]

Lenin was clear that discipline, hierarchy and control were necessary in a socialist society. He is scornful in his attack on the 'anti-authoritarians', and quotes with approval Engels's remarks on the need for hierarchy and co-ordination,

> 'Take a factory, a railway, a ship on the high sea, said Engels — is it not clear that not one of these complex technical establishments, based on the employment of machinery and the planned cooperation of many people, could function without a certain amount of subordination, and, consequently, without a certain amount of *authority or power?*'[42]

Under socialism this necessary domination and control is practised differently however — officials would be elected and liable to dismissal and their level of reward would not exceed that of ordinary workers.[43]

It is clear that this debate about the nature and origins of state bureaucracies within Marx's work, and amongst Marxists, is of relevance to a more general sociology of large scale organisations. Firstly, the debate considers the relationship between organisational structure (in this case bureaucratic structure) and societal types. A major area of interest is to what extent bureaucratic structures as they occur within Capitalism would, or should, be necessary under Socialism. It is with reference to this issue that Marx, Engels and later Lenin use the example of the Paris Commune to stress how existing bureaucratic structures must be destroyed and replaced by new forms of administrative structure:

'From the very outset the Commune was compelled to recognise that the working class, once come to power, could not go on managing with the old state machine: . . . this working class must, on the one hand, do away with the old repressive machinery previously used against itself, and on the other, safeguard itself against its own deputies and officials, by declaring them all without exception subject to recall at any moment'.[44]

In short, traditional bureaucratic forms are seen as inherently opposed to socialist priorities and as intrinsically oriented towards capitalist interests and values.

Secondly, the Marxists in their discussion of the optimum and necessary relationship between the party and the working class, can be seen to be involved in a discussion which has direct and obvious implications for more general explorations of organisational structures which build on, and emerge from, *members'* needs and interests but which do not rigidify into permanent structures of privilege and hierarchy, i.e. the debate about participation and democracy within organisations.

Thirdly, the Marxist approach to bureaucracy makes the highly pertinent point that bureaucratic activity, which is presented as above politics, as neutral, expert administration, is essentially and irredeemably political. The state itself, which is usually seen as '. . . an organ for the *reconciliation* of classes'[45] is in fact an organ of class rule. Because it is political, it must be smashed and replaced. This point needs particular emphasis, since by its very nature, bureaucracy is not only political in its activity and structure, it is also mystifying — presenting itself, and being seen as, beyond interests and sectional priorities, as mere administration. In pointing to the ideological nature of such notions and justifications of organisational structure and activity, and to the political implications of certain organisational forms Marx was establishing some of the essential elements of a radical sociology of organisations.

Finally, the debate touches on the question of the determinants of organisational structure, in that Marx and other Marxists attempted to separate the degree of control, hierarchy and coordination that stemmed from the nature of the task or technology, from that which followed from the capitalist nature of the organisation, or its activities. This remains a highly significant area of debate. As we shall see it is one that Marx gave more comprehensive attention to in his treatment of the relationship between work and capitalism.

Marx's analysis of the nature and role of the division of labour which is highly relevant to this analysis demonstrates considerable development from his early writings in the *Economic and Philosophical Manuscripts* to his more thorough and mature writings in *Capital*. It is his later writings that are most pertinent to this analysis. Marx maintains that the nature of capitalism has direct and unavoidable consequences for the division of labour and the structure of employing organisations. This follows from two interrelated features of capitalism. Under capitalism, labour *power* is purchased by the employer in order to achieve profit. Labour power is a commodity, a factor of production, to be used profitably. The employment relationship is determined by the employer's search for profit and the forces of the market. It is this that supplies the 'rationality' of capitalism and the 'rationality' of organisational structure and process.

By 'labour power' Marx refers to the 'aggregate of those mental and physical capabilities existing in a human being, which he exercises whenever he produces a use-value of any description'.[46] The significant aspect of this emphasis on labour *power* rather than mere labour itself is that it points to the crucial significance of management, direction, and control. If it is a potential, or capacity that is purchased by the employer, then it is necessary to organise, direct and design the way in which the potential is realized. The labourer, or employee, no longer, under capitalism, sells his labour incorporated in a commodity, but his labour power as a commodity. As

Marx notes, in order to sell commodities (other than labour power itself) the employer must have ownership or control of the other necessary factors of production — raw materials, capital, etc.

Secondly, the purchaser of labour power buys it to *use* it, to achieve profit. This has one crucial implication — the conflict of interest between the employee who sells his labour power and the employer who purchases and uses it in order to realise, and maximise, surplus value from it. The interests of employee and employer are inherently and essentially in conflict. It is these two features of work in capitalism which determine the structure and nature of the division of labour in capitalist societies. It is from these two features of capitalism: the purchase of labour power by the employer in order to achieve profit; that two basic features of the nature and design of work under capitalism derive. Firstly, '. . . the labourer works under the control of the capitalist to whom his labour belongs: the capitalist taking good care that the work is done in a proper manner . . .'[47] Secondly, '. . . the product is the property of the capitalist and not that of the labourer, its immediate producer . . . from his (the capitalist's) point of view, the labour-process is nothing more than the consumption of the commodity purchased, i.e., of labour power'.[48]

As a result, the design of work, and of organisations, reveals one highly significant feature which has considerable influence over a variety of organisational processes: the search for greater efficiency is inherently sectional, or political, irredeemably interrelated and involved with the search for more reliable and efficient forms of *control* and exploitation. Control, efficiency (from the employer's point of view) and exploitation become inseparable. Because, in capitalism, the organisation of work involves the purchase and use of labour potential for the achievement of profit for the owner — or his agents (thereby establishing a systematic conflict of interest between employer and employee) — the work of the employees must be strictly directed and coordinated; and since their commitment must be uncertain they must be exposed to constant discipline and surveillance by members of the organisation specially delegated to the task. As Marx puts it:

> The directing motive, the end and aim of capitalist production, is to extract the greatest possible amount of surplus-value, and consequently to exploit labour-power to the fullest possible extent. As the number of cooperating labourers increases, so too does their resistance to the domination of capital, and with it the necessity for capital to overcome this resistance by counter-pressure. The control exercised by the capitalist is not only a special function, due to the nature of the social labour-process, and peculiar to that process, but it is, at the same time, a function of the exploitation of a social labour-process, and is consequently rooted in the unavoidable antagonism between the exploiter and the living and labouring raw material he exploits.[49]

This interdependence and coincidence of efficiency and control has implications for a number of aspects of organisational structure and process; the three most important are: the degree and extent of the division of labour, the use of machinery, and technology, and the role of management. Each of these deserves attention.

For Marx the division of labour under capitalism demonstrated certain characteristic features directly related to the elements of capitalism described above. Under capitalism there is a tendency for the work of the employees, for the mass of the work force, to be de-skilled, for labour to be cheapened, to be reduced to the frequent repetition of a small number of processes or activities. Capitalism, writes Marx, revolutionises work, by converting the '. . . labourer into a crippled monstrosity, by forcing his detail dexterity at the expense of a world of productive capabilities and instincts'.[50] Discretion and skill are concentrated in a few employees, and systematically and purposively denied the rest — 'Intelligence in production expands in one direction, because it vanishes in many others. What is lost by the detail labourers, is concentrated in the capital that employs them'.[51] And this 'lordship of capital over labour' increases the productive power of labour at the expense of the employees concerned and serves to dominate and subjugate as it exploits. Marx is quite clear that under capitalism the extreme division of labour which involves the large scale de-skilling of jobs, and the consequent separation of hand and brain work — the former concerned with detailed execution of procedures designed by the latter — serves the goals of productivity, discipline and control. Even the concept of efficiency itself must be seen to contain ineradicably political — i.e. class — elements and interests, despite the efforts of the employers and their ideologies to present the division of labour and the objectives it serves as beyond politics or class, as aspects of an inevitable and desirable search for a generally beneficial level of efficiency and productivity. It is critical to stress, Marx writes, that 'Division of labour within the workshop implies the undisputed authority of the capitalist over men, that are but parts of a mechanism that belongs to him'.[52]

The class-based, political aspects of the structure of organisations and the division of labour also extend to Marx's analysis of the role and consequences of machinery in employing organisations. Machinery raises the degree of exploitation of labour; it also serves to cheapen and de-skill labour. Just as the extreme division of labour reduces the autonomy and skill of the mass of the employees while enabling control and direction to be concentrated in the hand of a small minority of the owners, or their agents, so the installation and use of machinery reduces skills, concentrates work decisions and permits a division of employees into '. . . workmen who are actually employed on machines (among whom are included a few who look after the engine) and into mere attending (almost exclusively children) of these workmen'.[53] An important consequence of the use of machinery (and of the extreme sub-division of labour) is the easy transferability of labour — 'Since the motion of the whole system does not proceed from the workman, but from the machinery, a change of persons can take place at any time without an interruption of the work'.[54]

The use of machinery also has implications for the employer's capacity to control and dominate the work force — as well as to regulate and direct it. Marx notes the role of machinery in strike breaking, and in facilitating the concentration of organisational decision-taking:

> . . . capital, in its true development, combines mass labour with skill, but in such a way that the former loses its physical power, and the skill resides not in the worker as a whole but in the machine and in the scientific combination of both as a whole in the factory.[55]

Marx's argument that the design of work and the use of machinery in large scale organisations can only be seen in terms of the employer's efforts to direct the labour power he purchases to cheapen labour and to achieve ever greater profits also applies to his analysis of the role of management. If, on the one hand, there is discernible a '. . . tendency to equalise and reduce to one and the same level everything that has to be done by the minders of the machines'[56] there is also a resultant expansion of the coordinating, supervising and controlling functions of management. The two processes are mutually interlocked: the 'mere appendage' can only play his part in a capitalist environment with the direction and supervision of management.

Marx does not claim that all management and coordination stems from the exigencies and elements of capitalism. He recognises that:

> All combined labour on a large scale requires, more or less, a directing authority, in order

to secure the harmonious working of the individual activities, and to perform the general functions that have their origin in the action of the combined organism, as distinguished from the action of the separate organs. A single violin player is his own conductor; an orchestra requires a separate one.[57]

However, he stresses that under capitalism management necessarily does more than merely coordinate and integrate the activities of those collectively involved in a cooperative activity. Under capitalism, management takes on new functions, functions which follow from the class nature of the employment relationship, and which are reflected in the class-based antagonisms between the detail labourer and the manager. Under capitalism, management works to ensure a satisfactory level of profitability and to increase it, to impose and maintain discipline on those whose labour is being used, to direct and determine their work activities and to regulate the speed and nature of their work operations, the standard of their work, etc. Capitalism, he writes, requires managers, as an army requires officers, to command in the name of the capitalist. The formal power of the manager comes not from the technical functions he serves but from his position as employer — or as agent of the employer. The form of organisation characteristic of capitalism — with its division of members into 'hand' and 'brain' workers, the former reduced to detailed operations, the latter allocated control, design, supervisory and coordinating functions — is not an inevitable or neutral phenomenon. It is '. . . a method employed by capital for the more profitable exploitation of labour, by increasing that labour's productiveness'.[58]

Despite the obvious differences between Marx's and Weber's approach to and analysis of large scale organisations, these two theorists can be seen to share certain interests in organisations, to ask similar questions of them and to focus attention on similar processes. These areas of common interest represent the basic parameters of a truly sociologic approach to organisations, an approach which has recently shown signs of re-emergence.

First, both theorists were concerned with describing and explaining general principles and features of organisational structure. They were more interested in the broad tendencies demonstrated by and within employing organisations than with small scale intra-organisational variations. This focus of interest makes them vulnerable to criticisms, from the less ambitious, empirically-minded student of organisations, that their models of organisations, or the processes isolated, show greater empirical variation than they seemed to appreciate. This line of attack is particularly common in recent American reactions to Weber's ideal type of bureaucracy.[59] Such criticisms miss the point. In drawing attention to certain basic features of large scale organisations (for Weber the elaborate, detailed and formal specification of authorities and responsibilities, supported by formal, 'bureaucratic' authority; for Marx the division between detail, 'hand' employees who execute procedures designed, controlled and coordinated by management — the 'brain' workers) both theorists are not only emphasising common and striking features of modern employing organisations (albeit features which may, in fact, demonstrate some degree of variability), they are also isolating those elements of large scale organisation which are *theoretically* significant, in terms of their theory of employing organisations in society. For both Marx and Weber their conceptualisation of organisation can only be understood in terms of their theoretical assessment of, and approach to, the nature and function of large scale organisations in modern, or capitalist society. To forget this leads to the sort of excessive, directionless empiricism which characterises much organisational analysis.

The second feature follows from the first. Both theorists sought to *understand* the major feature of organisational structures. Their explanations eschewed the available justifications and explanations of organisational analysis in terms of a neutral, apolitical conception of efficiency and replaced rhetoric with analysis. For both Marx and Weber the major elements of the structure of modern large scale organisations stem from the efforts of those who own, manage or design the organisation to achieve control over the members. For both writers the structure of modern organisations can only be understood in terms of control for sectional interests. For Weber, bureaucracy, which is not restricted to government administration, but is a *type* of organisation which is '. . . in principle applicable with equal facility to a wide variety of different fields',[60] depends on, and reflects in its structure and its process, the acceptance of certain ideas about the legitimacy of rational-legal control and power. Bureaucracy must be seen in terms of the form of authority which prevails in it and which determines, and is reflected in, bureaucratic structure. He remarks: 'Bureaucratic administration means fundamentally the exercise of control on the basis of knowledge'.[61] Weber's analysis is useful for emphasising the centrality of control and the importance, to senior members, of achieving ideological justification for the structure and function of the organisation.

For Marx the structure of modern employing organisations, and the design of work within them, characterised by extremes of sub-division and specialisation — the creation of 'detail' work — must be seen as a result of the capitalist's efforts to direct and coordinate the labour power of his employees to achieve profit: 'Division of labour within the workshop implies the undisputed authority of the capitalist over men, that are but parts of a mechanism that belongs to him'.[62]

Both writers insist, as noted, on the close relationship between 'efficiency' as defined by senior organisational members and processes of organisational control — an instance which has been largely forgotten, but which is evident in their analyses of many aspects of organisational design, structure and activity. Marx points to the control implications of management structures and of automation and technology. Weber notes the control functions of bureaucratic regulations, personnel and selection procedures, career structures, etc. Whereas many modern organisational analysts and researchers are prepared to regard these various aspects of organisations as discrete processes or elements which coalesce in various patterned forms as a result of pressures for efficiency (a concept which most writers regard with insufficient scepticism), Marx and Weber, in their delineation of a genuine sociology of organisations emphasised that *no* acceptable understanding of any feature of organisations — and especially those features which they saw as most typical and significant — could be achieved unless it proceeded from the realisation that organisations are, quintessentially, structures of control and domination, and that this control, and the goals it serves, are surrounded by ideological activity which strives to mask or neutralise the political nature of organisations by reference to generally acceptable values and ways of thinking — e.g. rationality, efficiency, etc.

But if organisations are structures of control, what is this control for? What interests or purposes are served by bureaucratisation, or minute sub-division and specialisation of work? And what efforts are made to legitimise these structures? It is a third common element in Marx and Weber's sociology of organisations that they both emphasised the necessity of seeing organisational structure and activity in terms of their social context, or their relationship with society.

It is clear that the two writers differed in their conception of the relationship with societal interests and values. For Marx, large scale employing organisations reflected capitalist priorities and sectional, class interests not merely in their activity, but in their structure. He was at pains to discuss the relationship between the division of labour within organisations, the nature, function, and size of management, and the design and use of technology and capitalism. While conceding that some degree of division and specialisation of labour was evident in pre-capitalist societies, he stressed that the extremes of specialisation and differentiation occurred under capitalism as a result of the priorities of the capitalist and the relationship with the employees — '. . . the most diverse division of labour in the workshop, as practiced by manufacture, is a special creation of the capitalist mode of production alone'.[63]

Weber too regarded the major elements of bureaucracy as significantly influenced by capitalism, and notes that modern capitalism '. . . strongly tends to foster the development of bureaucracy'.[64] But he argued that both socialism and capitalism rely upon bureaucratic organisations in numerous spheres — armies, governments, administrative agencies, economic enterprises, etc. For Weber, bureaucracy was not a feature of capitalism only, but was a key feature of the modern world, a world dominated by rationality. It was in their emphasis on rationality that bureaucratic organisations reflected key features of modern (as against capitalist) society.

But if Marx and Weber differed in their assessment of the most significant feature of modern organisations and their analysis of the societal roots and causation of such elements, they agreed in firmly locating their reorganisational analyses in terms of societal variables and the interests and purposes of those who own or run the organisations. 'The question is', remarks Weber, 'who controls the existing bureaucratic machinery?' For 'the bureaucratic apparatus is driven to continue functioning by the most powerful interests which are material and objective but also ideal in character'.[65] Similarly, their organisational analyses are firmly placed in their societal analyses and their discussions of processes of legitimation and mystification, although their assessment of the pertinent societal features differs.

In short, despite their differences, both Marx and Weber in their sociology of organisations isolated and emphasised those key elements in the structure of large scale organisations which were of most significance to their theoretical interest in processes of control and legitimation within organisations and the relationship between organisational structure and process and societal values and interests. Both stressed that organisational structure — the design of work and control — can only be seen in terms of general processes of organisational control initiated by, and in the interests of, those who ran or dominated the organisation. And both saw the purposes of organisations (or of those who dominated them) and the structures of work and control to which they gave rise, as reflecting more general processes, cultures, interests and priorities in the society at large. They firmly rejected the widely prevalent view that organisational structure follows from the application of neutral, apolitical priorities — such as efficiency, technology, etc. — and insisted that such concepts should be exposed for their political purposes and assumptions, and focused attention on the nature and function of organisational ideologies. These are the ingredients of a genuine sociology of organisations.

THE SOCIOLOGY OF ORGANISATION

It is possible to see various recent publications in industrial sociology and organisational analysis as containing some — or all — of these elements of such a sociology of organisations. Some of these writers clearly would not accept wholeheartedly the perspective outlined above; nevertheless their work does contribute to a genuine sociology of organisations.

Such work shows a major area of common interest: the description and analysis of organisational structure and the division and design of organisational work in terms of the societal context within which these organisations occur. This, for most writers, leads to a concern to consider organisational structure not as a response to neutral problems of efficiency, administration and technology, but as a result of the need to resolve problems of *control*. It sees organisational structure as a response to the problems, priorities and philosophies of senior organisational members, whose power — or authority — is backed up by, and based upon, extra-organisational resources and ideologies. It regards the goals of organisations as sectional and conflictful, and '. . . takes the rationalised organisation as an arbitrary model unevenly imposed upon events and insecure its hold'.[66] Such an approach relates organisational events and conflicts to extra-organisational interests and resources and goes beyond organisational definitions of organisational structure and process by investigating the nature of organisational ideologies of all sorts and their role in justifying or disguising organisational realities, including their representation in varieties of so-called organisation theory.

Recent analyses of the relationship between organisational structure and the division and design of organisational work and societal interests and values has occurred within both industrial and organisational sociology. Fox in an important work has sought to '. . . explore fundamental principles implicitly informing the ways in which men organise, regulate, and reward themselves for the production and distribution of goods and services, and the significance of these principles for their wider social relations'.[67] He finds that the major axis of job variation is discretion — trust — and argues that the design and distribution of 'high' and 'low' discretion organisational roles cannot be understood except in terms of class interests and class assumptions. His point is not simply that high and low discretion jobs (the latter being those to which the principles of Taylorism have been applied) tend to generate the very responses which are assumed in their design and allocation, but also that the proliferation of low trust jobs — and the problems this generates — is a systematic feature of capitalist society. In the concluding sections, Fox notes that no significant change in organisational structure can occur without drastic societal changes. In a later publication he goes further and argues for an even closer link between job discretion at work and capitalist assumptions, values and interests.[68]

The distinction Fox draws between the division of organisational work into high and low discretion jobs is a useful one. It parallels Marx's distinction between design and execution in work. The same distinction has been noted by a large number of writers on organisations as Hickson has pointed out.[69]

It is important to appreciate, as Deutsch emphasises, that this distinction between mental and manual labour is not apparent only in the organisation of work within manufacturing organisations with their explicit application of scientific management principles. It is also the keystone of bureaucratic organisation — 'The roots of bureaucracy . . . show themselves at the moment when the primitive community divides into the leaders and the led, the organisers and the organised, into the managers and the managed'.[70] The basic factor which is exemplified in bureaucracy, Deutsch continues, is '. . . the division of labour between intellectual work and manual labour, the gulf between the organisers and the organised. This contradistinction is in fact the prologue to class society'.[71]

The point about this distinction however is not simply that it is empirically significant in various organisational forms, but that it is critical in any understanding of the relationship between the structure of organisations and the design of organisational work and the capitalist nature of the society within which they occur. This point has been best made by Braverman. In his important work, *Labor and Monopoly*

Capital, Braverman argues that the major features of the division of labour within employing organisations — including office organisations and white collar employees — demonstrate a cheapening and degradation of work — a separation of the work of design and conceptualisation from the work of execution. Braverman argues that under capitalism, with labour power a commodity to be used profitably by the employer, it is natural for the employer to divide and sub-divide work, in a way that '. . . polarises those whose time is infinitely valuable and those whose time is worth almost nothing. This might even be called the general law of the capitalist division of labour'.[72] This law is represented in the 'principles' — and application — of Taylorism.[73] Braverman's main thesis is that organizational structure, and the design of organisational work, reveal, directly, the priorities, interests and 'problems' of capitalism. In particular the principles and practice of scientific management coincide with a number of fundamental changes in the structure and functioning of capitalism.

The same conception of organisational structure is presented in books by Beynon, and Nicholas and Armstrong.[74] These writers see the design of work and of organisational processes generally, as part of the continuing effort of management to direct, cheapen, and dominate the labour power of their innately recalcitrant employees. Under capitalism, these authors note, echoing Marx, the organisation of work, and the design of organisations generally, reflect the efforts of the managers to control the labour of their employees. This control, the form it takes and the goals it seeks, are intimately connected with capitalist priorities and problems.

Under capitalism, organisation necessarily requires a high degree of supervision, direction, co-ordination and surveillance; much greater than that necessitated by the fact of large scale co-operative endeavour *per se*. The result: '. . . the organisation of industry with all its complexities and diversities, ultimately revolves on a single process: the administrative process through which the employees' effort is controlled by the employer'.[75] This control may be achieved through a wide variety of mechanisms, some of which have been exposed by more conventional organisational analysts.

It is not only the design of work and the structure and distribution of organisational responsibilities and duties which have been analysed in terms of the inevitable problems and priority (in capitalism) of control and direction. Such analysis has also been applied to other aspects of organisational structure and functioning which have, traditionally, been presented as being concerned simply with neutral, apolitical questions of organisational efficiency and rationality — technology and management. The first of these — technology — is particularly important since within conventional organisational analysis, technology is frequently seen as a major determinent of organisational structure (see below).

The sociological analysis of organisational technology does not reject the argument from efficiency, but insists on asking not only whose interests are served by such efficiency, but on emphasising that within capitalism notions of efficiency can only be seen in terms of capitalist priorities, problems and interest. Gorz has noted that '. . . the capitalist division of labour is functional to a system that rests on forced labor and that therefore relies only on regimentation and hierarchical control, not on the workers' consent or cooperation'.[76] And Edwards makes a similar point when he argues that,

> Bureaucratic organisation promotes efficiency or rationality only within the context of managerial control. Bureaucratic organisation, with its reliance on multiple levels of authority and supervision and its emphasis on discipline and predictability, is probably the only way of ensuring efficient production using alienated labour.[77]

It is in this highly partial and political sense that the design, installation and selection of technology can be seen to be efficient: that it maximises the profitability of labour and intensifies the employer's control over the amount and direction of the employee's work activity, while cheapening labour. Technology means control. Technological innovation, as Dickson puts it, is a *management* technique. Or, as expressed by Braverman, '. . . machinery offers to management to do by wholly mechanical means that which it had previously attempted to do by organisational and disciplinary means'.[78]

A number of important recent works have stressed the political, i.e. sectional, implications of organisational technology and asserted the ideological status of these forms of organisation theory which see technology as the result of necessary, indeed inevitable, organisational application of scientific or mechanical innovations and achievements.[79] Also highly relevant to this debate are the arguments of Davis and Taylor, who on the basis of an extensive review of the evidence concerning 'structural and organisational behavioral concomitants of technology' conclude that '. . . there is considerable flexibility in the design of technology, which challenges the widely accepted notion of technological determinism'. And add that choices of technology are based on 'social system values and psychosocial assumptions'. It is worth quoting these authors' conclusions fully:

> Hypotheses held about the nature of man embedded within a technical system are operationalised in the design of the system . . . when the assumptions are held that a system is comprised of reliable technical elements and unreliable social elements, then in order to provide total system reliability, the technical design must call for parts of people as replaceable machine elements to be regulated by the technical system or by a superstructure of personal control.[80]

Clearly under capitalism such hypotheses about the nature of man are likely to take the form described by Fox, i.e., that 'lower level' working class employees are unreliable, bloody minded and of little personal consequence or value.

This same approach has been applied to the functions of organisational experts and managers. Their function has been seen not as a necessary feature of large scale organisation *per se* but of the exigencies and problems of such organisation in capitalism. A number of interrelated points have been made connecting the nature and function of managerial, administrative and expert members of organisations to the essentially capitalist nature of large scale organisations in capitalism. Works by Beynon, Nichols and Armstrong argue that management efforts to maintain and justify their 'right to manage' stem from the need, under capitalism, constantly to direct and dominate labour in terms of capitalist 'rationality' and the 'problems' and 'exigencies' that this subsumes: market fluctuations, motivational problems, pressure from head-office, etc.

Fox has contributed to this interpretation of management level organisational positions. He points out that different organisational positions — high versus low discretion jobs — reveal class-based assumptions about the nature, capacity, intelligence and reliability of the people concerned. He notes that such assumptions tend to be self-fulfilling, but emphasises the final location of these ideas, this knowledge, in the society outside the organisation. Similarly, the distribution of discretion in work and other more tangible work rewards and deprivations demonstrates and constitutes class inequalities at work. Particularly since, as Braverman and others, following Marx, have noted, the creativity and decision-making features of some organisational rôles are directly at the expense of repetitious, low-discretion work.

A genuine sociology of organisations will not take the existence and function of managers, technicians, administrators and experts as given which owe their existence simply to the exigencies of modern industrialism and to their own intelligence and achievements[81] but must consider the following questions, listed by Gorz:

> (1) (a) Is their function required by the process of material production *as such?* or (b) by capital's concern for ruling and for controlling the productive process from above? (2) (a) Is their function required by the concern for the greatest possible efficiency in production technology? or (b) does the concern for efficient production technology come second only to the concern for "social technology," i.e., for keeping the labour force disciplined, hierarchically regimented and divided? (3) (a) Is the present definition of technical skill and knowledge primarily required by the technical division of labour and thereby based upon scientific and ideologically neutral data? or (b) is the definition of technical skill and knowledge primarily social and ideological, as an outgrowth of the social division of labour?[82]

Gorz himself argues that the function of technical workers is only explicable in terms of capitalist priorities, and that their rôle is basically technical and ideological, i.e. concerned with maintaining the hierarchical structure of capitalist organisations and with ensuring that the maximum of surplus value is extracted and that control is achieved.

A broadly similar analysis of the rôle of management has been presented by Marglin.[83] The point here however is not simply to repeat the arguments of these and other radical analysts of the role of management and technical functions in organisations within capitalism but to stress the questions posed above by Gorz, that initiate these or any other form of sociology of organisations: questions which are strikingly absent in most conventional organisational analysis, where management rhetoric all too often passes for sociological analysis.

There are however some exceptions to this view. The conventional approach to organisational structure sees it as an inexorable consequence of some determinant variable — frequently technology. The choice of technology is, in turn, the result of the search for efficiency, as dictated by organisational rationality, objectives, work processes and products, etc. In this view, technology and organisational structure, are placed beyond debate or possibility of alteration, and are seen as inevitable and inexorable consequences of the organisation's need for efficiency within the constraints of product, market, work process, etc. Fox has stated this view succinctly:

> This conventional view sees the existing design of work and job patterns, along with their profound differences of discretion, autonomy, opportunities for personal growth and fulfillment, and all the associated class and status differences . . . as having been "created" by the scientific technological and organisational advances of the continuing Industrial Revolution . . . this technological and organisational thrust, developing in response to what was "necessary" or "appropriate" to the "demands" of the prevailing economic conditions, is in itself neutral.[84]

This view has been attacked on a number of fronts, by Fox and others. First, the relationship between technology and organisational structure may not be as tight as some writers have argued.[85] Secondly such relationships as do exist between technology and organisational structure may be correlational as much as causal. Organisational structure *and* technology may be chosen together as part of some overall strategy. Argyris, for example, remarks: 'The formal organisation is a cognitive strategy about how the designers intend the rôle to be played, given the nature of human beings'.[86] Or as Davis and Taylor remark on the basis of their empirical investigations, 'There are choices available based on social systems values and assumptions . . . nearly all technology is designed by exercising certain assumptions about people and work'.[87] Thirdly, and most significantly, even if technology — or other factors — are important as determinants of organisational structure, the sociologist who studies organisations should not regard the existence and nature of these determinant variables as universal givens, as emerging inexorably from the norm of efficiency or rationality. As Child has emphasised in an important paper, the dominant coalition within an organisation can make choices covering such things as '. . . the context within which the organisation is operating, to the standards of performance against which the pressure of economic constraints has to be evaluated, and to the design of the organisation's structure itself'.[88] In short, organisational structure, and the various so-called determinant variables, represent in structural or technological form, the preferences, priorities and indeed philosophies of those who own or run the organisation. These choices reflect current ideologies and the continuing priority of achieving organisational control.

A genuine sociology of organisations as presented in the relevant works of Weber and Marx would not stop with investigations or organisational structures, technology and the rôle of managements and experts. It would also cover various other topics, such as the nature and function of personnel practices and procedures, mechanisms of management control, the impact of organisational experience on members' attitudes and aspirations, and the nature and rôle of organisational ideologies. The significance of a sociological approach lies not in its subject matter but in its replacements of organisational statements, conceptualisations and explanations by a search for the real principles and priorities which lie behind and are revealed in, organisations, and their location and origin within the larger society.[89]

There is evidence that such an approach to organisations is finally developing and is mounting an increasingly effective critique of conventional organisation theory. Contributors to this 'critical' sociology of organisations are not members of a cohesive 'school' or movement; and their contributions display significant differences. Nevertheless, their contributions demonstrate certain elements and shared interests.

Elger, in an important paper, presents a systematic and thorough account of '. . . processes through which participants in industrial organisations, sustain and transform the patterns of social relations in which they are implicated and which constitute the organisation . . .'[90] This approach sees organisational structure as the emergent product of processes of conflict, negotiation, domination, resistance and acquiescence. The 'given-ness' and fixity of organisational structure is replaced by an emphasis on the emergent nature of organisational structure. Such an emphasis, though important, is not new, and Elger's article contains a thorough review of other organisational studies which have argued, or assumed, this approach. Where Elger's analysis is particularly important, however, is in its insistence that organisational structure must be seen in terms of conflict and struggle between organisational groups; that organisational goals, objectives, rationalities and structures are ideological. And that '. . . substantial resources buttress particular versions of organisational purpose'.[91] Elger would include much organisation theory as variants of such versions of organisational purpose.

Furthermore, in discussing the ways in which organisational members protect or advance their interests within the organisation, he emphasises the necessity to see such struggles, and the resources and ideologies they can deploy and their likelihood of achieving final success, in terms of the groups' positions not only within the organisation, but in the society at large. He remarks, for example,

The manner in which such "organisational objectives" as production plans or payment policies, designed by top management and mediated through the activities of middle-managers, are implemented on the shopfloor is an outcome of interaction between managers commanding resources buttressed by legal and customary prerogatives and workers commanding resources which flow from the character of their labour.[92]

In a recent article, Benson has also criticized conventional organisation theory for its preoccupation with senior members' definitions and problems, its uncritical acceptance of organisational structures, as inevitable and necessary, following the organisation's pursuit of desirable social goals, etc. Observed correlations between organisational features are presented as inevitable consequences of 'hypothetical social processes', most of them centering on questions of efficiency.

In contrast to this deficient organisation theory, Benson advances what he terms a 'dialectical analysis'. This stems from, but is not 'locked into', a Marxist approach to organisations. Like Elger, Benson emphasizes the processual aspect of organisational structure and functioning, and notes the significance of '. . . powerful forces which tend to occasion the re-production of the existing social structure. These include . . . the interests of particular groups of people and their power to defend their interests within an established order'.[93]

As well as noting the manner in which organisational structures emerge from, or are constructed by, processes of negotiation and struggle within organisations, Benson notes three other features of the dialectic approach: *totality,* which requires a focus on the whole organisation, and its constituent inter-connections; *contradiction,* which refers to the inevitable strains and conflicts contained in, though they may be masked by, apparent organisational stability; and *praxis,* which refers to the potential within organisational members actively to reconstruct their organisational experiences and the structure of the organisation of which they are members. Benson sees a dialectical approach to organisations as contributing to such reconstruction by de-mystifying organisational structure and separating a genuine theory of organisation from the ideologies of senior organisational members. This aspiration, like many of the elements of his approach, he has in common with others whose contributions are considered in this section.

Benson insists that a genuine theory of organisations should reject the common assumption that organisations can be abstracted from their relations with dominant groups, powerful resources, ideological structures, etc., in the surrounding society and be viewed '. . . as if it were autonomous or at least capable of filtering the environment through its input-output orifices'.[94] On the contrary, they must be studied in terms of these relationships with their social contexts. Only then will it be possible for a dialectic approach to consider alternative forms of organisation, alternative designs of work or of control.

A similar critique of established organisation theory has been advanced by Clegg, and Clegg and Dunkerley.[95] These writers also see established organisation theory as defective and misleading; as sharing, in its concepts, assumptions, and theories, the interests of management. In particular they assert the necessity for an organisation theory that 'sees the organisation as structurally embedded within the wider social context'. And they stress the links between the rationality of organisations — as deduced by organisation theorists and organisational spokesmen — and the context and demands of technological capitalism, as well as emphasising the ahistorical and unreflexive nature of conventional organisation theory.

A recent and ambitious article by Heydebrand in a volume of the *Sociological*

Quarterly entitled 'Organisational Analysis: Critique and Innovation' attempts to outline a 'Marxian Theory' of organisations.[96] While noting the ways in which organisation theory has been dominated by ideological forces and has successfully reproduced and legitimised the structure of capitalist society, Heydebrand focuses on the contradictions in organisational structure and process. These contradictions, which occur under both capitalism and state socialism, follow from the efforts to 'rationalise' labour, and to control it — to increase productivity and to retain the commitment (or avoid the alienation) of the work force whose surplus is being appropriated and whose time and lives are being wasted.

Allen's work *Social Analysis,* shares many of the elements outlined above. In the course of a thorough review of a variety of theories of organisation he emphasises that '. . . all the main approaches represent different models within a single analytical framework, and not distinct theories'.[97] The feature common to these theories is precisely that which has repeatedly been mentioned above — that organisation theory emphasises, and focuses on, '. . . the autonomy of organisations so that they could . . . be analysed independently of external environmental factors'.[98] Such preconceptions produce what Allen calls a 'static' conception of organisations, emphasising, celebrating, deriving from, the *status quo.* From such a starting point, the deficiencies noted above follow: organisational analysis, Allen notes, becomes organisational justification.

No doubt other writers could also be included here, but enough has been said to make the major point: conventional organisational analysis, for a number of reasons, demonstrates certain deficiencies and inadequacies, stemming in the main from an inability or unwillingness seriously to consider the relationship between internal organisational structure and process and the society within which the organisation occurs. Such deficiencies are all the more surprising because both Weber and Marx in their various — and very different — writings on organisations, bureaucracy and the division of labour, articulated some basic elements of what has been described here as a genuine sociology of organisations. However some recent publications do suggest a renaissance of interest in these issues, which is apparent in detailed studies of work processes, the rôle of management, in the implications of technology and technocrats, and in more general attempts to develop and justify a sociological approach to organisations. In both cases there is apparent a concern to separate organisational analysis from organisational rhetoric; to see organisational structure and process in relation to the extra-organisational interests, resources and priorities of organisational members, and to uncover and investigate the nature and origin of organisational ideologies.

NOTES

[1] M. Albrow: The Study of Organisations — Objectivity or Bias?', in J. Gould (ed.): *Penguin Social Sciences Survey, 1968,* Penguin Books, Harmondsworth, 1968, pp. 146-67; D. Silverman: *The Theory of Organisations,* Heinemann, London, 1970.

[2] R. Blackburn: 'A Brief Guide to Bourgeois Ideology' in R. C. Edwards, M. Reich and E. Weisskopf (eds.): *The Capitalist System,* Prentice-Hall, New Jersey, 1972, p. 42.

[3] P. Blau, and A. R. Schoenherr: *The Structure of Organisations,* Basic Books, New York, 1971, p. 355.

[4] K. Mannheim: *Ideology and Utopia,* Harcourt Brace, New York, 1936, p. 360.

[5] T. Shroyer: 'Towards a Critical Theory for Advanced Industrial Society' in H. P. Dreitzel (ed.): *Recent Sociology No. 2* Macmillan, New York, 1970, p. 212.

[6] M. Rose: *Industrial Behaviour,* Allen Lane, London, 1975, p. 277.

[7] S. Clegg and D. Dunkerley: *Critical Issues in Organisations,* Routledge & Kegan Paul, London, 1977, p. 3.

[8] ibid.

[9] A. Gouldner: *Patterns of Industrial Bureaucracy,* Free Press, New York, 1954; M. Crozier: *The Bureaucratic Phenomenon,* Tavistock, London, 1964; J. A. Elger: 'Industrial Organisations: a Processual Perspective' in J. B. McKinlay (ed.): *Processing People,* Holt Rinehart and Winston, London, 1975, pp. 91-149; R. Collins: *Conflict Sociology,* Academic Press, London, 1975; Clegg and Dunkerley: op. cit.; K. J. Benson: 'Organisations: A Dialectical View', *Administrative Science Quarterly,* Vol. 22, 1977, pp. 1-21.

[10] R. Brown: 'The Tavistock's Industrial Studies', *Sociology,* Vol. 1, 1967, pp. 33-60.

[11] D. Silverman: op. cit., 1970.

[12] Benson: op. cit., p. 2.

[13] T. Parsons: 'Social Systems' in O. Grusky and A. G. Miller (eds.): *Organisations,* The Free Press, New York, 1970, p. 81.

[14] C. Perrow: *Complex Organisations,* Scott, Foresman and Co., Glenview, Ill., 1972, p. 14.

[15] Silverman: op. cit., 1970.

[16] Benson: op. cit., p. 1.

[17] Silverman: op. cit., 1970; Albrow: op. cit., 1968.

[18] Benson: op. cit., p. 2.

[19] P. Blau and Scott: *Formal Organisations,* Routledge and Kegan Paul, London, 1963.

[20] Silverman: op. cit., 1970, p. 39.

[21] ibid.; see also Elger: op. cit.; Collins: op. cit.; V. L. Allen: *Social Analysis,* Longman, London, 1975; Benson: op. cit.; Clegg and Dunkerley: op. cit.

[22] Benson: op. cit.

[23] See for example, R. Hyman and R. Fryer: 'Trade Unions: Sociology and Political Economy' in McKinlay (ed.): op. cit., pp. 150-213; and Clegg and Dunkerley: op. cit. for support for this view.

[24] Allen: op. cit., p. 89.

[25] Elger: op. cit.

[26] Clegg and Dunkerley: op. cit.

[27] Gouldner: op. cit.

[28] Allen: op. cit.

[29] J. Child: 'Organisational Structure, Environment and Performance', *Sociology,* Vol. 6, No. 1, 1972, pp. 1-22.

[30] Elger: op. cit.; Allen: op. cit.

[31] M. Albrow: *Bureaucracy,* Macmillan, London, 1970, p. 43.

[32] M. Weber: *The Theory of Social and Economic Organisation,* translated by A. M. Henderson and T. Parsons, Free Press, New York, 1964, p. 337.

[33] Albrow: op. cit., 1970, pp. 61-66.

[34] ibid., pp. 63-64.

[35] Weber: op. cit., p. 216.

[36] ibid., pp. 338-339.

[37] Albrow: op. cit., 1970; J. E. T. Eldridge and A. D. Crombie: *A Sociology of Organisations,* Allen and Unwin, London, 1974. N. P. Mouzelis: *Organisation and Bureaucracy,* Routledge and Kegan Paul, London, 1967.

[38] Albrow: op. cit., 1970.

[39] Eldridge and Crombie: op. cit., p. 138.

[40] Eldridge and Crombie: op. cit.

[41] V. I. Lenin: *The State and Revolution,* Foreign Languages Press, Peking, 1965, p. 122.

[42] ibid., p. 73 (my emphasis).

[43] ibid., p. 92.

[44] Engels in Lenin: op. cit., p. 91.

[45] Lenin: op. cit., p. 8.

[46] K. Marx: *Capital,* Vol. 1, Lawrence and Wishart, London, 1954, p. 164.

[47] ibid., p. 180.

[48] ibid.

[49] ibid., p. 313.

[50] ibid., p. 340.

[51] ibid., p. 341.

[52] ibid., p. 336.

[53] ibid., p. 396.

[54] ibid., p. 397.

[55] ibid.

[56] ibid., p. 396.

[57] ibid., p. 313.

[58] ibid., p. 317.

[59] Albrow: op. cit., 1970.

[60] Weber: op. cit. p. 334.

[61] ibid., p. 339.

[62] Marx: op. cit., p. 336.

[63] ibid., p. 339.

[64] Weber: op. cit., p. 339.

[65] ibid., p. 338.

[66] Benson: op. cit., p. 60.

[67] A. Fox: *Beyond Contract: Power and Trust Relations,* Faber and Faber, London, 1974, p. 13.

[68] A. Fox: 'The Meaning of Work' in *People and Work* (DE351), Open University Press, 1976.

[69] D. J. Hickson: 'A Convergence in Organisation Theory', *Administrative Science Quarterly,* No. 11, 1966, pp. 224-37.

[70] I. Deutsch: 'Roots of Bureaucracy' in R. Miliband and J. Saville (eds.): *Socialist Register,* Merlin Press, London, 1969, p. 12.

[71] ibid., p. 15.

[72] H. Braverman: *Labour and Monopoly Capital,* Monthly Review Press, New York, 1974, p. 83.

[73] ibid., pp. 85-123.

[74] H. Beynon: *Working for Ford,* Allen Lane, London, 1973; T. Nicholls and P. Armstrong: *Workers Divided,* Fontana/Collins, Glasgow, 1976.

[75] W. Baldamus: *Efficiency and Effort,* Tavistock Publications, London, 1961, p. 1.

[76] A. Gorz: 'Technical Intelligence and the Capitalist Division of Labour', *Telos,* No. 12, 1972, p. 34.

77 R. C. Edwards: 'Bureaucratic Organisation in the Capitalist Firm' in Edwards *et al.* (eds.): op. cit., p. 118.

78 Braverman: op. cit., p. 195.

79 See D. Dickson: *Alternative Technology,* Fontana, Glasgow, 1974; S. A. Marglin: 'What Do Bosses Do?' in A. Gorz (ed.): *The Division of Labour,* Harvester Press, Sussex, 1976, pp. 13-54; Braverman: op. cit.; Fox: op. cit., 1976; Gorz: op. cit., 1972.

80 L. E. Davis and J. C. Taylor: 'Technology, Organisation and Job Structure' in R. Dublin (ed.): *Handbook of Work, Organisation and Society,* Rand McNally, Chicago, 1976, pp. 379-420.

81 C. Offe: *Industry and Inequality,* Edward Arnold, London, 1977.

82 Gorz: op. cit., 1972, p. 28.

83 Marglin: op. cit.

84 Fox: op. cit., 1976, p. 48.

85 Davis and Taylor: op. cit., 1976.

86 C. Argyris: *The Applicability of Organisational Sociology,* Cambridge University Press, 1972, p. 79.

87 Davis and Taylor: op. cit., 1976, pp. 410-411.

88 Child: op. cit., 1972, p. 2.

89 See Albrow: op. cit., 1968.

90 Elger: op. cit., p. 91.

91 ibid., p. 99.

92 ibid., p. 12.

93 Benson: op. cit., p. 3.

94 ibid., p. 12.

95 S. Clegg: *Power, Rule and Domination,* Routledge and Kegan Paul, London, 1975; Clegg and Dunkerley: op. cit.

96 W. Heydebrand: 'Organisational Contradictions in Public Bureaucracies: Towards a Marxian Theory of Organisations', *Sociological Quarterly,* Vol. 18, No. 1, 1977, pp. 83-108.

97 Allen: op. cit., p. 89.

98 ibid., p. 90.

2.   Understanding Organizational
Power: Building on the Weberian Legacy*

Kenneth McNeil

One of the most important, yet difficult, research issues facing social scientists today is to investigate the actual dynamics by which large-scale organizations gain dominating power in society. In only 60 years, the U.S. federal budget has risen from less than one billion dollars a year to a billion dollars a day; and General Motors has grown from a fledgling company to a corporation with a budget larger than that of many nations. On the surface, this massive trend may appear to be the fulfillment of the hope of the Enlightenment — the development of a harmonious society out of the Industrial Revolution by use of rational technique. But Max Weber spelled out a more unsettling result. He saw a "paradox of domination" that developed when rational technique became embodied in organizational form. To gain predictability in the inherently unstable markets of industrial capitalism, organizations had to develop strong power relationships over the people they served. Only through impersonal coercion and discipline of subordinates and clients could organizations achieve the coordination necessary for rational, i.e., quantitatively or logically calculable, action. He therefore suggested two central research problems for organizational analysis: (1) How do organizations develop asymmetrical power in concrete settings? and (2) How could this power be politically controlled?

Yet the sociology of organizations, which owes much to Weber, has not given priority to the study of organizational power. The past decade has seen major strides in quantifying such variables as task structure or formalization, but these variables cannot explain very much about the struggles involving powerful organizations that Perrow (1972) and others (Blau, 1974; Coleman, 1974) urge us to examine — the Pentagon, Congress, the huge conglomerates. Size, as measured by number of employees, has become the main explanatory variable in recent research (Blau and Schoenherr, 1971); but an examination of a list of the 15 United States organizations employing the largest number of people — such as General Motors, American Telephone and Telegraph, the U.S. Post Office, the Department of the Army — reveals that organizational sociologists have not seriously investigated any of them (Rehfus, 1973:87).

This neglect is basically due to conceptual models of organizational behavior that

---

* Reprinted from "Understanding Organizational Power: Building on the Weberian Legacy" by Kenneth McNeil, published in *Administrative Science Quarterly*, March 1978, vol. 23, no. 1, pp. 65–90, by permission of *The Administrative Science Quarterly*. Copyright © 1978 by Cornell University.

An early draft of this essay was presented at the American Sociological Association Meetings, New York, New York, September 2, 1976. A revision was presented at the series of "Colloquia and Symposia on Max Weber," University of Wisconsin-Milwaukee, February 3, 1977. An enormous intellectual debt is owed to Michael Aiken and John Myles for their encouragement and feedback throughout the development of this essay. Many others have offered helpful criticisms of this paper, but several deserve special acknowledgement: Richard Schoenherr, Joseph Elder, Erik Wright, Nancy DiTomaso, Donald Levine, Mayer Zald, Ira Cohen, and Murray Edelman.

emphasize how organizations *adapt* efficiently to the environment, rather than how they seek to control it. But as Perrow (1972: 199) has shown, organizations also use domination strategies:

> The environment of most powerful organizations is well controlled by them, quite stable, and made up of other organizations, ones they control. Standard Oil and Shell may compete at the intersection of two highways, but they do not compete in the numerous areas where their interests are critical, such as foreign policy, tax laws, import quotas, government funding of research and development, highway expansion, internal combustion, pollution restrictions, and so on.

That is, organizations use the power of the state to gain the same or more important ends than they could achieve by internal efficiencies alone. Both adaptation and domination strategies are used in large-scale organizations; yet most organizational sociologists, seeing no sinister plot to dominate, focus solely on the adaptation strategies. But this is just as unrealistic as concentrating solely on domination, for managerial elites must always make decisions as to whether to meet a goal, like greater profits, through more efficient internal adaptation or through power strategies, such as influencing Congress to pass favorable tax law.

By "domination," Weber did not mean that administrators have total control. Rather organizational domination implies that an imbalance of power exists which structures social action to such an extent that any understanding of the ultimate consequences of struggle would see that power as central. For Weber, domination strategies therefore did not even have to be successful in order to be important in explaining outcomes. This more complex view of domination also suggests that we must clarify the linkages between internal adaptation and external domination strategies if we are to answer the Weberian question of how organizations develop asymmetrical power, or how it can be politically controlled.

The purpose of this essay is to urge development of a theoretical perspective that links the study of internal control to that of external power relations, and in doing this to make clear the necessary elements of such a perspective. It is obvious that we must go considerably beyond Weber in order to analyze the concrete patterns of organizational power that exist today. But sociologists have more often erred in not appreciating enough the fruitfulness of both Weber's theory and methodology for examining questions of organizational power. Even if his actual polemic is flawed, his work does set forth the necessary elements for an adequate conceptualization of the dynamics of organizational power.

First, five key elements in Weber's work are discussed: (1) the sources of pressures to use external power strategies; (2) the strategies available for gaining power over the environment; (3) the mechanisms crucial in shaping the decisions of administrators to use potential power; (4) the implications of the model of organizational behavior for the dynamics of its political control, and (5) the kind of research methodology appropriate for examining variation in the actual exercise of power. The work of comparative structuralists, who predominantly adopt an adaptation model, is then examined to show why the absence of these five key elements constrains what they can say about power. Finally, several perspectives on organizations are analyzed which seek to integrate power and efficiency concerns. These include the work of Selznick, Zald, Benson, and the institutional economists. With these elements and Weber's development of them as a frame of reference, we will critically assess progress in developing an adequate conceptualization of the interplay among adaptation, domination, and the political control of organizational power.

WEBER'S ORIGINAL PERSPECTIVE

Weber proposed to study the dynamics of organizational power in a traditional way, first developing an abstract model of organizational behavior and then evolving a methodology for studying how organizational power was exercised in the real world. This simply provided a basic framework for later research, not an ultimate explanation of organizational power dynamics.

American theorists, however, have developed a dangerously limited interpretation of Weber's model of organizational behavior. They have typically classified Weber's perspective as a "tool view" (Thompson, 1967:5); that is, organizations are defined as *rational instruments to achieve goals*. A shibboleth of organizational sociology, this definition often leads to a focus on formal structure as the significant mechanism shaping organizational behavior. At first glance, this emphasis might seem to fit Weber, because his ideal-type bureaucracy showed the formal characteristics of modern organizations, but in itself failed to give any clue to the main problem confronting Weber: how rational organizational behavior could have such irrational consequences for specific social groups.

For Weber, this paradox could be understood only by grounding his view of organizational behavior in the historical context of Western industrial capitalism. The dynamics of this modern economic order involved the allocation of goods and services through the law of supply and demand, with the absence of political and status restrictions regarding entry or performance in the market. The classic form of modern rational organizations, the capitalist enterprise, only became dominant in this epoch. Weber (1961:207) defined it as "an establishment which determines its income yielding power by calculation according to the methods of modern bookkeeping and the striking of a balance."

Capitalist enterprise has existed before in ancient and medieval times, but its origins were independent of the rise of the specialized bureaucratic form of organization which his ideal-type describes (Weber, 1968:400). What characterizes the modern industrial order is the *fusion* of the capitalist enterprise with a bureaucratic form of organization. This fusion was made possible by the emergence of certain fundamental preconditions, among which Weber included calculable law; free labor, meaning persons not only free to sell their labor on the market, but economically compelled to do so; and appropriation of the physical means of production by the entrepreneur (Weber, 1961:208-209). Weber's last published lectures on general economic history (1961) elaborated on these preconditions.[1]

The significance of this fusion of bureaucracy and capitalistic enterprise is its pervasiveness. Weber pointed out that "if we imagine this form of organization taken away, the whole economic system would collapse" (1961:207). Modern governmental organizations, which took the rational form of economic organizations, also arose as part of the expanding dynamics of market capitalism. Only a high degree of rationally organized action could make exchange relationships and production techniques calculable enough to supply the demands of expanding national and international markets.

---

[1] Giddens (1970, 1971) has elaborated on the relationship between organizations and the economic system in Weber's thought.

SOURCE OF PRESSURE TO DOMINATE: THE TENSION
BETWEEN MARKET AND ADMINISTRATIVE LOGIC

Although there was a reciprocal relationship between the rise of complex organizations as management systems and the rise of capitalism as an economic system, there
was a fundamental tension in this relationship. The market logic of supply and
demand for labor, commodities, and capital is inherently unpredictable, yet the
administrative logic of economic organizations demands a high degree of calculability. The basic problem for administration is the management of this unpredictability.
Thompson (1967) pointed out that for administrative elites, the inner logic of
organizations, which demands predictable inputs, clashes with the uncertainty of the
environment.

   This tension became a source of pressure for administrative elites to dominate the
environment, because the discipline of the market would quickly drive any organization that failed to produce a profit out of business. For one result of the relationship
between rational economic organizations and the economic system is that "rational"
takes on a historically specific meaning, which is essentially the calculation of capital
(Behrendt, 1971:182).

   It is easy, but misleading, to confuse this form of rationality with efficiency,
especially in the light of well-known research in which Weber's ideal-type bureaucracy was criticized as being functionally inefficient (Merton, 1957; Stinchcombe,
1959). After extensive investigation of Weber's concept of bureaucracy, Albrow
(1970:65) concluded that Weber's use of rationality simply referred to the *means by
which* efficiency was *measured,* through the calculation of cost in terms of money,
time, or energy expended:

> Such calculations are formal procedures which do not in themselves guarantee efficiency,
> but are among the conditions for determining what level of efficiency has been reached.

The basic point is that to give organizations a basis for the calculability they so
desperately need, the achievement of goals is measured by criteria cast in economic or
legal terms and embodied in organizational procedures. These procedures should
create predictability in exchange relationships through abstract manipulation of either
quantitative information or complex legal rules, but they do not *automatically*
promote goals. In fact, Weber was concerned with precisely the negative case —
when organizations using such rational criteria have irrational consequences for
social groups they serve by dominating the environment.

   Using profit maximization for evaluation demands a high degree of discipline and
control. Unless administrative elites meet the profit maximization criterion, they will
lose their positions; so as partners in organizational transactions, they must abandon
any ethical or fraternal behavior that interferes with formal rationality:

> There is no possibility, in practice or even in principle, of any caritative (benevolent)
> regulation of relationships arising between the holder of a savings and loan bank mortgage
> and the mortgagee . . . or between a holder of a federal bond and a citizen taxpaper . . .
> stockholders and factory workers, or between industrialists and the miners who have dug
> from the earth raw materials used in the plants by the industrialists. The growing imperson-
> ality of the marketplace follows its own rules, disobedience to which entails economic
> failure and, in the long run, economic ruin . . . Such absolute depersonalization is contrary
> to all the elementary forms of human relationship (Weber, 1968: II, 585, 637).

It is not easy for administrators to enforce the abandonment of fraternal or benevolent relationships. Subordinates must be willing to forego personal pleasure and follow a rigid work schedule, which often demands close timing, concentration, and a mechanical following of orders to maintain the coordination necessary. In these rational instruments of transformation called organizations, Weber realized that rationality meant a discipline that caused deprivation (MacRae, 1974:77). Such discipline would be difficult enough to maintain in a stable environment. But the environment in which a capitalist enterprise is operating — that is, labor markets, commodity markets, capital markets, constant technological innovation — is so incessantly changing that strong pressures develop in organizations to create some system of power relationships over both subordinates and over exchange partners in the environment. Consequently, instead of efforts at efficiency, there are efforts at "efficiency of control" (Benello, 1969:268), which demand some form of power over reluctant parties.

Strategies for Mobilizing Power.   How, then, can managers gain enough power in organizations under Western capitalism to discipline subordinates and assure calculability within an unstable environment? Without understanding the sources of the power of managers, we cannot solve the problem of politically controlling it.

Weber's conception of this process involves a fascinating paradox. On the one hand, no single organization can totally control or change the macro forces of supply and demand, so the organization is always in a potentially passive position, merely adapting to market forces. On the other hand, an organization can strategically put these macro forces to its own use, and in the process greatly increase its otherwise limited resources. So the macro forces of a capitalist economic system that create uncertainty for the organization can also be strategically tapped for efficiency of control.

For Weber, much of management involved just that: the control of market forces so as to use their power for one's own ends. This control was effected by two main strategies: (1) internal bureaucratization and (2) stabilization of environmental forces through state regulation.

Internal bureaucratization.   This refers not only to lines of authority and communication, but also to the information that flows through these lines (Chandler, 1962:14). Through his ideal-type bureaucracy, Weber typified the structures and procedures that increased the ability of organizational elites to gain information about labor, commodity, and capital markets, and then take strategic advantage of them. These structures and procedures, which included setting up formal levels of hierarchy and formalized procedures, and hiring employees according to expertise, would maximize their chances of meeting calculable criteria such as profit maximization.

Using the strategic leverage that coordination gave them, administrative elites could anticipate market demands well enough to produce the right number of products at the right time. In many cases, however, the success of internal coordination in an organization was partly a function of a strong demand for its products. Automobiles, for instance, are a necessity for most people; consequently, a person has a limited power to resist buying a car even if he or she does not like some aspect of the design or pricing. The stronger the demand, the more likely that coordination would be successful. Likewise, elites could calculate how hard they could press workers. They could develop procedures which would anticipate and exploit labor market conditions, so that workers could not easily afford to resign or be fired for disobeying orders.

But to equate this formal bureaucratic structure with power is misleading. For

Weber, structure was only a necessary mechanism, not a sufficient condition, to promote efficiency of control. Fundamentally, internal structure is only capable of taking strategic advantage of coercive market forces that already exist. Without a labor market that would make disobeying orders costly, administrative procedures would probably not be very effective in maintaining control. Therefore, structure alone does not explain enormous differences in real power. Although General Motors and Chicken Delight, Inc., may both have rational administrative structures, General Motors seems to be tapping many more fundamental and powerful market forces than Chicken Delight.

Because internal bureaucratization is so dependent upon external market forces for success, it is always an incomplete process and often heightens internal struggles for control as conditions fluctuate. Because these struggles are usually related to larger market forces, internal bureaucratization is incapable of resolving them. Furthermore, these control struggles in turn disrupt rational calculability.

State Regulation.   Weber recognized that the only instrument ultimately very effective in regulating the macro forces of the market and institutionalizing market conflicts was the state itself. As a dominant political organization, the state's source of power was the "monopoly of the means of violence" in a given geographical territory (Weber, 1968: I, 56). So a second major organizational strategy for mobilizing power was to gain certain proprietary rights from the state; that is, ownership of state-guaranteed access to power over other parties. These rights could be enforced by the state's regulatory powers.

If one views capitalism as a purely market economy, state regulation could be considered interference, for emergent capitalism required a legal system that guaranteed freedom from arbitrary government action (Banton, 1972:87). But some governmental intervention was required to the extent of guaranteeing the enforcement of contract law so as to create flexibility and predictability in exchange relationships (Little, 1969).

The struggle to gain proprietary rights from the state became an important strategy. Even in a relatively passive role of enforcing contracts, the state greatly influenced the mobilization of organizational power. Although it played almost no role in setting the terms of the contract, once the contract was signed the state enforced the contract obligations on all parties. Although neutral in theory, this state intervention was not neutral in application. Without any state interference in the bargaining on behalf of weaker parties, the party with the stronger bargaining position in the market dictated terms of a contract. In labor-management relations, this occurred because of the vulnerable position of workers in the labor market. Once the workers signed a management-dominated contract, management increased its power; for the power of the state, as well as the market, began to enforce restrictions on labor. Part of Weber's active political life was spent fighting just such unjust contract law which allowed management to keep workers in a very disadvantageous position.[2] In what Macpherson (1966) has called a "double system of power," the state only reinforced the imbalance of power already existing in the marketplace. By not explicitly prohibiting exploitation in the making of contracts, the state was tacitly granting to private corporations extensive proprietary rights through contract law.

Weber was certainly aware of such exploitation in the period of American industrialization that occurred during his career. From the 1870s through the 1890s,

---

[2] For an analysis of the problems of contract law protecting consumers in their relationships with large production organizations, see Llewellyn (1931).

the clash between the demand for predictability in production and the instability of market forces became enormous. Industrial organizations responded by developing formalized management structures (Chandler, 1962) to anticipate changes in the market and make calculable responses to them; that is, they followed a strategy of internal bureaucratization. They also responded by such power strategies as mergers, collusive price setting, and monopolistic control over key raw materials. The use of such strategies of domination often resulted from intense demands upon managers to maximize profits and pay off the enormous investments in facilities. A close reading of *Economy and Society* (Weber, 1968) shows Weber's concern with such types of domination.

The state had to make deliberate decisions about whether such strategies were legal. If the state did not pass laws against these strategies, it was in effect granting proprietary rights to organizations to use them. Indeed, the central thrust of key legal principles emerging in the nineteenth century was to actively encourage "entrepreneurial choice" in the marketplace with very few restrictions (Hurst, 1956). In some instances, laws were even passed which gave steel, oil, or railroad companies specific proprietary rights to gain control over market forces.

As a result, the abuse of market through all sorts of arrangements was proceeding much faster than the legislative arena was willing or able to control it. With the market failing as a control mechanism, the courts began to intervene (Commons, 1968) in reaction to the new instabilities created by abusive market strategies. They did not necessarily keep organizations from using such power strategies to gain advantages as price-setting arrangements or monopoly of raw materials; instead, courts began to legalize these proprietary rights to the extent that they met some abstract justification that it was in the "general welfare." Along with judicial intervention came legislative actions which signaled a trend away from total laissez-faire and toward a "regulatory state" (Wilson, 1975), a shift which many businessmen welcomed at the time to ensure more calculability in the marketplace.

With this trend came the emergence of *abstract legal logic* which complemented profit maximization in creating more calculable exchange relationships. Like contract law, these legal principles were not neutral in application, even if neutral in theory. For instance, the early codification of corporation law granted corporations the rights of individuals without requiring any major social responsibility in the exercise of corporate power (Hurst, 1970), economic development being equated with the public interest. This has had enormous consequences for the freedom of corporations from legal control. Likewise, the standardization of commercial law cleared away a welter of local laws designed to protect local markets from outside competition. This allowed a corporation to sell nationally and greatly extend the range of its power (Hurst, 1956). Friedman (1965) documents the way in which contract law gave way in Wisconsin to a flood of special laws such as occupational licensing, which gave proprietary powers to certain labor groups so they could monopolize and control labor markets.

In effect, an artificial environment of abstract laws was being created to provide control and channeling for the powers of the labor, commodity, and capital markets. Collective-bargaining arrangements gave rights to labor to protect themselves from coercive discipline of the market (Commons, 1968). In fact, the state has constantly intervened to institutionalize the struggles that evolved out of the need for discipline and control in organizations. The state's role has been to institutionalize the struggles within the limits of calculability for economic organizations. The greater the reverberations of organizational struggles for power, the more the state intervened.

It is no surprise then, that Weber (1968) emphasized the search for proprietary rights granted by the state as a central strategy for gaining power over the environment. This was an important reason for his focus on the sociology of law. Naturally the power of governmental organizations themselves has become a focus of concern as they enforce legal obligations or handle social problems left unresolved in the private struggles for power. Accelerated in their growth by the rising democratic pressures, new "production systems" in the public sector — schools, hospitals, welfare agencies — must develop their own administrative control strategies. Their administrators must discharge business "precisely, unambiguously, continuously and with as much speed as possible," according to calculable rules "without regard for persons" (Weber, 1946:215). These government organizations face the same needs to stabilize environmental forces as do economic organizations.

ADMINISTRATIVE RATIONALITIES AS MECHANISMS FOR DETERMINING THE USE OF POWER

A theory must not only trace the strategies that give elites potential power; it must also suggest the mechanisms that shape the actual exercise of power. General Motors, for example, may have enormous potential power over any individual customer, but the significant problem is whether it exerts that power over a Cadillac buyer or a Chevrolet buyer.

In the case of General Motors, the decision as to how power will be allocated depends upon how administrative elites develop specific criteria by which profit, in the abstract, can be maximized. For instance, does a company maximize profit by improving the quality of its products, investing in more advertising, gaining more power over suppliers, or what? To some extent this is determined by financial criteria by which the relative effectiveness of each factor on the rate of return on investment is judged (Sloan, 1963:140-148). But in a larger sense, these are political decisions fought out among different administrative interests and decided largely in accordance with the rationalities of divisions that have mobilized the most strategic resources in the organization.

For Weber, the rationalities, or *modes of calculation,* of managerial elites were the main mechanisms shaping the actual use of power. There are several reasons why his research emphasis was on the origins and consequences of rationalities used by managerial elites.

First, Weber noted that those in power seek to justify their use of power (1968: III, 953). But exercise of power is an especially difficult problem for the elites of modern organizations, who are by definition "appointed salaried officials" (Weber, 1968: I, 48; Albrow, 1970:42). This managerial class is new in history and must justify its exercise of power both to owners and to subordinates (Child, 1969), so managers must rigidly adhere to the rationalities of profit maximization, abstract legal logic through which they tap the coercive power of the state, and scientific knowledge which enhances calculability in organizational procedures.

Second, management involves strategic decisions about transforming nature of society, decisions which demand a continual monitoring of managerial activities according to certain criteria to calculate success (Giddens, 1977:82). These criteria are also important for understanding how elites exercise power because they are the criteria by which managers are evaluated and disciplined. Another reason for Weber's emphasis is that administrators must combine their mode of evaluation with a control system *compatible* with achieving those calculable results. For instance, public education organizations must decide what specific criteria define successful education, then develop strategies of control to insure success in meeting those criteria. This process gives managers important discretionary power; their function is precisely that of translating the abstract general criteria such as profit maximization into specific criteria for unique management situations, and the developing control strategies for meeting those specific criteria. The multiple criteria that emerge, in production, marketing, or finance, may result in conflicting control systems, so that the design and use of these control systems is very political and affects how power is ultimately exercised.

This theme in Weber's work is being rediscovered. The role of rationalities in shaping efforts to actively "transform" the environment is dealt with at great length in Giddens's *New Rules of Sociological Methods* (1977). A recent analysis of Weber's conceptualization of rationality by Levine (1977) has uncovered several "forms" of rationality as the term is used by Weber. The theme of multiple rationalities in organizations is illustrated by Karpik (1972, 1977).

The emphasis upon the role of administrative rationalities does not exclude the influence of objective market, political, or strictly technical production factors on the system of control that emerges. It simply stresses that administrative rationalities are decisive in determining how elites translate potential power into the actual exercise of power. These rationalities become important because the constraints of markets, politics, and technology affect managers in very complex ways. Even sociologists in all their wisdom cannot predict these unique configurations or their impact on the future very accurately. Faced with the indeterminateness of these configurations, managers must assign some meaning to them in order to place some importance on them as predicting achievement of goals. Weber argued that this makes modes of calculation key mechanisms in determining how managers will use the power they can mobilize, because such rationalities do provide a means of assessing the meaning of events.

Likewise, an emphasis upon managerial rationalities does not imply that administrative intentions will in fact be carried out. Weber has been criticized by functional theorists for not seeing the "system maintenance needs" which create unanticipated consequences for managerial rationalities (Gouldner, 1954; Merton, 1957). But Weber did not insist that consequences had to be rational, only that consequences had to be traced back causally to modes of calculation in the heads of managerial elites. In deciding to merge with another company, a corporate board of directors might invite many unanticipated consequences, but causal analysis would have to take the rationality of the board into account, even though the board did not anticipate the consequences (Clegg, 1975). A different mode of calculation would create different organizational dynamics (Child, 1972).

IMPLICATIONS FOR THE POLITICAL CONTROL OF ORGANIZATIONAL POWER

If organizational power strategies are effective, they can give large-scale organizations enormous power. A conceptual model should give some insight into the problems and dynamics of controlling such power politically. For Weber, this issue was the main reason for his interest in the study of complex organizations. Viewing society as a power struggle, he focused his research on the *concrete* forms of dominating power relationships that developed in historically unique settings, and their implications for the interests and goals pursued. For Weber, it was the exercise of power through modern rational administration, rather than through patrimonial or charismatic structures of control, which was the new and unique element in Western capitalism. This concern with patterns of domination was grounded in Weber's philosophical view that human society is replete with irreconcilable values, which in turn demand political decisions as to what *costs* will be accepted for what *benefits*. It is *power,* the probability that one can carry out his or her will in a social relationship in spite of resistance, which ultimately determines whose values gain priority and who pays the costs.

Rational administration had immense potential for building structures of domination that could be controlled by small elites, particularly vested economic interests (Weber, 1968: III, 953). Only establishing political control over organizational power could prevent this, but such control presented several difficulties. First, the political process in democracy was unstable, involving constant struggle among competing interests. Like the tension between the inherent unpredictability of the market and the need for administrative predictability, organizational imperatives conflict with the unpredictability inherent in democratic control. Since administrative elites are disciplined by calculable criteria, they see power struggles as potentially undermining calculability. It is tempting for administrators to coalesce with powerful interest groups against weaker groups to maintain stability despite democratic pressures (Selznick, 1949; Lowi, 1969).

Second, the power factors of capitalism and bureaucracy are hardly open to the influence of institutional forms. This is small encouragement for those suggesting such technocratic reforms as innovative structures or more widespread use of human-relations techniques. For this reason, Weber encouraged strong political action by various economic interests (Bahrdt, 1971:105). He felt that the only way for individuals ultimately to maintain their freedom against the enormous power of large-scale organization was through constant political struggle. He thought that anything that maintained that struggle, whether strong parliamentary control of bureaucracy (Weber, 1968: III, 1381-1496), or private ownership to counteract the political leverage of state production units, was needed. The struggle is particularly important because of the sheer complexity of administrative power. Under traditional authority, one might regain control by simply dethroning the king, but rational-legal bureaucratic despotism is Hydra-headed, gaining power through a complex legal process that changed the structure of market forces but is not itself easily dismantled. If democratic control is not constantly reasserted, large-scale organizations, under the guise of rationality, make political decisions for individuals.

Therefore, any effort to get out of the "iron cage" of bureaucratic domination demands analysis by social scientists of the complex patterns of organizational power and its exercise. This did not assume a priori that bureaucratic power ruled out democratic control (Albrow, 1970). Rather he wanted to learn what concrete forms of control developed in each unique historical period. His general model of organizational power in Western capitalism was simply a point of departure. He left to future researchers the task of analyzing the factors leading to specific patterns in the exercise of power.

Once the specific dynamics of organizational power are uncovered, the researcher can then deal with two important issues of political control which Weber raised: (1) How does the state institutionalize — or bring within calculable limits — the struggles created by an imbalance of organizational power? and (2) What implications does such public policy have for the "stratification of access" to the benefits of organizational action?

The first question demands a focus on the mechanisms by which public policy institutionalizes a variety of struggles which affect the direction of social change:

labor-management conflict, business-consumer conflict, urban struggle in metropolitan planning efforts where an imbalance of power exists between major economic organizations in a city and inner-city residents, conflict between different organizational sectors where one sector holds an imbalance of power in exchange relations with the other.

The second question relates to the central role which Weber saw for social science: clarifying to the politician just what costs were being incurred for what benefits. It is certainly not axiomatic that costs and benefits are equitably distributed. Which labor groups benefit from labor policy more than others, and at what costs? Which consumers does public policy protect better than others in the marketplace? Which social groups benefit more from urban economic planning, and at what costs to other social groups? The social scientist cannot ultimately decide what the tradeoffs between costs and benefits will be, since those decisions ultimately lie with the politicians. But the social scientist can ensure that politicians understand the consequences of the tradeoffs made in public policy. This focus on stratification of access to benefits dealt directly with Weber's concern about the "irrational consequences" of "rational" organizational activity: namely, organizational actions may be beneficial only to certain groups, while quite harmful to others.

WEBER'S METHODOLOGY

Because Weber placed such great weight on researching concrete patterns of organizational power and their consequences, methodology became important in his program of action. Several of Weber's principles of methodological procedures have already become apparent: his comparative-historical viewpoint; his focus on economic and governmental linkages at the societal level as key variables shaping organizational power; and his view of causation, which dismissed any hope of capturing the dynamics of organizational power with abstract, ahistorical theories.

To test his hunch that without specific forms of managerial rationality organizational power would have been substantially altered, Weber had to devise some methodological tool to isolate this factor from the complex configuration of interacting factors in Western capitalism. The strategy he used for this was comparative analysis — finding cases very similar to one another in history, but different in one significant respect which gained exaggerated importance in an "ideal-type" (Weber, 1949; Simey, 1965; Dronsberger, 1971: Appendix B). The ideal-type was a kind of *extreme case* against which organizational patterns in different settings could be compared. To the degree that the formal rationality typified by Weber seemed more present in Western capitalism, and to the degree that the characteristics of control logically associated with modern organizations most closely approximated the extreme case of formal bureaucracy, Weber could suggest that formal rationality was indeed important for understanding organizations in Western capitalism. For example, Weber (1975) endorsed the value of abstract mathematical models of economic behavior, not because they represented reality, but because they typified the perceptions of managerial elites as they calculated their strategies in the market.

Weber's ideal-type of bureaucracy was an idealized system of control congruent with the model of calculation of a "typical" managerial elite. Canovan (1974:33) has captured some of the essence of Weber's intentions in her contrast of the Weberian depiction of bureaucracy as rational with Arendt's depiction of bureaucracy as irrational:

Her (Arendt's) view forms an interesting contrast to Weber's model of bureaucracy as a highly rationalized responsible form of government that works according to rules: but the difference is partly that Weber looked at bureaucracy *from the point of view of the official, from within* (italics added), whereas Hannah Arendt sees it much more from the point of view of the subject. Looked at from below, the striking characteristic of this kind of rule is its mysteriousness, secrecy, unpredictability and arbitrariness — its Kafkaesque qualities.

Weber preferred using an extreme case as a form of definition, to the diffuse and often contemptuous way in which the word "bureaucracy" was being used by his contemporaries (Albrow, 1970). In fact, it was partly his reaction to their careless definitions that motivated him to define bureaucracy in terms of specific control characteristics, even though he acknowledged that such a definition would eventually be outdated and would be unable to provide clarification in comparative analysis. But temporarily it would provide a "safe harbor in a stormy sea of facts" (Weber, 1949:104) until social scientists could get a better perspective on the concrete forms of organizational power. The bureaucratic ideal-type was not meant to represent the actual structure of all modern organizations; it was designed to *clarify* the role of formal rationality in bureaucratic control by the use of an extreme case. New ideal-types could be constructed to deal with more specific patterns of control.

Many criticisms can be made of Weber's conceptualization of organizational power. Hughes (1958:77) has pointed out that a number of Weber's contemporaries were much more systematic observers of internal structure and strategy than he was. For present-day researchers, Weber's theoretical ideas about the linkage of power and efficiency still lack some of the conceptual richness needed as a basis for a systematic research program. But the purpose of this essay is to compare the five major elements in Weber's work that have been discussed, with comparative structural analysis and other organizational perspectives that link power and efficiency. As a frame of reference, Weber serves as an illustration of new directions that need to be taken to integrate the study of internal control with external power relations.

The Neglect of Power in Comparative Structural Analysis.   While sociologists claim to be following Weber, the mainstream of sociological research is not. The search is now for ahistorical theoretical generalizations, not causal explanations of unique historical patterns. The rationalities of administrative elites are generally ignored as a causal element, while the unit of analysis becomes the organization as a whole. Recent theorists have accepted a view of the organization as a system *adapting* to external forces and internal structural needs, and consequently have abandoned concerns about organizational domination. As a result, several research groups (Udy, 1959; Hall, 1963; Aiken, 1967; Pugh *et al.*, 1969) have abandoned Weberian methodological principles for examining power. This trend is typified by the recent work of Blau and his students. While giving new insights into the variety of structural adaptation patterns, their research fails to present a picture of the power dynamics through which organizations gain control over their environment. By tracing their modification of Weber's five key elements, one can see what is lost in terms of explaining organizational power.

Blau's Conceptual Model.   Despite the familiarity of Blau's conceptualization and methodology, it is important to make explicit its limitations for examining power. Blau's work derives from the middle-range functionalism of Merton, whose students carved out complex organizations as a domain of sociological research. So it is not difficult to see why Blau and others looked at the Weberian legacy initially from a functionalist perspective, and so tended to divorce the study of organizations from the wider economic system, even though Merton's anthology (Merton *et al.*, 1952) on bureaucracy is still the most concerned with organizational power in society of any standard texts on organizational behavior. Second, these theorists were interested in developing a perspective of organizations as functional systems, and Weber's ideal-type represented what Blau has called an "implicit" functional system of interdependent structural characteristics (Blau, 1957).

Within this group, Merton (1957) and Gouldner (1954) began to elaborate the "dysfunctions" or irrelevance of rules and formal structure in the ongoing functional system known as the organization and emphasized the importance of studying informal structure, often through the case-study method. Blau himself began in this tradition with his famous monograph on informal structure in employment agencies (Blau, 1955).

But Blau soon abandoned the diffuse theoretical conceptualizations and the case-study methodology of the earlier functionalists. Reinterpreting Weber's ideal-type bureaucracy, he hypothesized that independent of individuals involved, certain structural configurations were functionally necessary for efficiency. Rather than insisting that Weber's bureaucratic ideal-type was either inappropriate or too rigid for efficiency, Blau, (1957:67) suggested that it be seen as a "hypothesis implied by Weber that administrative efficiency is the result of a combination of various characteristics in a bureaucracy." It was an empirical question as to what configurations were functional under what circumstances. But the conceptual linchpin for uniting the Weberian emphasis on formal structure with a functionalist perspective was the assumption that the ultimate function of an organization is efficiency. This, of course, ignored the Weberian linkage of power to efficiency. The functionalists had not only abandoned a societal and historical perspective for causation, but they also abandoned the emphasis upon the process by which administrative elites decided on control strategies. Instead, Blau (1957:66) labeled power struggles as social-psychological processes that could be empirically incorporated as intervening variables between formal structural characteristics and the ultimate outputs.

Evolution of Methodology.   Nevertheless, Blau's conceptualization was the basis for a comparative analysis of organizations, that is, the study of variation in the structural elements that led to efficiency in goal attainment. The configuration of structural factors — division of labor, hierarchy of offices, control and sanctioning mechanisms, official rules and regulations, personnel policies (Blau, 1957:66) — varied according to certain factors through which organizations could be compared, such as size, environmental resources, or age of the structure. Indeed it was then easy to measure the relative effectiveness of these factors by statistically sampling large numbers of organizations. Perhaps Lazarsfeld (1973: xxiv) summed up the euphoria of those frustrated by a vague Weberian legacy and diffuse functionalism in his foreword to Heydebrand's *Hospital Bureaucracy:*

> In the past, sociologists have been concerned with where to place their bets: quantification vs. case studies, micro- vs. macro-sociology, conceptual analysis vs. empirical propositions. Such controversies become more and more uninteresting. The plane on which mutual understanding develops most rapidly is the comparative study of organizations.

However, the structuralist adaptation model leaves structural theorists with very little theory or methodology for examining organizational domination. This does not mean that structural theorists are unconcerned with such issues. Blau and Schoenherr (1971:345-358) ended their comparative study of employment-security agencies with speculation on the "insidious forms of power." Furthermore, Blau, in his presidential address before the American Sociological Association, following Watergate, declared that the "challenge of the century" is to find ways to curb the power of organizations (Blau, 1974:634). The problem is that the structuralists abandoned much of Weberian conceptualization and methodology without developing a serious alternative research strategy for examining organizational power or its political control.[3]

The greatest conceptual problem for structural analysis at this point is tracing the systematic relationship between power and efficiency. In the functionalist perspective underlying present-day research, it is assumed that structure promotes efficiency, and in a democratic society, the more efficiency, the more everyone benefits. But this view fails to address the problem of power necessary to achieve that efficiency. As a result, structuralists are limited in what they can say about the political control of organizational power.

For example, researchers of formal structure are basically limited to attributing power relationships to structure itself, or abuse of authority by those in formal positions within organizations. Several explanations are commonly given to relate power to formal structure.

The first relates to the ability of managerial elites to manipulate the formal structure in ways that control subordinates' access to information (Simon, 1947). This "unobtrusive control" (Perrow, 1972:156) through the channeling of the flow of information allows managerial elites to structure both subordinate expectations and premises for making decisions. In this way, elites maintain power over subordinates.

A second explanation relates to the ability of subordinates to gain informal power through abuse of the formal authority of their positions. As the size of an organization increases, span-of-control problems also grow, resulting in more decentralization of actual decision making to subordinates (Blau and Schoenherr, 1971).

Third, power is related to formal structure through the mechanism of the "legitimacy" of formal rational authority. Subordinates follow orders simply because they believe managers have the legitimate right to give orders. Weber's focus on the legitimacy of rational authority in Western capitalism is sometimes used as the theoretical justification for this explanation.

The implication of these explanations for the political control of organizational behavior would be a technocratic solution — simply finding certain new structural arrangements which will make everyone more sensitive or share in the decision making.

But these explanations fail to address several aspects of Weber's work. First, Weber's emphasis upon the role of legitimacy, which could lead to abuse of power by those having formal authority, meant something subtly but profoundly different from the blind following of orders stated in legal-rational terms. Rather, the legitimacy of relationships of domination seems to arise over time as subordinates see that it would not be "rational," judged by criteria such as their own profit maximization, to disobey orders and still reach their own ends, under the political and market conditions present (Roth, 1968:lxxxiii).

Second, these arguments never seriously consider Weber's concept of structure as only a proximal condition of coordination, which implicitly draws upon outside power forces to be effective. Simon (1947) and others are correct in stating that formal structure shapes the kind of information subordinates have about the environment. In

---

[3]This does not imply that research on formal structure has been completely useless. A prominent Weberian scholar has suggested that such statistical analysis may be useful at a very preliminary stage of causal explanation (Rex, 1974:63).

itself, however, formal structure cannot account for the power differences inherent in the actions of a Department of Defense versus a toy manufacturer.

Furthermore, the structuralist explanations of power ignore a vast amount of information both in Weber's work and in the present-day world which suggests that organizations actively seek the support of the legal system, if not outright governmental subsidy, to control the unpredictability in their environments. Indeed, any casual content analysis of *Business Week, Forbes,* or the *Wall Street Journal* will make it clear that major corporations are not preoccupied, as is organization theory, with internal structure, but with the stabilization of economic contingencies through state regulation. To build a bridge between power and efficiency, students of formal structure would do well to integrate their research with a conceptual model that takes into account some of the elements of Weber's work discussed here.

POLITICAL PERSPECTIVES THAT LINK POWER AND EFFICIENCY

Researchers in several traditions are making an effort to link the study of internal organizational control with a broader analysis of external power relations. For example, Zald and Benson have been working in the traditional field of organization sociology, while institutional economists have been focusing on these concerns in their critique of current economic theory. Weber's five key elements provide valuable criteria against which to measure their progress toward a sophisticated view of organizational power. These new research perspectives are examined to discover elements that are as yet inadequately developed in their framework, and to judge how far the developed elements go beyond the Weberian research. But first, the Selznick-ian tradition is examined — the tradition of organizational sociology that first tried to integrate the study of organizational behavior with that of power in society (Selznick, 1949).

The Selznickian Tradition.   Although one of the earlier research traditions, Selznick's perspective comes closer than most to developing all five necessary elements for understanding organizational power. Impressed by how TVA, the "experiment in democratic control," was manipulated by managerial elites who were influenced by powerful interests, Selznick used the Tennessee Valley Authority example to point out the fundamental *source of tension* that led administrative elites to seek to dominate their environment. This tension was based in the dilemma of how to adapt to powerful interests in the environment, without causing uncontrollable conflict with those interests hurt by the displacement of the organization's original goals. Selznick analyzed key *strategies* that elites could draw upon in mobilizing power; specifically, the mechanisms of cooptation and protective ideology. He pinpointed leadership as the key mechanism for *implementing* power. Leaders delegated authority to subordinates but maintained their control of power through the infusion of "value" or "purpose" into the organization, creating an "organizational character" (Selznick, 1957). The model went further to suggest the central dynamics of political control; namely, the constant efforts by managerial elites to coopt the public. Selznick's methodology was greatly influenced by the heavy functionalist interpretation he placed on these organizational dynamics. Seeing the ultimate functional need as organizational survival, he felt that each organization would develop a very unique pattern of adaptation and control. This demanded a holistic case-study analysis of each organization, leaving little chance for much comparative analysis.

Perhaps Selznick's main conceptual problem was his view of the dynamics of political control. Although he stressed that concrete patterns of organizational domination might vary widely, what emerged from his model was a suggestion of the one best way to protect the public against being duped; namely, a kind of responsible, Burkean administrative leadership (Wolin, 1960). To correct this rather simplistic view, Selznick would have done well to draw upon Weber's concern with the dynamics of struggle, even in situations where an obvious imbalance of power exists. To do this, he could have incorporated Weber's focus on the concrete historical market tensions that created the source of unpredictability for TVA's managerial elites.

In the case of TVA, it was the electrical utilities which were resisting the government effort to use TVA as a "yardstick" measure to promote competition in the rural electrification market (McCraw, 1971). At stake were their proprietary rights to operate without competitive pressure from government. To counterbalance the political power of the electrical utilities industry, TVA elites sought to increase the proprietary rights of the Farm Bureau interests and others in the TVA program, in hopes of creating a more calculable environment for pursuing goals.

If the struggle is placed in the market context of the developing electrical utilities industry, it is easier to understand how TVA gained such a dominant position in the economic development of the southeastern United States. The present-day behavior of TVA illustrates something far more than survival, since it is involved in everything from domination of the Appalachian coal market to the building of controversial nuclear power plants. Once Selznick's conceptual model is put in this market context, it is possible to go beyond a simple model of political control, which relies upon responsible leadership as the best mechanism for protecting the public interest. Until a few years ago, for example, the three-member TVA executive board had never had an open meeting, and Selznick is the first to admit that their behavior is not always in the public interest.

Zald's Political-Economy Tradition.   Zald's political-economy tradition of organizational research (1970a, b; Walmsley and Zald, 1973) grew out of a case study that uncovered some of the defects in the Selznickian framework. Tracing the radical transformation of the YMCA in just a few decades from an evangelical organization to a secular social agency, Zald found that goal displacement was not mere survival but a conscious seeking out of new niches in the environment, responding to new demands for service in the urban industrial marketplace. So Zald began to move away from a strict adaptation model to a more aggressive entrepreneurial picture of managerial elites (Aldrich and Pfeffer, 1976). Zald also found much more variation in leadership mechanisms for exercising power than was indicated by the Selznickian model. The capture of leadership positions was essential for major goal changes, but the entrepreneurial efforts of different groups within the YMCA to gain autonomous resource bases led to a much more pluralistic model of decision making and the exercise of power. As a result, Zald suggested a methodology which would analyze systematic variation in patterns of leadership and in resource bases. He was particularly interested in the interplay between the political processes (goal formation) and economic processes (resource allocation) in organizations, in contrast to the Selznickian model which heavily emphasized a more one-directional impact of external resource allocation upon internal goal formation. In this respect, Zald's framework included the interrelationship between the Weberian strategies of internal bureaucratization and mobilization of external power to promote goals. His methodology was also compatible with Weber's in that he urged comparative analysis to uncover systematic differences in political struggles across organizations.

Zald's framework still needs the development of a general model of political control dynamics, which logically derives from his view of organizational behavior. Although the YMCA study implies a pluralistic picture of political control, it is not clear the consequences are pluralistic. One can envision groups of administrative elites using their entrepreneurial skills not only to find niches in the environment, but to dominate them. Such a balkanized social service environment could create serious problems of political control if there were unequal distribution of the benefits to various groups needing social services — for example, suburban youth in contrast to inner-city youth. To get at these issues, Zald's work could benefit from the same critique given to Selznick; namely, to deal more explicitly with the market dynamics of industrial capitalism and the effort of the state to regulate conflicts that they precipitate. In the YMCA case, for example, what kinds of demand and supply dynamics were operating within the general market for social services? How was the state intervening to institutionalize the conflicts created by these demands? How did the proprietary insulation of the voluntary service sector by the state facilitate this entrepreneurial pattern of funding which Zald found?

Government in the late nineteenth and early twentieth centuries was short of tax revenue needed to handle the growing demands for social services in cities, so it encouraged private associations through public policy to provide those services instead of the state (Hurst, 1956). This was an important factor underlying the entrepreneurial pattern of goal formation in the YMCA and other social service agencies. By the late 1960s however, major urban political struggles had developed in reaction to the stratification of access to the benefits provided by that pattern of voluntary service delivery. And the state was finding it quite difficult to institutionalize that struggle by coordinating those independent social service agencies (Zald, 1970c). Once the YMCA is placed in this context, one may have a better picture of the degree to which organizational change strengthened or weakened the historical stratification of access to social services. Zald's more recent work on the social control of industries (Wiley and Zald, 1968; Zald and Hair, 1972; Zald, 1978), deals more directly with strategies for stabilizing environmental forces through state regulation. In that analysis, he has set up a framework to aid in investigating how "norms of performance," or modes of calculation by which managers are disciplined, are set up and enforced.

Benson's Dialectical Analysis.   Benson's (1977) Marxian or dialectical model of organizational behavior concentrated on how tensions within organizations, created by societal forces, lead to constant transformation of structures and goals, a theme already present in Zald's work. But Benson sought to go beyond Zald in developing an appropriate methodology for examining the concrete dynamics of struggle within organizations. Benson's work has pointed to a serious shortcoming in present research methodology, i.e., its positivist nature. Such methodology leads researchers to examine what exists at a given time and then assume that the pattern is inevitable. But in this reification, the dynamics that will ultimately create sudden, dramatic change within organizations are overlooked. Benson's most severe criticism of this fallacy is reserved for researchers analyzing variation in formal characteristics of organizations, but he also sees this methodological fallacy in the work of Zald and other political perspectives.

Benson's work has not yet passed the early stages, for he has the major task of detailing the key sources of pressure to dominate the environment, the strategies used, and the mechanisms through which power might actually be exerted in the dialectical process. His failure to do this is rather glaring for one claiming a Marxist perspective, since there is a large literature on the apparent differences in the way Marx and Weber conceptualized these elements. In particular, Marxists have taken a different view from Weber on the dynamics of political control over organizational power, relating the pivotal conflicts and tensions to class struggle (Wright, 1975). Undoubtedly, however, a crude Marxism needs to be tempered by a much more sophisticated understanding of the interaction between social forces and internal organizational dynamics, as illustrated in Aiken's recent study of urban governments in Belgium (Aiken and Bacharach, forthcoming).

Institutional Economists.   Almost unnoticed by organizational sociologists is a research tradition half a century old which offers real promise for linking internal control to the dynamics of market and state power struggles. It is the field of institutional economics, an agglomerate of maverick economists emphasizing mechanisms through which industrial organizations gain control over environmental contingencies through state policy. The founding father, Thorstein Veblen, was impressed with the productive efficiency of organizational structure in the manner of Frederick Taylor. He recognized, however, that much of the real strategy to achieve profit maximization occurred through control by financial elites over the state apparatus (Veblen, 1965). Much of his life was spent in arguing against what he called the ''business system's'' control over the internal ''industrial system,'' gaining profits not by increasing productivity but by securing proprietary rights from the state.

It was Commons, a successor to Veblen in the institutional tradition and the originator of much New Deal legislation, who saw the analytical potential in Veblen's conceptualization. Taking Veblen's germinal idea, Commons conceptualized the economic organization as operating on two levels: the ''going plant'' and the ''going concern.'' The going plant operates in what Commons called an ''engineering economy,'' an internal system of allocation geared to produce goods more efficiently for output to the public, with a given amount of resources. The factors of production are routinized to use these resources to maximize productivity. In an analytical view close to the functionalism of some formal structuralists, Commons suggested that the ''aim of technological efficiency was achieved by a proper proportioning of the various factors of production'' (Gruchy, 1967: 194). At another analytical level, the corporation must be considered a going concern operating in a ''bargaining economy,'' a system of allocation external to the organization where strategy to gain control of the environment is crucial. This external bargaining economy does not involve an actual increase in productivity, but rather an allocation of scarce resources among competing interests. As a going concern, the corporation must depend upon predictability in its exchange relationships with allocators of strategic resources. Commons observed that these relationships develop through certain customs, habits, and working rules which are institutionalized at the state level through the legal system.

The fundamental source of tension leading to external power strategies was the need of the organization to develop predictable exchange relationships. Like Veblen before him, Commons pointed out that this could create conflict between the two economies. While this potential conflict had been held in check during the early stages of industrialization, the dynamics of the bargaining economy began to dominate with the rise of large corporations, which tried to stabilize the external environments through the control of the economy, a phenomenon he called ''banker capitalism.'' The state accepted this type of banker capitalism because of the need to stabilize production and thereby avoid chronic unemployment that would result from too much instability in the economy for the planning needs of big corporations. A serious issue of democratic control arose as a result, very similar to the one conceptualized by Weber. There would be an inherent tendency to maximize profits through gaining favorable proprietary rights from the state, rather than through increasing internal productivity. The state tended to concede to these demands by corporations, fearing that economic turmoil would otherwise result and cause political tensions to heighten. This led Commons to state the problem as emphatically as Weber: "Are democracy and representative governments able to manage these world-wide governments?" (Commons, 1961: 898). And like Weber, Commons felt the only solution was vigilant political action by a variety of interest groups (Commons, 1961: 903). Present-day writers who are working in this tradition include John Kenneth Galbraith, Warren Samuels, and Gunnar Myrdal.

The institutionalist school is sensitive to the fact that different industries must be analyzed differently, precisely because their labor markets, capital markets, and government regulation have evolved in different ways. While there may be certain generalizations about the structural forms of internal efficiency that might apply to all organizations, this would not be true of power relationships. In this sense, the methodology of institutional economists is more in the tradition of the German historical school. The close affinity between the work of Commons and Weber was noted by Lerner (1935) and Gruchy (1968). Martindale (1960: 405) felt it was unfortunate that Commons was classified as an economist, rather than a sociologist, and thus insulated from major influence on sociology.

The conceptualization of two economies does represent a step beyond Weber and makes it possible to begin integrating the traditional research of organization sociology with work done in such fields as business history, legal history, and political science. While sociologists have made almost no studies of the linkages between organizational behavior and the legal system, researchers in these other fields have. Hurst (1964) demonstrated the use of legal strategies by lumber companies almost a century ago in Wisconsin to stabilize their developing competitive environment. Those strategies have had enormous consequences for environmental protection ever since. Macaulay (1966) traced the effects of the legal system on the balance of power in exchange relationships between auto manufacturers and dealers. Stone (1975), studying corporate response to legal control, analyzed how the complexities of internal structure deflected the impact of external regulation. Hirsch (1975) documented how the pharmaceutical industry generated greater returns on profits than the recording industry, partly as a result of a regulatory environment that reduced its vulnerability to market forces. Franko (1974) indicated that internal bureaucratization to rationalize diversification has proceeded more slowly among European firms than U.S. firms, because the lax enforcement of antitrust laws in Europe allowed profits to be made through cartel pricing arrangements rather than through maximizing internal efficiencies. McNeil and Minihan (1977) have shown how the evolving regulation of medical device manufacturers has contributed to internal efficiency problems for hospitals in the face of technological innovations. Perhaps the best recent example of research which consciously links internal control to external power strategies is Blair's *The Control of Oil* (1976). Whether or not his policy conclusions are correct, his analysis shows the fruitfulness of an institutional economist's perspective.

The major benefit which institutional economists, legal historians, and others might gain from Weber in this new avenue of research is a healthy skepticism about the effectiveness of democratic control of economic power through state regulation.

Some institutional economists have assumed that since profits come mainly from proprietary control rather than from internal efficiencies, the state can easily manipulate organizations in the public interest through state regulation and national planning. But that must remain a question for research, not an assumption of fact. Tushnet's (1972, 1977) recent critiques of major works in legal history and Edelman's (1964, 1971, 1977) examinations of public policy demonstrate the subtle ways in which analysts can miss the realities of domination in a pluralistic environment.

CONCLUSION

In the continuing concern in organizational research for understanding the dynamics of organizational power in society, few research perspectives have fully developed a conceptualization of organizational behavior that includes five key elements treated by Weber: (1) the sources of pressure for managerial elites to dominate the environment, (2) the strategies available for mobilizing power, (3) the mechanisms that shape the actual exercise of power, (4) the implications of the model of organizational behavior for the dynamics of their political control, and (5) a methodology that can appropriately guide research on power. While not a complete and adequate guide to research, Weber's work provides an important frame of reference for measuring progress and guiding research, and provides a challenge to current researchers to incorporate a societal perspective in which organizational action is a part of a larger set of market and political dynamics.

   Concrete research upon specific industries and organizational sectors that have power over the environment may help researchers to focus more strategically on the mechanisms by which democratic control can be exercised. This research will demand systematic analysis of the interaction between the internal engineering economy of the organization and the external bargaining economy through which managerial elites gain proprietary rights from the state. In the short term, some synthesis of a Weberian perspective with key concepts from institutional economists may provide more narrow organizational research perspectives with a footing for dealing with the larger issues of political control of organizational power. But much new theoretical ground remains to be broken. Nevertheless, Bendix (1971: 155) may not have been overly optimistic in his hope of "linking the study of bureaucracy, with its historical and comparative approach, and the study of organizational power, to the benefit of both."

REFERENCES

Albrow, Martin
1970   Bureaucracy. New York: Praeger.
Aiken, Michael, and Samuel Bacharach
forthcoming
      "Organizational environment, permeability, and organizational structure: a study of forty-four local governments in Belgium." In Lucien Karpik (ed.), Organizations and Environment.

Aldrich, Howard, and Jeffrey Pfeffer
1976   "Environments of Organizations." In Annual Review of Sociology, Volume II: 79–105. Palo Alto: Annual Reviews, Inc.
Bahrdt, Hans
1971   "Discussion of Raymond Aron's 'Max Weber and power-politics.'" In Otto Stammer (ed.), Max Weber and Sociology Today: 103–109. Oxford:

Basil Blackwell.

Banton, Michael

1972   "Authority." *New Society*, 22, October 12: 86-88.

Behrendt, Richard

1971   "Discussion on Herbert Marcuse's 'industrialization and capitalism.'" In Otto Stammer (ed.), *Max Weber and Sociology Today:* 175-183. Oxford: Basil Blackwell.

Bendix, Reinhard

1971   "Bureaucracy." In Reinhard Bendix and Guenther Roth (eds.), *Scholarship and Partisanship: Essays on Max Weber:* 129-155. Berkeley: University of California Press.

Benello, George

1969   "Wasteland culture." In H. P. Dreitzel (ed.), *Recent Sociology, No. 1:* 263-291. London: Macmillan.

Benson, J. Kenneth

1977   "Organizations: a dialectical view." *Administrative Science Quarterly,* 22: 1-21.

Blair, John M.

1976   The Control of Oil. New York: Pantheon Books.

Blau, Peter

1955   *The Dynamics of Bureaucracy,* Chicago: University of Chicago Press.

1957   "Formal organization: dimensions of analysis." *American Journal of Sociology,* 63: 58-69.

1974   "Parameters of social structure." *American Sociological Review,* 39: 615-635.

Blau, Peter, and Richard Schoenherr

1971   *The Structure of Organizations.* New York: Basic Books.

Canovan, Margaret

1974   *The Political Thought of Hannah Arendt.* New York: Harcourt, Brace, Jovanovich.

Chandler, Alfred

1962   *Strategy and Structure.* Boston: M.I.T. Press.

Child, John

1969   *British Management Thought.* London: Allen & Unwin.

1972   "Organization structure, environment, and performance: the role of strategic choice," *Sociology,* 6: 1–22.

Clegg, Stewart

1975   *Power, Rule, and Domination.* Bos-

ton: Routledge and Kegan Paul.

Coleman, James

1974   *Power and the Structure of Society.* New York: Norton.

Commons, John R.

1924   *Legal Foundations of Capitalism* (1968 edition). Madison: University of Wisconsin Press.

1934   *Institutional Economics,* Volumes I and II (1961 edition). Madison: University of Wisconsin Press.

Dronsberger, Ilse

1971   *The Political Thought of Max Weber: In Quest of Citizenship.* New York: Appleton-Century-Crofts.

Edelman, Murray

1964   *The Symbolic Uses of Politics.* Urbana: University of Illinois Press.

1971   *Politics as Symbolic Action.* New York: Academic Press.

1977   *Political Language: Words that Succeed and Policies That Fail.* New York: Academic Press.

Franko, Lawrence

1974   "The move toward a multi-divisional structure in European organizations." *Administrative Science Quarterly,* 19: 493-506.

Friedman, Lawrence

1965   *Contract Law in America: A Social and Economic Case Study.* Madison: University of Wisconsin Press.

Giddens, Anthony

1970   "Marx, Weber, and the development of capitalism." *Sociology,* 4: 289-310.

1971   *Capitalism and Modern Social Theory: An Analysis of Marx and Durkheim and Weber.* London: Cambridge.

1977   *New Rules of Sociological Method.* London: Hutchinson.

Gouldner, Alvin

1954   *Patterns of Industrial Bureaucracy.* New York: Free Press.

Gruchy, Allan G.

1967   *Modern Economic Thought: The American Contribution.* New York: Augustus M. Kelley.

1968   *Contemporary Economic Thought.* New York: Augustus M. Kelley.

Hage, Jerald, and Michael Aiken

1967   "Relationship of centralization to other structural properties." *Administrative Science Quarterly,* 12: 72–92.

Hall, Richard
1963   "The concept of bureaucracy: an empirical assessment." *American Journal of Sociology,* 69: 32–40.

Hirsch, Paul M.
1975   "Organizational effectiveness and the institutional environment." *Administrative Science Quarterly,* 20: 327–344.

Hughes, H. Stuart
1958   *Consciousness and Society: The Reorientation of European Social Thought, 1890–1930.* New York: Knopf.

Hurst, J. Willard
1956   *Law and the Condition of Freedom in the Nineteenth Century United States.* Madison: University of Wisconsin Press.

1964   *Law and Economic Growth.* Cambridge, MA: Harvard University Press.

1970   *The Legitimacy of the Business Corporation in the Law of the United States, 1780-1970.* Charlottesville: University of Virginia Press.

Karpik, Lucien
1972   "Multinational enterprise and large technological corporations." *Revue Economique,* 23: 563–591.

1977   "Technological capitalism." In S. Clegg and D. Dunkerley (eds.), *Critical Issues in Organizations:* 41–70. London: Routledge and Kegan Paul.

Lazarsfeld, Paul
1973   "Foreword." In Wolf Heydebrand, *Hospital Bureaucracy: A Comparative Analysis of Organizations.* New York: Dunnellen.

Lerner, Max
1935   "Book review: John Commons, institutional economics." *Harvard Law Review,* 49: 360–365.

Levine, Donald
1977   "Rationality and freedom: Weber and beyond." Paper presented to symposium on Max Weber, University of Wisconsin-Milwaukee, May 5.

Little, David
1969   *Religion, Law, and Order.* London: Basil Blackwell.

Llewellyn, Karl
1931   "What price contract? an essay in perspective." *Yale Law Journal,* 40: 704–751.

Lowi, Theodore
1969   *The End of Liberalism.* New York: Norton.

Macaulay, Stewart
1966   *Law and the Balance of Power.* Madison: University of Wisconsin Press.

Macpherson, C. B.
1966   *The Real World of Democracy.* London: Oxford.

MacRae, Donald
1974   *Weber.* London: Woburn.

McCraw, Thomas
1971   *TVA and the Power Fight, 1933–1939.* Philadelphia: Lippincott.

McNeil, Kenneth, and Edmond Minihan
1977   "Regulation of medical devices and organizational behavior in hospitals." *Administrative Science Quarterly,* 22: 475–490.

Martindale, Don
1960   *The Nature of Types of Sociological Theory.* Boston: Houghton-Mifflin.

Merton, Robert
1957   "Bureaucratic structure and personality." In Robert Merton, *Social Theory and Social Structure* (1957 edition): 195-206. Glencoe: Free Press.

Merton, Robert, A. Gray, B. Hockey, and H. Selvin (eds.)
1952   *Reader in Bureaucracy.* New York: Free Press.

Perrow, Charles
1972   *Complex Organizations: A Critical Essay.* Glenview, IL: Scott, Foresman.

Pugh, D. S., D. J. Hickson, C. R. Hinings, and C. Turner
1969   "The context of organization structure." *Administrative Science Quarterly,* 14: 91–114.

Rehfus, John
1972   *Public Administration as Political Process.* New York: Scribners.

Rex, John
1973   *Sociology and the Demystification of the Modern World.* London: Routledge and Kegan Paul.

Roth, Guenther
1968   "Introduction." In Max Weber, *Economy and Society:* xxvii-civ. New York: Bedminster.

Selznick, Philip
1949   *TVA and the Grass Roots.* Berkeley: University of California Press.

1957   *Leadership in Administration.* New York: Harper and Row.

Simey, T. S.
1965   *Social Science and Social Purpose.* London: Constable, Ltd.

Simon, Herbert
1947   *Administrative Behavior.* New York: Macmillan.

Sloan, Alfred
1963   *My Years with General Motors.* New York: Doubleday.

Stinchcombe, Arthur
1959   "Bureaucratic and craft administration of production." *Administrative Science Quarterly,* 4: 168–187.

Stone, Christopher
1975   *Where the Law Ends: The Social Control of Corporate Behavior.* New York: Harper and Row.

Thompson, James D.
1967   *Organizations in Action.* New York: McGraw-Hill.

Tushnet, Mark
1972   "Commentary: lumber and the legal process." *Wisconsin Law Review,* 1972: 114–132.
1977   "Perspectives on the development of American law: a critical view of Friedman's 'A history of American law.'" *Wisconsin Law Review:* 81–109.

Udy, Stanley
1959   "'Bureaucracy' and 'rationality' in Weber's organization theory." *American Sociological Review,* 24: 791–795.

Veblen, Thorstein
1965   *The Theory of Business Enterprise* (revised edition). New York: Augustus M. Kelley.

Wamsley, Gary, and M. Zald
1973   *The Political Economy of Public Organizations.* Lexington, MA: Lexington Books.

Weber, Max
1946   "Bureaucracy." In Hans Gerth and C. Wright Mills (eds.), From Max Weber: *Essays in Sociology:* 196–244. New York: Oxford.

1949   *The Methodology of the Social Sciences* (1949 translation). New York: Free Press.
1961   *General Economic History* (Collier Books edition). New York: Collier.
1968   *Economy and Society: An Outline of Interpretive Sociology.* New York: Bedminster Press.
1975   "Marginal utility theory and 'the fundamental law of psychophysics.'" *Social Science Quarterly,* 56: 21-36.

Wiley, Mary, and Mayer Zald
1968   "The growth and transformation of educational accrediting agencies: an exploratory study in social control of institutions." *Sociology of Education,* 40: 36-56.

Wilson, James Q.
1975   "The rise of the bureaucratic state." *The Public Interest,* 41: 77-103.

Wolin, Sheldon
1960   *Politics and Vision.* Boston: Little, Brown.

Wright, Erik
1975   "To control or to smash bureaucracy: Weber and Lenin on politics, the state, and bureaucracy." *Berkeley Journal of Sociology,* 19: 69-108.

Zald, Mayer
1970a   *Organizational Change: The Political Economy of the YMCA.* Chicago: University of Chicago Press.
1970b   "Political economy: a framework for comparative analysis." In Mayer Zald (ed.), *Power in Organizations:* 221-261. Nashville: Vanderbilt University Press.
1970c   "The structure of society and social service integration." *Social Science Quarterly,* 50: 557-567.
1978   "On the social control of industries." *Social Forces* (forthcoming).

Zald, Mayer, and F. Hair
1972   "The social control of hospitals." In Basil Geogopoulous (ed.), *Organization Research on Health Institutions:* 51-82. Ann Arbor: University of Michigan, Institute of Social Research.

3.   The Goal Paradigm and Notes Towards a Counter Paradigm*

Petro Georgiou

Organizational analysts have in recent years conducted an intensive review of their field (cf. Scott, 1964; Etzioni, 1960; Gouldner, 1959; Blau, 1968; Thompson, 1968; McGuire, 1961; March and Simon, 1958). The conclusion usually reached is that "organizational theory" is an expression of aspiration rather than a reflection of reality. There is no generally accepted conceptualization of organizations that serves to define the facts, isolate the relevant problems, and prescribe the ways in which research ought to proceed. What exists is merely a heterogeneous accumulation of literature on organizations: "a number of more or less well developed conceptual schemes focussed on various aspects of organizations; a rapidly growing collection of empirical generalizations sometimes relevant to, but often uninformed by, the conceptual schemes; a handful of descriptive studies of concrete organizations and subunits of organizations; and, . . . material which deplores or defends some aspects, or the very existence of organizations or which offers how-to-do-it advice to the various types of organizational participants or aspirants" (Scott, 1964: 485).

By contrast, in the present article, the study of organizations is regarded as possessing an essential unity; as having been dominated since its inception by the conceptualization of organizations as goal attainment devices. The prevailing perception of the diffuseness of organizational analysis overlooks the significance of the fact that whatever conceptual scheme a student adheres to, whatever its claimed distinctiveness, whatever the disconnected piece of empirical research or conventional wisdom relating to organizations, indeed, "Whatever else authors have to say on the general subject, there seems general agreement . . . that it is the dominating presence of a goal that marks off an 'organization' from all other kinds of systems" (Gross, 1969: 227). It is this understanding of organizations as goal attaining instruments that constitutes the shared conceptualization reviewers claim their discipline lacks.

This conception, so fundamental that it is embodied in the very derivation of the word "organization" from the Greek term for a tool, is here designated the *goal paradigm*. "Paradigm" is preferred to either "theory" or "model," which are used interchangeably in the literature, on two grounds. Firstly, while there may be many conflicting models or theories in a particular field, competing for primacy and adherents, the term paradigm denotes an overwhelmingly accepted conceptualization. Secondly, a theory is understood to be tentatively held, subject to empirical

* Reprinted from "The Goal Paradigm and Notes Towards a Counter Paradigm" by Petro Georgiou, published in *Administrative Science Quarterly*, September 1973, vol. 18, no. 3, pp. 291-310, by permission of *The Administrative Science Quarterly*. Copyright © 1973 by Cornell University.

The ideas contained in this paper were first developed in seminars held by Leon Peres at the University of Melbourne, 1968. I also wish to thank Josef Szwarc for his invaluable assistance and Colin Rubenstein and Rudolf Plehwe for their substantive suggestions.

falsification. A paradigm, however, is an article of faith, rejected only when it loses its potency following the occurrence of a quasi-religious conversion experience (Kuhn, 1962: 150.)[1]

Evidence for a goal paradigm is readily available. Even a cursory examination of the literature on organizations illustrates, irrespective of the theory or model utilized, the primacy of organizational goals, but at the same time the extremely restricted scope of the study of goals (cf. however Albrow's 1968 sustained and insightful critique). Attention focusses almost exclusively on determining the degree to which organizations are effective in achieving their goals, how organizations can be made more effective, or the processes through which goals are achieved and succeeded, diverted, or displaced. Rarely are analysts concerned with the question of whether organizations can be said to have goals; their existence is an unquestioned and unquestionable assumption. The only difficulty, insofar as any is recognized, lies in determining precisely what the goals of any particular organization are. (For some of the discussions on goals, cf. Perrow, 1961, 1968; Etzioni, 1964: 5-19; Sills, 1957: 253-270; Warner and Havens, 1968; Simon, 1964; Parsons, 1956; Clark, 1956; Cressey, 1958; Cyert and March, 1963: 26-43; Thompson and McEwen, 1958).

Yet almost invariably, studies demonstrate the fruitlessness of understanding organizations as goal attaining devices. The paradigm retains its primacy not because of the insights it yields, but because it is embedded so deeply in our consciousness that it is a reality rather than a theoretical construct to be discarded when it ceases to enlighten. Intellectually exhausted, the goal paradigm has become a procrustean bed into which all findings are forced and even incipient counter paradigms absorbed, regardless of their promise of greater insight.

THE EVOLUTION OF THE GOAL PARADIGM

The Classical Goal Paradigm: Origins and Inadequacies.   The compelling quality of the goal paradigm rests fundamentally on its apparently logical extrapolation from the distinctive features of the modern organization — exemplified by the public bureaucracy and the business enterprise — as it developed in the nineteenth and twentieth centuries. Compared with other social groups, the modern organization was distinguished by its consciously created network of roles, division of labor, hierarchy of authority, and system of rules. These prominent characteristics led naturally to the view that organizations could best be understood as goal attainment devices.[2] How could the structure of roles be elaborated, the patterns of power determined, the labor divided, the rules devised, if there did not exist a preconceived goal, calling the organization into existence and determining its structure and operations? Accordingly, the organization was seen as "an instrument, a deliberate and rational means for attaining known goals. In some versions the goals are explicitly stated; in others,

---

[1] The paradigm concept is derived from Kuhn (1962). Kuhn equivocates (1962: 13) on whether paradigms exist in the social sciences, and while his hesitation appears generally well founded (cf. Friedrichs, 1970; Wolin, 1968; Holt and Richardson, 1970) organizational analysis, it is here argued, is an exception. This point and the factors contributing to the goal paradigm's hegemony are taken up by Georgiou (1970).

[2] The goal paradigm was not developed by any single individual but appeared in the writings of various contemporaries ranging from Weber, to the classical management theorists Taylor and Fayol, to such writers on public administration as Wilson and Goodnow (cf. Blau, 1968; Waldo, 1968).

the goals are assumed to be self evident as, for example, the assumption that the goal of the private business firm is to maximize profits'' (Thompson, 1968: 397).

The inadequacy of this classical version of the goal paradigm in understanding organizations has been made clear in empirical analyses. The stated goals of the organization have often been found to be vague, contradictory, or multiple, with no clear indication of their respective priorities: for example Shubik's (1961: 109-110) examination of company policy statements found that ''profit was supplemented or even replaced as an objective by commitments to consumers, the personnel of the firm, corporate growth, technological progress, and society in general'' (Albrow, 1968: 154). Even where the goals are explicit, they usually do not specify the means to be used in attaining them. For instance where profit making is the avowed goal, it is not clear whether ''quality or quantity is to be emphasised, whether profits are to be short run and risky or long run and stable'' (Perrow, 1961: 855). These difficulties are further exacerbated by the fact that the stated goals are often largely unrelated to organizational behavior; for example Michels (1962) showed that the stated goals of democratic political parties were substantially divorced from the actual functioning of these parties. Merton (1957) drew attention to the process by which goals were subordinated to means, as organizational members treated rules as ends rather than means for pursuing the substantive organizational goal. The ''human relations'' group (Roethlisberger and Dickson, 1939; Mayo, 1945) and many others found that' people in organizations were not one-dimensional ''officials'' or ''employees.'' They often resisted behavior formally prescribed for them. The resulting accommodations sometimes so changed the organization as to make the stated goals completely irrelevant to organizational behavior and always limited very considerably the degree to which organizations could be understood through their goals.

An Alternative Natural System Model? Gouldner, Selznick, and Parsons.   According to Gouldner (1959), the response to the shortcomings of this classical goal paradigm (which he designated the ''rational model'') was the emergence of an alternative ''natural system model,'' in which organizations are viewed as ''organisms.'' Although designed to achieve some goal, organizations generate needs of their own, the prime one being survival. The satisfaction of these needs results in the relegation of goals to a secondary position. Organizational change is not the product of any deliberate plan, but the spontaneous defence of the organization's equilibrium — a response prompted and directed by values deeply internalized by its members. In Gouldner's (1959: 406) view natural systems theorists ''tend to regard the organization as a whole as organically 'growing' with a 'natural history' of its own which is planfully modified only at great peril, if at all.'' However, an examination of Selznick and Parsons — the authors who Gouldner (1959: 406) considered ''best exemplified'' the natural system approach — provides little support for an actual, as distinct from a potential, bifurcation in the study of organizations. Rather, it indicates that the natural system and rational models are not conflicting conceptual schemes, but stages in the evolution of the goal paradigm.

The work of Selznick (1948, 1949, 1957) did indeed appear to signal a crisis for the goal paradigm. He argued that to view organizations as rational goal attainment devices was mistaken. Planners could never hope to eradicate the nonrational aspects of organizational behavior, the spontaneous patterns that invariably arose alongside the formally established organizational structure. ''Plans and programs reflect the freedom of technical or ideal choice, but organized action cannot escape involvement, a commitment to personnel, or institutions, or procedures which qualifies the initial plan'' (Selznick, 1948: 32). As informal structures become firmly established, the organization matures, "acquires a self, a distinctive identity" (1957: 21). It is transformed from an expendable, infinitely manipulable instrument into an institution valued by its members as an end in itself. Hence, organizations could best be understood as "natural communities," "adaptive social structures" — primarily concerned with self-maintenance and the preservation of their character rather than as technical instruments predicated on the pursuit of goals.

Gouldner (1955; 1959: 409-410) accused Selznick of a "conservative and antiliberal metaphysical pathos" because he emphasized the fragility of rational organizational striving to attain goals, especially liberal ones. Criticism of Selznick on these grounds is, however, misplaced, for Selznick's neo-Burkeanism is a facade (cf. Wolin, 1961: 412-414). Behind it resides a subtle but nonetheless committed proponent of the goal paradigm. The focus of his attack was on the assumption that organizational goals were "essentially unproblematic 'givens' in organization building and decision-making" (Selznick, 1957: 74). This he argued was an evasion of the critical organizational problem — setting and maintaining goals in a constantly changing internal and external situation — a "retreat to technology" which could only culminate in the cardinal organizational sin: "a history of uncontrolled, opportunistic adaptation . . ." (1957: 75). Treating organizations as inert tools requiring only the application of engineering principles similarly led to a distortion of goals by failing to comprehend and anticipate the changes which an organization, "a responsive, adaptive organism" (1957: 5) could wreak. The solution to these problems lay beyond technology and demanded a recognition of the recalcitrance of organizations and the significance of creative leadership. The responsibility of the administrative leader was "to define the ends of group existence, to design an enterprise distinctively adapted to these ends, and to see that the design becomes a living reality . . . by building purpose into the social structure of the enterprise, or . . . [T]ransforming a neutral body of men into a committed polity" (1957: 37, 90).

It is thus ironic that Selznick has been regarded as initiating a critical division in the study of organizations. His emphasis on the organismic dimension of organizational behavior was the prelude, not to a natural system model, but to a restatement and re-affirmation of faith in the paradigm. Underscoring the "recalcitrance of the tools of action" was an attempt to exorcise the paradigm's crudest and most mechanistic assumptions, because in practice, these threatened to undermine the essential character of organizations as goal attainment devices.

With reference to Parsons (1956: 64) his definition of organizations shows his fundamental accord with the goal paradigm: "As a formal analytical point of reference, *primacy of orientation to the attainment of a specific goal* is used as the defining characteristic of an organization which distinguishes it from other types of social systems."

In sum, the goal paradigm has always been the dominant conceptualization of organizations. The natural system model is nothing more than the sophistication and articulation of the goal paradigm, a response to the shortcomings of the classical version which absorbed contrary evidence while leaving its core untouched. The fact that stated goals disclosed little about organizational behavior has merely sparked off a search for real or operative goals. Organizations are still seen as tools, but the emphasis has shifted to their proclivity for turning in their masters' hands, to the processes of goal displacement and distortion. It has now become "one of the central problems in organizational analysis . . . to account for the tendency for some organizations to concentrate on activities and programs that contribute relatively little to the attainment of their major goals" (Warner and Havens, 1968: 540).

Indeed, even Gouldner, despite his belief in the hostile separation of the two models, argued (1959: 426) that a critical task facing analysts was to fuse them into a more powerful model — one that would ''aid in analyzing the distinctive characteristics of the modern organization as a rational bureaucracy, the characteristics which it shares with other kinds of social systems, and the relationship of these characteristics to one another.'' Such an operation could only drain the natural system model of what Gouldner regarded as its distinctive characteristics while requiring only marginal modifications in the goal paradigm.

Etzioni and Real Goals.   The task of synthesis Goulder suggested was undertaken by Etzioni. His work may be considered as exemplifying the process of sophistication which the goal paradigm has undergone. It is a salutary example of the ingenuity devoted to retaining the goal paradigm and the futility of the endeavour. Etzioni (1960, 1961, 1964) distinguished between the goal and system models. The goal model ''focusses on the study of goals and of organizations as their servants, obedient or otherwise . . . [and] has some distinct disadvantages both for studying and evaluating organizations'' (1964: 16). In response, Etzioni (1964: 17) advocated adoption of the system model, which ''constitutes a statement about the relationships which must exist for an organization to operate.'' Its advantage lay in viewing organizations as multifunctional units, involving various groups with different perspectives, thereby alerting the researcher to the dangers of a partisan viewpoint. ''In short,'' Etzioni (1960: 278) stated, ''the system model supplies not only a more adequate model but also a less biased point of view.''

There were two system subtypes, the survival and effectiveness models. The survival model specified the relationships necessary to allow the system to exist, and could answer only yes or no to questions about the functionality of any particular relationship. The effectiveness model, which Etzioni favored (1960: 271-272), ''defines a pattern of interrelationships among the elements of the system which would make it most effective in the service of a given goal.'' The question is, however, if organizations cannot be adequately analyzed as the servants of goals, how can any statements be made about effectiveness other than a positive or negative response to the question: is the organization surviving? How can there be an effectiveness variant of the system model? The answer, which Etzioni gives is his reason for espousing the effectiveness model (1960: 273), is that ''if . . . one accepts the definition that organizations are social units oriented toward the realization of specific goals, the application of the effectiveness model is especially warranted . . .'' (1960: 273). Why anyone, especially Etzioni, in the light of his criticisms of the goal model, should accept this definition is not discussed.

Etzioni thus assimilated the system model into the goal paradigm. However, he rejected stated goals because they are usually meant only for public consumption, and focussed on real goals (1964: 7), ''those future states toward which a majority of the organization's means and the major organizational commitments of the participants are directed.'' These real goals reflect the outcome of conflicts between individuals, departments and strata, and can only be established by ''an examination and extrapolation of on-going organizational processes'' (1961:72).

This concept appears to avoid the misplaced formalism of the classical goal paradigm. Yet in application it raises daunting problems, and its negative implications for the study of effectiveness go unrecognized. Etzioni claimed that having determined the real goals, the researcher, sensitized by the effectiveness model to the system needs of the type of organization he is studying, can judge ''how closely does the organization's allocation of resources approach optimum distribution'' (1960: 262), and how changes affect the organization's ability to ''serve its goals as compared to its earlier state or to other organizations of its kind'' (1964: 19). This looks suspiciously like a tautology which renders the whole question of effectiveness meaningless; at the very least, it prevents the analyst from saying anything consequential about organizational effectiveness.

If real goals are derived from the observation of "on-going organizational processes" (1964: 19) then the actual distribution of resources cannot be widely divergent from the optimal distribution. Further, any significant change in distribution means, by definition, that the real goals have changed. Thus either nothing can be said about how changes affect the ability of the organization to serve its goals as compared to an earlier state, because the organization now pursues new goals, or (and this is the choice Etzioni apparently makes) the real goals identified by the researcher at a particular point in time become sacrosanct. A real goal, reflecting the operation of the organization (and the interests of the dominant coalition) at point X, is transformed into the timeless, legitimate organizational goal. Subsequent changes in the operation of the organization and the consequent alteration of the real goals are referred to as subversion or displacement; the organization "substitutes for its legitimate goal some other goal for which it was not created, for which resources were not allocated to it, and which it is not known to serve" (Etzioni, 1964: 10).

Quite apart from these problems, there is a serious question about whether real goals can be determined. Is the concept operational, or more accurately, is it capable of being made so? Etzioni and others following his line of analysis (Price, 1968) have offered little in the way of workable guidelines. How does one "extrapolate from on-going organizational processes"?

The magnitude of the difficulties involved is evidenced by Etzioni's reversion to the classical goal paradigm's "self-evident" goals. Having declared commitment to the effectiveness model and expounded his notion of real goals, Etzioni (1964: 78-79) stated that "The organizational goal of private business is to make profits. The major means are production and exchange . . . When a professional orientation dominates, this tends to 'displace' the profit goal of privately owned economic organizations."

Perrow and Operative Goals.   A more elegant attempt to retain goals as the major variable in understanding organizations, while avoiding the difficulties inherent in stated goals, is Perrow's (1961: 855) concept of operative goals. These "designate the ends sought through the actual operating policies of the organization; they tell us what the organization is actually trying to do, regardless of what the official goals say are the aims." Operative goals are shaped by the "dominant group, reflecting the imperatives of the particular task that is most critical [to the organization], their own background characteristics (distinctive perspectives based on their training, career lines, and areas of competence) and the unofficial uses to which they put the organization for their own ends" (1961: 856-857).

This is a more satisfactory approach, in that operative goals refer to the ends of one particular group in the organization rather than to some abstracted set of organizational goals. It is also extremely valuable in its view of organizations as vehicles used by various groups to attain particularistic goals, its isolation of the factors that contribute to forming the goals of various groups, and finally in sketching the impact on organizational behavior which the primacy of one group rather than another can have. The fundamental flaw lies in its assumption that the goals of any group can effectively determine the operation of the organization.

All organizations, Perrow argues, must perform four basic tasks: obtain capital inputs, secure basic legitimation, marshall skills, and achieve internal and external coordination. These tasks are unlikely to be equally important simultaneously. The group which performs the most important task facing the organization at any particular time dominates, moulding the organization in its own image.

It is true that at any particular time, one task may have salience in the eyes of organization members. For instance, if all other tasks are being performed adequately and there is a difficulty in obtaining capital for enlarging facilities, those able to secure it may exercise greater influence than when financing was more easily raised or less highly desired. This increment in their power stems from the other contributors surrendering — either willingly or unwillingly — some portion of the rewards which they previously derived in return for the needed money. It is, however, fallacious to argue that any one task can be more important than any other. In a functional sense, all tasks are equally important — a failure to perform any one of them renders the performance of the other tasks difficult or impossible. The difficulty of a particular task, the fact that it is regarded as critical, does not mean that it is the most important, or that the significance of the other tasks is diminished.

The recognition of the equal importance of the various task areas and their mutual dependence is fundamental. Its neglect results in the concept of the dominant group, substantially regarded as independent of all other contributors who in turn are almost completely dependent upon it. Perrow (1961: 856, 861) vests nearly absolute power in the dominant group, defining dominance as "a more pervasive, thorough, and all embracing phenomenon than authority or power . . . . [It is] the ability to control all, or almost all of the actions of others."

Organizational behavior cannot be so fully determined by the goals of any one group. These goals are modified, conditioned and limited by the need to satisfy the demands of the other groups upon which the ostensibly dominant group is dependent to achieve its goals, or more accurately, some part of them.

This point is driven home by Perrow's example of hospitals. None of the three groups he discusses — trustees, administrators, or doctors — can achieve the degree of control required by a dominant group, because the goal attainment of each is firmly dependent on the resources possessed by the others. Herein lies the answer to Perrow's (1961: 859) slight puzzlement over the failure of doctors to dominate all hospitals, despite the "increasing complexity and specialization of the doctor's skills, their common professional background, the power of organized medicine, and the prestige accorded to the doctor in society." However formidable these assets, they fall short of the overwhelming control of time, money, prestige, and multiple skills, which could render them so independent of other contributors as to make them dominant in Perrow's sense. Moreover, power is distributed throughout the organization. Groups other than doctors, trustees, and administrators control resources which enable them to play a significant part in determining organizational behavior, the nursing staff for instance (cf. Scheff, 1961; Mechanic, 1962).

If operative goals were to be discerned through the extremely careful study that Perrow (1961: 856) suggests, including the analysis of "series of minor decisions," hospitals would probably be closer to what Perrow (1961: 860-861) describes as organizations with multiple leadership than organizations dominated by one group.

Blau and Scott: *Cui Bono?* The goal paradigm, it must be emphasized, is no mere appendix to the study of organizations, a residue from a less sophisticated period which can be readily severed to leave the bulk of analyses unscathed and a sound basis for understanding organizations. The concern with organization goals is more than a regrettable deflection of intellectual resources caused primarily by the desire to study the problem of organizational effectiveness.[3] It derives fundamentally from the belief that organizations are goal attainment devices, and that *ipso facto* the pursuit of goals is the critical variable determining organizational behavior. This is most clearly seen in the attempt to construct typologies based on a single taxonomic principle (Burns, 1967:119).

An example is the widely current Blau-Scott typology (1963) in which the criterion *cui bono* is used as the foundation of classification because "the identity of the prime beneficiary of the organization's operations has far-reaching consequences for its structural characteristics" (1963: 57). The rationale for this derives from Blau and Scott's (1963:1) adherence to the classical goal paradigm; organizations are "established for the explicit purpose of achieving certain goals." More precisely, they are created to serve the interests of a particular group, the prime beneficiary. On this basis, four types of organizations are differentiated: mutual-benefit associations, business concerns, service organizations and commonweal organizations, respectively benefiting primarily the membership, owners, client groups, and public at large. While emphasizing that all parties contributing to the organization derive certain benefits, Blau and Scott asserted (1963: 43) the utility of the concept of prime beneficiary on the grounds that "the benefits to one party furnish the reasons for the organization's existence, while the benefits to others are essentially a cost." The illustration they used to underscore the difference between the prime beneficiary and other groups is the business concern where "the prime beneficiary is the owner of the firm. He established it for the purpose of making a profit, and he will close it should it operate for long showing a loss" (1963:43).

The problem with the definition of the prime beneficiary is that almost all membership groups satisfy it. If the employees find it is not in their interest to work for the organization, or the customers to buy from it, then it would cease operation just as surely as if the owner's profits stopped. The existence of the organization is dependent on its ability to elicit contributions from various individuals, each making his own cost-benefit calculations. Hence organizational structure and functioning must reflect these calculations, if contributions are to continue.

Further, Blau and Scott recognized that often those who decide key questions of organization structure and functioning are not those whom their initial categorization of prime beneficiaries suggests, for example oligarchic unions and public corporations. Where this is so — and the studies of organizations classified as mutual-benefit associations: "political parties, fraternal organizations, clubs, veterans associations, professional organizations and religious sects" (1963:45) suggest that these are generally oligarchic — it is clear that the analytic value of the typology is severely restricted.

The attempt to overcome this difficulty aggravates rather than resolves it, for Blau and Scott are forced to argue that the locus of power must lie with the prime beneficiary. Thus, a change in the identity of the group with controlling power — for example, from the membership to an oligarchic leadership in the case of a mutual-benefit organization, or from the owners to top management in a business concern — means a change in the type of organization (1963:44). The typology, however, makes

---

[3] Even if it were only this, the severance could not be very clean. The problem of effectiveness has pervaded most studies. Price (1968: 3), for instance, used the concept of effectiveness as the basis for his summary of the empirical literature on the grounds that it was a "classical problem in the study of organizations. Its classical standing arises from the centrality of 'goals' in all definitions of organization . . . [and] is commonly an implied problem in this immense literature."

no allowance for such changes. In what categories do oligarchic unions and public corporations belong? Blau and Scott's argument is also vitiated by the concession, made at various points, that the group "intended to benefit" may still be benefiting despite the shift in the locus of power. Indeed, the coincidence of power and prime beneficiary may be harmful to the benefits which the prime beneficiary seeks. The reason "democratic controls are often sacrificed" in unions is because oligarchic leadership is "in the interests of promoting the effective accomplishment of objectives" (Blau and Scott, 1963:48).

If undemocratic unions are effective — whether the leaders are oligarchs from altruistic or self-interested motives — does this not suggest that the prime beneficiary has not changed? Like the union members, corporation shareholders may be content with the manager's exercise of power providing that it produces the desired rewards. But while the rewards these groups demand are thus extremely important, it is clear that the restraints they place on the organizational elites may be extremely vague and tolerant. Would they still remain the most significant group for studying organizational structure and change?

FOUNDATIONS OF A COUNTER PARADIGM

Organizational analysts have been unable to cope with the reality of organizations because their vision is monopolized by an image of the organization as a whole; an entity not merely greater than the sum of its parts, but so superior that it is effectively divorced from the influence of the parts. The whole is regarded not as the product of interaction between the parts, but as determining them. The organization is endowed with a personality while the individuals constituting it are depersonalized, role players in the service of the organization's goals. Although it is generally recognized that individuals participate in organizations to attain their own goals; that organizations must adapt to these ends if they are to persist; that adaptation is continuous as organization members exploit the opportunities they find and create for increasing their rewards; this recognition nonetheless has little impact on the basic conceptualization of organizations.

Barnard's Image of Organizations.   Barnard (1938) more than any other transcended the image of organizations as goal attaining instruments. He saw them as cooperative, incentive distributing devices. Individuals contributed their activities to organizations in return for incentives, the contribution of each in the pursuit of his particularistic ends being a contribution to the satisfaction of the ends of others. Instead of goals being the key to organizational behavior, Barnard regarded the motives of the individuals participating in organizations as the critical determinants. Only if these were satisfied could the organization continue to operate. He stated (1938:139) that

> The contributions of personal efforts which constitute the energies of organizations are yielded by individuals because of incentives. The egotistical motives of self-preservation and of self satisfaction are dominating forces; on the whole, organizations can exist only when consistent with the satisfaction of these motives, unless, alternatively, they can change these motives. *The individual is always the basic strategic factor in organization* [italics added].

Barnard certainly regarded purpose as an essential element of organization, but this concept, although ambiguous, has little resemblance to the notion of goals used by the authors already discussed. For him, the purpose of the organization, rather than being the end to which the organization was oriented, was the means to the personal satisfaction of its contributors; it described that activity to which the energies of individuals are given. Barnard (1938:154) took great pains, for example, to emphasize that the purpose of privately owned industrial enterprises was not profit, but production. More recently Katz and Kahn (1966) used a similar formulation, but differed from Barnard in making purpose the "basic strategic factor."

In Barnard's analysis, purpose is subordinate to the contributors' demands; to be ignored, discarded or altered if this is what the satisfaction of the contributors' incentives required. Organizational success in this view cannot be judged by the degree to which any organizational goal is achieved, but only by the "absolute test" of an incentive system — its capacity to survive through being able to elicit sufficient contributions from its participants by providing them with sufficient rewards.

Notwithstanding the limitations of Barnard's analysis, he supplied the foundations of a counter paradigm. If his perception of the organization as the medium through which individuals pursue a diversity of personal goals is developed, and the ambiguities and tensions in his work are resolved in accordance with this central insight, it can help the study of organizations break out of the conceptual impasse represented by the goal paradigm.[4]

Incentive Analysis and Goal Paradigm Compared. An incentive system paradigm could provide a far more realistic conceptual scheme for understanding organizations, developing generalizations about them and directing research more fruitfully. It would be capable of accommodating realities disclosed by empirical studies that have proved so intractable when examined on the basis of the goal paradigm. Organizational change, conflict, goal displacement and succession can be explained in terms consistent with the conceptualization of organizations as incentive systems, as outcomes of the primordial organizational process — the constant adjustments that must be made in the organization because of the striving of individuals and groups to increase, maintain, or exchange the rewards they get from the organization in return for their contributions to it.

The goal paradigm by contrast cannot cope with such problems. Goal displacement is the most extreme case. This phenomenon contradicts the fundamental postulate of the paradigm and thus cannot be explained in terms of the paradigm. Organizations as tools can only determine their goals if their masters allow them to slip in their hands. This is not to argue that analysts subscribing to the goal paradigm do not understand organizational change. Highly sophisticated explanations are given in terms of the differential rewards and interests of the various organizational participants. The point is that these explanations cannot be reconciled with the proposition that organizations are goal attainment devices. The very nature of the explanations emphasizes the necessity for an alternative conceptualization.

---

[4] Cf. Krupp's (1961: 91-107) critical discussion of Barnard. This however identifies Barnard a little too closely with Simon, to whom many of Krupp's criticisms are more directly applicable. Although Simon (1957, 1964) also utilizes the incentive system approach in his analysis, it is clearly harnessed to a highly rationalistic, goal oriented conception of organization. See also the initial emphasis on incentive analysis and its subsequent subordination to the goal paradigm by March and Simon (1958). The contrast between Barnard and Simon is highlighted by their different understanding of efficiency, a concept central to both their theories. For Simon (1957:39), efficiency requires "the greatest accomplishment of organizational objectives," whereas Barnard (1938:93) defines it as "the capacity to offer effective inducements in sufficient quantity" to enable the organization to survive.

Again, it must be stressed that the fact that those who hold to the goal paradigm have an appreciation of these aspects of organizational behavior, does not mean that the goal paradigm is a residue from a less sophisticated, more mechanistic period, and is no longer important. Adherence to the goal paradigm involves the disassociation of reality and conceptual schema, thus reducing the possibility of pay-offs from empirical research. More significantly, the paradigm distorts our view of the empirical findings. When generalizations about organizations are made, it is not the documented pursuit of individual and group interests that appear as primary determinants of organizational behavior, but the pursuit of organizational goals. So Etzioni (1961) in his impressive assessment of empirical findings, recognized the critical nature of compliance, and, by definition, the importance of resistance. Yet, in hypothesizing about the sources and direction of organizational change, he identified (1961:87) the "strain towards an effective type" and stated (1961:15) that "Congruent types are more effective than incongruent types. Organizations are under pressure to be effective. Hence, to the degree that the environment of the organization allows, *organizations tend to shift their compliance structure from incongruent to congruent types and organizations which have congruent compliance structures tend to resist factors pushing them towards incongruent compliance structures.*" (Etzioni's italics.) But he did not specify the forces pushing the organization to be effective. It was accepted as axiomatic that since organizations are goal attainment devices, they must therefore strive for effectiveness, which begs the question posed by Burns (1967:121), that "If there is so much pressure towards congruence, how do organizations get to be incongruent in the first place?"

Perrow (1967:205) argued that Barnardian analysis works well only for a "routine organization with a stable product environment . . . . Where non-routine activities are involved, however, the measurement of both inducements and contributions tends to be difficult, and little is gained by the model except the unenlightening assertion that if a person stays in the organization and produces, there must be some kind of inducement at least to match his contribution." The point about the difficulty of measurement is important; indeed, Barnard (1938:240-257) himself emphasized it; but it is unwarranted to conclude from this that the model is of little use. With the idea that organizations are groups of individuals pursuing their own rewards, the way is open to categorizing the kinds of rewards individuals pursue through organizations, and from there to an understanding of the sources and types of organizational conflict, the reasons for organizational change, and the direction it may take.

Clark and Wilson's Incentive Analysis: Potentialities and Limitations.   The explanatory power inherent in incentive system analysis is demonstrated by Clark and Wilson (1961). Developing Barnard, they postulated that the incentive system was the critical variable affecting organizational behavior. Using the "principal incentive" relied on by the organization to elicit contributions as the basis of classification, they put forward a threefold typology of organizations: utilitarian, solidary, and purposive.

Utilitarian organizations rely primarily on material incentives: "rewards that have a monetary value or can easily be translated into ones that have" (1961:134). The organization's preoccupation is recruiting material resources. The activities through which this is done are relatively flexible, and "relatively little attention is paid to the substantive goals implied by its activities" (1961:139). Insofar as statements about goals are made, they are ritualistic, oriented at gaining public legitimacy for the organization while having little influence on its behavior. Conflicts focus on the distribution of material resources rather than on the activities of the organization or its goals.

Solidary organizations are based on intangible incentives deriving essentially from "the act of associating and include such rewards as socializing, congeniality, the sense of group membership and identification, the status arising from membership . . . and so on" (1961:134). The emphasis is on obtaining solidary resources, for example through recruiting high-status or sociable individuals, and in return enhancing their prestige. Considerable attention is given to the formulation of goals for they are important in attracting contributors: goals must be socially acceptable, indeed socially applauded, for organizational prestige is of the essence. Nevertheless, goals are essentially secondary. Since they must be acceptable to contributors they are characterized by considerable ambiguity and often altered to satisfy present and potential contributors. It is the provision of solidary incentives that critically determines organization behavior and structure, both being geared to organizational prestige and attractiveness rather than to the achievement of goals. The basic conflicts are over the distribution of status and the inclusion of members who cannot contribute adequate solidary resources.

Purposive organizations rely on their stated goals as incentives: "the intrinsic worth or dignity of the ends themselves are regarded by members as justifying efforts" (1961:146). Precisely because of this, goals tend to be highly generalized, for any attempt to make them more specific threatens loss of membership. Consequently, purposive organizations often cannot act decisively and considerable attention is given to producing a frequently spurious sense of accomplishment: "rhetoric about 'moral victories' may often replace actual achievements, [for,] if tactical flexibility is not possible, moral victories have to replace actual accomplishments" (1961:148). In those purposive organizations where the goal can be specified, for example ideological political parties, membership commitment means that goal change or even tactical change leads to a loss of contributors who believe that their reason for being in the organization has disappeared. The major conflicts are over the statement of goals, the relationship between means and ends, and the responsibility for failure to attain the stated goals.

The major limitation of Clark and Wilson's analysis stems from a reluctance to accept completely the implications of its underlying premise. Although Clark and Wilson approved Barnard's (1938:139) statement that "the individual is the basic strategic factor," they stated (1961:131), "The point of view of this paper is that the most important thing to know about an organization is that it *is* an organization and that it seeks to persist." The individual is thereby reduced to a tactical factor while the key to organizations is made "persistence" or "survival," a concept that is not merely extremely difficult to define, but is in Clark and Wilson's (1961:164) own view, "too coarse" to cope with important aspects of organizational behavior. More particularly, the shift of perspective from the individual's pursuit of incentives through the organization, to the organization's persistence strivings, brings incentive analysis to a halt. The subordination of incentive to survival analysis is evident, as are the problems involved, when Clark and Wilson's treatment of the executive and power is examined.

The role of the executive — performed because he derives his "reputation and in some cases his livelihood and material success" (1961:134) from it — is the maintenance of the organization. The executive is in substance presented as omniscient and omnipotent, distributing incentives to contributors in accordance with their importance for organizational survival. The explanation for his control of incentives appears to lie in the distinction between activities, that is, the contributions of individuals to the organization, and incentives, the rewards generated by the organization (1961:133). The executive controls incentives because he mediates the process of exchange; it is through his efforts that contributions are elicited, coordinated and thereby transmuted into incentives. The generation of incentives is uniquely an organizational process, and the executive is the pivot of the organization, all exchanges being routed through him.

This apotheosis of the executive (and the preoccupation with survival) stems from an implicit concern with the problem of organizational order. Having accepted the individual as the basic strategic factor in organization, that he acts to minimize his costs and maximize returns, Clark and Wilson are hard pressed to explain how such collectivities of self-interested individuals can persist. Their solution is the executive, whom they define in such a way as to make him a man in whom self-interest, organizational interest, and power coincide.

The solution is neat, but creates two major problems. First, the equation of the executive's interest with the perpetuation of the organization *per se* is not justified. Like all other contributors, the executive usually values the organization not for itself, but for the rewards it provides him. Thus, he will participate only so long as these are forthcoming, and, in certain circumstances his commitment may well be lower than that of other individuals. (Contrast the unequivocal commitment to organizational survival characteristic of Clark and Wilson's executive with the conditional commitment of that not totally imaginary figure, the economists' entrepreneur.) Second, the analysis is faulty in that the exchange of incentives is regarded totally, or at the very least preponderantly, as channelled through and sanctioned by the executive, when in fact exchanges by-pass him, take place without his knowledge, and even against his wishes. The distinction between activities and incentives, made so the executive can be seen as the fount of organizational rewards, cannot be sustained. The activities of nonexecutive contributors are incentives for other individuals in the organization. These incentives may either be direct, valued as ends in themselves, or indirect in that they constitute means to some further ends.

The distinction between these types of incentives may be difficult to draw, but examples of direct incentives are: the exchange between a security guard allowing a worker to smuggle goods out from a factory in return for a share in these material rewards; a warder warning prisoners that a raid for contraband will be made, thus receiving solidary rewards — being considered a ''good Joe'' (Sykes, 1958:54-55); between workers maximizing solidary rewards and minimizing contributions by controlling rules and output (Roy, 1954-1955). Examples of indirect incentives are the cooperation between line foremen and workers against staff men in order to prevent the latter gaining power and diminishing the line's incentives (Dalton, 1950); the cultivation of secretaries because they control access to the boss (Wilensky, 1961:227-229).

These illustrations also highlight the limits of seeing power as determined by the executive's evaluation of ''the effect that any contributor's presence or absence may have on the survival of the organization'' (Clark and Wilson, 1961:154). They point to the need to locate and measure power in the relationships of organizational members to one another. With incentive analysis carried through to its conclusion, it is clear that the whole organization is a complex series of ramifying and crosscutting exchanges between individuals and groups aiming to maximize the rewards they derive from the organization. The power of contributors is dependent on the contributions which they make to other individuals and groups rather than on the executive's appreciation of their contribution to the survival of the organization. The executive is certainly a useful label to describe the particular person (or persons) controlling disproportionate amounts of incentives and greatly influencing the structure of the organizational market, but he still controls only a segment of the incentives available in the organization. Analytically, the executive is but one part of the incentive exchanging process, and does not warrant elevation to the unique status accorded him by Clark and Wilson.

NOTES TOWARDS A COUNTER PARADIGM

It may appear at this stage that the concept of organization as an analytically distinct social unit has been almost completely dissolved. To a considerable extent this has been the intention of the present paper, and this dissolution constitutes the central component of an alternative conception of organization. Other elements of the counter paradigm have emerged somewhat disconnectedly in the course of the critique of the goal paradigm and the examination of Clark and Wilson, and may now be drawn together.

Organization as arbitrary focus.   If organizational behavior and organizational change are to be understood, the concept of organization must be recognized as an arbitrarily defined focus of interest. Out of the network of social relationships of any society, one form of relationship, differentiated by its apparently enacted character and possession of formal rules, has been treated as if it possessed its own distinctive logic and motivation towards the attainment of some organizational goal. At least some of the responsibility for this lies with Max Weber (Gerth and Mills, 1946), for his ideal type bureaucracy has misled analysts. It is so much a one-sided accentuation (Weber, 1949:90) of the orientation to rational rules that, however useful as a historical comparison between the administrative arrangements corresponding with the various forms of legitimate authority, it is too far divorced from actual organizations to be used in analyzing them.

The modes of behavior in all social units, whether designated organizations or not, are fundamentally premised on the derivation and contribution of incentives, and organizations cannot be regarded as a form of interaction in which the exchange of incentives is embodied in formal rules.[5] Rules represent only one of the processes of exchange and they are constantly being enforced, altered, ignored, or applied differentially in accordance with the rewards desired by the various contributors, and their power to attain them. Moreover, rules exist in most forms of social interaction; it is in the *formality* of the rules that organizations differ, but this is a formalistic not an analytical distinction. (Even on this formalistic level, the distinction between crescive and enacted relationships (Blau, 1968: 298) tends to be tenuous, for crescive relationships themselves tend to formalize rules once they have persisted for a sufficient period of time.)

Nor can the distinctiveness of organizations be sustained on the grounds that organizations constitute systems. The rationale for considering an organization a

---

[5] Cf. Blau (1964: Ch. 8 and p. 260). While Blau provides an illuminating treatment of the nature of exchange between individuals and groups, in the case of organizations, he focusses almost exclusively on indirect change — the exchanges between the organization and the individual embodied in the formal rules and oriented to the achievement of the organizational goals. Direct exchanges between the members and behavior that cannot be understood from the standpoint of the organizational goal are relegated to the interstices of the organization. Blau's exchange theory thus culminates in the goal paradigm (see also Dahlstrom, 1966: 260-263).

system must be that the relationships falling within the boundaries of the organization are more significant for understanding the organization than those without. Yet boundaries have never been defined in such a way as to comply with this requirement. Even where the organization is designated an open system and intimations given about how and where boundaries may be drawn in an analytically meaningful way, ultimately the commonsense boundaries of organizations are accepted (with a marginal qualification that these might be misleading) and the conventionally defined organization is treated as an analytically valid system (Katz and Kahn, 1966).

In sum, organizations can only be defined by conventional usage: the organizational analyst's primary sphere of interest lies in understanding the behavior which takes place within what are commonly referred to as organizations. This is an arbitrary focus of interest, and while arbitrariness is acceptable to this point, if taken any further, it distorts analysis. The delimitation of an area of interest may not be transformed into a system — this term and "boundary" and "environment" may all be legitimately used as references to the focus of interest, but they ought not to be converted into analytically charged concepts. The relationships which must be examined in order to understand the behavior within the focus "organization" manifestly cannot be restricted to those falling within the ambit of the conventionally accepted boundaries of the organization. They must include those relationships that have a significant impact on organizational behavior, for in an analytical sense, these are just as much a part of the organization as are the relationships falling within the conventional boundaries.

Individual Basic in Organization.   The basic strategic factor in organization is the individual. Understanding behavior in the complex of relationships called "organization" can only be based on ascertaining the rewards which various individuals pursue through the organization.

This statement may seem pessimistic for generating typologies; but there is a middle road between the multitude of types implied by a literal individual approach, and the grossness of the organization as an entity in its own right upon which the goal paradigm foundered. The difficulties of the latter, even per medium of incentive analysis, are encountered by Clark and Wilson's principal incentive typology, and are acknowledged by these authors (1961:137), who stress the need for mixed incentives in some organizations. The most obvious problem is that even if the rewards sought by a majority are identified, significant power is wielded by minorities who are otherwise motivated. A related problem, alluded to by Clark and Wilson, is the need to distinguish between "principal" and "operative" incentives, that is, between incentives which may be the *sine qua non* of contributions but nevertheless not the relevant ones in understanding particular aspects of behavior. Barnard (1938:145), for instance, noted that beyond a certain point, material inducements ceased to be a dominating factor motivating individuals, and that from there on "the opportunities for distinction, prestige, personal power, and the attainment of dominating position" became the paramount motivations.

The most promising direction for refining the range of incentives, and characterizing their ordering and interaction within organizations, would appear to be through the analysis of categories of organizational members seeking the same sorts of rewards. Empirical studies of a wide variety of organizations already provide considerable material for identifying such categories, and would allow general statements to be made about how members of such categories are likely to behave in various organizations. In turn this would permit the classification of organizations in accordance with the configuration of categories involved, and the ways in which their members would be likely to restrict and modify the incentives and behavior of others.

The great many findings that have come from investigations of professionals suggest the possibilities. Much is known about the rewards sought by professionals in organizations and the consequences of these for the organization; the ways in which professionals' behavior is conditioned by the incentives sought by other organizational members; and the types of exchange arrangements which professionals will enter. Furthermore the category of professionals can be differentiated and refined into various types as with "cosmopolitans" and "locals" (Gouldner, 1957-1958).

Power and the Organizational Marketplace.   The organization is seen not as an incentive distributing device, abstracted from the relationships of its members, but as a marketplace in which incentives are exchanged. From this, power is regarded not as a relationship between contributors and the organization, but as a relationship between contributors. The possession of power is a function of the capacity of an individual to contribute incentives to one or many, or even all of the other contributors to the organization. Both the exchange of incentives and the possession of power are evident throughout the organization, every individual having some power because he contributes to the satisfaction of someone else's wants. Further it follows that power is both situational and mercurial (Riesman *et al.*, 1950: 257), and cannot be captured by either survival analysis or goal paradigm, but must be located in the context of the concrete exchange relationships entered into by contributors. Thus, whatever conclusion one reached about the relative contribution to survival made by an organizational member, his position in the organizational hierarchy, or his participation in the process of decision making, the conclusion as to his power would still have to be determined by various factors:

1. The member(s) with whom the exchange was taking place; for example, the power of a foreman would generally be different as against the men on the line, as against the general manager, or as against a worker who was his brother-in-law.

2. The issue involved; for instance, the general manager's ability to dismiss a man on the line would generally differ depending on whether the dismissal was made for an admitted misdemeanor or was arbitrary, in which case, the man might have union support.

3. The effects of time which would be relevant in two ways; the changes in members' evaluation of incentives, and the widely noted ability of subordinates to effectively resist and undermine the directives of their superiors, in accordance with their own incentives.

If the power of organizational members is seen as an expression of their ability to contribute incentives to other members, then the relative power possessed by the individuals in any particular relationship would seem to rest on their replaceability and dispensability.

Replaceability.   The power of any organizational member would be in part a function of the extent to which the organizational members to whom he contributes incentives could replace him with another who could provide these incentives "more economically." What is meant by "more economically" is often a complex problem as in the example of the general manager dismissing the worker. An employer's freedom to hire somebody to do "the same work" for a lower wage (that is, act rationally in a strict economic sense), is complicated by costs involved in (a) union opposition to the dismissal of the man, (b) the effects on productivity if the man is popular and his dismissal lowers morale, (c) contractual and industrial law obligations involved in the employer-employee relationship. Thus, the incentive-exchange relationship between the general manager and employee is not simply one of "wages-work" but has ramifications throughout the organization.

The considerable power usually associated with ownership or legal control of material assets is very much a result of the variable of replaceability. From the employees' point of view, it is not easy to replace the "boss," but it is certainly far from impossible. Governments are known to have taken over public utilities where these no longer satisfy more materially oriented private owners, and even to acquire firms against their owners' wishes.

Dispensability.[6]   The power of any organizational member will be partly a function of the extent to which the rewards he provides are valued by other organizational members. Where the first variable focussed on the particular person providing incentives and took the value of the incentives as a given, this variable focusses on the incentives themselves. This is simply to say that the more any member's contribution of incentives is valued by other members, the more they can be expected to concede in the process of exchange, assuming that they cannot achieve those incentives at less cost to themselves, that is, by replacement. The value assigned to any contribution by other organizational members must be assessed relative to other incentives and over time.

Power in organizations is thus highly complex. It reflects organization members' assessment of their own and others' dispensability and replaceability within an intricate network of exchanges, as contrasted with the goal paradigm's view that the distribution and exercise of power is to be understood in terms of the logic supplied by some superordinate goal. It should also be noted that the dominant conception of power (cf. Dahrendorf, 1959:157-173; Parsons, 1967; Weber, 1947:152; Lehman, 1969) parallels the goal paradigm in its emphasis on goal attainment. The difficulties the goal paradigm has faced in establishing organizational goals through which behavior in organizations can be satisfactorily comprehended suggests that the conceptualization of power as the achievement of intended ends through social action might warrant re-examination. The notion of power may have to be reformulated in recognition of the fact that the outcome of power relations cannot often be understood in terms of the attainment of preconceived, determinate goals — whether these be the consensually accepted "collective goals" of Parson's theory, or the particularistic, imposed goals of Dahrendorf's conflict analysis. The stress, for example, may have to be placed on the ways and the extent to which the goals pursued by individuals and groups, and the resources they bring to bear, condition the outcomes of their power relations, outcomes which frequently are unintended by any of the actors involved.

Conclusion.   Thus, the essential thrust of the counter paradigm is that the emergence of organizations, their structure of roles, division of labor, and distribution of power, as well as their maintenance, change, and dissolution can best be understood as outcomes of the complex exchanges between individuals pursuing a diversity of goals. Although the primary focus of interest lies in the behavior within organizations, and the impact of the environment on this, the reciprocal influence of the organization on the environment is also accommodated. Since not all the incentives derived from the processes of organizational exchange are consumed within the interpersonal relations of the members, organizational contributors gain resources

---

[6] This formulation of dispensability was sharpened by Emerson's (1962) discussion of "Power-Dependence Relations."

with which they can influence the impact of the environment. Some of this influence is exercised by the members in a private capacity. For example, the organizational distribution of material incentives to the contributors is relevant to their acting as consumers, investors, contributors to political parties, and so on.

More importantly, however, members of the organization will be able to utilize the resources contributed to the organization to bring about changes in the environment as representatives of the organizational marketplace. Executives, for instance, may take decisions affecting the structure of communities, determine whether plants are to be established or shut down and where, bargain with governments and set the price of goods, and so forth. Yet the capacity to make these decisions is firmly rooted in the exchange arrangements made by organizational members, and the nature of the decisions are to a significant degree outcomes of the complex process of accommodation and adjustment between the various ends sought through the organization. This does not imply that all the exchanges made throughout the organization must be analyzed in order to understand any particular decision. Which exchanges are viewed as particularly salient will depend on the area of interest and the facts of the particular case in hand. It does mean, however, that the more adequate analysis of intra-organizational exchange that the counter paradigm makes possible should assist in an understanding of the impact of organizations on their environment.

REFERENCES

Albrow, Martin
1968   "The study of organizations — objectivity or bias?" In J. Gould (ed.), *Penguin Social Sciences Survey 1968:* 146-167. Harmondsworth: Penguin.

Barnard, Chester I.
1938   *The Functions of the Executive.* Cambridge: Harvard University Press.

Blau, Peter M.
1964   *Exchange and Power in Social Life.* New York: Wiley.
1968   "Theories of organizations." In the *International Encyclopaedia of the Social Sciences,* II: 297-305. New York: Macmillan.

Blau, Peter M., and W. Richard Scott
1963   *Formal Organizations: A Comparative Approach.* London: Routledge and Kegan Paul.

Burns, Thomas
1967   "The comparative study of organizations." In Victor H. Vroom (ed.), *Methods of Organizational Research:* 113-170. University of Pittsburgh Press.

Clark, Burton R.
1956   "Organizational adaption and precarious values." *American Sociological Review,* 21: 327-336.

Clark, Peter B., and James Q. Wilson
1961   "Incentive systems: a theory of organizations." *Administrative Science Quarterly,* 6: 129-166.

Cressey, Donald R.
1958   "Achievement of an unstated organizational goal." *Pacific Sociological Review,* 1: 43-49.

Cyert, Richard M., and James G. March
1963   *A Behavioral Theory of the Firm.* Englewood Cliffs: Prentice-Hall.

Dahlström, Edmund
1966   "Exchange, influence and power." *Acta Sociologica,* 9: 237-284.

Dahrendorf, Ralf
1959   *Class and Class Conflict in an Industrial Society.* London: Routledge and Kegan Paul.

Dalton, Melville
1950   "Conflicts between staff and line managerial officers." *American Sociological Review,* 15: 342-351.

Emerson, Richard M.
1962   "Power-Dependence Relationships." *American Sociological Review,* 27: 34-41.

Etzioni, Amitai
1960   "Two approaches to organizational analysis: a critique and a suggestion."

Administrative Science Quarterly, 5: 257-278.

1961   *A Comparative Analysis of Complex Organizations*. Glencoe: Free Press.

1964   *Modern Organizations*. Englewood Cliffs: Prentice-Hall.

Friedrichs, Robert W.

1970   *A Sociology of Sociology*. New York: Free Press.

Georgiou, Petro

1970   "The paradigm of organizations." Paper presented at Annual Conference of the Australasian Political Studies Association, Canberra, August 1970.

Gerth, Hans H., and C. Wright Mills

1946   *From Max Weber*. New York: Oxford University Press.

Gouldner, Alvin W.

1955   "Metaphysical pathos and the theory of bureaucracy." *American Political Science Review*, 49 (June): 496-507.

1957-1958   "Cosmopolitans and locals: towards an analysis of latent social roles: I and II." *Administrative Science Quarterly*, 2: 280-306, 444-480.

1959   "Organizational analysis." In Robert K. Merton, Leonard Broom and Leonard S. Cottrell (eds.), *Sociology Today*: 400-428. New York: Basic Books.

Gross, Edward

1969   "The definition of organizational goals." *British Journal of Sociology*, 20: 277-294.

Holt, Robert T., and John M. Richardson

1970   "Paradigms in comparative politics." In Robert T. Holt and John E. Turner (eds.), *The Methodology of Comparative Research*: 20-71. New York: Free Press.

Katz, Daniel, and Robert L. Kahn

1966   *The Social Psychology of Organizations*. New York: Wiley.

Krupp, Sherman

1961   *Pattern in Organizational Analysis*. New York: Holt, Rinehart and Winston.

Kuhn, Thomas S.

1962   *The Structure of Scientific Revolutions*. Chicago: University of Chicago Press.

Lehman, Edward W.

1969   "Towards a macrosociology of power." *American Sociological Review*, 9: 453-465.

March, James G., and Herbert A. Simon

1958   *Organizations*. New York: Wiley.

McGuire, Joseph W.

1961   "The concept of the firm." *California Management Review*, 3: 64-88.

Mayo, Elton

1945   *The Social Problems of an Industrial Civilization*. London: Routledge and Kegan Paul.

Mechanic, David

1962   "Sources of power of lower participants in complex organizations." *Administrative Science Quarterly*, 7: 349-364.

Merton, Robert K.

1957   "Bureaucratic structure and personality." In his *Social Theory and Social Structure*: 195-206. Glencoe: Free Press.

Michels, Robert

1962   *Political Parties*. New York: Collier.

Parsons, Talcott

1956   "Suggestions for a sociological approach to the theory of organization: I and II." *Administrative Science Quarterly*, 1: 63-85, 225-239.

1967   "On the concept of political power." In his *Sociological Theory and Modern Society*: 297-354. New York: Free Press.

Perrow, Charles

1961   "The analysis of goals in complex organizations." *American Sociological Review*, 26: 854-866.

1967   "A framework for the analysis of complex organizations." *American Sociological Review*, 32: 194-208.

1968   "Organizational goals." In the *International Encyclopaedia of the Social Sciences*, II: 305-316. New York: Macmillan.

Price, James L.

1968   *Organizational Effectiveness: An Inventory of Propositions*. Homewood: Irwin.

Riesman, David, in collaboration with Reuel Denney and Nathan Glazer.

1950   *The Lonely Crowd: A Study of the Changing American Character*. New Haven and London: Yale University Press.

Roethlisberger, F. J., and W. J. Dickson

1939   *Management and the Worker*. Cambridge: Harvard University Press.

Roy, Donald

1954-1955   "Efficiency and 'the fix': informal intergroup relationships in a piecework machine shop." *American Journal of Sociology*, 60: 255-266.

Scheff, Thomas J.

1961   "Control over policy by attendants in a mental hospital." *Journal of Health and Human Behavior*, 2: 93-105.

Scott, W. Richard

1964   "Theory of organizations." in Robert E. L. Faris (ed.), *Handbook of Modern Sociology*: 585-629. Chicago: Rand McNally.

Selznick, Philip

1948   "Foundations of a theory of organizations." *American Sociological Review*, 13: 25-35.

1949   *TVA and the Grass Roots*. Berkeley and Los Angeles: University of California Press.

1957   *Leadership in Administration*. New York: Harper and Row.

Shubik, Martin

1961   "Approaches to the study of decision making relevant to the firm." *Journal of Business*, 34: 101-118.

Sills, David L.

1957   *The Volunteers: Means and Ends in a National Organization*. Glencoe: Free Press.

Simon, Herbert A.

1964   "On the concept of organizational goal." *Administrative Science Quarterly*, 9: 1-22.

1957   *Administrative Behavior: A Study of Decision-Making Processes in Administrative Organizations*. (Second Edition.) New York: Free Press.

Sykes, Gresham M.

1958   *The Society of Captives: A Study of a Maximum Security Prison*. Princeton: Princeton University Press.

Thompson, James D.

1968   "Models of organization and administrative systems." In *The Social Sciences: Problems and Orientations*: 395-405. The Hague: Mouton/ UNESCO.

Thompson, James D., and William J. McEwen

1958   "Organizational goals and environment." *American Sociological Review*, 23: 23-31.

Waldo, Dwight

1968   "Public administration." In the *International Encyclopaedia of the Social Sciences*, 13: 145-156. New York: Macmillan.

Warner, W. Keith, and A. Eugene Havens

1968   "Goal displacement and the intangibility of organizational goals." *Administrative Science Quarterly*, 12: 539-555.

Weber, Max

1947   *The Theory of Social and Economic Organization*. New York: Free Press.

1949   *The Methodology of the Social Sciences*. Glencoe: Free Press.

Wilensky, Harold L.

1961   "The trade union as a bureaucracy." In Amitai Etzioni (ed.), *Complex Organizations: A Sociological Reader*: 221-234. New York: Holt, Rinehart and Winston.

Wolin, Sheldon

1961   *Politics and Vision: Continuity and Innovation in Western Political Thought*. London: Allen and Unwin.

1968   "Paradigms and political theories." In Preston King and B. C. Parekh (eds.), *Politics and Experience: Essays Presented to Professor Michael Oakeshott*: 125-253. Cambridge: Cambridge University Press.

4. Managerial Strategies and the Worker: a Marxist Analysis of Bureaucracy*

Paul Goldman and Donald R. Van Houten

Systematic study of the sociology of organizations is almost absent in both the classical and modern Marxist traditions. Marxist scholars have given little attention to the bureaucratic aspects of the labor process and have thus left us without a sophisticated understanding of how managerial decision making and the institution of "bureaucratic rationality" have served the purposes of capital accumulation and social control of the work force during the capitalist epoch. This inattention has limited our knowledge of the structural contradictions of capitalist administrative practice.

For the most part Marxists have ceded this area of intellectual inquiry to professors of business administration and to sociologists who take the Weberian perspective as a point of departure. Both Giddens (1973) and Wright (1974) have described the disjunction between the Marxian and Weberian traditions in a fashion that is suggestive for the study of the industrial enterprise. Wright notes:

> Marxists have generally continued to focus on the dynamics and contradictions of capitalist
> society seen as a total system, while paying relatively little attention to the organizational
> dynamics of the state . . . Analysts in the Weberian tradition in contrast, have continued to
> treat organizations in isolation from the social contradictions in which they are embedded
> (1974:103).

We hope in this paper to begin to synthesize these divergent viewpoints, and subsume current bourgeois[1] administrative and sociological theory and research under the broader rubric of Marxist political economy. Recent research has shown the promise of a Marxist approach to bureaucracy. Marglin's (1974) analysis of hierarchy during the industrial revolution and Stone's (1973) discussion of the development of job ladders in the late nineteenth century steel industry show how changes in the division of labor stem as much from the desire to effect organizational control as from the need to apply continually advancing technology to production. Braverman (1974) and Edwards (1975), analyzing contemporary work organization, suggest that machinery and bureaucratic regulations in industry derive from managerial desires to

* "Managerial Strategies and the Worker: a Marxist Analysis of Bureaucracy" by Paul Goldman and Donald R. Van Houten, from *The Sociological Quarterly,* Vol. 18, Winter 1977, pp. 108-115. Copyright © 1977 by the Midwest Sociological Society. Reprinted by permission.

Reprints of this article may be obtained by writing the authors at the Department of Sociology, University of Oregon, Eugene, OR 97403.

We would like to thank Terry Hanford, Ken Kusterer, Jim Mulherin, and Dan Ross who read and commented on an earlier version of the paper.

[1] The use of the term "bourgeois sociology" in this paper is for descriptive purposes and refers to that sociology that accepts, as a given, the overall maintenance of the capitalist system.

effect substantial control over both labor market characteristics and the attitudes of workers. This research indicates that managerial thinking is attuned to the larger social, political, and economic setting, as well as to internal administration.

Other Marxist or quasi-Marxist research informs the study of bureaucracy, albeit in a more indirect fashion. Studies of economic elites, focusing particularly on interinstitutional relationships and the interpenetration of economics and politics, provide an alternative view of managerial behavior to that found in most literature on organizations (Melman, 1970; Lens, 1970; Domhoff, 1967, 1969, 1972).

Marxist theories of the state and of the differences between "productive" and "non-productive" labor raise new issues connecting political economy to bureaucratic administration (Gold, et al., 1975; O'Connor, 1973, 1976). Finally, research on current and past worker struggles (Aronowitz, 1973; Davis, 1975; Brecher, 1972; Palmer, 1975) and on the burgeoning workers' control movement (Hunnius, 1973; Jenkins, 1973) help emphasize both how workers make history and how bureaucratic arrangements are influenced by the political activities of organized and unorganized workers and not merely by executive decision.

Tentative Requirements for a Theory.   Any effort to develop new sociological theory, or to apply existing theory to new areas of social life, faces two complementary tasks: (1) integrating new concepts within a larger theoretical framework, in this case Marxist political economy, and (2) addressing issues that have been inadequately explained by alternate or competing theories. Past organizational theory has been unsuccessful in these endeavors since, with few exceptions, there has been little serious effort to fit bureaucratic organization into broader theories of society.[2] At the same time, even within the field, there is little consensus on critical issues, with each researcher concentrating on relatively narrow aspects of organizational life.

What Marxian concepts should inform the study of bureaucracy in order to provide it with the necessary theoretical foundation? Four in particular stand out: (1) the labor theory of value, (2) a focus on the forces and relations of production, (3) historical analysis regarding capitalism as a continually developing system at once resolving old contradictions and generating new ones, and (4) an emphasis on class structure and class struggle. These represent less a source of derivable propositions to be tested than a set of guidelines to be followed in analyzing bureaucratic behavior.[3]

The *labor theory of value,* of course, attempts to explain the generation of a commodity's value by the human labor involved in its production. The worker must, of course, sell his or her labor power to the capitalist in order to survive. A corollary is the capitalist's continuing effort to obtain and reinvest surplus value as a necessary mechanism within capitalist economies. There is little indication that this mechanism is less operative in contemporary monopoly capitalism than in the developing capitalism observed by Marx although new obstacles to successful accumulation and reinvestment have emerged (Baran and Sweezy, 1966; Galbraith, 1967; Leonard,

---

[2] The exceptions are, however, quite important within the history of sociology. Weber (1947) linked his analysis of bureaucracy to the historical process of rationalization within Western civilization. More recently, Parsons (1956) and Merton (1957) have attempted to use functionalism as a framework for examining bureaucracy.

[3] Blauner's (1964) and Zwerman's (1970) attempts to test derived hypotheses falter because they have not related their research to the larger context of the theory.

1969; Moore, 1962).[4] What we seek to do is emphasize how the drive to generate surplus value can be found in the structure and decision-making of bureaucracies. This rather obvious point cannot be emphasized too strongly. Capitalists and managers have a persistent interest in keeping labor costs down and have developed strategies — direct and indirect, short-term and long-run — devoted to this purpose. The nature of these strategies is discussed later in this paper.

For Marx the conscious production of the material necessities of life is the essence of the human condition (Marx, 1964). Within each historical epoch the existing *forces of production*[5] are forged into a set of typical *social relations* that allocates both the work to be done by and the rewards given to each member of society. The dominant class in each period determines (and maintains) the forms of ownership and control over the means of production (factories, machinery, etc.), the division of labor, the relationships between those working for a concern, and the socio-technical relations and procedures (Heydebrand, 1975). It is an emphasis on the generation of surplus value, however, rather than on the forces of production alone that determines capitalist social relations. The sense that new forces of production (technology for example) are developed to strengthen *existing* social relations of production is one presumption setting apart Marxist from bourgeois analyses of bureaucracy.

The *historical approach* within Marxism enables us to locate past sources of current managerial practices and stress fundamental continuities within the capitalist experience. Capitalists — entrepreneurs and managers alike — need to organize production in the face of a potentially recalcitrant labor force that may actively or passively resist control from above. Recent historical studies show how central this has been to managerial thinking and suggest that technology, the division of labor, bureaucratic rules, and management training and internal social mobility have been responsive to needs for labor discipline (Pollard, 1965). These trends began as early as 1770 in Wedgewood's pottery factories, and continued in Taylorist rituals at the turn of the century, in post-war incentive plans, and "humanistic" management. Capitalists no longer rely on physical coercion due to the trade union movement, labor law, and variations in the labor market. In unorganized, largely non-monopoly sectors of the economy, however, the labor process bears a strong similarity to the earlier period (Edwards, 1975; Mallet, 1975).[6] The continued trend towards automated machinery suggests further routinization in monopoly sectors (Braverman, 1974).

The fourth element in Marxist thought, *class struggle*, is firmly embedded in bureaucracies. Some non-Marxist conflict theories, notably Dahrendorf (1959), have dealt with this issue, although their model admits only to a permanent state of tension between management and labor, not to antagonistic and irreconcilable contradictions. It is necessary to go beyond the relationship between capitalist hegemony and worker

---

[4] The emphasis on growth in many of these works stresses the reinvestment aspect of the equation and tends to assume the need for accumulation. Starbuck's (1956) litany of executive motives also places an emphasis on growth and its correlates.

[5] The forces of production include the human abilities to perform physical and mental labor, rationality and science, and the physical implements used in production such as tools, instruments, machines, and technical innovations.

[6] Physical force, and the fears it engenders, is still a factor in "labor discipline" among farmworkers, especially migrants, and Appalachian coal miners.

struggle, using this structured contradiction to explain changes and developments within capitalism, and to discover whether they may lead to its ultimate transformation. This ambitious project faces numerous difficulties, most notably the apparent separation between industrial and electoral politics, at least in the United States. Nevertheless, widespread awareness of the corruption of business and political elites, the inability of the "system" to stem either inflation or unemployment, the growing disillusion and alienation on the part of the workers, and the domino effects of labor disputes might eventually bring industrial politics into the larger political arena.

Internal structural contradictions too may increase class conflict. The speed-up to a record assembly line pace at General Motors' Lordstown plant provoked a reaction similar to the first widespread implementation of Taylorism. The Lordstown events are indicative of a new militancy and class consciousness among predominantly young workers (Aronowitz, 1973; Davis, 1975; Georgakis and Surkin, 1975; Rothschild, 1973). Reactions to Taylorism, it should be recalled, contributed significantly to the growth of International Workers of the World (I.W.W.). New machinery in offices and retail stores has continued the proletarianization and routinization of much white collar work, especially that performed by women (Braverman, 1974; Tepperman, 1976). Organizing drives among these workers and the knowledge and experience gained by the women's movement may result in a new phase of class conflict.

The challenges posed by these issues have not been taken up by bourgeois sociologists studying organizations. The reasons for this are both ideological and situational. Conservatizing influences can be found in the close ties between sociology and business administration academics with the corporate and government worlds, in the privileged financial position of business schools within most universities, and in the academics' need for research access to business organizations.

These factors have contributed to five serious deficiencies in organizational analysis. Most have been commented upon by critics (Baritz, 1960; Benson, 1975; Hirsch, 1975; Mouzelis, 1967; Perrow, 1972; Wolin, 1960).[7] First, the field has been ahistorical with little attention given the ways in which a particular organization (or type of organization) has evolved or changed.[8] Even studies of change have a very brief time span. Second, the sociology of organizations has been isolated from issues of social class, social stratification, and social conflict. One consequence of this has been an anthropomorphic orientation where organizations "act" rather than individuals in social classes acting in defense of their class interests. Third, the field has emphasized microanalysis with either the work group or the single organization serving as the primary unit of analysis. Thus there is little discussion of how the economy, the political context, or the community affects day-to-day organizational life. Fourth, the field is elitist in the interests of capital and management rather than those of workers and in assuming that managerial behavior is more important, more variable, and more worthy of study than that of workers. Finally, the discipline, with the exception of the now unfashionable study of bureaucratic "dysfunctions," is undialectical, seldom seeing the roots of tomorrow in the reality of today.

There is, however, much of value for Marxists in this literature. Extensive

---

[7] A more complete overview of these characteristics of bourgeois organizational sociology can be found in Goldman (1976).

[8] One exception, widely admired but little emulated, is Stinchcombe's (1965) analysis of organizational development.

fieldwork and survey research, sometimes requiring reinterpretation, are the best available sources of organizational data. Moreover, the close tie between the profession and the business community is presumably based on mutual understanding and respect. Consequently, published work represents a potential guide to the intentions, concerns, and styles of corporate elites. Businss school students and managers take courses from organizational analysts, and the latter's books and articles, for example those of Peter Drucker, often have a significant following among businesspeople and therefore should be studied and taken seriously.

Big business and monopoly capitalism.   Managerial strategy for controlling the work force must be set within the context of a monopoly capitalist system in which industry has become progressively concentrated and oligopolistic.[9] Yet at the same time capitalists face an uncertain world as resources become scarcer, as nationalist movements remove areas of the world from imperial dependency, and as business cycles increase their frequency and intensity (Baran and Sweezy, 1966; Perlo, 1973). Even on a less global scale, potential changes in ownership and control, executive shake-ups, and mergers are everyday facts of life for capitalists and managers. Successful management, and managerial tenure, require minimizing uncertainties in areas other than labor including problems of obtaining capital and raw materials, political support in tax and labor legislation, zoning laws, government contracts, and sales of products whether to corporate clients or to the consuming public.

For Thompson (1967) maximizing certainties in the "technical core" of a firm is the primary organizational task, but a routinized technology and labor force is worth little if left vulnerable to the uncertainties of inputs and outputs, that is of supply schedules, customers' demands, new machinery and so on. Managers can buffer these by stockpiling raw materials, leveling supply and demand curves by differential rate schedules that induce corporate clients to buy or sell at specific times or in bulk quantities, rationing their product if demand exceeds supply and, these failing, predicting surplus or shortage and attempting to compensate. Their success at these endeavors can determine the stability and, often, the wage rates of the labor force (Edwards, 1975).

These strategies are most common for smaller corporations and those in highly competitive sectors. Conglomerates can more easily maintain contractual relationships with complementary firms or interlock with them through merger. This pays off in bulk rates and priority shipping. While the turn-of-the-century merger movement was designed to eliminate competition (and was only partially successful), the merger movement of the twenties saw the beginnings of vertical integration (Nelson, 1959). Mining concerns bought refineries; refiners purchased mines and oil fields. Sears Roebuck went first into direct retailing, then into manufacturing. In recent years conglomerates have purchased firms in new areas, domestic or foreign, where labor costs are lower. Managers and owners benefit significantly from monopoly or oligopoly power which allows them to undercut smaller rivals by subsidizing price wars, denying materials to producers who have no other suppliers to turn to, and by colluding with nominal rivals to fix prices. Monopoly pricing raises the ceiling on prices and gives managers greater flexibility in dealing with workers' wage demands.

Less formal cooperation between corporations serves a political and legitimation

---

[9] Between 1947 and 1968, the 200 largest manufacturing corporations increased their portion of total manufacturing assets from 47.1 percent to 60.4 percent (Blair, 1972).

function. Coalitions, trade associations, and superorganizations serve the interests of seeming competitors by masking joint action and presenting a public service image. Some such organizations are illegal cartels (MacAvoy, 1965), but more commonly they are trade associations that lobby at municipal, state, and federal levels, or engage in collective research and development (as in retailing), or collectively negotiate with large trade unions. Superorganizations in utilities integrate corporations and the state around such issues as nuclear power. Similarly large-scale retailers and the real estate and construction industries cooperate in urban redevelopment schemes. These umbrella organizations acquire a ''public'' image insulating them from grass roots pressures and dividing citizens between their roles as producers, consumers, and members of the community.

Merger and superorganization are probably, as Wycko (1975) and Boddy and Crotty (1974) suggest, responses to crises of low capital availability and natural reactions to certain stages of the business cycle. They may, however, generate new problems for individual corporations and contradictions for the system as a whole. According to Chandler (1962), General Motors, Sears, Dupont, and Standard Oil of New Jersey all encountered structural strains during expansion. Internal coordination becomes more problematic, and sub-units and their managing executives become dangerously competitive with each determining its own priorities (Rosenfeld, 1972). The demise of the Penn Central is an instance of this process although there the holding company pauperized the railroad to benefit their other subsidiaries (Fitch and Oppenheimer, 1970). Although his study focuses on short-run results, Pfeffer (1972) suggests that merger is not generally profitable despite the advantages of economies of scale, oligopolistic pricing, lessened competition, and increased lobbying. Mergers can have negative consequences for the economy as a whole even if individual conglomerates may profit. The first two major periods of mergers were ended by severe economic crises: the ''panic'' of 1907 and the crash of 1929. The post-war merger movement was followed by the continued recession of the seventies. Windfall profits and the tendency of the surplus to rise with monopoly pricing may serve individual firms, but they generate needs for investment typically satisfied by military spending and imperialist adventures (Baran and Sweezy, 1966).

CONTROLLING THE WORK FORCE: A SUMMARY OF MANAGERIAL STRATEGIES

Management is no less concerned with insuring certainty in the ''social relations of production'' within the firm. To assure such certainty involves dealing with workers, many of whose interests are in contradiction with those of management, and doing so in the context of potential class conflict — an underlying reality of which both parties are aware. The managerial orientation is towards obtaining as much work, with as little trouble, as they possibly can from the workers. These purposes — capital accumulation and social control — complement one another although their relative importance may vary with organized worker activity.

The managers' power to define the social relations of production, while not absolute, is substantial. Both policy creation and policy implementation are vested in executives who, through training and experience, share a common corporate ideology and who collectively appropriate a disproportionate amount of the surplus value generated by productive workers in the form of salaries, fringe benefits, expense accounts, stock options and so on. Moreover, their positions provide them with those opportunities that can come from access to political and other economic elites. Power comes not only from determining the social and technological division of labor within the firm, but also in determining "personnel policy." Control over hiring, firing, promotion, and reward reinforces their power over the technical sphere and is crucial to the maintenance of internal inequality. That this power may be inhibited by trade unions in industry could lead to our underestimating its centrality to the labor process. Management negotiating teams often compromise on wages and benefits (realizing that prices can usually be raised to match wage demands) in order to retain control over personnel matters.

Stability and predictability of work force behavior to serve "production" and "efficiency" have been capitalists' goals since the time of Wedgewood. Several complementary managerial ideologies have supported this orientation, from the Weberian ideal of bringing bureaucratic order to organizational chaos, to the Taylorist emphasis on the virtues of hard work (Merkle, 1968; Sutton, et al., 1956), to Fordism and complementary beliefs in the benefits of technology as a source of efficiency. Less frequently stated apprehensions underlie these ideological positions. Workers, particularly those with specialized skills or strong unions, can limit output or even stop production, and at times they have been recalcitrant. While violent strikes, sitdowns, lock-outs, and the invasion of electoral activity by industrial strife are far less common than in the pre-World War II era, recent wildcats at GM's Lordstown plant and in eastern coalfields suggest that corporate elites cannot entirely rule out the possibility of such actions. More commonly expressed concerns are with worker dissatisfaction, disaffection, and reduced quantity and quality in production (HEW, 1973; Gooding, 1972).

Despite the influence of the "new human relations" theorists, prevailing managerial attitudes towards workers are heavily laced with distrust. The latter are not expected to like their work — or any work — preferring instead to be lazy and uninterested in responsibility (McGregor, 1960). Managers often attribute resentment and organized resistance neither to alienating characteristics of the work setting nor to inequities of reward, but rather to the human inadequacies and inferiorities of the workers themselves.

The precise impact of managerial motivations on policies affecting the lives of workers is of course difficult to specify with any precision since unobtrusive access to the executive suite is almost impossible for Marxist scholars. Similarly it is unclear whether organizational practices result from real *intentionality* on the part of management, that is the degree to which their decisions are based on clearly thought out and rational assessments of worker attitudes rather than on tradition or imitation. Ruling class publications (*Fortune, The Wall Street Journal,* more specialized trade journals, especially in personnel management) give conflicting messages. *But* it is clear that current trends in organizing work do not differ markedly from those of a century ago in their focus on providing the worker with as little leverage as possible. There is a continual emphasis, usually through judicious application of mechanical technology to isolate and atomize the worker by making his or her work routine, narrow, and repetitive (Braverman, 1974). These practices reduce skills, increase the replaceability of workers, and thus make demands for worker control less and less easy to generate.

Strategies for implementing these goals have developed with considerable sophistication during the history of capitalism and it is to the specific analysis of them that we devote the remainder of this paper. Three techniques are recognizable to Weberian students of bureaucracy: (1) the division of labor into narrowly specific tasks, (2) organizational hierarchy, and (3) rules and procedures, although it is less well-known that Marx devoted two chapters of *Capital* (1967:Ch. 13, 14) to the division of labor and Engels (1959) made at least passing remarks on hierarchy.[10] The other two techniques, (4) secrecy and the hoarding of knowledge, and (5) systematic division of the labor force according to ascriptive characteristics, have been given little attention.

REFERENCES

Acker, Joan and Van Houten, Donald R.
1974 "Differential recruitment and control: the sex structuring of organizations," *Administrative Science Quarterly* 19:152-63.

Aronowitz, Stanley
1973 *False Promises: The Shaping of the American Working Class.* New York: McGraw-Hill.

Baran, Paul and Sweezy, Paul
1966 *Monopoly Capital.* Monthly Review Press.

Baritz, Loren
1960 *The Servants of Power.* Minneapolis: Greenwood Publishing Co.

Benson, Kenneth
1975 "On the measurement of organizational structure: methodological implications of a dialectical perspective." Paper presented to the August Meeting of the *American Sociological Association.*

Bernstein, Paul
1974 "Run your own business: worker-owned plywood firms." *Working Papers* 2:24-34.

Blair, John M.
1972 *Economic Concentration, Structure, Behavior and Public Policy.* New York: Harcourt, Brace, Jovanovich.

Blau, Peter M.
1955 *The Dynamics of Bureaucracy.* Chicago: University of Chicago Press.

Blau, Peter M. and Schoenherr, Richard A.
1970 *The Structure of Organizations.* New York: John Wiley.

Blau, Peter M. and Scott, W. Richard
1962 *Formal Organizations: A Comparative Approach.* San Francisco: Chandler.

Blauner, Robert
1964 *Alienation and Freedom: The Factory Worker and His Industry.* Chicago: University of Chicago Press.

Boddy, Raford and Crott, James
1974 "Class conflict, Keynesian policies and the business cycle." *Monthly Review* 26:1-17.

Bowles, Samuel and Gintis, Herbert
1975 "Schooling and the family: the long shadow of work." *The Insurgent Sociologist* 3:3-24.

Braverman, Harry
1974 *Labor and Monopoly Capital: The Degradation fo Work in the Twentieth Century.* New York: Monthly Review Press.

Brecher, Jeremy
1972 *Strike!* San Francisco: Straight Arrow Books.

Burns, Tom and Stalker, G.M.
1961 *The Management of Innovation.* London: Tavistock Publications.

Chandler, Alfred
1962 *Strategy and Structure.* Cambridge: MIT Press.

Chinoy, Ely
1955 *Automobile Workers and the American Dream.* Garden City, N.Y.: Doubleday.

Crider, Lynn Marie and Van Houten, Donald
1974 "Playing the consultant game." *Oregon Times* 4:16-21.

Crozier, Michel
1964 *The Bureaucratic Phenomenon.* Chicago: University of Chicago Press.

Cyert, Richard M. and March, James G.
1963 *A Behavioral Theory of the Firm.* Englewood Cliffs, N.J.: Prentice-Hall.

Dahrendorf, Ralf
1959 *Class and Class Conflict in Industrial Society.* Stanford: Stanford University Press.

Dale, Ernest
1960 *The Great Organizers.* N.Y.: McGraw-Hill.

---

[10] Weber's analysis is based on the Prussian bureaucracy staffed by career officials who accepted the values of the state. The same principles applied to workers have different implications.

Davis, Mike
1975   "The stop watch and the wooden shoe: scientific management and the Industrial Workers of the World." *Radical America* 9:69-95.

Domhoff, G. William
1972   *Fat Cats and Democrats.* Englewood Cliffs, N.J.: Prentice-Hall.
1969   *The Higher Circles.* New York: Random House.
1967   *Who Rules America.* Englewood Cliffs, N.J.: Prentice-Hall.

Edwards, Richard C.
1975   "The social relations of production in the firm and labor market structure." *Politics and Society* 5:83-108.

Engels, Frederick
1959   "On authority." Pp. 481-85 in Lewis S. Feuer (ed.). *Marx and Engels: Basic Writings on Politics and Philosophy.* Garden City, N.Y.: Anchor.

Fitch, Robert and Oppenheimer, Mary
1970   "Who rules the corporations." *Socialist Revolution* 4, 5, 6:73-108, 61-114, 33-94.

Friedmann, Georges
1961   *The Anatomy of Work.* New York: The Free Press.

Galbraith, John Kenneth
1967   *The New Industrial State.* Boston: Houghton-Mifflin.

Georgakis, Dan and Surkin, Marvin
1975   *Detroit – I Do Mind Dying: A Study in Urban Revolution.* New York: St. Martin's Press.

Giddens, Anthony
1973   *The Class Structure of the Advanced Societies.* New York: Harper & Row.

Gold, David, Clarence Y. H. Lo, Erik Olin Wright
1975   "Marxist theories of the state." *Monthly Review* 26:29-43, 36-51.

Goldman, Paul
1976   "Ideology, bureaucracy and socialogy: a critique of bourgeois organizational theory and research." Presented at the Annual Meeting of the *American Sociological Association,* New York, (August).
1973   "The organizational caste system and the new working class." *The Insurgent Sociologist* 3:41-52.

Gooding, Judson
1972   *The Job Revolution.* New York: Collier.

Goulder, Alvin W.
1954   *Patterns of Industrial Bureaucracy.* New York: The Free Press.

Hampden-Turner, Charles
1970   *Radical Man.* Cambridge: Schenkman.

Health, Education and Welfare, Department of
1973   *Work in America: Report of a Special Task Force to the Secretary of Health, Education, and Welfare.* Cambridge: MIT Press.

Heydebrand, Wolf
1975   "Organizational contradictions in public bureaucracy: towards a Marxian theory of organization." Paper presented to the Meeting of the *American Sociological Association.*

Hirsch, Paul
1975   "Organizational analysis and industrial sociology: an instance of cultural lag." *The American Sociologist,* 10: 3–12.

Hunnius, Gerry, G. David Garson and John Case (eds.)
1973   *Workers' Control: A Reader on Labor and Social Change.* New York: Random House.

Il Manifesto
1972   "Technicians and the capitalist division of labor," (trans. Kathy Brown), In *Socialist Revolution* 2(3): 65-84.

Jenkins, David
1973   *Job Power: Blue and White Collar Democracy.* Baltimore: Penguin Books.

Kanter, Rosabeth Moss
1975   "Women and the structure of organizations: explorations in theory and behavior." Pp. 34-74 in Marcia Millman and Rosabeth Kanter (eds.). *Another Voice: Feminist Perspectives on Social Life and Social Sciences.* Garden City, N.Y.: Anchor.

Kusterer, Ken
1976   "Working knowledge: the development of know-how in the workplace." Unpublished Ph.D. dissertation. Department of Sociology, Washington University, St. Louis.

Langer, Elinor
1970   "The women of the telephone company." *New York Review of Books,* 14 (5, 6): 16, 14.
1976   "Forum: why big business is trying to defeat the ERA: the economic implications of equality." *Ms.* 4: 64–6, 100–8.

Lens, Sidney
1970   *The Military-Industrial Complex.* Philadelphia: Pilgrim Press.

Leonard, William
1969   *Business Size, Market Power and Public Policy.* Englewood Cliffs, N.J.: Prentice-Hall.

MacAvoy, Paul W.
1965   *The Economic Effects of Regulation.* Cambridge: MIT Press.

McGregor, Douglas
1960   *The Human Side of Enterprise.* New York: McGraw-Hill.

Mallet, Serge
1975   *Essays on the New Working Class* (trans. and eds. Dick Howard and Dean Savage). St. Louis: Telos Press.

Mandel, Ernest
1973   "The Debate on Workers' Control." Pp. 344-73 in Gerry Hunnius, G. David Garson and John Case (ed.) *Workers' Control: A Reader of Labor and Social Change.* New York: Random House.

March, James G. and Simon, Herbert A.
1958   *Organizations.* New York: John Wiley.

Marglin, Stephen A.
1974   "What the bosses do? The origins and functions of hierarchy in capitalist production." *Review of Radical Political Economics,* 6: 60-112.

Marx, Karl
1967   *Capital* (trans. Samuel Moore and Edward Aveling: ed. Frederick Engels). New York: International Publishers.
1964   *Economic and Philosophical Manuscripts of 1844.* (ed. Dirk Struik). New York: International Publishers.

McKendrick, Neil
1962   "Josiah Wedgewood and factory discipline." *The Historical Journal* 4: 30-55.

Melman, Seymour
1970   *Pentagon Capitalism: The Management of the New Imperialism.* New York: McGraw-Hill.

Merkle, Judith
1968   "The Taylor strategy: organizational innovation and class structure." *Berkeley Journal of Sociology* 13: 59-81.

Merton, Robert
1957   *Social Theory and Social Structure.* New York: The Free Press.

Miller, George A.
1967   "Professionals in bureaucracy: alienation among industrial scientists and engineers." *American Sociological Review* 32: 755-68.

Moore, Wilbert E.
1962   *The conduct of the corporation.* New York: Random House.

Mouzelis, Nicos
1967   *Organization and Bureaucracy: An Analysis of Modern Theories.* Chicago: Aldine.

Nelson, Ralph L.
1959   *Merger Movements in American Industry, 1895-1956.* Princeton: Princeton University Press.

O'Connor, James
1975   "Productive and unproductive labor." *Politics and Society* 5: 297-336.
1973   *The Fiscal Crisis of the State.* New York: St. Martin's Press.

Palmer, Bryan
1975   "Class, conception and conflict: the thrust for efficiency, managerial views of labor and the working class rebellion." *The Review of Radical Political Economics* 7: 31-49.

Parsons, Talcott
1956   "Suggestions for a sociological approach to the theory of organizations." *Administrative Science Quarterly* 1: 68-85, 225-39.

Perlo, Victor
1973   *The Unstable Economy: Booms and Recessions in the U.S. Since 1945.* New York: International Publishers.

Perrow, Charles
1972   *Complex Organizations: A Critical Essay.* Glenview, Ill.: Scott, Foresman.

Pfeffer, Jeffrey
1972   "Merger as a response to organizational interdependence." *Administrative Science Quarterly,* 17: 382-93.

Priori, Michael J.
1975   "Notes for a theory of labor market stratification." Pp. 125-50 in Richard C. Edwards, Michael Reich and David M. Gordon (eds.) *Labor Market Segmentation.* Boston: D.C. Heath.

Pollard, Sidney
1965   *The Genesis of Modern Management: A Study of the Industrial Revolution in Great Britain.* Cambridge: Harvard University Press.

Reich, Michael
1972   "The economics of racism." Pp. 313-22 in Richard C. Edwards, Michael Reich and David M. Gordon (eds.) *The Capitalist System.* Englewood Cliffs, N.J.: Prentice-Hall.

Rosenfeld, Richard
1972   "Some unanticipated consequences of organizational expansion." Unpublished manuscript.
Rothschild, Emma
1973   *Paradise Lost: The Decline of the Auto-Industrial Age.* New York: Random House.
Sennett, Richard and Cobb, Jonathan
1972   *The Hidden Injuries of Class.* New York: Alfred Knopf.
Shostak, Arthur
1969   *Blue Collar Life.* Philadelphia: Philadelphia Book Co.
Sjoberg, Gideon and Paula Jean Miller
1973   "Social research on bureaucracy: limitations and opportunities." *Social Problems* 21: 129-43.
Starbuck, William
1965   "Organizational growth and development." Pp. 451-533 in James G. March (ed.) *Handbook of Organizations.* Chicago: Rand McNally.
Stellman, Jeanne and Daum, Susan
1973   *Work is Dangerous to Your Health.* New York: Pantheon.
Stinchcombe, Arthur L.
1965   "Social structure and organizations." Pp. 142-93 in James G. March (ed.) *Handbook of Organizations.* Chicago: Rand McNally.
Stone, Katherine
1973   "The origins of job structures in the steel industry." *Radical America* 7: 17-66.
Sutton, Francis X., Seymour E. Harris, Carl Kaysen and James Tobin
1956   *The American Business Creed.* Cambridge: Harvard University Press.
Tepperman, Jean
1976   "Organizing office workers." *Radical America* 10: 3-20.

Thompson, James D.
1967   *Organizations in Action.* New York: McGraw-Hill.
Wallick, Frank
1972   *The American Worker, An Endangered Species.* Westminister, Md.: Ballantine.
Watson, Bill
1971   "Counter-planning on the shop floor." *Radical America* 5: 77-85.
Weber, Max
1947   *The Theory of Social And Economic Organization* (trans. and ed. Talcott Parsons). New York: The Free Press.
Weir, Stan
1973   "Rebellion in labor's rank and file." Pp. 45-61 in Gerry Hunnius, G. David Garson and John Case (eds.) *Workers' Control: A Reader on Labor and Social Changes.* New York: Random House.
Wolin, Sheldon
1960   *Politics and Vision: Continuity and Innovation in Western Political Thought.* Boston: Little-Brown.
Wright, Erik Olin
1974   "To control or smash bureaucracy: Weber and Lenin on politics, the state and bureaucracy." *Berkeley Journal of Sociology* 19: 69-108.
Wycko, William
1975   "The work shortage: class struggle and capital reproduction." *The Review of Radical Political Economics* 7: 11-30.
Zimbalist, Andrew
1975   "The limits of work humanization." *The Review of Radical Political Economics* 7: 50-60.
Zwerman, William L.
1970   *New Perspectives on Organizational Theory: A Reconsideration of the Classical and Marxian Analyses.* Minneapolis: Greenwood Publishing Co.

5. New Organizational Perspectives:
Critiques and Critical Organizations*

Richard Colignon and David Cray

INTRODUCTION

Any area of study that has pretensions of building a coherent body of knowledge and theory requires continued criticism and evaluation of earlier work, but recently there has been a questioning of some of the basic assumptions of sociological thought in regard to complex organizations that seems to go beyond the usual intellectual skirmishing. In a 1974 survey of 22 organizational sociologists, Cornelis J. Lammers concluded that, "All in all the mood of organizational sociologists with respect to the future of their speciality can be characterized as restive" (Lammers, 1974: 427). However, his conclusion that the field would undergo a change in focus rather than a shift in paradigm is countered by critics who claim that the established paradigm, with its emphasis on goal achievement, administrative performance, and the interrelations of formal characteristics of the organization, is no longer adequate, if it ever was, for the research task.[1]

The established paradigm, which views the organization as a bounded, rational instrument for the achievement of specified goals, has been variously characterized as rational, goal-oriented, or, more narrowly, structural (Georgiou, 1973; Benson, 1977a). But these three labels only distinguish different approaches based on what we will call the rational paradigm. Under the rational paradigm the goals of an organization impose certain constraints that influence patterns of dominance, hierarchy, interaction, and resource allocation within the organization. Consequently, research in this paradigm has been directed toward the identification of clusters of factors that affect the efficiency of the organization. This research has largely taken the managerial point of view in the identification of important problems, the definition of central concepts, and the application of results.

Criticism of the rational paradigm has come from two distinctly different perspectives. The first criticizes the methods and conclusions of particular studies and, to a lesser extent, the concept of organizations that underlies them (Argyris, 1972; Perrow, 1972; McNeil, 1978). This perspective can be thought of as reformist in that the critiques are themselves grounded in the rational paradigm as are the proposed reforms. The second perspective, which has emerged more recently, argues that the deficiencies of the rational paradigm grow not out of its faulty elaboration but from its basic assumptions (Benson, 1977a, 1977b; Goldman and Van Houten, 1977; Wassenberg, 1977). Authors working from this perspective have criticized the field as a whole rather than particular studies and have done so from an intellectual base outside the rational paradigm.

* *Critical Organizations* by Richard Colignon and David Cray. Copyright © 1981 by Richard Colignon and David Cray. Reprinted by permission of the authors.

The authors thank Michael Aiken and the members, past and present, of the Social Organization Colloquium of the Department of Sociology, University of Wisconsin-Madison, for the comments and suggestions on various drafts of this paper.

We also wish to express our gratitude to Howard Aldrich for his invaluable assistance and suggestions on our earlier draft of this manuscript.

Despite their different orientations, each of these perspectives has fostered similar criticisms of the rational conception of the organization, making four basic points — hat it is passive, static, ahistorical, and does not place the organization in its social context.

The rational paradigm conceives of the organization as passive toward both internal and external forces. While the organization is seen as being molded by the environmental pressures that surround it, the possibility of the organization influencing or even shaping the environment is not considered. As a result, the impact of large organizations on all aspects of society has been a topic largely unexplored by those working within the rational paradigm. Similarly, the political processes by which particular groups within the organization accomplish their ends are ignored in favor of an idealized view of the unified organization working toward an agreed upon set of goals. This conception of the organization has encouraged researchers to accept definitions provided by managers or found in official documents as conceptual categories for the research process. The existence and influence of competing definitions of the situation are largely ignored.

The passive view is paralleled by the static view, which attempts to capture the relationship of different elements of the organization at a particular historical moment with scant regard for the processes by which those relationships are created, modified, and destroyed. Because the organization is viewed as a tool by which the administration attempts to accomplish a given set of goals, no further inquiry as to the generation of either goals or the mechanisms by which they are reached is deemed necessary. In a similar fashion those working within the rational paradigm have given little attention to the history of the organization. Neither the history of the organization's internal processes nor of its relations with the larger society have been systematically examined. Thus it is unclear whether the relationships observed between elements of the organization are idiosyncratic responses to present conditions or are of a more fundamental nature.

The final and perhaps most severe shortcoming of the work done within the rational paradigm is the failure to place the organization in its societal context. Despite acknowledging the importance of organizations for society, most researchers have neglected to investigate the reciprocal effects of the organization and different elements in the social fabric. Because the organization is seen as passive, the question of organizational effects on society is simply not germane. Even those studying interorganizational relationships have limited themselves largely to networks of organizations with similar interests. Connections to markets, labor organizations, financial interests, and other social institutions have remained unexplored.

As a result of this conceptualization the research done within the framework of the rational paradigm has a certain hermetic aspect. These theories reflect the preoccupation of researchers with the problem of organizational efficiency and their disinterest in the impact of organizations on society. Precisely because the view of the organization is passive and static, these studies have not revealed how organizations can be made to adapt to social needs or to the desires of the majority of those who live and work in the organization. Findings have had a distinctly elitist bias and are best suited to improving the productive or managerial efficiency of the organization. By remaining within this tightly restricted province, organizational sociology has remained aloof, not only from many social problems, but from a number of sociological problems as well.

Another outcome of the rational concept of organizations is the lack of research into the operations of large complex organizations, especially those which have the potential for substantial impact on society. This is entirely consistent with the rational concept of the organization, since the determinants of efficient goal accomplishment should not depend on the type of organization under consideration. This being assumed, it is natural that those organizations that are most stable and offer the easiest access are most often chosen as research sites. As a result, a disproportionate amount of the organizational research has been conducted within what Perrow calls "trivial organizations," those without particular social importance (Perrow, 1972:197-198). Therefore the bulk of the studies done under the rational paradigm do not illuminate, directly or by inference, the activities of important organizations.

The emphasis on trivial organizations is not simply a curious byproduct of the rational organizational paradigm. On the contrary, it arises from the fundamental assumptions of that system and reinforces them. If a new organizational paradigm is to be formed, this deficiency must be rectified, and rectified in a way that is an integral part of that new paradigm. In this selection we will examine some of the new approaches to organizational sociology in light of the criticisms outlined above. We will argue that these new approaches consistently fail to deal with the basic problem of which organizations should be studied. Finally, we will describe a type of organization, the critical organization, which is crucial to the development of social structure and examine the implications of this choice for organizational sociology.

NEW APPROACHES

Those advocating new approaches to the study of organizations can by roughly divided into three groups, the reformists, the Marxists, and the political economists. The reformist group is numerous and diverse, ranging from those who wish only to introduce a few new concepts into the field to those who believe it requires substantial redirection. In general, the reformists address themselves to one or two of the criticisms outlined above while retaining the basic orientation of the rational paradigm. It is impossible to give even a summary of the various reformist views so we will content ourselves with a few examples.

THE REFORMISTS

While examining the Weberian perspective on organizational power, McNeil (1978) addresses the problem of the link between the organization and its environment. McNeil argues that, though much of organizational research is nominally built on Weber's work, it ignores one of his basic concerns, the domination of society by powerful organizations. As a result, recent work in the field focuses almost exclusively on the distribution of power within the organization while ignoring the power that organizations wield in society. McNeil suggests that the strategies of control within the organization enable leaders to mobilize resources in the environment and make the organization an instrument of political power. The two processes of power accumulation are inextricably bound together.

By returning to the roots of organizational theory McNeil seeks to replace the organization in its societal context. He argues that powerful organizations are not passive with respect to their environment but constantly seek to control it. However, his view is still largely static and ahistorical. Elites are assumed to control the organization and hence influence its environmental position but the roots of this elite dominance are left unexamined. The link between power inside and outside the organization is analyzed but the process by which one is translated into the other is ignored. Nor are the particular elements in the environment which the organization may affect differentiated from less important forces. McNeil recognizes the importance of the organization as a power base but not the dynamic nature of power relations.

Hirsch (1975) is also concerned with the relation of the organization to its environment but focuses on a particular type of organization, the industrial firm, rather than a particular concept. Reflecting on the decline of industrial sociology as a major concern of sociologists, Hirsch suggests that some of the work being done by organizationalists, particularly that concerned with interorganizational analysis, could rejuvenate the study of industry. As Hirsch observes, "Most sociological studies of industrial firms consider these organizations neither in terms of their effect on other organizations and units in society, nor as having to adapt to external constraints and uncertainties" (Hirsch, 1975:5). He suggests three specific steps to link the study of economic organizations to the larger society. First, researchers should examine sets of firms rather than single units so as to highlight interfirm similarities. Second, the concept of the task environment of the organization should be expanded to include elements of the general social environment. Finally, Hirsch argues that industrial sociologists should be more aware of the institutional level of analysis and the research framework that it implies.

Hirsch attempts to turn sociologists from their fascination with trivial organizations by arguing that organizations should be only part of a more inclusive level of analysis. But this simply moves the problem to another level of abstraction. Even more seriously, it ignores the potential importance of the individual organization in setting the parameters for the activities of an industry. Hirsch attempts to replace the organization in its social setting without having a clear idea of the link between the two. This is partly due to his static and ahistorical view of the organization, which obscures the dynamics of the organization-society relationship.

One of those working in the interorganizational area is Jeffrey Pfeffer. In a number of influential articles he and his associates have attempted to outline a framework for the analysis of relations between business firms (Pfeffer, 1972a, 1972b; Pfeffer and Leblebici, 1973; Pfeffer and Nowak, 1976). Their basic thesis is that the pressures that impinge on the organization can be mitigated by a number of interfirm strategies which, if implemented, have consequences for the structure of the enterprise. But perhaps more importantly for our purposes is Pfeffer's examination of the organizational bases of social stratification (Pfeffer, 1977). While his categories are still firmly embedded in the rational paradigm and deal largely with the status of managers, his findings suggest that the effect of socio-economic origins on social status is mediated by organizational characteristics. This attempt to link organizational dynamics with larger social processes is virtually unique in the organizational literature.

In both areas of work Pfeffer postulates a dynamic process by which the organization actively confronts some elements in the social context. But the empirical test of these hypotheses reverts to the static approach of the rational paradigm. Interorganizational linkages are analyzed in terms of organizational structure and the industrial sector. The competing strategies within the organization which lead to one or another outcome are unexamined. Pfeffer's attempt to incorporate the organizational-environmental interface ultimately fails because he assumes the causal link rather than examining it. The interorganizational bonds are but a part of the organization's links with the environment. Finally, Pfeffer offers no means for distinguishing those organizations whose strategies are likely to affect the society as a whole from those whose importance is negligible.

The authors mentioned above and a number of others have recognized some of the shortcomings of the established paradigm and have proposed additions or corrections which they believe will allow it to address new or neglected problems. All three authors attempt to expand the scope of organizational sociology by placing the organization within the larger social context. McNeil and Pfeffer try to link processes within the organization to its relation with the environment while Hirsch argues that the industry must be linked to larger processes. Yet with the exception of McNeil, the authors seem to regard the organization as externally passive and all three ignore processes and competing cliques within the organization. This precludes a historical view of the organization. While some recognize categories of organization which should be studied, they do not suggest guidelines for the selection of a specific organization nor a means by which the choice could be related to a larger theory.

THE MARXISTS

The Marxists propose much more sweeping changes, arguing that an entirely new paradigm is needed to address questions of power distribution, class conflict, and social structure. For example, J. Kenneth Benson (1977a, 1977b) maintains that the new paradigm should not only contain new categories and concepts but also argues that these should be in the context of a dialectic rather than positivist logic. His dialectical approach would be based on four principles: social construction/ production, totality, contradiction, and praxis. The dialectical approach is intended to analyze the continuously evolving organization by examining the processes by which the organization is changed and maintained. In Benson's opinion this type of analysis will enable organizationalists to move beyond the static, passive, and ahistorical concept of the organization in order to see its non-linear development and its part in the parallel development of society. Because the organization is constantly changing, the dialectical approach focuses on the underlying forces that cause this change rather than the momentary clusters of characteristics that may emerge.

Benson does not claim that his logic of analysis constitutes a theory of organizations. "The dialectical view provides instead a critical-emancipatory stance toward organization studies" (Benson, 1977a:19). The dialectical perspective, if applied properly, would generate a dynamic, non-elitist, historical view of organizations in their social context. But Benson gives us little idea how such a theory might emerge or what it would resemble. While he claims to employ the dialectical approach associated with Marx's work, he fails to link it to substantive Marxist categories such as classes, class relations, or social formations. At the same time he believes that current theories, while unacceptable, can be subsumed under the larger dialectical process. Neither the theoretical nor the substantive starting point for such a dialectical analysis is clear since Benson falls into the rationalist trap of seeing all organizations as equally important theoretically while arguing that all organizations are unique. The societal context of the organization is thus considered without judging the importance of the organization in that context.

Goldman and Van Houten (1977) also draw on Marxist theory for their proposals but are much less interested in the logic of analysis than in its content. They too believe that current organizational research can be utilized within a Marxist paradigm but only to the extent that it gives content to the concepts of the labor theory of value, the forces and relations of production, contradictions, class struggle, and class structure. Unlike Benson, Goldman and Van Houten attempt to use the general

Marxist theory as the framework for their analysis. They are especially interested in the strategies of managerial control within the organization and its implications for class conflict.

While Goldman and Van Houten propose to study organizations from a Marxist perspective, their view is curiously static and ahistorical and does not rule out a continued emphasis on isolated and trivial organizations. Whereas Benson emphasized process and mislaid context, Goldman and Van Houten have enumerated categories but neglected to integrate them into a dynamic theory. Their focus on control is passive because it views the organization as a monolithic structure in which power emanates from the top. This focus on management control strategies, while sympathetic toward the worker, is little more than the elitist view in another guise. Their treatment has no historical dimension. In fact, the authors suggest that the logic of control in organizations has not changed in the last century, thus dismissing the historical struggle that has taken place both within the organization and outside it. Like Benson, they fail to take into account the differential importance of organizations, choosing to focus on many of the same bureaucratic characteristics that are found in the rational paradigm.

Heydebrand (1977) proposes yet another version of a Marxist theory of organizations. First, he points out that Marxists have traditionally recognized the importance of only one organization, the state, but should now appreciate the importance of other organizations. Then, using the two basic concepts of activity and outcome as embodied in the forces and relations of production, Heydebrand shows how they lead to contradictions that give rise to changes in the social and organizational structure. He applies this approach to United States federal courts, briefly discussing the conflict caused by the opposing forces of professionalism and production, the result of which is contradictions within the judiciary and a shift toward domination by powerful actors.

As with the other Marxist approaches, Heydebrand's discussion shows a certain disjuncture between the overarching theory and the specific application. Heydebrand assumes that Marxist categories conceived at the societal level are applicable at the organizational level though there is no *a priori* reason to believe this is so. Relying on this dubious theoretical connection, Heydebrand sees no need to examine the societal or historical relations of his empirical object to the rest of capitalistic society. Like those working in the rational paradigm, he links the organization to society only through theory. Therefore, any organization, no matter how trivial, is a worthy object of attention since it may yield important theoretical insights. The result, in this case, is a passive, ahistorical, isolated reconsideration of the Parsonian problem of the conflict between bureaucratic and professional tendencies in large organizations.

Despite their extensive use of the dialectical method and Marxist theories and concepts, those attempting to formulate a Marxist theory of organizations fall prey to many of the failures of the rational paradigm. They tend to view the organization as passive and isolated, ignoring the link between struggles within the organization and the relations between the organization and the class structure. Instead they assume that societal processes are reflected in the organization and that analysis appropriate at the societal level can be imposed on the organizational level. This simply leads to the study of many of the same elitist problems, especially control strategies of top management, that have been the concern of the rational paradigm. It also leads to analysis for the sake of theoretical rather than substantial results and the subsequent indiscriminate choice of trivial organizations as research sites. The historic apathy of Marxists toward organizational analysis has left some barriers which a mere grafting of Marxian theory onto the body of established research will not demolish.

THE POLITICAL ECONOMISTS

The political economists, many of whom work in Europe, have traditionally been interested in the interaction of organizations and society. Until recently they had concentrated on the state apparatus but lately have become more aware of the importance of private, especially economic, institutions. Touraine (1971) has emphasized the connection between different levels of the organization and its societal context. Each level constrains the options available to those below it and is constrained by those which are superior. Poulantzas (1973; 1975) has focused on the role that particular types of organizations play in contemporary class relations, but as yet these considerations have been marginal to the mainstream of his analysis.

Working within the political economy tradition, Callon and Vignolle (1977), attempt to identify particular mechanisms that operate in specific organizations. In this case, they employ the *logique d' action* framework proposed by Lucien Karpik (1978) to examine the conflict within a state-financed research center. What is important for our purpose is that the logics of action adopted by groups within the organization dictate the relation of these groups with other sectors of society. The passive view of the organization is decisively rejected. Equally important is the care with which Callon and Vignolle have placed the research center in its societal context.

> From this point of view the study of a technological center makes it possible clearly to determine how scientific activity fits into the action of a ruling class and tends to constitute a system of social domination through the relations between industry, science, and the State, the stakes of which are no other than the orientation of industrial development and the conditions for accumulation (p. 164).

Although the *logique d' action* framework provides Callon and Vignolle with the tools to examine the organization in process and to link it to its context, their pluralist orientation and ahistorical treatment of the organization inhibits the development of criteria for distinguishing trivial from important organizations. The identification of logics of action for groups in the organization and its environment emphasizes the organizational process, but a parallel concern with the history of these struggles and alliances is missing. Finally, while Callon and Vignolle come closest to specifying why a particular research object should be chosen, their criteria remain largely implicit. They defend their choice but provide no guidelines for further work.

All the authors discussed in this section deal with one or more of the criticisms outlined above. And while their emphases differ, all of them to some extent attempt to break out of the narrow limits of the rational paradigm and reconnect the organization with society, to reestablish it in its societal context. It is all the more surprising, therefore, that these same authors have failed to see the obverse of this criticism. If it is important to understand how the organization interacts with the larger society, it is also important to insure that the organization studied has significance for the society. There is little sense in placing the organization within its social context and analyzing its impact on society if that impact is likely to be minimal. What is needed is a means of identifying the organizations that are crucial to social change, preferably those contained within a larger framework. In the next section we will describe these types of important organizations and the means by which they can be identified.

CRITICAL ORGANIZATIONS

There are a number of different types of organizations that are important for society, but we wish to focus on those organizations which are crucial for the direction of societal development. Several authors have argued that some organizations are strategic arenas for societal decision making (Crozier, 1964; Allison, 1971; Touraine, 1971; Bell, 1973; Galbraith, 1973; Karpik, 1978). Far from assuming that all organizations are equally interesting, these authors have pointed to certain organizations as important for setting the constraints under which other elements of society operate (Perrow, 1972; McNeil, 1978). "The organization is seen not as the central theoretical object, but rather as the most expressive social reality in identifying the rules of functioning and evolution of general social processes." (Karpik, 1978:17). These organizations pose social questions, frame the alternatives available, and provide the arena in which socially powerful interests compete to influence important decisions. Thus, to understand societal development, not only the external effects but the internal processes of the organization must be examined (Callon and Vignolle, 1977).

The task for the remainder of this essay is to specify the general criteria for locating these critical organizations at the time that they assume a crucial importance for society. To some extent the designation of these important organizations is obvious. They are often large organizations with vast resources that may be readily deployed such as multinational enterprises, financial institutions, or portions of the state apparatus. But it is not sufficient that these organizations merely have the potential to affect the course of society. For our purposes, they only assume importance to the extent that they actually produce such effects. For example, General Motors is certainly an important organization in the United States today, but it is not currently exercising the leadership it did in the 1920s, when it was simultaneously introducing a new mode of transportation to the country and developing a new style of management structure that has since become standard for large organizations (Chandler, 1962). The role of shaping not only the technological but also the social basis has shifted recently to firms in the electronic and computer industries. Powerful organizations that serve to maintain the configuration of society are, of course, important objects of study and, as we have argued, have not been investigated to the degree that their importance demands (Castells, 1979). But the organizations that attract our attention are those which disrupt the status quo in an effort to reorganize the logic of accumulation and domination and consequently reshape society. For a new paradigm that hopes to examine the organization in its societal context, the investigation of these critical organizations must be a prime requisite.

The important organizations we wish to examine are those that have significant transformative effects on society. We focus on the relation to society rather than on a more limited characterization of the context of the organization because it provides a much more comprehensive picture of the forces confronting the organization. This moves beyond the more limited concept of the environment and allows us to consider more diverse forms of social organization such as social movements, the state, and stratification systems. It also helps to link the study of organizations to the wider problem of power and conflict in modern society (Mouzelis, 1967). What is required then, is a characterization of society that will allow us to address all these diverse social elements. Therefore, we will define a *critical organization as one which has significant transformative effects on the class relations of a society.*[2]

There are three elements in the definition of the critical organization that need further discussion: the specific organization, class relations, and the interrelation of the two. The concept of the organization inherent in our definition differs considerably from that of the rational paradigm. Rather than seeing the organization as a monolithic, unified entity moving toward a set of universally accepted goals, we visualize it as a collection of individuals brought together in structured relationships of domination and subordination who form alliances in order to influence the direction of the organization (Georgiou, 1973; Allison, 1971). This concept of the organization is neither abstract nor deterministic since it views the organization as the outcome of relationships and actions of individuals in concrete situations. Nor is this conception of the organization reductionistic. Critical organizations do not generate society, nor do they contain a microcosm of social relationships. Organizations and class relations are complementary, concrete social objects which must be understood in relation to one another.

The second component of our definition of critical organizations is class relations, that is, the relations among social groups defined by their relation to the mode of production in a historically determined social formation. Class relations refers to the relative capacities of classes or class segments such as those between competitive and monopoly capital, labor and the petty bourgeoisie, and labor and the unemployed.[3] As the societal referent for our definition of critical organizations, class relations offers several distinct advantages over other characterizations of the societal context. First, class relations as a characterization of society embodies all the theoretical distinctions in the literature on organizational environments. Second, it provides a systematic framework for locating the critical organization within the important sectors of society. Finally, class relations offers a logic of meaning for understanding the relations between the organization and structures and actors in society.

While the organization and class relations are central to the concept of the critical organization, it is the interrelation of the two that is the key to our analysis. It is through this relation that the critical organization is identified by its effects on class relations. If the relationship is stable, then the organization, though it may be important within the framework of class relations, is not critical. But if the relationship changes so that class relations are transformed, then the organization is critical. The shift in the specific relations also indicates the characteristics of the organization that should be the focus of analysis.

The relationship of the organization to class relations also has important implications for organizational theory. First, these relations are not consistently critical but become critical at a particular time and later cease to be critical. These relations are never determined or final but develop in a discontinuous manner through the history of the organization. Our analysis of these relationships focuses on these specific periods. Second, through their effect on this relationship, critical organizations change the fabric of class relations and thereby the terrain upon which noncritical organizations must operate. The effects of the new organizational arrangements inside the organization and the effects of the organization's interrelationship with class relations are thus spread throughout society.

The importance of critical organizations may be better understood by examining them in light of Touraine's (1971:139-192) scheme of analytical levels. He identifies four levels of organizational analysis: the operational, organizational, institutional, and the highest level, which he calls economic power. The operations level of which the literature on negotiated order and staff-client relations are examples, focuses on the informal processes within the organization. The organizational level has been the province of the structuralists, whose main interest is the identification of the most efficient organizational morphology. At the institutional level the relation of the organization to its immediate task environment is the chief interest of investigators. Critical organizations operate on all these levels and at the level of economic power, which represents a qualitatively different set of relationships between the organization and other elements in society. In this way they are enmeshed in the limits and opportunities relevant to their decision-making processes, which are created by class relations. This level also constrains the levels which it subsumes, affecting the institutional, organizational, and operational levels within the focal organization.

The relations between an organization and society can be decomposed into a number of different elements, any one of which can serve as a conduit for a critical impact on class relations. The economic, political, technological and cultural bases of a society are bound up in large organizations and can be shifted by them. In a capitalist society the economic element is concerned with the flow of capital through organizations and the generation and abstraction of surplus value. It must be discovered where capital originates, to whom capital accrues, and where the accumulated capital is invested. A shift in this pattern not only affects class relations among the segments of the capitalist class but also those involving the working class. For example, the consolidation of the North American steel industry was made possible by the power and capital of the Morgan finance group. Money accumulated largely as the result of the sale and manipulation of railroad securities funded the concentration of the steel industry, allowing the formation of a corporation that set a new standard for size and set the stage for the growth of vertically integrated firms (Corey, 1930). Besides the threats this posed for other capital groups, it also changed the social and productive circumstances of direct producers within the industry and had indirect effects on labor throughout the industrial sector.

The political aspect of an organization's relationship to society includes direct interference in the political process as well as shaping the framework within which the political life of a nation occurs. The state is often the focus of the struggle to alter or maintain a particular political element of class relations. Portions of the state apparatus become critical when they limit or expand the possible alternative strategies available to different organizations and class segments in society. The impetus for such a critical transformation may come from within the state structure or be effected by a group outside. Sometimes the political arrangements within an organization are altered in a way that makes an organization critical. When the strategies of social control within the oganization are substantially changed, either by employees seeking greater autonomy or by employers seeking increased control, the results may have critical effects for class relations. The great battles for unionization and the later growth of union bureaucracy can be interpreted in this light.

Often the opportunity for both political and economic changes arises from the impact of technological innovation. This may take a number of different forms: the introduction of new methods of production, the development of new products, or even the imposition of new methods of administration and management. An organization, whether profit-making or public, can obtain an advantage if it is able to introduce a technical innovation that provides higher profits or allows for the more efficient use of resources. Other organizations will then feel the pressure to emulate the innovating organization, and the terrain of an entire sector of the economy may quickly shift. The introduction of the transistor and later the printed circuit offer an excellent illustration of this type of effect. The ramifications are not confined to the relations between organizations or even industrial sectors. The individuals within the organization must adapt themselves to the new logic of production, often to their detriment (Braverman, 1974). In order to gain advantage under changing circumstances, the organization must make internal as well as external changes.

Finally, an organization becomes critical when it is able to alter values in a society by changing the definition of attitudes and actions. This can be done through allusion to a legitimating standard such as science, rationality, or collective interest (Poulantzas, 1973:37-41). The communication media and the educational system are important examples of the ideological effects of organizations on class relations (Bowles and Gintis, 1976). But quite often financial, commercial, and industrial organizations are able to foster a definition that is accepted by enough of the population to create an atmosphere that is favorable to specific interests. The introduction of new products and processes into less developed countries (LDC) by multinational corporations is an especially clear example of this impact. There is evidence that through extensive advertising campaigns, multinational corporations have altered for the worse eating habits in LDCs by making imported or processed foods more attractive than locally produced foodstuffs (Barnet and Muller, 1974:172-184). This not only funnels profits into the coffers of the foreign firms, but it also diverts funds from marginal local producers.

Naturally, an organization can be critical because it has important impact on more than one aspect of this relationship, and it is often difficult to disentangle the effects. But these elements of the relationship between organizations and class relations can serve to focus the analysis of a critical organization. They also prove that no organization can be critical in and of itself. It is only through the organization's interface with class relations that it can be critical. However much potential power the organization may have, it is of no interest to us as a critical organization until those resources have been utilized to produce significant changes in class relations. It is implicit in this definition that an organization may be critical or non-critical in different periods. After the change in class relations is in place, the organization is no longer critical. It is to this temporal element that we now turn our attention.

CRITICAL MOMENTS

Implicit in the definition of the critical organization is the idea that an organization is critical during a specific period of time. During this period, which we call the critical moment, the organization takes some action that significantly transforms class relations, shifts the interrelationship of the organization with class relations, and almost inevitably involves changes in the organization itself. Critical moments embody three general characteristics: capacity, structural context, and decision-making. First, the organization must have the discretionary power to mobilize available resources and implement innovative policies by transcending external constraints. Second, the pattern of obstacles and external constraints on the organization's maneuverability waxes and wanes. These limits on organizational behavior are influenced but never fully determined by the organization itself. The changing configuration of these limitations presents opportunities for the organization to dramatically affect its environment. Finally, the organization requires decision-makers who can apprehend contextual changes and mobilize the appropriate resources in order to seize the opportunity for the organization. This does not mean that the leaders set out to change class relations, only that they seek to improve the situation of the organization.

The idea of the critical organization embodies a very different view of organizational change than does the rational paradigm, which postulates an evolutionary process (Stinchcombe, 1965). As the resources, both material and social, become available in a society, various groups of organizations utilize them to adopt more complex organizational forms. The evolutionary perspective views new types of organizations as emerging when the social technology necessary for the performance of their tasks becomes available. The process of organizational change is seen as a largely passive adaptation to environmental factors.

The concepts of the critical organization and critical moment require a very different view. We argue that certain organizations are much better equipped to take advantage of opportunities to change class relations to their advantage. As Galbraith (1973:86) has argued with respect to large business firms:

> With the rise of the great corporation goes the power extensively to enforce its will on society — not only to fix prices and costs but to influence consumers, and organize the supply of materials and components, and mobilize its own savings and capital, and develop a strategy for handling labor, and influence the attitudes of the community and the actions of the state.

The evolutionary view ignores the fact that in industrialized societies the resources are very largely controlled by organizations that may dispose of them within certain limits. This is not to say that evolutionary change does not occur. Rather, the critical organization takes a qualitatively different path than the evolutionary change evident in non-critical organizations. As a result, the strategies which critical organizations pursue tend to have higher risks, involve more abrupt changes, and are geared toward reaping greater benefits. When the strategy is successful, that is, when the organization becomes critical, other organizations attempt to follow its lead so as to gain the same advantages. Instead of the gradual movement of numbers of organizations through the same progression, this disjunctive view of organizational change postulates an abrupt move by a single organization, which is imitated by others and which only appears smooth and evolutionary in retrospect.

Organizational processes, especially decision-making, are important points of analysis during the critical moments (Burns, 1961; Long, 1958; Zaldman, et.al., 1973). The process begins with differential perceptions of the opportunities or necessities that result in the formation of new goals and objectives by groups within the organization. To the extent that these group objectives diverge, conflict will develop. The groups will assess the costs and benefits of the various policies and will form coalitions with other groups in an effort to realize their choice (Zaldman, et al., 1973). Since the alternatives may have dramatic effects on class relations, interested parties inside and outside the organization will attempt to affect the outcome. As the consequences of the decisions are felt, the conflict may spread to other organizations or class segments, who may attempt to facilitate or deflect the consequences of the decisions or try to reverse them entirely. Eventually a resolution will take place either through negotiation or simple power politics.

The change in the relationship between the organization and class relations that occurs at the critical moment is usually reflected in the internal structure and processes of the critical organization. The internal power system may be altered by changes in the locus of decision-making, information flows, and the allocation of organizational resources (Harvey and Mills, 1970). Aspects of the formal structure such as the division of labor, technological base, methods of control and coordination, and the internal economy of the organization may also be changed (Harvey and Mills, 1970; Zald, 1970; Pfeffer, 1978). These changes may also be reflected in shifts of executive personnel or the processes by which they are selected (Zald, 1970; Soref and James, 1978). Finally, disjunctive changes in the relationship of the organization to society will be reflected in changing policies with respect to institutional and societal actors and processes (Zald, 1970; Karpik, 1978).

This process of perception, conflict, decision, further conflict, and resolution is one reason it is important to study critical organizations at the critical moment. At that time the operation of the political process centered in the organization is most visible to the researcher. The various strategies available to the organization and the groups within it are much more apparent. The advantages and disadvantages of these alternatives are contested, promoted, and criticized by parties inside and outside the organization. At the critical moment there is no need to accept managerial pronouncements on goals of the organization, since the commitment of resources to alternative plans demonstrates which alternatives are most beneficial for different interests.

Similarly, since the stakes are high at critical moments the various actors are under pressure to influence the outcome. Because these are real actors with concrete positions in the organization and class structure, the links between various actors and their class interests are made more clear than they would be in a non-critical situation. The effect of these pressures brings about what one author refers to as a "revelatory moment" (Burns, 1961). Conflicts that are manifest among the actors of the organization reflect the social interests they represent. The changes in the social structure and the organization represent attempts to manage these conflicts by adjusting the limits on the organization. The result is a temporary resolution of the conflict when the interests of one group prevail.

At critical moments the links between the power distribution in the organization and the parallel elements in the class structure are brought into sharp relief. In part this is due to the location of important actors and their class positions but it is also due to the actions of other groups within the class structure who react to the movements of the critical organization. The environmental constraints on the organization embodied in class relations are emphasized as the organization moves to transcend them and opposing elements seek to enforce them. The substance of the particular issue interacts with the structure of class relations to produce a clearer picture of the actors, interests, and the critical organization in the social configuration.

This, then, is the rationale for making the critical organization a major focus of organizational sociology and for studying it at its critical moment. First, critical moments are the point at which many important organizational changes take place. These changes may also be an important source of societal change. Throughout the process of the critical moment the important actors, their class positions, environmental constraints, and their relations to class relations and each other are highlighted. Of course, it will be argued that studying an organization in the process of the critical moment is inappropriate because this is not the "normal" state. But this is simply a restatement of the position of the rational paradigm. Unless we believe that all organizations are equally interesting and that they are passive in the face of environmental constraints, then those organizations that have the most important effects are the natural objects of study. Insisting on the "normal" state of the organization ignores the fact that no organization is ever completely stable; nor is the relationship between the organization and the class structure ever finally determined. Any static stage is simply a moment in the history of the organization. We prefer to concentrate, in that case, on critical moments. The idea that there are critical organizations and critical moments in society means that criteria can be established to determine which of these organizations should be studied.

The analysis of critical organizations and critical moments must be based on selective principles, otherwise indiscriminate attempts to relate organizational policy to social change will contribute little to a theory of purposive organizational behavior. To some extent the outline of these criteria are clear. We wish to examine organizations which set the pattern for changes in class relations and which limit the alternatives available to organizations and other elements in society. But the selection of precise criteria will obviously depend on the specific historical conditions that obtain in a society or region at a particular moment. The innovative economic, political, technological, or ideological mechanisms which are used to manipulate class relations will be specific to time and place although international and historical patterns will doubtless appear. The formulation of a set of general criteria is a continuing task that will be facilitated by work done in critical organizations.

CONCLUSION

The outline presented in this selection is not a theory of organizations but a set of analytic questions that allows one to identify critical organizations and the relationship that makes them critical. Because this relationship is particular to each organization and to each critical moment, a specific research agenda cannot be offered. To some extent the current organizational literature may be helpful for the study of critical organizations. While the key to the study of the critical organization is the organization-class relations interface, organizational structure and process are still important. Internal dynamics will influence the kinds of strategies available to the organization and the resources that can be mobilized to implement them. The interrelationship between the critical organization and class relations will indicate which characteristics of the organization are most important for that critical moment. The specific methods used in any particular study will naturally depend on the organization, the historical situation, and the research issue at hand. The framework suggests the use of multiple methods of analysis, including historical and statistical methods that would employ a range of data sources from archival to demographic.

Our discussion of critical organizations and critical moments suggests that research into these organizations must be on a case by case basis so that the particular historical and structural circumstances can be fully investigated. Case studies of critical organizations can create an interpretive model of important social relationships, a set of analytic tools, and theoretical questions (Karpik, 1978:3). As an interpretive model the case study can be used to suggest a framework which is, to a degree, generalizable. Thus we would argue that historical case studies of critical organizations should be concerned with the particular social functions of these organizations and at the same time serve as conceptual models toward general comparisons.

While the idea of the critical organization does attempt to provide a new approach to the study of organizations, it does not reject out of hand the work done under the rational paradigm. We suggest that a new organizational paradigm needs to take into consideration the relationship between organizations and society. Within this relationship we have argued for the importance of recognizing the timing and impact of certain powerful organizations on society. From this perspective we can begin to raise questions of how the main features of the organization relate to the principles, interests, and purposes that lie behind them. However, a great many of the problems posed by the rational paradigm such as hierarchy, the division of labor, mechanisms of control, etc., will also be central to the work done under any new paradigm. Furthermore, the techniques developed by those working under the rational paradigm may also be applicable to certain problems of a new paradigm. What will be different is that the expanded scope and historical orientation of a new paradigm will allow new interpretations of old issues and more adequately reflect the ways in which organizations can be instruments of societal dynamics.

Besides the implications for research, our discussion leads to some conclusions on a new direction for organizational sociology. The primary change is a renewed interest in organizations that have major importance for the social structure. The preference for studying organizations that are stable and offer easy access must give way to the fact that important organizations are often more intractable objects of study. Such organizations are likely to be viewed as unsuitable objects for study because they are not representative of all organizations. It is precisely because these organizations are unusual, and because they move to change the limits placed on all organizations, that they are necessary objects of research. The new paradigm must not only deal with changing organizations, it must also recognize them as agents of change.

All this is not to say, of course, that a new paradigm should focus only on critical organizations or even only those organizations with the potential to become critical. Small organizations, either singly or in groups, play important reproductive roles in society. But the crucial relation between important organizations and the society, which the rational paradigm has so successfully ignored, demands that critical organizations receive central significance in a new paradigm. Just as the critical organization affects the limits under which other organizations must exist, so the study of critical organizations will influence the research approaches to other important organizations. In this way the new paradigm will allow organizational sociology to once again become the study of organizations in society rather than simply a sociology of organizations.

NOTES

[1] We use paradigm here to mean a framework for the analysis of a class of objects shared by the majority of the practitioners in a sub-area of a discipline. This differs substantially from Kuhn's (1970) original definition, which is more rigorous and embraces all those working in a scientific field.

[2] For a more extensive discussion of critical organizations see Colignon and Cray (1980).

[3] Poulantzas's (1973:58-73) discussion of class relations is helpful in understanding this concept. Class relations, he argues, are relations among social groups and not elements of a structure. These social groups are defined by their relation in a historically determined social formation. The relation among classes is not only between capital and labor as in a pure mode of production, but as in any empirical social formation, there are overlapping modes of production which therefore present more classes.

REFERENCES

Allison, Graham
1971   *Essence of Decision.* Boston: Little, Brown and Company.
Argyris, Chris
1972   *The Applicability of Organizational Sociology.* Cambridge: Cambridge University Press.
Barnet, Richard, and Ronald Muller
1974   *Global Reach.* New York: Simon and Schuster.
Bell, Daniel
1973   *The Coming of Post-Industrial Society.* New York: Basic Books.

Benson, J. Kenneth
1977a   "Organizations: A Dialectical View," *Administrative Science Quarterly* 22:1-21.
1977b   "Innovation and Crisis in Organizational Analysis," *Sociological Quarterly* 18:3-16.
Bowles, S., and H. Gintis
1976   *Schooling in Capitalist America: Educational Reform and the Contradictions of Economic Life.* New York: Basic Books.

Braverman, Harry
1974   *Labor and Monopoly Capital*. New York: Monthly Review Press.
Burns, Tom
1961   "Micropolitics: Mechanisms of Institutional Change," *Administrative Science Quarterly* 6:257-281.
Callon, M., and J. Vignolle
1977   "Breaking Down the Organization: Local Conflicts and Societal Systems of Action," *Social Science Information* 16:147-167.
Castells, M., and F. Godard
1979   *Monopolville: The Corporation, the State and the Urban Process*. London: Macmillan.
Chandler, Alfred
1962   *Strategy and Structure*. Cambridge: MIT Press.
Colignon, Richard and David Cray
1980   "Critical Organizations," *Organization Studies* (in press).
Corey, Lewis
1930   *The House of Morgan*. New York: Brosset and Dunlop.
Crozier, M.
1964   *The Bureaucratic Phenomenon*. Chicago: University of Chicago Press.
Edwards, Richard
1978   "The Social Relations of Production at the Point of Production," *The Insurgent Sociologists* 8:109-125.
Galbraith, John Kenneth
1973   *Economics and the Public Purpose*. New York: Signet.
Georgiou, Petro
1973   "The Goal Paradigm and Notes Toward a Counter Paradigm," *Administrative Science Quarterly* 18:291-310.
Goldman, P., and D. Van Houten
1977   "Managerial Strategies and the Worker: A Marxist Analysis of Bureaucracy," *Sociological Quarterly* 18:108-125.
Harvey, Edward, and R. Mills
1970   "Patterns of Organizational Adaptation: A Political Perspective," in Mayer Zald (ed) *Power in Organizations*. Nashville: Vanderbilt University Press.
Heydebrand, Wolf
1977   "Organizational Contradictions in Public Bureaucracies: Toward a Marxist Theory of Organizations," *The Sociological Quarterly* 18:83-107.

Hirsch, Paul
1975   "Organizational Analysis and Industrial Sociology," *The American Sociologist* 10:3-12.
Karpik, Lucien
1978   *Organizations and Environment*. Beverly Hills: Sage.
Kuhn, Thomas
1970   *The Structure of Scientific Revolutions*. Chicago: University of Chicago Press.
Lammers, Cornelis J.
1974   "The State of Organizational Sociology in the United States: Travel Impressions From a Dutch Cousin," *Administrative Science Quarterly* 19:422-430.
Long, Norton
1958   "The Local Community as an Ecology of Games," *American Journal of Sociology* 64:251-261.
McNeil, Kenneth
1978   "Understanding Organizational Power: Building on the Weberian Legacy," *Administrative Science Quarterly* 23:65-89.
Mouzelis, Micos
1967   *Organizational and Bureaucracy*. Chicago: Aldine.
Perrow, Charles
1972   *Complex Organizations: A Critical Essay*. Glenview: Scott, Foresman and Company.
Pfeffer, Jeffrey
1972a   "Size and Composition of Corporate Boards of Directors: The Organization and its Environment," *Administrative Science Quarterly* 17:218-228.
1972b   "Merger as a Response to Organizational Interdependence," *Administrative Science Quarterly* 17:382-394.
1977   "Toward an Examination of Stratification in Organizations," *Administrative Science Quarterly* 22:563-567.
1978   "The Micropolitics of Organizations." In Marshall Meyer and Associates *Environments and Organizations*. San Francisco: Jossey-Bass.
Pfeffer, Jeffrey, and H. Leblebici
1973   "Executive Recruitment and the Development of Interfirm Organizations," *Administrative Science Quarterly* 18:449-461.

Pfeffer, Jeffrey, and P. Nowak
1976 "Joint Ventures and Interorganizational Interdependence," *Administrative Science Quarterly* 21:398-418.

Poulantzas, Nicos
1973 *Political Power and Social Classes.* London: New Left Books.
1975 *Classes in Contemporary Capitalism.* London: New Left Books.

Soref, Michael, and David James
1978 "The Unmaking of the Corporation President: Profit Constraints on Managerial Autonomy." Paper presented at the Annual Meeting of the *American Sociological Association,* San Francisco.

Stinchcombe, Arthur
1965 "Social Structure and Organizations." In James March *Handbook of Organizations.* Chicago: Rand McNally.

Touraine, Alain
1971 *The Post-Industrial Society* (trans. by Leonard Mayhew). New York: Random House.

Wassenberg, Arthur
1977 "The Powerlessness of Organization Theory." In S. Clegg and D. Dunkerly *Critical Issues in Organizations.* London: Routledge and Kegan Paul.

Zald, Meyer
1970 *Organizational Change: The Political Economy of the YMCA,* Chicago: University of Chicago.

Zaldman, G., R. Duncan, and J. Holbeck
1973 *Innovations and Organizations,* New York: Wiley.

II

Introduction To Micro-Emphases On Control And Power

Accompanying the strong critiques of the dominant perspectives in organization theory as summarized and illustrated in Part I, the reader could and should expect some alternative conceptualizations of organizations that avoid the specified criticisms. Such alternatives are offered in the selections of Part II, under the heading "Micro-Emphases on Control and Power." The heading is not meant to imply that only questions about power and control are important; rather it is simply that many of the alternative perspectives developed to date focus on these micro issues.

Common to the readings that follow is the idea that what have been called organizational structures — systems of control, coordination, incentives, rewards, etc. — are choices made by dominant coalitions. Hence, while these choices can be affected by worker attitudes and behavior, technology, culture, and external exigencies, they nevertheless are the consequences of human choices.

These readings also share an emphasis on such processes as negotiation, bargaining, coalition formation, domination, coercion, and manipulation. We have divided them into four sections: (1) the negotiated order perspective, (2) political perspectives, (3) Marxist micro-organizational perspectives (a label we use with some risk of contradiction in terms), and (4) organizations as loosely coupled systems.

NEGOTIATED ORDER PERSPECTIVE:

The negotiated order perspective as described by Strauss (1978, Selection 6) focuses, like the other perspectives in this part, on processes within organizations. The selection is part of his summary chapter in *Negotiations: Varieties, Contexts, Processes, and Social Order*. While the Marxian perspectives of Edwards (1978, Selection 8), Friedman (1977, Selection 9), and Goldman and Van Houten (1979, Selection 10) and the political perspective of Allison (1971, Selection 7) are also process approaches, none of these stress the importance of negotiations as explicitly as the negotiated order perspective. Strauss's primary assumption is that organizational arrangements are continually emerging through the negotiating interactions of participants in day-to-day encounters. The arrangements of structures established by these actions are hence seldom stable, and actors are continually renegotiating their circumstances in organizations. Strauss (1978:235) argues that social orders are, in some sense, always negotiated orders.'' He recognizes that there are other methods of getting things done such as ''coercion, persuasion, manipulation,'' etc. However, he advocates the primacy of analyzing processes in organizations such as these instead of ''outcomes, efficiency, decision-making,'' or other aspects of social order.

In an attempt to answer the criticism of the negotiated order perspective leveled by Benson and Day (1976) and Day and Day (1977) that it has been limited largely to interpersonal relations, Strauss elaborates various macro-structural level aspects of social order that this perspective has been used to analyze, thus demonstrating the possibility of its application to the study of collectivities ranging from the dyad to multinational corporations. Hence, his perspective includes both process and structure as reflected in key terms such as: ''subprocesses of negotiation,'' which includes tradeoffs, obtaining kickbacks, compromising towards the middle, paying off debts, and reaching negotiated agreements; ''structural contexts,'' within which negotiations take place; and the ''structural properties'' of social settings. The term ''negotiation context'' refers to the specific ''conditions'' of the negotiation process. In the selection included here, Strauss enumerates a dozen or more properties of the negotiation process that should serve to sensitize a researcher to key aspects of this approach.

Like Allison in his work on the Cuban missile crisis (see Selection 7), Strauss advocates the particularistic nature of each negotiated order and therefore presents arguments against attempts to construct a general theory of negotiations. His major argument against such an endeavor is the continually changing nature of each ''negotiation context,'' each ''structural context,'' and each ''historical context'' in which a negotiated order occurs.

There are similarities in the nature of the questions posed by Strauss and the questions that Allison recommends in his political model outlined later in this section. The set of questions that Strauss suggests for one working from his perspective include: Who is being included in the negotiation process? In what relationship does the negotiator stand to the represented? Are the represented aware that they are being represented? If they know, do they agree to the representation and to what degree? How much of the negotiator's representative actions are the represented aware of? How many parties are represented? A complete listing of his questions can be found on pages 245-246 of his book.

In the last part of his summary chapter (the text of which is not reprinted here), Strauss outlines the criticisms that have been raised against the negotiated order perspective. These criticisms are answered throughout the revisions of his perspective in the part of his book included here. However, those interested in a more in-depth understanding of the criticisms that have been made of the negotiated order perspective and Strauss's rebuttal may wish to examine the original source (1978:247-259).

The reader who is interested in micro-process approaches to organizations may also wish to examine the growing number of interesting and insightful works by symbolic interaction theorists who analyze negotiations and build on the negotiated order perspective: Bucher (1970), Bucher and Stelling (1969), Stelling and Bucher (1972), Morgan (1975), Martin (1976), and Gerson (1976).

While there could be more dissimilarities than similarities between this approach and others included in this part of the anthology, the concerns of the negotiated order perspective do seem to underlie the concerns of political process approach such as that of Allison (1971, Selection 7) and the Marxist approaches of Edwards (1978, Selection 8), Friedman (1977, Selection 9), and Goldman and Van Houten (1979, Selection 10). Hence this perspective should provide the reader with a sensitivity to those aspects of organizational dynamics that are presupposed by these other intraorganizational perspectives.

POLITICAL PERSPECTIVES

In this section we include the political perspective of Allison (1971, Selection 7). As will become readily apparent to the reader, this analysis has characteristics similar to Andrew Pettigrew's analysis of *The Politics of Organizational Decision-Making* (1973). It may help illustrate this work by discussing some of the characteristics of Pettigrew's works. These two authors pose some similar questions about organizational phenomena, but they differ in the scope of the phenomena addressed. Both are extraordinarily insightful and were taken from a set of works reflecting a political perspective on organizations dating back to the early 1960s: Wilson and Clark (1961), Long (1962), March (1962), Baldridge (1971), Wilson (1973), and Baldridge, *et al.* (1978). Recently, Bacharach and Lawler (1980) have integrated the social psychology of politics with the structural analysis of organizations to explain interorganizational politics.

In his book, Pettigrew analyzes the politics and innovative decisions in a department store in England. The central theme is that these innovative decisions generate conflicts and associated behaviors that can only be fully explained and understood if the present is understood in the context of past and future expectations. That is, the behavior of organizational actors is best understood in terms of the circumstances and pressures currently impinging on them, in terms of their past actions, and in terms of their hopes, aspirations, and desires for the future.

Pettigrew's conceptual framework of organizational power and control is essentially an extension and revision of March and Simon's (1958) and Cyert and March's (1963) decision-making models. While Pettigrew focuses on the individual as the unit of analysis and the expression of the individual's interests through groups, he also takes into consideration, more than most decision-making theorists, the structural, institutional, environmental, and societal constraints on actors. He recognizes that underlying a strategic choice model of behavior is the self-interest of each individual actor. He avoids an overly mechanical political approach by assuming that not all individuals act in their own best interests or seek rewards each time they engage in social behavior. Further, Pettigrew assumes that individual choices are often limited by human perceptions of the situation, the amount and kinds of information they possess, and by the lack of access to information that each person's location in the social structure imposes. He allows for people making errors that bring unintended consequences. His perspective includes both rational and irrational aspects of human behavior.

One of the most important characteristics of Pettigrew's perspective is his emphasis on the volitional behavior of actors in organizations. In pursuing their self-interests, actors make choices. While they are limited and constrained in some ways by organizational structures, they are also activists in molding that structure over time. This part of Pettigrew's perspective is analogous to Strauss's concern for actors continually renegotiating their situation within social settings. Pettigrew (1973:4) further elaborates that ''[the] individual's ability to achieve this molding is very much a function of his ability to generate sufficient power and influence to impose his will on others in the face of opposition.'' While this may seem to be a fairly straightforward and unproblematic view of organizational behavior, the consequences of applying it consistently in the study of organizations are far-reaching.

From the work of Cyert and March (1963:27), Pettigrew also adopts the view of organizations as coalitions of decision-makers and their view of the ubiquitiousness of conflict because of sub-goal differentiation and the resultant actions of coalitions. Indeed, conflict is an essential and ubiquitious aspect of the power relationships in organizations, and bargaining and coalition formation are paramount features of Pettigrew's approach to organizations.

In short, Pettigrew generates a broad definition of power and control in organizations by (1) criticizing the limited approaches that define power as authority (Parsons, 1967:319); (2) advocating the importance of the role of communication, internal structure of the organizations, the membership of the bargaining groups within the coalitions, the complex and changing task environment and its effects on uncertainty in decision-making, differential interdependencies of subgroups, differential attitudes and values, and intergroups' conflicts of subgroups; and (3) realizing the importance of informal power such as leadership, "office politics," and "bureaucratic gamesmanship" (Strauss, 1962), line/staff relationships (Dalton, 1959), and the subordinates' technical control of strategic uncertainties (Crozier, 1964). He further realizes that such resources can be mobilized by organization members in different groups, subgroups, and levels throughout the organization. Finally, citing Giddens (1968:264), Pettigrew notes that an analysis of power that does not "bring into play a multiplicity of possible strategies of coercion, deceit, and manipulation which can be used either to acquire or to hold on to power is blatantly inadequate."

As should be clear, Pettigrew's imagery of organizations is considerably different from the comparative structural and structural contingency approaches to the study of organizations. Rather than "throwing men [people] out," as some structural theorists have proposed, it places the actor, his or her motivations, personal goals, skills, and choices at the very heart of the analysis.

The political perspective on organizations included here is taken from *Essence of Decisions: Explaining the Cuban Missile Crisis* (1971) by Graham Allison. In his book Allison develops three models of organizational behavior. The first is a classical bureaucratic model; the second is an organization process model; and the third, which is reprinted in this volume, is a political model. In addition to examining major intriguing questions about the Cuban missile crisis, Allison presents alternative images of organizations in terms of the basic assumptions, categories of knowledge used, and basic vision of the organization. This work is an excellent example of various methods of organizational analysis as applied to national security.

Allison (1971, Selection 7) begins by recognizing, as does Pettigrew, that the classical decision-making models of March and Simon (1958) and Cyert and March (1963) cannot adequately explain organizational decision-making. First, participants in decision-making processes are not "monolithic groups"; that is, there is no unitary group possessing consensus of values and therefore goals. Like Pettigrew, Allison defines the individual as the unit of analysis, and each individual in the group plays the game based on his or her own interests, values, and attitudes. The game is politics and the process is that of bargaining. While the rational models of decision-making deal with only one issue at a time, Allison views decision-makers as dealing with many diverse issues simultaneously. They act in terms of what they define as national, organizational, group, and personal objectives; but their objectives and actions alone do not make *the* difference. Rather the "resultant" or outcome is a consequence of the "pulling and hauling that is politics." The decision-making arena is made up of political leaders from the top levels of various governmental agencies and thus is decentralized, because each person has a different power base with different responsibilities and different interests. This process yields conflicting recommendations because people with different responsibilities share power. This results in negotiations, conflicts, decisions, and foul-ups — political processes.

Allison (1971:146) makes the point that an analysis of political processes is particularistic and must deal with the unique situation: "To explain why a particular formal government decision was made, or why one pattern of governmental behavior emerged, it is necessary to identify the games and players, to display the coalitions, bargains, compromises, and to convey some feel for the confusion." Finally, and perhaps most importantly, Allison deflates what he considers to be the public image and "academic orthodoxy" — that political outcomes are based on objective decisions. Concurrently, he negates the assumption that the actors involved are above "playing politics with national security."

Using his "bureaucratic politics" paradigm, Allison analyzes a particular event — the Cuban missile crisis. The model proceeds inductively in the manner outlined in the introduction to Part I above. It is individual, action-oriented, and process-based. Power and influence are central to his analysis. He begins by defining the basic unit of analysis as "governmental *action* as *political resultants*" (emphasis added) and then moves to asking the analytical questions of "Who plays? What determines each player's stand? What determines each player's relative influence? How does the game combine the players' stands, influence, and moves so as to yield governmental decisions and actions?" (1971:164)

As has been demonstrated, both Allison and Pettigrew offer strikingly different images of organizations in comparison to organization theorists who work in the structural contingency and comparative structural traditions. Individual actors and the volitional aspects of their behavior, the political process of organizational behavior, and outcomes in organizations conceived as political outcomes are central features of their approaches that distinguish them from sociological approaches that are currently dominant in organizational analysis.

MARXIAN MICRO-ORGANIZATIONAL PERSPECTIVES

Each of the next three selections — 8, 9, and 10, by Edwards (1978), Friedman (1977), and Goldman and Van Houten (1979), respectively — use a Marxian perspective in analyzing manager control of workers in contemporary capitalist society. They are included here because they emphasize micro-processes of power and control in organizations. However, they would be equally appropriate examples of the macro-societal Marxian perspectives included in Part III, since the larger perspective from which they are derived is essentially a macro-societal one.

These articles constitute a reaction to and critique of the rationalization of the work process that has accompanied industrialization in advanced capitalist societies, although one of them (Edwards, Selection 8) is additionally a reaction to Braverman's (1974) *Labor and Monopoly Capital*. The authors of these selections would all disagree with Weber's general thesis about the trends toward rationalization in advanced capitalism and would favor Marx's thesis that such processes are intimately connected with the rise of capitalist accumulation and its consequences. Marx leaves no doubt that contemporary forms of organization in capitalist societies are for the purpose of exploitation of the labor force (Marx, 1967:284) when he writes: "The simple elements of the labor process are (1) purposeful activity, that is, work itself, (2) the object on which the work is performed, and (3) the instruments of that work." Marx then proceeds to show how all three of these elements are stripped from the laborer in capitalist society. As Goldman and Van Houten (1979:130) have argued, "modern bureaucracy was forged as much from the need to respond to class conflict as it was from the need to 'coordinate' large numbers of people engaged in material production. Insofar as bureaucracy is a 'necessity' of capitalist industry, it is largely due to the continuing need to deny workers control over their productive lives."

The informing thesis of the Edwards book, *Contested Terrain: The Transformation of the Workplace in 20th Century America* (1979), from which Selection 8 is taken, is one of Marx's elemental ones — that the relationship between a capitalist employer and the worker is and will always be antagonistic. As Edwards puts it, "workers must provide labor power . . . they must show up for work; but they need not necessarily provide labor, much less the amount of labor that the capitalist desires to extract." And as long as they do not control how they work and what they produce, "any extraction beyond the minimum needed to avert boredom will be in the worker's interest." On the other hand, for the capitalist the more work which can be wrung from the labor power purchased, the greater the capitalist's profit. This conflict of interests is rooted in the very nature of our society. Capitalists are constantly plagued by the problem of how to organize work — what pace to establish, what environment to provide for the greatest productivity and profit. They have developed successive strategies to control workers, one of the most recent being the bureaucratization of the relations of production. Edwards feels that this type of social conduct will eventually be the undoing of capitalism.

Edwards (1979:110) sees the production process, in particular, as fraught with uncertainties resulting from the two tasks of employers: (1) the coordination of social production, which is the conscious direction of the meshing of the labor of all workers and (2) the compelling of workers to produce goods from which the capitalists will profit. This second task is the more difficult because "capitalists must seek to convert the labor power they have purchased in the marketplace into useful labor under conditions in which the possessor of the labor power has little to gain from providing useful labor." Capitalism makes this compulsion an economic necessity.

Edwards documents how capitalists have attempted over the centuries to organize production in such a way as to minimize workers' opportunities for resistance. Recently capitalists have even attempted to alter the worker's perception of the desirability of opposition. Considering this, one should ask: What are the relations between workers and employers in the firm? What system of control prevails? Edwards (1978:112) defines three elements of management control: (1) the directions of work tasks; (2) the evaluation of the work done, and (3) the rewarding and disciplining of workers. He also defines three historically important and essentially different ways of organizing these three elements. The first is *simple control,* in which capitalists exercise power openly, arbitrarily, and personally (or through hired bosses who act in much the same way). This method of control was predominant in the nineteenth century. The second is *technical control,* in which the control mechanism is embedded in the physical apparatus of the firm. The third is *bureaucratic control,* which is embedded in the social organization of the enterprise, in the contrived social relations of production at the point of production. Edwards further sees the technical and bureaucratic methods of control as *structural* in the sense that the exercise of power becomes institutionalized in the very structure of the firm and is thus made impersonal.

Just as capitalism has proceeded from a competitive to a monopolistic phase, so the organization of workers in regard to production and circumstances of their work has changed from requiring simple to requiring structural methods of control. Edwards views structural control, both the physical (technology) and the social structure, as more consciously contrived, less visible to the worker, more covert, and more institutional than other methods. He sees this control as a product, not of capitalist employment relations, but rather of modern industry, with capitalists determining the work flow speed and quality. Thus this method of control is not technologically determined; rather, the workers' loss of control of the pace and sequence of tasks is "understood to be the result of the *particular* [*capitalist*] *design* of the technology and not as an inherent characteristic of machinery in general" (Edwards, 1978:115). Thus Edwards, like Marglin (1974), rejects any technological determinism explanation of social relations. Technology does not "cause" organizational structure or the nature of work design. At most it places limits upon it. These limits are always constructed from within the context of the dialectical relationship of the productive forces of technology and the social relationships associated with them. The Marxian perspective maintains that both technology and organizational structure have developed out of need for capital accumulation and through the control of capitalists and their managers.

Edwards (1978:117) notes that technological control alone is neither sufficient nor pervasive enough to control all the aspects of a firm. Although it progressively directs the worker to further tasks, it does little to change the second and third elements of "evaluating work performance" and "enforcing compliance." Thus capitalists have felt the need for broader and more extensive controls than are afforded by mechanization and automation — controls inherent in the social or organizational structure of the firm, that is, "bureaucratic control."

Edwards (1978:120) defines four methods of bureaucratic control that have been developed, which are further elaborated by Goldman and Van Houten (1979) in the next selection. First, the power relations of hierarchical authority were made invisible, "submerged and embedded in the structure and organization of the firm, rather than visible and openly manifest in personal, arbitrary power." Second, bureaucratic control, through its emphasis on formal structure and status distinctions, made it possible to differentiate jobs more finely, which tended to erode the bases of common work oppositions. Thus the workers increasingly faced the impersonal and massive organization alone; the possibilities of uniting worker's actions against the capitalists declined. Third, supervisory roles were transformed from instigator, director, and overseer of work to monitor and evaluator of performance according to the established criteria. Likewise, the supervisors' work was subject to more extensive evaluation and control. Fourth, numerous mechanisms were used to tie the worker to the employing firm; job ladders were available only to those who would stay in the firm and work their way through the career ladder to prove that they deserved organizational rewards such as salary raises, tenure, and promotions.

The second Marxian selection is taken from Andrew Friedman's *Industry and Labor: Class Struggle at Work and Monopoly Capitalism.* In this insightful and provocative work Friedman first notes the limitations of applying Marx's analysis to contemporary society. Marx did not systematically take into account the possibility that changes might occur under capitalism in response to the contradictory forces created by capitalist accumulation. In particular, Marx did not analyze the means by which the capitalist would co-opt the worker unions and movements. Friedman writes: "On examining the day-to-day operation of worker resistance and managerial counter pressure one finds that the proletariat, rather than forming a revolutionary class (a class for itself rather than simply in itself), often appears to be fighting among itself. Worker resistance is unevenly developed among different groups of workers, and managers use these divisions to maintain their authority and to subdue overall resistance." Responsible autonomy (a term explained in the following paragraph) is one method of dividing and controlling workers.

Friedman supplements and extends Edwards' elaboration of the types of control in the capitalistic firm by defining not only bureaucratic control but also professional control, which has become increasingly prominent in recent years. Friedman begins by defining two basic types of control: (1) coordination of functional areas and (2) control of workers. He defines as "direct control" such techniques of social control as division of labor, hierarchy of authority, and control of knowledge and information; and he differentiates it from a second technique of social control that he labels "responsible autonomy," which is a strategy in which capitalists attempt to harness the adaptability of labor power by giving workers leeway and encouraging them to adapt to changing situations in a manner that is, of course, beneficial to the firm. In this strategy, managers give workers status, authority, and responsibility. By manipulating employees with such techniques, top managers attempt to win the loyalties of workers and co-opt them and worker unions to the ideologies of the firm (Friedman, 1977:78). Responsible autonomy techniques have been used in human relations approaches as well as in job enrichment theories while direct control strategies have been used primarily in scientific management and classical management approaches. Direct control limits the scope of labor power through coercive threats, close supervision, and minimizing individual autonomy.

Both strategies have been applied by capitalists throughout history, but Friedman also sees these strategies applied differentially to a class situation. The responsible autonomy strategy has been applied most consistently to privileged workers, that is, those with higher rank, status, or education. Direct control strategies have been reserved for unskilled or less skilled workers of the lower economic class. Friedman sees managerial strategies under monopolistic capitalism turning to responsible autonomy strategies in order to co-opt and deal with organized worker resistance. He criticizes Braverman and some other Marxists for not differentiating adequately between these two types of managerial strategies. Friedman argues that one should not lose sight of the fact that loosening of control over the operative tasks of workers reduces worker resistance, but this is still a control technique. Reduction of worker resistance is a part of the job of management, but this kind of "good" management in essence strengthens management's control over productive activities. Top management still controls the overall work activities, and the product of the workers' labor still belongs to the capitalist. The only thing that is changed in the strategy of responsible autonomy is that the worker has power within his or her work activity.

The final Marxian selection by Goldman and Van Houten (Selection 10) is an extension and elaboration of themes developed by them in an article that appeared in the Winter, 1977 issue of *The Sociological Quarterly,* which was devoted to Marxist and alternative approaches to the study of organizations. In this article Goldman and Van Houten define three interrelated mechanisms by which management controlled labor between 1880 and the beginning of World War I. At their origin and during their establishment, these processes were described by management as methods by which organizations became more rational and efficient. They did in fact increase efficiency, but they also served to further the subordination of workers to management. Goldman and Van Houten's analysis of the interrelations of (1) detailed division of labor and the "degradation of skills," (2) hierarchy of authority, and (3) the monopolization of knowledge at the management and technician levels unveils the decisions of management as they overtly and covertly control workers and labor organizations. Thus these processes are not natural, inevitable, historical, rational processes as Chandler (1977) and others might have us believe, but rather they are manifestations of a political struggle between workers and employers. Management's realization that labor needs to be controlled is reinforced by: (1) the power of intensive labor organization, protests, and strikes; (2) the astronomical rate of labor turnover; and (3) the persistence of the skilled workers' and foremen's control over the everyday production process. Goldman and Van Houten demonstrate a deep concern for the latter of these management problems. Workers' knowledge and skills provide solidarity and autonomy to their possessors and as they have increased have consequently reduced the control of foremen.

The *detailed division of labor* after 1880 progressed from occupational specialization, in which people produced certain types of products, to a division of labor based on certain types of tasks, to work factionalization and the performing of a single activity. This factionalization was paralleled by the process of mechanization. Together, factionalization and mechanization enabled management to gain higher predictability of quality and quantity of the product and greater control of the worker through the following steps: institution of continuous work with few rest periods; implementation of job analysis and job descriptions; easy substitution and replacement of workers, lowering of wages through the elimination of skilled laborers; separation of workers into specialized groups so that none utilized a full range of skills, which resulted in the degradation of labor; and finally, the decrease of the value of *each* worker, not only to the organization but to him or herself. Overt control was easily implemented because activities of workers were individualized and easily observable; thus management took on the function of evaluation of the worker which had previously been the prerogative of first-line supervisors, a peer-like evaluation.

The factionalization of labor did not fully guarantee the performance of the worker; therefore, *hierarchical gradations* were instituted to ensure performance by: emphasizing the subordination of the worker to management through an extensive chain of command; regularizing communication; instituting evaluations at every level through the routinization of worker supervision, which gave management the power to reward the worker not only for work performance but also for loyalty and living style; developing job ladders that were tied to the differential wage scale, which changed the reward structure from one linked to selling price to one consisting of management-created steps on a promotion ladder and at the same time gave management greater control of the profits; adding personnel departments with personnel managers equipped with aptitude and placement measures; establishing rules and job descriptions for each task performed, thus further limiting the worker's autonomy; and finally, legitimizing authority at every level.

The detailed division of labor that minimized the skill of the worker and the extensive hierarchy of authority that legitimized the power of management were reinforced by the monopolization of knowledge and information. Through *control of knowledge and information* management was able to mystify the technical knowledge generated by the process of mechanization; generate a legitimizing process based on expertise and later on professionalization that claimed sole right to this technical knowledge; substitute labor with machine power; institute cost accounting departments and research and development departments to find ways to control labor through cost accounting; utilize technology to eliminate the jobs of workers who were organizing, striking, or in other ways diminishing the control of management. Finally, by the turn of the century a three-way alliance was formed between the business community, academia, and the emerging engineering profession, each branch supplying resources for the expansion of the others and at the same time ensuring management's continued control of innovation, skills, and knowledge related to both technical and human control in the production process.

There are obvious similarities in the arguments of Goldman and Van Houten to the arguments of (1) Braverman (1974), that managers used classical management theory to concentrate knowledge in their own hands in order to control production techniques; (2) Edwards (1978, Selection 8), that management modified "simple hierarchy" to form "bureaucratic control" and gain supervisory control to fight the growth of trade unionism; and (3) Friedman (1977), that management gained control through responsible autonomy. Taken together these arguments make a convincing case for management's struggle to gain complete control of work organizations and the work process at the expense of the workers. Goldman and Van Houten's quote from Gordon (1976:20) expresses this best: "There are no universally efficient forces and relations of production. . . . Capitalism has developed a production process which can not only deliver the goods, but also control its workers." In sum, efficiency of technique, however necessary it was for dramatic increases in production, was not sufficient to accomplish that goal unless accompanied by equal attention to problems of social control. Thus, Goldman and Van Houten concur with other Marxian theorists that technological determinism is not an adequate explanation of the bureaucratization of American industrial society.

Some other recent works in this tradition include David Gartman's (1978) article entitled "Marx and the Labor Process: An Interpretation," Stephen A. Marglin's (1974) "What Do Bosses Do?," David Noble's (1979) "Social Choice in Machine Design: The Case of Automatically-Controlled Machine Tools, a Challenge for Labor," Katherine Stone's (1974, Selection 18) "The Origins of Job Structures in the Steel Industry," as well as selections from the March 1977 issue of *The Sociological Quarterly* edited by Kenneth Benson.

ORGANIZATIONS LOOSELY COUPLED

The final selection in Part II is Karl E. Weick's (1976) description of loosely coupled systems. This selection does not delineate new and different methods of organization control or question the origin and justice of the existing methods of organization control. Rather Weick questions the very existence of tightly controlled, rationally structured organizations of the types described in Weber's essay on bureaucracy. Thus the validity of all perspectives that rest on the assumption that intraorganizational characteristics are identifiably and predictably interrelated is questioned. If we can assume that loosely structured images of organizations are better fits with reality, we will quickly realize that the prevailing ideas and organizational perspectives "do not shed much light on how such 'soft' structures develop, persist, and impose crude orderlines among these elements." In other words, organization theorists have treated the existence of well defined goals, integrated technologies, consistent and well ordered power relationships, and extensive rules and regulations as the defining characteristics of organization. Weick argues that the existence of such an organization is more likely to be the exception than the rule. The rule is that organizations are sloppily structured and loosely coupled. Organizational analysis should be concerned with understanding this type of organizational arrangement because it is pervasive and has real consequences for human existence. (This view of organizations as being loosely coupled is advocated and exemplified in John W. Meyer and Brian Rowan's (1977) perspective of organizations as institutionalized myth in Selection 15 below.)

Like the other selections in the second part of this anthology, Weick's (1976) provides us with an alternative image of organizations, an appropriate and helpful corrective to some of the overly rational images of organizational stucture and functioning that characterize some contemporary works on organizations. But his view of organizations as loosely coupled is not innovative. Again, like many of the selections in this part, his work is based in the classics, specifically his ideas are an elaboration of those of March and Simon (1958) presented in the sixth chapter of *Organizations*.

BIBLIOGRAPHY

Allison, Graham T.
1971 "Model III: governmental politics." Chapter 5 in *Essence of Decision: Explaining the Cuban Missile Crisis.* Boston: Little, Brown and Company.

Bacharach, Samuel B. and Edward J. Lawler
1980 *Power and Politics in Organizations.* San Francisco: Jossey-Bass Publishers.

Baldridge, J. Victor
1971 *Power and Conflict in the University.* New York: John Wiley and Sons, Inc.

Baldridge, J. Victor, David V. Curtis, George Ecker, and Gary L. Riley
1978 *Policy Making and Effective Leadership.* San Francisco: Jossey-Bass Publishers.

Benson, Kenneth
1977 'Organizations: A dialectical view," *Administrative Science Quarterly* 22:1-21.

Benson, J. Kenneth, and J. Day
1976 "On the limits of negotiation: A critique of the theory of negotiated order." Paper presented at the Annual Meeting of the American Sociological Association, New York.

Braverman, Harry
1974 *Labor and Monopoly Capital.* New York: Monthly Review Press.

Bucher, R.
1970 "Social process and power in a medical school." In M. Zald (ed.) *Power and Organizations.* Nashville, Tenn.: Vanderbilt University Press.

Bucher, R., and J. Stelling
1969 "Characteristics of professional organizations," *Journal of Health and Social Behavior* 10:3-15.

Chandler, Alfred D. Jr.
1977 *The Visible Hand: The Managerial Revolution in American Business.* Cambridge, Massachusetts: The Belknap Press of Harvard University Press.

Clark, Peter B., and James Q. Wilson
1961 "Incentive systems: A theory of organizations," *Administrative Science Quarterly.* 6:129-166.

Crozier, M.
1964 *The Bureaucratic Phenomenon.* Chicago: University of Chicago Press.

Cyert, R. M., and J. G. March
1963 *A Behavioral Theory of the Firm.* Englewood Cliffs, N.J.: Prentice-Hall.

Dalton, M.
1959 *Men Who Manage.* New York: Wiley.

Day, R., and J. Day
1977 "A review of the current state of negotiated order theory," *Sociological Quarterly* 18:126-142.

Edwards, Richard C.
1978 "The social relations of production at the point of production," *The Insurgent Sociologist* 8:109-125.

1979 *Contested Terrain: The Transformation of the Workplace in the 20th Century.* New York: Basic Books.

Friedman, Andrew
1977 "Management — preliminary argument." Chapter 6 in *Industry and Labor: Class Struggle at Work and Monopoly Capitalism.* London: The Macmillan Press.

Gartman, David
1978 "Marx and the labor process: An interpretation," *The Insurgent Sociologist* 8 (Fall):97-108.

Gerson, E.
1976 "On the quality of life," *American Sociological Review* 4:266-279.

Giddens, A.
1968 "Power in the recent writings of Talcott Parsons," *Sociology* 2,3:257-272.

Goldman, Paul, and Donald R. Van Houten
1977 "Managerial strategies and the worker: A Marxist analysis of bureaucracy," *Sociological Quarterly* 18 (Winter): 108-125.

1979 "Bureaucracy and domination: Managerial strategy in turn-of-the-century American industry." Chapter 5 in *The International Yearbook of Organization Studies.* London: Routledge and Kegan Paul.

Gordon, David M.
1976 "Capital efficiency and socialist efficiency," *Monthly Review* 28 (July-August):19-39.

Heydebrand, Wolf
1977 "Organizational contradictions in public bureaucracy: Toward a Marxian theory of organization," *Sociological Quarterly* 18 (Winter): 83–107.

Hymer, Stephen
1972 "The multinational corporation and the law of uneven development." Pages 113-140 in J. Bahagwati (ed.) *Economic and World Order from the 1970's to the 1990's.* New York: Collier-Macmillan. Printed in pages 37-62 in Hugo Radice (ed.) *International Firms and Modern Imperialists.* London: Penguin Books.

Long, Norton
1962 "The administrative organization as a political system." In Sidney Mailick and Edward H. Van Ness (ed.) *Concepts and Issues in Administrative Behavior.* Englewood Cliffs, N.J.: Prentice-Hall, Inc.

March, James G.
1962 "The business firm as a political coalition," *The Journal of Politics* 24:262-278.

March, James G., and Johan P. Olsen
1976 *Ambiguity and Choice in Organizations.* Bergen: Universitelsforlaget.

March, J. G., and H. A. Simon
1958 *Organizations.* New York: Wiley.

Martin, W.
1976 *The Negotiated Order of the School.* Canada: Macmillian of Canada, MacLean-Huner Press.

Marglin, Stephen
1974 "What the bosses do: The origin and functions of hierarchy in capitalist production," *Review of Radical Political Economics,* 6 (Summer): 6–112.

Marx, Karl
1967 *Capital.* (trans. Samuel Moore and Edward Aveling: ed. Frederick Engles) New York: International Publishers.

Mechanic, David
1962 "Sources of power of lower participants in complex organizations," *Administrative Science Quarterly* 7: 349-364.

Meyer, John, and Brian Rowan
1977 "Institutionalized organizations: Formal structure as myth and ceremony," *American Journal of Sociology* 83, 2:440-463.

Morgan, D.
1975 "Autonomy and negotiation in an industrial setting," *Sociology of Work and Occupations* 2:203-226.

Noble, David F.
1979 "Social choice in machine design: The case of automatically-controlled machine tools, and a challenge for labor." *Case Studies on the Labor Process.* New York: Monthly Review Press.

Parsons, Talcott
1967 *Sociological Theory and Modern Society.* New York: Free Press.

Pettigrew, Andrew
1973 "Conceptual orientation" and "Decision-making as a political process." Chapters 1 and 2 in *The Politics of Organizational Decision-Making.* London: Tavistock.

Stelling, J., and R. Bucher
1972 "Autonomy and monitoring on hospital wards," *Sociological Quarterly* 13:431-466.

Stone, Katherine
1974 "The origins of job structures in the steel industry," *The Review of Radical Political Economics* 6:113-173.

Strauss, Anselm
1962 "Tactics of lateral relationships: The purchasing agent," *Administrative Science Quarterly* 7:161-186.
1978 "Summary, implications, and debate." Pages 234-239 in *Negotiations: Varieties, Contexts, Processes and Social Order.* San Francisco: Jossey-Bass.

Weick, Carl E.
1976 "Educational organizations as loosely coupled systems," *Administrative Science Quarterly* 12:1-11.

Touraine, Alain
1971 "The firm: power, institutions, and organizations." Pages 139-192 in *Post-Industrial Society.* New York: Random House.

Wilson, James Q.
1973 *Political Organizations.* New York, Basic Books, Inc.

6.   Summary, Implications and Debate*

Anselm Strauss

What has been the central argument of this book? What data and interpretations have supported the argument? And why should there be argument at all, rather than a straightforward presentation of data and theory? Answering that general line of questioning allows a quick summary of the book's contents; it also allows, in a later section, focused consideration of both pertinent and not so pertinent objections raised by critics of a "negotiated order perspective." Engaging in that debate should help to fill in whatever detail may be missing elsewhere in these pages, as well as to correct any further misreading of what is implied in this approach to the study of negotiations and negotiated social orders.

SUMMARY

In this book, negotiation has generally stood for one of the possible means of "getting things accomplished" when parties need to deal with each other to get those things done. Negotiation is not merely one specific human activity or process, of importance primarily because it appears in particular relationships (diplomacy, labor relations, business transactions, and so on), but is of such major importance in human affairs that its study brings us to the heart of studying social orders. As argued in the preface to this book, a given social order, even the most repressive, would be inconceivable without some forms of negotiation.

The implication is that social orders are, in some sense, always negotiated orders. The phrase "in some sense" is a guard against asserting that negotiation explains "everything," for it is always found in conjunction with other processes, other alternatives to getting things done — notably coercion, persuasion, manipulation, and the like. Most research on negotiation has either focused rather narrowly on substantive areas of negotiation, such as those just mentioned, or, if taken as a relatively universal phenomenon, nevertheless tends to approach the phenomenon from relatively rationalistic, efficiency perspectives (as in game theory or in the work of economists who have written about negotiation). I have argued that issues of outcome, efficiency, decision making, and the like are secondary to issues pertaining first to how negotiation is related to other modes of action and second to varying kinds of social order.

I have also argued that larger structural considerations need to be explicitly linked with microscopic analyses of negotiation processes. Negotiations always take place within social settings. The various structural conditions of the settings affect the actions of the negotiating parties, the aims they pursue through negotiation and alternative modes of action, their tactics during the negotiations, and, undoubtedly,

---

the outcomes of the negotiations themselves — which in turn may affect not only future courses of action but also the social settings themselves.

Furthermore, if negotiations are indeed relatively universal, then our conceptualizations should deal with the whole range of the phenomenon or at least with their great variation. That implies the need for examining a variety of structural contexts and their associated courses of negotiation. It also implies that either a general theory of negotiation should be developed or that at least (as I have done) a paradigm should be offered that other researchers can qualify, amend, add to, and work over, so that eventually a theory of negotiation might get developed.

A subsidiary argument was that researchers' conceptions of social order — and their usually implicit assumptions about and theories of negotiation — generally lead them to overlook or misconstrue their data on negotiations; also, that close examination of those data would raise some sharply critical questions about both their conceptions of social order and some of their research conclusions.

In examining the research of a number of well-known social scientists (Goffman, Blau, Gouldner, Banfield, Riker, Coleman and Morse), whose perspectives included functionalism, political pluralism, interactionism, and so on, the following questions were asked. "Can the research actually affect the general theory (or theoretical framework) if the researcher does not see negotiation in terms of theory? What happens if the researcher sees negotiation 'in the data' but does not build theoretically on those particular data? What kind of description is offered — or what kind of substantive theory? Or, blinded by theoretical preconceptions, do researchers actually overlook the negotiations that are there in the collected data? What would happen if they, or we, found negotiations in their data and took them seriously? How would that affect what was offered us by way of descriptions, substantive theories and theoretical conceptions?"

With due respect to their other virtues, these researchers generally did not score high on the special test offered by my questions. I concluded that my scrutiny had supported the following points. First, looking at the data on negotiations in a researcher's work can afford a very useful critique of the theorizing done on the basis of the research itself; negotiations are not just another interesting phenomenon or special area for research. Second, if researchers are going to analyze negotiations, then they need to do so in relation to questions of social order — and with an eye on their own implicit theories of negotiation. Third, negotiation processes are entwined with manipulative, coercive, and other processes, and they all must be studied together, although the researcher's main focus may be on one or another. I concluded, too, that each researcher had raised interesting and valid theoretical questions, but I doubted whether those could be answered without careful studies of a varied set of interlocked processes, including the negotiation processes. The larger issue implied, of course, is whether social orders can be properly analyzed without building negotiation into the analysis. Or, said another way, are there any social orders that are not also negotiated orders?

In Part Two, I addressed that issue, attempting to cast doubt on the efficacy of conceptualizing about organizations, groups, institutions, and so on, without also analyzing their implied negotiation processes. Part Two — the longest and perhaps most important section of the book — consisted essentially of analyses of negotiation cases drawn from various research publications. Eleven cases were presented, paired in six chapters, to bring out similar or contrasting features around a central issue raised by a paradigm, with an emphasis both on structural or social setting considerations and on the negotiation itself: (1) negotiating working relations in organizations, (2) legal and illegal negotiations in the political arena, (3) negotiating cooperative international structures, (4) negotiating compromises within social orders, (5) antagonistic negotiations and changing structural contexts, and (6) organizational functioning and the silent bargain.

Clearly, a considerable variety of social settings and the associated types of negotiation were examined. The organizational scale of the cases varied greatly, the negotiating parties ranging from individuals and small groups to large nations. The settings varied from face-to-face ones to those that are international, from relatively simple or routine ones to the most complex and unpredictable. Time scales also varied greatly — from immediate transactions to those occurring over long periods of time.

In analyzing those cases of negotiation and their embeddedness in social settings, a paradigm was utilized. Its key terms include *subprocesses of negotiation,* of which examples were making tradeoffs, obtaining kickbacks, compromising toward the middle, paying off debts, and reaching negotiated agreements; and *structural context,* "within which" negotiations take place in the largest sense. Hence for each case of negotiation it is necessary to bring out some of the salient *structural properties* of the social setting. (One important structural property consists of respective parties' theories of negotiation, which bear on the negotiation.) The term *negotiation context* refers specifically to the structural properties entering very directly *as conditions* into the course of the negotiation itself. The many specific kinds of negotiation contexts pertaining to interaction among negotiating parties are related to permutations of the following properties of any negotiation context:

- The *number* of negotiators, their relative *experience* in negotiating, and whom they *represent*
- Whether the negotiations are *one-shot, repeated, sequential, serial, multiple,* or *linked*
- The relative *balance of power* exhibited by the respective parties *in* the negotiation itself
- The nature of their respective *stakes* in the negotiation
- The *visibility* of the transactions to others; that is, their overt or covert characters
- The *number* and *complexity* of the *issues* negotiated
- The *clarity of legitimacy* boundaries of the issues negotiated
- The *options* to avoiding or discontinuing negotiation; that is, the alternative modes of action perceived as available

I wish to emphasize that the final item, options, is of particular relevance in understanding both the decision to embark on negotiation and the course of negotiation itself. If the potential or actual parties to negotiation perceive that they can attempt persuasion, make an appeal to authority, manipulate political or social events, and so forth, then their choices of these alternative modes will either prevent them from entering negotiation, or if they choose that also, then their choices will affect what transpires during the course of the negotiation.

When introducing this paradigm, I argued that a steady focus on both structural and negotiation contexts, and on their respective properties, would increase the likelihood that the analysis of specific courses of negotiation would be carefully located in relationship to the larger social structure. (No reification was intended by the term *social structure.*) In short, social order considerations were vital to any analysis of negotiation. Also, we could see that the structural context is larger, more encompassing than negotiation context; but the lines of impact might run either way. That is, changes in the former might impact on the latter, and vice versa. Outcomes of negotiation itself could contribute to changes in negotiation contexts relevant to future negotiations; although they are less likely to affect the structural context except as repeated or combined with other negotiations and other modes of action, perhaps thereby having a cumulative impact.

I further argued, there, that some approaches to negotiation tend to concentrate closely on negotiations themselves but leave unattended or implicit the relations of negotiations to social structural considerations, and sometimes even to negotiation contextual considerations (as shown already in Part One). On the other hand, like many social science approaches that tend not to bother with microscopic analyses of interaction, some accounts of negotiation settle for essentially narrative description or an emphasis on overall bargaining relations rather than for an analysis of the bargaining itself. In both approaches, little attention frequently is paid to the development character of much negotiation, some of which is underlined in the case studies of Part Two. An additional richness was added to the paradigmatic analysis insofar as each case illustrates somewhat different combinations of subprocesses of negotiation that are explainable by the type of negotiation under examination.

FURTHER USES OF THE PARADIGM

In this section, I wish to supplement the earlier discussion of the paradigm's use for analyzing and commenting on other people's data. Here, the first question might be "How can the paradigm be useful to researchers whose main concerns are not with negotiation in general, but either with negotiations in a given substantive area or only with that area itself?"

First, the paradigm can sensitize them to possibilities in their data that otherwise might go quite unnoticed. Thus they can become sensitized to negotiations, actors, interactions, tactics, subprocesses of negotiation, and consequences that have been overlooked or left relatively unanalyzed in the data. Second, grasp of the paradigm can force them to analyze the negotiation aspects of their data. Researchers will ask themselves if they have enough data on negotiation and along various contextual dimensions. They will be forced to compare the kinds of negotiations being witnessed or interviewed about, as well as the range of negotiations being studied, to other kinds that they know about — to the end of forcing themselves to think more intensively and systematically about the former negotiations. Systematic pursuit of negotiation data should force consideration of relationships between the negotiations under study and the major substantive matters under study. That is, analytically speaking, the researcher will have to relate the negotiation properties to other substantive properties.

A third use of the paradigm is that it can help researchers discover which contextual properties of negotiation are salient for their specific substantive materials. Once a researcher senses that certain properties are relevant, "fit" the reality of the data, then a systematic exploration of the implications of these contextual properties will check out the researcher's sense of their fitness.

A fourth use of the paradigm pertains to its possibilities as a predictive guide. What I have in mind is that, if the researchers begin to grasp the general structural properties of the substantive areas under study, they will begin to make informed guesses about the most salient contextual properties of negotiations and about the associated negotiation events; that is, they will make better predictions about negotiations and their outcomes. Conversely, there is a feedback from the negotiation materials to phenomena other than negotiation. During the course of the research, then, there is a crucially important interplay between achieving an increasingly better awareness of relevant structural conditions and getting more accurate predictions about the negotiation phenomena. Or, as reiterated throughout this book, insofar as the researcher is interested in social order, he or she must be concerned with negotiated order.

In the early stages of a study, a researcher is handicapped by how relatively little he or she knows about the structural conditions bearing on the phenomenon under study. It takes time to know them. The researcher has not been around long enough to be familiar enough with what everyday events may signify, or for important events and behaviors to have transpired, or to have hit on the most important documentary data. And the researcher certainly has not yet done sufficient data analysis to have the kind of grasp of structural conditions that will lead to relatively accurate predictions about negotiations. So the more structural conditions one can anticipate, the better the predictions about the main features of both the associated negotiations and the variations in their patterning. The kind of paradigm offered here should help researchers in their theoretical sampling (Glaser and Strauss, 1967) by forcing them to ask "What would happen if . . . under this or that condition?" Then they must look for or inquire about that "if."

One difficulty about predicting outcomes accurately is that the structural context may change, thus changing the relationships of negotiation to alternate modes of action among which actors may choose, as well as changing the elements of the negotiation context itself. That condition of long-run and often radical change does not eliminate the probability of relatively accurate predictions about negotiation outcomes; but, presumably, the more unexpected the radical change, the less accurate the prediction. (This issue will be discussed apropos of general theory in the next section.) Despite those changes, the paradigm should be of continued use. By directing attention to the relationships of current structural properties to contextual properties and by periodically requiring new soundings about changes in either context, clues can then be found about new directions of change — with their consequential impact on the outcomes of negotiation and on alternative modes of action.

Another issue: "Is there a difference in procedure between the researcher who is interested primarily in substantive negotiations and the researcher who is interested primarily in a substantive phenomenon and so concerned with negotiations only as a means for better understanding it?" Their principal procedures are probably the same. The differences have to do mainly with their major focus — with implications for their respective apportionment of time and effort and for how detailed and elaborate their respective analyses of negotiation itself will be.

On this latter point, an example will perhaps be useful. In a study titled *Military Lawyers, Civilian Courts, and the Organized Bar* (1972), a legal scholar, Raymond Marks, traces what happened when the armed forces decided to attempt an experimental program for expanding the nature and scope of legal assistance to servicemen and dependents. This program raised a problem because special permission was required in the various American states for "foreign lawyers" to practice in the local courts. Marks shows that, as the result of varied kinds of negotiations, the program got implemented in a considerable variety of ways in the different states. Marks is primarily interested in the outcomes of the negotiations (that is, what finally was permitted or arranged), rather than in the negotiations themselves. Nevertheless, he offers considerable information on the negotiations. The detail and clarity of his discussion of the negotiations depends less on his interest in them than on the ease or difficulty which the armed forces encountered in making arrangements and on the amount of compromising they had to do in terms of what they had originally requested. In fact, this researcher has more data on negotiation in his files than he cared to analyze, since negotiation was distinctly secondary in focus. He obtained as much on negotiation as he did in part because it was clearly a part of the primary topic in focus. One implication of his unanalyzed negotiation data — and the data of other researchers in similar situations — is that if he cares to analyze those data he could certainly write separately about the negotiations themselves.

Turning to a fifth potential use of the paradigm, one implicit in various cases reviewed in Part Two, the paradigm can be useful to researchers who are interested in how negotiated order is destroyed or even prevented from forming. I have in mind not the specific structural conditions that prevent successful, linked negotiations, but the strategies and tactics of parties who are not necessarily involved directly in the negotiations. An instance that springs vividly to mind is how the fragile alliance that made Allende the head of the Chilean government for a short while was undoubtedly destroyed not simply by the course of events or the falling out of the various parties to the coalition but also by an effective combination of various modes of action: use of force, threat, persuasion, manipulation of events, money, various resources, and also, undoubtedly, covert negotiations among the various parties who wished to see the Allende alliance destroyed. The ability and the desire to break up or prevent a given order is, of course, not confined to political affairs. The paradigm can remind us that we should not be interested merely in successful or unsuccessful negotiations and how those are managed but also in the wider structural and contextual issues in any substantive area we study. Some case analyses presented earlier undoubtedly suffered because the respective researchers did not offer (they rarely do) good data on how opponents outside the negotiation situation attempt to play those related antagonistic games.

In rounding off the suggestions made in this section about the further uses of the paradigm, it may be useful to emphasize again that a vital part of the concept of structural context is that of the negotiating parties' "theories of negotiation." Hence all of my suggestions also direct researchers to gather data on those theories. One of the considerable deficiencies of studies of negotiation to date is precisely either that researchers fail to collect data about those theories or, if they do have some data bearing on them, that they do not analyze their significance. I urge the necessity to do just that.

IS A GENERAL THEORY OF NEGOTIATION POSSIBLE?

What about the use of such a paradigm for those who are genuinely interested in a general or "formal" theory of negotiation per se? Before attempting to answer that question, I should state my position on the possibility of formulating general theory, for I have, after all, insisted we must take into account that negotiations take place within changing structural contexts — within historically changing social orders. The question of whether general theory is possible has been variously answered by different scholars. Some take extreme historical positions, denying the possibility of universal propositions about social life. Others, such as Simmel and Weber, whose discussions and formulations of general theory continue to stimulate social scientists, nevertheless had a profound respect for historical matters. However, many contemporary social scientists apparently believe that, regardless of the particularities of historical moment, the formulation of general theory is entirely feasible.

Concerning the possibility of negotiation theory, my own view is related to the distinctions drawn earlier between structural and negotiation contexts. I have argued and attempted to demonstrate that the features of a specific negotiation context cannot be properly analyzed except in conjunction with a clear specification of the relevant structural context. In a historical perspective, structural conditions, including actors' theories of negotiation, do change, and therefore new types of negotiation contexts do evolve — while old ones may disappear, should pertinent structural conditions vanish (for example, in the Kenya case and the Li case). This means that old contextual properties of negotiation may disappear, while new ones emerge and while their combinations with each other also change. The changes brought about by "the workings of history" do not at all signify that a general theory of negotiation is impossible. They only mean that no such theory can ever predict all the future permutations of negotiation context. This kind of theory, however, can predict by theoretical sampling (Glaser and Strauss, 1967) the possibility that such combinations may emerge at a future time ("What if this property were to change to . . . ?"). It can likewise predict backward in time, directing us to look for times long vanished but concerning which we may have good data, when different types of negotiation context were in operation from those to which we are now accustomed.

I turn now to the original question: "What about the uses of the paradigm, as developed in this book, for those who are genuinely interested in a general theory of negotiation?" Several answers are possible, according to the interests of different groups of scholars. First, there are those who while doing substantive research find also they can contribute to a general theory of negotiation. They would do this in entirely conventional ways. Thus, they might elaborate sections of the paradigm that are sparse or underdeveloped — as by working through the implications of an additional negotiation contextual property, by following out in more detail a property already noted by me or any other theorist, by focusing intensively on different subprocesses and types of negotiation interaction, or by treating the same ones more elaborately. Another conventional and entirely necessary possibility is to qualify the formulated theory, since some of its parts are inadequate or inaccurate. Those qualifications can, of course, be either minor or very considerable.

Researchers whose chosen concerns are with the development of substantive negotiation (whether labor bargaining, economic transactions, diplomatic negotiation, and so on) are currently more likely to make major contributions to the development of a general theory of negotiation; but certainly any researcher into substantive phenomena might make a useful contribution, provided he or she is interested in that particular theoretical enterprise. Perhaps the latter researchers can then make very interesting contributions precisely because their data will be drawn from nontraditional areas concerning the analysis of negotiation.

Finally, another group of social scientists might be interested in general theory of negotiation for its *own* sake. I envision that their elaborations and qualifications of a negotiation theory would proceed by further theoretical sampling of data from extant negotiation literature in many different substantive areas. This secondary analysis could greatly — and probably quickly — help to further a general theory. For instance, someone might be interested in elaborating the contextual property of the negotiator as a "representative" and hence do theoretical sampling of varied data concentrating systematically on various properties of representativeness itself.

As a brief illustration of how that might work, I offer a few beginning steps for such an analysis. First, there is the question of *who* is being represented. The negotiator can represent himself, another person, a group, an organization, a faction in the organization or a majority group, a government, and so on. (Note that the government itself represents another "party" — but that is an additional complexity.) Second, in *what relationship* does the negotiator stand to the represented? Is the negotiator appointed, commanded, elected, self-selected, and so on? Third, we must ask about the *recognition* by the represented, of the representative: Do they know or understand, are they aware when they are not being represented? Fourth, if they know, do they *agree* to such representation or do they not, and to what degree? Fifth, of which or how much of the negotiator's actual negotiating interactions are the represented parties actually *aware?* How quickly do they become aware? What control do they have over his or her actions? Are all of the represented or just some of them aware? Sixth, *how many parties* are actually represented by the negotiator? If more than one, are their interests, for any given issue being negotiated, in conflict, not connected, commensurate, and so on? Does the negotiator actually know the details accurately? Do the respective parties recognize all the details? All these questions and more should immediately suggest to the theorist-researcher questions about resultant strategies, tactics and consequences. For instance, there may be a struggle among members of an organization to have certain persons represent them in negotiations, and that struggle may be different in established structures (such as labor unions) from the struggle in more emergent ones (say, in black organizations during the late 1960s); of course, these struggles will bear differently on representativeness in ensuing negotiations with outsiders.

Turning to the relationships between the negotiators themselves concerning their representativeness, one could look at the forgoing questions in reverse. Thus, what does each know about the representativeness of the other? How accurate or incorrect is their assessment of that representativeness? How accurate is the presentation of his or her own representativeness by each to the other? Are they suspicious and discounting, or do they take the other's presentation at face value? Or, more specifically, there are such questions as "How clear is it whom the other is actually representing? Does he really represent himself rather than those he is supposed to be representing? Can he be induced to represent himself rather than them? At least on this particular issue? Is he representing some faction rather than the whole organization (government, group)? Or is all that, or some of that, unclear, ambiguous, clouded?"

Those questions can lead to a fairly complex issue of analyses, when one considers that the larger analysis must also include the strategies, tactics, consequences, and so forth pertaining to those questions that the negotiators themselves are asking about each other. For instance, how do the negotiators check out whether they can induce the others to double-cross or sell out their represented parties? Whom can the negotiators choose to represent themselves in checking out both that particular possibility and the consequent negotiation about the double-cross? My suggested questions about representativeness are, of course, only initial steps in an inquiry about that important contextual property of negotiation, but I believe that thinking about negotiations along those lines — and collecting the necessary comparative data — would take us along the path toward a general theory of negotiation.

One could analyze the cases presented in Part Two systematically for "representativeness" or for any other contextual property itemized in the guiding paradigm. Then the analysis would have to be done in terms not of each case as such but in terms of their total theoretical yield. I did not choose to do that in this book. To build a general theory would take many more cases of negotiation and a determinedly comparative stance toward those data. I have wanted to put my emphases elsewhere.

REFERENCES

Banfield, E.
1962 *Political Influence.* New York: Free Press.
Benson, J.
1977 "Innovation and Crisis in Organiza-

tional Analysis." *Sociological Quarterly,* 18:3-16.
Blau, P.
1955 *The Dynamics of Bureaucracy.*

Chicago: University of Chicago Press.

Coleman, J.
1973   "Loss of Power." *American Sociological Review,* 38:1-17.
1974   *Power and the Structure of Society.* New York: Norton.

Glaser, B., and Strauss, A.
1967   *The Discovery of Grounded Theory.* Chicago: Aldine.

Goffman, E.
1961a   "On the Characteristics of Total Institutions." In E. Goffman, *Asylums.* Garden City, N.Y.: Doubleday.
1961b   "The Underlife of a Public Institution: A Study of Ways and of Making Out in a Mental Hospital." In E. Goffman, *Asylums.* Garden City, N.Y.: Doubleday.
1974   *Frame Analysis.* New York: Harper & Row.

Gouldner, A.
1954a   *Industrial Bureaucracy.* New York: Free Press.
1954b   *The Wildcat Strike.* Yellow Springs, Ohio: Antioch Press.

Marks, R.
1972   *Military Lawyers, Civilian Courts and the Organized Bar.* Chicago: American Bar Foundation.

Morse, E.
1976   "The Bargaining Structure of NATO: Multi-Issue Negotiations in an Interdependent World." In I. W. Zartman (Ed.), *The Fifty Percent Solution.* Garden City, N.Y.: Doubleday.

Riker, W.
1962   *The Theory of Political Coalitions.* New Haven, Conn.: Yale University Press.

7. Model III: Governmental Politics*

Graham T. Allison

Model II's grasp of government action as organizational output, partially coordinated by a unified group of leaders, balances the classical model's efforts to understand government behavior as choices of a unitary decision-maker. But the fascination of Model II analysis should not be allowed to blur a further level of investigation. The "leaders" who sit on top of organizations are not a monolithic group. Rather, each individual in this group is, in his own right, a player in a central, competitive game. The name of the game is politics: bargaining along regularized circuits among players positioned hierarchically within the government. Government behavior can thus be understood according to a third conceptual model, not as organizational outputs but as results of these bargaining games. In contrast with Model I, the Governmental (or Bureaucratic) Politics Model sees no unitary actor but rather many actors as players — players who focus not on a single strategic issue but on many diverse intra-national problems as well; players who act in terms of no consistent set of strategic objectives but rather according to various conceptions of national, organizational, and personal goals; players who make government decisions not by a single, rational choice but by the pulling and hauling that is politics.

* From Graham T. Allison, *Essence of Decision: Explaining the Cuban Missile Crisis,* pp. 144-147, 162-184. Copyright © 1971 by Graham T. Allison, Reprinted by permission of Little, Brown and Company.

The apparatus of each national government constitutes a complex arena for the intra-national game. Political leaders at the top of the apparatus are joined by the men who occupy positions on top of major corporations to form a circle of central players. Those who join the circle come with some independent standing. Because the spectrum of foreign policy problems faced by a government is so broad, decisions have to be decentralized — giving each player considerable baronial discretion.

The nature of foreign policy problems permits fundamental disagreement among reasonable men about how to solve them. Analyses yield conflicting recommendations. Separate responsibilities laid on the shoulders of distinct individuals encourage differences in what each sees and judges to be important. But the nation's actions really matter. A wrong choice could mean irreparable damage. Thus responsible men are obliged to fight for what they are convinced is right.

Men share power. Men differ about what must be done. The differences matter. This milieu necessitates that government decisions and actions result from a political process. In this process, sometimes one group committed to a course of action triumphs over other groups fighting for other alternatives. Equally often, however, different groups pulling in different directions produce a result, or better a resultant — a mixture of conflicting preferences and unequal power of various individuals — distinct from what any person or group intended. In both cases, what moves the chess pieces is not simply the reasons that support a course of action, or the routines of organizations that enact an alternative, but the power and skill of proponents and opponents of the action in question.

This characterization captures the thrust of the bureaucratic politics orientation. If problems of foreign policy arose as discrete issues, and decisions were determined one game at a time, this account would suffice. But most "issues" — e.g., Viet Nam, or the proliferation of nuclear weapons — emerge piecemeal over time, one lump in one context, a second in another. Hundreds of issues compete for players' attention every day. Each player is forced to fix upon his issues for that day, deal with them on their own terms, and rush on to the next. Thus the character of emerging issues and the pace at which the game is played converge to yield government "decisions" and "actions" as collages. Choices by one player (e.g., to authorize action by his department, to make a speech, or to refrain from acquiring certain information), resultants of minor games (e.g., the wording of a cable or the decision on departmental action worked out among lower-level players), resultants of central games (e.g., decisions, actions, and speeches bargained out among central players), and "foul-ups" (e.g., choices that are not made because they are not recognized or are raised too late, misunderstandings, etc.) — these pieces, when stuck to the same canvas, constitute government behavior relevant to an issue. To explain why a particular formal governmental decision was made, or why one pattern of governmental behavior emerged, it is necessary to identify the game and players, to display the coalitions, bargains, and compromises, and to convey some feel for the confusion.

This conception of national security policy as political resultant contradicts both public imagery and academic orthodoxy. Issues vital to national security are considered too important to be settled by political games. They must be "above" politics: to accuse someone of "playing politics with national security" is a most serious charge. Thus, memoirs typically handle the details of such bargaining with a velvet glove. For example, both Sorensen and Schlesinger present the efforts of the ExCom in the Cuban missile crisis as essentially rational deliberation among a unified group of equals. What public expectation demands, the academic penchant for intellectual elegance reinforces. Internal politics is messy; moreover, according to prevailing doctrine, politicking lacks intellectual substance. It constitutes gossip for journalists rather than a subject for serious investigation. Occasional memoirs, anecdotes in historical accounts, and several detailed case studies to the contrary, most of the foreign policy literature avoids bureaucratic politics.

The gap between academic literature and the experience of participants in government is nowhere wider than at this point. For those who participate in government the terms of daily employment cannot be ignored: government leaders have competitive, not homogeneous interests; priorities and perceptions are shaped by positions; problems are much more varied than straightforward strategic issues; management of piecemeal streams of decisions is more important than steady-state choices; making sure that the government does what is decided is more difficult than selecting the preferred solution.*

The primary source of the paradigm is the model implicit in Neustadt's work, though his concentration on Presidential action has been generalized to a concern with action as a resultant of political bargaining among a number of independent players, the President being only a "superpower" among many lesser but considerable powers.[64] The paradigm takes seriously Schilling's contention that the substantive problems are so inordinately difficult that differences about goals, alternatives, and consequences are inevitable. Thus the process of conflict and consensus building described by Hilsman becomes crucial. Characterization of the techniques employed starts from Huntington's insight that the activity resembles bargaining in legislative assemblies, though his contention that the process is "legislative" overemphasizes participant equality as opposed to the hierarchy that structures the game.[65]

I. BASIC UNIT OF ANALYSIS: GOVERNMENTAL ACTION AS POLITICAL RESULTANT

The decisions and actions of governments are intranational political resultants: *resultants* in the sense that what happens is not chosen as a solution to a problem but rather results from compromise, conflict, and confusion of officials with diverse interests and unequal influence; *political* in the sense that the activity from which decisions and actions emerge is best characterized as bargaining along regularized channels among individual members of the government. Following Wittgenstein's employment of the concept of a "game," national behavior in international affairs can be conceived of as something that emerges from intricate and subtle, simultaneous, overlapping games among players located in positions in a government. The

---

* The tendency of participants in American government to understand these facts when thinking about an issue within the U.S. government, but to downgrade them and rely instead on Model I concepts and logic when thinking about other national governments, is well illustrated by an anecdote told by Henry S. Rowen. Shortly after taking a job in the U.S. government, Rowen attended a meeting of twelve representatives from different agencies on the problem of desalination in the Middle East. After more than an hour of discussion of U.S. policy, no one was in doubt about the fact that each of the representatives favored a policy that conflicted sharply with the policies of the others. Moreover, several of the agencies were carrying out directly contradictory courses of action. But when the group turned to the next item on the agenda, everyone proceeded to talk about "the Israeli policy on desalination" as if a consistent course of action had been chosen by a single rational individual in the light of broad national goals.

hierarchical arrangement of these players constitutes the government.* Games proceed neither at random nor at leisure. Regular channels structure the game; deadlines force issues to the attention of incredibly busy players. The moves, sequences of moves, and games of chess are thus to be explained in terms of the bargaining among players with separate and unequal power over particular pieces, and with separable objectives in distinguishable subgames.

In analyzing governmental actions — for example, U.S. government efforts to retard the spread of nuclear weapons — one must examine all official actions of the U.S. government that affect this outcome. U.S. government actions affecting the spread of nuclear weapons include the State Department's efforts to gain adherence to the Nonproliferation Treaty, Presidential offers of guarantees to non-nuclear nations against nuclear blackmail; Atomic Energy Commission (AEC) tests of nuclear explosives for peaceful purposes (that consequently provide a convenient shield for non-nuclear powers' development of nuclear devices); withdrawal of U.S. forces from the Far East (which may increase the concern of some Japanese and Indians about their national security); statements by the AEC about the great prospects for peaceful nuclear weapons (designed to influence AEC budgets); an AEC commissioner's argument, in the absence of any higher level decision, to a Brazilian scientist about the great virtues of peaceful nuclear explosives; and U.S. government refusal to confirm or deny the reported presence of nuclear weapons aboard ships calling in foreign ports. As this list suggests, it is important to recognize that governmental actions relevant to some issues are really an agglomeration or collage composed of relatively independent decisions and actions by individuals and groups of players in a broader game, as well as formal governmental decisions and actions that represent a combination of the preferences and relative influence of central players or subsets of players in more narrowly defined games. For purposes of analysis, it will often be useful to distinguish among: (1) governmental actions that are really agglomerations of relatively independent decisions and actions by individuals and groups of players, (2) *formal* governmental decisions or actions that represent a combination of the preferences and relative influence of *central* players in the game, (3) formal governmental decisions and actions that represent a combination of the preferences and relative influence of a special *subset* of players in the game.

II. ORGANIZING CONCEPTS

The organizing concepts of this paradigm can be arranged as strands in the answers to four interrelated questions: Who plays? What determines each player's stand? What determines each player's relative influence? How does the game combine players'

---

* The theatrical metaphor of stage, roles, and actors is more common than this metaphor of games, positions, and players. Nevertheless, the rigidity connoted by the concept of "role" both in the theatrical sense of actors reciting fixed lines and in the sociological sense of fixed responses to specified social situations makes the concept of games, positions, and players more useful for this analysis of active participants in the determination of national foreign policy. Objections to the terminology on the grounds that "game" connotes nonserious play overlook the concept's application to most serious problems both in Wittgenstein's philosophy and in contemporary game theory. Game theory typically treats more precisely structured games, but Wittgenstein's examination of the "language game" wherein men use words to communicate is quite analogous to this analysis of the less specified game of bureaucratic politics. Wittgenstein's employment of this concept forms a central strand in his *Philosophical Investigations*. See also Thomas C. Schelling, "What Is Game Theory?" in James Charlesworth, *Contemporary Political Analysis*, New York, 1967.

stands, influence, and moves to yield governmental decisions and actions?

A. Who plays?   That is, whose interests and actions have an important effect on the government's decisions and actions?

1. *Players in Positions.*   The governmental actor is neither a unitary agent nor a conglomerate of organizations, but rather is a number of individual players. Groups of these players constitute the agent for particular government decisions and actions. Players are men in jobs.

   Individuals become players in the national security policy game by occupying a position that is hooked on to the major channels for producing action on national security issues. For example, in the U.S. government the players include *Chiefs:* the President, the Secretaries of State, Defense, and Treasury, the Director of the CIA, the Joint Chiefs of Staff, and, since 1961, the Special Assistant for National Security Affairs;[66] *Staffers:* the immediate staff of each Chief; *Indians:* the political appointees and permanent government officials within each of the departments and agencies; and *Ad Hoc Players:* actors in the wider government game (especially "Congressional Influentials"), members of the press, spokesmen for important interest groups (especially the "bipartisan foreign policy establishment" in and out of Congress), and surrogates for each of these groups. Other members of the Congress, press, interest groups, and public form concentric circles around the central arena — circles that demarcate limits within which the game is played.*

   Positions define what players both may and must do. The advantages and handicaps with which each player can enter and play in various games stem from his position. So does a cluster of obligations for the performance of certain tasks. The two sides of this coin are illustrated by the position of the modern Secretary of State. First, in form and usually in fact, he is a senior personal adviser to the President on the political-military issues that are the stuff of contemporary foreign policy. Second, he is the colleague of the President's other senior advisers on problems of foreign policy, the Secretaries of Defense and Treasury, and the Special Assistant for National Security Affairs. Third, he is the ranking U.S. diplomat in negotiations with foreign powers. Fourth, he serves as the primary representative of the administration's foreign policy in Congress. Fifth he is an educator of the American public about critical issues of foreign affairs and a defender of the actions of the administration. Sixth, he serves as an administration voice to the outside world. Finally, he is Mr. State Department or Mr. Foreign Office, "leader of officials, spokesman for their causes, guardian of their interests, judge of their disputes, superintendent of their work, master of their careers."[67] But he is not first one and then the other: all these obligations are his simultaneously. His performance in one affects his credit and power in the others. The perspective he gets from the daily work he must oversee — the cable traffic by which his department maintains relations with other foreign offices — conflicts with the President's requirement that he serve as a generalist and coordinator of contrasting perspectives. The necessity that he be close to the President restricts

---

* For some purposes, organizations and groups can be treated as players. In treating an organization or group as a player, it is important to note the differences among (1) summarizing the official papers that emerge from an organization as coherent calculated moves of a unitary actor; (2) treating the actions of the head of an organization, whose goals are determined largely by that organization, as actions of the organization; and (3) summarizing the various actions of different members of an organization as coherent strategies and tactics in a single plan.

his ability to represent the interests of his department. When he defers to the Secretary of Defense rather than fighting for his department's position — as he often must — he strains the loyalty of his officialdom. In the words of one of his Indians: "Loyalty is hilly, and it has to go down if it is going to go up."[68] Thus he labors under the weight of conflicting responsibilities.

A Secretary of State's resolution of these conflicts depends not only upon the position, but also upon the player who occupies it. For players are also people; men's metabolisms differ. The hard core of the bureaucratic politics mix is personality. How each man manages to stand the heat in *his* kitchen, each player's basic operating style, and the complementarity or contradiction among personalities and styles in the inner circles are irreducible pieces of the policy blend. Then, too, each person comes to his position with baggage in tow. His bags include sensitivities to certain issues, commitments to various projects, and personal standing with and debts to groups in the society.

B. What determines each player's stand?   What determines his perceptions and interests that lead to a stand?

1. *Parochial Priorities and Perceptions.*   Answers to the question "What is the issue?" are colored by the position from which the question is considered. Propensities inherent in positions do not facilitate unanimity in answering the question "What must be done?" The factors that encourage organizational parochialism also exert pressure upon the players who occupy positions on top of (or within) these organizations. To motivate members of his organization, a player must be sensitive to the organization's orientation. The games into which the player can enter and the advantages with which he plays enhance these pressures. Thus propensities and priorities stemming from position are sufficient to allow analysts to make reliable predictions about a player's stand in many cases. But these propensities are filtered through the baggage that players bring to positions. Some knowledge of both the pressures and the baggage is thus required for sound predictions.

2. *Goals and Interests.*   The goals and interests that affect players' desired outcomes include national security interests, organizational interests, domestic interests, and personal interests. Some national security objectives are widely accepted — for example, the interest in U.S. avoidance of foreign domination and the belief that if the United States were to unilaterally disarm other nations would use military force against it and its allies with serious adverse consequences. But, in most cases, reasonable men can disagree about how American national security interests will be affected by a specific issue. Thus other interests as well affect an individual's stand on an issue of national security or foreign policy. Members of an organization, particularly career officials, come to believe that the health of their organization is vital to the national interest. The health of the organization, in turn, is seen to depend on maintaining influence, fulfilling the mission of the organization, and securing the necessary capabilities. While many bureaucrats are unconcerned with domestic affairs and politics and do not ask themselves how a proposed change in policy or behavior would affect domestic political issues, the President and senior players will almost always be concerned about domestic implications. Finally, a player's stand depends on his personal interests and his conception of his role.

3. *Stakes and Stands.*   Games are played to determine decisions and actions. But decisions and actions advance and impede each player's conception of the national interest, his organization's interests, specific programs to which he is committed,

the welfare of his friends, and his personal interests. These overlapping interests constitute the *stakes* for which games are played. *Stakes* are an individual's interests defined by the issue at hand. In the light of these stakes, a player decides on his *stand* on the issue.

4. *Deadlines and Faces of Issues.*   "Solutions" to strategic problems are not found by detached analysts focusing coolly on *the* problem. Instead, deadlines and events raise issues and force busy players to take stands. A number of established processes fix deadlines that demand action at appointed times. First, in the national security arena, the budget, embassies' demands for action-cables, requests for instructions from military groups, and scheduled intelligence reports fix recurring deadlines for decision and action. Second, major political speeches, especially Presidential speeches, force decisions. Third, crises necessitate decisions and actions. Because deadlines raise issues in one context rather than in another, they importantly affect the resolution of the issue.

When an issue arises, players typically come to see quite different *faces of the issue*. For example, a proposal to withdraw American troops from Europe is to the Army a threat to its budget and size, to the Budget Bureau a way to save money, to the Treasury a balance-of-payments gain, to the State Department Office of European Affairs a threat to good relations with NATO, to the President's congressional adviser an opportunity to remove a major irritant in the President's relations with the Hill. (Chiefs, especially, tend to see several faces of the issue simultaneously.) But the face of the issue that each player sees is not determined by his goals and interests alone. By raising an issue in one channel rather than in another, deadlines affect the face an issue wears.

C. What determines each player's impact on results?

1. *Power.*   Power (i.e., effective influence on government decisions and actions) is an elusive blend of at least three elements: bargaining advantages, skill and will in using bargaining advantages, and other players' perceptions of the first two ingredients. The sources of bargaining advantages include formal authority and responsibility (stemming from positions); actual control over resources necessary to carry out action; expertise and control over information that enables one to define the problem, identify options, and estimate feasibilities; control over information that enables chiefs to determine whether and in what form decisions are being implemented; the ability to affect other players' objectives in other games, including domestic political games; personal persuasiveness with other players (drawn from personal relations, charisma); and access to and persuasiveness with players who have bargaining advantages drawn from the above (based on interpersonal relations, etc.). Power wisely invested yields an enhanced reputation for effectiveness. Unsuccessful investments deplete both the stock of capital and the reputation. Thus each player must pick the issues on which he can play with high probability of success.

D. What is the game?   How are players' stands, influence, and moves combined to yield governmental decisions and actions?

1. *Action-channels.*   Bargaining games are neither random nor haphazard. The individuals whose stands and moves count are the players whose positions hook them on to the action-channels. An action-channel is a regularized means of taking governmental action on a specific kind of issue. For example, one action-channel for producing U.S. military intervention in another country includes a recom-

mendation by the ambassador to that country, an assessment by the regional military commander, a recommendation by the Joint Chiefs of Staff, an evaluation by the intelligence community of the consequences of intervention, a recommendation by the Secretaries of State and Defense, a Presidential decision to intervene, the transmittal of an order through the President to the Secretary of Defense and the JCS to the regional military commander, his determination of what troops to employ, the order from him to the commander of those troops, and orders from that commander to the individuals who actually move into the country. Similarly, the budgetary action-channel includes the series of steps between the Budget Bureau's annual "call for estimates," through departmental, Presidential, and congressional review, to congressional appropriation, Presidential signature, Bureau of Budget apportionment, agency obligation, and ultimately expenditure.

Action-channels structure the game by preselecting the major players, determining their usual points of entrance into the game, and distributing particular advantages and disadvantages for each game. Most critically, channels determine "who's got the action" — that is, which department's Indians actually do whatever is decided upon.

Typically, issues are recognized and determined within an established channel for producing action. In the national security area, weapons procurement decisions are made within the annual budgeting process; embassies' demands for action-cables are answered according to routines of consultation and clearance from State to Defense and White House; requests for instructions from military groups (concerning assistance all the time, concerning operations during war) are composed by the military in consultation with the Office of the Secretary of Defense, the Secretary of State, and the White House; crises responses are debated among White House, State, Defense, CIA, Treasury and ad hoc players.

2. *Rules of the Game.*   The rules of the game stem from the Constitution, statutes, court interpretations, executive orders, conventions, and even culture. Some rules are explicit, others implicit. Some rules are quite clear, others fuzzy. Some are very stable; others are ever changing. But the collection of rules, in effect, defines the game. First, rules establish the positions, the paths by which men gain access to positions, the power of each position, the action-channels. Second, rules constrict the range of governmental decisions and actions that are acceptable. The Constitution declares certain forms of action out of bounds. In attempting to encourage a domestic industry — for example, the computer industry — to take advantage of certain international opportunities, American players are restricted by antitrust laws to a much narrower set of actions than, for example, are players in Japan. Third, rules sanction moves of some kinds — bargaining, coalitions, persuasion, deceit, bluff, and threat — while making other moves illegal, immoral, ungentlemanly, or inappropriate.

3. *Action as Political Resultant.*   Government decisions are made, and government actions are taken, neither as the simple choice of a unified group, nor as a formal summary of leaders' preferences. Rather, the context of shared power but separate judgments about important choices means that politics is the mechanism of choice. Each player pulls and hauls with the power at his discretion for outcomes that will advance his conception of national, organizational, group, and personal interests.*

---

* How each player ranks his interests as they are manifest as stakes at particular points in the game is a subtle, complex problem. In one sense, players seem to have gone through a Model I

Note the *environment* in which the game is played: inordinate uncertainty about what must be done, the necessity that something be done, and the crucial consequences of whatever is done. These features force responsible men to become active players. The *pace of the game* — hundreds of issues, numerous games, and multiple circuits — compels players to fight to "get others' attention," to make them "see the facts," to assure that they "take the time to think seriously about the broader issue." The *structure of the game* — power shared by individuals with separate responsibilities — validates each player's feeling that "others don't see my problem," and "others must be persuaded to look at the issue from a less parochial perspective." The *law of the game* — he who hesitates loses his chance to play at that point and he who is uncertain about his recommendation is overpowered by others who are sure — pressure players to come down on one side of a 51 to 49 issue and play. The *reward of the game* — effectiveness, i.e., impact on outcomes, as the immediate measure of performance — encourages hard play. Thus, most players come to fight to "make the government do what is right." The strategies and tactics employed are quite similar to those formalized by theorists of international relations.

Advocates fight for outcomes. But the game of politics does not consist simply of players pulling and hauling, each for his own chosen action, because the terms and conditions of players' employment are not identical. Chiefs and Indians are often advocates of particular actions. But staffers fight to find issues, state alternatives, and produce arguments for their Chiefs. Presidential staffers — ideally — struggle to catch issues and structure games so as to maximize both the President's appreciation of advocates' arguments and the impact of Presidential decision. Chiefs sometimes function as semi-staffers for the President. The President's costs and benefits often require that he decide as little as possible, keeping his options open (rather than coming down on one side of an uncertain issue and playing hard).

When a governmental or Presidential decision is reached, the larger game is not over. Decisions can be reversed or ignored. As Jonathan Daniels, an aide to Franklin Roosevelt, noted:

> Half of a President's suggestions, which theoretically carry the weight of orders, can be safely forgotten by a Cabinet member. And if the President asks about a suggestion a second time, he can be told that it is being investigated. If he asks a third time, a wise Cabinet officer will give him at least part of what he suggests. But only occasionally, except about the most important matters, do Presidents ever get around to asking three times.[69]

And even if not reversed or ignored, decisions still have to be implemented. Thus formal governmental decisions are usually only way-stations along the path to action. And the opportunity for slippage between decision and action is much larger than most analysts have recognized. For after a decision, the game expands, bringing in more players with more diverse preferences and more independent power.

Formal decisions may be very general or quite specific. In some cases, the players who reach a formal decision about some action that the government should

---

analysis. American culture tends to legitimize national interests and to render "political considerations" beyond the pale. This makes it difficult for many players to articulate, even to themselves, the priorities that their behavior suggests.

take will have no choice about who will carry it out. But in other cases, there will be several subchannels leading from decision to action. For example, negotiations with foreign governments are usually the concern of the State Department but can be assigned to a special envoy or to the intelligence services. Where there are several subchannels, players will maneuver to get the action into the channel that they believe offers the best prospect for getting their desired results.

Most decisions leave considerable leeway in implementation. Players who supported the decision will maneuver to see it implemented and may go beyond the spirit if not the letter of the decision. Those who opposed the decision, or opposed the action, will maneuver to delay implementation, to limit implementation to the letter but not the spirit, and even to have the decision disobeyed.

III. DOMINANT INFERENCE PATTERN

If a nation performed an action, that action was the *resultant* of bargaining among individuals and groups within the government. Model III's explanatory power is achieved by displaying the game — the action-channel, the positions, the players, their preferences, and the pulling and hauling — that yielded, as a resultant, the action in question. Where an outcome was for the most part the triumph of an individual (e.g., the President) or group (e.g., the President's men or a cabal) this model attempts to specify the details of the game that made the victory possible. But with these as with "orphan" actions, Model III tries not to neglect the sharp differences, misunderstandings, and foul-ups that contributed to what was actually done.

IV. GENERAL PROPOSITIONS

The difficulty of formulating Model III propositions about outcomes can be illustrated by considering the much simpler problems of a theorist attempting to specify propositions about outcomes of a card game he has never seen before but which we recognize as poker. As a basis for formulating propositions, the analyst would want information about (1) the rules of the game: are all positions equal in payoffs, information, etc., and if not, what are the differences? (2) the importance of skill, reputation, and other characteristics that players bring to positions: if important, what characteristics does each player have? (3) the distribution of cards, i.e., the advantages and disadvantages for the particular hand; (4) individual players' valuation of alternative payoffs, e.g., whether each simply wants to maximize his winnings or whether some enjoy winning by bluffing more than winning by having the strongest cards. This partial list suggests how difficult the problem is, even in this relatively simple, structured case.* The extraordinary complexity of cases of bureaucratic politics accounts in part for the paucity of general propositions. Nevertheless, as the paradigm has illustrated, it is possible to identify a number of relevant factors, and, in many cases, analysts can acquire enough information about these factors to offer explanations and predictions.

A. Political Resultants.   A large number of factors that constitute a governmental game intervene between "issues" and resultants.

---

* An analogous difficulty is faced by economists trying to formulate propositions in oligopoly theory.

1. The peculiar preferences and stands of individual players can have a significant effect on governmental action. Had someone other than Paul Nitze been head of the Policy Planning Staff in 1949, there is no reason to believe that there would have been an NSC-68. Had MacArthur not possessed certain preferences, power, and skills, U.S. troops might never have crossed the narrow neck.
2. The advantages and disadvantages of each player differ substantially from one action-channel to another. For example, the question of economic directives for Germany was considered by the U.S. government in a military context. If the issue had arisen through international monetary channels, players in the Treasury would have had more leverage in pressing their preferences.
3. The mix of players and each player's advantages shift not only *between* action-channels but also *along* action-channels. Chiefs dominate the major formal decisions on important foreign policy issues, but Indians, especially those in the organization charged with carrying out a decision, may play a major role thereafter.

B. Action and Intention.   Governmental action does not presuppose government intention. The sum of behavior of representatives of a government relevant to an issue is rarely intended by any individual or group. Rather, in the typical case, separate individuals with different intentions contribute pieces to a resultant. The details of the action are therefore not chosen by any individual (and are rarely identical with what any of the players would have chosen if he had confronted the issue as a matter of simple, detached choice). Nevertheless, resultants can be roughly consistent with some group's preference in the context of the political game.
1. Most resultants emerge from games among players who perceive quite different faces of an issue and who differ markedly in the actions they prefer.
2. Actions rarely follow from an agreed doctrine in which all players concur.
3. Actions consisting of a number of pieces that have emerged from a number of games (plus foul-ups) rarely reflect a coordinated government strategy and thus are difficult to read as conscious "signals."

C. Problems and Solutions.
1. "Solutions" to strategic problems are not discovered by detached analysts focusing coolly on *the* problem. The problems for players are both narrower and broader than *the* strategic problem. Each player focuses not on the total strategic problem but rather on the decision that must be made today or tomorrow. Each decision has important consequences not only for the strategic problem but for each player's stakes. Thus the gap between what the player is focusing on (the problems he is solving) and what a strategic analyst focuses on is often very wide.
2. Decisions that call for substantial changes in governmental action typically reflect a coincidence of Chiefs in search of a solution and Indians in search of a problem. Confronting a deadline, Chiefs focus on an issue and look for a solution. Having become committed to a solution developed for an earlier, somewhat different and now outmoded issue, Indians seek a problem.[70]

D. Where you stand depends on where you sit.[71]   Horizontally, the diverse demands upon each player shape his priorities, perceptions, and issues. For large classes of issues — e.g., budgets and procurement decisions — the stance of a particular player can be predicted with high reliability from information about his seat. For example, though the participants in the notorious B-36 controversy were, as Eisenhower put it, "distinguished Americans who have their country's good at heart," no one was surprised when Admiral Radford (rather than Air Force Secretary

Symington) testified that "the B-36, under any theory of war, is a bad gamble with national security," or when Air Force Secretary Symington (rather than Admiral Radford) claimed that "a B-36 with an A-bomb can take off from this continent and destroy distant objectives which might require ground armies years to take and then only at the expense of heavy casualties."[72]

E. Chiefs and Indians.   The aphorism "Where you stand depends on where you sit" has vertical as well as horizontal application. Vertically, the demands upon the President, Chiefs, Staffers, and Indians are quite distinct, first in the case of policymaking, and second in the case of implementation.

The foreign policy issues with which the President can deal are limited primarily by his crowded schedule. Of necessity, he must deal first with what comes next. His problem is to probe the special face worn by issues that come to his attention, to preserve his leeway until time has clarified the uncertainties, and to assess the relevant risks.

Foreign policy Chiefs deal most often with the hottest issue *du jour,* though they can catch the attention of the President and other members of the government for most issues they take to be very important. What they cannot guarantee is that "the President will pay the price" or that "the others will get on board." They must build a coalition of the relevant powers that be. They must "give the President confidence" in the choice of the right course of action.

Most problems are framed, alternatives specified, and proposals pushed, however, by Indians. Indians' fights with Indians of other departments — for example, struggles between International Security Affairs of the Department of Defense and Political-Military of the State Department — are a microcosm of the action at higher levels. But the Indians' major problem is how to get the *attention* of Chiefs, how to get an issue on an action-channel, how to get the government "to do what is right." The incentives push the Indian to become an active advocate.

In policymaking, then, the issue looking *down* is options: how to preserve my leeway until time clarifies uncertainties. The issue looking *sideways* is commitment: how to get others committed to my coalition. The issue looking *upward* is confidence: how to give the boss confidence to do what must be done. To paraphrase one of Neustadt's assertions, the essence of *any* responsible official's task is to persuade other players that his version of what needs to be done is what their own appraisal of their own responsibilities requires them to do in their own interests.[73]

For implementation of foreign policy decisions, vertical demands differ. The Chief's requirements are two, but these two conflict. The necessity to build a consensus behind his preferred policy frequently requires fuzziness: different people must agree with slightly different things for quite different reasons; when a government decision is made, both the character of the choice and the reasons for it must often remain vague. But this requirement is at loggerheads with another; the necessity that the choice be enacted requires that footdragging by the unenthusiastic, and subversion by the opposed, be kept to a minimum. Nudging the footdraggers and corraling the subversives constitute difficult tasks even when the decision is clear and the watchman is the President. And most oversight, policing, and spurring is done not by the President but by the President's men or the men who agree with the government decision. Men who would move the machine to act on what has been decided demand clarity.

F. The 51—49 Principle.   The terms and conditions of the game affect the time that players spend thinking about hard policy choices and the force and assurance with which they argue for their preferred alternative. Because he faces an agenda fixed by hundreds of important deadlines, the reasonable player must make difficult policy choices in much less time and with much less agonizing than an analyst or observer would. Because he must compete with others, the reasonable player is forced to argue much more confidently than he would if he were a detached judge.

G. Inter- and Intra-national Relations.   The actions of one nation affect those of another to the degree that they result in advantages and disadvantages for players in the second nation. Thus players in one nation who aim to achieve some international objective must attempt to achieve outcomes in their intra-national game that add to the advantages of players in the second country who advocate an analogous objective.

H. The Face of the Issue Differs From Seat to Seat.   Where you sit influences what you see as well as where you stand (on any issue). Rarely do two sets of eyes see the same issue. President Truman never saw the issue of defense in the military budget of 1950. Arguments about security and the forces required to support our foreign policy appeared purely as military strategies for expanding the budgets of the services concerned.

I. Misperception.   The games are not played under conditions of perfect information. Considerable misperception is a standard part of the functioning of each government. Any proposal that is widely accepted is perceived by different men to do quite different things and to meet quite different needs. Misperception is in a sense the grease that allows cooperation among people whose differences otherwise would hardly allow them to coexist.

J. Misexpectation.   The pace at which the multiple games are played allows only limited attention to each game and demands concentration on priority games. Thus players frequently lack information about the details of other players' games and problems. In the lower priority games, the tendency to expect that someone else will act in such a way that "he helps me with my problem" is unavoidable. In November 1950, each man expected that someone else would go to the President to get MacArthur's orders changed.

K. Miscommunication.   Both the pace and the noise level merge with propensities of perception to make accurate communication difficult. Because communication must be quick, it tends to be elliptic. In a noisy environment, each player thinks he has spoken with a stronger and clearer voice than the others have actually heard. At the Key West meeting of March 1947, the Chiefs understood Forrestal to say that the President had decided to purchase a flush deck carrier. Forrestal head the Chiefs' acceptance of the President's decision as their approval of the merits of a flush deck carrier. These differences came to light only when the issue was reopened.[74]

L. Reticence.   Because each player is engaged in multiple games, the advantages of reticence — i.e., hesitant silence and only partially intended soft-spokenness — seem overwhelming. Reticence in one game reduces leaks that would be harmful in higher priority games. Reticence permits other players to interpret an outcome in the way in which the shoe pinches least. It gives them an ill-focused target of attack. Reticence between Chiefs and Staffers or Indians permits each Indian to offer a charitable interpretation of the outcome — the proposal that simply never moves, for example, or the memo that dies at an interagency meeting of Chiefs. And at least it reduces explicit friction between a Chief and his men. Neustadt's example of the reticence of various Chiefs in speaking to Truman about leashing MacArthur is classic.

M. Styles of Play.   There are important differences in the behavior of (1) bureaucratic careerists, whether civilian or military, (2) lateral-entry types, and (3) political appointees. These differences are a function of longer-range expectations. The bureaucrat must adopt a code of conformity if he is to survive the inevitable changes of administration and personnel, whereas the lateral entry type and the political appointee are more frequently temporary employees, interested in policy. The political appointees have a very limited tenure in office and thus impose a high discount rate, that is, a short-time horizon on any issue. Careerists know that presidents come and presidents go, but the Navy . . .

Style of play is also importantly affected by the terms of reference in which a player conceives of his action. Some players are not able to articulate the bureaucratic politics game because their conception of their job does not legitimate such activity. On the other hand, Acheson maintained that the Secretary of State works "in an environment where some of the methods would have aroused the envy of the Borgias." The quality he distinguished from all others as the most necessary for an effective American Secretary of State was "the killer instinct."[75]

V. SPECIFIC PROPOSITIONS

A. Nuclear Crises

1. A decision to use nuclear weapons is less likely to emerge from a game in which a political leader (whose position forces upon him the heat of being a Final Arbiter) has most of the chips than from a game in which the military have most of the chips.
2. The probability of the U.S. government making a decision to use more military force (rather than less) in a crisis increases as the number of individuals who have an initial, general, personal preference for more forceful military action increases in the following positions: President, Special Assistant for National Security Affairs, Secretaries of Defense and State, Chairman of the JCS, and Director of the CIA.
3. In a nuclear crisis, the central decisions will be hammered out *not* in the formal forums, e.g., the National Security Council, but rather by an *ad hoc* group that includes the President, the heads of the major organizations involved, plus individuals in whom the President has special confidence.
4. These individuals' perception of the issue will differ radically. These differences will be partially predictable from the pressure of their position plus their personality.

B. Military Action

1. For any military action short of nuclear war, decision and implementation will be delayed while proponents try to persuade opponents to get on board.
2. Major decisions about the use of military tend not simply to be Presidential decisions, or majority decisions, but decisions by a large plurality.
3. No military action is chosen without extensive consultation of the military players. No decision for a substantial use of force, short of nuclear war, will be made

against their advice, without a delay during which an extensive record of consultation is prepared.

VI. EVIDENCE

Information about the details of differences in perceptions and priorities within a government on a particular issue is rarely available. Accurate accounts of the bargaining that yielded a resolution of the issue are rarer still. Documents do not capture this kind of information. What the documents do preserve tends to obscure, as much as to enlighten. Thus the source of such information must be the participants themselves. But, *ex hypothesis,* each participant knows one small piece of the story. Memories quickly become colored. Diaries are often misleading. What is required is access, by an analyst attuned to the players and interested in governmental politics, to a large number of the participants in a decision before their memories fade or become to badly discolored. Such access is uncommon. But without this information, how can the analyst proceed? As a master of this style of analysis has stated, "If I were forced to choose between the documents on the one hand, and late, limited, partial interviews with some of the principal participants on the other, I would be forced to discard the documents."[76] The use of public documents, newspapers, interviews of participants, and discussion with close observers of participants to piece together the bits of information available is an art. Transfer of these skills from the fingertips of artists to a form that can guide other students of foreign policy is this model's most pressing need.

THE GOVERNMENTAL POLITICS MODEL APPLIED

A Model III approach to problems considered in earlier chapters accents new dimensions. The Soviet Union's simultaneous purchase of ABMs and pursuit of detente emerge as separate resultants of different bargaining games. A full understanding would require specific information about the players, their advantages, and the overlapping games from which relevant decisions and actions resulted. In the absence of this information, however, one can consider more general characteristics of the Soviet national security game.

The dominant feature of bureaucratic politics in the Soviet Union is the continuous "struggle for power." An occupant's position in the central game is always uncertain and risky. Members of the Politburo and Central Committee are aware of the historical tendency for one man to become preeminent. Thus while a central problem of life for the leader is managing to stay on top, a large part of the problem for Politburo members is how to keep the leadership collective. This fact yields a relevant proposition: policy issues are inextricably intertwined with power plays. Reorganizations, or shifts in resources, constitute redistributions of advantages and disadvantages in the central game.

Presidium and Central Committee Secretariat members have typically risen through, and assumed special responsibility for, various departments and subdepartments. These organizational associations color players' perspectives and priorities. Individuals in these organizations constitute each player's power base. Because of personal histories and constituent pressures, a number of central players must have taken visible stands for ABM deployment, and for detente. In the absence of a deadline forcing a decision in the central Soviet game between ABM and detente, it seems likely that advocates of each have been allowed to tend their own gardens. (Indeed, if one assumes that the Soviet government is analogous to the U.S. government, advocates of the two tracks argue that there is really no conflict between the two.) Thus the two courses of action probably emerged, and are likely to be sustained.

A necessity for budgetary cuts or a requirement to respond to a strong American initiative for an agreement limiting ABM deployment might present an opportunity for advocates of detente to interfere with the established programs and procedures of the PVO. Indeed, stopping deployment of ABMs would constitute a major defeat for several central players and a redistribution of the power base of certain ministers and Presidium members. It is important to recognize, however, that this conflict would arise from unavoidable choices on concrete issues rather than by internal disagreement about the consistency of strategic policies.

Nuclear Strategy.   In thinking about the problem of deterrence, a Model III analyst begins from the proposition that if a nuclear attack occurs, it will have emerged as a resultant of bargaining in the attacking government. Rather than Model I's focus on balance and stability, or Model II's focus on organizational routines, a Model III analyst is concerned with the features of the internal politics of a government that might produce this decision.

First, which players can decide to launch an attack? Whether the effective power over this action is controlled by an individual, a minor game, or the central game is critical.

Second, though Model I's confidence in deterrence relies on the assumption that, in the end, nations will not commit suicide, Model III recalls historical precedents. Admiral Yamamoto, who designed the Japanese attack on Pearl Harbor, told the members of the Japanese government accurately: "In the first six months to a year of war against the U.S. and England I will run wild, and I will show you an uninterrupted succession of victories; I must also tell you that, should the war be prolonged for two or three years, I have no confidence in our ultimate victory."[77] But Japan attacked. Such a precedent suggests three key questions. One: Could any member of the government solve *his* problem by attack? What patterns of bargaining could yield attack as a resultant? The major difference between a stable balance of terror and a questionable one may simply be that most members of the government appreciate fully the consequences of attack in the case of the former and are thus on guard against this decision. Two: What stream of decisions might lead to an attack? At what point in that stream do the potential attacker's politics lie? If members of the U.S. government had known more about the succession of decisions from which the Japanese attack on Pearl Harbor emerged, they would have been aware of a considerable probability of that attack. Three: How might miscalculation and confusion generate foul-ups that yield attack as a resultant? For example, in a crisis or after the beginning of conventional war, what happens to the information available to, and the effective power of, members of the central game?

A final element of importance in thinking about nuclear attacks is the probable differences in perceptions and priorities of central leaders. Pressures encourage both the Soviet Chairman and the U.S. President to feel the distance between their own responsibilities and those of other members of their central games. Each lives with the daily responsibility for nuclear holocaust. Neither will be overly impressed by differences between the death of one million and one hundred million of his own citizens when choosing to take, or to refrain from taking, a risk. Each will be more sensitive to the other's problem than is any other member of the central game. Both may well appreciate the extent to which the "kings" are partners in the game against nuclear disaster. Both will be interested in private communication with each other. If channels can be arranged, such communication offers the most promising prospect of resolution of a crisis.

NOTES

[1] Walter Millis (ed.), *Forrestal Diaries,* New York, 1951.

[2] Richard Neustadt, *Presidential Power,* New York, 1960.

[3] Ibid., p. 33. Emphasis added.

[4] Ibid., p. 10. Emphasis added.

[5] Richard Neustadt, "Whitehouse and Whitehall," *The Public Interest,* No. 2, Winter 1966, p. 64. Emphasis added.

[6] Neustadt, Testimony, U.S., Congress, Senate, Committee on Government Operations, Subcommittee on National Security and International Operations, *Conduct of National Security Policy,* 89th Congress, 1st Session, June 29, 1965, p. 126. Emphasis added.

[7] Neustadt, *Presidential Power,* p. 2. Emphasis added.

[8] Ibid., p. 184. Emphasis added.

[9] Neustadt, Testimony, p. 126. Emphasis added.

[10] See Neustadt, Testimony, U.S., Congress, Senate, Committee on Government Operations, Subcommittee on National Security Staffing, *Administration of National Security,* 88th Congress, 1st Session, March 25, 1963; Testimony, 1965; "Afterword: 1964" to *Presidential Power; Alliance Politics,* New York, 1970.

[11] Arthur Schlesinger, Jr., *A Thousand Days: John F. Kennedy in the White House,* Boston, 1965, p. 859. Neustadt's *Alliance Politics* contains a brief, summary account of the Skybolt episode.

[12] Neustadt, *Presidential Power,* pp. 123 ff.

[13] Ibid., p. 124.

[14] Memoirs of Harry S. Truman, Vol. 2, *Years of Trial and Hope,* Garden City, N.Y., 1956, p. 341, quoted by Neustadt in *Presidential Power,* p. 123.

[15] Neustadt, *Presidential Power,* p. 126.

[16] Ibid., p. 139.

[17] Ibid., p. 140.

[18] Ibid., p. 144.

[19] Ibid.

[20] Ibid.

[21] Ibid., p. 145.

[22] Ibid.

[23] Gabriel Almond, *The American People and Foreign Policy,* New York, 1950.

[24] Compare, for example, David Truman, *The Governmental Process,* New York, 1951.

[25] Charles E. Lindblom, "Bargaining? The Hidden Hand in Government," RM-1434-RC, Rand Corporation, February 22, 1955; "The Science of 'Muddling Through,' " *Public Administration Review,* Vol. 19, Spring 1959; *The Intelligence of Democracy,* New York, 1965. See also Charles E. Lindblom and D. Braybrooke, *A Strategy of Decision,* Glencoe, Ill., 1963.

[26] This notion is developed in *The Intelligence of Democracy* as "partisan mutual adjustment." The critical differences between the analysis developed in this essay and that of Lindblom are two. First, whereas Lindblom's focus of attention is the actual process by which policy is *made,* the Governmental Politics Model concentrates on *explanations* of policy outcomes. Second, while Lindblom's examination of the process of partisan mutual adjustment

by which policy is made is harnessed with a defense of this process as the best mechanism for making decisions, the Governmental Politics Model is neutral on the merits of the process.

[27] Warner Schilling, "The Politics of National Defense: Fiscal 1950," in W. Schilling. P. Hammond, and G. Snyder, *Strategy, Politics, and Defense Budgets*, New York, 1962.

[28] Ibid., pp. 21-24.

[29] Ibid., pp. 25-26.

[30] Ibid., p. 191.

[31] Ibid., p. 199.

[32] Ibid., pp. 216-22.

[33] Samuel Huntington, *The Common Defense*, New York, 1961. See Huntington's earlier statement of this idea, "Strategy and the Political Process," *Foreign Affairs*, Vol. 38, January 1960.

[34] Huntington, *The Common Defense*, p. ix.

[35] Ibid., p. 146.

[36] Ibid.

[37] Ibid.

[38] Ibid., p. 153.

[39] Ibid., p. 128.

[40] Ibid., p. 158.

[41] Ibid., p. 162.

[42] Ibid., p. 163.

[43] Ibid., p. 164.

[44] Ibid., p. 165.

[45] Roger Hilsman, *To Move a Nation*, New York, 1967.

[46] R. Hilsman, "Congressional-Executive Relations and the Foreign Policy Consensus," *American Political Science Review*, September 1958; "The Foreign-Policy Consensus: An Interim Research Report," *Journal of Conflict Resolution*, Vol. 3, No. 4, December 1959.

[47] Hilsman, *To Move a Nation*, pp. 13, 562.

[48] As the title of Hilsman's first chapter asserts, "Policy Making Is Politics" *(To Move a Nation).*

[49] Ibid., p. 553.

[50] Ibid., p. 554.

[51] Ibid., pp. 554-55.

[52] Ibid., p. 561.

[53] Ibid., p. xviii. Emphasis added.

[54] Ibid.

[55] Ibid., p. 6.

[56] Ibid.

[57] Ibid., p. 8. See also Morton Halperin, "The Gaither Committee and the Policy Process," *World Politics*, Vol. 13, April 1961.

[58] Hilsman, op. cit., p. 8. This constituted considerably less than a victory in the major battle, since leaked reports rarely make the most powerful ammunition.

[59] See, for example, H. Stein (ed.), *American Civil-Military Decisions*, Birmingham, Ala., 1963; H. Stein (ed.), *Public Administration and Policy Development*, New York, 1952; and the Inter-University Case Program. The Institute of War and Peace Studies at Columbia University, and especially William T. R. Fox, have played an important role in developing bureaucratic politics studies.

In almost every area of foreign policy and international relations reviewed in our earlier characterization of Model I, there are now scholars at work using a version of a Model III perspective. In diplomatic history, see, for example, Ernest R. May, *The World War and American Isolation,* Cambridge, Mass., 1966; "Bombing for Political Effects," unpublished paper; and *The Washington Naval Conference,* forthcoming; Richard H. Ullman, *Anglo-Soviet Relations, 1917–1921,* Princeton, N.J., Vol. 1, 1961, Vol. 2, 1968; Samuel R. Williamson, *The Politics of Grand Strategy,* Cambridge, Mass., 1969.

For strategy, see Graham Allison and Morton H. Halperin, "Bureaucratic Politics: A Paradigm and Some Policy Implications," in *World Politics,* special issue, 1971; and A. W. Marshall and Graham Allison, "Strategic Nuclear Deterrence: Do We Understand the Behavior of the Black Box?" forthcoming. For Sovietology, see A. W. Marshall, unpublished papers; and Thomas W. Wolfe, "Policymaking in the Soviet Union: A Statement with Supplementary Comments," P-4131, Rand Corporation, June 1969.

For Sinology, see Allen Whiting, "U.S.-Chinese Political Relations," an unpublished paper presented at the Conference on the Foreign Policy of Communist China, January 4-8, 1970.

For American foreign policy, see Morton H. Halperin and Tang Tsou, "U.S. Policy Toward the Offshore Islands," *Public Policy,* 1966; Morton H. Halperin, *Bureaucratic Politics and Foreign Policy,* forthcoming; and John Steinbruner, *The Mind and the Milieu of Policy Makers,* forthcoming.

[60] Paul Hammond, "Directives for the Occupation of Germany," in H. Stein (ed.), *American Civil-Military Decisions.*

[61] Ibid., p. 427.

[62] Paul Hammond, "Super Carriers and B-36 Bombers," in H. Stein (ed.), op. cit.

[63] Paul Hammond, "NSC-68: Prologue to Rearmament," in Schilling, Hammond, Snyder, op. cit.

[64] This comparision was noted by N.J. Spykman, *America's Strategy in World Politics,* New York, 1942. See also Roger Hilsman, "The Foreign-Policy Consensus," op. cit., p. 368; and *To Move a Nation;* also Warner Schilling, "The Politics of National Defense: Fiscal 1950." Both Schilling and Hilsman credit William T. R. Fox.

[65] On hierarchical bargaining, see Herbert Simon, *Models of Man,* New York, 1957, pp. 66-68; Robert Dahl and Charles Lindblom, *Politics, Economics, and Welfare,* New York, 1953, pp. 341-44; N. E. Long, "Public Policy and Administration," *Public Administration Review,* Winter 1954; Richard Fenno, *The President's Cabinet,* Cambridge, Mass., 1959, ch. 6.

[66] Inclusion of the President's Special Assistant for National Security Affairs in the tier of Chiefs rather than among the Staffers involves a debatable choice. In fact he is both super-Staffer and near-Chief. His position has no statutory authority. He is especially dependent on good relations with the President and the Secretaries of Defense and State. Nevertheless, he stands astride a genuine action process. The decision to include this position among the Chiefs reflects my judgment that the function that McGeorge Bundy served is becoming institutionalized.

[67] These points are drawn from Neustadt, Testimony, 1963; see especially pp. 82-83.

[68] Hilsman, *To Move a Nation,* p. 81.

[69] Daniels, *Frontier on the Potomac,* New York, 1946, pp. 31-32.

[70] This proposition was formulated by Ernest R. May.

[71] This aphorism was stated first, I think, by Don K. Price.

[72] P. Hammond, "Super Carriers and B-36 Bombers," op. cit.

[73] Neustadt, *Presidential Power,* ch. 3.

[74] P. Hammond, "Super Carriers and B-36 Bombers," op. cit.

[75] Dean Acheson, "The President and the Secretary of State," in D. Price (ed.), *The Secretary of State,* New York, 1960.

[76] Richard Neustadt.

[77] Roberta Wohlstetter, *Pearl Harbor: Warning and Decision,* Stanford, Calif., p. 350.

8.   The Social Relations of Production at the Point of Production*

Richard C. Edwards

For the last several years, discussions of the labor process have tended to take as their starting point Harry Braverman's *Labor and Monopoly Capital*. Most writers have accepted Braverman's thesis of the degradation of work; a few have criticized it. Yet despite the book's brilliant insights, the weaknesses in its analysis are becoming increasingly visible. Most important are the following:

1. The book fails to take account of labor responses to the new forms of "degraded" work that employers have developed. In Braverman's story, new, fragmented, de-skilled methods of work are developed and implemented by capitalists, with drastic effects on workers but with little apparent resistance. No impact results from what resistance does occur. Unions play no role, and there is no class struggle.

2. The book accepts or seems to accept writings on management theory as evidence for actual developments on the shop or office floor. The most important example is Braverman's reading of Frederick Taylor's writings as though they described real processes rather than simply Taylor's thinking and theories. The book has therefore taken what are clearly ideological sources of information and treated them as though the processes they describe were real.

3. The book's basic premise of "de-skilling" remains problematical. It seems clear that de-skilling has occurred in the traditional craft trades, including the machinists' tradition out of which Braverman himself came. It also seems correct to emphasize the tendency for capitalists to replace high-skill (or more precisely, high-wage) labor with low-skill (low-wage) labor whenever possible. Nonetheless, the development of both the forces and relations of production continually throw up new products, new technologies, and a demand for re-skilled, especially educated labor as well as de-skilled labor. Thus accumulation must be seen as simultaneously de-skilling and re-skilling the labor force. Rather than the simple, one-way process that Braverman describes, we must recognize this more complicated, two-way movement.

Admitting this point immediately changes our analysis of the trends in the composition of the American working class. The historical tendency can no longer be the simple one of the creation of an ever-increasing mass of unskilled or low-skilled workers. Rather, craft work declines, educated labor emerges, and the overall impact on the working class — whether it is becoming more homogeneous or more differentiated — is at least ambiguous.

4. The book fails to be clear as to whether modern techniques of production (carrying with them their inherent de-skilling, degradation of work, etc.) are inevitable consequences of technical economies of scale. The most consistent reading of the

---

*"The Social Relations of Production at the Point of Production" taken from *Contested Terrain: The Transformation of the Workplace in America,* by Richard C. Edwards, © 1979 by Basic Books, Inc., Publishers, New York. Reprinted by permission.

book, I would argue, would necessarily interpret the new methods of production as more efficient. In part, of course, the new methods simply permit (in Braverman's theory) the use of low-skill workers, but this begs the central question of whether such techniques do not also result in higher productivity. If this reading is accurate, then the demise of craft and other production in which workers have a knowledge of the entire production process is sad but "progressive." Capitalism is only the messenger, the vehicle for these necessary advances in society's productive capacity. Yet this reading seems quite at odds with the vitriol that Braverman displays when he records management's quest for control, and his suggestion, in several places, that degradation results from the specifically capitalist organization of production.

5. The book fails to make any distinctions between monopoly capital and non-monopoly capital. Indeed, the "monopoly capital" of the title turns out to be monopoly capital*ism,* i.e., capitalism in the present period. Yet how the book's analysis relates to monopoly capitalism rather than simply to capitalism remains entirely unclear. There is no evidence or reasoning introduced to suggest that monopoly capital in particular impinges upon the labor process in any way different from contemporary non-monopoly capital — or, for that matter, different from an earlier competitive capital. Of course the more recent managers are more sophisticated than (e.g.) their 19th-century counterparts, but the transition to monopoly capitalism does not seem to have altered the *logic* of the labor process.

6. While the book appears to provide an historical argument, starting with the development of management ideas in the 19th century and pursuing their realization in the present, in fact there exists no real historical content to the analysis. For example, between Taylorism and the present came, among other historical processes, the organization of workers in the mass production industries into industrial unions. This historic achievement, the goal of the labor and left-wing movements for the preceding several decades, does not in any way impinge on Braverman's "historical" argument.

These six omissions (and others) are serious flaws indeed in any analysis of the labor process. Just as Paul Baran and Paul Sweezy in *Monopoly Capital* excise the sphere of production from their analysis of modern capitalism, so it seems Harry Braverman has left class conflict out of his analysis of the labor process. The relations of production simply unfold as ever more systematic (and horrifying) applications of the Babbage principle. This rather mechanical logic is all the more surprising since it was Braverman himself who insisted that Marx's distinction between labor and labor power (between work done and the capacity to do work) was the essential starting point for any analysis of the labor process. But surely the relevance of this distinction is precisely the workers' ability — individually, in small groups, and collectively — to resist and in consequence to re-shape employers' schemes to transform labor power into labor. Workers do not have unlimited power, but then neither do capitalists, and Braverman's story needs to be amended to take account of the real constraints on capitalists.

In this paper I cannot deal with all these issues, but I will try to suggest an alternative formulation of the dynamics of the labor process which begins to get at some of the problems in Braverman's analysis.[1] The central departure from Braverman's analysis can be quite simply stated. Whereas Braverman concerned himself primarily with the *technical* aspects of the development of the labor process — "technical" in the sense of workers' relations to the physical process of production — my analysis will focus on the developing *social* relations of production at the point of production. This analysis, rather than contradicting Braverman's work, instead incorporates and builds upon it. The 20th century has witnessed the emergence of two divergent tendencies: (1) the development of production technology has tended to abolish old craft skills and obliterated distinctions among work tasks, and thereby also reducing skills distinctions among workers; but (2) the development of the social relations of the workplace has tended to create new divisions (and institutionalize pre-existing ones) based on the social organization of the workplace. As a result, the working class has become both more homogeneous as a mass of machine operatives and re-divided by the social organization of production. What Braverman leaves out is the capitalist firm as a social system, one embodying technical and social relations of production. This is what must be studied if we are to understand the dynamics of the labor process and the formation of the modern American working class. The rest of this paper is devoted to providing a sketchy and schematic framework for such an investigation.

1. THE LABOR PROCESS

Capitalists are in business to make profits, and to do that they organize society's production. They begin by converting their funds for investment (money capital) into the raw materials, labor, machinery, etc., needed for production; they organize the labor process itself, whereby the constituents of production are transformed into useful products or services; and then, by selling the products of labor, they re-convert their property back to money form. If the money capital obtained at the end of this cycle exceeds that invested initially, the capitalists have earned a profit.

Each step in this sequence is fraught with uncertainties, and none more so than production itself. In organizing the labor process, employers seek to carry out two very different tasks. The first is what might be termed the coordination of social production. Any production process that involves many persons must be consciously directed so that each person's labor meshes with or contributes to the labor of the other producers. Such coordination is required in all societies.

The second task derives more particularly from the class nature of the capitalist labor process. Employers not only coordinate, they must also compel. They must compel because, while workers produce the firm's output, it is capitalists who own or appropriate the output. Capitalists must therefore convince workers, through means subtle or brutal, to produce goods that they (the capitalists) will profit from. That is, capitalists must seek to convert the labor power they have purchased in the marketplace into useful labor under conditions in which the possessor of the labor power has little to gain from providing useful labor. Indeed, competition among capitalists makes such compulsion not merely a matter of individual choice or greed but rather an economic necessity. Capitalists are forced to extract as much useful labor from their workers as possible; those employers who fail to do so or do it badly will usually be driven out of business.

What employers strive to achieve is minimum *per unit* costs of production. After all, it is the total unit cost that is deducted from the selling price to yield the "residual," the capitalist's profit. Profit maximizing, particularly if it is intensified and enforced by market competition, thus sets in motion a continuing search for new methods of production, new sources of labor, new ways of organizing the labor process that will reduce unit costs. In this search, the capitalist has few biases: whatever reduces unit costs and increases profits is seized upon.

It must be noted, however, that de-skilling and the increasing use of low-skill, low-wage labor is only *one* avenue for reducing unit costs. Consider in particular that portion of total unit costs that derives from the labor input, i.e., the unit labor cost. This portion of the firm's costs clearly depends upon two quantities: the price (wage) or labor power, and the productivity of labor power. Minimizing one of these elements (e.g., the wage) does not minimize their ratio. Specifically, it may pay the firm to pay a wage higher than the least possible wage if the result is a more than proportionate increase in productivity. Of course, if wages can be reduced with effect on, or with an increase in, productivity, then cutting wages will be profit-maximizing; but if lower wages bring forth lower productivity, then the profit-maximizing strategy depends on the magnitudes involved.

This distinction between minimizing wages and minimizing per unit labor costs is not simply a point in theory; as should become clear below, the history of the labor process in the 20th century cannot be understood without it. This distinction assumes such importance because labor, unlike all the other ingredients of production, does not come available to capitalists as a purchasable commodity. Labor power can be bought, but between the purchase of labor power and the real appropriation of useful labor comes a wedge; the will, motivation, and consciousness of the worker drastically affect the work force's productivity. Hence the employer's second task in organizing production: the extraction of labor from labor power.

This second task must be understood as one which applies primarily to the firm's workforce at large, or at least to substantial portions of it. For any individual or any small group of workers, wider market mechanisms come into play. Any worker who produces significantly less than the "norm," or indeed who produces less than the most eager substitute among the unemployed, will simply be replaced; here, the market and the "reserve army" enforce production levels. But as I argue below, the use of the reserve-army sanction as a "first-resort" mechanism for extracting labor has produced resistance to the limitations on capitalists as well as obedience from workers. In all cases the employer's prerogative to hire and fire remains the ultimate sanction, but, especially among big employers, different methods serve to organize work on a day-to-day basis.

In some cases, the second task may be trivial. It is trivial, for example, if employers can directly contract for labor rather than labor power. If it is possible to specify in advance all of the duties to be performed, then the employer can simply purchase the product or service of labor. Likewise, employers may pay only for work actually done if each worker's output is independent; here, piece-rate pay may compel adequate production. Other workplace schemes may be directed towards the same end.

In general, however, capitalists have found it neither practical nor profitable to rely on such devices. Only rarely can every worker's duties be exhaustively specified when the worker is hired. Piece-rate pay has limited application and frequently engenders conflict over the rates themselves. In both cases, evaluation of whether the contracted work was properly done raises further problems. Moreover, such workers are likely to be using company-provided tools or machinery, so even if a "slow" worker receives a low wage, the capitalist cannot be indifferent to the under-utilization of the capital. Other schemes (profit sharing, distributing company stock to workers, more elaborate incentive schemes) also fail. Most importantly, all these devices founder because their targets, the workers, retain their ability to resist. Typically, then, the second task — extracting work from employees who have no direct stake in profits — remains to be carried out in the workplace itself.

The social division into workers and capitalists thereby lays the foundation for continuing conflict in the labor process, as employers attempt to extract the maximum effort from workers necessarily resist their bosses' impositions. Conflict ensues over how work shall be organized, what work pace shall be established, what conditions producers must labor under, what "rights" workers shall enjoy, how the various employees of the enterprise shall relate to each other. The workplace becomes a perpetual battleground.

The struggle in the workplace has a closely-intertwined parallel in the bargaining that goes on in the marketplace. Here conflict concerns wages, as labor and capital contend over the reward for the laborer's time. Sometimes this bargaining occurs collectively (e.g., between unions and industry representatives); at other times it takes an individual form (between job applicant and employer). At times wage bargaining creates a crisis; at other times it assumes an entirely pacific form. But here too the clash of interests persists.

Thus, in the old slogan, "a fair day's work for a fair day's pay," both elements become matters of conflict. "A fair day's work" is as much an issue for bargaining, resistance, and struggle as is the "fair day's pay." The old Wobbly demand said it more cogently if less completely: "Good Pay or Bum Work!"

The "war" on the shop and office floor may take many forms. At times it is open warfare, mutually joined; more commonly, it is a cold war, or some variant of guerrilla operations and peaceful co-existence. Frequently it is not consciously recognized as battle at all. The combatants sometimes perceive the clash in class terms, but more often they view it within an individual or small-group framework. But whether acute or dormant, the conflict remains.

Conflict in the labor process occurs under definite historical circumstances — or, what is the same, within a specific economic and social context. Most importantly, production is part of the larger process of capital accumulation, i.e., the cycle of investment of prior profits, organization of production, sale of produced commodities, realization of profits (or loss), and reinvestment of new profits. This process constitutes the fundamental dynamic of a capitalist economy. But capital accumulation, while it remains the basic theme, gets played out with substantial variations. A whole set of factors — the degree of competition among capitalists, the size of corporations, the extent of trade union organization, the level of class consciousness among workers, the impact of governmental policies, the speed of technological change, and so on — influence the nature and shape and pace of accumulation. Taken together, these various forces provide both possibilities and constraints for what can occur within the workplace. What was possible or successful in one era may be impossible or disastrous in another. Conflict at work, then, must be understood as a product both of the strategies or wills of the combatants and of definite conditions not wholly within the grasp of either workers or capitalists. As Marx put it,

> People make their own history, but they do not make it just as they please; they do not make it under circumstances chosen by themselves, but under circumstances directly found, given, and transmitted from the past.[2]

Conflict occurs within definite limits imposed by a social and historical context, yet this context rarely yields a precise determination of work organization. After technological constraints, the discipline of the market, and other forces have been taken into account, there remains a certain indeterminacy to the labor process. This "space" for the working out of workplace conflict is particularly evident within the large corporation, where "external" constraints have been reduced to a minimum. Here especially, the essential question remains: how shall work be organized?

Outside the firm, relations between capitalists and workers take the form of demanders and suppliers of the commodity "labor power;" that is, the "equality" of market relations prevails. Inside the firm, relations between capitalists and workers take the form of boss and bossed; that is a *system of control* prevails. Any system of control must embody three elements:

1. the direction of work tasks;
2. the evaluation of the work done; and
3. the rewarding and disciplining of workers.

I distinguish below between three historically important and essentially quite different ways of organizing these three elements. The first is what I term "simple control:" capitalists exercise power openly, arbitrarily, and personally (or through hired bosses who act in much the same way). Simple control formed the organizational basis of 19th century firms and continues today in the small enterprises of the more competitive industries. The second is "technical control:" the control mechanism is embedded in the physical technology of the firm, designed into the very machines and other physical apparatus of the workplace. The third is "bureaucratic control:" control becomes embedded in the social organization of the enterprise, in the contrived social relations of production at the point of production. These last two systems of control constitute "structural" forms of control, in the sense that the exercise of power becomes institutionalized in the very structure of the firm and is thus made impersonal. Structural control, as explained below, provides the rationale for the organization of workplace in big corporations today.

This typology of control embodies both the pattern of historical evolution and the array of contemporary methods for organizing work. On the one hand, each form of control corresponds to a definite stage in the development of the "representative" or most important firms, and so the systems of control correspond to or characterize stages of capitalism. On the other hand, capitalist production has developed unevenly, with some sectors pushing far in advance of other sectors, and so each type of control exists alongside the others in the economy today.

Since the transformation of the workplace in the 20th century is largely a story of the organization of work in large corporations in the advanced countries, I restrict the discussion below to that topic. Workers in small firms, as well as most large corporations' employees in Third World countries, continue to face older, more direct, less institutionalized forms of control.

The labor process becomes an arena of class conflict. Faced with chronic resistance to their efforts to compel production, employers over the years have attempted to resolve the matter by reorganizing, indeed revolutionizing, the labor process itself. Their goal remains profits; their strategies aim at establishing structures of control at work. That is, capitalists have attempted to organize production in such a way as to minimize workers' opportunities for resistance and even to alter workers' perceptions of the desirability of opposition. Work has been organized, then, to contain conflict. In this endeavor employers have sometimes been successful.

2. TOWARDS NEW SYSTEMS OF CONTROL

The conditions of work in capitalist enterprises have changed as capitalism itself has changed. In both cases, evolution has not overturned the fundamental relations that exist between capitalist and worker. But just as capitalism has proceeded from a competitive to a monopoly phase, so also have the organization of workers in production and the circumstances of their employment passed from one developmental stage to another. And it is important to note that the latter process has occurred largely as a result of the class nature of capitalist production, rather than as the result of anything ''inevitable'' or ''natural'' in either technology or the operation of large organizations.

During the 19th century much production was still carried on by skilled craftsmen, who established their own working conditions, protected the quality of their products, and limited access to their industry through craft rules, customs, apprenticeships, and the like. They were subject to market forces, of course, yet within the unit of production they themselves or their craft traditions served to organize the labor process. But as a population dependent on wages emerged, capitalists could increasingly out-compete petty producers by taking control of the labor process directly. Production itself, as well as the sale of commodities, became organized by capitalists.

Most 19th century businesses were small and subject to relatively tight discipline from competition in their product markets. The typical firm had few resources and little energy to invest in creating more sophisticated management structures. A single entrepreneur, usually flanked by a small coterie of foremen and managers, ruled the firm. They exercised power personally, intervening often in the labor process to exhort workers, bully and threaten them, reward good performance, hire and fire on the spot, favor loyal workers, and generally act as despots, benevolent or otherwise. They had a direct stake in promoting production, and they combined both incentives and sanctions in an idiosyncratic and unsystematic mix. There was little structure to how power was exercised, and workers tended to be treated arbitrarily. Since workforces were small and the boss was both close and powerful, workers had little chance collectively to oppose his rule. Generally, workers could do little more than attempt to protect dying craft traditions or engage in informal efforts to restrict output.

In terms of the three elements of a control system listed above, analysis shows that each element tended to reveal simply another feature of the personal relation between capitalist (or other bosses) and workers. In specifying what tasks were to be done, the boss directly delineated the jobs and assigned workers to them. Where production involved unstandardized or batch-type processes, this direction typically involved continuous supervision, as in gang-labor. Where production was routinized, personal direction still involved assignment and reassignment of workers to different work stations. Evaluations also occurred continuously and could scarcely be distinguished from direction; certainly few separate evaluation procedures existed. Rewarding and disciplining tended to be somewhat more structured (firms often established wages schedules, for example), yet even here the arbitrary and unconstrained power of the capitalist to punish workers meant that workers were constantly subject to personal rule. Control was, in effect, a system of direct and immediate tyranny, from which little relief was possible. Indeed, those outside the factory gates — the reserve army — stood as ready replacements for any workers who rebelled against such tyrannical power.

This system of *simple control* survives today in the small-business sector of the American economy. It has necessarily been amended by the passage of time and by borrowings of management practices from the more advanced corporate sector, but it retains its essential principles and mode of operation. We readily see it in the mom-and-pop grocery store, but it is also apparent in small manufacturing concerns. For example, a small guitar factory in Kansas employs some 50-60 workers, all of whom know the owner well. Indeed, the owner acts as ''head workman'' in some cases, occasionally building the specialized one-of-a-kind guitars ordered by show-business celebrities. The workers build the more standardized instruments, each doing a small operation on the 10 or so guitars produced every day. In directing their labor, in evaluating their performance, in rewarding and disciplining them, the owner (and the few other bosses present) rely on the personal relations of the factory to control work. The impact of simple control can also be seen in a Boston-area electronics plant, a plant employing some 500 workers. As described by Ann Bookman, the owner and the top-level foreman rule the roost in direct personal ways, exhorting or threatening workers to produce more, watching closely how hard workers work, assigning workers to easy or tough work stations depending on the foreman's fancy, and handing out or withholding pay raises, permission to take time off, overtime, etc., as rewards and disciplines.[3] Once again, personal despotism rules the workplace.

The system of simple control is not the principal organizing device in today's corporate sector. Toward the end of the 19th century, tendencies toward concentration of capital undermined the practice; some firms grew too large for effective simple control. As firms began to employ thousands of workers, the distance between capitalists and workers expanded and the intervening space was filled by growing numbers of foremen, general foremen, supervisors, superintendents, and other petty managers. The unplanned, willy-nilly expansion of intermediate bosses produced an exaggerated harshness on the shop floor — what one observer has aptly termed "the foreman's empire."[4] Here, foreman and hired bosses ruled nearly without restraint, assuming most of the powers formerly exercised by the entrepreneur. They hired and fired, assigned work, set pay rates, disciplined recalcitrants, and drove the work pace. They acted as petty tyrants, dispensing and withholding the various sanctions at their command.

But whereas immediate tyranny had been more or less successful when conducted by entrepreneurs (or foremen close to them), the system did not work well when staffed by hired bosses. The new bosses were caught in the middle of intensifying workplace conflict. On one side, foremen came into conflict with the employers. The new bosses exercised many of the workplace powers of entrepreneurs, but they nonetheless remained hired hands, not capitalists. The interests of capitalists and petty bosses diverged, and foremen began to use their power for their own ends. Owners experienced increasing difficulty in controlling production through these unreliable intermediaries. Sometimes termed "organizational uncoupling," substitution of the foremen's interests for those of the capitalist understandably destroyed the foreman's allegiance to the system.

On the other side, and undoubtedly more serious, the foremen also came into increasingly serious conflict with the workers. Intensified competition — "cut-throat" competition, as it was known — among manufacturers led them to press ever harder in their efforts to extract greater production from their workers. But the firm's workforce had grown much bigger, and with expansion and speed-up came increased consciousness. Then, too, the entrepreneur had profited directly from increased productivity, and a small capitalist's success often derived as much from eliciting cooperation and loyalty from his employees as from exercising the whip. But for foremen, no comparable incentive existed, and the historical evidence demonstrates that simple control via hired bosses produced brutal, severe punishment, abusive supervision, and few positive compensations. The industrial regime had become harsher, and the mix of incentives and sanctions had swung to nearly total reliance on the negative.

These developments inside the firm both reflected and interacted with a broader reorganization occurring throughout the American economy: the transition from the small-business, competitive capitalism of the 19th century to the corporate monopoly capitalism of the 20th. The driving force of capital accumulation pushed successful firms first to merge and then to attempt to make their new positions profitable. This tendency toward centralization increasingly produced a dichotomy in the economy's industrial structure. Big firms with great market power dominated most major industries, while small firms with little market power survived in their interstices and along their periphery. The dual economy was born.

The transition also unleased powerful oppositional forces. The maturing labor movement and an emergent Socialist Party organized the first serious challenge to capitalist rule. From the Homestead and Pullman strikes at the beginning of the period to the great 1919-1920 steel strike that closed it, workers fought with their bosses over control of the actual process of production. Intensifying conflict in society at large and the specific contradictions of hierarchical control in the workplace combined to produce an acute "crisis of control" on the shop floor.

The large corporations fashioned the most far-reaching response to this crisis. During the conflict, big employers joined small ones in supporting direct repression of their adversaries. But the large corporations also began to move in systematic ways to reorganize work. They confronted the most serious problems of control, but they also commanded the greatest resources with which to attack the problems. Their size and substantial market power released them from the tight grip of short-run market discipline and made possible for the first time planning in the service of long-term profits. Their initial steps — welfare capitalism, scientific management, company unions, industrial psychology, etc. constituted experiments, trials with serious errors inherent in them, but useful learning experiences nonetheless. In retrospect, these efforts appear as beginnings in the corporations' larger project of establishing more secure control over the labor process.

The new methods of organization that big employers developed were more formalized, more consciously contrived, more structured; they were, in fact, *structural* forms of control. Two possibilities existed: the more formal, consciously-contrived controls could be embedded either in (1) the physical structure (technology) of the labor process, or in (2) its social structure. In time, employers used both. They found the advantages of structural control (whether in its technical or social variant) to be two-fold. On the one hand, it made the control system less visible to workers, more hidden and institutional; control became a product not of capitalist employment relations, but rather of "technology" or the scale of "modern industry." On the other hand, structural control provided a means for controlling the "intermediate layers," those extended lines of supervision and power.

Technical control tended to emerge out of the employer's attempts to control conflict in the "bluecollar" or production operations of the firm, whereas bureaucratic control grew out of similar conflicts in the burgeoning "white-collar" or administrative functions. Yet, as I argue below, no such simple identification is possible today. The incompleteness of technical control and the increasingly factory character of administrative work has largely obliterated such distinctions.

3. TECHNICAL CONTROL

How something is produced is in large part dictated, of course, by the nature of the product and by the known and available technologies for producing it. Thus lumbering tends to be dispersed in the forests while auto assembly is concentrated indoors, building jet-liners tends to involve a stationary work-object while radio-assembly uses a moving line. In this sense, considerations of the physical efficiency of a technique — for example, the number of times steel has to be reheated as it is processed — distinguish superior from inferior methods. Yet these types of technical considerations by themselves are insufficient for determining what technologies will actually be used.

It is well known that most industries face a variety of possible techniques, and that the relative costs of required inputs will influence which technology is chosen. For example, steel-making can be performed in huge automated factories with much machinery and little labor, as can be seen now in the advanced countries where labor is expensive; or it can be produced in primitive hearths, with greater labor inputs and less machinery, as, for example, in some underdeveloped countries today or in the advanced countries 75 years ago, where machinery is or was expensive. Thus, *within* the known and available technologies, considerable choice is possible.

What is less well known is that there is an important social element in the development and choice of technique as well. Just as it is true that firms confront a range of techniques which tend to provide greater or lesser possibilities for control over their workforces. That is, capitalists may prefer one technique over another because it gives them a strengthened hand in transforming labor power into useful labor. The preferred technique need not be more efficient, but it must be more *profitable*. What is profitable depends on the extent to which purchased commodities (including labor power) result in salable output. Consider, for example, two production techniques, A and B. Technique A is highly efficient, permitting three workers to produce 10 units per day, but it also gives workers substantial power to set their own pace. Technique B is less efficient, permitting three workers to produce at most 8 units per day, but the technology establishes this pace as an invariant daily rate. The two techniques are identical with respect to the per unit use of other inputs. If we take as the "labor input" the labor actually done, the first technique is more efficient. However, if technique A's workers use their control over the labor process to limit how much useful labor they tender in each working day, they do not affect the efficiency of the technique but they do affect the level at which it can be run. For example, they may actually produce only 7 units a day. Technique A remains the more efficient one, but technique B becomes more profitable, since for the same *purchased* inputs, the capitalist winds up with more output in technique B.

Thus, while it remains true that capitalists undoubtedly seek those technologies which are most profitable, we now must admit that there are several considerations which enter into the calculations of profitability. One is physical efficiency, the ratio of the physical output to the material inputs; another is the cost of the various inputs and the value of outputs; yet a third is the extent to which any technology provides managers leverage in transforming labor power into labor done. The way in which the third consideration — control — came to be considered is revealing of the whole process which has revolutionized work in the capitalist era.

Technical control involves designing machinery and planning the flow of work to minimize the labor/labor-power problem. This process occurs simultaneously with the attempt to maximize the purely physically-based possibilities for achieving efficiencies. Thus a social dimension — the inherent class nature of capitalist production — is added to the evolution of technology.

Technical control is "structural" in the sense that it is embedded in the technological structure or organization of production. Technical control can be distinguished from simple mechanization, which merely increases the productivity of labor without altering the elements of control. Thus, for example, use of an electric rather than manual typewriter increases the speed with which a secretary works, but it does not alter how the secretary is directed to the new task, how his or her work is evaluated, or what the rewards or disciplining will be. Mechanization often brings with it technical control, as the worker loses control of the pace or sequence of tasks, but this consequence must nearly always be understood to be the result of the *particular* (capitalist) design of the technology and not as an inherent characteristic of machinery *in general*.

Technical control may also be distinguished from simple machine pacing, although the latter may be considered simply as technical control applied to the individual worker. Machine pacing occurs whenever a worker must respond to, rather than set, the pace at which the machinery is being operated. Building a production pace into machinery has long been a tactic used by employers to try to gain control of the labor process. Yet so long as the machinery affects just one worker or one work team, the conflict over pace and rhythm continues to revolve around and focus on these workers and their boss. For example, such machinery typically can in fact be operated at various speeds, and in this sense it requires bonus schemes, piece-rates, incentive pay, etc., to set the pace. Even where machinery has only one speed, boss and workers can nonetheless agree to turn it off for rest periods, if the machinery in question utilizes only workers in this workplace. The social organization surrounding such machine pacing continues to be that of simple control.

Technical control only emerges when the entire production process of the plant, or large segments of the plant, are based on a technology which paces and directs the labor process. In this case, the pacing and direction of work transcend the particular workplace and are thus beyond the power of even the immediate boss; control here is truly "structural."

Toward the end of the 19th century, the crisis created by the contradictions of simple control set off a search for more powerful and sophisticated mechanisms. This experimentation, often identified with "scientific management" or "Taylorism," both went far beyond the theories and stopped far short of the often silly applications put forward by Frederick Taylor and his followers. In essence, although the scientific management movement self-consciously adopted the rhetoric of mechanical engineering, the actual contribution of Taylor and his followers to the design of machinery was quite small. Yet in the plants and offices of the large corporations, the notion of technical control was by no means ignored. The advantages of continuous flow production beckoned.

While all the corporations at the turn of the century groped toward new structures to control their workers, each firm and each industry faced somewhat different circumstances. In some, the product — whether blast furnace heat, a harvester, or a railroad sleeping car — seemingly involved single-unit or small-batch production; here employers saw little chance to exploit technical possibilities for control, although they did engage in a titanic struggle to break the power of the skilled crafts workers. In these industries simple control was solidified, and the corporations turned to the bribes of bonus schemes, incentive pay, and welfare capitalism to create a more sophisticated control structure. But in other industries, notably meat-packing, electrical products, and autos, the flow of production was more direct. There technology was first recognized as a basis for wider, *structural* control.

Textile manufacturers in the 19th century had developed the basis for technical structuring of the first of the three elements of any control system, the technical direction of the work tasks. The other elements of the control system were less well worked out. In these mills, workers found themselves yoked to machinery which determined their work pace. There was little room for resistance in the workplace, and, lacking a strong union, the workers accepted the work or left.

Meat-packing was another early industry to adopt continuous-flow production —

this time as a disassembly line. When Swift, Armour, and other Chicago packers began using refrigeration to revolutionize slaughtering and meat packing, the old shop-based, small-batch techniques of the abattoir gave way to continuous flow. Investigating the packing houses for a British medical journal, one observer put it as follows:

> . . . outside the big factory buildings there are long, inclined, boarded passages up which the animals are driven. Thus the pigs are brought up to the height of the second floor. As they enter the main building each pig is caught by one of the hind legs. With rope and loop-knot and hook it is slung up, the head downwards and the neck exposed, at a convenient height for the slaughterer to strike. With great rapidity the suspended pigs are pushed on to a sort of passage about four feet broad where their throats are slashed open as they pass along . . . . Within less than a minute the dying pig reaches a long tank full of scalding water and in this the palpitating body is thrown . . . Standing in the damp and steam men armed with long prongs push the swine along. By the time when the hogs have floated down to the other end of the boiling-water tank they are sufficiently scalded for the bristles to be easily extracted. They are now put on a moveable counter or platform and as the hogs pass along other workers scrape the bristles off their backs . . . . At a subsequent stage the body is opened and the intestines are removed.[5]

From the perspective of control, the benefits of such production were immediate and obvious. By establishing the pace at which hogs were driven up the passages and onto the slaughter platform, managers could set the pace of work for the entire workforce. There were, of course, limits, both physical and worker-imposed ones, but each supervisor no longer has primary responsibility for directing the workers. Instead, the line now determined the pace, and the foreman had merely to get workers to follow that pace. Our observer makes this point quite explicit:

> . . . when [the animal is] strung up, the machinery carries [it] forward and men have to run after it to cut its throat, while others follow with great pails to catch the blood; and all this without interrupting the dying animal's journey to . . . the next process of manufacture . . . . On they go from stage to stage of manufacture and the men have to keep pace with them . . .[6]

Thus by 1905 the essentials of continuous flow production, including the possibilities for controlling workers, were established in meat-packing.

With each worker fixed to a physical location in the production process, contact between and among workers nearly ceased. Whereas before workers had made the workday pass more quickly by talking, reading to each other, etc., now each worker simply tended his or her machine. Of particular interest to their employers was the fact that workers had little opportunity to discuss common grievances, compare foremen, exchange views on pay rates or job conditions, etc. Thus, despite their physical proximity, workers had little chance to communicate.

But if continuous flow production appeared first in textiles, meat-packing, lamp-production, and elsewhere, it was the Ford assembly line which brought the technical direction of work to its fullest potential. The automobile industry had its origin in the bicycle plants, where each team (a skilled mechanic and his helpers) performed all the operations necessary to assemble bicycles from separate parts. Carried over into auto plants, this organization slowly gave way as the assembly process began to be broken into parts; each team now added only a limited range of parts to the product, which was then passed on to another team. But it was not until the Highland Park plant opened in 1913 that the endless conveyor finally abolished the craft pretensions of the Ford workers.

The Ford line resolved technologically the essential first task of any control system: it provided unambiguous direction as to what operation each worker was to perform next, and it established the pace at which the worker was forced to work. Henry Ford himself emphasized this aspect of the line by stating as one of his three principles of "progressive manufacture:"

The delivery of work instead of leaving it to the workmen's initiative to find it.[7]

Ford might well have added that the line's "delivery of work" also relieved his foremen of having to push work onto the workers, as was the case in simple control. H.L. Arnold studied the plant in great detail in 1914, and his report provides an excellent source for understanding how the new methods worked out in practice. Ford introduced the first chain-driven "endless conveyor" to assemble magnetos, and Arnold (and co-author L.F. Faurote) wrote,

The chair drive [i.e., continuous assembly] proved to be a very great improvement, hurrying the slower men, holding the fast men back from pushing work on to those in advance, and acting as an all-around adjustor and equalizer.[8]

The Ford line created a "technological necessity" in the sequence of tasks which were to be performed. Despite the fact that many assembly sequences were physically possible, no choice attached to the order in which workers did their jobs: the chassis or magneto or engine under construction came past a worker's station, lacking the part inventoried at that station; it would soon move on to other stations where it would gain every other part. The obvious necessity of adding the part in question at this station was thus established. Arnold and Faurote expressed this point as follows:

Minute division of operations is effective in labor-cost reducing in two ways: first, by making the workmen extremely skillful, so that he does his part with no needless motions, and secondly, by training him to perform his unvaried operation with the least possible expenditure of will-power, and hence with the least brain fatigue.[9]

Thus the line hemmed in the worker, establishing a situation in which only one task sequence was possible.

Similarly, the line established a "technological presumption" in favor of the line's work pace. Struggle between workers and bosses over the transformation of labor power into labor done was no longer a simple and direct *personal* confrontation; now the conflict was mediated by the production technology itself. Workers had to oppose the pace of the line, not the (direct) tyranny of their bosses. The line thus established a technically-based and technologically-repressive mechanism to be used to keep workers at their tasks.

The substitution of technical for human direction and pacing of work simultaneously revolutionized the relation between foreman and workers. Arnold and Faurote explained that

[The Highland Park plant] has applied team work [i.e., division of labor] to the fullest extent, and by this feature in conjunction with the arrangement of successive operations in the closest proximity, so as to minimize transportation and to *maximize the pressure of flow of work, it succeeds in maintaining speed without obtrusive foremanship.*[10]

The line eliminated "obtrusive foremanship," that is, close supervision in which the foreman simultaneously directed production, inspected and approved work, and disciplined workers. In its place, the line created a situation in which the foreman was relieved of responsibility for the first element of the control system. This change marked an important first step away from the simple control model which granted the foreman all the prerequisites of an ''entrepreneur'' within his own shop. Instead, the line brought with it the first appearance of structural control.

The importance of this change is indicated by the small number of ''straw-bosses'' and foremen needed to supervise the Ford workplace. In 1914 about 15,000 workers were employed at all the Ford plants. Leaving aside the top management, this large force was overseen by just 255 men ranking higher than ''workman,'' including:

11 department foremen,
62 job foremen,
84 assistant foremen, and
98 sub-foremen (straw-bosses).

Thus there was one foreman (all ranks) for each 58 workers, an impossible ratio except in a situation in which the foremen no longer directed the sequence of pacing of work.[11]

The foreman in technical control is thus transformed into an *enforcer* of the requirements and dictates of the technical structure. On the assembly line he or she monitors workers to keep them at their tasks — the foreman no longer is busy initiating tasks. The foreman penalizes exceptions to the normal flow of work, rather than personally directing that flow. Moreover, this enforcement is seen as being required by the larger structure. Exceptional circumstances aside, the foreman cannot personally be held responsible for the oppressiveness of the production process. If the legitimacy of the line is accepted, then the necessity for the foreman's job follows. The actual power to control work is thus vested in the line itself rather than in the person of the foreman, and the power relations are made more invisible. Instead of control appearing to flow from boss to workers, control emerges from the much more impersonal ''technology.''

Technical control has since come to be based upon a much more sophisticated technology, of course, than that which was available when the Ford line was introduced. The most dramatic changes in technology have occurred as a result of the invention of new devices to control or ''program'' machinery, including the increasingly pervasive linking of mini- or micro-computers to machines. Yet rather than producing qualitative differences, this new technology is best understood as simply expanding the potential contained in the concept of technical control.

But technical control by itself was not a sufficient advance over simple control to resolve the crisis of control within the firm, and it is not difficult to see why. Technical control provided the possibility of embedding in the technical structure the first element of all control systems (progressively directing the worker to further tasks), but it did little to change the second and third elements (evaluating work performance and enforcing compliance). In early forms of technical control, for example, supervisors had the power to discharge workmen immediately and at will. The second and third elements of control changed little.

Thus technical control by itself was not destined to be the ultimate wrinkle in corporate control. For one thing, it still left open the issue of how to motivate workers. If anything, the Ford plants represented a step *backwards* on this score, since the massive layoffs needed to ''discipline'' those workers who failed to produce according to the line's speed provoked increasingly intense hostility and resistance. The carrot was largely absent, the stick ever-present. The chief weapon, often even a first-resort disciplining device, was the ''reserve army of the unemployed.'' Less drastic penalties (docking pay, suspension, etc.) also existed, but their usefulness varied directly with the potency of the supervisor's major sanction, dismissal. The only real motivator in this system was the worker's fear of being sacked.

But if dismissal was to be feared, either as a threat or as a fact, it was necessary that there be many substitute workers able and available to fill the jobs. The lack of plausible replacements was precisely what had given the old skilled workers their power, and had led, by way of reaction, to their demise. Similarly, in times of tight labor markets (such as during war), workers were relatively confident both that replacements could not easily be found and that, if fired, workers could find other jobs.

Thus, in technical control no less than in simple control, employers had a powerful incentive to make their workers as interchangeable and substitutable as possible. The continuing mechanization eroded the need for skills anyway, making the workforce more uniformly composed of unskilled and semi-skilled machine operatives. But the strictly *control* aspects of work reorganization contributed a further impetus to the homogenizing process.

The tendency to create a common (and degraded) status for all workers was evident in the labor policies of the early Ford plants. The famous Five Dollar Day which Ford announced in 1914 seemed to be a real advance, since $5 was substantially above other wages being paid to factory labor. Yet the higher wage was not essential for filling the company's vacancies; although it did create an enormous labor surplus. The day after the announcement there were 10,000 people outside the gates clamoring for jobs; for months afterward, as Francesca Maltese reports, the job-seekers "continued to clog the entrances to Ford's employment offices."[12] The lesson was not lost on the people employed inside the gates: the Company would have no trouble finding replacements for recalcitrant workers.

Similarly, other Ford labor policies attempted to generate a "ready reserve" of surplus labor. Thus it is no coincidence that the first large-scale entry of blacks into northern industrial employment was in the Ford plants. By 1926 Ford employed 10,000 black workers, over 90 percent of Detroit's black industrial labor force. The Company cast its net even further, drawing into potential employment the physically handicapped (generously labelled "substandard men"), young boys, and others. It was energetic in establishing a recruiting bureau to attract workers from other cities. Thus technical control both continued the need for surplus labor as a ready disciplinarian, and strengthened its derivative, the increasing substitutability and homogenizing of the labor force.

The attempt to generate highly visible pools of surplus labor was a response to the crisis of control on the shop floor, and it affected primarily the blue-collar workers. But technical control's influence extended also to the lower-level clerical staff, and here technical control introduced a new stimulus towards homogenization.

The corporation in part addressed the problem of controlling the white-collar staff by reorganizing their work along the lines of technical control. The routinization of clerical work has been extensively investigated elsewhere, and it need not be repeated here.[13] The essential point is that many clerical workers — those performing key-punching, typing of forms, and other standardized operations — were transformed into operatives of simple machines. Given the nearly universal nature of high school education by 1930, they could easily be replaced, and they became subject to the discipline of the reserve army. They had been reduced to the level of homogeneous labor.

But even as the new system solved some of the corporation's labor problems, it created other and more serious ones. Technical control yoked the entire firm's labor force (or each of the major segments thereof) to a common pace and pattern of work set by the productive technology. In so doing, technical control resolved for the individual workplace and the individual foreman the problem of translating labor power into labor. But it did so at the cost of raising this conflict to the plant-wide level. Thus the basic conflict was *displaced,* not eliminated.

At first this displacement was not realized. Throughout the 1910's and even more so during the relatively conflict-free 1920's, technical control appeared to have decisively turned the power balance in favor of the capitalists. Individual sabotage, disputes between workers and their foremen, and grumbling over wages continued, of course, but these could be managed and the power of technology drove the work pace.

The flaw in this naivete was exposed dramatically and at heavy costs to the capitalists. Irving Bernstein describes what happened in the auto plants.

> On December 28 [1936] a sudden sit-down over piece-rate reductions in one department in Cleveland swept through the plant and 7000 people stopped work; Chevrolet body production came to a complete halt.
>
> On December 30 the workers in Flint sat down in the huge Fisher One and the smaller Fisher Two plants. Combined with the stoppage in Cleveland, this forced the closing of Chevrolet and Buick assembly operations in Flint. On December 31 the UAW sat down at Guide Lamp in Anderson, Indiana . . . By the end of the first week of the new year, the great General Motors automotive system had been brought to its knees.[14]

The cost of lifting the shop-floor conflict out of the individual workplace and raising it to the plant-wide level was not apparent. Technical control linked together the plant's workforce, and when the line stopped, every worker necessarily joined the strike. Moreover, in a large, integrated manufacturing operation, such as auto production, a relatively small group of disciplined unionists could cripple an entire system by shutting down a part of the line.

Technical control thus took relatively homogeneous labor — unskilled and low-skilled workers — and technologically linked them together in production. This combination proved to be exceptionally favorable for building unions. The Flint strike was not the first sit-down, nor were such strikes confined to plants with moving lines. But the sit-downs were most effective in the mass-production industries of autos, electrical products, rubber, and textiles. More broadly, "quickie" sit-downs (strikes of a few minutes or an hour or two), sabotage, wildcats, and other labor actions were much more effective in plants organized according to technical control.

The CIO success of the 1930's clearly resulted in part from wider factors not considered here: the depression, the increasing concentration of industry, the conscious activity of militant union organizers. Yet the rise of industrial unionism was also significantly a response to technical control, and it marked the beginning of an effective limitation on that system.

These limits were nowhere more clearly revealed than at GM's Lordstown (Ohio) Vega plant several decades later.[15] GM had come to Lordstown with the intention of achieving a dramatic speedup in output. Its strategy was two-pronged. First, GM re-designed the plant and machinery to accommodate production at roughly 100 cars per hour (one every 36 seconds); this rate represented a 40 percent increase over the one-a-minute average that prevailed in most of its plants. Second, the company recruited a new labor force, one without long traditions of struggle to restrict industrial output. The plan didn't work.

The 1972 revolt at Lordstown gained much publicity and even notoriety, and justifiably so, but mostly the event attracted attention for the wrong reasons. On one side, Lordstown was declared atypical (and hence not really worrisome) because of the youthfulness of the workers (average age 24), because of the plant's counter-culture ambience, and because of the workforce's lack of industrial experience and discipline. On the other side, Lordstown was heralded as the new wave of working-class revolt for precisely the same reasons. Yet what really should have been noted was that Lordstown may have represented technical control's final gasp as an ascendant control system. The most advanced industrial engineering went into the design of the plant, but only resistance and the breakdown of control came out. Undoubtedly youth, counter-culture, and lack of industrial conditioning contributed to GM's problems, but it is precisely for such populations that technical control is designed.

Machine-pacing and de-skilling through use of "smart" machines continue, and it is even expanding in the lower-level clerical occupations. Moreover, in the "new" areas of investment — the U.S. South and the Third World, for example — technical control remains a first principle for factory organization. Equally, in the economy's small-firm periphery such organization remains important. But technical control can never again by *itself* constitute an adequate control system for the core firm's main industrial labor force.

Indeed, in its principal areas of application, technical control has evolved into a more mixed system, with unions playing a decisive (even if limited) role. The second and third elements of control become *jointly* administered by management and unions (with unions as junior partners). Evaluation and reward/discipline become matters for mutual determination in accordance with collectively bargained rules, procedures, and protections. Arbitrary dismissal and other punishments are limited by arbitration and grievance machinery; job "rights" become contractual obligations rather than "privileges" dispensed by bosses; wages and benefits are established within an overall contract structure. Technical control thus becomes supplemented, in the unionized sector of industry, by the elaborate administrative mechanisms achieved by unions to protect workers from the ravages of the earlier, more pure system of technical control.

The resistance engendered by technical control set off a new search for methods of controlling the workplace. In firms like IBM, Polaroid, Xerox, Gillette, and others, management devised a different system of structural control, this time based on the social or organizational structure of the firm. The result is what is here termed *bureaucratic control*.

4. BUREAUCRATIC CONTROL

The defining feature of bureaucratic control is the institutionalization of hierarchical power. "Rule of law" — the firm's law — replaces "rule by supervisor command" in the direction of work tasks, in the principles for evaluation of those tasks, and in the exercise of the firm's power to enforce compliance. Work activities become defined and directed by a set of work criteria: the rules, procedures, and expectations governing particular jobs. Thus for the individual worker, his or her job tends to be defined more by formalized job descriptions or "work criteria" attached to the job (or, more precisely, by the interpretation given to those criteria by his or her supervisor and higher levels of supervision) than by specific orders, directions, and whims of the supervisor. Moreover, it is against those criteria that the worker's performance is measured. Finally, company rules and procedures carefully spell out the penalties for poor performance and, more importantly, the rewards for adequate performance.

The criteria contain both written and unwritten requirements, and the essential characteristic is just that the worker is able to ascertain them and that they are highly stable. The firm no longer alters the worker's tasks and responsibilities by having the supervisor tell the worker to do something different; rather, it "creates a new job" or "redefines the job." From these criteria derive the "customary law" notions of "equity" or "just cause" in firing, promotion, and job assignment.

Top-echelon management retain their control over the enterprise through their ability to determine the rules, set the criteria, establish the structure, and enforce compliance. For the latter concern (enforcing compliance), bureaucratic organization again marked a departure from simple control. In simple control, power is vested in individuals and exercised arbitrarily according to their discretion, but with bureaucratic control power becomes institutionalized by vesting it in official positions or roles and permitting its exercise only according to prescribed rules, procedures, and expectations. Rules governing the exercise of power become elements of the work criteria defining supervisor's jobs. Superiors as well as subordinates become accountable to top-down control; the system thus broadens its reach to the "intervening layers" of petty officials.

Work activities can never be completely specified by job criteria in advance, and "rule of law" can never completely replace "rule of command" in an hierarchical enterprise. Some situations or problems always arise which need to be handled in an *ad hoc,* particularistic way, and so supervisors can never be content merely to evaluate and never to instigate. The shift to bureaucratic control must therefore be seen as a shift toward relatively greater dependence on institutionalized power, and bureaucratic control comes to exist alongside and be reinforced by elements of simple control. Bureaucratic control becomes, then, the predominant system of control, giving shape and logic to the firm's organization, although not completely eliminating elements of simple control.

The imposition of bureaucratic control in the monopoly firm had four specific consequences for the social relations of the firm.

1. The power relations of hierarchical authority were made invisible, submerged and embedded in the structure and organization of the firm, rather than visible and openly manifest in personal, arbitrary power.
2. Bureaucratic control, because of its emphasis on formal structure and status distinctions, made it possible to differentiate jobs more finely. Organizational as well as technical (i.e., production) aspects of jobs defined their status. Each job appeared more unique and individualized by its particular position in the finely graded hierarchical order, by the job criteria which specified work activities, and by its distinct status, power, responsibilities, and so on. Elements of the social organization of the firm which differentiated between jobs were emphasized, while those which created commonality diminished.

These two changes tended to erode the bases for common worker opposition. Increasingly the individual worker came to face an impersonal and massive organization more or less alone. In general, the work environment became less conducive to unions and strike or other opposition activities. In those bureaucratized industries where unions remained (or were subsequently organized), more and more the unions accepted the organization of work and directed their energies toward non-control issues (wages, fringe benefits, and procedures for promotion, hiring, and firing). Even where unions turned their attention to the work activities themselves, their efforts were mainly defensive, directed toward making the job criteria more explicit and openly articulated; while this tended to undermine the authority of arbitrary foremen, it strengthened the legitimacy of the overall structure. As the common bases of work experience declined, so did the possibility for united worker action concerning control over work.

3. The role of the supervisor was transformed from that of active instigator, director, and overseer of work activities to that of monitor and evaluator of the worker's performance. The superior now judged the subordinate's work according to the work criteria. Moreover, the supervisor's own work — his or her use of sanctions, for example — became subject to much greater evaluation and control from above.

4. Bureaucratic control has made possible, and indeed fostered, career ladders and institutional rewards for tenure and seniority within the firm — that is, what labor market economists have called "internal labor markets." These mechanisms by which job vacancies are filled — for example, job bidding systems, regularized promotion procedures requiring periodic supervisors' evaluations, customs restricting job access to apprentices or assistants, and "management development" programs — all tend to tie the worker to continued employment in the firm. Good jobs up the job ladder become available only for workers who stay with the firm. In all these ways, the firm structures relations so that identification with the company pays off, while resistance is penalized.

This new system of control appears in modified or partial form in many corporations, but it is seen most clearly in the "modern management" firms that have consciously planned it. Polaroid is a good illustration.[16]

Each job within the Polaroid plants has been analyzed and summarized in an "approved description" (or, in the case of salaried employees, an "exempt compensation survey"). Such descriptions, in addition to stating pay, location, and entry-requirement characteristics for each job, set forth in considerable detail the tasks which the worker must perform. That is, the company writes down in these descriptions the rules, procedures, and expectations that I have referred to more broadly as "work criteria."

One such description is that for the job of a machine operator who assembles SX-70 film. All the regular duties of such operatives are set forth in considerable detail, including the operation of the "automatic assembly machine," responsibility for "clearing jams" and making adjustments, monitoring the machine's output, maintaining the machine, etc. In addition, precise direction is given for responsibilities in the event of the crew chief's absence (the operative is responsible). Finally, even the "irregular" duties are spelled out: training new operators, conducting special tests for management to improve productivity or quality, and so on.

It might be thought that the company would find it profitable to make such a careful listing of duties and responsibilities only for management or skilled positions. But the job description indicates that "SX-70 Film Assembly Operator" is rated only at the level of PCV-13; from the company's wage schedule one can see that roughly half of the hourly workers — not to mention the salaried employees — have higher-level jobs.

The content of each job, what the worker is supposed to do while at work, is thus formalized and made explicit and routine in these "approved descriptions." In contrast to simple control, where bosses assign work tasks by command, or to technical control, where sequencing is engineered into the machinery, bureaucratic control at Polaroid directs production through work criteria. In large part these are *written* rules and directives. They may also include unwritten procedures that the company inculcates during training programs. But what is central is that whatever their form, they emanate from the contrived formal organizational structure of the firm.

Of course bureaucratic control never fully replaces direct and personal command, and Polaroid's compensation manual is careful to point out that any approved description

> does not attempt to define all elements of a position. It defines Main Function, Regular Duties, and Irregular Duties.

Implicitly, irregular Irregular Duties or even the occasional Exceptional Circumstances may require efforts outside the job description, and as we shall see, the evaluation procedure permits plenty of scope for supervisors to reinforce cooperation in such matters.

Yet the fact that bureaucratic specification of tasks is less than complete should not obscure the tremendous importance of what it does do. The fine division and stratification of Polaroid's workers, in combination with the carefully articulated job descriptions (work criteria), establish each job as a distinct slot with clearly defined tasks and responsibilities. A presumption of work and its specific content — that is, a presumption of what constitutes a "fair day's work" — has been established.

Directing the worker is only the first control-system element. At Polaroid, great attention is given to the second element as well. Polaroid appraises every worker's performance on a regular schedule. Undoubtedly supervisors on the job consistently monitor, assess, and reprimand or praise workers as production occurs. Yet more formally, at least once per year, supervisors must evaluate each worker's performance.

Polaroid's bureaucratic control immediately provides the structure for evaluation. Workers are evaluated on the tasks and duties laid out in the job description. Although (e.g.) the significance of any particular task or the severity of the assessment undoubtedly varies with the supervisor, the job description provides a limited, explicit, and set basis for rating each worker's performance.

The criteria, and what the worker is supposed to do on the job, are known by both worker and boss; so also is the evaluation. Evaluation is an open process, with the final supervisor's rating available for the worker's inspection.

Formalizing and making explicit the basis for evaluation also in turn permit Polaroid's first-line and intermediate supervisors to be evaluated themselves. Their appraisals of subordinates can be subjected to higher-up scrutiny.

For example, a "production manager" at Polaroid normally supervises ten to 25 production workers. In addition to directing and monitoring production, he or she must

> interpret and administer personnel policies. Select, train, and evaluate individual and team performance. Initiate actions on merit increases, promotions, transfers, disciplinary measures.

Yet in all these activities the production manager reports to a "general supervisor — production" whose job it is to

> select and train first-line supervisors. Evaluate performance of supervisors and determine actions on salary and promotion. Review and approve supervisor determinations on merit increases, promotions, disciplinary measures.

Hence the first-line supervisor's room for maneuver is restricted by the imposition of inspection by higher command.

The content as well as the form of Polaroid's evaluation provides insight into its control system. Each worker is rated in each of four equally important categories on a seven-point scale, with the seven levels defined as performances appropriate to the seven pay steps built into each job classification. Of the four categories, only the fourth ("skill and job knowledge") deals with whether the employee is capable of doing the assigned job. One category treats the quantity of work done. The remaining two categories — "quality" (meaning the worker's dependability and thoroughness) and "work habits and personal characteristics" — are concerned with work behavior rather than actual production achieved. These categories rate the degree to which the employee is responding appropriately to the work criteria and to the bureaucratic organization of the workplace.

A separate category in the evaluation checks up on "attendance and punctuality." Here mere judgments are not enough, and the form demands more precise information: a space is left for percentages and frequencies. Once again Polaroid is not measuring output but instead compliance with rules.

The formal system of evaluation does not perfectly mirror the actual system, of course, and personality clashes, favoritism, and personal jealousies often occur. Yet formalizing evaluation — making it periodic and written, basing it on established criteria, opening it to the employee's inspection, subjecting it to higher scrutiny — tends to limit and constrain the arbitrariness of the system.

Within the bureaucratic control system, as in any control system, it is insufficient simply to set out the tasks and later check to see whether they have been done; capitalists require rewards and sanctions to elicit or compel behavior in accord with their needs. Polaroid's policies demonstrate the considerable advance in sophistication and subtlety which bureaucratic control allows over prior systems.

The company's power to hire and fire underlies its ability to get purchased labor power transformed into labor done. This power comes into play in a couple of ways. Insubordination and other explicit "violations of company rules and of accepted codes of proper behavior" (to use the company's language) can trigger immediate dismissal. Dismissal also threatens workers who get bad evaluations. The company states that the evaluations are designed to weed out "mediocrity," and, of course, "mediocre" job performance is determined by how faithfully the worker fulfills the work criteria. In addition to periodic reviews — new employees after three months, older workers at least once a year — both old and new workers are on almost continuous probation. So the penalty for failing to comply with stated performance standards is readily evident.

Yet even though bureaucratic control at Polaroid continues the historic capitalist right to deprive workers of their livelihood, this power has been re-shaped by the bureaucratic form. Exceptional violations aside, workers can be dismissed only if, after receipt of written warnings specifying the improper behavior, they continue to "misbehave." Moreover, higher supervisory approval is required and any grievance can be appealed. Thus even the process of dismissal has become subjected to the rule of (company) law.

If bureaucratic control has re-shaped the power to fire (and other negative sanctions), it has brought even greater change by introducing elaborate positive rewards to elicit cooperation from the workers. At Polaroid, the structure of rewards begins with the seven possible pay steps within each job. Each of these steps represents a five-percent increment over the previous pay. After having been hired into a particular job, the worker is expected in a period of months to pass through the first two ("learning") steps. What is actually to be learned is not so much job skills as "work habits, attendance, attitude, and other personal characteristics" which

Polaroid sees as necessary for dependable performance. Moreover, the learning may occur more on the side of the company (learning whether the new worker has acquired the proper work habits through prior schooling or jobs) than on the part of the employee.

As he or she demonstrates "mastery" of the "normal work routine," the worker moves up into the middle three ("experienced") pay steps. At these levels, work "quality can be relied on," the worker is "reliable," and "good attendance [has been] established;" or more simply, "personal characteristics are appropriate to the job." Progress is by no means automatic, but the worker who tries reasonably hard, who makes little trouble, and is an "average performer" moves, in time, through these steps.

Finally, there remain the final two ("exceptional") pay steps for workers who set "examples . . . to others in methods and use of time" and who suggest ways of "improving job methods" and "increasing effectiveness of the group." These workers need to show "cooperation, enthusiasm, [and exceptional] attitude." Supervisors are reminded that there must be "special justification for 'outstanding' ratings such as these."

The pay steps within each job classification thus establish a clear reward (up to 30 percent higher pay) for workers who obey the rules, follow the work criteria, cooperate, and in general do their jobs without creating difficulty. Yet the pay scales within job classifications are merely a prelude to rewards available to those who move up the corporate hierarchy — that is, who transfer to new job categories.

"It is [Polaroid's] general policy to fill job openings by promotion from within the Company . . ." The mechanism for filling jobs is a posting system. The company lists each job, along with skill requirements and other job characteristics, on bulletin boards. Employees wishing to move to the new job can "bid" for the job, setting in motion a process of application, interview, and selection. Unlike many union plants, Polaroid's selection is not based solely on seniority, although "seniority should always be considered." Instead, jobs are filled by "the persons considered to be among the most qualified;" qualifications include, among other things, work habits and attendance.

Thus, through the posting system, Polaroid's 15 hourly and ten salaried grades of jobs come to represent a second scale of rewards for the enterprising employee. Although no employee can realistically expect to start at the bottom and rise to the top — such stories better support myth than represent reality — the salary differential nonetheless suggests the range of rewards available to the employee who accepts the system: the top pay, at $160,644 annually (in 1975), is over 28 times the lowest pay of $5678 per year. More to the point, the top hourly pay ($9.26) more than triples the bottom ($3.01), and the pay of the 30-35 percent of the firm's workforce which is salaried rises from the top hourly pay.

Yet even the within-job and between-job differentials do not complete the positive incentives which Polaroid dangles before its workers. Every employee who stays at the job for five years earns an additional five-percent bonus. Seniority is also a factor in being able to obtain job transfers and promotions. Finally, the company's lay-off policy is based on an elaborate "bumping" system in which seniority is the key criterion. For example, during the 1975 recession nearly 1600 employees were laid off; employees in departments where there was no work bumped less senior workers in other departments or even in other plants.

Polaroid's structure thus provides tremendous rewards — higher pay, more rights, greater job security — to workers who accept the system and seek, by individual effort, to improve their lot within it. Moreover, the considerable rewards to workers who stay long periods at Polaroid insure that this identification will be a long-term affair. Organizing efforts to build a union at Polaroid have failed due in large measure to this structure.

To be understood fully, Polaroid's organization of its workers must be seen as a system — a structure in which power is institutionalized and the various elements of control fit together. Most importantly, it is the system which directs work, monitors performance, and rewards cooperation or punishes recalcitrance. Insofar as it works, people only carry out roles that the system assigns them, with circumscribed responsibilities and "proper" modes of behavior. By contrivance, Polaroid's exercise of power has been embedded in the firm's social relations.

One of the clearest manifestations of the systematic character of control is the elimination of arbitrary and capricious rule by bosses. Most importantly, supervisors' treatment of their underlings, including their evaluation of workers' performance, is subjected to scrutiny and is regulated by higher-ups. That treatment is also constrained from below, as workers have rights: they can file a grievance when they feel the rules are not being followed, they can inspect their supervisors' evaluations of them, they can demand explanations when they have been passed over for a job they bid on. Except for the highest echelons (where people can change the system itself), superiors as well as subordinates are enmeshed in the system.

A second feature of Polaroid's system is worth emphasizing. As its major way of motivating workers, the company has explicitly moved away from reliance on negative sanctions, on penalizing failure, and moved toward positive incentives, toward rewarding cooperation. All elements of control — not only rewards but the very structure of jobs and the process of evaluation as well — have been bent to make these incentives efficacious. This feature is especially striking relative to prior systems of control. Of course for troublemakers or chronic slackers the sack is still always available; but the attractions of the sophisticated range of promotions, step pay raises, seniority bonuses, and other positive rewards work for most employees.

The positive incentives, the relief from capricious supervision, the right to appeal grievances and bid for jobs, the additional job security from seniority — all these make the day-by-day worklife of Polaroid's workers more pleasant. They function as an elaborate system of bribes, and like all successful bribes, they are attractive. But they are also corrupting. They push workers to pursue their self-interests in a narrow way as individuals, and they stifle the impulse to struggle collectively for those same self-interests.

All this elaboration of job titles and rules and procedures and rights and responsibilities is, of course, neither accidental nor benevolent on Polaroid's part. It is simply a better way to do business. As workers are isolated from each other and as the system is made distinct from the bosses who supervise it, the basic capitalist-worker relation tends to shrink from sight. The capitalist's power has been effectively embedded in the firm's organization.

For a time, bureaucratic control appeared to have resolved the problem of control — it was the first system without contradictions. Indeed, at present the corporations that have carried it furthest have been quite successful in forestalling unionism and in containing worker resistance. Yet this success is deceptive. While the opposition to bureaucratic control remains more a potential than a pressing reality, it is growing and already we can begin to see the main lines of attack. This opposition appears as the demand for workplace democracy.[17]

Workers' response to bureaucratic control, in the U.S. at least, has resulted primarily in individual and small-group discontent rather than collective action. This individualistic opposition emerges in part from the failure of the labor movement to challenge new forms of control. In the absence of a well-articulated critique, the systemic roots of experiences producing individual resentment remain obscure. The lack of a collective response can also be partially traced, however, to the inherent properties of bureaucratic control; its stratification and re-division of workers makes collective action more difficult. Workers' failure to respond collectively is, then, a measure of bureaucratic control's success in dividing workers. Together with the lack of a self-conscious movement challenging it, bureaucratic control has resulted in individual, not collective, opposition.

Thus bureaucratic control has created among American workers vast discontent, dissatisfaction, resentment, frustration, and boredom with their work. We do not need to recount here the many studies measuring alienation: the famous HEW-commissioned report, *Work in America,* among other summaries, has already done that. It argued, for example, that the best index of job satisfaction or dissatisfaction is a worker's response to the question: "What type of work would you try to get into if you could start all over again?" A majority of both white-collar workers and blue-collar workers — and an increasing proportion of them over time — indicated that they would choose some different type of work. This overall result is consistent with a very large literature on the topic.[18] Rising dissatisfaction and alienation among workers, made exigent by their greater job security and expectation of continuing employment with one enterprise, directly create problems for employers (most prominently, reduced productivity).

Individual or small-group opposition cannot by itself, however, seriously challenge employer control. Such opposition has existed throughout the history of capitalism without posing a real problem. Only the *collective* power of workers can effectively threaten the organized power of capitalists. Moreover, productivity loss by itself is not so serious either, since capitalists depend on average, not peak, productivity. What makes the rising individual frustration with capitalist control a source of potentially revolutionary change is the fact that an *alternative, higher-productivity* method of organizing work beckons. That truth emerges from the many experiments with worker self-management. An astonishingly high proportion of such experiments result in (a) relaxing of management's prerogative to make the rules, and (b) higher productivity.[19] The former is the peril that capitalists face in introducing workers' management; the latter is the lure, and it has proved to be a powerful attraction.

Capitalists themselves are led, even forced, to introduce the very schemes that threaten their grip. They have been the most important force behind actual experiments in workplaces. They have sponsored innumerable efforts in job enrichment, job enlargement, Scanlon Plans, worker self-management, worker-employer co-management, etc. Thus the logic of accumulation increasingly drives capitalists to try to unlock the potential productivity which lies inside economically secure producers who both identify with their enterprise and govern their work activities themselves. They try to obtain this higher output "on the cheap," by granting limited amounts of each of the needed components: some security within the overall capitalist context of insecurity, partial identification with work within the relations of private ownership, and limited self-government within authoritarian enterprise.

The trouble is that a little is never enough. Just as some job security leads to demands for guaranteed lifetime wages, so some control over workplace decisions raises the demand for industrial democracy. Thomas Fitzgerald, Director of Employee Research and Training at GM's Chevrolet Division and a former GM first-line supervisor, stated this point directly; Fitzgerald explained to the readers of the *Harvard Business Review* that, once workers begin participating, the subjects of participation . . . are not necessarily restricted to those few matters that management considers to be of direct, personal interest to employees . . . . [A plan cannot] be maintained for long without (a) being recognized by employees as manipulative or (b) leading to expectations for wider and more significant involvement — "Why do they only ask us about plans for painting the office and not about replacing this old equipment and rearranging the layout?" Once competence is shown (or believed to have been shown) in say, rearranging the work area, and after participation has become a conscious, officially sponsored activity, *participators may very well want to go to topics of job assignment, the allocation of rewards, or even the selection of leadership. In other words, management's present monopoly [of control] can in itself easily become a source of contention.*[20]

That this concern is no idle threat is evident from an incident in the 1960's at Polaroid. The company set up a special worker-participation project involving some 120 film-pack machine operators. The production requirements did not seem especially promising for the experiment; making the new film packs called for high-quality operation of complex machinery in the face of a pressing deadline. Workers on the project spent one hour each day in special training, two hours doing coordinating work, and five hours operating the machinery. According to Polaroid's "organization development" consultant, the film was brought into production on time, and "most people think we would never have gotten it out otherwise." Nonetheless, the experiment was liquidated, not for efficiency reasons but rather because democracy got out of hand. Ray Ferris, the company's training director, explained:

[The experiment] was *too* successful. What were we going to do with the supervisors — the managers? We didn't need them anymore. Management decided it just didn't want operators that qualified.[21]

5. THE PRESENT SITUATION

The social relations of the workplace can only be understood as a product of an on-going dialectic. The unfolding logic of the accumulation process creates new circumstances for both capitalists and workers, circumstances embodying both new constraints and new possibilities. On the one hand, capitalists are pushed by competition to seek new ways to reduce unit labor costs at the same time that the concentration of capital gives them new resources with which to conduct this search. On the other hand, workers are subject to new forms of control while they continually press for their needs based on what they experience, what they perceive, what they think possible. Together, capitalists and workers clash in the sphere of production over the general issue of the transformation of labor power into labor. More concretely, capitalists and workers struggle over the pace of work, workplace "rights," issues of safety, relief from the immediacy of the reserve army sanction, and myriad other specific aspects of capitalist production.

This history of accumulation and class conflict provides and "transmits from the past" definite circumstances which impinge upon the present. Contemporary labor processes are subject to three quite distinct sets of the social relations of production at the point of production: simple control, technical control, and bureaucratic control. Each system contains within it important variations on the general theme of the exploitation of wage-labor.

The existence of distinct systems of control in the labor process has far-reaching implications for the formation of the modern American working class. For one thing, the nature of workers' resistance to workplace tyranny differs markedly depending upon the organization of the workplace. In simple control, workers tend to struggle against the effects of boss's personal despotism. In technical control with joint management/union administration, workers resist the technically-imposed production pace as well as struggle for expansion and enforcement of the collectively-bargained "rights." In bureaucratic control, workers are beginning to press for the introduction of workplace democracy. Thus, in these workplace-specific struggles, the needs and demands of workers turn out to be quite different because the manner of the workers' exploitation also differs.

The effects of these divisions in the labor process extend far beyond the workplace. They provide an immediate basis for the oft-noted segmentation of labor markets and the more widely observed division (or "fractionalizing") of the American working class. They even, I argue elsewhere, impart a new (i.e., post-1945) dynamic to American politics.[22]

This, then, is the element of the labor-process dialectic that Braverman misses. Technical aspects of production — de-skilling, degradation of work, creation of a mass of machine-operatives, etc. — can only be understood within this simultaneous development of the social relations of production. For, fundamentally, capitalism is not driven by technology but rather by the imperatives of appropriating surplus labor.

NOTES

[1] See my *Contested Terrain: The Transformation of the Workplace In the 20th Century* (forthcoming from Basic Books) for a more extended treatment.

[2] Karl Marx, *The Eighteenth Brumaire of Louis Bonaparte,* in Robert C. Tucker, ed., *The Marx-Engels Reader* (New York: Norton, 1972), p. 457.

[3] Ann Bookman, *The Process of Political Socialization Among Women and Immigrant Workers* (unpublished Ph.D. thesis, Harvard University, 1977).

[4] Daniel Nelson, *Managers and Workers* (Madison, Wisconsin: University of Wisconsin Press, 1975), Chapter III.

[5] *The Lancet,* No. 4246 (January 14, 1905), p. 120.

[6] *Ibid.,* p. 122.

[7] Henry Ford, "Progressive Manufacture," *Encyclopedia Britannica* (Cambridge: Cambridge University Press, 1927).

[8] H.L. Arnold and L.F. Faurote, *Ford Methods and the Ford Shops* (New York: The Engineering Magazine Co., 1915).

[9] *Ibid.,* p. 245.

[10] *Ibid.,* pp. 6, 8 (emphasis added).

[11] *Ibid.,* pp. 2, 46.

[12] Francesca Maltese, "Notes Towards a Study of the Automobile Industry," in R. Edwards, M. Reich, and D. Gordon, eds. *Labor Market Segmentation* (Lexington, Mass.: D.C. Heath, 1975).

[13] See Harry Braverman, *Labor and Monopoly Capital* (New York: Monthly Review Press, 1974).

[14] Irving Bernstein, *Turbulent Years: A History of the American Worker, 1933-1941* (Boston: Houghton Mifflin, 1970), pp. 524-525.

[15] Stanley Aronowitz, *False Promises* (New York: McGraw-Hill, 1972), Chapter 1.

[16] All quotations, data, etc., concerning Polaroid are taken from internal documents that the company made available to me.

[17] I consider here only the workplace-oriented opposition. In *Contested Terrain* (op. cit.) I consider the broader and potentially more revolutionary opposition, rooted in bureaucratic control, that appears in the political sphere.

[18] See, for example, Special Task Force to the Secretary of Health, Education, and Welfare. *Work in America* (Washington, D.C.: U.S. Government Printing Office, 1972), and Harold Sheppard and Neal Henick, *Where Have All the Robots Gone?* (New York: Free Press, 1972).

[19] See David Jenkins, *Job Power* (New York: Doubleday, 1973), and Juan Espinosa and Andrew Zimbalist, *Economic Democracy* (New York: Academic Press, 1978).

[20] Thomas Fitzgerald, "Why Motivation Theory Doesn't Work," *Harvard Business Review*, July-August 1971, p. 42 (emphasis added).

[21] In Jenkins, op. cit., pp. 313-315.

[22] See my *Contested Terrain* (op. cit.).

9.   Management — Preliminary Argument*

Andrew Friedman

1. TYPES OF MANAGERIAL STRATEGIES

Management[1] under the capitalist mode of production has always involved two rather different, but closely related functions.

First, there is the co-ordination of the various activities undertaken by the firm. Flows of input materials and instruments of labour must find their way to workers at well-timed intervals for each activity. Finances must be available from sales and borrowings to pay for labour power, materials and tools. The final output must be marketed. This job of co-ordination is part of any complicated economic process.

Second, there is the exercise of authority over workers. This second function of management is peculiar to productive activity in class-divided societies. Under capitalism, the capitalist buys labour power from the worker as he would buy any other commodity. But labour power is peculiar in that it is possible for labour power to create more value in the labour process than it costs to produce that labour power. When the capitalist buys labour power he buys the *possibility of exploitation*, because whatever is produced in the labour process legally belongs to the capitalist. Also, legally, the capitalist controls what the worker does in the labour process, within broad socially defined limits. As pointed out in Chapter 2, the capitalist is *encouraged*

---

* "Management — Preliminary Argument" by Andrew Friedman from *Industry & Labor: Class Struggle at Work and Monopoly Capitalism*. Copyright © 1977 by Andrew Friedman. Reprinted by permission of the Macmillan Administration Ltd., London and Basingstoke, and Humanities Press, Inc., New Jersey.

to realise this possibility as much as he can because of his avarice and because of competition. Marx described co-operation, division of labour and mechanisation as methods by which capitalists *might technically realise* the possibility for exploitation represented by the act of labour power purchase.

The final ingredient for exploitation is the theory and practice of exercising capitalist authority over labour power in the labour process. The capitalist or the manager may order the worker to do something, but how can he actually get the worker to do that thing, and to do it well and quickly? Certainly capitalists have often exercised their legal right to fire the worker who does not perform well, but the capitalist's problem would remain if the replacement worker also performed unsatisfactorily. Also many capitalists have considered the performance of all their employees to be unsatisfactory.

While the capitalist may turn to outside judicial or military power to discipline recalcitrant workers, even this may not achieve the obedience desired. To extend an old saying, you can lead a horse to water, you can even whip it for not drinking, but you still cannot force it to drink.

Marx emphasised this managerial problem under capitalism by calling labour power "variable capital." When the capitalist buys tools or raw materials he can determine their value in the labour process with a precision which is impossible when dealing with human beings. The capitalist knows that a certain portion of his outlay on constant capital will be transferred to each unit of production and he can account for this capital in terms of lay-out costs or depreciation. But when the capitalist buys labour power, he buys what is on the one hand a potentially malleable commodity, but what is on the other hand a commodity ultimately controlled by an independent and often hostile will. The exercise of managerial authority over labour power may be subdivided into two aspects. First, top managers try to mould labour power to fit in with changes in overall organisation or techniques more or less dictated by market conditions. Second, top managers try to subdue or limit workers' independent control over their actions once particular tasks have been assigned or general orders given.

These two aspects are closely related. It may be that top managers will try to reorganise the labour process in order to reduce workers' exercise of independent action, as well as simply to fit in with increasing relative surplus value as when machinery is introduced. Nevertheless it will be useful to separate worker resistance to reorganisations of the labour process planned by top managers from worker resistance to existing organisation. To put it another way, managerial attempts to realise more of the potential surplus value represented by their variable capital may be separated from attempts to retain the planned or expected value of that variable capital.

Broadly, there are two major types of strategies which top managers use to exercise authority over labour power — Responsible Autonomy and Direct Control. The Responsible Autonomy type of strategy attempts to harness the adaptability of labour power by giving workers leeway and encouraging them to adapt to changing situations in a manner beneficial to the firm. To do this top managers give workers status, authority and responsibility. Top managers try to win their loyalty, and co-opt their organisations to the firm's ideals (that is, the competitive struggle) ideologically. The Direct Control type of strategy tries to limit the scope for labour power to vary by coercive threats, close supervision and minimising individual worker responsibility. The first type of strategy attempts to capture benefits particular to variable capital, the second tries to limit its particularly harmful effects and treats workers as though they were machines.[2]

Both these types of strategies have characterised management throughout the history of capitalism, but generally the Responsible Autonomy type of strategy has been applied most consistently to privileged workers and the Direct Control type of strategy to the rest.

What has changed with the coming of Monopoly Capitalism? With the rising size and complexity of firms' operations, the rise of well-organised worker resistance among less skilled workers; and the incorporation of science directly into capitalist productive activity, management has become a more conscious, a better organised, and a more scientific activity. With the growth of monopoly power top managers have been able to experiment with new managerial techniques with less fear that failure will surely lead to financial ruin. Thus with Monopoly Capitalism came managerialism, meaning the proliferation of theories of how best to manage firms which have been based on some trace of scientific method.[3] Also, with the coming of Monopoly Capitalism, top managers have had to deal more specifically with *organised* worker resistance. This has meant a rise in relative importance of the Responsible Autonomy strategy, particularly increased use of techniques to co-opt worker organisations.

Marx concentrated on the pressure of the industrial reserve army, which allowed capitalists to maintain harsh disciplinary procedures to enforce managerial authority over the majority in factories. But given organised worker resistance among the less skilled, direct, harsh disciplinary methods may simply disrupt productive activity. Internal labour markets have grown in importance. Within these markets top managers have found co-option of certain groups and conciliation to be more effective than blanket coercion. Within large firms in particular, financial incentives and other concessions have been offered to encourage worker effort and to ensure compliance with changing managerial directives. Also systems by which managerial authority has been delegated have become increasingly complex. Hobsbawm stated, "Capitalism in its early stages expands, and to some extent operates, not so much by directly subordinating large bodies of workers to employers, but by subcontracting exploitation and management" (1968:297). But this delegation of managerial authority has continued long beyond capitalism's early stages. What was once carried out via quasi-market transactions in the form of subcontracting is now carried out through complex bureaucratic structures incorporating many layers of middle managers, and often several layers of trade union bureaucrats and a fat book on Procedure. (Of course the benefits top managers gain from union organisation and established Procedure arise from managerial adaptations to worker resistance, and therefore benefit can quickly turn to bane for top managers.)

A more detailed discussion of Direct Control and Responsible Autonomy strategies and their limitations may be found in Chapter 7, Sections 3 and 4, and Chapter 8, Section 1. These strategies are also discussed in Friedman [1977].

2. MANAGEMENT AND MARXIST THEORY

Marxists have generally treated the Direct Control strategy as *the* theory and practice of capitalist control over the labour process. In fact Lenin argued for the introduction of Taylorian scientific management into Soviet organisation of production in 1918. He found in scientific management "a number of the greatest scientific achievements in the field of analysing mechanical motions during work, the elimination of superfluous and awkward motions, the elaboration of correct methods of work, the introduction of the best system of accounting and control, etc." (1918:259).

Recently, in an extremely important book, Harry Braverman [1974] has reminded us that Taylor's system was not a method for elaborating correct methods of work. It was a system for increasing the rate of exploitation of alienated labour and, one should add, of counteracting worker resistance.

Braverman correctly criticises Lenin for confusing social relations in productive activity specific to exploitation in the capitalist mode of production with technological factors or forces of production which are more independent of the mode of production (though they are shaped by the mode of production). ·Lenin confused authority during productive activity with co-ordination of complex processes. Both are managerial functions in the capitalist labour process, but only the latter is general to all modes of production. But Braverman too must be criticised for confusing one *particular strategy* for exercising managerial authority in the capitalist labour process with *managerial authority* itself.

Just as strict disciplinary rules were a particularly popular managerial strategy of top managers in the early years of the first industrial revolution, so strict work measurement and minute division of tasks have been popular managerial strategies, particularly during the first decades of the twentieth century. But Taylorian scientific management is not the only strategy available for exercising managerial authority, and given the reality of worker resistance, often it is not the most appropriate strategy from top managers' point of view (see Section 3 of the next chapter for a detailed discussion of Taylor's theory of scientific management).

Let us trace Braverman's arguments in detail. Braverman begins by distinguishing human from animal labour following Marx (*Capital,* vol. 1, pp. 173-4). Human labour is conscious and purposive, while other animal labour is instinctive. Human labour is guided by conceptual forethought. While human labour in the abstract involves both conception and execution, in its particular social form conception may be separated from execution. 'The conception must still precede and govern execution, but the idea as conceived by *one* may be executed by *another*' (Braverman 1974:51). The unity of conception and execution, thus dissolved from the standpoint of the individual, would then be reasserted in the larger organisation or community which contained the individuals concerned. Braverman's major theme is that, as the capitalist labour process develops, conception is gradually separated from execution and conceptual activities are progressively concentrated among fewer and fewer people. Why should this occur?

Braverman notes the uncertainty and variability which labour power presents to the capitalist because ultimately it is controlled by the subjective state of the workers (p. 57). For Braverman the antagonism between worker and capitalist in the labour process is important primarily because of its exacerbation of this variability and uncertainty characterising labour power. For Braverman the problem of management is the problem of reducing this uncertainty by capturing control over the labour process

The principal weapon by which management captures this control is to separate conception from execution through the division of labour and mechanisation. This progressively reduces the skill and imagination concerning individual tasks required of the mass of workers. This separation through de-skilling, which was an unconscious tendency of capitalist production in early years, becomes a conscious and systematic strategy of management with the development of scientific management. With each worker performing only a simple task, conceptual activities and scientific development would be concentrated in the hands of managers (pp. 120-1). While scientific management seeks to increase managerial control by separating conception from execution, assuming a given technology, the technical development of machinery has also been shaped by this desire. As machines have become more automatic and more complex, the degree of judgement and control exercised by the machine operator over the labour process has declined. Knowledge of the machine becomes a specialized trait segregated from the actual machine operators. The pace at which the machine operates becomes a clearer managerial prerogative as control over that pace is centralised and often removed from the site of production to the planning office (pp. 187, 194-5).

For Braverman Taylorian scientific management *is* the fundamental practice of management in twentieth-century advanced capitalism.

> The popular notion that Taylorism has been ''superseded'' by later schools of industrial psychology or ''human relations,'' that it ''failed'' . . . represent[s] a woeful misreading of the actual dynamics of the development of management.
>
> Taylor dealt with the fundamentals of the organisation of the labour process and of control over it. The later schools of Hugo Munsterberg, Elton Mayo, and others of this type dealt primarily with the adjustment of the worker to the ongoing production process as that process was designed by the industrial engineer (p. 86).

Here Braverman's inadequate treatment of organised worker resistance is evident. First, labour power is variable both because individual human beings are intelligent and guided by subjective states, and because workers are alienated from the labour process and actively build organisations to resist managerial authority. These two aspects of labour power present top managers with two qualitatively different problems. Worker resistance does not simply make labour more uncertain, taking uncertainty to imply randomness. Top managers are often reasonably certain that if they were to do certain things (such as to dismiss someone for a reason which workers consider grossly unfair, or to change manning levels in some crucial way without prior negotiations) it would provoke a work stoppage. In a sense, the first sort of variability is so complex that employers cannot calculate probabilities as to its immediate prospect, while against the second sort of variability top managers can calculate reasonably good probabilities of occurrence. This is the distinction between uncertainty and risk made popular in economics literature by Frank Knight [1921]. The separation of conception from execution by division of labour, mechanisation or scientific management is not necessarily the best strategy for management in organising the labour process when confronted with worker resistance. Techniques which reduce managerial reliance on worker goodwill may not be most appropriate for insuring against the effects of determined worker resistance or for directly reducing expressions of that resistance.

Disadvantages of the Direct Control strategy are discussed in the next chapter. These disadvantages are particularly evident when demand is fluctuating widely (necessitating lay-offs), or when technical change is rapidly occurring.

Braverman suggests a strict division between design of the work process and selection, training, manipulation, pacification, and adjustment of the worker to fit that design. But management is not a two-tier process where work organisation designed by engineers is sacrosanct and primary, and the exercise of managerial counter-pressure to worker resistance is secondary. Both are managerial problems and are measured in terms of profits. If the costs of scientific management in terms of worker resistance or lost flexibility are too great, alternative strategies will be tried and these will involve changes in the organisation of work processes.

3. ON CONTROL

The word 'control' has caused confusion when applied to productive activity because it has been used both in an absolute sense, to identify those 'in control', and in a relative sense, to signify the degree of power which people have to direct work. This confusion has become particularly evident in discussions of workers' control. On the one hand, one wants to make clear that recent schemes for participation in the managerial decision-making apparatus or group technology do not confer workers' control in an absolute sense because the fundamental capitalist relations of production remain. Top managers are still 'in control' in that they, in their role as representatives of capital, continue to initiate changes in work arrangements and continue to exercise authority over the work activity of others. Also the products of workers' labour still belong to the capitalists. On the other hand, one wants to allow the possibility that changes in organisation of work or decisions about work may increase the power which workers may exercise to act within production according to their own judgement and their own will (over such things as their work pace, the particular tasks they do and the order in which they do that work). One wants to allow for shifts in the 'frontier of control', in spite of the continuation of the capitalist mode of production (Goodrich [1920]), and in spite of the continuation of managerial control in the absolute or identifying sense.

The notion of control by management in the absolute sense is further complicated by a possible confusion of control with creation. To control is to exercise restraint or direction upon the action of a force or thing. The force or thing, when referring to productive activity under the capitalist mode of production, is separate from its controller. It stands apart from the capitalists and the managers as well as the workers. People are not free to create their own history consciously, according to their needs and abilities, because capitalist society is class divided. The society, the mode of production and the associated labour process at any point in time, is created out of the dynamic of class conflict and the competitive struggle. Top managers are constrained in their power over productive activity by pressure to accumulate and the need to counteract worker resistance. While top managers are clearly 'in control' of productive activity, their freedom to create and recreate this activity is severely limited by the relations of capitalist production.

If workers' control implies the possibility of those participating in productive activity exercising this creative sort of freedom, then workers' control could never be realised under the capitalist mode of production. Also its content would be very different from managerial control under capitalism. It could not mean a simple change in personnel 'in control'.

The notion of relative control is also complicated by the desire to identify 'progressive' changes from the workers' point of view. The difficulty is, of course, that workers sold their labour power out of economic necessity in the first place, rather than as part of a choice expressing their will and judgement. The overall organisation of work in capitalist enterprise is not a matter of worker choice. Nevertheless some changes are fought for and won by the workers and this means some increase in the power of workers to resist further managerial initiatives. On this point it may be useful to distinguish changes in work organisation and decision making which workers have fought for, and those which managers have initiated. Changes which top managers have initiated which increase workers' relative control over productive activity are likely to represent attempts to counteract, contain, or co-opt worker resistance, particularly when labour power markets are tight. Changes in work organisation in Swedish car factories may be viewed in this way. Faced with high labour turnover and absenteeism in Volvo and Saab car factories (encouraged by the scarcity of white male workers in Sweden's near full employment economy over the past few years), the car firms have made great publicity over their attempts to 'humanise' car assembly work. This has been 'achieved' by replacing long assembly lines with small working groups who assemble entire components or sub-assemblies together. Apparently these 'experiments' have been more limited in scope than the Swedish publicity implies.

At Fiat similar experiments were tried, but the impetus came from the workers and the changes were won only after long struggles. Eventually worker initiatives concerning work organisation within certain plants were superseded by initiatives concerning Fiat's overall investment policy and particularly its activity in southern Italy.

The different source of initiatives in the Swedish situation compared with the Italian one may be crucial in deciding whether the changes in relative control were progressive from the workers' point of view. The mere fact that the changes came out of victorious struggle in the Fiat case strengthens worker resistance and encourages further initiatives. Also changes conceived by the workers are more likely to be controlled by them in their detailed implementation. In the Fiat case managerial control over productive activity was weakened.

In both cases monotony was reduced and workers' relative control or autonomy over precisely what they do at any particular moment and the speed at which they do that work was increased. In the Swedish case, however, managerial control over productive activity as a whole was increased by loosening top managers' *direct* control over worker activity in order to reduce worker resistance. This conclusion makes sense only if one explicitly recognises the management of worker resistance to be an integral part of managerial control over productive activity.

Authority over workers, direction of worker activity and co-ordination of flows of materials, products and cash are all necessary aspects of managerial control over productive activity within the capitalist mode of production. If top managers decide to reduce their direct control over the direction of worker activity and the co-ordination of materials flows in order to increase their authority over workers, success in implementing this strategy will result in greater managerial control over productive activity as a whole, greater managerial control, given the reality of worker resistance. This will not occur if top managers have made a mistake. But mistakes, while possible, are a complication which may be ignored when speaking generally.[4]

So top managers may loosen direct control over work activity as part of a strategy for maintaining or augmenting managerial control over productive activity as a whole (Responsible Autonomy), or they may be forced to loosen direct control as part of a general shift in control over productive activity in favour of the workers. In this book I shall be focusing on the former situation because it has been the more common.

NOTES

[1] Management is taken to mean the process or activity of managing economic enterprises or firms, rather than the group of top managers who direct those enterprises. To manage originally meant to handle or to train a horse in its paces.

[2] While it may seem confusing to enumerate these different categories, the value of the distinctions stems from the different approaches which top managers take toward different groups of workers at different times, largely in response to different forms and strengths of their resistance. Also the distinction will help to clear up what I believe to be a major error of Marxist analysis of the labour process, discussed in Section 2 of this chapter.

[3] Scientific method is taken to mean the formulation of general laws or hypotheses based on systematic observations.

[4] This ignores more than simply managerial mistakes. I am not dealing explicitly with the general contradiction of capitalism at the moment: that the basic interests of capitalists and workers are opposed to each other because of exploitation, and that masking that opposition or dampening worker resistance by financial concessions, more pleasant working conditions or ideological persuasion all create expectations of the system which become increasingly difficult

to satisfy — particularly as safety valves outside the capitalist mode of production come to be incorporated. The problem with leaving the story at this highly abstract level is that the growth of worker resistance tends to be treated as a homogeneous development in which one strategy or tactic appears to be as good as another and all developments appear progressive because progress towards 'the revolution' is assumed to be inevitable and inexorable. Once we admit that the world's date for changing the mode of production is not fixed for some particular future moment, we must accept that some moves by workers can be regressive *and* that some moves by top managers may successfully forestall fundamental change (see Armin [1975]). The managerial strategies described in this chapter are concerned with attempts to forestall fundamental change and get on with the business of accumulation, not with affecting the probability of revolution in some ultimate sense. I am avoiding dealing with the latter issue.

REFERENCES

Braverman, H.
1974 *Labor and Monopoly Capital.* New York: Monthly Review Press.
Friedman, A. L.
1977 "Responsible Autonomy Versus Direct Control Over the Labour Process," *Capital and Class,* 1.
Goodrich, C. L.
1975 *The Frontier of Control.* London: Pluto.
Hobsbawm, E. J.
1968 *Labouring Men.* London: Weidenfeld & Nicholson.

Knight, F.
1921 *Risk, Uncertainty and Profit.* Boston: Houston Mifflin.
Lenin, V. I.
1916 *Imperialism, the Highest Stage of Capitalism.* Moscow: Progress.
1918 "The Immediate Tasks of the Soviet Government," in *Collected Works.* London: Lawrence & Wishart, 1962.
Marx, K.
1867 *Capital, vol. 1.* London: Lawrence and Wishart, 1970.

10.   Bureaucracy and Domination: Managerial Strategy in Turn-of-the-century American Industry[1]*

Paul Goldman and Donald R. Van Houten

Modern industrial bureaucracy in the United States has its historical foundations in the period between the 1890s and the beginning of the First World War, when manufacturing establishments were transformed from chaotic, ad hoc factories to

* "Bureaucracy and Domination: Managerial Strategy in Turn-of-the-century American Industry" by Paul Goldman and Donald R. Van Houten from *International Yearbook of Organizational Studies* edited by Dunkerly and Salaman. Copyright © 1980 by Routledge & Kegan Paul Ltd., London, Boston and Henle. Reprinted by permission.

rationalized, well-ordered manufacturing settings.[2] Economic histories of the period focus on industry's rapid growth, on merger and combination, and on technological innovation in the productive process. Labor histories emphasize the continual strife between capital and labor. While perhaps more subdued than in the two previous decades, labor conflict was substantial. The interplay between these two forces — management's desires and labor's struggles — established a framework for industrial bureaucracy that persists to this day.

In this paper we hope to probe for the roots of three interrelated mechanisms as they emerged after 1890: (1) detailed division of labor and the "degradation of skills," (2) labor discipline through hierarchical relations, and (3) the monopolization of knowledge at the management and technician levels. Each of these strategies developed as employers sought to integrate efficiency on the shop floor, that is to match labor power with machine power maximizing productivity at the lowest possible cost, and social control, that is motivation of workers who, overtly and covertly, resisted the then oppressive conditions of factory life. We suggest that bureaucratic technique came not just from "natural" evolution towards increased rationalization, but from a political dialectic in which the struggle between workers and employers played a major role.[3]

Aside from intensive labor organization and protest, including highly publicized strikes, two problems specific to workplace organization caused employers deep concern. First were the astronomical rates of labor turnover, often reaching as high as 100 percent (Nelson, 1975:86-7). Workers, skilled and unskilled, native-born and immigrant, frequently left their jobs in good times and even during recessions. Business periodicals discussed labor turnover in hundreds of articles per year (Bilbut, 1959:356).[4] The phenomenon persisted throughout the first two decades of the century and managers were constantly forced to seek mechanisms either to reduce turnover substantially or to organize work in a fashion that diminished its increasingly high cost.[5]

A second source of concern was the persistence of skilled worker and foreman control over the everyday production process. Working knowledge and skill, and the solidarity that frequently accompanies it, gave workers greater autonomy on the shop floor than many employers felt they could tolerate. Even unskilled workers, when acting collectively, could exercise significant control over the quantity of output and the time required for each task. As Montgomery (1976:486) suggests, "working people clung to their traditional, spasmodic, task-oriented styles of work and to a social code which was less tightly disciplined, less individualistic and less exploitative than that which industrialization was imposing upon them." Skilled workers, particularly, were often able to resist, even if temporarily, the institution of new machinery that threatened either their jobs or their craft (Stone, 1975; Yellowitz, 1977a:198; 1977b).[6]

Employers were only partially prepared to deal with such difficulties or to devise appropriate organizational solutions to them. During the last third of the nineteenth century, both the size and the nature of industrial firms increased beyond immediate comprehension. While in 1870 few companies operated plants employing more than 500 workers, thirty years later there were more than a thousand such firms. Growth rates were particularly sharp for producers of capital equipment, for their sales increased twice as fast as those making consumer goods (Faulkner, 1951:117). Mergers and the general trend towards industrial concentration reinforced rapid growth. Moreover, growth and innovative technology mutually stimulated one another. Anticipating later growth (and contemporary research on the effects of large size on modern organizations[7]), Marx suggested that quantitative expansion of the workplace would lead to qualitative changes in it social relationships. As he describes the process, "even without an alteration in the system of working, the simultaneous employment of a large number of laborers effects a revolution in the material conditions of the labor-process" (Marx, 1967:324).

Despite the prevailing managerial view that horse-sense combined with practical experience prepared employers to face ever-changing conditions, organizational expertise and labor relations "technique" lagged behind productive capacity (Baritz, 1960:18; Korman, 1967:65). One historian characterizes the administrative techniques of the day as "chaotic, confused and wasteful" (Litterer, 1963:370). Another describes the managerial climate as follows:

> Consider the setting at the turn of the century. . . . The science of management was in its infancy. Management lacked systemization. . . . There was a noticeable absence of written instructions to executives and workmen. Internal management was reminiscent of an earlier era. An inventory of management around 1900 would show that there was [little concern for] departmental coordination of efforts to raise employee efficiency (Wood, 1960:405).

In short, employers struggled to organize production in a more systematic fashion (Palmer, 1975:34; Chandler, 1962:10). Litterer (1963:373ff.) suggests that employers faced the problem of "organizational uncoupling," whereby the growing division of labor and fractionation of work at headquarters and on the shop floor progressed more rapidly than did the newly required coordination and reintegration of these tasks. Without the latter, full advantage of the former could not be realized.

Employers, however, were by no means immobilized. Within a relatively brief period they confronted the challenges posed by workers, and many of them implemented effective organizational change. Some changes were refinements of earlier strategies, some frankly emulated successful innovations of other firms, some were drawn from the business and technical periodicals which began to discuss managerial issues, and others resulted from the ideas of reformers and consultants such as Frederick Taylor and his disciples (Hawkins, 1963). One principle was clear and constant in all innovation: no change was to erode employers' traditional prerogatives. A manifesto by the National Metal Trades Association in 1899 preached "management's sole right to conduct a business, refusal to deal with striking employees, absolute freedom to discharge, unilateral determination of wages, and establishment of apprenticeship rules" (Bernstein, 1960:155). But whether or not employers overestimated their power and underestimated the contribution made by formal and informal actions of workers, many saw that effective policy had to align methods of social control with the drive towards efficiency.

EFFICIENCY, SOCIAL CONTROL AND THE EMERGENCE OF BUREAUCRACY

The quest for efficiency, and its relationship to emergent bureaucracy, is central to both Marxist and functionalist treatments of industrial modernization. Functionalist sociologists and historians, drawing only on aspects of the Weberian legacy, see rationalization of the workplace as an inevitable part of the logic of historical progress. Bureaucracy is the structural instrument by which productive efficiency can be guided. Jacoby (1973:148) exemplifies this general position in the following passage:

> The development of bureaucracy . . . has its roots in the efforts of industrial society to establish an efficient structure, to realize technical objectivity, and to integrate man into a

mechanized system. The decisive factor in the advance of bureaucratic organization has always been its purely *technical* superiority over any other system (emphasis in original).

Formal organization, including the division of labor, hierarchy of authority, standardized procedures, and so on, is a technical solution to the administrative confusion resulting from rapid growth (Litterer, 1961, p. 473). Many innovative turn-of-the-century businessmen shared this view as they attempted to apply the same scientific principles to management that had been used to develop new tools and machinery.

This functionalist perspective is incomplete rather than incorrect. Generally, proponents underestimate or ignore the coercive nature of the bureaucratization process and the degree to which conflicts with labor helped determine the shape of industrial bureaucracy. Recent Marxist scholarship on the historical evolution of the labor process has addressed this issue. Marglin (1974), for example, suggests that during the English industrial revolution employers developed and maintained hierarchical structures in order to guarantee themselves an essential role in the production process. Edwards (1975:7-11) notes that bureaucratic control replaced "simple hierarchy" as more subtle mechanisms than arbitrary supervision were needed to mitigate growing trade union organizations. Braverman (1974:85-139) indicates that managers used Taylorism to concentrate working knowledge in management's hands in order to control productive technique more authoritatively, a view shared by Aiken (1960:77, 164), McKelvey (1952:17ff.), Montgomery (1977:98), and Yellowitz (1977b:5).[8] Montgomery (1976:507) sees the managerial response to the control workers did have over the production process as *"enforced* standardization of method, *enforced* adoption of the best and *enforced* cooperation."

What these writers share is a widespread agreement that bureaucratic reforms were in part generated by employers' reaction both to the power and the cost of labor, especially skilled labor. This perspective is supported by other historians and contemporary commentators such as Drury (1916:23), Bernstein (1960:49), Brody (1965:58, 147), Ozanne (1967:61) and Wiebe (1967:210). The general response to this pressure, and the thrust of many bureaucratic innovations, was management's attempt to free itself from uncertainty in the labor market (Yellowitz, 1977b). Despite employers' relative success in this endeavor, labor resisted their efforts vigorously throughout the era (Aiken, 1960; Davis, 1975; Montgomery, 1976; McKelvey, 1952; Nadworney, 1955; Yellowitz, 1977a).

There is little doubt that rationalization improved industrial efficiency in a purely technical sense or that it lowered the unit costs of production.[9] A recent study of the carriage and wagon industry in Cincinnati provides an example of the financial advantages resulting from changing labor practices. Buggies costing 45.67 dollars to produce by hand in 1865 cost only 8.10 dollars with machine production in 1895. The machine-made buggy required 116 workers and 40 hours of labor compared to 6 workers and 200 hours for the hand-made product (Duggan, 1977:312). Scientific management, with its adherents' desire to make "machines of men as cannot err," symbolizes but does not fully explain the drive towards efficiency. It had its basis in hard-headed financial logic: if the production process can be so structured that workers use only minimal and routine skills, labor can be paid lower average wages. Therefore, high turnover is less costly; workers who do not accept jobs on employers' terms can be easily discharged. The emergence of bureaucracy itself has a political dimension that is often neglected by those writing in modern Weberian tradition.

An emphasis on efficiency alone, however, tends to assume that human activity, especially that of workers, is constant and predictable. There is a second current to the

Marxist approach to industrial development that deals with this issue. If the advantages of new technology specifically, and the efficiency movement generally, were to be realized, workers had to be rendered unwilling (or unable) to resist capitalist hegemony. The dwindling market for traditional skills and the labor surplus resulting from massive immigration eroded the worker's individual and collective bargaining position. More important, detailed division of labor and associated bureaucratic mechanisms encouraged workers to internalize the values and structures of the industrial workplace. To the degree that this occurred, employers were successful in creating a climate of greater social control. Gordon (1976:22) suggests that this, too, is efficient:

> A production process is qualitatively (most) efficient if it maximizes the ability of the ruling class to reproduce its domination of the social process of production and minimizes producers' resistance to ruling class domination of the production process.

In the same essay, he suggests that "there are no universally efficient forces and relations of production . . . capitalism has developed a production process which not only delivers the goods, but also controls its workers" (Gordon, 1976:20). In sum, efficiency of technique, however necessary it was for dramatic increases in production, was not sufficient to accomplish that goal unless accompanied by equal attention to social control.

The more thoughtful managers of the day were no doubt aware that social control was a spin-off of industrial bureaucracy. Others may have discovered it as a (largely) unanticipated, though welcome, consequence. But employers could not limit their efforts to the shopfloor alone. Some businessmen also instituted humanistic practices under the general rubric of "welfare work." These included pensions, insurance, recreation centers, classes, and sometimes even profit-sharing. While such programs partially resulted from employers' sincere concern for their workers' welfare, they were also motivated by the belief that satisfied, secure workers would be more highly motivated by goals of increased productions.[10] A pamphlet issued by Metropolitan Life ("Welfare Work," 1917:27) also referred to the problem of turnover in explaining that their welfare programs were designed to "increase the permanency of the working force in order to secure loyalty and interest on the part of the employees." Employers differed in their motivation, and some perhaps were ambivalent. William Tolman (1909:1) suggested that "some employers . . . felt they owed their operatives something more than wages. . . . Others again improved the condition of their operatives because it paid in actual dollars and sense." This view of contradictory motives is shared by several recent students of business history (Derber, 1970:206; Ozanne, 1967:245; Hagedorn, 1958:137). In an acerbic passage, Hagedorn (1958:134) notes that businessmen were indeed frightened: "to read the pleas of the social engineers for sanitary drinking cups and decent ventilation is to realize how assiduously welfare workers followed the trail of class warfare, the doctrines of which they sometimes seem to have confused with the germ theory." The potentially wide scope of welfarism, however, was limited by its cost and only large firms could afford substantial efforts.[11] The programs themselves, in fact, became relatively bureaucratized, as did the personnel, employment, and welfare departments that came to administer them.

The major contribution of recent Marxist approaches to American industrial history is the hypothesis that managerial consciousness of its own needs for social control was systematically applied to problems of shopfloor management. The interrelationships between efficiency and social control have been hinted at in general terms by Edwards (1975), Gordon (1976), Marglin (1974), Palmer (1975), and Stone (1975). Only the latter, however, has attempted to focus on specific bureaucratic methods. Palmer (1975:34, 40) speaks of the need to secure both stability and productivity and of management's difficulties in securing hegemony at a time when they lacked control over basic work processes. Both Palmer and Gordon, however, note a potential contradiction between stability and productivity since emphasis on one strategy may conflict with the other.[12] In his study of International Harvester, Ozanne (1967:175) asserts that its managers themselves clashed over the competing approaches of the "iron fist" versus the "velvet glove." In examining specific management practices, we contend that the two strategies were generally not in conflict, and that each was successful to the degree that they were complementary and mutually reinforcing.

Employers, as they came to realize the limits of the heavy-handed approach to labor, became necessarily more interested in winning the "hearts and minds of workers" if this could be done without sacrificing productivity and profits. The financial and public-relations costs of bitter labor disputes were simply too high, and threatened not only the individual capitalists but the system as a whole.[13] Thus, as Edwards (1978:195-7) suggests, employers moved away from the implicit coercive aspects of traditional hierarchy to bureaucratic control, vesting power in positions rather than people and unifying the organization by formal, almost legalistic standards. The shift emphasized long-term stability and growth rather than immediate profits and, according to Chandler (1977:10), was a dominant feature of the emerging managerial synthesis of the day. Efficiency in the technical sense was always a fundamental consideration, but successful employers were equally cognizant of the impact of these changes on workers. As clothing magnate Joseph Feiss (1916:29) stated, "scientific management will not have completed its mission when it has determined in each industry the best method of handling materials and equipment . . ., but when it has determined also the principles which underly correct methods of handling men."

Specifically bureaucratic mechanisms, notably the detailed division of labor-formalized hierarchy, and the isolation of technical knowledge from workers, proved the most successful means of effecting both social control and efficiency. As an industrial strategy bureaucracy had predated late-nineteenth-century America; in fact Wedgewood had refined formal procedures in his English pottery works more than a century earlier (McKendrick, 1961; Finer and Savage, 1965). But modern bureaucratic technique only became widespread in the United States around the turn of the century. Even then it was not universal. The instances we cite in the subsequent sections come largely from manufacturing in the North and in the upper Midwest, from extractive industries in the south. Larger firms, more complex and with more resources, tended to be most innovative. Each company moved at its own pace, but that increased for most that survived.

DETAILED DIVISION OF LABOR AND THE DEGRADATION OF SKILL

The social division of labor as a means for increasing human productivity is a legacy from prehistoric men and women. Its primary advantage is occupational specialization, enabling workers to concentrate upon and develop those skills necessary to produce particular items or types of product, for example shoes, glassware, or cutlery. The detailed division of labor divides these larger crafts, and the workers who perform them, into far more narrow and interdependent tasks within a workshop or factory. Braverman (1974:72-3) suggests that "the division of labor in the workshop is a special product of capitalist society . . . imposed by planning and control." It adds to the advantage of specialization the benefits of sequential ordering of operations and minimization of set-up time for each task.

Detailed division of labor is particularly appropriate to mass-production manufacturing wherein goods are produced in quantity and intended for a broad market rather than the luxury trade. For example, as Wedgewood widened his selling activities in the 1770s, he also divided and trained the 278 workers in his Etruria pottery works into 40 different job specialties (McKendrick, 1961:33). Yet, each of these workers, like those in most American factories a hundred years later, performed a variety of tasks. Mass-production techniques at the end of the nineteenth century resulted in far more extreme division of labor, and the typical worker came to carry out repeatedly one or only a very few operations.

The assembly line epitomized work fractionation, although the general principles were applied to other tasks as well. Assembly (or, in the specific case, disassembly) practices were apparently first employed on a large scale in the meat-packing industry just after the Civil War (Giedion, 1948:93). Several decades later, Upton Sinclair's epic description of the progress of a newly slaughtered pig through a packing plant provided an image of emerging industrial methods:

> It was sent upon a trolley ride, passing between two lines of men, who sat on a raised platform, each doing a certain single thing to the carcass as it came to him. One scraped the outside of the leg; another scraped the inside of the same leg. One with a swift stroke cut the throat; another with two swift strokes severed the head, which fell to the floor and vanished through a hole. Another made a slit down the body; a second opened the body wider; a third with a saw cut the breast-bone; a fourth loosened the entrails; a fifth pulled them out. . . . There were men to scrape each side and men to scrape the back; there were men to clean the carcass inside, to trim and wash it . . . (Sinclair, 1906:40-1).

This process differed fundamentally from the ways in which the farmer or the butcher would have slaughtered and dressed pork to prepare it for consumption. Meat packing on a large scale was faster and cheaper (per finished animal) than the skilled work of professional meat cutters. In this respect it conformed to Henry Ford's description of mass production:

> the focusing upon a manufacturing project of the principles of the power, accuracy, economy, system, continuity and speed. And the normal result is a productive organization that delivers in quantities a useful commodity of standard material, workmanship and design at minimal cost (Faulkner, 1951:121).

Mechanization and detailed division of labor went hand-in-hand in late-nineteenth-century industry and allowed management to attain a higher ratio of material output per given invested dollar. In short the combination resulted in greater efficiency. The trend towards increed use of machines seemed inexorable. The ratio of horsepower to wage earners rose from 2.1 in 1889 to 2.8 ten years later and 3.2 in 1914 (Rosenblum, 1973:65). Machines were costly, but in most cases not exorbitant. A careful study of technological innovation in the nineteenth century characterizes typical investment in the metal trades as follows:

> Around 1880 the value of machinery . . . per worker in a plant manufacturing interchangeable mechanisms was between $300 and $350. The most accurate machine tool known at this time, the automatic pinion cutter of the Hampden Watch Company cost $4,000. In the 1890's, flat-turrent lathes sold for about $1,000; the first high-precision Norton grinding

machine was designed to sell for $2,500; and the cost of building the first multiple-spindle automatic lathes was about $500 each (Strassmann, 1959:145).

The investment in machinery paid handsome dividends, at least for those firms large enough to afford them. Moreover, according to Yellowitz (1966b:18), "they allowed employers to pay good wages and cut prices, something that was impossible when hand labor dominated industry." But as we shall see below, higher relative wages accrued to unskilled and semi-skilled workers and skilled craftsmen's wages declined relatively. A final advantgae of machinery came in its ability to overcome human limitations. As Rosenberg (1976b:131-3) points out, machine processes, especially when compared to our finite human capabilities, are susceptible to continuous and indefinite improvements in both speed and accuracy. Machines did, however, eliminate a substantial proportion of the back-breaking labor performed by unskilled laborers.

The acquisition of machinery encouraged employers to refine the division of labor within the factory and to rationalize productive operation. Aiken (1960:4) contends that scientific management itself was devised primarily to exploit the potential of new machines, especially cutting tools which could be run two to four times faster than previous implements.[14] Rosenberg (1976a:64) agrees tha the signal characteristic of "modern industry" was the sophistication with which employers divided the production process. Most advances became associated with a machine process to which scientific knowledge and bureaucratic procedure might be applied. Specialization took on a more limited meaning, referring not to workers' skills but to their activities. Walker (1967:93) describes how the marriage of machinery and specialization requied each worker to perform a task that is predetermined, endlessly repetitive, paced by mechanical means, and demands only minimal skills and surface attention. One employer told William Tolman (1909:2) that "I want machines so simple in their operation that any fool can run them."

Because of their relative expense, all tools and equipment had to be run continuously since down time represented waste and lost opportunity. Workers had to labor harder and faster than ever and this took a heavy toll. Under the Taylor system the pace was intense; one typical worker reported that it was "a great strain on my nerves . . . by the time I get through I am not able to do anything else when I get home" (Aiken, 1960:216). One immigrant wrote home the following about his "good" twelve-hour job: "work all time, go home, sleep" (Brody, 1965:100). Management was aware of the rigors of the work they offered. Ford foreman James O'Connor noted that 'there were a lot of people who wouldn't even try. They thought they couldn't do it," but production superintendent Max Wollering remarked that "if the first man can't come up to . . . standard, try another. That was Henry's scheme of the thing." (Russell, 1978:39, 35).

The demands and potentialities of machines had purely bureaucratic consequences as well. They encouraged the growth of job analysis and job descriptions. These were generally prepared by white-collar staff (located, in firms using scientific management, in the "planning and laying-out" departments). Thus managers could instruct workers with increased precision (Litterer, 1961:475; Nelson, 1975:151). Workers could be moved from job to job with relative ease. Indeed Joseph Feiss (1916:48) suggested that it was important for them to learn "to perform more than one kind of work. In this way they can be used to help out in cases of emergency, some of which occur daily in every large establishment because of absences and other reasons." New workers could be hired and broken-in with a minimum of fuss. With a decreased demand for skilled (and sometimes even semi-skilled) labor and the diminished need for constant communication and cooperation among workers, management found a suitable strategy for usefully employing the millions of non-English-speaking job seekers then immigrating to the United States.

Mechanization and detailed division of labor increased efficiency not only through intrinsic advantages but because they could minimize the economic impact of labor turnover, even without affecting the turnover rates themselves. Moreover, they provided rationalization in the form of greater predictability. The worker became the functional equivalent of a general purpose machine who, when tied to a given task, could provide a predictable quantity of output during the course of the working day. Thus, the nature of labor and the exchange value of labor power were fundamentally changed. Labor power became more of a quantitative unit, instead of a capacity that embodied the qualitative dimensions of judgment and skill. Writing in "The Annals," Ernest Martin Hopkins (1916:58) summed up the effects of the "gigantic accomplishment" of industrial efficiency but added his worries about "the necessary struggle for uniformity and system [that] has involved the limitation of individualism to standardized types to an extent that raises some serious questions."

Embedded in these developments was an awareness of how efficiency could be wedded to internal social control and external legitimacy. Efficiency could easily be tied to the virtues of order, science and hard work in the lexicon of turn-of-the-century ideology (Haber, 1964:ix; Merkle, 1968:1). Rodgers (1978:73) quotes Secretary of Labor Carroll D. Wright who felt that observing a "complex automatic machine at work was to absorb intuitively lessons in science, harmony, and beauty." Rodgers (1978:73) further points to the popularity of the view that "by bringing workers for the first time under constant, systematic supervision, the factories had imposed moral order upon a moral chaos" and found "the ideal behind the material shell of life." Capital investment itself became a basis for legitimacy. As management argued during the epic Homestead steel dispute in 1892,

> We had put in new improvements in some departments which increased the output and reduced the work, and we thought we were entitled to some of the benefits . . . we had also invested more money in the machinery to do that work than our competitors (Brody, 1965:53-4).

The benefits in this case included not only the right to lower wages but the sanction to exercise full control over the labor process.

An even more formidable aspect of social control was the separation of the worker from his (or her) ability to utilize fully time-honored skills associated with particular crafts. While Braverman's concept of "degraded labor" is perhaps extreme, there is little question that it became more and more difficult for workers to pass on a craft tradition to a new generation. Skilled workers often continued to ply their craft because skill implied general competence in several associated tasks rather than deep specialization. In fact, many found their way into supervision, design, and even management (Duggan, 1977:37). But younger workers had neither the opportunity nor the incentive to devote years of apprenticeship to learning skills that were fast becoming obsolete. Before the end of the century many skilled trades became virtually extinct because of mechanization. Among them were cigar-makers, stone-cutters, glass-blowers and barrel-makers (Yellowitz, 1977b:65ff.). Some tasks could not be fully routinized and bureaucratized, but mechanization allowed management to assert a much greater degree of control.[15] Generally, new machinery and work fractionation were instituted in intricate and complex, rather than simple jobs, for here existing workers' control and high unit costs could be mitigated (Rodgers, 1978:66).

Aside from discouraging a crafts orientation, fractionation also served, of course, to decrease the intrinsic value of each worker and the self-worth associated with it. Added to the generally alienative effects of semi-coercive appropriation of labor power and suplus value, this increased the effectiveness of social control.[16] Marx (1964:106-19) discussed this general consequence in his famous 1844 essay on Esranged Labor, but also treated it in some detail in the first volume of "Capital" (1967:350). He noted that

> manufacture begets, in every handicraft that it seizes upon, a class of so-called unskilled laborers, a class which handicraft strictly excluded. If it develops a one-sided specialty into perfection, at the expense of the whole man's working capacity, it also begins to make a specialty of the absence of all development.

In the same chapter, he suggests that the process "converts the laborer into a crippled monstrosity, by forcing his detail dexterity at the expense of a world of productive capabilities and instincts" (Marx, 1967:360). An implication in these passages is that a worker confined to fractionated work is not only limited in exercising potential capabilities in the workplace, but also is less able to carry out organized political activity. It is unclear whether this is in fact the case, just as it is uncertain whether employers' motives consistently reached that level of sophistication.

Associated with the declining proportion of skilled jobs was the decrease in remuneration for skilled workers. Traditionally, crafts wages had been quite high in the United States, at least relative to unskilled workers and to comparable crafts workers in England. It has been suggested, in fact, that many mid-nineteenth-century American innovations in machinery were in direct response to the prevailing high cost of labor, although this hypothesis is a controversial one (Habukkuk, 1962; Saul, 1970). In any case, the differential between skilled and unskilled wages in the glass, steel, and woolen industries narrowed in the decades before the First World War (Shergold, 1977:486). In a comprehensive study of wage structures in Pittsburgh, an almost ideal-typic industrial town of the era, Shergold (1977:488ff.) discovered a substantial decrease in the wage differential for bakers, printers, and railway workers between 1899 and 1907; between 1907 and 1914, the process continued for bakers and printers and included steelworkers and brewers as well. At the same time the differential remained stable or only slightly decreased in other industries and, in two (mining and the building trades between 1899 and 1907) the differential actually increased. The general trend suggests that little premium was placed on skilled labor and that detailed division of labor could successfully increase the productivity of unskilled workers (Shergold, 1977:504).

At times the relative wages paid skilled workers induced some companies to fire them and use unskilled labor instead. At International Harvester wage specialist Frank Ericsson developed policies to save the company money by firing skilled machinists, millwrights, and patternmakers whenever possible (Ozanne, 1967:61-9). In describing this process, Braverman (1974:79-83) notes that Babbage had promulgated it as early as 1832. Yellowitz (1977b:128) suggests that changes in production technology, by reducing the protection of skill, allowed immigrants to challenge those already at work. Generally wages remained stagnant. Paul Douglas's (1930) massive study of real wages between 1890 and 1926 showed fluctuation but no real gains before 1917 in most industries. According to Faulkner (1951:251) most economists agree with this assessment and with the finding that income was not adequate to support most working-class families decently.

Detailed division of work had an additional social control function. It individualized aspects of the labor process to a hitherto unknown degree. Invididual work stations allowed management to focus attention on the activities of each worker, making it far easier to assess the quantity and quality of individual performance. At the same time, highly routinized work limited the emergence of positive worker visibility. Since quality is standardized, noticeable deviations are negative. In effect, workers were reduced specifically to their labor and management could regard them impersonally, without reference to individual needs or abilities.[17] The works of Bendix (1963:57) and Nadworney (1955:81) suggest that these conditions allowed a refined development of the rather vague concept of "individual responsibiity." In a 1912 edition of "Engineering Magazine," C. B. Going felt the process incorporated "the germ of a great idea: separate consideration of every job, separate observation of every man; standards and records — the beginnings of the restoration of individuality" (Rodgers, 1978:47). Individual "accountability" was furthered by the incentive wage and the payment by piece rates rather than hourly rates. Between 1875 and 1920, various piece-rate systems not only began to dominate specific industries such as metal work, machinery, and railroad repair, but also influenced every facet of the private sector. A Conference Board survey in the early 1920s found that just under one half of manufacturing workers were paid by the piece (Rodgers, 1978:51-2). The impact of Taylor was clearly felt in this area.

The effect of work fractionation on workers, while perhaps exaggerated by Braverman and others, was nonetheless enormous and indicates the probability that social control was a primary consequence. Skill sharing and skill growth necessarily diminished as control over job assignment and evaluation came to be the prerogative of management and not fellow workers. Isolation could result not only from the lack of physical proximity, but also from the enormous noise generated by machinery in continuous operation and strictures on physical mobility within the plan. A significant proportion of workers were doubtless demoralized by these conditions and did not take full advantage of the opportunities that did exist for communication with other workers and for involvement in organizing or other union activities. In so far as many contemporary workers may be apathetic and uninvolved (admittedly a debatable contention), the roots of this phenomenon lie partially in the managerial strategies of the progressive era. The detailed division of labor may have increased efficiency, but the extent of its implementation probably exceeded the point of marginal utility if this area alone is considered. Specialization is technically efficient when workers learn a job well enough to perform at full capacity, when materials flow is constant, and when set-up time requires the least possible fraction of the working day, not when a worker carries out the same simple processes day-in and day-out (Marglin, 1974). Job rotation, job bidding and the like are not incompatible with work fractionation, but they do lessen control. It is suggestive, to say the least, that the moving assembly line was heralded not only for its technical advantages, but also because it provided the means to control workers by technological means (Nelson, 1975:24).

The political dimensions of work fractionation were not lost on workers. Individual workers, and particularly the well-organized crafts unions, recognized that the detailed division of labor threatened existing skill structures, the traditional, collective nature of much industrial work, and the meaning of that work itself. Gompers, for example, was concerned that workers could become merely a mechanized adjunct of the production process and thereby would be robbed of creative interest in their work (McKelvey, 1952:17). Workers resisted the introduction of skill-breaking machinery and scientific management, and continued to struggle against fractionated work once it was in place. Aiken's (1960) study of Watertown Arsenal and Nadworney's (1955) analysis of union response to scientific management amply demonstrate the depth and breadth of labor's struggles. Gutman (1976:23) points out that specialization first generated an attitude of anxiety on the part of Jewish glove-makers, but soon begat resistance even though fractionation of work promised higher wages. Similarly, lasters in the shoe industry tried to control the implementation of the Matzelinger machine which mechanized the sizing of footwear although, ultimately, their union accepted the equipment when management guaranteed wages (Yellowitz, 1977a:197-201). Davis's (1975) study of the IWW's struggle against scientific management and their citation of Taylor's maxims as reverse propaganda suggests that the reaction to new departures in dividing work was not confined to skilled workers. The dehumanization and degradation of work that followed these managerial strategies evokes particularly strong opposition at the time they were being introduced, as the implications of deskilling were obvious to workers experiencing the changeovers. The articulation of this reaction recalls earlier struggles in England when the industrial revolution virtually dragged workers from depressed farmlands into dank factories. The period of transition apparently calls forth the greatest conflict.[18]

Both mechanization and subdivided labor lend themselves to caricature. As effective as they are, they do not reduce the worker to an abject, isolated automaton. Workers do communicate during beaks, when equipment slows down or breaks down, and in those frequent work situations where a small number of individuals work side-by-side even though their tasks are not interdependent. On these occasions, and after work in taverns, skills are shared and knowledge and suggestions passed on. And more important, some of the skills required for ostensibly unskilled and routine jobs may be in fact substantial. Sometimes unreliable machinery, cumbersome rules and the high outputs required by supervisors force workers to develop sophisticated, if unrecognized, methods of makeshift adjustment if they are to get the work out at all (Kusterer, 1978).

HIERARCHY AND LABOR DISCIPLINE

By itself, the detailed division of labor did not fully guarantee that workers would perform the tasks assigned to them, much less internalize "appropriate" values. A sophisticated system of hierarchical gradations, however, helped large firms to realize the social control potential of fragmented work. As divided labor routinized new horizontal distinctions among workers, hierarchy served a similar function in formalizing a new set of vertical distinctions. Vertical differentiation was of two types: one instituted internal stratification among workers themselves, another established a caste-like separation between managers and workers (Goldman, 1973:41-2). In symbol and in fact, hierarchical distinctions served the political function of highlighting the worker's subordination and in increasing social distance within the industrial firm.[19] A new stratum of managers and technicians was inserted as an intermediary between the owners of capital and those whose labor was exploited.

The advantages of hierarchical organization, less obvious than those associated with the division of labor, are quite real. They are symbolized by the Weberian concept of imperative coordination. A clear chain of command, limited jurisdictions, and, most important, a well-informed, competent managerial force who can set and carry out policy with a reasonable amount of predictability characterize its main tenets. Hierarchy represents a division of labor at all levels coupled with the power to enforce decisions made at the top. A fixed chain of command allowed early entrepreneurs to expand their businesses while leaving day-to-day operations at dispersed sites to trained and usually highly paid subordinates. Chandler (1977:7-8) notes that American industry was only able to effect efficiency and profitability when managerial hierarchies and administrative coordination began to characterize business firms. Hierarchical organization regularizes, even if imperfectly, both communication and evaluation. In the Weberian formulation, they also assume legitimacy, but we should remember that Weber's model was primarily defined by government bureaucracies. In business, hierarchy rests not only on legitimacy but on a combination of mistrust and economic incentives (Etzioni, 1961:31-6).

Hierarchical structures provided a template onto which the requirements of both efficiency and social control could be forged simultaneously. In Volume I of "Capital," Marx alluded to the relationship between completing necessary industrial tasks and controlling the inevitable resentment of workers.

> The work of directing, superintending, and adjusting becomes one of the functions of capital. . . . As the number of cooperating laborers increases, so too does their resistance to the domination of capital, and with it, the necessity for capital to overcome this resistance by counter pressure (Marx, 1967:331).

In a subsequent passage, it is clear that these responsibilities will evolve into a quasi-bureaucratized, hierarchical structure.

> An industrial army of workmen, under the command of a capitalist, requires, like a real army, officers (managers), and sergeants (foremen, overlookers), who, while the work is being done, command in the name of the capitalist. . . . He treats the work of control made necessary by the cooperative character of the labor process as identical with the different work of control, necessitated by the capitalist character of that process and the antagonism of interests between capitalist and laborer (Marx, 1967:332).

By the end of the century in which Marx wrote, hierarchy and the bureaucratic mechanisms sustaining it had achieved great subtlety.

Differential job statuses and wages for workers were an integral component of the hierarchical nature of the industrial pyramid. On the surface this appears to be a rational device allowing management the option to reward workers according to their skill levels or seniority. Ford, for example, divided his workers into seven categories, each with a different wage (Nelson, 1975:44). Rates were based on the planning department's analysis of each job's requirements, but Ford, like other employers of the day, used them to reward loyalty and clean living as well as (or sometimes in place of) performance (Sward, 1948:58ff.). This practice structured the workplace both for already employed workers and for new workers who might be hired.

Job ladders in the steel industry developed, according to both Brody (1960:80ff.) and Stone (1975:65ff.), in order to control workers through a sophisticated system of rewards and to break the power of strong crafts unions in the industry. In steel a structured hierarchy also undercut the special position held by contractors, who operated functionally as businessmen with small shops on the plant floor, and had control over work processes and the quality and quantity of production. Moreover, job ladders enabled managers to rationalize and control wages, since their control over more aspects of production made it easier to ignore the time-honored practice of pegging wages to the selling price of finished steel.

Job ladders and differential wage scales served well as mechanisms of social control. They allowed, even encouraged, limited social mobility within the plant and operationalized an internal labor market. At the same time, however, they increased competition between workers for better paying and/or less undesirable jobs. As contemporary journalist John Fitch put it, "in every department of mill work there is a more or less rigid line of promotion. Every man is in training for the next position above . . . thus the working force is pyramided and is held together by the ambition of the men lower down" (Stone, 1975:42). This description coincides with the overt philosophy of the John Dewey-inspired McCormick whose founder felt that "every man [should] be given an opportunity to prepare himself for some higher quality of work than the lowering of a lever and the occasional adjustment of a jig" (Ozanne, 1967:41).[20] The specific job, not jobs in general, became a scarce resource for workers and potentially eroded one basis for solidarity among them. Group concerns could fragment by individual and status-specific interests and thereby lessen the attractiveness of collective activity.

A hierarchy of job statuses allowed firms to rationalize recruitment and promotion policies. In fact, it was during this period that employment and personnel management departments began to play a role in industrial administration (Eilbut, 1959). Testifying before the U.S. Commission on Industrial Relations in 1914, John D. Rockefeller noted that "hitherto executive control in business has had three main branches: finance, manufacturing and sales. . . . There has not developed a fourth major division, namely, the supervision of personnel or employment management"(Leiserson, 1928:35). Personnel management, aside from adding a new level of hierarchy, was a necessary requirement for managing the graded system of jobs and the internal labor market thereby created. Performance and attitude could not be better measured and rewarded and vacant positions could be filled from within the firm rather than by external recruitment. In short, hierarchy enabled firms to formalize the labor market segmentation that divided workers from one another (Edwards, 1975; Reich et al., 1973).

New hierarchical arrangements also affected the process of routine worker supervision. Traditionally, supervision had been only one of the many functions carried out by the foreman. He was responsible for personnel policy and its implementation since he did the hiring, training, motivating, and disciplining of the workers, as well as organizing work activities and making decisions about tools, materials, timing, and process. Generally his role was similar to that of the general foreman or even plant superintendent of today, and was constrained only by overall labor costs and the speed and quality of the work (Nelson, 1975:34-40). Foremen were at times autocratic and arbitrary and their power was often not amenable to control from above.[21] As the size and complexity of the industrial workplace increased and operations became more rationalized, the job grew too large for a single individual (Eilbut, 1959:360). Taylor's attempt to create "functional foremen" reflected managerial thinking of his time, but a more typical solution was to confine the foreman to supervision and to locate his other functions elsewhere in administration (Litterer, 1963:376-7).

The bureaucratic solution was to assign recruiting, hiring, and promotion to employment officers located away from the shopfloor who would be less affected by daily problems of labor relations and more "rational" in the assignment of workers to jobs. By the beginning of the First World War, personnel departments' mandate increased to include worker safety, welfare, and training (Eilbut, 1959:346ff.). These changes were designed to enhance management's control over operations and, by limiting his power, to insure that the foreman's actions conformed to policy. They also allowed a greater standardization of labor practice itself (Wiebe, 1968:165).

Apparently there was an evolving opinion that the typical foreman was underqualified relative to his traditional power and these changes effectively removed him from the ranks of management. Ultimately this sharpened the caste line between blue- and white-collar work and between shopfloor and office.

What remained of the foreman's role was nonetheless critical. In a time where obedience was highly valued, the foreman took on the role of disciplinarian (Palmer, 1975:37). In some shops, his effective span of control was cut sharply so that he could closely supervise workers. At Goodyear, which had given up the attempt to cut turnover, there was one supervisor for every ten workers (Montgomery, 1977:99). The hierarchical principle was reinforced by the proliferation of rules and procedures that were instituted to aid him in this responsibility. Many of these were prescriptive and dealt with what the planning department saw as the proper way to do a job, to increase the speed of work, or to improve safety. The aim of others, however, was to enhance social control. For example, Ford prohibited his men from leaving their stations during work breaks, from socializing with one another and from smoking (Sward, 1948:360).[22]

Many of these rules were enforced irregularly, operating only to the extent the foreman wished to exert his authority (Nelson, 1975:44). Despite the drive towards industrial efficiency, the pattern of "strategic leniency" described by Gouldner (1954:45-56) has always played a role in American industry. Even where the foreman did not fully control the promotion process, he could use the existing rules to influence it and reaffirm the principles of hierarchical organization. As Brody (1965:87) describes the situation, "managers held out unlimited prospects for advancement. . . . Insecure and ambitious, [the steel hands] came to identify their fortunes with the good will of their particular boss, and they behaved accordingly." Thus rules, combined with hierarchy, gave employers some additional leverage with which they could enforce cooperation and enforce discipline. Strict rules may have seemed particularly necessary in dealing with individualistic American workers. Both the native-born and immigrants who had broken away from their homelands had (from the managerial perspective) too little of the traditional respect for authority and the accompanying acceptance of discipline that apparently characterized European factories (Gutman, 1976:53). Korman (1967:2) notes, however, that religious authority could still be effective and that priests were frequently used in Milwaukee plants to encourage workers to follow safety regulations.

Rules and enforcement practices were a frequent source of worker grievance. Nelson (1975:56) contends that the procedures associated with scientific management were of greater concern to workers than even the fabled stopwatch itself. There is no question that workers, and the union officials representing them, felt hemmed in by the rapid incursion of bureaucratic rules upon worker autonomy (Barbash, 1967:65; Nadworney, 1955). In time, work rules would become a subject of labor management negotiations.

But what of the managers themselves? The burgeoning hierarchy was as critical to administrative as it was to shop management. Most managers were segregated from workers by background as well as duties. Managerial positions came to require either a middle-class background or a college education (or both) and were denied to workers whose own aspirations had to be subordinated onto hopes for their children. The growth of a caste system around the turn of the century distinguished that period from an earlier one when smaller factories, widespread apprenticeships, and greater emphasis on skills encouraged the belief that every workman was a potential businessman awaiting his opportunity. As Noble (1977:168) suggests, "the integration of formal education into the industrial structure weakened the traditional link between work experience and advancement, driving a wedge between managers and managed and separating the two by the college campus.''

Hierarchy in management was fundamental to efficient factory operation. Rapid growth had generated frequent breakdowns in coordination and planning. Necessary information was too complex to be mastered by those few officers lodged in a central headquarters. In the past problems had been exacerbated by poor relationships between top and lower management and the meager abilities of the latter (Litterer, 1963:373ff.). Hierarchy and standardized procedures allowed top management to ''eliminate confusion, oversight and neglect; coordinate efforts, return firm control to the top people in the organization'' (Litterer, 1961:473). Hierarchical distinctions between managers, while somewhat fluid, suggested invidious comparisons and encouraged high aspirations and steady work.

Hierarchy within the administrative ranks was not without its own contradictions for capitalist firms. Like workers, management loyalties were tempered by fear. As one worker, Wyndham Mortimer (1971:29) described the situation in 1906, managers too were subject to the demands of high production:

> Men were kept in a state of fear; workers were fired on the slightest pretext, or for no reason at all. Nor was the fear confined to the worker; it extended up through supervision and even to higher officials, such as plant managers. Pittsburgh issued orders to produce more ''or else'' which were sent down through a chain of command until they reached the foremen and the workers in the mill.

At the same time, however, managers were gaining more power as they gradually took over the functions formerly handled by capitalists themselves. The ''managerial revolution'' may have had little impact on the actual content of decisions made by large firms, but the growth of hierarchies among managers and staff personnel created a new power base in many companies.[23] The new structures often affected lower management's consciousness. Aiken (1960:120) notes the irony of Tayloristic practice that made executives perceive themselves as being in control over plant activities: ''every person playing a supervisory role under the Taylor system of management tended, when describing his job, to exaggerate his own importance and indispensability.''

In sum, hierarchy and standardization of procedures rationalized production and administration. They enabled top management to allocate and control expenditures authoritatively and to plan effectively. As a consequence, they certainly made factory production more orderly and efficient. As strategies, hierachy and standardized procedures had a profound effect on the character of work at all levels. Their strongest impact, however, was felt by workers whose labor, already alienated, was subjected to an authoritative, and often authoritarian, regime largely stripped of the paternalistic concern that characterized mid-nineteenth century industrial development. Once established, hierarchy is invariably self-maintaining and subject to oligarchical tendencies. For employers, hierarchy highlights and legitimates their ''unique''role in the production process (Marglin, 1974). For workers, it encourages a belief in status rather than class thereby contributing to social control.

MONOPOLIZATION OF KNOWLEDGE

Knowledge is power in organizational settings. A characteristic of turn-of-the-century managerial strategy was the creation of new knowledge and the attempt to capture from workers existing knowledge of production technique and locate it within the ranks of an emerging technical and administrative staff. This transfer and transformation of knowledge minimized one source of workers' leverage, and reinforced the trend towards hierarchy discussed above. At the same time, it encouraged the growth of white-collar occupations of all types.

The principles of scientific management reflect the dominant trend of the period, even in factories where management showed little interest in pursuing Taylor's system. Rationalization of production allowed management to remedy a situation in which "foremen and superintendents . . . know that their own knowledge and personal skill falls far short of the combined knowledge and dexterity of all the workmen under them" (Taylor, 1967:31-2). Detailed division of labor, of course, served to minimize workers' skills. Hierarchy generated, among other consequences, the partial legitimacy of authority. Monopolization of knowledge reinforced structural changes by mystifying much of the emerging technical (and other) knowledge and by generating a legitimation process based on expertise.

There were three facets to this process: 1) the stripping of productive knowledge from workers; 2) the use of this knowledge by management; and 3) the invention process itself. In the first instance, the worker was often not allowed to use all of the skills he or she had learned through years of experience and had little incentive for passing these skills on to younger workers and for continuing crafts traditions as they had previously existed. As Taylor (1967:36) describes it, managers "gather together traditional knowledge which in the past has een possessed by workmen and [classifies, tabulates and reduces] the knowledge to rules, laws and formulae." Braverman (1974:113) concludes that this process resulted in the "dissociation of the labor process from the skills of the worker." To put it more strongly, the existing and potential knowledge of workers, like their labor, was appropriated by the capitalists.[24] The result, as Montgomery (1977:98) suggests, was that "the skill and knowledge required by manufacturing occupations were embodied not in their training but in the technical organization of the factory itself. The mental component of their labor was not their property, but their employer's."

The second facet concerns the actual utilization of productive knowledge. Once centralized at managerial levels, it can be employed both to plan and organize the production process and to control it step-by-step. Taylorism was an extreme form of this process and reflects a general process of separating conception from execution. More generally, mental and manual labor became increasingly separated from one another as steps in the production process were laid out on paper well before they were actually implemented on the shop floor (Braverman, 1974:114-26). Workers often see new plans and machinery only when they are actually operational.

While centralized knowledge has obvious implications for social control, it doubtless made day-to-day operations more efficient. Specialization of technical and administrative tasks allowed routinization of previously haphazard activities such as the collection of cost figures, inventory, the status of orders and the like (Litterer, 1961:474). Chandler (1977:247) notes that as early as 1886, the Lyman Mills in Holyoke, Massachusetts "began to analyze unit costs for their specific products. Then . . . these cost data became managerial tools. They were used to rationalize internal operations, to check on the productivity of the worker, . . . and to check the efficiency of minor improvements in machinery or plant design." Centralization of information improved the short- and medium-range planning that had become a necessity for growing firms producing a larger line of products. Furthermore engineers and other technical staff were needed to monitor market conditions and, more important, to keep abreast of rapidly evolving technology so that modifications in product and process could be effected. Management hoped that the monopolizaton of knowledge would help achieve the ideal goal of "control over the entire job situation, exercised in such a way that a predictable increase in output would certainly result" (Noble, 1977:264).

The growth of technical staff positions, moreover, provided a new source of social control. Scientists and technicians developed productive knowledge inaccessible to even the most sophisticated worker. Few workers were trained to understand fully the scientific principles embodied in some of the newer, more complex machines. Even where they might have comprehended these principles, information was often packaged in a format — technical language, formulae, blueprints — that could only be consumed after explanation by a "translator."

Invention itself constituted a third facet of the monopolization of knowledge. It is difficult to document the relationship between rapid development of scientific capability and management's desire to limit workers' skills and bargaining power. Many managers do seem to have been aware of the potential relationship between invention and labor and to have planned with it in mind. According to one historian, labor-saving devices were introduced because managers were determined to engage in rational long-term planning. This was impossible as long as the possibility of strikes by indispensable skilled workers hung like a sword of Damocles over their heads (Rosenberg, 1976b:124). During the nineteenth century in England, there were several cases where employers hurriedly developed new technology in the context of immediate labor disputes. The riveting machine was invented as a result of a work stoppage by Manchester boilermakers, and grooved rollers for musket barrels were a consequence of a strike by gun-skelp forgers, who were then superseded (Rosenberg, 1976b:1192-0). Henry Ford was fond of telling a perhaps apocryphal story about how his friend, from Edison, had "invented" his way out of a difficult labor situation. Faced with a new organization of skilled labor, Edison quickly invested in a machine which eliminated their jobs and destroyed the union at birth (Sward, 1968:114). Such dramatic incidents were probably not common and became less so once major (and expensive) breakthroughs occurred. Citing Charlotte Erickson, Rosenblum (1973:128) notes that few, if any, employers could develop or introduce new machinery sufficiently quickly actually to break a strike (in fact, this reverses the direction of usual causal order). He goes on to say, however, that in times of growth new firms could emerge with technologies that decreased the ratio of skilled to unskilled workers. Thus, there was some relation between invention, technology, and social control. Andrew Ure, a famous mid-nineteenth century manufacturer, summed it up as follows: "when capital enlists science in her service, the refractory hand of labor will always be taught docility" (Rosenberg, 1976b:118).

Another area in which emerging knowledge, of at least a quasi-scientific nature, could be put to work was in personnel administration. As industry became larger and more complex and the dictatorial authority of shop foremen was reduced, personnel departments gained greater and greater control over routine dealings with workers. Like other staff specialties, personnel administration was unknown in the nineteenth century (Nelson, 1975:34). By 1900, many firms began using employment agents and welfare workers and, within a few years, larger corporations chartered full-fledged personnel departments to carry out recruitment, selection and training of new workers (Eilbut, 1959). The social control implications are obvious. In the steel industry, employers established a new training program, called the "short course," to replace union-controlled apprenticeships (Stone, 1975:56-8). The personnel department's duties extended beyond the shopfloor. As one prominent personnel manager described their activities, "the employment department keeps in touch with

the newly appointed·employees by interviewing them at least once a month"
(Williams, 1917:85). In hiring, the personnel department screened workers for
subversive attitudes and generally favored men and women with families to support.
According to one highly involved industrial psychologist, Professor A. J. Snow of
Northwestern University, those doing the hiring were well-advised to pass over
workers with "too much intelligence" since they would prove to be difficult employees constantly looking for ways to escape industrial labor (Baritz, 1960:66).
Eventually, intelligence and personality tests were used to screen potential employees, although this was largely a post-First World War phenomenon (Baritz,
1960:60-2).

Refinements in the personnel process specifically, and the greater reliance on
"administration" generally, had a marked, but subtle, effect on workers' ability to
understand and deal with the actions of their employers. Workers had learned to
manipulate, to some degree at least, even the most autocratic and arbitrary traditional
foreman, for he was an autonomous individual whose aberrations were partially
understandable. The establishment of rules and procedures governing not only work
but also hiring and promotion made managerial decisions, and the criteria on which
they were based, more distant from, and less comprehensible to, workers. While the
supervisor retained the power to administer and interpret rules, he had become an
intermediary. The insecurity of his new status allowed him to be arbitrary, but
simultaneously made him more accountable to management even if workers were less
than fully aware of this. In the pre-war period, these rules invariably served management, although a generation later union contracts and a more effective shop steward
system allowed workers to use formal rules for bureaucratic protection.[25]

The concentration of knowledge in the hands of managers and staff in the growing
technical and personnel professions helped resolve one set of managerial problems
during the period between the 1890s and 1917. It matched the division of labor on the
factory floor with a comparable division of labor at plant or corporation headquarters.
Managerial recruitment came more and more from college-educated men, and
academicians of all kinds, not just scientists and engineers, began to have an impact
on large-scale businesses. This trend was noticed as early as 1895 and reported in the
first volume of the "American Journal of Sociology" (Henderson, 1895:386). An
offshoot of the scientific management movement was the greater willingness of
corporate executives to use the ideas and services of university professors (Baritz,
1960:31; Mulherin, 1976). At the same time, universities themselves started offering
courses in both general management and even in specialized areas such as personnel
administration (Eilbut, 1959:353). The developing structures of higher education
generally denied workers access to such information.

In fact, as David Noble (1977) has persuasively argued, links between the
business community, the academy, and the emerging engineering profession became
ever closer in the first years of the century. The establishment of research laboratories
and industrial fellowships helped cement this relationship, as did recruitment
mechanisms that drew engineers directly from the universities into corporate firms,
especially the larger ones (Noble, 1977:112ff., 168ff.). Engineering education itself
became geared to producing not just technicians, but businessmen who were prepared
to adopt the values of business enterprise. This included "human relations" as well as
the operation of machines. As Noble (1977:xxiv) suggests, the engineers "consciously undertook to structure the labor force and foster the social habits demanded
by corporate capitalism." These understandings led many of the engineers to aspire to
top management positions where science could be applied to human organization

(Jenks, 1960:44). One study of career patterns found that two-thirds of engineering graduates became managers within fifteen years of receiving their degrees during the 1884-1924 period (Noble, 1977:41).

These developments were not without their own problems and contradictions. Technological advance and employment of specialists concentrated new knowledge at intermediate ranks within firms.[26] Comparative autonomy and high wages were often sufficient to guarantee loyal performance by engineers and staff administrators. In most companies, these positions required considerable discretion and the attitudes of professionals and bureaucrats came close to those of their employers. Differentiation and the isolation of knowledge helped legitimate the system at both the middle and lower levels. But many technical personnel were locked into staff positions and had their ambitions blocked. The disillusionment and potential alienation of engineers was noted by Veblen (1971:438-45) as early as 1921. It remains a persistent, if not serious, problem a half-century later.[27]

RECAPITULATION

As capitalists and managers reacted to the dual pressures of capital accumulation and class conflict, administrative strategies necessarily stressed both efficiency and social control. We have suggested that specific tactics, notably detailed division of labor, labor discipline through extended hierarchies, and monopolization of knowledge, gained currency because they served both requirements simultaneously.

Each of these mechanisms contributed to the growing bureaucratization of industry. Without unduly stretching Weber's (1946:196-202) famous characterization of bureaucracy in government, it is easily seen how closely the tactics described above parallel his description of such areas as the "fixed and official jurisdictional areas," the "levels of graded authority," the degree to which management (and technical staff) positions "presupposes thorough and expert training," and the notion that the "position of the official [and of the worker] is held for life." During the turn-of-the-century period, management became a bureaucratized system rather than an arbitrary and sometimes idiosyncratic set of specific practices unique to each firm. From this base, bureaucracy grew within individual companies and from one firm to the next.

Contemporary sociologists and historians view the emergence of bureaucratic practices in this period as a natural and rational evolution of the practice of industrial management. Their analysis is not entirely incorrect, but it is essential to recognize that modern bureaucracy was forged as much from the need to respond to class conflict as it was from the need to "coordinate" large numbers of people engaging in material production. Insofar as bureaucracy is a "necessity" of capitalist industry, it is largely due to the continuing need to deny workers control over their productive lives and by the monopolistic tendencies of the capitalist system which result in gigantic, relatively centralized corporations operating on a world-wide scale.

One final issue merits comment. The thrust of this paper has been in analyzing tendencies in the capitalist system as they were played out in the years before the First World War, giving some attention to the consciousness of capitalists and managers whose policies resulted in the bureaucratization of the industrial workplace. Recent studies by Weinstein (1968), Kolko (1963) and others provide a persuasive argument that at least some corporate elites consciously set out to influence and direct public policy formation.[28] It is not unreasonable to expect that the same awareness would be applied to their immediate domains in industry where problems were at least as complex and subtle. Wood (1960:419) suggests that management had conscious strategies for long- and short-run planning that went beyond the pressures generated by workers and their unions. He indicates that they were motivated by the desire to promote efficiency and to fight unions, but that they also attempted to sway public opinion and influence legislation. According to Wiebe (1968:169), The National Association of Manufacturers proposed that employers should have full control over hiring, firing, apprenticing, and all details of production, thus intimating that its leadership both recognized the nature of the threats facing them and had a clear strategy in response. Management journals and the management movement as a whole grew during this period, as did the use of academic social scientists as consultants. One retail executive even persuaded six competitors that they needed a common research bureau and training institute (Baritz, 1960:40).

We have hoped, in this paper, to raise the issue of managerial consciousness and to indicate that bureaucratic innovation was in part a strategic response to workers and not merely a rational evolution of technique nor an adjustment to developing market forces. As a consequence, our presentation resembles the instrumentalist position laid out in recent debates about the nature of the modern capitalist state (Gold et al., 1975). We do not wish to dwell here on this important conceptual issue, but might point out that, as bureaucracies, business firms differ from the state in some essential qualities. They maintain no claims of democratic process and are only slightly limited in internal operations by claims of outsiders. More important, they are, compared to the state apparatus, both centralized and relatively small, certainly during the period we analyze. Thus, the owners, directors, and managers can usually effect internal changes at their own discretion, basing them on their readings of the needs, constraints, and opportunities that face the firm.

No doubt strategies of individual firms, and of managers within them, differed. The craft of modern management was in its infancy and consensus on technique was some years into the future. Nevertheless, bureaucratization as evinced by division of labor, hierarchy, and monopolization of knowledge grew in large-scale industry. While it never guaranteed complete industrial efficiency and failed fully to control workers, it rationalized and systematized management strategies in an enduring pattern.

NOTES

[1] Portions of an earlier draft of this paper were read at the Annual Meetings of the American Sociological Association in San Francisco, August 1978. A number of friends and colleagues in Eugene and elsewhere read, and provided critical comment, on previous versions. Their help was appreciated even where, perhaps unwisely, their counsel was not fully incorporated into the final version. They include Howard Aldrich, Nancy Chodorow, Mimi Goldman, Heidi Hartmann, Judy Merkle, Jim Mulherin, Carla Orcutt, Daniel Pope, and Michael Reich.

[2] Historians disagree on the precise dating of the period when critical changes occurred. Nelson (1975) prefers the forty years between 1880 and 1920, which incorporates the massive wave of immigration, Taylor's full working life and influence, and the First World War. Jenks (1960) and Litterer (1963) believe that massive changes began just at the turn of the century as employers and writers interested in economics and management began to codify and share their ideas in print. Palmer (1975) dates the period from 1903 to 1922, reflecting the common types of labor struggles occurring then. Wiebe (1967) and Galambos (1970) focus on the 1890-1910 era. While any designation is arbitrary (and perhaps pedantic as well), we tend to look at the early 1890s, marked by the end of a two decade recession, as a starting point, and 1917, when

labor relations were affected by the cessation of immigration and demands for wartime production, as an end point.

[3] Chandler (1977) uses the self-organization of management as a major theme of his recent treatise on American business development. However, he gives no attention whatever to labor relations and the uncertainty it generated as a contributory source of emergent industrial bureaucracy.

[4] Turnover statistics from the early twentieth century confirm the basis of employer concern. Nelson (1975:86-7) reports that contemporary studies show that turnover often reached 100 per cent. Prior to instituting the five dollar day, Ford noted that he had to employ 53,000 men annually in order to maintain a labor force of 14,000 (Flink, 1976:90). These figures were no doubt exceptional, although a 1912 study found that 35 per cent of autoworkers had been with their employers for less than six months (Russell, 1978:39).

[5] Such costs could be enormous. A.G. Bondie, head of Ford's Employment Office, cited a figure of 38 dollars to break in a new worker. Taking this amount, Russell (1978:40) estimates that the 1913 cost at Ford was about two million dollars.

[6] In our focus on managerial strategies below, it is sometimes easy to overlook the extent to which employers were reactive rather than "rational." Bureaucratization was accompanied by the use of external resources they could bring to the struggle. These included spies and provocateurs, the sympathetic power of the state which incorporated both legislation and, at times, armed forces, the power of the press, and cooperative arrangement between firms, as well as the ability to marshall internal forces authoritatively and to reward management well. Moreover, the prevailing work ideology of the period gave sanction to whatever efforts were initiated by management (Haber, 1964; Rodgers, 1978).

[7] Haire (1959) suggests with a biological analogy that the weight carried by large size requires geometrically increasing administrative skeleton. Melman (1951) takes the same view. More systematic research summarized by Hall (1977:104-19) and Blau (1974) disputes that conclusion.

[8] Braverman's monumental "Labor and Monopoly Capital" (1974:59-152) has served as a template for discussions of the labor process in turn-of-the-century American capitalism. We feel that its deserved influence has contributed to some confusion about the nature of Scientific Management. Taylorism, as a system, was installed in relatively few plants and often for only short periods of time. It proved too rigid, on its own merits, for the majority of managers. The general trend towards mechanization and the fractionation of work developed independently of Taylor, even though he helped publicize it and exemplified it in a most extreme form. Braverman may have exaggerated the impact of Scientific Management in identifying it with the larger trend. Palmer (1975) substantially shares this view, while de Kadt (1976) and Gordon (1976) agree in part.

[9] As Haber (1964:ix) points out, efficiency can have several meanings: (1), "social efficiency" or the relationship of social harmony, (2), individual efficiency as a personal trait, (3) the emergency-input ratio of a machine, and (4) the efficiency of enterprise, especially the input-output ratio of dollars. As we use the term, it is primarily in the latter sense, conforming to contemporary usage among businesspeople.

[10] Rudin (1972:66) suggests that managerial intentions in initiating welfare work were even broader:

> In essence, the attempt was to build an alternative to working class culture. The industrial reformers stressed specialization of labor, workers prided themselves as artisans; the industrial reformers emphasized efficiency, workers stressed craftsmanship; the proponents of uplift spoke of morality and the sublimation of "morbid cravings," the workers enjoyed a night at the bar and a morning of leisure; finally, conservative reformers worked for amelioration through legislation and company paternalism, while the worker sought a better life through his union. In short, the leaders of the industrial reform movement wanted social control much more than social justice.

[11] Welfare projects could be expensive. Ozanne (1967:88) reports that International Harvester spent $100,000 in 1908, although he notes that corporate profits were $10.5 million. By the 1920s, costs rose dramatically as exemplified by the $10 million expended yearly by US

Steel (Brody, 1968:154). Brody (1968:161) also finds that it was a "minority phenomenon, limited to the large, prosperous firms." We compared a list of firms with extensive early welfare programs (Nelson, 1975:116) to the 1977 "Fortune 1000" (Fortune, 1977a, 1977b). Thirty-one per cent of the listed firms survived under the same name for more than sixty years. A list of companies using Scientific Management (Nelson, 1975:71) provides a useful comparison. Only 3 per cent (one firm, in fact) lasted to the present day, at least without having been absorbed in a larger firm or changing its name. See also Nelson and Campbell (1972). The latter suggests that welfare work requires "a large enough number of employees to justify a systematic welfare program, and the wherewithal to pay for it. At times welfare work could itself generate revenue" (Goldman and Wilson, 1977).

[12] Gordon (1976:24) calls attention to what he calls a "strong" Marxist formulation: that "quantitative and qualitative efficiency tend somewhat to conflict in capitalist societies. The requirements of labor control tend to push capitalists . . . toward production processes which are less quantitatively efficient than other (technically) possible processes." He prefers a "weak" proposition that "capitalist production processes maximize qualitative efficiency subject to the constraint that they are quantitatively efficient."

[13] Between 1880 and 1900, there were no less than 23,000 strikes (Brandes, 1976:1). Boyer and Morais (1971) and Brecher (1972) provide brief summaries of this period of labor history, and Foner (1947-65), Taft (1957), and Commons et al. (1926-35) more detailed general histories.

[14] In any given factory, it seems probable the increased division of labor occurred simultaneously with the installation of new machines. In a later passage, Aiken also implies that acquisition of machines followed the decision to use Taylorism. Watertown Arsenal purchased 55,000 dollars' worth of equipment in the foundry and $26,000 in machinery for the machine shop in fiscal 1911 after they hired Taylor's associate Carl Barth. In fiscal 1910 they had only ordered a total of $385 in new equipment for both departments (Aiken, 1960:190).

[15] Some of this control had to be delegated not only to those who designed and engineered complex machinery, but probably also to those who had the highly specialized maintenance and repair skills. While there is little evidence of the dynamics of this process, more recent studies, notably Crozier (1964), suggest that such knowledge gives mechanics unusual power in industrial plants.

[16] Empirical studies of worker alienation as it results from detailed division of labor have been as numerous in the past two decades as they were scarce sixty years ago. Blauner's (1964) examination of powerless, meaningless, social isolation and self-estrangement as they occur in industrial settings has set the tone for much of this research which has attempted to support, refute, or modify his argument. Also see Nash (1976). No one, to our knowledge, however, has argued that fractionated work is good for the soul.

[17] This tendency was built into the growing impersonality of the factory. Noble (1977:58) suggests that it may have been exacerbated by the "alien ways of the immigrants [which] widened the gap between the worker and the manager, and better enabled the latter to treat the former as simply another object of 'scientific' study."

[18] The oft-cited super-speed-up at General Motors' Lordstown plant in 1972 suggests that militant reactions to mechanized technique are not limited to the historical past (Aronowitz, 1973:21-50; Rothschild, 1973:97-119).

[19] This process is at the root of Marglin's (1974) analysis of "what the bosses do." He suggests that the hierarchical division of labor was the result of early capitalists' search for a structure that would guarantee them, even though they performed no labor, an essential role in the production process.

[20] This institute, however, was an adjunct of International Harvester Company and received company funds only because it promised to be an antidote to unionism during the first decade of the century (Ozanne, 1967:40-2).

[21] The foreman was also a symbol to employees and assumed new importance in larger, more impersonal corporations. Henry Dennison (1917:17) asserted that "to the employee the foreman is the company. I do not care how splendidly humanitarian the head of the company may be . . . the connection of the employee with the company is the connection of the employee with his foreman." Thus, the task came to incorporate a public or labor relations aspect.

[22] William Tolman, an influential early "theorist" of social relations felt that efficiency promotion was largely a function of the extensiveness and explicitness of rules. Many of his examples came from white-collar organizations, particularly insurance, banking, and retail sales where literacy was relatively high, but he assumed that the principle held for manufacturing as well. He was especially enthusiastic about Marshall Field's rule book which contained 111 pages and "fit comfortably into a man's pocket" (Tolman, 1909:16).

[23] Scientific Management itself highlighted one of the contradictions stemming from a new locus of power. The necessary authority vested in the planning department, as well as that of outside experts, removed a degree of control from the employers establishing it (Haber, 1964:25).

[24] As Jim Mulherin pointed out to us, it is easy to overestimate the extent to which workers "lost" or "never developed" some sophisticated technical skills. Manual "hobby culture," including wood, machine, electronic, and auto working has always been a part of working-class culture. The point is, rather, that skills were not valued, utilized, or compensated by employers.

[25] The most sophisticated discussion of the bureaucratic functions of rules in post-Second World War firms is found in Gouldner (1954). In the plant he studied, workers have a fairly complete knowledge of the content and intent of the bureaucratic rules governing their work lives.

[26] These developments were a second generation solution to the problem of delegating managerial authority. Pollard (1965) notes that educated clerks and bookkeepers were hired by entrepreneurs before 1850 in Great Britain.

[27] See Miller (1967) for an empirical study of engineers and Ehrenreich (1977) for a theoretical interpretation. Much of the debate about the "new working class" has centered on the actual and potential political behavior of skilled technicians, although it is evident that American engineers are more thoroughly integrated into the managerial value-system than are their European counterparts.

[28] Workers too developed class consciousness around some of the same issues. Their attention was, if anything, more concentrated since the dangers to them were more obvious (Aiken, 1960; McKelvey, 1952; Nadworney, 1955).

REFERENCES

Aiken, Hugh G. J.
1960   *Taylorism at Watertown Arsenal: Scientific Management in Action, 1908-1915,* Cambridge, Mass.: Harvard University Press.

Aronowitz, Stanley
1973   *False Promises: The Shaping of American Working Class Consciousness,* New York: McGraw-Hill.

Barbash, Jack
1967   "Technology and labor in the twentieth century," in Melvin Kranzberg and Carroll W. Pursell, Jr. (eds.), *Technology in Western Civilization,* New York: Oxford University Press, Vol. 2, pp. 64-76.

Baritz, Loren
1960   *The Servants of Power,* Minneapolis: Greenwood.

Bendix, Reinhard
1963   *Work and Authority in Industry: Ideologies of Management in the Course of Industrialization,* New York: Harper & Row.

Bernstein, Irving
1960   *The Lean Years: A History of the American Workers, 1920-1933,* Boston: Houghton-Mifflin.

Blau, Peter M.
1974   "Parameters of social structure," *American Sociological Review,* Vol. 39 (October), pp. 615-39.

Blauner, Robert
1964   *Alienation and Freedom: The Factory Worker and His Industry,* Chicago: University of Chicago Press.

Boyer, Richard O. and Herbert M. Morais
1971   *Labor's Untold Story,* New York: United Electrical, Radio and Machine Workers of America.

Braverman, Harry
1974   *Labor and Monopoly Capital: The Degradation of Work in the Twentieth Century,* New York: Monthly Review Press.

Brecher, Jeremy
1972   *Strike!* San Francisco: Straight Arrow Books.

Brody, David

1960   *Steelworkers in America: The Nonunion Era,* New York: Harper & Row.

1965   *Labor in Crisis: The Steel Strike of 1919,* New York: Lippencott.

1968   "The rise and decline of welfare capitalism," in John Braeman et al. (eds.), *Change and Continuity in Twentieth-Century America: The 1920's,* Columbus: Ohio State University, pp. 147-78.

Chandler, Alfred D.

1962   *Strategy and Structure: Chapters in the History of Enterprise,* Cambridge, Mass.: MIT.

Chandler, Alfred D., Jr.

1977   *The Visible Hand: The Managerial Revolution in American Business,* Cambridge, Mass.: Harvard University Press.

Commons, John R. et al.

1926-   *History of Labor in the United*
35   *States,* 4 vols., New York: MacMillan.

Crozier, Michel

1964   *The Bureaucratic Phenomenon,* Chicago: University of Chicago Press.

Davis, Mike

1975   "The stop watch and the wooden shoe: scientific management and the industrial workers of the world," in *Radical America,* Vol. 9 (Jan.-Feb., 1975), pp. 69-95.

deKadt, Maarten

1975   "A review of labor and monopoly capital," in *Review of Radical Political Economics,* Vol. 7 (Spring), pp. 84-90.

Dennison, Henry

1917   "What the employment department should be in industry," in *Bulletin of the United States Bureau of Labor Statistics,* No. 227, Employment and Unemployment Series: No. 7, pp. 77-81.

Derber, Milton

1970   *The American Idea of Industrial Democracy, 1865-1965,* Urbana, Illinois: University of Illinois Press.

Douglas, Paul H.

1930   *Real Wages in the United States, 1890-1926,* New York: Houghton-Mifflin.

Drury, Horace B.

1916   "Democracy as a factor in industrial efficiency," *The Annals of the American Academy of Political and Social Science,* Vol. 65 (May), pp. 15-27.

Duggan, Edward P.

1977   "Machines, markets, and labor: the carriage and wagon industry in nineteenth-century Cincinnati," *Business History Review,* Vol. 51 (Autumn), pp. 308-25.

Edwards, Richard C.

1975   "The social relations of production the firm and labor market structure," *Politics and Society,* Vol. 5 (Summer), pp. 83-108.

1978   "Systems of control in the labor process," in Richard C. Edwards et al., *The Capitalist System,* Englewood Cliffs, N.J.: Prentice-Hall, pp. 193-200.

Ehrenreich, Barbara and John Ehrenreich

1977   "The professional managerial class," in *Radical America,* Vol. 11 (March-April), pp. 7-31.

Eilbut, Henry

1959   "The development of personnel management in the United States," *Business History Review,* Vol. 33 (Autumn), pp. 345-64.

Etzioni, Amatai

1961   *A Comparative Analysis of Complex Organizations,* New York: Free Press.

Faulkner, Harold U.

1951   *The Decline of Laissez-Faire, 1897-1917,* New York: Holt, Rinehart & Winston.

Feiss, Richard A.

1916   "Personal relationship as a basis of scientific management," *The Annals of the American Academy of Political and Social Science,* Vol. 65 (May), pp. 27-57.

Finer, Ann and George Savage (eds.)

1965   *The Selected Letters of Josiah Wedgwood,* London: Cory, Adams, & MacKay.

Flink, James J.

1976   *The Car Culture,* Cambridge, Mass.: MIT Press.

Foner, Philip S.

1947-   *The History of the Labor Movement*
65   *in the United States,* 4 vols., New York: International Press.

Fortune
1977a   "The Fortune directory of the 500 largest U.S. industrial corporations," *Fortune* (May), pp. 364-91.
1977b   "The Fortune directory of the second 500 largest U.S. industrial corporations, *Fortune* (June), pp. 204-32.

Galambos, Louis
1970   "The emerging organizational synthesis in modern American history, *Business History Review*, Vol. 44 (Autumn), pp. 279-90.

Giedion, Sigfried
1948   *Mechanization Takes Comand,* New York: Oxford University Press.

Gold, David et al.
1975   "Marxist theories of the state," *Monthly Review*, Vol. 26 (October), pp. 29-43.

Goldman, Paul
1973   "The organization caste system and the new working class," *The Insurgent Sociologist,* Vol. 3 (Winter), pp. 41-51.

Goldman, Robert and John Wilson
1977   "The rationalization of leisure," *Politics and Society,* Vol. 7, No. 2 (Spring), pp. 157-87.

Gordon, David M.
1976   "Capitalist efficiency and socialist efficiency," *Monthly Review,* Vol. 28 (July-August), pp. 19-39.

Gouldner, Alvin W.
1954   *Patterns of Industrial Bureaucracy,* Chicago: Free Press.

Gutman, Herbert G.
1970   "The worker's search for power labor in the gilded age," in H. Wayne Morgan (ed.), *The Gilded Age: A Reappraisal,* Syracuse: Syracuse University Press, pp. 31-54.
1976   *Work, Culture and Society in Industrializing America,* New York: Knopf.

Habakkuk, H. J.
1962   *American and British Technology in the Nineteenth Century,* Cambridge: Cambridge University Press.

Haber, Samuel
1964   *Efficiency and Uplife: Scientific Management in the Progressive Era,* Chicago: University of Chicago Press.

Hagedorn, Homer H.
1958   "A note on the motivation of personnel management," *Explorations in Entrepreneurial History,* Vol. 10 (April), pp. 134-9.

Haire, Mason
1959   "Biological models and empirical histories of the growth of organizations," in Mason Haire (ed.), *Modern Organization Theory.* New York: John Wiley.

Hall, Richard H.
1977   *Organizations: Structure and Process,* Englewood Cliffs, N.J.: Prentice-Hall.

Hawkins, David F.
1963   "The development of modern financial reporting practices among American manufacturing firms," in *Business History Review,* Vol. 37, pp. 135-68.

Henderson, C. R.
1895   "Businessmen and social theorists," in *American Journal of Sociology,* Vol. 1 (Jan.), pp. 385-97.

Hopkins, Ernest Martin
1916   "A functionalized employment department as a factor in industrial efficiency," *The Annals of the American Academy of Political and Social Science,* Vol. 65 (May), pp. 67-75.

Jacoby, Henry
1973   *The Bureaucratization of the World,* Berkeley: University of California Press.

Jenks, Leland H.
1960   "Early phases of the management movement," *Administrative Science Quarterly,* Vol. 5 (December), pp. 420-47.

Kolko, Gabriel
1963   *The Triumph of Conservatism, 1900-1916,* New York: Quadrangle.

Korman, Gerd
1967   *Industrialization, Immigrants and Americanizers: The View From Milwaukee, 1866-1921,* Madison: The State Historical Society of Wisconsin.

Kusterer, Kenneth
1978   *Know-how on the Job,* Boulder, Colo.: Westview.

Leiserson, W. M.
1928   "Personnel management," *Wertheim Papers on Industrial Relations,* Cambridge: Harvard University, pp. 125-64.

Litterer, Joseph A.
1961   "Systematic management: the search for order and integration," *Business History Review,* Vol. 35 (Winter), pp. 461-76.

1963   "Systematic management: design for organization coupling in American manufacturing firms," *Business History Review,* Vol. 37 (Winter), pp. 369-91.

McKelvey, Jean Trepp
1952   *AFL Attitudes toward Production, 1900-1932,* Ithaca: Cornell University Press.

McKendrick, Neal
1961   "Josiah Wedgewood and factory discipline," *The Historical Journal,* Vol. 4, pp. 30-55.

Marglin, Stephen A.
1974   "What the bosses do: the origins and functions of hierarchy in capitalist production," *The Review of Radical Political Economics,* Vol. 6 (Summer), pp. 60-112.

Marx, Karl
1964   *The Economic and Philosophical Manuscripts of 1844,* New York: International.
1967   *Capital,* New York: International.

Melman, Seymour
1951   "The rise of administrative overhead in manufacturing industries in the United States, 1899-1947," *Oxford Economic Papers,* Vol. 3 (New Series), pp. 62-112.

Merkle, Judith
1968   "The Taylor strategy: organizational innovation and class structure," *Berkeley Journal of Sociology,* Vol. 13, pp. 59-81.

Miller, George A.
1967   "Professionals in bureaucracy: alienation among industrial scientists and engineers," *American Sociological Review,* Vol. 32 (October), pp. 755-67.

Montgomery, David
1976   "Workers' control of machine production in the nineteenth century," *Labor History Review,* Vol. 17 (Fall), pp. 485-509.
1977   Immigrant workers and managerial reform, in Richard Erlich (ed.), *Immigrants in Industrial America, 1850-1920,* Charlottesville: University Press of Virginia, pp. 96-110.

Mortimer, Wyndham
1971   *Organize! My Life as a Union Man,* Boston: Beacon.

Mulherin, James P.
1976   "The development of the sociologi-

cal fields which study work organization — a preliminary description." Paper presented at the Meetings of the American Sociological Association, New York.

Nadworney, Milton J.
1955   *Scientific Management and the Unions, 1900-1952: A Historical Analysis,* Cambridge: Mass.: Harvard University Press.

Nash, Al
1967   "Job satisfaction: a critique," in B. J. Widick (ed.), *Autowork and Its Discontents,* Baltimore: Johns Hopkins Press, pp. 61-88.

Nelson, Daniel
1975   *Managers and Workers: Origins of the New Factory System in the United States, 1880-1920,* Madison: University of Wisconsin Press.

Nelson, Daniel and Stuart Campbell
1972   "Taylorism versus welfare work in American industry: H. L. Gantt and the Bancrofts, *Business History Review,* Vol. 46 (Spring), pp. 1-16.

Noble, David F.
1977   *America by Design: Science, Technology and the Rise of Corporate Capitalism,* New York: Knopf.

Ozanne, Robert
1967   *A Century of Labor-Management Relations at McCormick and International Harvester,* Madison: University of Wisconsin Press.

Palmer, Bryan
1975   "Class, conception and conflict: the thrust for efficiency, managerial views of labor and the working class rebellion," *The Review of Radical Political Economics,* Vol. 7 (Summer), pp. 31-49.

Pollard, Sidney
1965   *The Genesis of Modern Management: A Study of the Industrial Revolution in Great Britain,* Cambridge, Mass.: Harvard University Press.

Reich, Michael et al.
1973   "A theory of labor market segmentation," *American Economic Review,* Vol. 64 (May), pp. 359-65.

Rosenberg, Nathan
1976a "Marx as a student of technology," *Monthly Review,* Vol. 29 (July-August), pp. 56-77.
1976b *Perspectives on Technology,* New York: Cambridge University Press.

Rosenblum, Gerald
1973   *Immigrant Workers: Their Impact on American Labor Radicalism,* New York: Basic Books.
Rodgers, Daniel T.
1978   *The Work Ethic in Industrial America, 1850-1920,* Chicago: University of Chicago Press.
Rothschild, Emma
1973   *Paradise Lost: The Decline of the Auto-Industrial Age,* New York: Random House.
Rudin, Bradley
1972   "Industrial betterment and scientific management as social control, 1890-1920," *Berkeley Journal of Sociology,* Vol. 17, pp. 59-77.
Russell, Jack
1978   "The coming of the line: the Ford Highland Park plant, 1910-1914, *Radical America,* Vol. 12 (May-June), pp. 29-45.
Saul, S. B.
1970   *Technological Change: The United States and Britain in the 19th Century,* London: Methuen.
Shergold, Peter R.
1977   "Wage differentials based on skill in the United States, 1899-1914: a case study, *Labor History,* Vol. 18 (Fall), pp. 485-508.
Sinclair, Upton
1906   *The Jungle,* New York: Doubleday, Page & Co.
Strassman, W. Paul
1959   *Risk and Technological Innovation: American Manufacturing Methods during the Nineteenth Century,* Ithaca, N.Y.: Cornell University Press.
Stone, Katherine
1975   "The origins of job structures in the steel industry," in Richard C. Edwards et al. (eds.), *Labor Market Segmentation,* Lexington, Mass.: D. C. Heath, pp. 27-84.
Sward, Keith
1968   *The Legend of Henry Ford,* New York: Holt, Rinehart & Winston.
Taft, Philip
1957   *The A.F. of L. in the Time of Gompers,* New York: Harper.

Taylor, Frederick W.
1967   *The Principles of Scientific Management,* New York: Norton.
Tolman, William H.
1909   *Social Engineering: A Record of Things Done by American Industrialists Employing Upwards of One and One-Half Million People,* New York: McGraw-Hill.
Veblen, Thorstein
1971   *The Portable Veblen,* ed. by Max Lerner, New York: Viking.
Walker, Charles R.
1967   "The social effects of mass production," in Melvin Kranzberg and Carroll W. Pursell, Jr. (eds.), *Technology in Western Civilization,* New York: Oxford University Press, Vol. 2, pp. 91-103.
Welfare Work
1917   *The Welfare Work of the Metropolitan Life Insurance Company for its Industrial Policy-holders and Employees: Reports for 1917,* New York: Metropolitan Life Insurance Company.
Weinstein, James
1968   *The Corporate Ideal in the Liberal State,* Boston: Beacon.
Wiebe, Robert H.
1967   *The Search for Order, 1877-1920,* New York: Hill & Wang.
1968   *Businessmen and Reform: A Study of the Progressive Movement,* Chicago: Quadrangel.
Williams, Jane C.
1917   "The reduction of labor turnover in the Plimpton Press, *Bulletin of the United States Bureau of Labor Statistics,* No. 227, Employment and Unemployment Series: No. 7, pp. 82-91.
Wood, J. Norman
1960   "Industrial relations policies of American management, 1900-1933, *Business History Review,* Vol. 34 (Winter), pp. 403-20.
Yellowitz, Irwin
1977a "Skilled workers and mechanization: the lasters in the 1880's, *Labor History,* Vol. 18 (Spring), pp. 197-213.
1977b *Industrialization and the American Labor Movement, 1850-1900,* Port Washington, N.Y.: Kennikat.

11. Educational Organizations as Loosely Coupled Systems[1]

Karl E. Weick

Imagine that you're either the referee, coach, player or spectator at an unconventional soccer match: the field for the game is round; there are several goals scattered haphazardly around the circular field; people can enter and leave the game whenever they want to; they can throw balls in whenever they want; they can say "that's my goal" whenever they want to, as many times as they want to, and for as many goals as they want to; the entire game takes place on a sloped field; and the game is played as if it makes sense (March, personal communication).

If you now substitute in that example principals for referees, teachers for coaches, students for players, parents for spectators and schooling for soccer, you have an equally unconventional depiction of school organizations. The beauty of this depiction is that it captures a different set of realities within educational organizations than are caught when these same organizations are viewed through the tenets of bureaucratic theory.

Consider the contrast in images. For some time people who manage organizations and people who study this managing have asked, "How does an organization go about doing what it does and with what consequences for its people, processes, products, and persistence?" And for some time they've heard the same answers. In paraphrase the answers say essentially that an organization does what it does because of plans, intentional selection of means that get the organization to agree upon goals, and all of this is accomplished by such rationalized procedures as cost-benefit analyses, division of labor, specified areas of discretion, authority invested in the office, job descriptions, and a consistent evaluation and reward system. The only problem with that portrait is that it is rare in nature. People in organizations, including educational organizations, find themselves hard pressed either to find actual instances of those rational practices or to find rationalized practices whose outcomes have been as beneficent as predicted, or to feel that those rational occasions explain much of what goes on within the organization. Parts of some organizations are heavily

---

[1] Reprinted from "Educational Organizations as Loosely Coupled Systems" by Karl E. Weick, published in *Administrative Science Quarterly*, March 1976, vol. 21, no. 1, pp. 1-11, 19, by permission of *The Administrative Science Quarterly*. Copyright © 1976 by Cornell University.

This paper is the result of a conference held at La Jolia, California, February 2-4, 1975 with support from the National Institute of Education (NIE). Participants in the conference were, in addition to the author, W. W. Charters, Center for Educational Policy and Management, University of Oregon; Craig Lundberg, School of Business, Oregon State University; John Meyer, Dept. of Sociology, Stanford University; Miles Meyers, Dept. of English, Oakland (Calif.) High School; Karlene Roberts, School of Business, University of California, Berkeley; Gerald Salancik, Dept. of Business Administration, University of Illinois; and Robert Wentz, Superintendent of Schools, Pomona (Calif.) Unified School District. James G. March, School of Education, Stanford University, a member of the National Council on Educational Research and members of the NIE staff were present as observers. This conference was one of several on organizational processes in education which will lead to a report that will be available from the National Institute of Education, Washington, D.C. 20208. The opinions expressed in this paper do not necessarily reflect the position or policy of the National Institute of Education or the Department of Health, Education, and Welfare.

rationalized but many parts also prove intractable to analysis through rational assumptions.

It is this substantial unexplained remainder that is the focus of this paper. Several people in education have expressed dissatisfaction with the prevailing ideas about organizations supplied by organizational theorists. Fortunately, they have also made some provocative suggestions about newer, more unconventional ideas about organizations that should be given serious thought. A good example of this is the following observation by John M. Stephens (1967:9-11):

> [There is a] remarkable constancy of educational results in the face of widely differing deliberate approaches. Every so often we adopt new approaches or new methodologies and place our reliance on new panaceas. At the very least we seem to chorus new slogans. Yet the academic growth within the classroom continues at about the same rate, stubbornly refusing to cooperate with the bright new dicta emanating from the conference room . . . [These observations suggest that] we would be making a great mistake in regarding the management of schools as similar to the process of constructing a building or operating a factory. In these latter processes deliberate decisions play a crucial part, and the enterprise advances or stands still in proportion to the amount of deliberate effort exerted. If we must use a metaphor or model in seeking to understand the process of schooling, we should look to agriculture rather than to the factory. In agriculture we do not start from scratch, and we do not direct our efforts to inert and passive materials. We start, on the contrary, with a complex and ancient process, and we organize our efforts around what seeds, plants, and insects are likely to do anyway. . . . The crop, once planted, may undergo some development even while the farmer sleeps or loafs. No matter what he does, *some* aspects of the outcome will remain constant. When teachers and pupils foregather, some education may proceed even while the Superintendent disports himself in Atlantic City.

It is crucial to highlight what is important in the examples of soccer and schooling viewed as agriculture. To view these examples negatively and dismiss them by observing that "the referee should tighten up those rules," "superintendents don't do that," "schools are more sensible than that," or "these are terribly sloppy organizations" is to miss the point. The point is although researchers don't know what these kinds of structures are like but researchers do know they exist and that each of the negative judgments expressed above makes sense only if the observer assumes that organizations are constructed and and managed according to rational assumptions and therefore are scrutable only when rational analyses are applied to them. This paper attempts to expand and enrich the set of ideas available to people when they try to make sense out of their organizational life. From this standpoint, it is unproductive to observe that fluid participation in schools and soccer is absurd. But it can be more interesting and productive to ask, how can it be that even though the activities in both situations are only modestly connected, the situations are still recognizable and nameable? The goals, player movements, and trajectory of the ball are still recognizable and can be labeled "soccer." And despite variations in class size, format, locations, and architecture, the results are still recognized and can be labeled "schools." How can such loose assemblages retain sufficient similarity and permanence across time that they can be recognized, labeled, and dealt with? The prevailing ideas in organization theory do not shed much light on how such "soft" structures develop, persist, and impose crude orderliness among their elements.

The basic premise here is that concepts such as loose coupling serve as sensitizing devices. They sensitize the observer to notice and question things that had previously been taken for granted. It is the intent of the program described here to develop a language for use in analyzing complex organizations, a language that may highlight features that have previously gone unnoticed. The guiding principle is a reversal of the common assertion, ''I'll believe it when I see it'' and presumes an epistemology that asserts, ''I'll see it when I believe it.'' Organizations as loosely coupled systems may not have been seen before because nobody believed in them or could afford to believe in them. It is conceivable that preoccupation with rationalized, tidy, efficient, coordinated structures has blinded many practitioners as well as researchers to some of the attractive and unexpected properties of less rationalized and less tightly related clusters of events. This paper intends to eliminate such blindspots.

THE CONCEPT OF COUPLING

The phrase ''loose coupling'' has appeared in the literature (Glassman, 1973; March and Olsen,1975) and it is important to highlight the connotation that is captured by this phrase and by no other. It might seem that the word coupling is synonymous with words like connection, link, or interdependence, yet each of these latter terms misses a crucial nuance.

By loose coupling, the author intends to convey the image that coupled events are responsive, *but* that each event also preserves its own identity and some evidence of its physical or logical separateness. Thus, in the case of an educational organization, it may be the case that the counselor's office is loosely coupled to the principal's office. The image is that the principal and the counselor are somehow attached, but that each retains some identity and separateness and that their attachment may be circumscribed, infrequent, weak in its mutual affects, unimportant, and/or slow to respond. Each of those connotations would be conveyed if the qualifier loosely were attached to the word coupled. Loose coupling also carries connotations of impermanence, dissolvability, and tacitness all of which are potentially crucial properties of the ''glue'' that holds organizations together.

Glassman (1973) categorizes the degree of coupling between two systems on the basis of the activity of the variables which the two systems share. To the extent that two systems either have few variables in common or share weak variables, they are independent of each other. Applied to the educational situation, if the principal-vice-principal-superintendent is regarded as one system and the teacher-classroom-pupil-parent-curriculum as another system, then by Glassman's argument if we did not find many variables in the teacher's world to be shared in the world of a principal and/or if the variables held in common were unimportant relative to the other variables, then the principal can be regarded as being loosely coupled with the teacher.

A final advantage of coupling imagery is that it suggests the idea of building blocks that can be grafted onto an organization or severed with relatively little disturbance to either the blocks or the organization. Simon (1969) has argued for the attractiveness of this feature in that most complex systems can be decomposed into stable subassemblies and that these are the crucial elements in any organization or system. Thus, the coupling imagery gives researchers access to one of the more powerful ways of talking about complexity now available.

But if the concept of loose coupling highlights novel images heretofore unseen in organizational theory, what is it about these images that is worth seeing?

COUPLED ELEMENTS

There is no shortage of potential coupling elements, but neither is the population infinite.

At the outset the two most commonly discussed coupling mechanisms are the technical core of the organization and the authority of office. The relevance of those two mechanisms for the issue of identifying elements is that in the case of technical couplings, each element is some kind of technology, task, subtask, role, territory and person, and the couplings are task-induced. In the case of authority as the coupling mechanism, the elements include positions, offices, responsibilities, opportunities, rewards, and sanctions and it is the couplings among these elements that presumably hold the organization together. A compelling argument can be made that *neither* of these coupling mechanisms is prominent in educational organizations found in the United States. This leaves one with the question what *does* hold an educational organization together?

A short list of potential elements in educational organizations will provide background for subsequent propositions. March and Olsen (1975) utilize the elements of intention and action. There is a developing position in psychology which argues that intentions are a poor guide for action, intentions often follow rather than precede action, and that intentions and action are loosely coupled. Unfortunately, organizations continue to think that planning is a good thing, they spend much time on planning, and actions are assessed in terms of their fit with plans. Given a potential loose coupling between the intentions and actions of organizational members, it should come as no surprise that administrators are baffled and angered when things never happen the way they were supposed to.

Additional elements may consist of events like yesterday and tomorrow (what happened yesterday may be tightly or loosely coupled with what happens tomorrow) or hierarchial positions, like, top and bottom, line and staff, or administrators and teachers. An interesting set of elements that lends itself to the loose coupling imagery is means and ends. Frequently, several different means lead to the same outcome. When this happens, it can be argued that any one means is loosely coupled to the end in the sense that there are alternative pathways to achieve that same end. Other elements that might be found in loosely coupled educational systems are teachers-materials, voters-schoolboard, administrators-classroom, process-outcome, teacher-teacher, parent-teacher, and teacher-pupil.

While all of these elements are obvious, it is not a trivial matter to specify which elements are coupled. As the concept of coupling is crucial because of its ability to highlight the identity and separateness of elements that are momentarily attached, that conceptual asset puts pressure on the investigator to specify clearly the identity, separateness, and boundaries of the elements coupled. While there is some danger of reification when that kind of pressure is exerted, there is the even greater danger of portraying organizations in inappropriate terms which suggest an excess of unity, integration, coordination, and consensus. If one is nonspecific about boundaries in defining elements then it is easy — and careless — to assemble these ill-defined elements and talk about integrated organizations. It is not a trivial issue explaining how elements persevere over time. Weick, for example, has argued (1974:363-364) that elements may appear or disappear and may merge or become separated in response to need-deprivations within the individual, group, and/or organization. This means that specification of elements is not a one-shot activity. Given the context of most organizations, elements both appear and disappear over time. For this reason a theory of how elements become loosely or tightly coupled may also have to take account of the fact that the nature and intensity of the coupling may itself serve to create or dissolve elements.

The question of what is available for coupling and decoupling within an organization is an eminently practical question for anyone wishing to have some leverage on a system.

STRENGTH OF COUPLING

Obviously there is no shortage of meanings for the phrase loose coupling. Researchers need to be clear in their own thinking about whether the phenomenon they are studying is described by two words or three. A researcher can study "loose coupling" in educational organizations or "loosely coupled systems." Ths shorter phrase, "loose coupling," simply connotes things, "anythings," that may be tied together either weakly or infrequently or slowly or with minimal interdependence. Whether those things that are loosely coupled exist in a system is of minor importance. Most discussions in this paper concern loosely coupled systems rather than loose coupling since it wishes to clarify the concepts involved in the perseverance of sets of elements across time.

The idea of loose coupling is evoked when people have a variety of situations in mind. For example, when people describe loosely coupled systems they are often referring to (1) slack times — times when there is an excessive amount of resources relative to demands; (2) occasions when any one of several means will produce the same end; (3) richly connected networks in which influence is slow to spread and/or is weak while spreading; (4) a relative lack of coordination, slow coordination or coordination that is dampened as it moves through a system; (5) a relative absence of regulations; (6) planned unresponsiveness; (7) actual causal independence; (8) poor observational capabilities on the part of a viewer; (9) infrequent inspection of activities within the system; (10) decentralization; (11) delegation of discretion; (12) the absence of linkages that should be present based on some theory — for example, in educational organizations the expected feedback linkage from outcome back to inputs is often nonexistent; (13) the observation that an organization's structure is not coterminus with its activity; (14) those occasions when no matter what you do things always come out the same — for instance, despite all kinds of changes in curriculum, materials, groupings, and so forth the outcomes in an educational situation remain the same; and (15) curricula or courses in educational organizations for which there are few prerequisites — the longer the string of prerequisites, the tighter the coupling.

POTENTIAL FUNCTIONS AND DYSFUNCTIONS OF LOOSE COUPLING

It is important to note that the concept of loose coupling need not be used normatively. People who are steeped in the conventional literature of organizations may regard loose coupling as a sin or something to be apologized for. This paper takes a neutral, if not mildly affectionate, stance toward the concept. Apart from whatever affect one might feel toward the idea of loose coupling, it does appear a priori that certain functions can be served by having a system in which the elements are loosely coupled. Below are listed seven potential functions that could be associated with loose coupling plus additional reasons why each advantage might also be a liability. The dialectic generated by each of these oppositions begins to suggest dependent variables that should be sensitive to variations in the tightness of coupling.

The basic argument of Glassman (1973) is that loose coupling allows some portions of an organization to persist. Loose coupling lowers the probability that the organization will have to — or be able to — respond to each little change in the environment that occurs. The mechanism of voting, for example, allows elected officials to remain in office for a full term even though their constituency at any moment may disapprove of particular actions. Some identity and separateness of the element "elected official" is preserved relative to a second element, "constituency,'' by the fact of loosely coupled accountability which is measured in two, four, or six year terms. While loose coupling may foster perseverance, it is not selective in what is perpetuated. Thus archaic traditions as well as innovative improvisations may be perpetuated.

A second advantage of loose coupling is that it may provide a sensitive sensing mechanism. This possibility is suggested by Fritz Heider's perceptual theory of things and medium. Heider (1959) argues that perception is most accurate when a medium senses a thing and the medium contains many independent elements that can be externally constrained. When elements in a medium become either fewer in number and/or more internally constrained and/or more interdependent, their ability to represent some remote thing is decreased. Thus sand is a better medium to display wind currents than are rocks, the reason being that sand has more elements, more independence among the elements, and the elements are subject to a greater amount of external constraint than is the case for rocks. Using Heider's formulation metaphorically, it could be argued that loosely coupled systems preserve many independent sensing elements and therefore "know" their environments better than is true for more tightly coupled systems which have fewer externally constrained, independent elements. Balanced against this improvement in sensing is the possibility that the system would become increasingly vulnerable to producing faddish responses and interpretations. If the environment is known better, then this could induce more frequent changes in activities done in response to this "superior intelligence."

A third function is that a loosely coupled system may be a good system for localized adaptation. If all of the elements in a large system are loosely coupled to one another, then any one element can adjust to and modify a local unique contingency without affecting the whole system. These local adaptations can be swift, relatively economical, and substantial. By definition, the antithesis of localized adaptation is standardization and to the extent that standardization can be shown to be desirable, a loosely coupled system might exhibit fewer of these presumed benefits. For example, the localized adaptation characteristic of loosely coupled systems may result in a lessening of educational democracy.

Fourth, in loosely coupled systems where the identity, uniqueness, and separateness of elements is preserved, the system potentially can retain a greater number of mutations and novel solutions than would be the case with a tightly coupled system. A loosely coupled system could preserve more "cultural insurance" to be drawn upon in times of radical change than in the case for more tightly coupled systems. Loosely coupled systems may be elegant solutions to the problem that adaptation can preclude adaptability. When a specific system fits into an ecological niche and does so with great success, this adaptation can be costly. It can be costly because resources which are useless in a current environment might deteriorate or disappear even though they could be crucial in a modified environment. It is conceivable that loosely coupled systems preserve more diversity in responding than do tightly coupled systems, and therefore can adapt to a considerably wider range of changes in the environment than would be true for tightly coupled systems. To appreciate the possible problems associated with this abundance of mutations, reconsider the dynamic outlined in the preceding discussion of localized adaptation. If a local set of elements can adapt to local idiosyncracies without involving the whole system, then this same loose coupling could also forestall the spread of advantageous mutations that exist somewhere in the system. While the system may contain novel solutions for new problems of adaptation, the very structure that allows these mutations to flourish may prevent their diffusion.

Fifth, if there is a breakdown in one portion of a loosely coupled system then this breakdown is sealed off and does not affect other portions of the organization. Previously we had noted that loosely coupled systems are an exquisite mechanism to adapt swiftly to local novelties and unique problems. Now we are carrying the analysis one step further, and arguing that when any element misfires or decays or deteriorates, the spread of this deterioration is checked in a loosely coupled system. While this point is reminiscent of earlier functions, the emphasis here is on the localization of trouble rather than the localization of adaptation. But even this potential benefit may be problematic. A loosely coupled system can isolate its trouble spots and prevent the trouble from spreading, but it should be difficult for the loosely coupled system to repair the defective element. If weak influences pass from the defective portions to the functioning portions, then the influence back from these functioning portions will also be weak and probably too little, too late.

Sixth, since some of the most important elements in educational organizations are teachers, classrooms, principals, and so forth, it may be consequential that in a loosely coupled system there is more room available for self-determination by the actors. If it is argued that a sense of efficacy is crucial for human beings, then a sense of efficacy might be greater in a loosely coupled system with autonomous units than it would be in a tightly coupled system where discretion is limited. A further comment can be made about self-determination to provide an example of the kind of imagery that is invoked by the concept of loose coupling.

It is possible that much of the teacher's sense of — and actual — control comes from the fact that diverse interested parties expect the teacher to link their intentions with teaching action. Such linking of diverse intentions with actual work probably involves considerable negotiation. A parent complains about a teacher's action and the teacher merely points out to the parent how the actions are really correspondent with the parent's desires for the education of his or her children. Since most actions have ambiguous consequences, it should always be possible to justify the action as fitting the intentions of those who complain. Salancik (1975) goes even farther and suggests the intriguing possibility that when the consequences of an action are ambiguous, the stated *intentions* of the action serve as surrogates for the consequences. Since it is not known whether reading a certain book is good or bad for a child, the fact that it is intended to be good for the child itself becomes justification for having the child read it. The potential trade-off implicit in this function of loose coupling is fascinating. There is an increase in autonomy in the sense that resistance is heightened, but this heightened resistance occurs at the price of shortening the chain of consequences that will flow from each autonomous actor's efforts. Each teacher will have to negotiate separately with the same complaining parent.

Seventh, a loosely coupled system should be relatively inexpensive to run because it takes time and money to coordinate people. As much of what happens and should happen inside educational organizations seems to be defined and validated outside the organization, schools are in the business of building and maintaining categories, a business that requires coordination only on a few specific issues — for instance, assignment of teachers. This reduction in the necessity for coordination results in fewer conflicts, fewer inconsistencies among activities, fewer discrepancies between categories and activity. Thus, loosely coupled systems seem to hold the costs of coordination to a minimum. Despite this being an inexpensive system, loose coupling is also a nonrational system of fund allocation and therefore, unspecifiable, unmodifiable, and incapable of being used as means of change.

When these several sets of functions and dysfunctions are examined, they begin to throw several research issues into relief. For example, oppositions proposed in each of the preceding seven points suggest the importance of contextual theories. A predicted outcome or its opposite should emerge depending on how and in what the loosely coupled system is embedded. The preceding oppositions also suggest a fairly self-contained research program. Suppose a researcher starts with the first point made, as loose coupling increases the system should contain a greater number of anachronistic practices. Loosely coupled systems should be conspicuous for their cultural lags. Initially, one would like to know whether that is plausible or not. But then one would want to examine in more fine-grained detail whether those anachronistic practices that are retained hinder the system or impose structure and absorb uncertainty thereby producing certain economies in responding. Similar embellishment and elaboration is possible for each function with the result that rich networks of propositions become visible. What is especially attractive about these networks is that there is little precedent for them in the organizational literature. Despite this, these propositions contain a great deal of face validity when they are used as filters to look at educational organizations. When compared, for example, with the bureaucratic template mentioned in the introduction, the template associated with loosely coupled systems seems to take the observer into more interesting territory and prods him or her to ask more interesting questions.

METHODOLOGY AND LOOSE COUPLING

An initial warning to researchers: the empirical observation of unpredictability is insufficient evidence for concluding that the elements in a system are loosely coupled. Buried in that caveat are a host of methodological intricacies. While there is ample reason to believe that loosely coupled systems can be seen and examined, it is also possible that the appearance of loose coupling will be nothing more than a testimonial to bad methodology. In psychology, for example, it has been argued that the chronic failure to predict behavior from attitudes is due to measurement error and not to the unrelatedness of these two events. Attitudes are said to be loosely coupled with behavior but it may be that this conclusion is an artifact produced because attitudes assessed by time-independent and context-independent measures are being used to predict behaviors that are time and context dependent. If both attitudes and behaviors were assessed with equivalent measures, then tight coupling might be the rule.

Any research agenda must be concerned with fleshing out the imagery of loose coupling — a task requiring a considerable amount of conceptual work to solve a few specific and rather tricky methodological problems before one can investigate loose coupling.

By definition, if one goes into an organization and watches which parts affect which other parts, he or she will see the tightly coupled parts and the parts that vary the most. Those parts which vary slightly, infrequently, and aperiodically will be less visible. Notice, for example, that interaction data — who speaks to whom about what — are unlikely to reveal loose couplings. These are the most visible and obvious couplings and by the arguments developed in this paper perhaps some of the least crucial to understand what is going on in the organization.

An implied theme in this paper is that people tend to overrationalize their activities and to attribute greater meaning, predictability, and coupling among them than in fact they have. If members tend to overrationalize their activity then their descriptions will not suggest which portions of that activity are loosely and tightly coupled. One might, in fact, even use the presence of apparent overrationalization as a potential clue that myth making, uncertainty, and loose coupling have been spotted.

J.G. March has argued that loose coupling can be spotted and examined only if one uses methodology that highlights and preserves rich detail about context. The necessity for a contextual methodology seems to arise, interestingly enough, from inside organization theory. The implied model involves cognitive limits on rationality and man as a single channel information processor. The basic methodological point is that if one wishes to observe loose coupling, then he has to see both what is and is not being done. The general idea is that time spent on one activity is time spent away from a second activity. A contextually sensitive methodology would record both the fact the some people are in one place generating events and the fact that these same people are thereby absent from some other place. The rule of thumb would be that a tight coupling in one part of the system can occur only if there is loose coupling in another part of the system. The problem that finite attention creates for a researcher is that if some outcome is observed for the organization, then it will not be obvious whether the outcome is due to activity in the tightly coupled sector or to inactivity in the loosely coupled sector. That is a provocative problem of interpretation. But the researcher should be forewarned that there are probably a finite number of tight couplings that can occur at any moment, that tight couplings in one place imply loose couplings elsewhere, and that it may be the *pattern* of couplings that produces the observed outcomes. Untangling such intricate issues may well require that new tools be developed for contextual understanding and that investigators be willing to substitute nonteleological thinking for teleological thinking (Steinbeck, 1941:chapt. 14).

Another contextually sensitive method is the use of comparative studies. It is the presumption of this methodology that taken-for-granted understandings — one possible "invisible" source of coupling in an otherwise loosely coupled system — are embedded in and contribute to a context. Thus, to see the effects of variations in these understandings one compares contexts that differ in conspicuous and meaningful ways.

Another methodological trap may await the person who tries to study loose coupling. Suppose one provides evidence that a particular goal is loosely coupled to a particular action. He or she says in effect, the person wanted to do this but in fact actually did that, thus, the action and the intention are loosely coupled. Now the problem for the researcher is that he or she may simply have focused on the wrong goal. There may be other goals which fit that particular action better. Perhaps if the researcher were aware of them, then the action and intention would appear to be tightly coupled. Any kind of intention-action, plan-behavior, or means-end depiction of loose coupling may be vulnerable to this sort of problem and an exhaustive listing of goals rather than parsimony should be the rule.

Two other methodological points should be noted. First, there are no good descriptions of the kinds of couplings that can occur among the several elements in educational organizations. Thus, a major initial research question is simply, what does a map of the couplings and elements within an educational organization look like? Second, there appear to be some fairly rich probes that might be used to uncover the nature of coupling within educational organizations. Conceivably, crucial couplings within schools involve the handling of disciplinary issues and social control, the question of how a teacher gets a book for the classroom, and the question of what kinds of innovations need to get clearance by whom. These relatively innocuous questions may be powerful means to learn which portions of a system are tightly and loosely coupled. Obviously these probes would be sampled if there was a full description of possible elements that can be coupled and possible kinds and strengths of couplings. These specific probes suggest, however, in addition that what holds an educational organization together may be a small number of tight couplings in out-of-the-way places.

REFERENCES

Bateson, Mary Catherine
1972   *Our Own Metaphor*. New York: Knopf.

Cohen, Michael D., and James G. March
1974   *Leadership and Ambiguity*. New York: McGraw-Hill.

Glassman, R. B.
1973   "Persistence and loose coupling in living systems." *Behavioral Science*, 18:83-98.

Heider, Fritz
1959   "Thing and medium." *Psychological Issues*, 13:1-34.

March, J. G., and J. P. Olsen
1975   *Choice Situations in Loosely Coupled Worlds*. Unpublished manuscript, Stanford University.

Meyer, John W.
1975   *Notes on the Structure of Educational Organizations*. Unpublished manuscript, Stanford University.

Mitroff, Ian I.
1974   *The Subjective Side of Science*. New York: Elsevier.

Mitroff, Ian, I., and Ralph H. Kilmann
1975   *On Organizational Stories: An Approach to the Design and Analysis of Organizations Through Myths and Stories*. Unpublished manuscript, University of Pittsburgh.

Salancik, Gerald R.
1975   *Notes on Loose Coupling: Linking Intentions to Actions*. Unpublished manuscript, University of Illinois, Urbana-Champaign.

Simon, H. A.
1969   "The architecture of complexity." Proceedings of the American Philosophical Society, 106:467-482.

Steinbeck, John
1941   *The Log from the Sea of Cortez*. New York: Viking.

Stephens, John M.
1967   *The Process of Schooling*. New York: Holt, Rinehart, and Winston.

Weick, Karl E.
1974   "Middle range theories of social systems." *Behavioral Science*, 19:357-367.

III

Introduction To Macro-Societal And Historical Emphases

Selections in this third part emphasize macro-societal and historical studies of organizations. Each gives explicit recognition to the larger societal forces that impinge on or are affected by organizations, although the way each author characterizes those societal forces and relates them to the study of organizations varies. In some cases the questions motivating the author's study have more to do with an issue about society and how it changes than with organizations, although organizations are clearly involved in such processes (for example Hymer, 1972, Selection 14; and Stone, 1974, Selection 18). In other selections specific mechanisms by which societal forces have an impact on organizations are defined and examined. For example, Zald, (1970, Selection 12) uses a political economy approach to the study of organizations. What is common to all, however, is the focus on societal forces and their relationships with organizational dynamics.

Some readers may question why Part III is not titled simply "The Organization and Its Environments," since this phrase is commonly used in organizational analysis to refer to forces outside organizations that affect them. As noted in the introduction to Part I of this anthology, such a heading would implicitly legitimize organizations as appropriate units of analysis while characterizing everything else external to them as environment, which would be misleading and inappropriate for these selections. For example, Hymer (1972, Selection 14) is concerned about the impact of multinational corporations in the world economic system and how the private polity of such organizations affects the distribution of power, wealth, talent, and rewards in cities and nation-states within the world system. In Selection 17, Alfred Chandler (1962) analyzes four stages in the history of large American industrial enterprises and the relationships of these stages to management strategies. Katherine Stone (1974, Selection 18) brilliantly describes the strategy of management in the steel industry during the period 1890-1920 and explains how management was able to change the existing labor system by introducing new labor-saving technology, imposing a new control system on the production process, and institutionalizing this new labor system, thus ensuring control over the production process. In each of these examples the author has addressed some major societal issue in which the dynamics were played out in organizations. While each of these is clearly an organizational study, none was initiated as a study of organizations per se. In each instance the author has asked very broad, often historical questions about society and has incorporated insights about organizational behavior that provide helpful answers to these questions.

A number of the selections included in this section were stimulated directly or indirectly by the macro-societal theories of Karl Marx (see Benson, 1977, Selection 13; Hymer, 1972, Selection 14; Stone, 1974, Selection 18) or Max Weber (see Gallie, 1978, Selection 16; and Karpik, 1978, Selection 20). There is a significant trend in the recent study of organizations of returning to the classical theorists as inspiration for organizational analysis. If this trend continues it could result in a much tighter linkage between studies of organizations and the classical theoretical origins of sociology, thus creating a stronger theoretical underpinning for organizational analysis and possibly integrating organizational analysis more closely with other fields in the discipline.

If one reflects on the theoretical structure underlying much of the literature about organizations in the field of sociology during the past twenty years, one sees that the most ostensible link to classical sociological theory focuses on the work of Max Weber. But as McNeil (1978, Selection 2) argues, the linkage of organizational theory to Weber's work most often centers on Weber's description of the ideal type of bureaucracy and excludes the full range of his societal concerns and details of his methodology. Hence these works represent an opportunistic reading, or perhaps misreading, of the theoretical concerns of Weber, but such a use of Weber's essay was probably essential for such theorists to link their work to Weber's and thus legitimize their research.

If the true roots of the sociological study of organizations are in classical theories, a logical question is what was the theoretical impetus for much of the sociological work on organizations over the past twenty years? The answer is too complicated to deal with in detail here, but certainly it would have to include a discussion of the pervading influence of functional theory in the 1950s and 1960s as well as the coalescence of the interests of students of management techniques with those of quantitatively oriented organizational researchers. This coalescence of interests may have run its course by now. A bifurcation seems to be occuring among researchers, dividing those essentially interested in questions related to better management from those wanting to ask broader questions about organizations in society. As is illustrated in the introduction to Part I, the outcome of this process is likely to be an increasing polarization in the kinds of studies that are conducted — managerial-oriented research versus critical societal analyses that examine the role of organizations as agents of social change, agents of social control in society, and agents of domination for the ruling classes. The selections included here reflect concern with these larger societal questions; they provide few answers to the student seeking clues to better management techniques, but they may presage a new era of organizational studies from the societal perspective.

POLITICAL ECONOMY PERSPECTIVES

The term "political economy" is probably as old as social science and through the years has taken on different colorations of meaning depending on the author using it. For example, in his book, *A Contribution to the Critique of Political Economy,* first published in 1859, Karl Marx criticized the political economy perspectives of classical economists such as Adam Smith and David Ricardo. However, Marx himself used the term in developing his materialistic theory of history, and a number of Marxist scholars have used this term to refer to their perspectives. More recently some social scientists have referred to "public choice" perspectives on public administration as "political economy" perspectives.

Zald (1970, Selection 12) uses the term "political economy" to depict the essence of his perspective as "the intersection of the polity structure and political life of organizations with the economy and economic life within organizations." Within a set of four categories reflecting the internal and external polity and economy of organizations (i.e., internal polity, internal economy, external polity, and external economy), he outlines a number of concepts, propositions, and variables that researchers should utilize in the study of organizations. For example, factors that are included in the internal polity include the amount and distribution of power, processes of demand aggregation, processes of conflict-resolution, and succession systems and processes. The factors that are key elements of the internal economy include the division of labor, technologies, and interunit exchanges; mechanisms and criteria for allocating resources; and incentive economies and their consequences. The external polity includes relationships with similar organizations, major suppliers, or buyers and regulatory agents, while external economy has to do with the characteristics of markets, suppliers of raw materials, clienteles, and the like.

Zald's selection is more of a framework, i.e., a set of categories or factors to be used to examine an organization, than a systematic theory. However, the approach advocated here does avoid some of the criticisms of the structural perspectives outlined in the introduction to Part I. For example, Zald's approach sensitizes the researcher to the needs, aspirations, and motivations of organizational actors, to the subtle and nuance relationships among them, and to both internal and external processes of change and development in organizational systems. Further, his concerns with organizational constitutions and with incentive systems in organizations squarely confront issues of ideology and values and their impact on organizational actors. Also, this approach calls for a historical understanding of the origins and development of the political economy of organizations.

Zald has utilized this perspective to good advantage in an insightful study of the Young Men's Christian Association (see *Organizational Change: The Political Economy of the YMCA,* 1970). In addition, he and Wamsley have applied the framework to public organizations in an extended essay (see Gary L. Wamsley and Mayer N. Zald, *The Political Economy of Public Organizations*). Although the framework has not been used extensively by other scholars, it is patently a rich and comprehensive tool for the analysis of organizations and will probably be used more often as the field of organizational analysis moves toward a more macro-societal perspective.

Very recently Benson (1975) has used the term "political economy" in his essay on interorganizational networks and their environments. Like Zald, Benson outlines a series of categories to be examined instead of presenting a systematic theory, but unlike Zald, he uses as the unit of analysis an interorganizational network, not a single organization. He identifies the key resources important to interorganizational networks as money and authority, and he suggests a number of possible dimensions for the study of the environments of interorganizational networks (see "The Interorganizational Network as Political Economy"). While Benson's framework is not as comprehensive as Zald's and does not have the advantage of a concrete application as does Zald's, it is nevertheless an important theoretical statement because it focuses on networks of organizations in their societal setting.

MARXIAN MACRO-SOCIETAL PERSPECTIVES

Until recently, the Marxian perspective has had little impact on the field of organizational studies. There appear to be several reasons for this. First, there was a hegemony of structural functional images in the field of sociology in general, and in organizational studies in particular, during the 1950s and early 1960s as exemplified in the works of Merton, Selznick, Gouldner, and Blau. Secondly and perhaps more importantly, the Marxian perspective is a societal perspective in which organizations serve as centers of production and objects of control by the bourgeoisie. However, there is little in Marxian theory that pertains to internal organizational dynamics. Hence, to the extent that conceptions of organizations focus on internal arrangements or environments that impinge on them, there is little or nothing in the Marxian perspective that would be informative for such approaches. Only as the questions asked about organizations and the imagery of them have begun to change has the Marxian perspective become more relevant. That is, as organizational analysts have begun to address societal issues of social change, social control, the consequences of domination of powerful economic organizations, class relations, and the like, the Marxian perspective has become increasingly relevant and important.

It is noteworthy, however, that many of the Marxian selections included here are not written by people who have been identified with the field of organizational studies, but rather by Marxian scholars asking important questions about strategies used by management to control the workforce, strategies used to extract greater profits, and the role of technology in this process. In other words, the relevance of these Marxian perspectives for organizational analysis depends to a great extent on the degree to which the agenda of organizational researchers is changing and the degree to which societal emphases come to occupy a key place in organizational studies.

In Selection 13, entitled "Organizations: A Dialectical View," Benson (1977) defines the essence of the Marxist dialectical perspective on organizations and contrasts this with what he calls the "conventional approaches." Particularly noteworthy is his emphasis on social process, exemplified by the statement that "the social world is in a continuous state of becoming — social arrangements which seem fixed and permanent are temporary, arbitrary patterns and any observed social patterns are regarded as one among many possibilities" (1977:3). Benson also points out that powerful organizations are viewed as instruments of domination in advanced industrial societies; thus he establishes the salience of power issues in this perspective. Benson centers most of his discussion on the four key principles of the Marxian dialectical approach: social construction, totality, contradiction, and praxis.

Selection 14, entitled "The Multinational Corporation and the Law of Uneven Development," is most noteworthy for Hymer's (1972) application of the Marxian insights in analyzing the role and consequences of multinational corporations (MNCs) in the world order. In a few pages at the beginning of the article he insightfully sketches the history of the development of MNCs and the factors contributing to their growth. The essence of this article is contained in his discussion of the contributions of MNCs to the uneven development of nation-states within the world economic system. Extrapolating from a three-level model of organizational administration often used in organizational analysis, Hymer shows how the centralization of control within MNCs creates a concentration of talent, wealth, and social amenities in a few privileged nation-states and is ultimately responsible for the disparity in economic development among nation-states. In other words, he shows how the decisions made by a relatively few powerful economic organizations affect the relative affluence or deprivation of nation-states within the world system. Readers who find Hymer's arguments intriguing should examine his earlier but related article "The Efficiency (Contradictions) and Multinational Corporations" (Hymer, 1970).

While these are the only two Marxian selections we included in this section, we have included a number of selections elsewhere that could have appropriately been included here. For example, we have included three Marxian selections in Part II above (see Edwards, 1978, Selection 8; Friedman, 1977, Selection 9; and Goldman and Van Houten, 1979, Selection 10). We included these under the heading "Marxian Micro-Organizational Perspectives" because they all focus on issues of social control of workers in organizations, but such a label is almost a contradiction in terms since the theoretical underpinnings of each of these selections is Marxian and therefore macro-societal.

In the case of the Friedman selection, the opening part of his book, *Industry and Labor: Class Struggle at Work and Monopoly Capitalism,* from which this selection was taken, is devoted to an outline of the Marxist framework and a discussion of monopolistic capitalism. The Stone piece (1974, Selection 18), included in a subsequent group of historical organizational analysis selections, could also be appropriately included here because of its explanation of how managerial strategies in the steel industry during the period 1890-1920 altered the labor process and enabled employers to achieve a more effective system of social control over the work force.

ORGANIZATIONS AS ARENAS OF LARGER SOCIETAL ACTION

The selections in this section are distinguished by their conceptualization of organizations as arenas in which larger societal forces are played out. On first reflection this concept may appear to differ little from that of perspectives that focus on internal organizational structures and processes; but the range of social, economic, and political forces brought to attention under this concept makes these selections clearly distinctive from structural perspective works.

The first selection in this section is by John Meyer and Brian Rowan and is entitled "Institutionalized Organizations: Formal Structure as Myth and Ceremony" (1977, Selection 15). These authors contend not only that organizations are arenas in which the actions of society are played out (a perspective which is consistent with the works of the French sociologist Alain Touraine), but that in modern society, formal organizational structures originate from and arise in the highly institutionalized contexts of society. In other words, organizations are born out of institutional definitions. Institutionalized products, services, techniques, policies, and programs are powerful myths that can influence organizations in two ways: first, they can define domains of activity and formal organizations, then emerge in these domains; second, they can arise in existing domains of activity within organizations, with the consequence that the organization must expand its formal structure to include the new myths.

Meyer and Rowan see the power of institutionalized myths increasing in post-industrial society and leading to an even greater proliferation of supporting organizations. Not only do these myths account for the expansion of organizations but also for the increased complexity of organizations. This complexity is problematic because within organizations these myths exist alongside concerns for rational efficiency, technical production, and exchange. More often than not these myths decrease the rationality and efficiency of organizations, but they must be incorporated and supported in order to ensure the legitimization of the organization in and to society. Thus organizations are faced with finding ways to deal with these contradictions. One way recommended by Meyer and Rowan is loose coupling of the formal structure to the activities of the institutionalized myths. For explanations of loose coupling see Weick (1976, Selection 11, above) and March and Olsen (1976).

Another selection in this section, "Managerial Strategies, the Unions and the Social Integration of the Work Force" by Duncan Gallie (1978, Selection 16), is the concluding chapter in his book *In Search of the New Working Class: Automation and Social Integration Within the Capitalist Enterprise*. Gallie's major concern is to examine the impact of technology, specifically automation, on worker integration in industrial enterprises. In the opening chapter he contrasts two differing theories of the impact of automation on worker integration. The first is that of Robert Blauner (1964), which maintains that the introduction of automated technologies in industries will result in a greater social integration of workers in the enterprise. In her work on organizations and technology, Joan Woodward (1965) made similar arguments. This view is contrasted with the perspective of Serge Mallet (1960:11), a French industrial sociologist, who argues that, on the contrary, the effect of automation will eventually lead to "a new form of revolutionary consciousness that aims at the overthrow of the existing pattern of social relations in the enterprise." After comparing these two theories Gallie (1978:36-37) defines the fundamental questions of his study:

> Does the growth of a highly automated sector of industry have major implications for the social integration of the work force, for the structure of managerial power, and for the nature of trade unionism? Or, alternatively, does the highly automated sector become assimilated into the predominant patterns of the wider society in which it emerges, in such a way that the degree of social integration of the work force depends on cultural and institutional factors deriving from the broader pattern of historical development of the specific society?

In attempting to answer the specific questions outlined above, Gallie conducted a survey of 800 workers in four oil refineries, two in France and two in Britain, all belonging to British Petroleum. Like Touraine (1965, 1971) and Goldthorpe and his colleagues (1968, 1969, 1970) in their studies of the affluent worker, he uses the Weberian perspective, which stipulates the importance of taking into account the values, beliefs, and intentions of actors in order to understand their behavior. Among the many intriguing findings of his study, one of the most striking is his finding of markedly different attitudes and orientations of French and British workers toward management and social control techniques used by management, even though these workers were working for the same multinational corporations in plants with comparable technologies. He concludes that the broader cultural and social structural factors and the historical circumstances leading to their genesis may provide greater clues about the attitudes and orientations of the working class than do the constraints emanating from technology. This is consistent with the social action perspective outlined above and with the rejection of technological determinism exemplified by the works of Edwards (1978, Selection 8) and Goldman and Van Houten (1979, Selection 10).

HISTORICAL ANALYSES

A number of the selections already discussed either point to the importance of a historical approach for the understanding of organizations or are themselves historical analyses. For example, Edwards (1978, Selection 8), Friedman (1977, Selection 9), Goldman and Van Houten (1979, Selection 10), and Hymer (1972, Selection 14) all emphasize the importance of a historical perspective for the understanding of organizations from a macro-societal perspective.

There is nothing inherent in perspectives of organizations such as the comparative structural and structural contingency approaches, which focus on internal organizational characteristics of structure and their interrelationships, that would sensitize them to examine organizations from a more long-term viewpoint, and most of them do not. Perrow's (1963) analysis of goals in hospitals, Zald's (1970) study of the YMCA, and the recent work of Meyer and Rowan (1977) are notable examples of the few sociological studies of organizations that develop a historical perspective. Two selections included here that exemplify the insights that can be derived from historical analyses of organizations are Chandler's (1962, Selection 17) work on the development of the multi-divisional structure in modern corporations and Stone's (1974, Selection 18) examination of managerial strategies for control of the work force.

Selection 17 is the concluding chapter of the work by Alfred D. Chandler, Jr., (1962) entitled *Strategy and Structure: Chapters in the History of the American Industrial Enterprise*. In this well-known book Chandler distinguishes *strategic* decisions or those concerned with the long-term viability of the enterprise from *tactical* decisions or those concerned with "day-to-day activities necessary for the efficient and smooth operation" of the firm. Defining strategy as "long-term goals and objectives of the enterprise" and structure as "the design of organization through which the enterprise is administered," he develops a thesis of structure following strategy (1962:19) that is consistent with the political and social action perspectives outlined throughout this anthology. His thesis maintains that once leaders have defined their long-term goals and objectives, they develop administrative arrangements that are most likely to permit them to achieve these objectives efficiently and effectively. Through detailed historical case studies of four corporate giants (DuPont, General Motors, Standard Oil of New Jersey, and Sears Roebuck and Company), he traces the evolution of various administrative structures that resulted from strategies of expansion of volume or production, geographical expansion, vertical integration, and diversification. In his concluding chapter he briefly summarizes the implementation of these strategies through four stages. He shows that the leaders of firms like DuPont and General Motors eventually had to develop multi-divisional administrative structures in order to cope with the centrifugal consequences of these strategies.

We considered including a selection from Chandler's more recent book, *The Visible Hand: The Managerial Revolution in American Business* (1977), in which he chronicles the history of modern management, i.e., the "visible hand," its professionalization, and the development of what he calls managerial capitalism. However, we felt that the thesis of that work, while it provided considerable amplification of many of the insights in his earlier work, was less appropriate for illustrating the themes developed in this anthology.

In "The Origins of Job Structures in the Steel Industry," Katherine Stone (1974, Selection 18) analyzes the development of labor market structures in the steel industry during the period 1890-1920. Her thesis is that the changes that took place during this period represented deliberate strategies on the part of capitalism to destroy the traditional labor system that gave workers considerable autonomy over their work lives. One strategy was to first break the unions and then introduce new technologies that would totally alter the nature of work and the control that workers had over it. To counter the labor problems that ensued, other strategies were developed to undermine any unity and cohesion among workers and thus prevent effective resistance to these new control procedures on the part of the employers. Among such strategies were (1) the development of wage incentive schemes such as the Halsey Premium Plan and the

Differential Piece Rate system of Frederick W. Taylor, which not only induced workers to work harder but also differentiated the workers and undermined their solidarity; (2) new promotion policies such as the development of job ladders, which once again introduced differentiated work structures into the firm and also had the effect of separating workers from one another and hence undermining their potential for resistance; and (3) welfare programs, which Stone interprets as another mechanism to ensure more effective control on the part of employers.

Stone also charts the process by which employers developed new methods for managing their work forces; these processes included the alteration of job definitions, retraining of foremen, and recruitment of managers from the ranks of young, educated men from the universities. Her arguments are both intriguing and convincing. There are a number of important implications of her work that are noteworthy. First, there is the implication that "the institutions of the labor market were not the inevitable result of modern technology or complex social organization." Rather, they were *choices* made by top managers and owners that would permit them to control the production process more effectively and hence to extract greater profits from their enterprises. Second, there is the implication that hierarchical and other types of administrative control systems that currently exist in modern organizations are by no means adaptations to the exigencies of technology or complex environments, but rather the products of the same kinds of human choice. In other words, her analysis is consistent with a strategic choice or political perspective on organizations. A third implication is that only by attempting a careful historical reconstruction of processes can these aspects of current situations that are accepted as inevitable by structuralist thinking be illuminated, i.e., shown to be outcomes of human choices and power conflicts within organizational arenas.

HISTORICAL AND POLITICAL PERSPECTIVE ON ORGANIZATIONS

In the final section of this anthology we include two selections that outline the historical and political perspective of Lucien Karpik, a French sociologist who heads the Center of the Sociology of Innovation at the Ecole des Mines in Paris, one of the prestigious "grandes ecoles" of the French educational system. His perspective on organizations is contained in five different articles, two of which have not been translated into English. No one of them gives a comprehensive overview of his perspective; therefore, we have included a synthetic and interpretative essay by Joseph W. Weiss, Selection 19, which brings together in a few pages the essential elements of Karpik's approach. We also include a portion of Karpik's article entitled "Organizations, Institutions and History" (1978, Selection 20), in which he outlines his concepts of logics of action and strategies and in which he discusses his conception of the internal and external power relations of the firm.

Many of the elements in Karpik's framework are not new. For example, his view of organizations as political arenas of bargaining and compromise and the essence of his ideas about logics of action can be found in the work of Cyert and March (1963), Strauss (1978), and Pettigrew (1973). What is new and distinctive about his work, however, is the incorporation of a political, historical, and societal perspective on organizations in a single approach. The starting point for his perspective is the orientations and objectives of individual actors, their identity of common objectives, the formation of coalitions, and the ensuing political processes in the firm. He makes the distinction between *objectives* of actors, which are the phenomenological definitions of actors' intentions, and *logics of action*, which are rationalities attributed to them by an external observer based on the observer's interpretation of their words and deeds. This distinction between ends that actors define and ends that an outside observer attributes to them is most helpful in attempting to understand the various approaches to the study of goals in organizations, since one implication of making this distinction is that the "goals" of organizations are in reality the private ends of the coalition that controls the organization.

So Karpik's perspective presents organizations as political systems in which actors and coalitions of actors engage in bargaining and exchanges, although this political process is obviously constrained by factors such as the control and coordination strategies of the dominant coalition, technologies in the firm, and the like. In addition to his concern with political processes in organizations, his approach is also essentially a macro-societal one. He conceives the arenas of action as ever-widening circles of activity: a subunit of the organization, the organization itself, a sub-set of comparable organizations, the industrial sector in which they are located, the larger economy, etc. As one progresses through each level, one sees larger societal forces increasingly incorporated into the analysis.

Karpik's perspective is also historical in that he distinguishes technological capitalism (as exemplified by multinational corporations in the most technologically advanced sectors of the economy such as aerospace, chemicals, pharmaceuticals, etc.) from merchant and industrial capitalisms. By historically examining the evolution of science and invention and their recent monopolization by the technologically most advanced MNC's, he is able to show which multinationals are exemplars of technological capitalism from earlier forms.

Finally, his perspective is characterized by an insistence on studying that which is particular and unique to organizations in addition to that which is common and generalizable to them. Consequently, the content of some of his concepts applies only to multinationals. This is not to suggest, however, that his perspective is an esoteric study of only MNC's. On the contrary, what is important about his approach is the conceptualization of organizations as political systems, a concern with their historical origins, and a concern with their interrelationships with larger societal forces. In other words, his approach can be generalized and the principles of his analysis can be applied to other organizations. Callon and Vignolle (1977), for example, successfully utilized Karpik's perspective in their study of an industrial research center in France.

BIBLIOGRAPHY

Benson, J. Kenneth
1975   "The interorganizational network as a political economy," *Administrative Science Quarterly* 20 (June): 229-249.
1977   "Organizations: A dialectical view," *Administrative Science Quarterly* 22: 1-21.

Braverman, Harry
1974   *Labor and Monopoly Capital.* New York: Monthly Review Press.

Callon, Michel, and Jean-Pierre Vignolle
1977   "Breaking down the organization: Local conflicts and societal systems

of action," *Social Science Information* 16, 2: 147-167.

Chandler, Alfred D., Jr.
1962   "Chapters in the history of the American industrial enterprise." *Strategy and Structure.* Cambridge, Mass.: The MIT Press.
1977   *The Visible Hand: The Managerial Revolution in American Business.* Cambridge, Mass.: The Belknap Press of Harvard University Press.

Cyert, Richard, and James March
1963   *A Behavioral Theory of the Firm.* New York: Prentice-Hall.

Edwards, Richard C.
1978   "The social relations of production at the point of production," *The Insurgent Sociologist* 8: 109-125.
1979   *Contested Terrain: The Transformation of the Workplace in the 20th Century.* New York: Basic Books.
Friedman, Andrew
1977   "Management — preliminary argument." Chapter 6 in *Industry and Labor: Class Struggle at Work and Monopoly Capitalism.* London: The Macmillan Press.
Gallie, Duncan
1978   *In Search of the New Working Class: Automation and Social Integration within the Capitalist Enterprise.* Cambridge, England: Cambridge University Press.
Goldman, Paul, and Donald R. Van Houten
1977   "Managerial strategies and the worker: A Marxist analysis of bureaucracy," *Sociological Quarterly* 18 (Winter).
1979   "Bureaucracy and domination: Managerial strategy in turn-of-the-century American industry." Chapter 5 in *The International Yearbook of Organization Studies.* London: Routledge and Kegan Paul.
Goldthorpe, John H., David Lockwood, Frank Bechhofer, and Jennifer Platt
1968   *The Affluent Worker: Political Attitudes and Behavior.* Cambridge, England: Cambridge University Press.
1969   *The Affluent Worker in the Class Structure.* Cambridge, England: Cambridge University Press.
1970   *Industrial Attitudes and Behavior.* Cambridge, England: Cambridge University Press.
Hymer, Stephen
1970   "The efficiency (contradictions) of multinational corporations." Papers and proceedings, *American Economics Review:* 441-453.
1972   "The multinational corporation and the law of uneven development." Pages 113-140 in J. Bahagwati (ed). *Economic and World Order from the 1970's to the 1990's.* New York: Collier-Macmillan.
Karpik, Lucien
1972a   "Sociologie, economie, politique et buts des organisations de production," *Revenue Francais de Sociologie* 13: 299-324.
1972b   "Les Politique et les logiques d'action de la grande entre prise industrielle," *Sociologie du Travail* 13: 82-105.
1972c   "Multinational enterprises and large technological corporations," Translated from *Revue Economique* 23: 1-46.
1972d   "Technological Capitalism," Translated from *Sociologie du Travail* 13: 2-34.
1978   "Organizations, institutions and history." In Lucien Karpik (ed.) *Organization and Environment: Theory, Issues and Reality.* Beverly Hills, Calif.: Sage.
Mallet, Serge
1975   *Essays on the New Working Class* (trans. and ed. Dick Howard and Dean Savage). St. Louis: Telos Press.
March, James G., and Johan P. Olsen
1976   *Ambiguity and Choice in Organizations.* Bergen: Universitelsforlaget.
Marx, Karl
1904   *A Contribution to the Critique of Political Economy.* Chicago: International Liberal Publishing Company.
McNeil, Kenneth
1978   "Understanding organizational power: building on the Weberian legacy," *Administrative Science Quarterly* 23, 1: 65-90.
Meyer, John, and Brian Rowan
1977   "Institutionalize organizations: Formal structure as myth and ceremony," *American Journal of Sociology* 83, 2: 440-463.
Meyer, Marshall, and M. Craig Brown
1977   "The process of bureaucratization," *American Journal of Sociology* 83 (September): 364-385.
Perrow, Charles
1963   "Goals and Power Structures." Pages 112-146 in Elit Friedson (ed). *The Hospital in Modern Society.* New York: The Free Press.
Pettigrew, Andrew
1973   *The Politics of Organizational Decision Making.* London: Tavistock.
Stone, Katherine
1974   "The origins of job structures in the steel industry," *The Review of Radical Political Economics* 6: 113-173.
Strauss, Anselm
1978   *Negotiation: Varieties, Contexts, Processes and Social Order.* San Francisco: Jossey-Bass.

Touraine, Alain
1965 *Sociologie de l'Action.* Paris: Editions du Seuil.
1971 *The Post-Industrial Society.* New York: Random House.
1977 *The Self-Production of Society.* Chicago: The University of Chicago Press.
Weick, Karl E.
1976 "Educational organizations as loosely coupled systems," *Administrative Science Quarterly* 21 (March): 1-19.
Woodward, Joan
1965 *Industrial Organizations: Theory and*
Practice. London: Oxford University Press.
Zald, Mayer N.
1970a *Organizational Change: The Political Economy of the YMCA.* Chicago: University of Chicago Press.
1970b "Political economy: A framework for comparative analysis." In Mayer N. Zald (ed.) *Power in Organizations.* Nashville, Tenn.: Vanderbilt University Press.

12.   Political Economy: A Framework for Comparative Analysis*

Mayer N. Zald

The publication of the *Handbook of Organizations* (March 1965) confirmed what many students of complex organizations already knew: although a vast number of studies, concepts, and approaches have been developed for the study of organizations, there is little apparent unity among them. The absence of unity is in part a function of the number of "basic" and "applied" disciplines involved — e.g., psychology, sociology, political science, and economics; industrial management, operations and systems analysis, public administration, etc. As Victor Thompson (1966) has emphatically noted, the disunity is also a function of the absence of integrative frameworks guiding and giving focus to the disparate strands of research.

One such integrative framework is provided by the political-economy approach to the study of organizations. Starting from analogies to the nation-state and national economies, the political-economy framework focuses on the intersection of the polity structure and political life of organizations with the economy and economic life within organizations.

The political-economy approach to the study of organizations was originally developed to help explain the direction and processes of organizational change. It proved, I think, very fruitful in explaining the transformation of the Young Men's Christian Association in America over the last one-hundred-twenty years and the more recent transformation of the YMCA of Metropolitan Chicago (Zald, 1970). The advantages, as compared with other theories, of the political-economy approach for the study of major organizational change have been stated elsewhere (Zald, 1968) and need not be detailed here.

In brief, the political-economy approach focuses on proximal internal and external determinates of change; thus it retains focus. It links change to organizational structure *and* goals as opposed to leaping from internal problems to leadership decisions; thus, it spells out a rather complete causal and contingent chain. Because it assumes that organizational character shapes decision premises, it allows room for both "rational" and "irrational" decision premises to enter into organization choices; thus, it avoids the biases of rationalistic and irrationalistic approaches to organizational change.

But this approach also has the advantage of being useful as a *middle-range, integrative,* theoretical framework for the *comparative* study of organizations. The framework is of the "middle range" because it assumes many of the assertions or concepts of social-system analysis and the general theory of action. Instead of dealing with "universals" and completely general propositions, it attempts to develop concepts, propositions, and variables that will order a range of specific organizational forms and processes.

The approach used here provides an *integrative* framework because it specifies the interrelation of a range of organizational dimensions and types of organizations. Some of these dimensions have been central concerns of other students of organizations, but their interrelation with other important dimensions has been left unspecified. It is also an integrative framework, because it brings within one over-all framework and language system a wider range of *types* of organizations than is usual, e.g., it is not restricted to bureaucratic organizations or businesses, etc.

Because the framework states the range of variation between organizations on crucial (in the sense of pervasive and powerful) variables, it is useful for comparative work. It is useful for the comparative study of major types of organization *and* for the comparative study of organizations *within* major types. For example, government departments may all have major bureaucratic components yet differ significantly on dimensions contained within the framework.

This paper emphasizes the usefulness of the framework for integrative and comparative purposes. It is a "working paper," for, as will become apparent, I am still developing the concepts and analytic distinction.

THE BASIC CONCEPT

In its most generic sense, political economy is the study of the interplay of power, the goals of power-wielders, and productive exchange systems (Cf. Buchanan, 1964). As used here, political economy is neutral to the question of the market's value as a mechanism for registering preferences, producing goods, and distributing income. In its nineteenth-century meaning, of course, political economy referred to that system in which politics or government was so ordered as to encourage the free play of market forces in determining the allocation of resources. In its more general sense, however, political economy refers only to the relations between political and economic structures and processes.

When applied to nations, the term refers to description and analysis of the interplay between the institutions of government and law, fortified by coercive power, and the economy, or the system of producing and exchanging goods. James Willard Hurst's monumental *Law and Economic Growth: The Legal History of the*

Lumber Industry in Wisconsin, 1836 to 1915 (1964), for example, relates how government's initial desire for rapid economic development brought about legal policies for disposal of public lands in Wisconsin, how the laws of property and contract led to certain patterns of private usage and, finally, how changing goals and conceptions of the public good influenced regulations of property-usage and the use of state money (conservation) in relationship to this property.

As this capsule summary of Hurst indicates, political economy is more than the study of a power structure as it affects economic structure. Also involved is a study of the *ends* desired and enshrined in the economy and polity. In these terms laissez faire economics was a normative system of political economy which, given the advantages of the division of labor, with profit as an incentive, strove to maximize overall production of material goods. By allowing market forces to determine profit and production, society would capitalize on the benefits of the division of labor.

Both in political science and sociology, conceptualization (although not empirical study) of the polity has focused on this goal-determining aspect of government and the political process. For instance, Norton Long (1962) points to the value of analyzing community constitutions that is, to the study of community rule and the ethos or values of dominant groups as a way of answering the central questions raised by Aristotle for the study of politics.

In sociology Talcott Parsons has also focused on the political process as the major arena of goal-determination and allocation for a society. His relevant point is that study of an organization's political economy must be concerned with the goal-shaping aspects of goals as these are embodied in dominant groups. *Whose* goals are maximized and with *what* consequences must be a central concern.

Beyond a study of an organization's goals and powers, what else is implied in taking a political-economic approach to organizations? There must be a form of institutional analysis focusing on the interaction of values and control groups with the supply of resources and demand for services of clients and funders. The term economy focuses both on the internal allocation of men, money, and facilities and on the external supply of resources and clients. Internally, of course, the mechanisms for allocating men, facilities, and money are carried out by traditional rules of thumb, intergroup bargaining, and hierarchical assignments. The internal economy of no organization can be described as functioning precisely according to pure market processes. (This empirical fact makes it harder to separate the internal political processes of organization from those of the internal economy.)

The term economy should not be conceived narrowly as limited to the exchange of money for services. Rather what is exchanged is a number of goods, or incentives, that bind men to each other. Following Barnard (1938:134-181) and derivatively Wilson and Clark (1961), a wide range of incentives can be explicated. Men are bound to organizations by promises of values fulfilled and promises of friendship and prestige, as well as by monetary contracts for the exchange of goods and services.

That this framework deals with the major political and economic factors in an organization does not rule out attention to many traditional concerns of the sociology of organization; professions and professional socialization, role relations and role conflict, and even the "fit" between personality and role can be included. Basing this analysis on political economy, however, suggests that these more traditional concerns must be subordinated and intermeshed with the dominant concern for the political-economic interactions and structure. For example, the attitudes and values of professional staff in an organization are not important as indicators of satisfaction, or morale, or even as a reflection of organizational ideology: they are only important as they articulate with the polity and economy. In a sense then, the political-economy approach abstracts for analysis two key sectors of a social system. Processes of socialization and pattern-maintenance are not dismissed but are treated only as they affect the political economy.

If the approach is to be more than a guiding metaphor, it is necessary to elaborate its major components. What are the major political and economic processes and structures of organization? How do they relate to each other? What is the variation among organizations on each of the central dimensions? What are some of the propositions about organizations that can be generated from these concepts and dimensions?

ORGANIZATIONAL CONSTITUTIONS

Just as nation-states and primitive societies have constitutions, so do complex organizations. These constitutions guide (constrain) the operation of the ongoing political economy. An organization's constitution is its fundamental normative structure. The constitution of an organization or, for that matter, of any enduring social system, is a set of agreements and understandings which define the limits and goals of the group (collectivity) as well as the responsibilities and rights of participants standing in different relations to it.

The term "constitution" is often used in both a narrower and a broader sense than we use it here. Narrowly, it refers to a specific, usually written, set of agreements as to the structure and rights of actors (collective and individual). Yet constitutions need not be written and written constitutions need not be binding. Broadly, the constitution sometimes refers to a total pattern of organization and the relationship among its parts (cf. Stinchcombe, 1960; Bakke, 1959). In the sense we use it, the constitution of an organization is more limited than the pattern of social organization since it refers to a conceptually defined normative order; the pattern of social organization contains elements which are neither normative nor conceptually defined. By constitution we will refer to a historic and conceptually defined normative order.

Organizational constitutions regulate behavior in at least four normative sectors: incentive exchanges, the range of discretion of positions, organizational "ownership," and collective goals and means. First, constitutional norms vary according to the norms binding individuals into the organization (that is, according to the "contract" or terms of exchange existing between organizations and their individual members). These norms of exchange determine the amount of energy, time, and commitment that the organization can expect from different members. They also determine the exent to which organizations have discretion over wide ranges of members' behavior.

"Incentive theory" and "compliance theory" have their major interest in the variations among organizations in the terms of exchange. Wilson and Clark (1961) distinguished between material, solidary, and purposive organizations in terms of three different kinds of incentives that bring about three different kinds of commitments. Etzioni's (1961) categories (coercive, utilitarian, and normative) overlap Wilson and Clark's and have much the same focus. An organization has a fragile polity if its norms of exchange are fundamentally weak and non-binding.

Second, constitutional norms specify the range of discretion and the decision responsibilities of officers, groups, and units. Rights and responsibilities are deeply imbedded in different kinds of functional, territorial, and hierarchical units. The federated-corporate distinction may be the broadest distinction in this regard, but even within corporate structures, questions of functional responsibility, autonomy, and levels of centralization may become basic constitutional parameters having great import for the polity's operation. It is quite clear that many crucial changes in modern society involve these constitutional norms regarding the rights and responsibilities of different groups. To cite only one widely known example, the range and rights of management as contrasted with unions involve the central constitutional norms of business corporations.

Third, constitutional norms are deeply embedded in the relationship of an organization to the society of which it is a part. These norms involve such basic premises as: To whom is the organization responsible? Under what conditions? The norms linking these organizations to society may undergo change during crisis periods. For example, an organization's right to use business property for profit may be modified in wartime. Moreover, the norms linking an organization to the larger society may be relatively unstated or even unknown except during such periods of crisis as wars and disasters (Thompson and Hawkes, 1962).

Finally, constitutional norms specify the focuses of collective action (that is, concerns falling inside or outside the zone of indifference of the organization and its subgroups). These include goals, target groups (clientele), and technologies (means). The clarity, specificity, and breadth of these focuses of collective action become involved in the ongoing political life of the organization as groups contend for their actual definition.

It should be clear that constitutional norms differ from organization to organization, not only substantively, but also in their import and intensity. Some organizations may change clientele groups or even goals with but little consequence if the former have few attachments to the latter.

Constitutional norms set limits for behavior, and it may be rare for participants even to be aware of the norms. One way to illustrate a constitutional norm is to ask what would happen if it were violated. For instance, what would happen if an NAACP leader asked his members to support the Ku Klux Klan? Stunned disbelief and accusations of insanity! (When Reverend Bevel said he would support James Earl Ray, the first response of many was that he was having a nervous breakdown.)

Constitutional norms set zones of expectation (zones of indifference). These indifference sectors may be broad or narrow. However, all zones of indifference need not be constitutional. If, for instance, the zone of indifference is merely habitual, few sanctions will be invoked by its violation; little power will be mobilized for its protection.

Empirically one recognizes constitutional norms by two kinds of indicators. Negatively, violation of basic norms leads to withdrawal of resource-commitment (including members) and/or major conflict, accompanied by *perceptions* of violations of major norms. Positively, basic norms are indicated by their reaffirmation and articulation by spokesmen for the collectivity.

Many comparative typologies of organizations are constructed out of the polar extremes of each of the constitutional dimensions. Numerous typologies are founded on basic differences in the terms of exchange (Wilson and Clark, 1961; Etzioni, 1961; Warriner, 1965; Gordon and Babchuck, 1959), difference in goals (Zald, 1963; Bidwell and Vreeland, 1963), rights and responsibility of groups and units (Sils, 1957). Also, they have been constructed out of conditions of responsibility (Blau and Scott, 1962), and the common sense classification of "public-private."

There is no special merit in showing that these constitutional dimensions have had traditional value in typological exercise. (All that would necessarily demonstrate is the ability to construct a concept of a constitution out of the history of sociological research. In fact, the dimensions were developed over time by pondering inductively-intuitively basic organizational "agreements" needed for an organization to function — they were not "derived" from a more general system framework. It is possible that they could be.) What is important to note is that the four dimensions are addressed to four fundamental problems of social systems:

(1) The motivational bases of individual commitment or participation in collectivities. (And what are the consequences of differences in these bases?) (2) The distribution of decision prerogative with the organization — the internal power-distribution. (3) The distribution of decision prerogative between the organization and the outside world — the external power relation. (4) The collective focus of the organization — what its work shall be.

I will not argue that there might not be other dimensions of constitution. I will argue that analysis of organizational constitutions will always include at least these four dimensions.

Note that organizations exhibiting all combinations of positions on all constitutional dimensions are unlikely to be found. For instance, because federated constitutions allow independent spheres of action, organizations are unlikely both to have federated constitutions (internal-polity dimension) and to be constitutionally responsible to a single major external decision center (external-polity dimension). Or again, organizations based on solidary incentive norms are unlikely to have also highly differentiated task norms, because such differentiation of task destroys or interferes with cohesion required for maintenance of solidary norms.

The congruence of organizational constitutional dimensions deserves further elaboration. Another topic deserving elaboration is the "sources" of basic norms. Some, for instance, will be rooted in the social structures of society. More important for our task is the implication of constitutional norms in the ongoing operation of the political economy.

THE OPERATING POLITICAL ECONOMY

The operating power system and the operating economy of an organization are constrained by and contain constitutional norms. We consider the power system the actual means by which decisions are influenced. There need not be much difference between the constitution and the actual power system, but it is a fundamental postulate of sociology and political science that, in a changing social system, there is likely to be a continuous state of tension and adjustment between them.

The actual power system is the patterned use of social influence in an organization. Use of the term "polity" or "power system" indicates that we wish to include more actors in this pattern than simply those who formally make and execute decisions. In its more inclusive form, a polity refers to the whole web of groups and individuals, internal or external to an organization, that possess resources to sanction decisions.[1]

---

[1] Following the usage current in political science, we use the term polity to refer only to those groups or positions having an active and somewhat organized influence on the process of decision-making. Certainly, upper level staff are included within the boundary of a polity. Also included would be groups holding major sanctions, such as unions or professional associations. In the national polity individual voters (i.e., those who register preferences relatively passively, intermittently, and without direct interaction with decision-makers) are the outer edge of the polity, but interest groups which speak for an articulate mass interest are certainly part of the polity. Similarly, for organizations, individual workers and/or stockholders become important to the political process as their interests aggregate to affect decisions, and so do the aggregations of interests of suppliers of major inputs (e.g., labor, capital, raw materials, facilities).

Polity analyses examine the institutionalized and authoritative patterns of decision control as well as the less regular and even "illegitimate," but systematic, influence processes. Analysis of polity focuses on the ends of decisions that are made, the channels to utilizing influence, the characteristics of influence-holders, and the distribution of power.

Where the polity is the power-and-control system of an organization, the economy is the productive exchange system of an organization. By definition organizations are less inclusive than societies. They have relative specific "products" or services which they offer in exchange for support by members of society. Just as an organizational polity has an internal and external aspect, so too, does an organization's economy. Although it is somewhat unusual to discuss an economy *within* an organization (Parsons would call it the "adaptive system"), our usage is consistent with its usage in the phrase "political economy" and is, we think, easily justified.

It will be convenient to analyze political economies into the structure processes and interaction of four broad sectors: external political environment, economic environment, internal polity structure and process, and internal economic structure and process. Figure 1 illustrates these sectors.

The over-all framework is undergirded by a very general and very weak assumption — that processes originating in any one of the sectors may impinge in some organizational cases on any of the other sectors.

We assume that the internal polity affects and/or is affected by the internal economic structure and process. And we also assume that some organizations to some extent can affect the external political and economic environments in which they are involved. However, for many there are some elements of both economic and political environment that are highly impervious to organizational action. For example, the economist's pure competitive market (homogeneous products, many suppliers, many buyers, low barriers to entry), leaves no room for an organization to affect the market and its position in it. Similarly, governmental constraints (an external political process) on an organization's internal economy through safety laws and regulations are, in the short run, impervious to action. In the long run, of course, organizations may coalesce to attempt to change such regulations.

Figure 1. Major Components of Political Economy

	Environment Structure and Process	Internal Structure and Process
POLITY	Associations of similar organizations (trade associations)	Power-distribution and major value constellations
	Relationship with major suppliers and buyers of factor inputs	Demand-aggregation
	Regulatory agents	Succession system
	Indirect parties	
ECONOMY	Characteristics of factor "markets" (labor, capital, etc.)	Allocation rules / Accounting-information systems
	"Raw materials" supply	Incentive system
	Characteristics of demand and clientele "Industry structure"	Task- and technology-related unit differentiation

Although in this last example the external polity effects the internal economy, a complete behavioral chain would have external-polity processes affecting internal polity, which transmits rules and allocates resources to the internal economy. That is, power-holders could (and sometimes do), refuse to comply with governmental regulation, thus eliminating a constraint over the internal economy. Interconnections between environmental and internal processes are elaborated below.

POLITICAL AND ECONOMIC ENVIRONMENTS

There are both distinctive differences and a degree of overlap in consequences between the environmental political and economic relations. The distinctive difference is that political relations involve attempts to influence the decision premises of the parties to the relationships. Organizations, in attempting to achieve ends, form external alliances, curry favor, and conform to the requirements of agents having greater power. On the other hand, strictly economic relations in the environment involve no attempt to change organizational goals; instead the willingness to buy a product or sell labor represents a registering of preferences. Only as these preferences are aggregated by the decision centers do they influence goals and operating procedures (e.g., the buyer shopping for a Cadillac registers a preference; he does not, by himself, influence design.)

Where individual buyers and suppliers represent minor proportions of organizations' exchange relations, they can be considered economic. But where they become "significant" proportions of an organization's supply sources or product-users, these relations may take on political connotations, and promises and threats (overt and covert bargaining) may be used to influence decision premises. As these relations stabilize, and as structural mechanisms, such as co-ordinating and consultative committees, are developed, formal political structures emerge.

External Polity.   The extent to which external political negotiations and relations develop into stable structures, including sanctions for nonconformity, is important for several reasons. First, *the greater the sanction and resource control of the other party, or the coalitional alliance, the less the autonomy of the focal organization* (the organization that is the object of analysis).

Second, *the more a focal organization is bound into a stable external political structure, the more areas of internal policy-setting are influenced by the coalition.*

Possibly more important than the *extent* of external political involvement are the types of relationships. First, political relations develop "horizontally" among organizations having similar "products." Horizontal relations have two focuses: control of relations *among* the similar units — price-fixing, establishing territories — and control of relations between the organizations as a group and agents in the impinging environment — government, unions, etc.

Second, political relations develop "vertically" among suppliers of resources, distributors, and buyers of products (Palamountain, 1955). These include suppliers of labor, raw materials and facilities, and capital.

Typically, we have thought of the relationship of large suppliers of capital (major stockholders, banks, government) as different in kind from the suppliers of other resources, because capital suppliers have, in capitalistic countries, a different legal status. They sometimes have rights of "ownership," and rights of ownership are associated with rights of appointing executive leaders, formulating goals, etc. But under some conditions user and supplier groups may claim these rights. For instance, student-power advocates emphasize their rights to have a voice in appointing professors or even presidents of universities, and in other countries "ownership" may pass to either the state or the workers — suppliers of labor. Either vertical or horizontal political relations may lend to a de facto transfer of "ownership" — that is, to a change in legitimate usage and discretion.

The external political relations discussed above are between groups having a *direct* stake in organizational interrelationships and exchanges. Even such groups as the National Council of Churches or the Western Railway Men's Association have a stake in the constituent organizations' contributions to them and to their constituent organizations' conformity with the "umbrella" organization's policies.

But sometimes direct stake is muted or diffuse. First, organizations attempt to influence or co-opt people or groups indirectly affecting the flow of resources, whether legitimacy, capital, or sales. DuPont gives professors educational tours, politicians befriend editors, pharmaceutical houses pay for trips of aspiring doctors, heads of correctional institutions befriend judges and editors.

Second, a major component of an organization's external political involvement lies in its relation to the state. Obviously, nation-states vary dramatically in the extent of control exercised over organizations. Within nation-states different organizational sectors are subject to varying degrees of regulation. Both points apply to all types of organizations — utilitarian, solidary, or purposive; churches, businesses, or social clubs. One might expect that the more centralized the state, the greater the range of organizations coming under state supervision. Furthermore, the more "important" are organizational goals and procedures, the more likely is the development of state regulatory provisions.

Description and comparison of external political relations force us to study the tangled web of external supporters, competitors, and enemies of an organization, focusing on the alliances, commitments, and structural mechanisms through which organizations relate to the power nodes of their environment. Attention is paid not only to the structure of the political environment, but to the level of politicalization as well. Terryberry (1968) has argued that organizational environments are becoming increasingly populated by other organizations. The important facet lies in its implications for goal-setting and influence processes.

Economic Environment.   In this framework, the description and comparison of economic environment draws heavily on concepts developed by economists in the theory of the firm, price theory, and in institutional economics.

Price theory emphasizes the interaction of utility, income level, supply and demand, and the elasticity of supply and demand in relation to price. The theory of the firm relates the combination of the factors of production, fixed and variable, to marginal and average cost curves and to profit; it focuses on internal allocational and production decisions. Since the theory of the firm is usually characterized as a "quasi-stationary equilibrium model," it is limited from the point of view of those interested in institutional growth and change. Institutional economists, especially industry specialists, tend to focus, although with less analytic precision, on the more dynamic change factors in industrial environments.

The historical changes in the quality and aggregate levels of factor inputs and in technology for *industries* are related to attempts to change the external polity of organizations. For instance, the oil industry historically was faced with increasing demand and increasing supply. But it was also faced with cyclical discoveries of crude oil and stepwise technological advances that led to surges in capacity and drastically fluctuating fixed costs and profits. Recourse to government quota-setting and monopoly practices changed the ability to absorb fluctuations (Chazeau and Kahn, 1959).

Institutional economists also tend to be more descriptive of the social-system characteristics of the environment — what are the special characteristics of buyers and sellers that affect organizational decisions? What are the distribution chains? On the input side, organizations deal with a variety of specific markets — labor, raw materials, capital — each with its own internal differentiation and supply-demand characteristics. On the output side, organizations vary in the number of products they offer and in the structural characteristics of product markets.

Social scientists other than economists have become increasingly concerned with aspects of economic environments. For instance, Lorsch and Lawrence (1968), building on the work of James D. Thompson, have related the *heterogeneity* and *instability* of environments to the internal structures and co-ordinating mechanisms of organizations. Although sociologists have begun to pay more attention to economic environments, there has been no apparent integration of their work with the theory of the firm and price theory. As a consequence, all of the problems of the economies of scale, and fixed and variable costs as related to demand and supply levels and rates of change have been ignored. Yet, it is here that the impetus to organizational change, the resources for growing salaries and other "minor" features of organizational life are found.

Students of social-movement organizations have long been concerned with problems caused by the changing level of demand. (Messenger, 1955; Zald and Ash, 1966). But economic environments of other kinds of organizations should also be studied. For instance, sociological studies of mental hospitals and prisons, even though dealing with the historical development of internal structures and goals, rarely focus on the supply of patients and prisoners. This literature has focused on internal staff-patient/prisoner relations. Yet, at least for the mental hospitals, there is tremendous flux in the input-output and processing procedures; there have been massive changes in technology, the speed of processing patients, the characteristics of those in the hospital and those outside, and the distributional network of patients.

Although the supply-demand matrix is relevant to almost all organizations, many nonprofit organizations have a fundamental dichotomy between who pays for service and who directly receives the service. Whether the client of the mental hospital is considered to be the state or the patient, the separation of payee from receiver means that pricing preference mechanisms are somewhat irrelevant (Etzioni, 1958). In a "welfare-service" state they are a growing edge of organizations. And the language of political economy is a relevant language for these indirect-service organizations.

Finally, many topics treated as economic ones by economists are political ones for us. Economists emphasize the pricing policies of monopolists or oligopolists, but for us the goal-setting and influence process of monopolists and monopsonists, oligopolists and oligopsonists may be even more important.

The dimensions of any organization's external political economy are in large part determined by its position on the fundamental dimensions of organizational constitutions discussed earlier. For example, except for social movements with well-insulated support bases, most social-movement organizations are subject to radical shifts in demand, depending upon issue-arousal.

Again, the particular constellation of interest groups, attitudes about them, and funding arrangements, which have led to prison's peculiar modes of organizational change, are tied to fundamental expectations about what prisons are supposed to accomplish, who has responsibility for them, and what should be the relations among groups within them. Since these constitutional dimensions are related to the external political economy of an organization, it is our expectation that the comparative approach suggested in our discussion of constitutions will illuminate important differences in external political economies.

The political economic environment directly impinges on, and interacts with, the internal political economy. It imposes constraints and presents opportunities to an organization. Goals and procedural choices tie an organization into a web of users, suppliers, distributors, and to a set of influences, relationships, alliances, and hostile antagonists.

Some aspects of the external political economy exert influence through impinging on decision-makers' perception of opportunity in the environment. Others, such as state laws, impose rigid constraints, and still others exert pressure on role effectiveness, which in turn leads to pressures for changing internal rights and responsibilities.

INTERNAL POLITICAL ECONOMY

The internal polity is the system of control and influence. One of the things it controls is the system of transforming "raw material" into finished products. In this conception every organization has a productive task, subject to a greater or lesser division of labor and requiring the combination of the factors of production to satisfy performance criteria. The statement holds whether describing a manufacturing corporation selling auto parts, a prison managing prisoners, an insurance company managing money in relation to claims, or a social-movement organization managing membership sentiment and effecting change in its environment.

The general analytic distinction between polity and economy is clear; but, both conceptually and empirically, specific polity and economy processes may be difficult to disentangle. However, there will be little difficulty in showing how these processes operate and are connected to the rest of the political economy.

Internal Polity.   The internal polity is an organization's internal power system: the systematic manner in which power is distributed, mobilized, utilized, and limited. As in any social system (and to repeat our earlier discussion), power is utilized to achieve or to maintain a set of goals and values. These ends may be personal or collective.

Three aspects of internal polities have proved to be extremely important for both empirical and theoretical work. First, examining the *amount and distribution* of power reveals a central structural aspect of a polity. One aspect of analyzing the distribution of power is to reveal its sources. Second, because of differences in constitutions, economies, and power-distributions, organizations vary widely in their processes of *demand-aggregation* and in *conflict-resolution*. Third, an important aspect of a political system is the manner in which change occurs in central positions. Related to resource control, changing goals, and power structure, *succession systems and processes* are a fundamental political reality.

Amount and Distribution of Power.   Any comparative approach to organizational politics must analyze variation in power structures. Whether one is doing comparative research within a subclass of organization — such as among utilitarian organizations (constitutional dimension of incentives) or hospitals (goal dimension), or between different types[2] such as comparing social-movement organizations and utilitarian ones, the question of power *distribution* is raised. Less common, though we think equally important, is the question of the *amount* of power mobilized in a social system (Huntington, 1963; Tannenbaum, 1962).

Power is the ability of a person or group, for whatever reason, to affect another person's or group's ability to achieve its goals (personal or collective). In Emerson's (1962) convenient formulation, if A and B are in fact in a social relation, it is likely that B also can affect A's goals, and the empirical problem becomes that of specifying relative resource control. The distributional question involves examining the relative ability of one group or position to control resources (including legitimate decisions) vis-à-vis others. The question of the *amount* of power in the system involves the over-all resources utilized to influence other groups.

Distribution of Power.   Two main questions concerning the distribution of power have been traditional:

1. What affects the distribution of power among functional groups or positions?
2. What are the differences in the *vertical* distribution of power between and within organizations?

Students of manufacturing firms, department stores, governmental bureaucracies, hospitals, correctional institutions, and mental hospitals have described and attempted to explain the sources of power of formally equivalent groups. (The "equivalence" comes only from the fact that no formal or authoritative — that is, explicit, accepted symbolic authorization — legitimation is given to the unequal distribution of power.)

There would seem to be two major *sources* of difference in the horizontal distribution of power; on the one hand, the contribution and functional importance of a particular group in the *work-flow* processing of the organization's raw materials to achieve organizational goals may be a strong economic source of differential power. On the other hand, horizontal differences may be attributable to a group's position in *defining* the internal information flow, rules of the game, and external environment relevant to control and evaluation of the internal economic system. Comptroller's offices, research and development units, budget offices, and long-range planning units gain their power from controlling information and definitions relevant to functioning. Sapolsky (1966), for instance, attributes to the unprogrammability of "taste," that vital ingredient of department-store buying, the inability of department-store comptrollers to raise their influence level effectively.

Where the source of horizontal power often flows directly from a unit's or position's role in the processing of raw materials, variation in the vertical distribution of power more often relates to polity sources, ownership, and legitimate authority. The internal economic structure may put limits upon and force a shift in the structure of vertical power, but it does so through challenging the effectiveness of the control system.

The literature contains a number of concepts that refer to aspects of the vertical

---

[2] Most comparative research studies that collect data on several organizations typically study variation within a major subtype, e.g., Lorsch and Lawrence (1968), businesses; Street, Vinter, and Perrow (1966), correctional institutions; Georgopoulos and Mann (1962), hospitals. However, the more strictly theoretical comparative works — e.g., Etzioni (1961), Clark and Wilson (1961), Babchuck and Gordon (1959) — find it useful to use a broader palette. Their theoretical strategy is to identify major variables, while the empirical work demands comparability of measures and control of many organizational parameters.

distribution of power — e.g., span and hierarchy of control. Characterization of the over-all distribution of power in organization is found in the concepts of centralization-decentralization and federated-corporate. Similarly, the literature on church polity focuses on "episcopal," "connectional," and "congregational" structures. The polar types refer to the relation of a "center," or executive office, to a periphery, or constituent units.

Although these polar types have in common a concern with the vertical dimension of power-distributions, they are not parallel concepts. For instance, the question of centralization-decentralization largely applies *within* a corporate structure: it refers to the degree of delegation — parceling out — of the "executives'" legitimate powers. On the other hand, the federated-corporate distinction has to do with whether there are fundamental *unit* rights and constraints on the over-all collectivity. In congregational church polities, the powers of the center are even conceived as being illegitimate or, at best, delegated by the constituent units.

Note that the literature on social-movement organizations pays little attention to the vertical dimensions of organizations. Because of the weakness of the incentive bases, most meliorist movements have little control over their members, leaders are in a weak position vis-à-vis members, and formal hierarchies may have few powers attached to them. Only as we examine political parties which combine a variety of incentives does a vertical dimension emerge (Duverger, 1954). Thus, although the vertical distribution of power can be described for all organizations, there is wide variation both within and between types of organizations.

In discussing the sources of the vertical distribution of power, one must account for the amount of vertical differentiation *and* for the distribution of power among the positions. The concept of an effective span of control is one important way of accounting for the amount of vertical differentiation. Effective spans of control combined with over-all "size" of productive work force determine the number of vertical levels. The range of effective spans of control is related at the production level to characteristics of technology and raw material as well as to devices for evaluating performance. But ideological factors and the cultural history of a group enter in as well.

Four main factors appear to affect the relative distribution of power between centers and constituent units: (1) Historical ideology of organizational elites. The founders and developers of organizations carry with them "theories" of proper authority structure. In the case of the founders of protestant denominations many were rebelling against the hierarchy of the Roman Catholic Church. Changing ideologies of management has also affected the level of centralization of business firms. (2) The resources controlled by central-peripheral units. Where the constituent unit controls vital resources — stemming from legal positions or from their relative self-sufficiency and alternatives — constituent units have great autonomy (much as professors with high market values have greater autonomy than those getting raises at the sufferance of their chairmen). Sills (1954), reports that a formally corporate structure was transformed into a perceptually federated one because of dependence on local commitment. (3) Task requirements encourage varying degrees of centralization or decentralization. The hostile environment of conspiratorial parties leads to high centralization. On the other hand, for business organizations, great complexity of product output and market is usually believed to press away from a centralized structure (Chandler, 1962). Vertical and horizontal sources of power-distribution may be closely linked in a particular case. For example, doctors became dominant in hospitals because of their functional skills (horizontal) *and* because they often owned or founded the hospitals, or were perceived as legitimate rulers there. Their position was translated into constitutional prerogative. The transformation of both the capital base of hospitals and the skills needed for administration have eroded both their vertical and horizontal power positions. (4) Amount of power. Two organizations might have similar distributions of power — that is, profiles of power-measurements over similar positions might be exactly parallel — and yet be very different in the overall *amount* of power mobilized in the system. An organization has a "low" power system if there are few resources mobilized to influence others, if units or positions conduct their affairs with few explicit attempts at influence from other units. A high power system (internally directed power) is characterized by a great number of influence-attempts. An example will clarify:

The phrase "the politicization of the University" essentially refers to the transformation of the traditional autonomy of departments and administrative offices into the center of influence-attempts from previously supine groups. (One university president told me that decisions which had always been left solely to his office's discretion had become a center of controversy. Local bar associations began pressing him about the law school deanship appointment, student groups wanted to influence the choice of the manager of the student union, etc.)

What are the sources of amount of power in a system? The over-all level of influence in an organization is a function of the level of non-routinized interdependence and/or the perception by groups or positions of the control of their own reward-deprivation balance by other groups or positions. The perception of a reward-deprivation balance controlled by others is in part a function of goals; the group or person who likes the status quo is unlikely to use his time, energy, and resources for influence unless there is a threat to the status quo.

The extent of nonroutine interdependence is a function of both goals and technology. In a study of correctional institutions for delinquents, for example, we found great differences between two institutions dedicated to treatment goals, because one of them focused on milieu-treatment and the other on individual counseling (Zald, 1962). The emphasis on manipulating the milieu led to a great number of meetings and consultation between clinical staff and cottage parents and, hence, to many more influence-attempts.

Differences between organizations in the amount and distribution of power can be described in static and structural terms. But the topic also bears on fundamental aspects of organizational change and conflict-resolution.

Demand-Aggregation and Mechanisms for Resolving Conflicts.   There is a curious hiatus in the literature on organizations. Social conflict is linked to social change in studies of society, but in studies of organizations conflict and change are often treated as relatively unconnected subjects. An exception is industrial sociology where union-management conflict is linked to social change. Much of the literature on organizations takes a short-time perspective and deals with enduring structural bases of conflict. Furthermore, much of the literature on organizational change starts from the *introduction* of the change and asks about the effect on (a) organizational structure or (b) individual morale (Mann and Hoffman, 1960). Thus, the intersection of large-scale change and conflict is bypassed. "Why do elites or members initiate change?" and "What is the social process of change?" are topics that are lightly treated.

Obviously, the political-economy approach can be used in describing enduring structural conflicts and their resolutions. Staff-line conflict, interprofessional relations, superior-subordinate conflicts, and interdivisional conflict, all smack of the stuff of competition for scarce resources, relative power positions, and the like. One of the distinctive advantages of the political-economy approach, however, is its illumination of the *processes* of change.

One of the central points made by students using the "systems" approach to the study of politics is that institutionalized political systems are the focus of aggregated demands for collective outputs. Through politics, individuals and groups attempt to change both individual and collective rewards. In this approach the distinctive feature of politics is that people who have grievances attempt to redress them not directly (although power may be used in this way) but through demands on authoritative officeholders. Officeholders are more or less responsive depending upon the resources they control, the competitive definitions of collective policy, and their own goals and values.

Organizational change, as distinct from sheer increase or decrease in size, involves changes in policy, products, goals, market, technology, and interunit relations. Whether or not the change is "irrational" or "rational," it involves a process in which (a) the current state of the organization or some aspect of it is in some sense unsatisfactory; (b) some unit or group proposes an alteration in the unsatisfactory state; (c) the proposal is or is not translated into a decision and an organization's program or policy; and (d) the new policy does or does not reduce dissatisfaction with the state of affairs. Variations in political structure — vertical and horizontal power-distributions and "amount" of power mobilized — help account for the patterns of organizational change and conflict.

Several propositions, some truisms, are useful in presenting a political model of demand-aggregation and organizational change: (1) Specific dissatisfaction within an organization and the formulation of an issue occurs in the group or section whose interests are hurt by the status quo, e.g., assembly-line workers, not stockholders, complain about assembly-line speedups; stockholders and upper management gripe about profit levels, growth, and dividend payments; upper executives criticize functional departmentalization and press for radical decentralization. External to organizations, "issue entrepreneurs" (e.g., Ralph Nader) mobilize demand for change.

(2) If an organization is highly centralized and power is concentrated in a small executive core, change depends either upon aggregating fractionated external and internal power sources into a unified opposition, or upon capturing the ear of the "elite." On the other hand, the more there is a dispersal of power in an organization, the more likely are forms of coalitional politics. Federated organizations, like some unions, or bodies of collegial equals, like the New York Stock Exchange, have forms of parliamentary politics. If they require unanimity or near unanimity for adoption of any changes, then the intensity of the motivating issue must indeed be strong. In the most radically dispersed organizations, social-movement organizations, in which the executive cadre control members *only* by dint of persuasion, or in confederations in which collective decisions (assembly votes) are considered only as advisory — e.g., Baptist assemblies, the early phase of the national YMCA movement — the adoption of change-proposals is essentially based on consensus. Among confederated organizations, the greater the homogeneity of elite perspectives and of environmental conditions, the more rapid the adoption of proposals for change.

John Q. Wilson's (1966) model of organizational innovation suggests that the greater the decentralization of an organization the more *proposals* for change will be initiated, for decentralization gives people a greater stake and sense of involvement. But he also suggests that highly decentralized organizations will also have a low rate of proposal-adoptions because each unit must get others to consent and none has more power than others. On the other hand, in highly centralized organizations, fewer proposals for change will be initiated, but those that are can be adopted easily ("by a wave of the King's wand"). Wilson argues essentially that the balance of a large number of proposals and a high rate of adoptions occurs in neither radically centralized nor decentralized organizations; he restricts himself to collectivity-wide proposals. It is likely that decentralized and federated organizations have a much greater rate of *individual unit* changes than centralized organizations; for the power to initiate and adopt internal changes is located in each unit.

How are collective demands generated in organizations? How is a perception of an issue translated into a social process of contending parties? When we are studying organizational conflict among small groups of managers, the social psychology of coalition-formation may be most appropriate, and for tactical lessons we may turn to Machiavelli. But where we are talking about the aggregation of diverse and dispersed individuals into relative coherent pressure groups, social-movement analysis is most appropriate.

Within organizations, several factors would seem to be conducive to social-movement formation. First, the greater the group solidarity and self-esteem, stemming from social status and/or professional homogeneity, the more likely a collective identity is to be found (Sayles, 1958). Since professional and highly skilled groups often have universalistic standards of performance, when the status quo departs from these standards collective action is likely to take place.

Second, if a subordinate group is to make collective demands, it must be insulated from repressive action on the part of the superordinates. The Wagner Act helped industrial unions in this country by controlling the ability of employers to retaliate against employees involved in union-building. In academia, liberal norms of freedom of expression *and* professors' absolute dependence on the good will and commitment of their graduate and undergraduate students have conditioned the response to internal social movements.

Finally the task structure and exigencies that facilitate communication and the development of grievances may be conducive to social-movement phenomena (Burks, 1961).

Some demands for change result in new policies which effectively solve the problem or reduce dissatisfaction. Other internal strains and conflicts are chronic, based on enduring fissures in the body politic, and their solution is based more on ways of channeling and handling conflict than on removing the causes of conflict.

Organizations develop a number of institutional mechanisms for resolving what could be disruptive conflicts. Capital-allocation committees use criteria of equity rather than economic standards; review procedures are institutionalized; appeal boards and collective-bargaining procedures come into existence. A general hypothesis: the more superordinates are dependent on subordinates, and the more vertical power is equally divided among several groups, the better-developed are criteria of equity and quasi-judicial mechanisms (Cf. Scott, 1965; Pondy, 1964).

Succession Systems and Political Behavior. Organizational changes occur not only through the aggregation of demand; they also occur through succession processes, leading to the systematic selection of new perspectives into executive office. Unfortunately, students of organizational leadership have been enamored with the personality styles of leaders or, slightly better, with the expectation pattern of subordinates and the superordinate-subordinate role-interactions (Grusky). The broader systemic implications of succession choices, except in a few studies (Grusky, 1963; Guest, 1962; Levinson, 1964; Carlson, 1962), have been ignored.

Yet it is patent that (1) how key executives are chosen varies with the internal political structure of organizations and (2) the outcome of succession choices may, under specific external and internal conditions, have a large impact on organizational directions and policies.

Organizational succession systems range from crown-prince systems, in which the chief executive chooses and trains his own replacement, to elective *leadership* systems in which executives serve on the short-time sufferance of a politicized, conflict-ridden, and involved electorate. Succession systems range from regularized ones, allowing for a chain of successors to be established, to those that take place through spasmodic and clandestine organizational coups d'état.

Let us specify the structures and processes of political economies that affect succession systems. At least three main factors must be considered in understanding recruitment and succession to higher office: (1) the distribution of power; (2) the degree of consensus about performance adequacy and the location in the power system of perceptions of inadequacy; (3) the career channels of "standard" and "deviant" executive leadership.

Who chooses key officeholders is, in most organizations, a fundamental aspect of constitutions, closely related to constitutional prerogatives attached to specific offices or groups. Constitutional provisions often specify not only who chooses the chief executive, but conditions of tenure in office and the timing and process of selection. In general, the more the constitution vests power in a broad-based "electorate," the more tenure in office is explicitly limited and defined. Examples of short-tenure electoral systems are found in Protestant congregational polities.

The higher the concentration of power, the more likely are "crown-prince" systems. Such is the case in larger corporations with either family ownership, or highly dispersed ownership that effectively concentrates control in the chairman's hand.

Systematic conflict and, indeed, regularized competition are most likely in federated organizations or in organizations that have several powerful but disparate nodes of power. Edelstein (1967) has persuasively argued that competition for office in trade unions is most likely when the constituent units have histories of autonomy. (This analysis of the relation of power-distribution to succession rules is somewhat superficial, for it ignores many interesting mixed cases: e.g., highly centralized systems with democratic succession principles attached to the upper levels — the Roman Catholic Church and that perennial favorite of sociologists, the "democratic system with oligarchic tendencies.")

Although, as noted above, "crown-prince" systems depend upon a high concentration of power, there is one difference between the two cases cited — family-owned corporations and dispersed ownership. The family-owned corporation is, hypothetically, in a position to ignore market and economic considerations, up to and including bankruptcy. On the other hand, where ownership is widely dispersed, inadequate profit-performance depresses stock prices and leads, potentially, to accumulation of blocs of stocks by investors who see recovery possibilities. Similarly, in business corporations with contending blocs of stockowners, minor fluctuations in their economic status may be the occasions for votes of confidence and attempts to win over previous backers of the incumbents. I cite these cases to indicate the interdependence of power systems, succession processes, and performance adequacy.

Performance adequacy is evaluated in most organizations along several dimensions. The causes of inadequacy may be internal or external and may be more or less subject to executive control. Regardless of whether the causes of inadequacy are under executive control, since key offices are charged with responsibility for the collective, replacement is most likely at times of inadequate performance. Latent conflicts are brought to the fore at such times, and competition for office is exacerbated. (Voluntary organizations may differ here: the low rewards of a failing organization may discourage office-seeking.) Also, where a crown prince has been established, we suspect that the discreditation of the regime may discredit the crown prince.

Not only does performance inadequacy lead to dismissal of incumbents, but continuing inadequacies lead to high rates of turnover. High rates of turnover in key positions, of course exacerbate inadequacy.

Performance adequacy or inadequacy is also related to the selection of candidates with "standard" or "deviant" careers. From a political-economy perspective (as contrasted with traditional social-psychological ones) a career is a labor-market mechanism that, over time, combines occupational and social backgrounds to "fit" specific job requirements. Most relatively stable organizations develop standard patterns of recruiting key executives. Career routes leading to high office develop, with options. The standard pattern is determined both by the perceived requirements of competence of top officers and the opportunities to develop those competencies provided in organizations. American Civil Liberties Union executives are recruited from liberal lawyers, railroad executives from operating railroad men, etc. Standard patterns filter out those with marginal skills or deviant career paths.

The standard pattern is affected by the internal political economy of an organization. For example, small organizations may not have sufficient internal divisions of labor to provide training for executive succession. They then have to rely on contact with other, similar organizations for identifying new executives (Carlson, 1962).

When performance has been "inadequate," however, whatever groups control succession may develop perspectives that lead away from standard pattern choices; the choosing of a successor becomes a period of political reassessment and deviant career patterns become relevant to executive choice. Thus, for instance, as the railroads became bankruptcy-prone and later merger-oriented, legal skills became relevant and traditional operating skills were downgraded. Or, in the Young Men's Christian Association, confronting the urban crisis led to an emphasis on program imagination rather than business efficiency (Zald, 1965). The point is that the careers of individuals intersect with an organization's changing political economy.

Internal Economics Structure and Process.   The internal polity articulates with the internal economic system in several ways. First, authoritative power centers make choices among "product" lines, technology, and the system of integrating roles and units. Second, both in inducing factors of production into the organization and in maintaining their usage once committed, political-economic choices are made which reflect the balance of resources in the organization and the relative power of different units. Commitments to a division of labor, to a grouping of roles into higher order units, and to technology become the basis for the development of group identity and solidarity, the development of strategic control of resources, and therefore, power.

Three aspects of internal economies merit systematic attention:
(1)   the division of labor, technologies, and interunit exchanges;
(2)   mechanisms and criteria for allocating resources and recording costs and information about performance adequacy; and
(3)   incentive economies and their consequences.

It is fairly easy to see the division of labor and product-processing as being an essential part of the internal economy. But the accounting-information and incentive systems might analytically be treated as part of the polity. The accounting-information system is established by authoritative power centers and functions to provide authoritative information. It serves as an internal substitute for a price system. Once the accounting system is established, the variable data, monetary and otherwise, recorded in it signal to participants efficiency and effectiveness vis-à-vis other units and the outside world. I argue below that the *choice* of accounting rules is based on political-economic considerations, and that once in operation the accounting rules operate like a sloppy price system to guide the allocation of resources.

A similar point can be made about incentive economies. Barnard's (1938) original argument was that different organizations have stocks of different kinds of incentives which they exchange for labor-commitment. In this sense, an economy exists; but authoritative power-wielders not only control stocks, they make choices about how they should be allocated, thus rewarding and depriving different groups. An incentive system is both economic and political in actual operation.

Division of Labor, Technologies, and Inter-Unit Relationships.   Economies are systems for producing and exchanging goods. Basic to any economy, whether free market or centrally controlled, are considerations of specialization, role differentiation, and division of labor. Specialization and differentiation within an organization are, in turn, largely functions of the state of the arts (technology) for producing a specific "product," the variety of "products" offered by the organization, the scale (size) of the organization "required" both to produce and to distribute production to the "market," and the organization's geographic dispersion.

Each of these factors has consequences for the amount of role and unit differentiation, as well as independent effects on the political structure and difficulties facing organizations. For example, holding other things constant, as differentiation increases, span of control decreases, as does organizational loyalty. Greater complexity (holding size constant) requires more supervision and administrative personnel (Anderson and Warkov, 1961; Rushing, 1967). Further, the more nonroutine the tasks, the more discretion must be left to lower level personnel (Thompson and Bates, 1957). In addition, a unit's weight in organizational counsels varies directly as it controls or is perceived as involved in the organization's functionally most difficult subtasks (Perrow, 1961; Crozier, 1963). Finally routinization and stabilization of output processes facilitate increased centralization and reduce coordinating problems.

These problems of the relation of the "socio-technical" system to the distribution of intra- and interunit power, to supervisory strains, and to problems of group cohesion have been a central concern of sociologists for the last twenty years. One advantage of the political-economy framework is that it treats the "socio-technical" system itself as a dependent variable.

The socio-technical system in most organizations is not rigidly fixed. It changes as a function of competitive pressures, the profit potential and capital investment requirement of an innovation, and the innovative orientations of the executive elite (Mansfield, 1968). Similarly, as labor costs increase, pressures to mechanize increase. Adopting new technologies may require large capital expenditures, changing both external political and economic commitments (long-term debt) and changing the scale of market required to utilize efficient production. Similarly, adoption of a new technology and related role differentiation changes the social relations internal to the organizations.

Just as, within the political-economy framework, the adoption of technology can be treated as a substantive problem, so, too, can that historic problem of increase of administrative personnel. Sociologists typically treat increases of administrative personnel as a response to internal complexity and co-ordination, a control-of-economy problem. They have ignored the goals-and-choice aspect. As Williamson

(1964) and Pondy (1969) indicate, however, managerial elites may have a "taste" for profits or increased staff (and I would add for short-range and long-range profits). Thus, Pondy shows that industries having higher percentages of owner-managers have lower staff ratios compared to industries having lower percentages of owner-managers, controlling for size and technology. This line of argument ties into the debate over managerial capitalism associated with Berle and Means (1934) and recently continued by Galbraith (1967).

The topic of the shape of the internal economy has been most fully developed for utilitarian organizations; for complex, large, and finely tuned internal economies do not exist to any great extent where organizations do not have control over their members regularly and for long periods of time. Although social-movement organizations do have internal divisions of labor and role differentiation, they are of simpler types. Only as social movements change does analysis of skill competence and division of labor become especially interesting. For social-movement organizations, the central economic problem is finding a set of incentives to ensure member participation; so often the stock controlled by the organization is extremely weak (Zald and Ash, 1966).

Incentive Allocations.   One component of the internal economy is the distribution of rewards and sanctions to motivate role performance. It was asserted earlier that one central normative principle of organizational constitutions is a set of exchange terms. What is to be gained by joining an organization? Analytically, this is a problem in the relation of an organization to the external environment. Even *within* major types of organizations, organizations differ in the *amount* of incentive *resources* they control. Their ability to retain and motivate members will depend upon their stock or supply.

The incentive necessary to maintain a member's motivation may well differ from that necessary to obtain his initial membership (e.g., a person joining an organization for purposive values may stay because of solidary relations). And it is probably the distinctive contribution of the human relations school to have emphasized the "extra-contractual" and "extra-monetary" incentives that bind men to utilitarian organizations.

This approach goes beyond that of the human relations school. Since I conceive of incentives as part of a comparative political-economy approach, eventually I must be able to treat within this framework monetary and non-monetary incentive systems, including symbolic ones. Incentives vary not only in the "needs" they satisfy but in their tangibility, their divisibility, and their pervasiveness. Furthermore, incentives are defined in a social and political matrix and are associated with particular kinds of social structures.

The effects of differences in incentive bases for organizations with similar goals has been nicely demonstrated by James Q. Wilson (1961). In "The Economy of Patronage" he poses the questions of under what conditions political parties are more likely to be ideologically riven by factions and when they can resemble a bureaucratic or patrimonial machine. The core of his analysis has to do with the number of patronage positions (material incentives), controlled by the "leader." He estimates that Chicago has three to four times as many patronage positions for districts of comparable size as does New York. He then argues that the material base of these positions allows the mayor to be able to mobilize more party workers without persuasion than the mayor of New York. To a greater extent, people in New York have to be attracted by purposive incentives, but in our society these are relatively weak, and in a complex situation each group attaches a different weight to issues. Thus, the party tends to be fractionated and faction-ridden.

Incentive analysis is important not only for comparing different kinds of organizations but for studying organizational change. Major change usually upsets the balance of incentives, affecting participant motivation. It is obvious that rising and declining incentive stocks affect the expectations and comparison-level alternatives of members. Moreover, within an organization, allocation of incentive to one group or unit affects the satisfaction/dissatisfaction levels of members in other units, contributing to patterns of mobility within the organization and affecting, possibly, decisions to remain with an organization.

Within organizations, incentives are allocated to motivate performance. From the point of view of organizational elites, incentives, like other resources (capital expenditures), are allocated in terms of the elites' perceptions of organization tasks and enhancement of their own values and performance. They are aided in their allocational work by various accounting and forecasting mechanisms which summarize both the internal and external state of the organization. Many of these information summary and transmittal mechanisms may be informal and based on direct observation. But others are based on quite extensive, formalized, accounting-information systems.

Information Systems: Budgeting and Accounting Systems.   Information systems are created by accountants, quality-control experts, and other specialists in measurement as "readings on the current state of the organization." By comparing past readings and projecting future ones, the relative satisfaction/dissatisfaction level of elites and relevant audiences can be affected. They are created for, and largely used by, influence-wielders.

In this sense they are part of the polity. But for the most part they represent indexes of the state of various aspects of the productive exchange system, and in this respect "stand for" the economy. Furthermore, rules developed by organizational elites and powerful external authorities operate to channel the flow of resources with the organization.

It is not too important whether the budget and accounting and information systems are considered as largely part of the economy (because they represent it) or as part of the polity (because they are used by its agents). Possibly they should be treated as important connecting tissues of political economy. It *is* important to understand the way in which these information-accounting systems are developed, used, and fit into organizational structure.

Unfortunately, until very recently sociologists and political scientists of a behaviorist persuasion largely ignored information systems. Like the sociologist of medicine who never questions the doctor's diagnosis, the sociologist of organization has tended to accept accounting systems as given — as professionally and abstractly dictated. Except for a few political scientists and economists interested in tax policy, these topics have been seen as "boring, dry topics for narrow-minded money-grubbers."

The irony is, of course, that these systems often are major bones of contention within and without organizations. We can modify Lasswell's famous phrase "who gets what, when, how" to "who is charged with what, when, how." Anyone following the debates over the financial statements of conglomerate corporations in 1968 and 1969 knows that the emergence of this form of corporate organization is related to tax and accounting rules, subject to debate and discretion, and that, if conglomerates decline, it will be because external authorities (including the Securities Exchange Commission) impose rules for their regulation.

If our discussion seems to overemphasize the use of information systems in business organizations, one need only turn to universities and churches to find parallel examples. Indeed, the statistical records of established denominations are used by staff to evaluate ministerial performance, production targets are established in relation to various goals (e.g., missionary giving, Sunday school attendance, and the like), and among the cognoscenti a debate goes on over the interpretation of membership statistics.

It may be that social scientists have ignored accounting systems because by the time they personally experience them they have become deans and chairmen, no longer doing research! In any event, who controls what budget, what shared costs are allocated, what a teaching charge is, what a fellowship change is are matters of no small import in universities.

Concern with the budgeting and accounting processes in government, and with the political effect of such innovations as PPBS (Program-Planning-Budgeting System) provides one step in the direction I am proposing (Wildavsky, 1964; Wilavsky, 1967). Furthermore, some accountants and "management-science" experts have become interested in the behavioral effects and sources of these systems (Gynther, 1967).

At this point I can at best propose a paradigm for investigation. Resource-allocation within organizations is a function of traditional rules, intergroup bargaining, mechanics for deciding conflict, and elite perception of new areas of growth, change, or defense. One level of investigation would be an examination of the *structural mechanisms* for reaching decisions. For example, following Pondy's (1964) lead, we might study institutional structures and the organizational rules used to reach decisions on allocating resource capital for investment and major facility change.

A second level of investigation is suggested by the *history and development* of the accounting and allocating rules themselves. For example, what factors encouraged the development of charging units a fixed interest cost on loans or allocating costs in a given ratio to different functions? On what basis do social-movement organizations determine staff salaries or percent of membership income to be shared between national and local units (e.g., in the National Association for the Advancement of Colored People or the American Civil Liberties Union)?

A third level of investigation would be the *consequences* of different allocational and accounting procedures. Who benefits? Which functions are supported and which slighted? Where are different information and account functions located in the organizations? Which departments gain in importance, and which lose because they do or do not control the information system or have special access to information from the system? The introduction of computerized information systems has only made more obvious the existence of a potential relation between the control of information systems and the control of key decisions. An increase in organizational complexity is reflected in the strategic importance of information systems and the offices that manage them.

Accounting systems reflect the ethos of organization as well as the internal power system. Organizations have choices between "conservative" and "radical" accounting rules (e.g., in charging depreciation, setting up reserves, and the like). The accounting system may favor short-run efficiency over long-run risk-taking (rules for capitalizing or treating research and development costs as current expense), or, in the YMCA, efficiency versus program-service.

Finally, organizational change reflects itself in the resources allocated to different functions and in the system used for processing information. For essentially stable organizations, it will become apparent that allocation rules are made up of traditional accounting procedures with a percentage increase or decrease depending upon total income projected for a given year (or whatever period is used). Crecine (1966), studying municipal government, has found that department heads request and receive a budget based on last year's expenditures plus or minus the percentage increase (decrease) in revenue projected by the municipal executives' financial office. Only as new programs are initiated or old programs expanded is this formula changed. For other organizations, (particularly those in rapid flux), resource-allocation and criteria for allocation will constitute central concerns of organizational elites. And the nature of the information system itself will be subject to change as organizational ethos changes.

The political-economy framework was initially developed because organizational analysis seemed inelegant and diffuse when utilized to study the causes and dynamics of organizational changes. Any general social-system approach to organizational change must include a host of variables, some of which will be political and economic, to explain change.

My focus on the political-economic variables is intended to provide a more *efficient* and *illuminating* approach than is possible with a more general framework. This approach postulates that economic and political forces, structures, pressures, and constraints (1) are among the most significant motivators of change and (2) are the key factors shaping directions of change. The political-economy approach is efficient because it concentrates investigation on two key processes and structures and their interrelation; a general social-system approach is too diffuse.

This approach is illuminating, I think, because it allows a greater explication of political and economic processes and structures within organizations than most sociologists and political scientists have heretofore provided. It forces the researcher to a more finely wrought conceptualization of organizational polity and economy than has been the norm. Virtually all students interested in organizations (not decision-making) utilize some concepts of power and exchange, as well as their synonyms and related terms. Without explicit focus on polity and economy as the central objects of analysis, however, a rich set of distinctions and analytic units has not been developed.

Although the political-economy framework was originally developed for the study of organizational change, here I have emphasized its utility as an integrative framework for comparative work. Major independent variables in many comparative studies have been shown to be aspects of a political economy. By systematically tracing out their position in a political economy and by paying attention to other major components, oversimplified explanations can be avoided; yet at the same time a delineated range of interlocking variables can be explored.

As a first step in developing our approach, I have turned, whenever possible, to the fields of economics and political science. The concepts used by these disciplines (at the most general level) are often applied to whole societies or to nation-states. However, since political scientists are centrally concerned with the aggregation, structure, mobilization, utilization, and limitations of power and economists with the consequences of differing exchange systems and terms, it has been useful to scan these disciplines for concepts and ideas applicable to organizations.

No claim is made that this essay presents a "complete" political-economy approach. At this point our concept of an internal polity is more fully developed than other aspects. For some purposes, different concepts or aspects of polity and economy might be elaborated. For example, there has recently been an interest in the judicial and internal legal systems of corporations. What appeals system, if any, do employees or members have? What rights are vested in the individual, and how are

260   Macro-Societal and Historical Emphases

individual rights protected? For a battery of concepts relevant to analyzing an organization's legal system, the student might well turn to that part of political science which examines judicial processes and comparative legal structure.

What of the theoretical status of my framework? At least two generations of social scientists have been nurtured in a model of the scientific enterprise that perceives formal theory and experiment as science's exemplar. Some philosophers and historians of science (e.g., the late Norwood Russell Hansen, 1958) would argue, however, that these models are only formalizations of "truths" emerging from a much looser pattern of discovery.

Even if the hypothetical-deductive method constitutes a late stage in the establishment of scientific truth, few would deny its value for clarifying the logical status of concepts and providing economical explanations. The political-economy framework can be used to generate specific predictions and in one case has already demonstrated its predictive values (Wood, 1967). No claim is made, however, that this framework has reached an advanced state of development.

The political-economy framework is not a substitute for decision theory, the human relations approach, or the concept of organizational rationality. It does claim to have organic connections to these approaches when they are used for empirical research. If, for example, organizations are conceived as rational instruments, the political-economy approach suggests that their rationality depends upon specifying rationality for what groups, or elites, with what kinds of incentives and normative legitimacy as support. In this approach all organizations have political economies: the model bureaucracy has a form of rule and ethos as does a school system "outside of politics." Politics and political economy are endemic to all forms of organizational life, not just the conflictual part that occasionally shows.

REFERENCES

Anderson, Theodore, and Seymour Warkov
1961 "Organizational Size and Functional Complexity: a Study of Administration in Hospitals." *American Sociological Review* 26:23-28.
Bakke, E. Wright
1959 "Concept of the Social Organization." Pg. 16-75 in Mason Haire (editor), *Modern Organization Theory.* New York: John Wiley.
Barnard, Chester F.
1938 *The Functions of the Executive.* Cambridge, Mass.: Harvard University Press.
Berle, Adolph A., and Gardiner C. Means
1934 *The Modern Corporation and Private Property.* New York: Macmillan.
Bidwell, Charles E., and Rebecca S. Vreeland
1963 "College Education and Moral Orientation." *Administrative Science Quarterly* 8:166-191.
Blau, Peter M., and W. Richard Scott
1962 *Formal Organization.* San Francisco:

Chandler Publishing Co.
Buchanan, James A.
1964 "What Should Economists Do?" *Southern Economic Journal* 30:213-222.
Burks, Richard V.
1961 *The Dynamics of Communism in Eastern Europe.* Princeton, N.J.: Princeton University Press.
Carlson, Richard O.
1962 *Executive Succession and Organizational Change: Place Bound and Career Bound Superintendents of Schools.* Chicago: Midwest Administration Center.
Chandler, Alfred Dupont, Jr.
1962 *Strategy and Structures: Chapter in the History of the Industrial Enterprise.* Cambridge, Mass.: MIT Press.
Chazeau, Melvin G., and Alfred E. Kahn
   Integration and Competition in the Petroleum Industry. New Haven, Conn.: Yale University Press.

Crecine, John P.

1966   *A Computer Simulation Model of Municipal Resource Allocation.* Unpublished Doctoral Dissertation, Carnegie-Mellon University, Pittsburgh, Pa.

Crozier, Michel

1963   *The Bureaucratic Phenomenon.* Chicago: The University of Chicago Press.

Duverger, Maurice

1954   *Political Parties.* New York: John Wiley.

Edelstein, J. David

1967   "An Organizational Theory of Union Democracy." *American Sociological Review* 32:19-31.

Emerson, Richard M.

1962   "Power-Dependence Relation." *American Sociological Review* 27:41-55.

Etzioni, Amitai

1958   "Administration and the Consumer." *Administrative Science Quarterly* 3:251-264.

1961   *A Comparative Analysis of Complex Organizations.* New York: Free Press of Glencoe.

Galbraith, John K.

1967   *The New Industrial State.* Boston: Houghton Mifflin.

Georgopoulos, Basil S., and Floyd C. Mann

1962   *The Community General Hospital.* New York: Macmillan.

Gordon, C. Wayne, and Nicholas Babchuk

1959   "A Typology of Voluntary Associations." *American Sociological Review* 24:22-79.

Grusky, Oscar

1963   "Managerial Succession and Organizational Effectiveness." *American Journal of Sociology* 64:21-31.

Guest, Robert H.

1962   *Organizational Change: The Effect of Successful Leadership.* Homewood, Ill.: Irwin-Dorsey.

Gynther, Reginald S.

1967   "Accounting Concepts and Behavioral Hypotheses." *Accounting Review* 42:274-290.

Hanson, Norwood R.

1958   *Patterns of Discovery: An Inquiry into the Conceptual Foundations of Science.* Cambridge, England: Cambridge University Press.

Huntington, Samuel

1966   "The Political Modernization of Traditional Monarchies." *Daedalus* 95:763-788.

Hurst, James Willard

1964   *Law and Economic Growth: The Legal History of the Lumber Industry in Wisconsin, 1836 to 1915.* Cambridge, Mass.: Belknap Press.

Levenson, Bernard

1964   "Bureaucratic Succession." Pp. 362-376 in A. Etzioni, editor, *Complex Organizations.* New York: Holt, Rinehart, and Winston.

Long, Norton A.

1962   *The Polity.* Chicago: Rand McNally.

Lorsch, Jay W., and Paul R. Lawrence

1968   *Environmental Factors and Organizational Integration.* Paper read at American Sociological Meeting. Boston, Massachusetts.

Mann, Floyd C., and L. R. Hoffman

1960   *Automation and the Worker: A Study of Social Change in the Power Plants.* New York: Holt, Rinehart and Winston.

Mansfield, Edwin

1968   *Industrial Research and Technological Innovation: An Econometric Analysis.* New York: W. W. Norton.

March, James G. (editor)

1965   *Handbook of Organizations.* Chicago: Rand McNally.

Messenger, Sheldon

1955   "Organizational Transformation: A Case Study of a Declining Social Movement." *American Sociological Review* 70:3-10.

Palamountain, J. C., Jr.

1955   *The Politics of Distribution.* Cambridge, Mass.: Harvard University Press.

Pondy, Louis

1964   "Budgeting and Inter-Group Conflict in Organizations." *Pittsburgh Business Review* 34:1-3.

1969   "Effect of Size, Complexity, and Ownership on Administrative Intensity." *Administrative Science Quarterly* 14:47-61.

Rushing, William

1967   "The Effects of Industry Size and Division of Labor on Administration." *Administrative Science Quarterly* 12:273-295.

Sapolsky, Harvey
1966   *Decentralization and Control: Problems in the Organization of Department Stores.* Unpublished dissertation, Harvard University, Cambridge, Mass.

Sayles, Leonard R.
1958   *Behavior of Industrial Work Groups.* New York: John Wiley.

Stinchcombe, Arthur
1960   "The Sociology of Organization and the Theory of the Firm." *Pacific Sociological Review* 3:75-82.

Street, David, Robert D. Vinter, and Charles Perrow
1966   *Organization for Treatment.* New York: The Free Press.

Tannenbaum, Arnold S.
1962   "Control in Organizations: Individual Adjustment and Organizational Performance." *Administrative Science Quarterly* 7:236-257.

Terreberry, Shirley
1968   "The Evolution of Organizational Environments." *Administrative Science Quarterly* 12:590-613.

Thompson, James D., and Fred L. Bates
1957   "Technology, Organization and Administration." *Administrative Science Quarterly* 2:325-342.

Thompson, James D., and Robert W. Hawkes
1962   "Disaster, Community Organization, and Administrative Process." Pp. 268-300 in *Man and Society in Disaster,* edited by George Baker and Dwight Chapman. New York: Basic Books.

Thompson, James D., and William J. McEwen
1958   "Organizational Goals and Environment: Goal Setting as an Interaction Process." *American Sociological Review* 23:23-31.

Thompson, Victor A.
1966   Review of Handbook of Organizations. *American Sociological Review* 31:415-416.

Warriner, Charles K.
1965a   "The Problem of Organizational Purpose." *The Sociological Quarterly* 6:139-146.

1965b   "Four Types of Voluntary Associations." *Sociological Inquiry* 35:138-148.

Wildavsky, Aaron
1964   *Politics of the Budgetary Process.* Boston: Little, Brown.

Williamson, Oliver E.
1964   *The Economics of Discretionary Behavior: Managerial Objectives in a Theory of the Firm.* New York: Prentice-Hall.

Wilson, James Q.
1961   "An Economy of Patronage." *Journal of Political Economy* 69:369-380.

1966   "Innovation in Organizations: Notes Towards a Theory." Pp. 193-217 in *Approaches to Organization Design,* edited by James D. Thompson. Pittsburgh: University of Pittsburgh Press.

Wilson, James Q., and Peter B. Clark
1961   "Incentive Systems: A Theory of Organizations." *Administrative Science Quarterly* 6:129-166.

Wood, James R.
"Protestant Enforcement of Racial Integration Policy: A Sociological Study in the Political Economy of Organization." Unpublished dissertation, Vanderbilt University, Nashville, Tenn.

Zald, Mayer N.
1962   Organizational Control Structures in Five Correctional Institutions. *American Journal of Sociology* 68:335-345.

1965   "Who Shall Rule? A Political Analysis of Succession in a Large Welfare Organization." *Pacific Sociological Review* 8:52-60.

1968   *Organizational Change: The Political Economy Approach.* Paper delivered at Meeting of Southern Sociological Society, Atlanta, Georgia.

1970   *Organizational Change: The Political Economy of the YMCA.* Chicago: University of Chicago Press (forthcoming).

Zald, Mayer N., and Robert Ash
1966   "Social Movement Organizations: Growth, Decay, and Change." *Social Forces* 44:327-341.

13.   Organizations: A Dialectical View[1]

J. Kenneth Benson

The study of complex organizations has been guided by a succession of rational and functional theories and by positivist methodology. These efforts have proceeded on the basis of an uncritical acceptance of the conceptions of organizational structure shared by participants. The distinctions between divisions, departments, occupations, levels, recruitment and reward strategies, and so forth, through which participants arrange their activities have become scientific categories. Likewise, the participants' explanations for the structure of the organization have been formalized as scientific theories.

As a result of these tendencies the sociology of organizations has failed to develop a critical posture. The theoretical constructs of the field are tied to and tend to affirm the present realities in organizations. Radical transformations of organizations would undermine the corresponding theories.

The basic problem may be seen clearly considering two divergent assessments of the future of organizational life in industrial societies. Howton (1969) envisioned the extension of the core processes of rationalization and functionalization to whole societies; thus, in his view the society would become a large organization with carefully articulated parts contributing to overall objectives. Such a development would permit the continued relevance of rational-functional theories of organizations, indeed would extend the range of those theories. Yet, the process through which this new organizational society emerges would remain outside rational-functional theories, although these theories may describe adequately the operation of such a society.

Simpson (1972) provided an opposing assessment of the future which raises the same theoretical problem. He suggested the possibility of the demise of rationality in organizations and a resurgence of emotional and moralistic bases of decision. The demise of organizational rationality would also spell the end of theories tied to it. As with the Howton example, the process giving rise to and/or undermining the realities to which the theories refer remains outside the theories. Dialectical analysis provides a way of reaching beyond these limits.

Dialectical theory, because it is essentially a processual perspective, focuses on the dimension currently missing in much organizational thought. It offers an explanation of the processes involved in the production, the reproduction, and the destruction of particular organizational forms. It opens analysis to the processes through which

[1] Reprinted from "Organizations: A Dialectical View" by Kenneth Benson, published in *Administrative Science Quarterly*, March 1977, vol. 22, no. 1, pp. 1–21, by permission of *The Administrative Science Quarterly*. Copyright © 1977 Cornell University.

Revision of a paper presented at the Sixty-eighth Annual Meeting of the American Sociological Association, New York, N.Y., August, 1973. I gratefully acknowledge comments on earlier drafts of this paper by Howard Aldrich, Eliot Freidson, Peter M. Hall, Wolf Heydebrand, James Mulherin, Charles Perrow, Richard Riddle, Stephen Turner, Robert A. Day, Mayer Zald, and students in my bureaucracy and theory seminars at the University of Missouri-Columbia. In preparation of this draft I have particularly benefited from extensive conversations with Mark Wardell and Robert Hagan. None of these are to be blamed for flaws remaining in the argument, and some have disagreed substantially with my position.

actors carve out and stabilize a sphere of rationality and those through which such rationalized spheres dissolve. Thus, dialectical theory can explain the empirical grounding of conventional organization theories because it deals with the social processes which conventional theories ignore.[2]

This article draws upon a general Marxist perspective on social life to develop a dialectical view of organizational theory. This approach to organizational studies has few close parallels. (For related efforts see Heydebrand, 1977; Goldman and Van Houten, 1977.) Marxists have rarely been interested in organizational analysis except to criticize the entire field; and organization scientists, for their part, have made minimal use of Marxist thought.

The dialectical view challenges the theoretical and methodological orthodoxies currently prevalent in the field. The established approaches, although varying in details, share a structure of reasoning or problematic which has been characterized as the "rational selection model" (Benson, 1971), the "goal paradigm" (Georgiou, 1973), and the "tool view" (Perrow, 1972). According to this problematic, much of what occurs in the organization is understood as a result of goal pursuit and/or need fulfillment. This view has been coupled with a methodological stance which accepts the conventionally understood components of the organization as scientific categories. The combination has uncritically accepted existing organizational arrangements and adapted itself to the interests of administrative elites. As a consequence organizational analysis has been dominated by issues of administrative concern. Its primary research questions have been administrative issues one step removed.

Despite this, all existing work will not be categorically rejected. Even work thoroughly within the conventional mode may be valuable. More important, a substantial amount of prior work has remained partially free of the dominant model — focusing on such phenomena as alternative power structures, strategic contingencies, political economy, negotiated order, and co-optative mechanisms — and may be usefully incorporated in a dialectical analysis. Thus, this article builds upon existing work while going beyond it at certain crucial points.

THE DIALECTIC AS SOCIAL PROCESS

The dialectical view is a general perspective on social life which can be extracted from the Marxist analysis of economic structure and its ramifications.[3] Marx's analysis of the capitalist economy is an application of the general perspective. The general perspective is, then, expressed through Marx's analyses of capitalism but not locked

---

[2] There have been a few efforts to develop dialectical analyses of organizational phenomena. Blau and Scott (1962: 222-253) for example devoted a chapter to ongoing processes through which dilemmas are confronted and partly resolved only to be confronted again in modified form. Also see Weinstein, Weinstein, and Blau (1972) and Lourenço and Gildewell (1975).

[3] In formulating a position I have been influenced most heavily by proponents of a dialectical Marxism, specifically Lukács (1971), Lefebvre (1968, 1971), Markov íc (1974), Goldmann (1969), Birnbaum (1969, 1971), and Habermas (1970, 1971, 1973). In addition, I have drawn occasional insights from such structural Marxists as Althusser (1970; Althusser and Balibar, 1970) and Godelier (1972). Finally, there are a number of places where I have drawn upon phenomenological sociologies, especially Berger and Luckmann (1966). I have consciously tried to work within a dialectical Marxist problematic and to draw upon other perspectives selectively where they provide insights which may be assimilated to the dialectical position.

into the specific categories and arguments of that analysis. Rather, a more general perspective running through Marx's work may be discerned.[4]

A dialectical view is fundamentally committed to the concept of process. The social world is in a continuous state of becoming — social arrangements which seem fixed and permanent are temporary, arbitrary patterns and any observed social pattern are regarded as one among many possibilities. Theoretical attention is focused upon the transformation through which one set of arrangements gives way to another. Dialectical analysis involves a search for fundamental principles which account for the emergence and dissolution of specific social orders.

There are four principles of dialectical analysis — social construction/ production, totality, contradiction, praxis. These constitute a perspective on the fundamental character of social life. A dialectical view of any particular field of study must be guided by an application of these principles.

Social Construction/Production.   The transformation of the social world is rooted in fundamental characteristics of human social life. People are continually constructing the social world. Through their interactions with each other social patterns are gradually built and eventually a set of institutional arrangements is established. Through continued interactions the arrangements previously constructed are gradually modified or replaced.

The construction of social arrangements is not a wholly rational-purposeful process, although the Marxist vision is that someday it might be. Social arrangements are created from the basically concrete, mundane tasks confronting people in their everyday life. Relationships are formed, roles are constructed, institutions are built from the encounters and confrontations of people in their daily round of life. Their production of social structure is itself guided and constrained by the context.

An important constraint is, of course, the existing social structure itself. People produce a social world which stands over them, constraining their actions. The production of social structure, then, occurs within a social structure. There are powerful forces which tend to occasion the reproduction of the existing social structure. These include, as prominent elements, the interests of particular groups of people and their power to defend their interests within an established order. Nevertheless, the efforts of people to transcend their present limits bring them eventually into conflict with the established arrangements and lead to social change. Sometimes the process is not planned and coherent, for example, where in reaching for higher levels of material productivity people go beyond the limits of present social arrangements. Sometimes, however, people may come to understand the limits of social structure and purposely rearrange it, a process termed "negation of the negation" (Marković, 1974: 24).

Totality.   Another important commitment of dialectical thought is that social phenomena should be studied relationally, that is, with attention to their multiple interconnections. Any particular structure is always seen as part of a larger, concrete whole rather than as an isolated, abstract phenomenon.

---

[4] My procedure is not one of relying upon dialectical laws of nature such as the transformation of quantity into quality, the interpenetration of opposites, and the like. The notion of dialectical laws located in nature and expressed both in society and in physical phenomena has been rightly criticized by Mills (1962: 129-130) and many others. Rather I have tried to utilize some general features of Marx's model and method of analysis, as did Mills himself (1962: 36-40).

The basis for this claim lies in the concept of social construction/production itself. People produce social structure, and they do so within a social context. The produced social world always constitutes a context which influences the ongoing process of production. Components of the social structure then become intertwined in complex ways. Divisions between components are not clear-cut or clean. Analysis must deal with the complex interlocking through which components are built into each other. This involves a search for dominant forces or components without resort to a deterministic argument.

The linkages between components are not complete nor wholly coherent. Rather, the processes of social construction take place in unique, partially autonomous contexts. These varying contexts are not centrally controlled and regulated except in rare cases. Thus, dialectical analysis, while looking at wholes, stresses the partial autonomy of the components. The principle of totality, then, expresses a commitment to study social arrangements as complex, interrelated wholes with partially autonomous parts. Analysis pursues the major breaks or divisions of the social structure which occasion divergent, incompatible productions, and the relations of dominance between sectors or layers of the social structure.

Because social construction is an emergent, partially autonomous process; the realities accepted by participants at any particular time may be continually undermined by ongoing acts of social construction. Even powerful actors may be unable to maintain an orderly, rationalized system of social relations in the face of this ongoing process. The totality, conceived dialectically then, includes newly emerging social arrangements as well as those already in place.

Contradiction.   Contradiction in the social order is a third principle of a Marxist dialectical view. The social order produced in the process of social construction contains contradictions, ruptures, inconsistencies, and incompatabilities in the fabric of social life. Radical breaks with the present order are possible because of *contradictions*. Some of these are necessary features of a particular order. For example, an integral part of capitalist social formations is that they are antithetical to the interests of labor, yet the functioning system maintains or reproduces this contradiction.

Other contradictions, by contrast, are system-destructive, that is, their presence undermines the system and destroys it. In classical Marxist analysis, the contradiction between the forces of production and economic relations is of this type. The advancement of the productive forces brings these into contradiction with the established system of economic relations. Economic systems pass from the scene as a consequence of this contradiction. (See Godelier, 1972.)

The ongoing process of social construction produces social formations. Once produced, these develop a seemingly autonomous, determinate structure. The structure may be studied and orderly relations between its components may be observed as if it were not a human product. Hence, conventional, theoretical approaches and positivistic methodologies may contribute to the description of these orderly patterns.

The dialectical approach differs from conventional strategies in treating these orderly patterns as created, produced arrangements with latent possibilities which can be transformed. The dialectical vision of the future is not one of continuous, predictable development through an extension or consolidation of the present order; rather, the future has many possibilities and the final determination depends upon human action or praxis (Marković, 1974: 210).

Contradictions grow out of social production in two ways. First, there is in any social setting a contradiction between ongoing production and the previously established social formation. The production of new patterns must always go against these established interests.

Second, the production process is carried out in differentiated social contexts producing multiple and incompatible social forms. The contexts vary in regard to the conditions affecting and limiting the process of production. There is in most instances little coordination between the multiple contexts within which construction takes place. Attempts to tightly regulate the process through authoritative direction or ideological manipulation are only partly successful, whether in political empires or organizational regimes. At the societal level the production processes in separate institutional sectors are partially autonomous. Likewise, at the level of organizations, the multiple levels and divisions form differentiated contexts within which social production proceeds in a partially autonomous manner. As a result the fabric of social life is rent with contradictions growing out of the unevenness and disconnectedness of social production.

Social contradictions have important effects upon production. (1) They may occasion dislocations and crises which activate the search for alternative social arrangements; (2) they may combine in ways which facilitate or in ways which thwart social mobilization; (3) they may define the limits of change within a particular period or within a given system. Consciousness of these limits may permit the ultimate negation of the limits; but in the interim the contradictions may be quite constraining.

Praxis.   The final principle is praxis or the free and creative reconstruction of social arrangements on the basis of a reasoned analysis of both the limits and the potentials of present social forms.

The commitment to praxis is both a description — that is, that people under some circumstances can become active agents reconstructing their own social relations and ultimately themselves on the basis of rational analysis — and an ethical commitment — that is, that social science should contribute to the process of reconstruction, to the liberation of human potential through the production of new social formations.

Dialectical analysis contributes to this process in part by dereifying established social patterns and structures — points out their arbitrary character, undermines their sense of inevitability, uncovers the contradictions and limits of the present order, and reveals the mechanisms of transformation.

An important dimension of such analysis is the critique of theories which affirm the present order or which deal only with minor adjustments or variations upon that order. From a dialectical perspective, the practice of social science is, like other human activities, a process of production imbedded in a social context. The social scientist uses the tools and raw materials at hand to construct realities.

The next section explores the implications of each of the general principles for the analysis of organizational phenomena. This involves the formulation of a conceptual apparatus and a methodology appropriate to the dialectical study of complex organizations.

THE SOCIAL PRODUCTION OF ORGANIZATIONAL REALITY

An organization as part of the social world is always in a state of becoming; it is not a fixed and determinate entity. Its major features — goals, structural arrangements, technology, informal relations, and so on — are the outcroppings of the process of social construction. The dialectical perspective focuses attention upon this process through which a specific organizational form has been produced, the mechanisms through which an established form is maintained (or reproduced), and its continuous reconstruction.

The organization is a product of past acts of social construction. As a product, it has some orderly, predictable relationships among its components at any particular point in time. These relationships may be studied scientifically and empirical generalizations may be framed to describe the order. In fact, this is the focus of much sociological research on organizations — for example, Perrow (1967), Woodward (1965; 1970), Zwerman (1970), and others found correlations between the technologies and the power structures of organizations. The demonstration of such relations, however, is not the end of inquiry but the beginning. Rather than treating such relationships as determinate, causal connections, for instance, arguing that technology determines social structure, the dialectician investigates the social process through which the orderly, predictable relations have been produced and reproduced.

There is a tendency in much organizational research to interpret observed correlations in terms of a hypothetical social process. For example, Blau and Schoenherr (1971) formulated some possible processes through which executives decide to increase organizational differentiation. Actual historical research tracing the sequence of events, however, has been rare. (See Chandler, 1962, for an exception.) The usual explanatory strategy, as with Blau and Schoenherr, is to formulate a hypothetical sequence involving actors who make rational or functional decisions, for example, fitting structure to technology in order to achieve efficiency.

Dialectical explanations observe or reconstruct sequences on the basis of historical evidence. The alternatives conceived by actors are explored; the constraints upon their decisions discovered; and the power bases of various actors uncovered. Once a pattern of organizational life is discovered, the processes through which it is maintained and/or modified are studied. Thus, an orderly pattern is taken to be a crystallized but temporary outcome of the process of social construction whose emergence and maintenance demands explanation. Several principles of social construction may be ventured as tentative guidelines for such investigations.

Ideas and Actions.   The consciousness of organizational participants is partially autonomous from the contextual situations in which they exist (Murphy, 1971). They are not in any simple sense captives of the roles, official purposes, or established procedures of the organization. The participants fill these "forms" with unique "content." Sometimes they may do so in an automatic, unreflective way; in other periods they may become very purposeful in trying to reach beyond the limits of their present situation, to reconstruct the organization in accord with alternative conceptions of its purposes, structures, technologies, and other features. Zald and McCarthy (1975) and Strauss and others (Strauss et al., 1964; Bucher and Stelling, 1969; Bucher, 1970) have provided examples of this phenomenon.

Interests.   The process of social construction proceeds through the mediation of interests in which the participants' perspectives are affected by the present structure of advantages and disadvantages built into the organization. This is not to say that a perfect correspondence between interests and ideas will prevail at all times — rather, over time the structure of interests will gradually influence the formation of ideas. In crisis periods, when thoroughgoing change is possible, participants may see their interests more clearly and conform their ideas and actions closely to them.

Power.   The ideas which guide the construction of the organization depend upon the power of various participants, that is, their capacity to control the direction of events. Some parties are in dominant positions permitting the imposition and enforcement of their conceptions of reality. Others are in positions of relative weakness and must act in conformity with the definitions of others. (See Silverman, 1971, for a similar analysis.)

Power in the organization derives to some extent from the official authority structure. Those occupying positions of authority have power to establish and enforce a model. They can design the organization as an instrument in the service of specific purposes. They can articulate its parts, adjust its technology and motivate its participants with certain ends in view. Once the organization is stabilized, they can use their power to maintain it as a rationally articulated structure by resisting interference from outside and opposing sources of resistance inside. (See Bendix, 1956, for a particularly valuable documentation of such processes.)

In most organization theories this state of affairs is assumed and is outside the area of inquiry. The organization is assumed to be an instrument designed for a purpose, and research focuses on the structural consequences flowing from that and on the technical adjustments necessary to enhance goal pursuit. The power base of the leadership is not examined; alternative systems based on different power bases are not considered. Perrow (1972) explicitly recognized that the organization is a tool in the hands of powerful actors; but he did not provide a framework for analyzing the struggle to control the tool. Rather, he asserted that organizational analysis should permit us to assess the effectiveness of organizational instruments for reaching specific objectives.

An examination of the power base of authority figures would generally extend beyond the boundaries of the organization itself and this is perhaps why most organization theorists have avoided the problem. The grounding of organizational authority in larger systems — interorganizational networks, political-economic power blocs, legal systems, and the like — is important to the dialectical approach. Crises in the universities in the late 1960s and the ultimate reliance of university administrators upon military and police forces to maintain order have demonstrated the importance of such investigations.

The sources of power to resist and ultimately to overturn the official authority structure of organizations are also important foci of dialectical analysis. How are some groups better able than others to extract advantages and privileges from the organization? How are some groups better able than others to influence the major decisions affecting the direction of the organization? Analyses of control over uncertainty by Crozier (1964; 1972; 1973); Pfeffer (1972; 1973; Pfeffer and Leblebici, 1973; Pfeffer and Salancik, 1974; Salancik and Pfeffer, 1974; Pfeffer, Salancik, and Leblebici, 1976) and Hickson (Hickson *et al.*, 1971; Hinings *et al.*, 1974) have provided important beginnings on such questions. Yet, these insightful analyses must be placed within a more encompassing framework with a critical-reflexive component, otherwise, this line of investigation breaks down easily into a technocratic effort to reduce irrational bases of resistance to authority. Also, analyses of "negotiated order" by Strauss, Bucher, and others (Strauss *et al.*, 1963; Bucher, 1970) may provide valuable elements of an explanation, even though their efforts are faulty in giving the impression that everything of importance is currently negotiable. (See Benson and Day, 1976, for a critique.) Likewise, the arguments of Bell (1973), Galbraith (1967), and Touraine (1971) stressing the centrality of occupations to the core technology of the organization as a basis of power should be explored, being careful not to accept the deterministic, functional explanations implicit in some of these analyses (particularly those of Bell and Galbraith).

The mobilization of participants to pursue their interests and to reach out for alternative structural arrangements is also a significant component of a dialectical analysis of power. Occupational groups, racial groups, social classes, and others may envision alternatives and become actively committed to their achievement. Such mobilization of commitment and resources will greatly enhance their power in the organization. It is intriguing that mobilization has been given little thought in organizational theory despite its obvious significance in the labor movement. Although mobilization has been prominent in other fields such as collective behavior, race relations, and politics, it seems to lie outside the paradigm of organizational studies. A few observers with analytical roots in these other fields have analyzed mobilization in organizations (Gamson, 1975; Bachrach and Baratz, 1970), as have students of social movement organizations (Zald and Ash, 1966). These efforts, however, are clearly outside the mainstream of organizational studies.

THE ORGANIZATION AS A TOTALITY

In a dialectical analysis the organization must be studied as a whole with multiple, interpenetrating levels and sectors. This means conceptualizing the organization as a concrete total phenomenon and attending to the intricate ways in which its components are tied together. The conventional, taken-for-granted distinctions should be rejected as the boundaries of inquiry. For example, abstracting a ''formal structure'' from the flux of ongoing social life is an unacceptable move for the dialectician; for concrete social life consists of an intricate interplay between form and content, between structure and process, and the like. Similarly, abstracting a sphere of ''rational action'' from the daily round of events is an equally serious error. Organizational phenomena must be understood as wholes in all of their interpenetrating complexity.

The principle of totality also directs us to see the intricate ties of organizations to the larger society — not only to macro-structural features such as economic and political systems but also to the everyday activities of people. Again, the arbitrary but conventional boundaries between phenomena must be distrusted. The conventional separation between organization and environment must be critically examined. The essential continuity, the relational character of social life must itself be analyzed and not overlooked in a search for analytical boundaries and units of analysis. The processes through which such conventional boundaries are produced and sustained must be pursued. The interests and power relations on which the conventional boundaries rest must be examined.

The presently established approaches to organization theory, by contrast, rely upon abstraction. Their abstractions correspond closely to the conventional administrative view and function as an ideology justifying, rationalizing administrative actions as well as a normative model or goal of administrative actions. That the model corresponds to our experience and seems reasonable is an indicator of our indoctrination with the administrative perspective and of the success of administrators in constructing a world in this image.

The history of organization theory may be seen, in part, as a process in which a series of ''nonrational factors'' have been conjured up only to be subdued by the rationalizing core. Thus, in the 1930s human relations theory arose as a champion of the informal structure. The trust of human relations theory, however, was to harness and control the informal in the interest of rationality. Later, the environment emerged as an important challenge in the work of Selznick (1949) and others. Yet through the years the trend has been toward extending the tentacles of rationalization to this sphere as well. Thus, recent theorists like March and Simon (1958), Lawrence and Lorsch (1967), and the school termed "neo-Weberians" by Perrow (1972) espouse a refined rationalism in which the sources of irrationality internal and external to the organization can be contained. This corresponds; incidentally, with an era of organizational monsters which Perrow (1972) warns control their environments and in which principles of rationalization and functionalization are being extended to wider spheres of social life (Howton, 1969).

Dialectical analysis is not to be restricted to the narrow, limited, conventional reality promulgated by administrators. Its focus is the total organization from which this limited segment has been wrenched. It analyzes the intricate ways in which the organization as a rationally articulated structure is linked to its unrationalized context; it explores and uncovers the social and political processes through which a segmental view becomes dominant and is enforced; and, it anticipates the emergence of new arrangements based on shifting power relations. Thus, the dialectical view takes the rationalized organization as an arbitrary model unevenly imposed upon events and insecure in its hold. The strategy for developing this kind of analysis here includes the recognition of two levels of organizational reality — morphology and substructure.

Organizational Morphology.   Morphology refers to the officially enforced and conventionally accepted view of the organization. It refers to the organization as abstracted from its concrete, intricate relations with other aspects of social life. This is the administrators' vision of the organization, the form which they try to impose upon events. Since they are partly successful, the morphology may also be somewhat accurate as a description of organizations.

Four aspects of organizational reality at the level of morphological analysis must be distinguished.

1. **The paradigm commitments of an organization** — specifically, its commitments to a domain, a technology, and an ideology. These commitments provide, respectively, a definition of the objectives of the organization, a specific set of techniques for pursuing objectives, and a set of ideas interpreting and justifying the organization's activities.
2. **The officially recognized and legitimate structural arrangements of the organization** — specifically, the network of social roles and role sets in the organization. This includes characteristics such as differentiation, centralization, bureaucratization, and so on.
3. **The constitution of the organization** — specifically, the bases of participation and involvement in the organization. These concern the terms on which participation and compliance of individuals and groups are effected. (On organization "constitutions" see Zald, 1970a, 1970b.)
4. **The organization-environment linkages** — specifically, the patterning or structuring of relations with organizations and individuals external to the focal organization.

One may, of course, construct organizational analysis on the correlated variability between morphological components like most organization theorists. Their efforts generally proceed by: (1) demonstrating an empirical regularity in organizations, such as a correlation between number of hierarchical levels and number of separate divisions, (2) establishing the types of organizations within which the relationship holds, and (3) inferring a rational or functional linkage between the correlated factors (for example, see Etzioni, 1961; Perrow, 1967; Blau and Schoenherr, 1971).

The research undertaken by Blau and associates (Blau, 1968, 1973; Blau, Heydebrand and Stauffer, 1966; Blau and Schoenherr, 1971) in the Comparative Organization Research Program exemplifies the pattern. The research relies upon summary indicators of structural patterns based on documents such as organization charts and on interview reports of structural patterns. From these data measures for structural features such as hierarchy, differentiation, and so forth are derived. These are correlated with each other and with other factors such as size and technology. The pattern of correlations is then explained as a result of a rational or functional arrangement of the organization's parts. The actual process of adjustment, the sequence of events producing the pattern has not been observed but has been inferred to be one of rational or functional adjustment. Thus, the entire explanatory effort remains within the confines of an abstracted organization ripped from its historical roots and societal context and innocent of its deeper-lying power struggles and negotiations. Thus, the research itself is drawn into the presuppositions of the order under study. The extra-rational processes — internal and external to the rationally conceived organization — remain out of focus, beyond the periphery of the investigators' vision. (See Turner, 1977, for a related critique.)

A dialectical analysis, by contrast, should attend to the underlying process which produced and sustained the observed regularities. The systematic relationships among parts of the organization's morphology must be explained by reference to a more fundamental substructure such as a power structure which generates changes within the morphology. This too involves finding an empirical base for organizational measurement, this is, continuously analyzing how the primary data sources such as organization charts are produced and sustained.[5]

This does not mean that morphological research is worthless. On the contrary, the description of regularities at this level is a necessary step in a dialectical analysis. These efforts must, however, be integrated in a larger explanatory program. Most important, morphological studies should not be allowed to define the parameters of the field and thereby limit its explanatory capacity.

Even appeals to rational or functional selection processes may have a continuing importance. One certainly cannot argue a priori that such processes are of no consequence. Such processes, however, should not be invoked as final arbiters, as the ultimate basis of organizational analysis; rather, actual event sequences must be examined. When rational or functional processes appear to be operating, such processes must themselves be grounded, that is, one must inquire about the production process through which rational or functional selection criteria are established and maintained. This, of course, may lead us beyond the conventional boundaries of the organization to larger systems of dominance.

Organizational Substructure.   The substructural network provides the basis for transformation of the organization's morphology. The substructure is in part a nonrationalized sphere of organizational action, a complex network of relations linking participants to each other and to the larger social world in a multiplicity of

---

[5] The substructure consists of the network of social relations through which the morphology is produced and reproduced. Here one encounters the bases of power, the dominance relations which establish and maintain the morphology of the organization. The orderly sequences of development, the predictable relations between components at the morphological level are grounded in and ultimately explained by this substructure.

unregulated ways. Administrative rationalizers try and have been partly successful at containing or harnessing the energy flowing from these ties. Much of organizational analysis, of course, has been supportive of such rationalizing moves by élites. Because it is only partly rationalized, the substructure provides the social basis for a latent social system forming within the established order and threatening its hegemony. For example the cleavage between sexual or racial groups, where coterminous with administrative divisions, could provide a cutting edge for consciousness formation (Gordon, 1972; Crozier, 1964). On the basis of substructural linkages people may act to overthrow the established morphology.

The substructure includes linkages to the larger societal system. These include the bases of recruitment of organizational élites; the framework of interests in the larger society setting limits upon the operations of the organization; the power structure controlling the flow of resources into organizations and through interorganizational networks; the ties of the organization to social classes, racial groups, ethnic groups, sexual groups, and others in the society; the institutionalized dominance patterns of professions in their spheres of practice; and so on. Developments within the organization often appear to be intricately related to events occurring in the larger society. In many ways the organization is a part of these larger patterns. Yet, the prevailing analytical strategy is to abstract the organization from these relations and treat it as if it were autonomous or at least capable of channeling or filtering the environment through its input-output orifices. (For exceptions see especially Zald, 1970a, 1970b; Warren, Rose, and Bergunder, 1974.) Dialectical analysis, by contrast, focuses attention upon the relations.

The substructure also includes bases of dominance that are intraorganizational. Included here are structures of control over strategic resources giving some departments, divisions, occupations, and so forth, advantages, vis-à-vis others. The centrality of an occupation to the core technology of an organization or the capacity of some departments to control uncertainty affecting significantly the welfare of other departments might provide leverage for exercising power in the main reality-defining arenas of the organization. These and other sources of power might be explored within a dialectical framework.

There is a large body of literature dealing with these issues that may be incorporated in a dialectical analysis. This includes the work of Crozier (1964, 1972, 1973), Hickson and others (Hickson et al., 1971; Hinings et al., 1974) on strategic contingencies, Pfeffer (1972, 1973; Pfeffer and Salancik, 1974; Salancik and Pfeffer, 1974; Pfeffer, Salancik, and Leblebici, 1976) and Aldrich (1972, 1976; Whetten and Aldrich, 1975) on resource dependence, and that of Zald and Wamsley (Zald, 1970a, 1970b; Wamsley and Zald, 1973) on political economy. While none of these works are cast within a dialectical framework, they grapple with the underlying, non-rationalized bases of control within the organization. There is a tendency within some of these efforts, especially those of Zald and Wamsley, to see these underlying power-dependence relations as the foundation of organizational goals paradigmatic commitments, and authority structures.[6]

---

[6] Since some of my argument here has been anticipated in the work on strategic contingencies, resource dependencies, and political economy, it seems important to suggest the ways in which a dialectical perspective incorporates but goes beyond these earlier efforts. The major difference is that these contributions represent partial perspectives which can be incorporated in a variety of more encompassing arguments. The dialectical view is instead a more nearly complete explanatory framework into which the more limited theories may be drawn. Work on strategic contingencies, for example, has been framed at times within an overall functionalist framework by assuming that the

ORGANIZATIONAL CONTRADICTIONS

The organizational totality, as conceived dialectically, is characterized by ruptures, breaks, and inconsistencies in the social fabric. To these we apply the general term "contradiction," while recognizing that such rifts may be of many different types. Many theorists see the organization as a reasonably coherent, integrated system, rationally articulated or functionally adjusted. This view, of course, is an abstraction. If one looks at the organization concretely and pays attention to its multiple levels and varied relations to the larger society, contradictions become an obvious and important feature of organizational life. (See Heydebrand, 1977.)

The Production of Contradictions.   Social construction-production is not a rationally guided centrally controlled process. Despite the efforts of administrations to contain and channel the process, some elements in the organization and outside of it remain beyond the reach of rationalization. Beyond this, the rationalization process produces structures which then resist further rationalization.

Some contradictions are generated within the organization — growing out of the divisions, reward structures, control structures, and other separation points in the organization. These define distinct, semi-autonomous spheres of social action, which are divergent contexts for social construction-production. The people occupying particular locations will tend to develop models of organizational structure based on their peculiar priorities and problems — from a specific occupational or departmental standpoint. Thus, across a range of sectoral divisions or levels the organization generates opposing models or images of organizational morphology. Beyond this, the subgroups created by sectoral divisions, levels, and the like may be sufficiently autonomous to implement their opposing models to some degree. In any case, a large, complex organization is likely at any given time to harbor a number of structural inconsistencies, for example, some departments organized along professional lines;

---

organization will grant power to those segments most crucial to its work (see especially Hickson *et al.*, 1971). The recent work by Pfeffer and Aldrich on resource dependence has produced a set of testable propositions floating free of any larger analytical system. In fact, they (Aldrich and Pfeffer, 1976) have recently tried to integrate their work with an evolutionary model. Thus, both the theoretical and practical connections of this body of thought are indeterminate. Drawing it into a dialectical framework provides a more general set of principles to guide analysis. We are directed to the role of contradictions, to the larger totality, to the importance of praxis, reflexivity, and the like. Thus, the tendency to fall into evolutionist, functionalist, or positivist stances is counteracted.

The work of Zald, Wamsley, and others within a political economy perspective presents a more difficult problem. Clearly, I have been heavily influenced by the political economy view; my previous work on interorganizational networks (Benson, 1975) takes a political economy stance. Further, the work of Zald (1970a, 1970b) and Wamsley and Zald (1973) constitute a very ambitious effort to grapple with the issues addressed in the present paper. Their work grounds goals, technologies, constitutions, and other features of the organization in more basic power relations. They are sensitive to the latent, unregulated social networks (termed substructure here) beneath the superficial realities addressed by most conventional theories. Overall, their work constitutes the closest parallel within the existing literature. Yet, they do not characterize their work as dialectical or Marxian. In part my effort is to establish a link suggesting how this important body of work may be incorporated in a dialectical view.

Beyond this, however, there are some important differences. The proponents of political economy, resource dependence, strategic contingencies, and the like remain committed to a basically positivist methodology. They have adopted an uncritical, unreflexive stance toward organizational realities. They fail to see or at least to grapple with the tentativeness, the arbitrariness of the phenomena they describe. They do not examine how these phenomena are produced. Instead

others, more bureaucratized. Many sociologists have analyzed inconsistencies of this kind, but few have recognized their basis as being a fundamental social process.[7]

Beyond this, the ongoing process of social construction in all sectors of the organization will continually generate alternatives to the presently established morphology. This may occur at all stratified levels. Even authorities may frequently generate innovations which are contradictory to the established patterns. Increased use of computers for purposes of coordination and control, new budgeting procedures, and other innovations from above may stand in opposition to previously constructed arrangements. Thus, the organization as established constitutes a structure which may resist its own further development. This should not be seen as a mysterious occurrence, but as a result of the rooting of present arrangements in a concrete structure of advantages, interests, commitments, and the like.

Contradictions may be generated also in the larger society and imposed upon the organization. An organization may be charged with multiple, contradictory functions, for instance, the prison's dual purposes of rehabilitation and protection. This may produce inconsistent moves within the organization yielding contradictory structures, competing interest groups, and occasional periods of crisis. Or, an organization may be made dependent upon support or cooperation from opposing sources. For example, a manpower program might be dependent both upon employers with a conservative ideology regarding work and militant advocacy groups with a radical ideology. The manpower agency may internalize the conflict by developing contradictory components to deal with those opposed publics (Schmidt and Kochan, 1976).

Some contradictions within the organization may directly reflect the fundamental features of the larger economic-political system. Management-labor conflict, for example, is a basic feature of capitalist societies which is reproduced by the workings of those societies. This conflict leads to the production of contradictory arrangements inside all of the work organizations in the society. This sets limits upon structural innovations, ideological formulations, morale levels, and other features within the organizations (Krupp, 1961).

The Structure of Contradictions.   The organization is typically the scene of multiple contradictions. The ongoing processes of social construction internal and external to the organization produce a complex array of interrelated contradictions. The combinations are contingent upon the ways in which components of the organization and the society are engaged. Contradictions become overlaid in unique clusters or patterns depending upon the ways in which different groups become involved in

---

they pursue the description and analysis of a particular kind of order — characterized by resource dependencies. Dialectical analysis must go beyond this to deal with the processes through which this kind of order is produced and maintained. Clearly the political economy model is historically and contextually limited. Its accuracy, predictive utility, and so on are contingent. This complication cannot be ignored by the dialectician.

As with other theories we must seek the connection between interests and theoretical orientations. In some instances work of this type has been funded extensively by government agencies with an apparent interest in smoothing interorganizational coordination, overcoming resistance to change, and creating more flexible organizational apparatuses. Thus, we must pursue the possibility that such work formalizes a perspective and interest that are institutionally isolable and limited. This may involve a program of technocratic rationalization through planning for, bargaining with, and manipulating organizations.

[7] Benson (1973) for an analysis of bureaucratic-professional conflict which elaborates this point.

their production. Every organization is, then, a unique case because of the contingencies affecting social construction-production.[8]

Consider, as an example, the knitting together of authority level and racial status as bases of social construction. Where a racial minority is subordinate in the organization's authority structure, the resulting patterns of contradiction may be different from otherwise comparable situations lacking the overlay of race upon authority. Recent crises in some state prisons have reflected the overlay of race and authority. The largely black populations of the prisons have increasingly seen the organization as an instrument of white oppression. Black inmates have created structures based upon racial antagonism, used a racial ideology, and linked their cause to that of racial liberation in the larger society.

Contradictions may be combined in ways which exacerbate conflict or in ways which contain it. Some combinations may constitute what Althusser (1970) terms a "ruptural unity," that is, a combination that permits a drastic reorganization of the system. Other combinations may tend to fragment the organization in a series of overlapping, partially competitive interest groups.

Participants may try to reach their objectives by managing or manipulating the combinations of contradictions. It has been argued, for example, that corporate élites have purposely created secondary labor markets for minorities and women as a device for maintaining control over jobs and dividing the labor movement (Gordon, 1972). Of course, combinations produced for one purpose may later produce perverse outcomes. The coincidence of race and occupation produced heightened racial tensions in the 1960s.

The Production of Change.   Contradictions feed into the social construction-production process in several ways. (1) Contradictions provide a continuing source of tensions, conflicts, and the like which may, under some circumstances, shape consciousness and action to change the present order. (2) Contradictions set limits upon and establish possibilities for reconstruction at any given time. (3) Contradictions may produce crises which enhance possibilities for reconstruction. (4) Contradictions are important, finally, as defining limits of a system. Some contradictions may be crucial features of a particular organizational order. Other contradictions of lesser significance may be eroded without changing the fundamental character of the organization. The fundamental contradictions tend to be reproduced in the organization by its normal operation as a system and by its linkages to a larger network. These contradictions define limits which must be exceeded in order to transform an organization.

The most basic, generic contradiction is that between the constructed social world and the ongoing process of social construction. The reification of the organization as a determinate thing standing over against people is contradictory to the ongoing process of production. This contradiction is the essence of social and political alienation. As people become conscious of this contradiction and act to overcome it, they rationally reconstruct the present order and overcome its limitations. Thus, we arrive at praxis.

---

    [8] It is not possible in a programmatic statement of this kind to specify a catalogue of contradictions weighted according to their importance. This is because (1) the combinations of contradictions operating in a particular organization is a unique, contingent structure, and (2) the ongoing process of social production continuously generates new contradictions.

TOWARD ORGANIZATIONAL PRAXIS

Dialectical theory attends to the interplay between practical interests and scholarship. The study of organizations is seen as a product of social construction — that is, theories have been produced by particular groups of people acting within a limited context on the basis of their practical concerns. Theories, then, reflect the social context in which they were created and the practical concerns of their creators (not simply the authors but the larger group of people whose actions produced the theories). In turn, theories are inextricably involved in the construction of organizations. Theories guide actors in their efforts to understand and control the organization. Theories provide models to be implemented, illuminate problems to be solved, reveal controls to be exercised, and so on. There is, then, a dialectical relation between organizational arrangements and organizational theories. The use of theories as guidelines for administrative control and as programs for organizational revolutions should be the object of study. This involves a "reflexive" moment within dialectical analysis and parallels the kind of analysis proposed by Gouldner (1970), Friedrichs (1970), and others.

The Critique of Limited Perspectives.   Many theories of organizations can be understood as formalized solutions of certain actors (usually administrators or other dominant figures) to the technical, practical problems posed by the organization's dialectical character. Such a theory formalizes a way of dealing with (controlling or adjusting to) the multilevel, contradictory complexity of the organization. Devices such as socializing, monitoring, rewarding, adjusting, structuring, and negotiating provide solutions to concrete problems encountered by participants. Theorists pull these devices together into coherent systems which then may be adopted within organizations, sometimes as a result of aggressive social movements. Such theories provide sets of procedures, movements, routines which may be employed to pursue an objective by cancelling, controlling, or capitalizing upon the contradictory complexity of organizational life.

From a dialectical perspective, then, specific theories are not in any simple sense to be set aside. Rather, they are to be superceded in a more encompassing framework. Human relations, structural-functional, decision, and open systems theories may each provide accurate predictive statements about some aspects of organizational structure and process within delimited time periods and institutional locations. The dialectician goes beyond such formulations to inquire into the relationships between organization theories and organizational realities — considering the "reality-defining" potential of a theory of administration, the linkage between administrator and theoretician, and the connection of social theories to social movements of various kinds. Such issues have been raised regarding human relations theories (see Carey, 1967; Krupp, 1961; Perrow, 1972; Mills, 1970) but, this type of critique must be broadened to include other theories as well. For example, open systems theories appear to be linked in time to the growing prominence in administrative circles of cybernation and its application to the organization structure and not merely to production technology. In this situation, the open systems theories have considerable intuitive appeal and have provided the intellectual foundation for a number of textbooks on management, industrial sociology, and complex organizations. Indeed, such theories may have some predictive power within this new institutional setting. However, it is important from dialectical perspective to recognize that open systems theories and theorists are deeply enmeshed in the social process creating the new administrative situation. The new administrative realities and the new administrative theories have emerged hand-in-hand. The theories and theorists are, then, part of the reality they describe. Their plausibility and predictive power may be derived from and circumscribed by this historically and institutionally delimited phenomenon. Furthermore, the entire "package" of events may be linked inextricably to larger and more fundamental processes of societal transformation such as the emergence of dominance patterns within which technology and science serve as legitimating ideologies (cf. Habermas, 1970; Karpik, 1972).

Similarly, theories of "negotiated order," which the author finds intuitively more appealing than open systems theory, must be subjected to the same mode of unrelenting critical examination. This perspective has been the creation of analysts working mainly in professional organizations (mostly medical settings). The perspective does seem intuitively to have a high degree of correspondence to events in those settings, particularly to the interactional patterns characterizing everyday life among professional staff members (Strauss *et al.*, 1963; Strauss *et al.*, 1964; Bucher and Stelling, 1969). Some questions that should be pursued about this perspective include the following: Is "negotiated order" a general theory of order or a theory of a specific kind of order existing within a narrowly delimited class of organizational settings? What issues are generally non-negotiable and thus ignored by or taken as defining boundaries by negotiated order theorists? Are the proponents of negotiated order theory engaged in dispensing its insights to practitioners in professional organizations? Do negotiated order theorists merely articulate and conceptualize the perspectives of insightful actors in the settings under study? (See Benson and Day, 1976.)

The task of the dialectician, then, is neither to reject these theories out of hand nor to accept their accuracy uncritically. Rather, it is to understand the connection between theory and reality by analyzing the social context.

The Construction of Alternatives.   Dialectical analysis must go beyond reflexivity; it has an active as well as reflexive moment. It must be concerned with the active reconstruction of organizations. This reconstruction is aimed toward the realization of human potentialities by the removal of constraints, limitations upon praxis. This task involves both the critique of existing organizational forms and the search for alternatives. The search for alternatives is based on the view that the future is not necessarily a projection of the present order; rather, the future is full of possibilities and one of them has to be made. This is not an unrealistic or utopian task; rather, it must be tied to an empirically grounded understanding of limits and possibilities in the present.

The commitment to social reconstruction is toward the freeing of the process of social construction from blockages and limitations occasioned by dominance. The larger objective is the realization of a social situation in which people freely and collectively control the direction of change on the basis of a rational understanding of social process (Marković, 1974; Habermas, 1971, 1973).

A dialectical analysis of organizations, then, should be concerned with conditions under which people may reconstruct organizations and establish social formations in which continuous reconstruction is possible. This provides guidance regarding the selection of research questions. Some important issues are the humanization of work processes, the development of systems of participation (self-management), the discovery of alternatives to bureaucracy, the removal of systems of dominance, the provision for the utilization of expert knowledge without creating technocratic élites, removing the resistance of organizations to more rational arrangements (for example, overcoming resistance to the development of rationally arranged systems of organization). These are, of course, difficult problems and the task is complicated by the possibility that contradictions will develop between them, for example, creating rational systems may undermine self-management. Thus, the prospect is for a continuous process of reconstruction.

CONCLUSION

Organizations constitute important instruments of domination in the advanced industrial societies. Any effort to change these societies must deal with the organizational dimension. Likewise, efforts to construct alternative social arrangements within or in the place of the present order must grapple with the problem of organization. (See Schurman, 1968, for an examination of the organizational problems posed in Communist China.)

Despite the central importance of organizations to thoroughgoing social reconstruction, the study of organizations has not developed a capacity to deal with fundamental change. Instead, established approaches tend to affirm present organizational realities and to deal with relatively minor adjustments within the present order.

This article has attempted to begin the process of constructing an emancipatory alternative approach by proposing a dialectical view of organizations committed to the centrality of process. Four basic principles of dialectical analysis — social production, totality, contradiction, and praxis — are developed and applied to organizational studies. The principles of dialectical analysis provide a guiding perspective for organizational studies grounded in a view of human social life. The principles do not constitute a developed substantive theory of organizations nor a conceptual framework to guide research. The dialectical view provides instead a critical-emancipatory stance toward organizational studies. Much work remains to be done in developing the implications of this perspective within substantively based theory and research.

REFERENCES

Aldrich, Howard
1972   "An organization-environment perspective on cooperation and conflict in the manpower training system." In A. Negandhi (ed.), *Interorganization Theory:* 49-70. Kent, Ohio: Center for Business and Economic Research.
1976   "Resource dependence and interorganizational relations: local employment service offices and social services sector organizations." *Administration and Society 7,* 4:419-454.

Aldrich, Howard, and Jeffrey Pfeffer
1976   "Environments of organizations." *The Annual Review of Sociology,* 2:79-106.

Althusser, Louis
1970   *For Marx.* Trans. by Ben Brewster. New York: Vintage, a division of Random House.

Althusser, Louis, and Etienne Balibar
1970   *Reading Capital.* Trans. by Ben Brewster. New York: Pantheon.

Bachrach, Peter S., and Morton S. Baratz
1970   *Power and Poverty, Theory and Practice.* New York: Oxford University Press.

Bell, Daniel
1973   *The Coming of Post-Industrial Society: A Venture in Social Forecasting.* New York: Basic Books.

Bendix, Reinhard
1956   *Work and Authority in Industry.* New York: Harper and Row.

Benson, J. Kenneth
1971   *Models of Structure Selection in Organizations: On the Limitations of Ra-*

tional Perspectives. Paper presented at the Annual Meeting of the American Sociological Association, Denver, Colorado, August.

1973 "The analysis of bureaucratic-professional conflict: functional versus dialectical approaches." *The Sociological Quarterly,* 14:376-394.

1975 "The interorganizational network as a political economy." *The Administrative Science Quarterly,* 20:229-249.

Benson, J. Kenneth, and Robert A. Day

1976 "On the Limits of Negotiation: a Critique of the Theory of Negotiated Order." Paper presented at the 71st Annual Meeting of the American Sociological Association. New York, New York, September.

Berger, Peter L., and Thomas Luckman

1966 *The Social Construction of Reality.* Garden City, N.Y.: Doubleday.

Blau, Peter M.

1968 "The hierarchy of authority in organizations." *The American Journal of Sociology,* 73:453-467.

1973 *The Organization of Academic Work.* New York: Wiley.

Blau, Peter M., Wolf V. Heydebrand, and Robert E. Stauffer

1966 "The structure of small bureaucracies." *The American Sociological Review,* 31, 2:179-191.

Blau, Peter M., and Richard A. Schoenherr

1971 *The Structure of Organizations.* New York and London: Basic Books.

Blau, Peter M., and Richard Scott

1962 *Formal Organizations.* San Francisco: Chandler.

Birnbaum, Norman

1969 *The Crisis of Industrial Society.* New York: Oxford University Press.

1971 *Toward a Critical Sociology.* New York: Oxford University Press.

Bucher, Rue

1970 "Social process and power in a medical school." In Mayer N. Zald (ed.), *Power in Organizations:* 3-48. Nashville, Tenn.: Vanderbilt University Press.

Bucher, Rue, and J. Stelling

1969 "Characteristics of professional organizations." *The Journal of Health and Social Behavior,* 10:3-15.

Carey, A.

1967 "The Hawthorne studies: a radical criticism." *The American Sociological Review,* 32, 3:403-416.

Chandler, Alfred D., Jr.

1962 *Strategy and Structure: Chapters in the History of the Industrial Enterprise.* Cambridge, MA: MIT Press.

Crozier, Michel

1964 *The Bureaucratic Phenomenon.* Chicago: University of Chicago Press.

1972 "The relationship between micro and macrosociology, a study of organizational systems as an empirical approach to problems of macrosociology." *Human Relations,* 25, 3:239-251.

1973 *The Stalled Society.* New York: Viking Press.

Etzioni, Amitai

1961 *A Comparative Analysis of Complex Organizations.* New York: Free Press.

Friedrichs, Robert W.

1970 *A Sociology of Sociology.* New York: Free Press.

Galbraith, John Kenneth

1967 *The New Industrial State.* Boston: Houghton-Mifflin.

Gamson, William A.

1975 *The Strategy of Social Protest.* Homewood, IL: Dorsey Press.

Georgiou, Petro

1973 "The goal paradigm and notes towards a counter paradigm." *The Administrative Science Quarterly,* 18:291-310.

Godelier, Maurice

1972 "Structure and contradiction in capital." In Robin Blackburn (ed.), *Ideology in Social Science:* 334-368. New York: Vintage Books.

Goldman, Paul, and Donald R. Van Houten

1977 "Managerial strategies and the worker: a Marxist analysis of bureaucracy." *The Sociological Quarterly,* 18: in press.

Goldmann, Lucien

1969 *The Human Sciences and Philosophy.* Trans. by Hayden V. White and Robert Anchor. London: Jonathan Cape.

Gordon, David M.

1972 *Theories of Poverty and Underemployment.* Toronto and London: D. C. Heath.

Gouldner, Alvin W.

1970 *The Coming Crisis in Western Sociology.* New York: Basic Books.

Habermas, Jürgen

1970   *Toward a Rational Society.* Trans. by Jeremy J. Shapiro. Boston: Beacon Press.

1971   *Knowledge and Human Interests.* Trans. by Jeremy J. Shapiro. Boston: Beacon Press.

1973   *Theory and Practice.* Trans. by John Viertel. Boston: Beacon Press.

Heydebrand, Wolf

1977   "Organizational contradictions in public bureaucracies: toward a Marxian theory of organizations." *The Sociological Quarterly* 18:1: in press.

Hickson, D. J., C. R. Hinings, C.A. Lee, R. E. Schneck, and J. M. Pennings

1971   "A strategic contingencies' theory of intraorganizational power." *The Administrative Science Quarterly,* 16:216-229.

Hinings, C. R., D. J. Hickson, J. M. Pennings, and R. E. Schneck

1974   "Structural conditions of intraorganizational power." *The Administrative Science Quarterly,* 19:22-44.

Howton, F. William

1969   *Functionaries.* Chicago: Quadrangle Books.

Karpik, F. Lucien

1972   *Le Capitalisme. Technologique I:* 2-34.

Krupp, Sherman

1961   *Pattern in Organization Analysis.* New York: Holt, Rinehart and Winston.

Lawrence, Paul R., and Jay W. Lorsch

1967   *Organization and Environment.* Boston: Graduate School of Business Administration, Harvard University.

Lefebvre, Henri

1968   *Dialectical Materialism.* Trans. by John Sturrock. London: Jonathan Cape.

1971   *Everyday Life in the Modern World.* Trans. by Sacha Rabinovitch. New York: Harper and Row.

Lourenço, Susan V., and John C. Glidewell

1975   "A dialectical analysis of organizational conflict." *The Administrative Science Quarterly,* 20:489-508.

Lukács, Georg

1971   *History and Class Consciousness.* Studies in Marxist Dialectics. Trans. by Rodney Livingstone. Cambridge, MA: MIT Press.

March, James, and Herbert Simon

1958   *Organizations.* New York: Wiley.

Markovıc, Mihailo

1974   *From Affluence to Praxis.* Ann Arbor: University of Michigan Press.

Mills, C. Wright

1962   *The Marxists.* New York: Dell.

1970   "The contribution of sociology to studies of industrial relations." *Berkeley Journal of Sociology,* 15:11-32

Murphy, Robert F.

1971   *The Dialectics of Social Life.* New York: Basic Books.

Perrow, Charles

1967   "A framework for the comparative analysis of organizations." *The American Sociological Review,* 32:3:194-208.

1972   *Complex Organizations: A Critical Essay.* Glenview, IL: Scott, Foresman.

Pfeffer, Jeffrey

1972   "Size and composition of corporate boards of directors: the organization and its environment." *The Administrative Science Quarterly,* 17:218-228.

1973   "Size, composition, and function of hospital boards of directors: a study of organization-environment linkage." *The Administrative Science Quarterly,* 18:349-364.

Pfeffer, Jeffrey, and Huseyin Leblebici

1973   "Executive recruitment and the development of interfirm organizations." *The Administrative Science Quarterly,* 18:449-461.

Pfeffer, Jeffrey, and Gerald R. Salancik

1974   "Organizational decision-making as a political process: the case of a university budget." *The Administrative Science Quarterly,* 19:135-151.

Pfeffer, Jeffrey, Gerald R. Salancik, and Huseyin Leblebici

1976   "The effect of uncertainty on the use of social influence in organizational decision-making." *The Administrative Science Quarterly,* 21:227-245.

Salancik, Gerald R., and Jeffrey Pfeffer

1974   "The bases and use of power in organizational decision-making: the case of a university." *The Administrative Science Quarterly,* 19:453-473.

Schmidt, Stuart M., and Thomas A. Kochan

1976   "An application of a 'political economy' approach to effectiveness. Employment service-employer exchanges." *Administration and Society,* 7:455-474.

Schurman, Franz
1968   *Ideology and Organization in Communist China:* enlarged Edition. Berkeley and Los Angeles: University of California Press.
Selznick, Phillip
1949   *TVA and the Grass Roots.* Berkeley, California: University of California Press.
Silverman, David
1971   *The Theory of Organizations, a Sociological Framework.* New York: Basic Books.
Simpson, Richard L.
1972   "Beyond rational bureaucracy: changing values and social integration in post-industrial society." *Social Forces,* 51:1-6.
Strauss, Anselm, Leonard Schatzman, Rue Bucher, Danuta Ehrlich, and Melvin Sabshin
1964   *Psychiatric Ideologies and Institutions.* New York: Free Press.
Strauss, Anselm, Leonard Schatzman, Danuta Ehrlich, Rue Bucher, and Melvin Sabshin
1963   "The hospital and its negotiated order." In Eliot Freidson (ed.), *The Hospital in Modern Society:* 147-169. London: Free Press of Glencoe.
Touraine, Alain
1971   *The Post-Industrial Society.* Trans. by Leonard F. X. Mayhew. New York: Random House.
Turner, Stephen P.
1977   "Blau's theory of differentiation: is it explanatory." *The Sociological Quarterly,* 18: in press.
Wamsley, Gary, and Mayer N. Zald
1973   *The Political Economy of Public Organizations.* Lexington, MA: Lexington Books, D.C. Heath.
Warren, Roland L., Stephen M. Rose, and Ann F. Bergunder
1974   *The Structure of Urban Reform. Community Decision Organizations in Stability and Change.* Lexington, MA: Lexington Books, D.C. Heath.
Weinstein, Michael, Deena Weinstein, and Peter M. Blau
1972   "Blau's dialectical sociology and dialectical sociology: comments." *Sociological Inquiry,* 42:173-189.
Whetten, David, and Howard Aldrich
1975   Predicting Organization Set Size and Diversity. Paper presented at the Annual Meeting of the American Sociological Association, San Francisco, California.
Woodward, Joan
1965   *Industrial Organization: Theory and Practice.* London: Oxford University Press.
1970   *Industrial Organization: Behavior and Control.* London: Oxford University Press.
Zald, Mayer N.
1970a "Political economy: a framework for comparative analysis." In Mayer N. Zald (ed.), *Power and Organizations:* 221-261. Nashville, Tenn.: Vanderbilt University Press.
1970b *Organizational Change: The Political Economy of the YMCA.* Chicago: University of Chicago Press.
Zald, Mayer N., and Roberta Ash
1966   "Social movement organizations: growth, decay, and change." *Social Forces,* 44:327-341.
Zald, Mayer N., and John D. McCarthy
1975   "Organizational intellectuals and the criticism of society." *Social Service Review,* 49, 3:344-362.
Zwerman, William L.
1970   *New Perspectives on Organization Theory.* Westport, Connecticut: Greenwood Press.

14. The Multinational Corporation and the Law of Uneven Development*

Stephen Hymer

The settler's town is a strongly-built town, all made of stone and steel. It is a brightly-lit town; the streets are covered with asphalt, and the garbage-cans swallow all the leavings, unseen, unknown and hardly thought about. The settler's feet are never visible, except perhaps in the sea; but there you're never close enough to see them. His feet are protected by strong shoes although the streets of his town are clean and even, with no holes or stones. The settler's town is a well-fed town, an easy-going town; its belly is always full of good things. The settler's town is a town of white people, of foreigners.

The town belonging to the colonized people, or at least the native town, the Negro village, the medina, the reservation, is a place of ill fame peopled by men of evil repute. They are born there, it matters little where or how; they die there, it matters not where nor how. It is a world without spaciousness: men live there on top of each other, and their huts are built one on top of the other. The native town is a hungry town, starved of bread, of meat, of shoes, of coal, of light. The native town is a crouching village, a town on its knees, a town wallowing in the mire. It is a town of niggers and dirty arabs. The look that the native turns on the settler's town is a look of lust, a look of envy . . .

Fanon,
The Wretched of the Earth.

We have been asked to look into the future towards the year 2000. This essay attempts to do so in terms of two laws of economic development: the Law of Increasing Firm Size and the Law of Uneven Development.[1]

Since the beginning of the Industrial Revolution there has been a tendency for the representative firm to increase in size from the *workshop* to the *factory* to the *national corporation* to the *multi-divisional corporation* and now to the *multinational corporation*. This growth has been qualitative as well as quantitative. With each step, business enterprises acquired a more complex administrative structure to coordinate its activities and a larger brain to plan for its survival and growth. The first part of this essay traces the evolution of the corporation stressing the development of a hierarchical system of authority and control.

The remainder of the essay is concerned with extrapolating the trends in business enterprise (the microcosm) and relating them to the evolution of the international

---

*Reprinted with permission of Macmillan Publishing Co., Inc. from "The Multinational Corporation and the Law of Uneven Development" by Stephen Hymer from *Economics and World Order from the 1970's to the 1990's,* edited by Jagdish N. Bhagwati. Copyright © 1972, Macmillan Publishing Co., Inc.

[1] See Marx (1867), chapter XXV, "On the General Law of Capital Accumulation," chapter XII, "Cooperation" and chapter XIV, part 4, "Division of Labour in Manufacturing and Division of Labour in Society"; and (1894), chapter XXIII.

economy (the macrocosm). Until recently, most multinational corporations have come from the United States, where private business enterprise has reached its largest size and most highly developed forms. Now European corporations, as a by-product of increased size, and as a reaction to the American invasion of Europe, are also shifting attention from national to global production and beginning to 'see the world as their oyster'.[2] *If* present trends continue, multinationalization is likely to increase greatly in the next decade as giants from both sides of the Atlantic (though still mainly from the US) strive to penetrate each other's markets and to establish bases in underdeveloped countries, where there are few indigenous concentrations of capital sufficiently large to operate on a world scale. This rivalry may be intense at first but will probably abate through time and turn into collusion as firms approach some kind of oligopolistic equilibrium. A new structure of international industrial organization and a new international division of labour will have been born.[3]

What will be the effect of this latest stage in the evolution of business enterprise on the Law of Uneven Development, i.e. the tendency of the system to produce poverty as well as wealth, underdevelopment as well as development? The second part of this essay suggests that a regime of North Atlantic Multinational Corporations would tend to produce a hierarchical division of labour between geographical regions corresponding to the vertical division of labour within the firm. It would tend to centralize high-level decision-making occupations in a few key cities in the advanced countries, surrounded by a number of regional sub-capitals, and confine the rest of the world to lower levels of activity and income, i.e. to the status of towns and villages in a new Imperial system. Income, status, authority, and consumption patterns would radiate out from these centres along a declining curve, and the existing pattern of inequality and dependency would be perpetuated. The pattern would be complex, just as the structure of the corporation is complex, but the basic relationship between different countries would be one of superior and subordinate, head office and branch plant.

How far will this tendency of corporations to create a world in their own image proceed? The situation is a dynamic one, moving dialectically. Right now, we seem to be in the midst of a major revolution in international relationships as modern science establishes the technological basis for a major advance in the conquest of the material world and the beginnings of truly cosmopolitan production.[4] Multinational corporations are in the vanguard of this revolution, because of their great financial and

---

[2] Phrase used by Anthony M. Salomon (1966), p. 49.

[3] These trends are discussed in Hymer and Rowthorn (1970).

[4] Substituting the word *multinational corporation* for *bourgeois* in the following quote from *The Communist Manifesto* provides a more dynamic picture of the multinational corporation than any of its present day supporters have dared to put forth:

'The need of a constantly expanding market for its products chases the multinational corporation over the whole surface of the globe. It must nestle everywhere, settle everywhere, establish connections everywhere. The bourgeoisie has through its exploitation of the world-market given a cosmopolitan character to production and consumption in every country. To the great chagrin of Reactionists, it has drawn from under the feet of industry the national ground on which it stood. All old-established national industries have been destroyed or are daily being destroyed. They are dislodged by new industries, whose introduction becomes a life and death question for all civilized nations, by industries that no longer work up indigenous raw material, but raw material drawn from the remotest zones; industries whose products are consumed, not only at home, but in every quarter of the globe. In place of the old wants, satisfied by the production of the country, we find new wants, requiring for their satisfaction the products of distant lands and climes. In place of the old local and national seclusion and self-sufficiency, we have intercourse in every direction, universal interdepen-

administrative strength and their close contact with the new technology. Governments (outside the military) are far behind, because of their narrower horizons and perspectives, as are labour organizations and most non-business institutions and associations. (As John Powers, President of Charles Pfizer Corporation, has put it, 'Practice is ahead of theory and policy.') Therefore, in the first round, multinational corporations are likely to have a certain degree of success in organizing markets, decision making and the spread of information in their own interest. However, their very success will create tensions and conflicts which will lead to further development. Part III discusses some of the contradictions that are likely to emerge as the multinational corporate system overextends itself. These contradictions provide certain openings for action. Whether or not they can or will be used in the next round to move towards superior forms of international organization requires an analysis of a wide range of political factors outside the scope of this essay.

PART I THE EVOLUTION OF THE MULTINATIONAL CORPORATION

The Marshallian Firm and the Market Economy.   What is the nature of the 'beast'? It is called many names: Direct Investment, International Business, the International Firm, the International Corporate Group, the Multinational Firm, the Multinational Enterprise, the Multinational Corporation, the Multinational Family Group, World Wide Enterprise, La Grande Entreprise Plurinationale, La Grande Unité Interterritoriale, La Grande Entreprise Multinationale, La Grand Unité Pluriterritoriale; or, as the French Foreign Minister called them, 'The US corporate monsters' (Michel Debré quoted in *Fortune*, August 1965, p. 126).

Giant organizations are nothing new in international trade. They were a characteristic form of the mercantilist period when large joint-stock companies, e.g. The Hudson's Bay Company, the Royal African Company, the East India Company, to

---

dence of nations. And as in material, so also in intellectual production. The intellectual creations of individual nations become common property. National one-sidedness and narrow-mindedness become more and more impossible, and from the numerous national and local literatures there arises a world literature.

'The multinational corporation, by the rapid improvement of all instruments of production, by the immensely facilitated means of communication, draws all, even the most barbarian, nations into civilization. The cheap prices of all its commodities are the heavy artillery with which it batters down all Chinese walls, with which it forces the barbarians' intensely obstinate hatred of foreigners to capitulate. It compels all nations, on pain of extinction, to adopt the bourgeois mode of production, it compels them to introduce what it calls civilization into their midst, i.e., to become bourgeois themselves. In a word, it creates a world after its own image.

'The multinational corporation has subjected the country to the rule of the towns. It has created enormous cities, has greatly increased the urban population as compared with the rural, and has thus rescued a considerable part of the population from the idiocy of rural life. Just as it has made the country dependent on the towns, so it has made barbarian and semi-barbarian countries dependent on the civilized ones, nations of peasants on nations of bourgeois, the East on the West.

'The multinational corporation keeps more and more doing away with the scattered state of the population, of the means of production, and of property. It has agglomerated population, centralized means of production, and has concentrated property in a few hands. The necessary consequence of this was political centralization. Independent, or but loosely connected provinces, with separate interests, laws, systems of taxation, and governments, became lumped together in one nation, with one government, one code of laws, one national class-interest, one frontier, and one customs tariff'.

name the major English merchant firms, organized long-distance trade with America, Africa and Asia. But neither these firms, nor the large mining and plantation enterprises in the production sector, were the forerunners of the multinational corporation. They were like dinosaurs, large in bulk, but small in brain, feeding on the lush vegetation of the new worlds (the planters and miners in America were literally *Tyrannosaurus rex*).

The activities of these international merchants, planters and miners laid the groundwork for the Industrial Revolution by concentrating capital in the metropolitan centre, but the driving force came from the small-scale capitalist enterprises in manufacturing, operating at first in the interstices of the feudalist economic structure, but gradually emerging into the open and finally gaining predominance. It is in the small workshops, organized by the newly emerging capitalist class, that the forerunners of the modern corporation are to be found.

The strength of this new form of business enterprise lay in its power and ability to reap the benefits of cooperation and division of labour. Without the capitalist, economic activity was individualistic, small-scale, scattered and unproductive. But a man with capital, i.e. with sufficient funds to buy raw materials and advance wages, could gather a number of people into a single shop and obtain as his reward the increased productivity that resulted from social production. The reinvestment of these profits led to a steady increase in the size of capitals, making further division of labour possible and creating an opportunity for using machinery in production. A phenomenal increase in productivity and production resulted from this process, and entirely new dimensions of human existence were opened. The growth of capital revolutionized the entire world and, figuratively speaking, even battered down the Great Wall of China.

The hallmarks of the new system were *the market* and *the factory* representing the two different methods of coordinating the division of labour. In the factory, entrepreneurs consciously plan and organize cooperation, and the relationships are hierarchical and authoritarian; in the market, coordination is achieved through a decentralized, unconscious, competitive process.[5]

To understand the significance of this distinction, the new system should be compared to the structure it replaced. In the pre-capitalist system of production, the division of labour was hierarchically structured at the *macro* level, i.e. for society as a whole, but unconsciously structured at the *micro* level, i.e. the actual process of production. Society as a whole was partitioned into various castes, classes, and guilds, on a rigid and authoritarian basis so that political and social stability could be maintained and adequate numbers assured for each industry and occupation. Within each sphere of production, however, individuals by and large were independent and their activities only loosely coordinated, if at all. In essence, a guild was composed of a large number of similar individuals, each performing the same task in roughly the same way with little cooperation or division of labour. This type of organization could produce high standards of quality and workmanship but was limited quantitatively to low levels of output per head.

The capitalist system of production turned this structure on its head. The macro

---

[5] See R. H. Coase (1952) for an analysis of the boundary between the firm and the market: 'outside the firm, price movements direct production which is coordinated through a series of exchange transactions on the market. Within the firm these market transactions are eliminated and in place of the complicated market structure with exchange transactions, is substituted the entrepreneur coordinator who directs production'.

system became unconsciously structured, while the micro system became hierarchically structured. The market emerged as a self-regulating coordinator of business units as restrictions on capital markets and labour mobility were removed. (Of course the State remained above the market as a conscious coordinator to maintain the system and ensure the growth of capital.) At the micro level, that is the level of production, labour was gathered under the authority of the entrepreneur capitalist.

Marshall, like Marx, stressed that the internal division of labour within the factory, between those who planned and those who worked (between 'undertakers' and labourers), was the 'chief fact in the form of modern civilization, the "kernel" of the modern economic problem'.[6] Marx, however, stressed the authoritarian and unequal nature of this relationship based on the coercive power of property and its anti-social characteristics. He focused on the irony that concentration of wealth in the hands of a few and its ruthless use were necessary historically to demonstrate the value of cooperation and the social nature of production.[7]

Marshall, in trying to answer Marx, argued for the voluntary cooperative nature of the relationship between capital and labour. In his view, the market reconciled individual freedom and collective production. He argued that those on top achieved their position because of their superior organizational ability, and that their relation to the workers below them was essentially harmonious and not exploitative. 'Undertakers' were not captains of industry because they had capital; they could obtain capital because they had the ability to be captains of industry. They retained their authority by merit, not by coercion; for according to Marshall, natural selection, operating through the market, constantly destroyed inferior organizers and gave everyone who had the ability — including workers — a chance to rise to managerial positions. Capitalists earned more than workers because they contributed more, while the system as a whole provided all its members, and especially the workers, with improved standards of living and an ever-expanding field of choice of consumption.[8]

---

[6] 'Even in the very backward countries we find highly specialized trades; but we do not find the work within each trade so divided up that the planning and arrangement of the business, its management and its risks, are borne by one set of people, while the manual work required for it is done by higher labour. This form of division of labour is at once characteristic of the modern world generally and of the English race in particular. It may be swept away by the further growth of that free enterprise which has called it into existence. But for the present it expands out for good and for evil as the chief fact in the form of modern civilization, the "kernel" of the modern economic problem'. Marshall (1962), pp. 74-5. Note that Marshall preferred to call businessmen Undertakers rather than Capitalists (p. 74).

[7] 'Division of labour within the workshop implies the undisputed authority of the capitalist over men that are but parts of a mechanism that belongs to him . . . The same bourgeois mind which praises division of labour in the workshop, life-long annexation of the labourer to a partial operation, and his complete subjection to capital, as being an organization of labour that increases its productiveness — that same bourgeois mind denounces with equal vigour every conscious attempt to socially control and regulate the process of production, as an inroad upon such sacred things as the rights of property, freedom and unrestricted play for the bent of the individual capitalist. It is very characteristic that the enthusiastic apologists of the factory system have nothing more damning to urge against a general organization of the labour of society, than that it would turn all society into one immense factory'. Marx (1867), p. 356.

[8] The following analysis by E. S. Mason (1958), of current attempts to justify hierarchy and inequality by emphasizing the skill and knowledge of managers and the technostructure is interesting and of great significance on this connection:
'As everyone now recognizes, classical economics provided not only a system of analysis, or

The Corporate Economy.   The evolution of business enterprise from the small workshop (Adam Smith's pin factory) to the Marshallian family firm represented only the first step in the development of business organization. As total capital accumulated, the size of the individual concentrations composing it increased continuously, and the vertical division of labour grew accordingly.

It is best to study the evolution of the corporate firm in the United States environment, where it has reached its highest stage.[9] In the 1870s, the United States industrial structure consisted largely of Marshallian type, single-function firms, scattered over the country. Business firms were typically tightly controlled by a single entrepreneur or small family group who, as it were, saw everything, knew everything and decided everything. By the early twentieth century, the rapid growth of the economy and the great merger movement had consolidated many small enterprises into large national corporations engaged in many functions over many regions. To meet this new strategy of continent-wide, vertically integrated production and marketing, a new administrative structure evolved. The family firm, tightly controlled by a few men in close touch with all its aspects, gave way to the administrative pyramid of the corporation. Capital acquired new powers and new horizons. The domain of conscious coordination widened and that of market-directed division of labour contracted.

According to Chandler (1961), the railroad, which played so important a role in creating the national market, also offered a model for new forms of business organization. The need to administer geographically dispersed operations led railway companies to create an administrative structure which distinguished field offices from head offices. The field offices managed local operations; the head office supervised the field offices. According to Chandler and Redlich (1961), this distinction is important because 'it implies that the executive responsible for a firm's affairs had, for the first time, to supervise the work of other executives'.[10]

This first step towards increased vertical division of labour within the management function was quickly copied by the recently-formed national corporations which faced the same problems of coordinating widely scattered plants. Business developed

---

analytical 'model', intended to be useful to the explanation of economic behaviour but also a defense — and a carefully reasoned defense — of the proposition that the economic behaviour promoted and constrained by the institutions of a free-enterprise system is, in the main, in the public interest.

'It cannot be too strongly emphasized that the growth of the nineteenth-century capitalism depended largely on the general acceptance of a reasoned justification of the system on moral as well as on political and economic grounds.

'It seems doubtful whether, to date, the managerial literature has provided an equally satisfying apologetic for big business.

'The attack on the capitalist apologetic of the nineteenth century has been successful, but a satisfactory contemporary apologetic is still to be created. I suspect that, when and if an effective new ideology is devised, economics will be found to have little to contribute. Economists are still so mesmerized with the fact of choice and so little with its explanations, and the concept of the market is still so central to their thought, that they would appear to be professionally debarred from their important task. I suspect that to the formulation of an up-to-date twentieth-century apologetic the psychologists, and possibly, the political scientists will be the main contributors. It is high time they were called to their job.

[9] This analysis of the modern corporation is almost entirely based on the work of Chandler (1961), and Barnard (1938).

[10] Chandler and Redlich (1961), pp. 103-28.

an organ system of administration, and the modern corporation was born. The functions of business administration were sub-divided into *departments* (organs) — finance, personnel, purchasing, engineering and sales — to deal with capital, labour, purchasing, manufacturing, etc. This horizontal division of labour opened up new possibilities for rationalizing production and for incorporating the advances of physical and social sciences into economic activity on a systematic basis. At the same time a 'brain and nervous' system, i.e. a vertical system of control, had to be devised to connect and coordinate departments. This was a major advance in decision-making capabilities. It meant that a special group, the Head Office, was created whose particular function was to coordinate, appraise, and plan for the survival and growth of the organism as a whole. The organization became conscious of itself as organization and gained a certain measure of control over its own evolution and development.

The corporation soon underwent further evolution. To understand this next step we must briefly discuss the development of the United States market. At the risk of great oversimplification, we might say that by the first decade of the twentieth century, the problem of production had essentially been solved. By the end of the nineteenth century, scientists and engineers had developed most of the inventions needed for mass producing at a low cost nearly all the main items of basic consumption. In the language of systems analysis, the problem became one of putting together the available components in an organized fashion. The national corporation provided *one* organizational solution, and by the 1920s it had demonstrated its great power to increase material production.

The question was which direction growth would take. One possibility was to expand mass production systems very widely and to make basic consumer goods available on a broad basis throughout the world. The other possibility was to concentrate on continuous innovation for a small number of people and on the introduction of new consumption goods even before the old ones had been fully spread. The latter course was in fact chosen, and we now have the paradox that 500 million people can receive a live TV broadcast from the moon while there is still a shortage of telephones in many advanced countries, to say nothing of the fact that so many people suffer from inadequate food and lack of simple medical help.

This path was associated with a choice of capital-deepening instead of capital-widening in the productive sector of the economy. As capital accumulated, business had to choose the degree to which it would expand labour proportionately to the growth of capital or, conversely, the degree to which they would substitute capital for labour. At one extreme, business could have kept the capital-labour ratio constant and accumulated labour at the same rate they accumulated capital. This horizontal accumulation would soon have exhausted the labour force of any particular country and then either capital would have had to migrate to foreign countries or labour would have had to move into the industrial centres. Under this system, earnings per employed worker would have remained steady and the composition of output would have tended to remain constant as similar basic goods were produced on a wider and wider basis.

However, this path was not chosen, and instead capital per worker was raised, the rate of expansion of the industrial labour force was slowed down, and a dualism was created between a small, high-wage, high-productivity sector in advanced countries, and a large, low-wage, low-productivity sector in the less advanced.[11]

---

[11] Neoclassical models suggest that this choice was due to the exogenously determined nature of technological change. A Marxist economic model would argue that it was due in part to the increased

The uneven growth of per capita income implied unbalanced growth and the need on the part of business to adapt to a constantly changing composition of output. Firms in the producers' goods sectors had continuously to innovate labour-saving machinery because the capital output ratio was increasing steadily. In the consumption goods sector, firms had continuously to introduce new products since, according to Engel's Law, people do not generally consume proportionately more of the same things as they get richer, but rather reallocate their consumption away from old goods and towards new goods. This non-proportional growth of demand implied that goods would tend to go through a life-cycle, growing rapidly when they were first introduced and more slowly later. If a particular firm were tied to only one product, its growth rate would follow this same life-cycle pattern and would eventually slow down and perhaps even come to a halt. If the corporation was to grow steadily at a rapid rate, it had continuously to introduce new products.

Thus, product development and marketing replaced production as a dominant problem of business enterprise. To meet the challenge of a constantly changing market, business enterprise evolved the multidivisional structure. The new form was originated by General Motors and DuPont shortly after World War I, followed by a few others during the 1920s and 1930s, and was widely adopted by most of the giant US corporations in the great boom following World War II. As with the previous stages, evolution involved a process of both differentiation and integration. Corporations were decentralized into several *divisions,* each concerned with one product line and organized with its own head office. At a higher level, a *general office* was created to coordinate the division and to plan for the enterprise as a whole.

The new corporate form has great flexibility. Because of its decentralized structure, a multidivisional corporation can enter a new market by adding a new division, while leaving the old divisions undisturbed. (And to a lesser extent it can leave the market by dropping a division without disturbing the rest of its structure.) It can also create competing product-lines in the same industry, thus increasing its market share while maintaining the illusion of competition. Most important of all, because it has a cortex specializing in strategy, it can plan on a much wider scale than before and allocate capital with more precision.

The modern corporation is a far cry from the small workshop or even from the Marshallian firm. The Marshallian capitalist ruled his factory from an office on the second floor. At the turn of the century, the president of a large national corporation was lodged in a higher building, perhaps on the seventh floor, with greater perspective and power. In today's giant corporation, managers rule from the top of skyscrapers; on a clear day, they can almost see the world.

US corporations began to move to foreign countries almost as soon as they had completed their continent-wide integration. For one thing, their new administrative structure and great financial strength gave them the power to go abroad. In becoming national firms, US corporations learned how to become international. Also, their large size and oligopolistic position gave them an incentive. Direct investment became a new weapon in their arsenal of oligopolistic rivalry. Instead of joining a cartel (prohibited under US law), they invested in foreign customers, suppliers and competitors. For example, some firms found they were oligopolistic buyers of raw materials produced in foreign countries and feared a monopolization of the sources of

---

tensions in the labour market accompanying the accumulation of capital and the growth of large firms. This is discussed further in Hymer and Resnick (1970).

supply. By investing directly in foreign producing enterprises, they could gain the security implicit in control over their raw material requirements. Other firms invested abroad to control marketing outlets and thus maximize quasi-rents on their technological discoveries and differentiated products. Some went abroad simply to forestall competition.[12]

The first wave of US direct foreign capital investment occurred around the turn of the century followed by a second wave during the 1920s. The outward migration slowed down during the depression but resumed after World War II and soon accelerated rapidly. Between 1950 and 1969, direct foreign investment by US firms expanded at a rate of about 10 per cent per annum. At this rate it would double in less than ten years, and even at a much slower rate of growth, foreign operations will reach enormous proportions over the next 30 years.[13]

Several important factors account for this rush of foreign investment in the 1950s and the 1960s. First, the large size of the US corporations and their new multidivisional structure gave them wider horizons and a global outlook. Secondly, technological developments in communications created a new awareness of the global challenge and threatened established institutions by opening up new sources of competition. For reasons noted above, business enterprises were among the first to recognize the potentialities and dangers of the new environment and to take active steps to cope with it.

A third factor in the outward migration of US capital was the rapid growth of Europe and Japan. This, combined with the slow growth of the United States economy in the 1950s, altered world market shares as firms confined to the US market found themselves falling behind in the competitive race and losing ground to European and Japanese firms, which were growing rapidly because of the expansion of their markets. Thus, in the late 1950s, United States corporations faced a serious 'non-American' challenge. Their answer was an outward thrust to establish sales production and bases in foreign territories. This strategy was possible in Europe, since government there provided an open door for United States investment, but was blocked in Japan, where the government adopted a highly restrictive policy. To a large extent, United States business was thus able to redress the imbalances caused by the Common Market, but Japan remained a source of tension to oligopoly equilibrium.

What about the future? The present trend indicates further multinationalization of all giant firms, European as well as American. In the first place, European firms, partly as a reaction to the United States penetration of their markets, and partly as a natural result of their own growth, have begun to invest abroad on an expanded scale and will probably continue to do so in the future, and even enter into the United States market. This process is already well under way and may be expected to accelerate as time goes on. The reaction of United States business will most likely be to meet

---

[12] The reasons for foreign investment discussed here are examined in more detail in Hymer (1968), pp. 949-73, and in Hymer and Rowthorn (1970).

[13] At present, US corporations have about 60 billion dollars invested in foreign branch plants and subsidiaries. The total assets of these foreign operations are much larger than the capital invested and probably equal 100 billion dollars at book value. (American corporations, on the average, were able to borrow 40 per cent of their subsidiaries' capital requirements locally in the country of operation.) The total assets of the 200 largest non-US firms are slightly less than 200 billion dollars. See US Department of Commerce (1969), and Fortune list of the 500 largest US corporations and 200 largest non-American.

foreign investment at home with more foreign investment abroad. They, too, will scramble for market positions in underdeveloped countries and attempt to get an even larger share of the European market, as a reaction to European investment in the United States. Since they are large and powerful, they will on balance succeed in maintaining their relative standing in the world as a whole — as their losses in some markets are offset by gains in others.

A period of rivalry will prevail until a new equilibrium between giant US firms and giant European and Japanese firms is reached, based on a strategy of multinational operations and cross-penetration.[14] We turn now to the implications of this pattern of industrial organization for international trade and the law of uneven development.

PART II UNEVEN DEVELOPMENT

Suppose giant multinational corporations (say 300 from the US and 200 from Europe and Japan) succeed in establishing themselves as the dominant form of international enterprise and come to control a significant share of industry (especially modern industry) in each country. The world economy will resemble more and more the United States economy, where each of the large corporations tends to spread over the entire continent, and to penetrate almost every nook and cranny. What would be the effect of a world industrial organization of this type on international specialization, exchange and income distribution? The purpose of this section is to analyse the spatial dimension of the corporate hierarchy.

A useful starting point is Chandler and Redlich's scheme for analysing the evolution of corporate structure. They distinguish 'three levels of business administration, three horizons, three levels of task, and three levels of decision making . . . and three levels of policies'. Level III, the lowest level, is concerned with managing the day-to-day operations of the enterprise, that is with keeping it going within the established framework. Level II, which first made its appearance with the separation of head office from field office, is responsible for coordinating the managers at Level III. The functions of Level I — top management — are goal-determination and planning. This level sets the framework in which the lower levels operate. In the Marshallian firm, all three levels are embodied in the single entrepreneur or undertaker. In the national corporation, a partial differentiation is made in which the top two levels are separated from the bottom one. In the multidivisional corporation, the differentiation is far more complete. Level I is completely split off from Level II and concentrated in a general office whose specific function is to plan strategy rather than tactics.

The development of business enterprise can therefore be viewed as a process of centralizing and perfecting the process of capital accumulation. The Marshallian entrepreneur was a jack-of-all-trades. In the modern multidivisional corporation, a powerful general office consciously plans and organizes the growth of corporate

---

[14] At present unequal growth of different parts of the world economy upsets the oligopolistic equilibrium because the leading firms have different geographical distributions of production and sales. Thus, if Europe grows faster than the United States, European firms tend to grow faster than American firms, unless American firms engage in heavy foreign investment. Similarly, if the United States grows faster than Europe, US firms will grow faster than European firms because Europeans have a lesser stake in the American market. When firms are distributed evenly in all markets, they share equally in the good and bad fortunes of the various submarkets, and oligopolistic equilibrium is not upset by the unequal growth of different countries.

capital. It is here that the key men who actually allocate the corporation's available resources (rather than act within the means allocated to them, as is true for the managers at lower levels) are located. Their power comes from their ultimate control over *men* and *money* and although one should not overestimate the ability to control a far-flung empire, neither should one underestimate it.

> The senior men could take action because they controlled the selection of executive personnel and because, through budgeting, they allocated the funds to the operating divisions. In the way they allocated their resources — capital and personnel — and in the promotion, transferral and retirement of operating executives, they determined the framework in which the operating units worked and thus put into effect their concept of the long term goals and objectives of the enterprise . . . Ultimate authority in business enterprise, as we see it, rests with those who hold the purse strings, and in modern large-scale enterprises, those persons hold the purse strings who perform the functions of goal setting and planning.[15]

What is the relationship between the structure of the microcosm and the structure of the macrocosm? The application of location theory to the Chandler-Redlich scheme suggests a *correspondence principle* relating centralization of control within the corporation to centralization of control within the international economy.

Location theory suggests that Level III activities would spread themselves over the globe according to the pull of manpower, markets, and raw materials. The multinational corporation, because of its power to command capital and technology and its ability to rationalize their use on a global scale, will probably spread production more evenly over the world's surface than is now the case. Thus, in the first instance, it may well be a force for diffusing industrialization to the less developed countries and creating new centres of production. (We postpone for a moment a discussion of the fact that location depends upon transportation, which in turn depends upon the government which in turn is influenced by the structure of business enterprise.)

Level II activities, because of their need for white-collar workers, communications systems, and information, tend to concentrate in large cities. Since their demands are similar, corporations from different industries tend to place their coordinating offices in the same city, and Level II activities are consequently far more geographically concentrated than Level III activities.

Level I activities, the general offices, tend to be even more concentrated than Level II activities, for they must be located close to the capital market, the media, and the government. Nearly every major corporation in the United States, for example, must have its general office (or a large proportion of its high-level personnel) in or near the city of New York, because of the need for face-to-face contact at higher levels of decision making.

Applying this scheme to the world economy, one would expect to find the highest offices of the multinational corporations concentrated in the world's major cities — New York, London, Paris, Bonn, Tokyo. These along with Moscow and perhaps Peking, will be the major centres of high-level strategic planning. Lesser cities throughout the world will deal with the day-to-day operations of specific local problems. These in turn will be arranged in a hierarchical fashion: the larger and more important ones will contain regional corporate headquarters, while the smaller ones

---

[15] Chandler and Redlich (1961), p. 120.

will be confined to lower level activities. Since business is usually the core of the city, geographical specialization will come to reflect the hierarchy of corporate decision making, and the occupational distribution of labour in a city or region will depend upon its function in the international economic system. The 'best' and most highly paid administrators, doctors, lawyers, scientists, educators, government officials, actors, servants and hairdressers, will tend to concentrate in or near the major centres.

The structure of income and consumption will tend to parallel the structure of status and authority. The citizens of capital cities will have the best jobs — allocating men and money at the highest level and planning growth and development — and will receive the highest rates of remuneration. (Executives' salaries tend to be a function of the wage bill of people under them. The larger the empire of the multinational corporation, the greater the earnings of top executives, to a large extent independent of their performance.[16] Thus, growth in the hinterland subsidiaries implies growth in the income of capital cities, but not vice versa.)

The citizens of capital cities will also be the first to innovate new products in the cycle which is known in the marketing literature as trickle-down or two-stage marketing. A new product is usually first introduced to a select group of people who have 'discretionary' income and are willing to experiment in their consumption patterns.[17] Once it is accepted by this group, it spreads, or trickles down to other groups via the demonstration effect. In this process, the rich and the powerful get more votes than everyone else; first because they have more money to spend, second, because they have more ability to experiment, and third, because they have high status and are likely to be copied. This special group may have something approaching a choice in consumption patterns; the rest have only the choice between conforming or being isolated.

The trickle-down system also has the advantage — from the centre's point of view — of reinforcing patterns of authority and control. According to Fallers (1963),[18] it helps keep workers on the treadmill by creating an illusion of upward mobility even though relative status remains unchanged. In each period subordinates achieve (in part) the consumption standards of their superiors in a previous period and are thus torn in two directions: if they look backward and compare their standards of living through time, things seem to be getting better; if they look upward they see that their relative position has not changed. They receive a consolation prize, as it were, which may serve to keep them going by softening the reality that in a competitive system, few succeed and many fail. It is little wonder, then, that those at the top stress growth rather than equality as the welfare criterion for human relations.

In the international economy trickle-down marketing takes the form of an international demonstration effect spreading outward from the metropolis to the hinterland.[19] Multinational corporations help speed up this process, often the key motive for direct investment, through their control of marketing channels and communications media.

The development of a new product is a fixed cost; once the expenditure needed for

---

[16] See Simon (1957).

[17] Gervasi (1964).

[18] Fallers (1963), pp. 208-216.

[19] See Vernon (1966).

invention or innovation has been made, it is forever a bygone. The actual cost of production is thus typically well below selling price and the limit on output is not rising costs but falling demand due to saturated markets. The marginal profit on new foreign markets is thus high, and corporations have a strong interest in maintaining a system which spreads their products widely. Thus, the interest of multinational corporations in underdeveloped countries is larger than the size of the market would suggest.

It must be stressed that the dependency relationship between major and minor cities should not be attributed to technology. The new technology, because it increases interaction, implies greater interdependence but not necessarily a hierarchical structure. Communications linkages could be arranged in the form of a grid in which each point was directly connected to many other points, permitting lateral as well as vertical communication. This system would be polycentric since messages from one point to another would go directly rather than through the center; each point would become a centre on its own; and the distinction between centre and periphery would disappear.

Such a grid is made *more* feasible by aeronautical and electronic revolutions which greatly reduce costs of communications. It is not technology which creates inequality; rather, it is *organization* that imposes a ritual judicial asymmetry on the use of intrinsically symmetrical means of communications and arbitrarily creates unequal capacities to initiate and terminate exchange, to store and retrieve information, and to determine the extent of the exchange and terms of the discussion. Just as colonial powers in the past linked each point in the hinterland to the metropolis and inhibited lateral communications, preventing the growth of independent centres of decision making and creativity, multinational corporations (backed by state powers) centralize control by imposing a hierarchical system.

This suggests the possibility of an alternative system of organization in the form of national planning. Multinational corporations are private institutions which organize one or a few industries across many countries. Their polar opposite (the antimultinational corporation, perhaps) is a public institution which organizes many industries across one region. This would permit the centralization of capital, i.e. the coordination of many enterprises by one decision-making centre, but would substitute regionalization for internationalization. The span of control would be confined to the boundaries of a single polity and society and not spread over many countries. The advantage of national planning is its ability to remove the wastes of oligopolistic anarchy, i.e. meaningless product differentiation and an imbalance between different industries within a geographical area. It concentrates *all* levels of decision-making in one locale and thus provides each region with a full complement of skills and occupations. This opens up new horizons for local development by making possible the social and political control of economic decision-making. Multinational corporations, in contrast, weaken political control because they span many countries and can escape national regulation.

A few examples might help to illustrate how multinational corporations reduce options for development. Consider an underdeveloped country wishing to invest heavily in education in order to increase its stock of human capital and raise standards of living. In a market system it would be able to find gainful employment for its citizens within its *national boundaries* by specializing in education-intensive activities and selling its surplus production to foreigners. In the multinational corporate system, however, the demand for high-level education in low-ranking areas is limited, and a country does not become a world centre simply by having a better educational system. An outward shift in the supply of educated people in a country, therefore, will not create its own demand but will create an excess supply and lead to emigration. Even then, the employment opportunities for citizens of low-ranking countries are restricted by discriminatory practices in the centre. It is well-known that ethnic homogeneity increases as one goes up the corporate hierarchy; the lower levels contain a wide variety of nationalities, the higher levels become successively purer and purer. In part this stems from the skill differences of different nationalities, but more important is the fact that the higher up one goes in the decision-making process, the more important mutual understanding and ease of communications become; a common background becomes all-important.

A similar type of specialization by nationality can be expected within the multinational corporation hierarchy. Multinational corporations are torn in two directions. On the one hand, they must adapt to local circumstances in each country. This calls for decentralized decision making. On the other hand, they must coordinate their activities in various parts of the world and stimulate the flow of ideas from one part of their empire to another. This calls for centralized control. They must, therefore, develop an organizational structure to balance the need for coordination with the need for adaptation to a patch-work quilt of languages, laws and customs. One solution to this problem is a division of labour based on nationality. Day-to-day management in each country is left to the nationals of that country who, because they are intimately familiar with local conditions and practices, are able to deal with local problems and local government. These nationals remain rooted in one spot, while above them is a layer of people who move around from country to country, as bees among flowers, transmitting information from one subsidiary to another and from the lower levels to the general office at the apex of the corporate structure. In the nature of things, these people (reticulators) for the most part will be citizens of the country of the parent corporation (and will be drawn from a small, culturally homogeneous group within the advanced world), since they will need to have the confidence of their superiors and be able to move easily in the higher management circles. Latin Americans, Asians and Africans will at best be able to aspire to a management position in the intermediate coordinating centres at the continental level. Very few will be able to get much higher than this, for the closer one gets to the top, the more important is 'a common cultural heritage'.

Another way in which the multinational corporations inhibit economic development in the hinterland is through their effect on tax capacity. An important government instrument for promoting growth is expenditure on infrastructure and support services. By providing transportation and communications, education and health, a government can create a productive labour force and increase the growth potential of its economy. The extent to which it can afford to finance these intermediate outlays depends upon its tax revenue.

However, a government's ability to tax multinational corporations is limited by the ability of these corporations to manipulate transfer prices and to move their productive facilities to another country. This means that they will only be attracted to countries where superior infrastructure offsets higher taxes. The government of an underdeveloped country will find it difficult to extract a surplus (revenue from the multinational corporations, less cost of services provided to them) from multinational corporations to use for long-run development programmes and for stimulating growth in other industries. In contrast, governments of the advanced countries, where the home office and financial centre of the multinational corporation are located, can tax the profits of the corporation as a whole as well as the high incomes of its management. Government in the metropolis can, therefore, capture some of the surplus generated by the multinational corporations and use it to further improve their infrastructure and growth.

In other words, the relationship between multinational corporations and underdeveloped countries will be somewhat like the relationship between the national corporations in the United States and state and municipal governments. These lower-level governments tend always to be short of funds compared to the federal government which can tax a corporation as a whole. Their competition to attract corporate investment eats up their surplus, and they find it difficult to finance extensive investments in human and physical capital even where such investment would be productive. This has a crucial effect on the pattern of government expenditure. For example, suppose taxes were first paid to state government and then passed on to the federal government. What chance is there that these lower level legislatures would approve the phenomenal expenditures on space research that now go on? A similar discrepancy can be expected in the international economy with overspending and waste by metropolitan governments and a shortage of public funds in the less advanced countries.

The tendency of the multinational corporations to erode the power of the nation state works in a variety of ways, in addition to its effect on taxation powers. In general, most governmental policy instruments (monetary policy, fiscal policy, wage policy, etc.) diminish in effectiveness the more open the economy and the greater the extent of foreign investments. This tendency applies to political instruments as well as economic, for the multinational corporation is a medium by which laws, politics, foreign policy and culture of one country intrude into another. This acts to reduce the sovereignty of all nation states, but again the relationship is asymmetrical, for the flow tends to be from the parent to the subsidiary, not vice versa. The United States can apply its anti-trust laws to foreign subsidiaries or stop them from 'trading with the enemy' even though such trade is not against the laws of the country in which the branch plant is located. However, it would be illegal for an underdeveloped country which disagreed with American foreign policy to hold a US firm hostage for acts of the parent. This is because legal rights are defined in terms of property-ownership, and the various subsidiaries of a multinational corporation are not 'partners in a multinational endeavor' but the property of the general office.

In conclusion, it seems that a regime of multinational corporations would offer underdeveloped countries neither national independence nor equality. It would tend instead to inhibit the attainment of these goals. It would turn the underdeveloped countries into branch-plant countries, not only with reference to their economic functions but throughout the whole gamut of social, political and cultural roles. The subsidiaries of multinational corporations are typically amongst the largest corporations in the country of operations, and their top executives play an influential role in the political, social and cultural life of the host country. Yet these people, whatever their title, occupy at best a medium position in the corporate structure and are restricted in authority and horizons to a lower level of decision making. The governments with whom they deal tend to take on the same middle management outlook, since this is the only range of information and ideas to which they are exposed.[20] In

---

[20] An interesting illustration of the asymmetry in horizons and prospectives of the big company and the small country is found in these quotations from *Fortune*. Which countries of the world are making a comparable analysis of the Multinational Corporation?

'A Ford economist regularly scans the international financial statistics to determine which countries have the highest rates of inflation; these are obviously prime candidates for devaluation. He

this sense, one can hardly expect such a country to bring forth the creative imagination needed to apply science and technology to the problems of degrading poverty. Even so great a champion of liberalism as Marshall recognized the crucial relationship between occupation and development.

> For the business by which a person earns his livelihood generally fills his thoughts during the far greater part of those hours in which his mind is at its best; during them his character is being formed by the way in which he uses his facilities in his work, by the thoughts and feelings which it suggests, and by his relationship to his associates in work, his employers to his employees.[21]

PART III THE POLITICAL ECONOMY OF THE MULTINATIONAL CORPORATION

The viability of the multinational corporate system depends upon the degree to which people will tolerate the unevenness it creates. It is well to remember that the 'New Imperialism' which began after 1870 in a spirit of Capitalism Triumphant, soon became seriously troubled and after 1914 was characterized by war, depression, breakdown of the international economic system and war again, rather than Free Trade, Pax Britannica and Material Improvement.

A major, if not the major, reason was Great Britain's inability to cope with the byproducts of its own rapid accumulation of capital; i.e., a class-conscious labour force at home; a middle class in the hinterland; and rival centres of capital on the Continent and in America. Britain's policy tended to be atavistic and defensive rather than progressive, more concerned with warding off new threats than creating new areas of expansion. Ironically, Edwardian England revived the paraphernalia of the landed aristocracy it had just destroyed. Instead of embarking on a 'big push' to develop the vast hinterland of the Empire, colonial administrators often adopted policies to slow down rates of growth and arrest the development of either a native capitalist class or a native proletariat which could overthrow them.

As time went on, the centre had to devote an increasing share of government activity to military and other unproductive expenditures; they had to rely on alliances with an inefficient class of landlords, officials and soldiers in the hinterland to

---

then examines patterns of trade. If a country is running more of an inflation than its chief trading partners and competitors and its reserves are limited it is more than a candidate; it is a shoo-in. His most difficult problem is to determine exactly when the devaluation will take place. Economics determines whether and how much, but politicians control the timing. So the analyst maintains a complete library of information on leading national officials. He tries to get 'into the skin of the man' who is going to make the decision. The economist's forecasts have been correct in sixty-nine of the last seventy-five crisis situations.

'DuPont is one company that is making a stab in the direction of formally measuring environmental incertainty, basically as a tool for capital budgeting decisions. The project is still in the research stage, but essentially the idea is to try to derive estimates of the potential of a foreign market, which is, of course, affected by economic conditions. The state of the economy in turn is partly a function of the fiscal and monetary policies the foreign government adopts. Policy decisions depend on real economic forces, on the attitudes of various interest groups in the country, and on the degree to which the government listens to these groups.

maintain stability at the cost of development. A great part of the surplus extracted from the population was thus wasted locally.

The new Mercantilism (as the Multinational Corporate System of special alliances and privileges, aid and tariff concessions is sometimes called) faces similar problems of internal and external division. The centre is troubled: excluded groups revolt and even some of the affluent are dissatisfied with the roles. (The much talked about 'generation gap' may indicate the failure of the system to reproduce itself.) Nationalistic rivalry between major capitalist countries (especially the challenge of Japan and Germany) remains an important divisive factor, while the economic challenge from the socialist bloc may prove to be of the utmost significance in the next thirty years. Russia has its own form of large-scale economic organizations, also in command of modern technology, and its own conception of how the world should develop. So does China to an increasing degree.[22] Finally, there is the threat presented by the middle classes and the excluded groups of the underdeveloped countries.

The national middle classes in the underdeveloped countries came to power when the centre weakened but could not, through their policy of import substitution manufacturing, establish a viable basis for sustained growth. They now face a foreign exchange crisis and an unemployment (or population) crisis — the first indicating their inability to function in the international economy, and the second indicating their alienation from the people they are supposed to lead. In the immediate future, these national middle classes will gain a new lease on life as they take advantage of the spaces created by the rivalry between American and non-American oligopolists striving to establish global market positions. The native capitalists will again become the champions of national independence as they bargain with multinational corporations. But the conflict at this level is more apparent than real, for in the end the fervent nationalism of the middle class asks only for promotion within the corporate structure and not for a break with that structure. In the last analysis their power derives from the metropolis and they cannot easily afford to challenge the international system. They do not command the loyalty of their own population and cannot really compete with the large, powerful, aggregate capitals from the centre. They are prisoners of the taste

---

'In the fiscal and monetary part of their broad economic model, the DuPont researchers have identified fifteen to twenty interest groups per country, from small landowners to private bankers. Each interest group has a 'latent influence', which depends on its size and educational level and the group's power to make its feelings felt. This influence, subjectively measured, is multiplied by an estimate of 'group cohesiveness': i.e. how likely the group is to mobilize its full resources on any particular issue. The product is a measure of 'potential influence'. This in turn must be multiplied by a factor representing the governments' receptivity to each influence group'.
Rose (1968), p. 105.

[21] This quote is taken from the first page of Marshall's *Principles of Economics*. In the rest of the book, he attempted to show that the economic system of laissez-faire capitalism had an overall positive effect in forming character. As we noted above, his argument rested upon the existence of competitive markets (and the absence of coercion). Because multinational corporations substitute for the international market they call into question the liberal ideology which rationalized it. (See footnote 8 above, quoting Mason.)

[22] A. A. Berle, Jr., (1967), has put the problem most succinctly: 'The Industrial Revolution, as it spread over twentieth-century life, required collective organization of men and things . . . As the twentieth century moves into the afternoon, two systems — and (thus far) two only — have emerged as vehicles of modern industrial economics. One is the socialist commissariat, its highest organization at present in the Soviet Union; the other is the modern corporation, most highly developed in the United States' (p. ix).

patterns and consumption standards set at the centre, and depend on outsiders for technical advice, capital, and when necessary, for military support of their position.

The main threat comes from the excluded groups. It is not unusual in underdeveloped countries for the top 5 per cent to obtain between 30 and 40 per cent of the total national income, and for the top one-third to obtain anywhere from 60 to 70 per cent.[23] At most, one-third of the population can be said to benefit in some sense from the dualistic growth that characterizes development in the hinterland. The remaining two-thirds, who together get only one-third of the income, are outsiders, not because they do not contribute to the economy, but because they do not share in the benefits. They provide a source of cheap labour which helps keep exports to the developed world at a low price and which has financed the urban-biased growth of recent years. Because their wages are low, they spend a moderate amount of time in menial services and are sometimes referred to as underemployed as if to imply they were not needed. In fact, it is difficult to see how the system in most underdeveloped countries could survive without cheap labour since removing it (e.g. diverting it to public works projects as is done in socialist countries) would raise consumption costs to capitalists and professional elites. Economic development under the Multinational Corporation does not offer much promise for this large segment of society and their antagonism continuously threatens the system.

The survival of the multinational corporate system depends on how fast it can grow and how much trickles down. Plans now being formulated in government offices, corporate headquarters and international organizations, sometimes suggest that a growth rate of about 6 per cent per year in national income (3 per cent per capita) is needed. (Such a target is, of course, far below what would be possible if a serious effort were made to solve basic problems of health, education and clothing.) To what extent is it possible?

The multinational corporation must solve four critical problems for the underdeveloped countries, if it is to foster the continued growth and survival of a 'modern' sector. First, it must break the foreign-exchange constraint and provide the underdeveloped countries with imported goods for capital formation and modernization. Second, it must finance an expanded programme of government expenditure to train labour and provide support services for urbanization and industrialization. Third, it must solve the urban food problem created by growth. Finally, it must keep the excluded two-thirds of the population under control.

The solution now being suggested for the first is to restructure the world economy allowing the periphery to export certain manufactured goods to the centre. Part of this programme involves regional common markets to rationalize the existing structure of industry. These plans typically do not involve the rationalization and restructuring of the entire economy of the underdeveloped countries but mainly serve the small manufacturing sector which caters to higher income groups and which, therefore, faces a very limited market in any particular country. The solution suggested for the second problem is an expanded aid programme and a reformed government bureaucracy (perhaps along the lines of the Alliance for Progress). The solution for the third is agri-business and the green revolution, a programme with only limited benefits to the rural poor. Finally, the solution offered for the fourth problem is population control, either through family planning or counter-insurgency.

It is doubtful whether the centre has sufficient political stability to finance and organize the programme outlined above. It is not clear, for example, that the West has

---

[23] Kuznets (1966), pp. 423-4.

the technology to rationalize manufacturing abroad or modernize agriculture, or the willingness to open up marketing channels for the underdeveloped world. Nor is it evident that the centre has the political power to embark on a large aid programme or to readjust its own structure of production and allow for the importation of manufactured goods from the periphery. It is difficult to imagine labour accepting such a re-allocation (a new repeal of the Corn Laws as it were[24]), and it is equally hard to see how the advanced countries could create a system of planning to make these extra hardships unnecessary.

The present crisis may well be more profound than most of us imagine, and the West may find it impossible to restructure the international economy on a workable basis. One could easily argue that the age of the Multinational Corporation is at its end rather than at its beginning. For all we know, books on the global partnership may be the epitaph of the American attempt to take over the old international economy, and not the herald of a new era of international cooperation.

CONCLUSION

The multinational corporation, because of its great power to plan economic activity, represents an important step forward over previous methods of organizing international exchange. It demonstrates the social nature of production on a global scale. As it eliminates the anarchy of international markets and brings about a more extensive and productive international division of labour, it releases great sources of latent energy.

However, as it crosses international boundaries, it pulls and tears at the social and political fabric and erodes the cohesiveness of national states.[25] Whether one likes this or not, it is probably a tendency that cannot be stopped.

Through its propensity to nestle everywhere, settle everywhere, and establish connections everywhere, the multinational corporation destroys the possibility of national seclusion and self sufficiency and creates a universal interdependence. But the multinational corporation is still a private institution with a partial outlook and represents only an imperfect solution to the problem of international cooperation. It creates hierarchy rather than equality, and it spreads its benefits unequally.

In proportion to its success, it creates tensions and difficulties. It will lead other institutions, particularly labour organizations and government, to take an international outlook and thus unwittingly create an environment less favourable to its own survival. It will demonstrate the possibilities of material progress at a faster rate than it can realize them, and will create a worldwide demand for change that it cannot satisfy.

The next round may be marked by great crises due to conflict between national planning by governments and international planning by corporations. For example, if each country loses its power over fiscal and monetary policy due to the growth of multinational corporations (as some observers believe Canada has), how will aggregate demand be stabilized? Will it be possible to construct super-states? Or does multinationalism do away with Keynesian problems? Similarly, will it be possible to

---

[24] See Polanyi (1944) on the consequences after 1870 of the repeal of the Corn Laws in England.

[25] See Levitt (1970) and Girvan and Jefferson (1968).

fulfill a host of other government functions at the supranational level in the near future? During the past twenty five years many political problems were put aside as the West recovered from the depression and the war. By the late sixties the bloom of this long upswing had begun to fade. In the seventies, power conflicts are likely to come to the fore.

Whether underdeveloped countries will use the opportunities arising from this crisis to build viable local decision-making institutions is difficult to predict. The national middle class failed when it had the opportunity and instead merely reproduced internally the economic dualism of the international economy as it squeezed agriculture to finance urban industry. What is needed is a comple change of direction. The starting point must be the needs of the bottom two-thirds, and not the demands of the top third. The primary goal of such a strategy would be to provide minimum standards of health, education, food and clothing to the entire population, removing the more obvious forms of human suffering. This requires a system which can mobilize the entire population and which can search the local environment for information, resources and needs. It must be able to absorb modern technology, but it cannot be mesmerized by the form it takes in the advanced countries; it must go to the roots. This is not the path the upper one-third chooses when it has control.

The wealth of a nation, wrote Adam Smith two hundred years ago, is determined by 'first, the skill' dexterity and judgement with which labour is generally applied; and, secondly by the proportion between the number of those who are employed in useful labour, and that of those who are not so employed'.[26] Capitalist enterprise has come a long way from this day, but it has never been able to bring more than a small fraction of the world's population into useful or highly productive employment. The latest stage reveals once more the power of social cooperation and division of labour which so fascinated Adam Smith in his description of pin-manufacturing. It also shows the shortcomings of concentrating this power in private hands.

---

[26] See Smith (1937 edition), p. 1.

REFERENCES

Barnard, C.
1938 *The Functions of Executives.* Harvard University Press.

Berle, A. A. Jr.
1967 Foreword to E. S. Mason (ed.), *The Corporation in Modern Society.* Atheneum, New York.

Chandler, A. D.
1961 *Strategy and Structure.* Doubleday.

Chandler, A. D., and Redlich, F.
1961 "Recent Developments in American Business Administration and Their Conceptualization," *Business History Review,* Spring.

Coase, R. H.
1952 "The Nature of the Firm," reprinted in G. J. Stigler and K. E. Boulding (eds.), *Readings in Price Theory.* Richard D. Irwin.

Fallers, L. A.
1963 "A Note on the Trickle Effect," in P. Bliss (ed.), *Marketing and the Behavioural Sciences.* Allyn & Bacon.

Gervasi, S.
1964 "Publicité et Croissance Économique," *Economie et Humanisme.* November-December.

Girvan, N., and Jefferson, O.
1968 "Corporate vs. Caribbean Integration," *New World Quarterly,* vol. IV, no. 2.

Hymer, S.
1968 "La Grande Corporation Mul-

tinationale," *Revue Économique,* vol. XIX, no. 6, November.

Hymer, S., and Resnick, S.
1970 "International Trade and Uneven Development," in J. N. Bhagwati, R. W. Jones, R. A. Mundell and J. Vanek (eds.) *Kindleberger Festschrift,* MIT Press.

Hymer, S., and Rowthorn, R.
1970 "Multinational Corporations and International Oligopoly: The Non-American Challenge," in C. P. Kindleberger (ed.), *The International Corporation,* MIT Press.

Kuznets, S.
1966 *Modern Economic Growth.* Yale University Press.

Levitt, K.
1970 *Silent Surrender: The Multinational Corporation in Canada.* Macmillan Company of Canada.

Marshall, A.
1962 *Principles of Economics.* Macmillan, 8th edition.

Marx, K.
1867 *Capital,* vol. I, Foreign Languages Publishing House, Moscow (1961).
1894 *Capital,* vol. III, Foreign Languages Publishing House, Moscow (1966).

Mason, E. S.
1958 "The Apologetics of Managerialism."

The Journal of Business of the University of Chicago, vol. XXXI, no. 1, January.

Polanyi, K.
1944 *The Great Transformation,* Farrar & Rinehart.

Rose, S.
1968 "The Rewarding Strategies of Multinationalism." *Fortune,* September 15.

Salomon, A. M.
1966 *International Aspects of Antitrust,* "Part I: Hearings before the Sub-Committee on Antitrust and Monopoly of the Senate Committee on the Judiciary," April.

Simon, H. A.
1957 "The Compensation of Executives," *Sociometry,* March.

Smith, A.
1937 *The Wealth of Nations,* The Modern Library, New York.

US Department of Commerce
1969 *Survey of Current Business,* September.

Vernon, R.
1966 "International Investment and International Trade in the Product Cycle," *Quarterly Journal of Economics,* vol. LXXX, May.

15. Institutionalized Organizations: Formal Structure as Myth and Ceremony[1]

John M. Meyer and Brian Rowan

Formal organizations are generally understood to be systems of coordinated and controlled activities that arise when work is embedded in complex networks of technical relations and boundary-spanning exchanges. But in modern societies formal organizational structures arise in highly institutionalized contexts. Professions,

[1] "Institutionalized Organizations: Formal Structure as Myth and Ceremony" by John W. Meyer and Brian Rowan from *The American Journal of Sociology,* Vol. 83, No. 2, 1977, pp. 340-363. © 1977 by The University of Chicago. All rights reserved.

Work on this paper was conducted at the Stanford Center for Research and Development in Teaching (SCRDT) and was supported by the National Institute of Education (contract no. NE-C-00-

policies, and programs are created along with the products and services that they are understood to produce rationally. This permits many new organizations to spring up and forces existing ones to incorporate new practices and procedures. That is, organizations are driven to incorporate the practices and procedures defined by prevailing rationalized concepts of organizational work and institutionalized in society. Organizations that do so increase their legitimacy and their survival prospects, independent of the immediate efficacy of the acquired practices and procedures.

Institutionalized products, services, techniques, policies, and programs function as powerful myths, and many organizations adopt them ceremonially. But conformity to institutionalized rules often conflicts sharply with efficiency criteria and, conversely, to coordinate and control activity in order to promote efficiency undermines an organization's ceremonial conformity and sacrifices its support and legitimacy. To maintain ceremonial conformity, organizations that reflect institutional rules tend to buffer their formal structures from the uncertainties of technical activities by becoming loosely coupled, building gaps between their formal structures and actual work activities.

This paper argues that the formal structures of many organizations in postindustrial society (Bell 1973) dramatically reflect the myths of their institutional environments instead of the demands of their work activities. The first part describes prevailing theories of the origins of formal structures and the main problem the theories confront. The second part discusses an alternative source of formal structures: myths embedded in the institutional environment. The third part develops the argument that organizations reflecting institutionalized environments maintain gaps between their formal structures and their ongoing work activities. The final part summarizes by discussing some research implications.

Throughout the paper, institutionalized rules are distinguished sharply from prevailing social behaviors. Institutionalized rules are classifications built into society as reciprocated typifications or interpretations (Berger and Luckmann 1967, p. 54). Such rules may be simply taken for granted or may be supported by public opinion or the force of law (Starbuck 1976). Institutions inevitably involve normative obligations but often enter into social life primarily as facts which must be taken into account by actors. Institutionalization involves the processes by which social processes, obligations, or actualities come to take on a rulelike status in social thought and action. So, for example, the social status of doctor is a highly institutionalized rule (both normative and cognitive) for managing illness as well as a social role made up of particular behaviors, relations, and expectations. Research and development is an institutionalized category of organizational activity which has meaning and value in many sectors of society, as well as a collection of actual research and development activities. In a smaller way, a No Smoking sign is an institution with legal status and implications, as well as an attempt to regulate smoking behavior. It is fundamental to the argument of this paper that institutional rules may have effects on organizational structures and their implementation in actual technical work which are very different from the effects generated by the networks of social behavior and relationships which compose and surround a given organization.

3-0062). The views expressed here do not, of course, reflect NIE positions. Many colleagues in the SCRDT, the Stanford Organizations Training Program, the American Sociological Association's work group on Organizations and Environments, and the NIE gave help and encouragement. In particular, H. Acland, A. Bergesen, J. Boli-Bennett, T. Deal, J. Freeman, P. Hirsch, J. G. March, W. R. Scott, and W. Starbuck made helpful suggestions.

PREVAILING THEORIES OF FORMAL STRUCTURE

A sharp distinction should be made between the formal structure of an organization and its actual day-to-day work activities. Formal structure is a blueprint for activities which includes, first of all, the table of organization: a listing of offices, departments, positions, and programs. These elements are linked by explicit goals and policies that make up a rational theory of how, and to what end, activities are to be fitted together. The essence of a modern bureaucratic organization lies in the rationalized and impersonal character of these structural elements and of the goals that link them.

One of the central problems in organization theory is to describe the conditions that give rise to rationalized formal structure. In conventional theories, rational formal structure is assumed to be the most effective way to coordinate and control the complex relational networks involved in modern technical or work activities (see Scott 1975 for a review). This assumption derives from Weber's (1930, 1946, 1947) discussions of the historical emergence of bureaucracies as consequences of economic markets and centralized states. Economic markets place a premium on rationality and coordination. As markets expand, the relational networks in a given domain become more complex and differentiated, and organizations in that domain must manage more internal and boundary-spanning interdependencies. Such factors as size (Blau 1970) and technology (Woodward 1965) increase the complexity of internal relations, and the division of labor among organizations increases boundary-spanning problems (Aiken and Hage 1968; Freeman 1973; Thompson 1967). Because the need for coordination increases under these conditions, and because formally coordinated work has competitive advantages, organizations with rationalized formal structures tend to develop.

The formation of centralized states and the penetration of societies by political centers also contribute to the rise and spread of formal organization. When the relational networks involved in economic exchange and political management become extremely complex, bureaucratic structures are thought to be the most effective and rational means to standardize and control sub-units. Bureaucratic control is especially useful for expanding political centers, and standardization is often demanded by both centers and peripheral units (Bendix 1964, 1968). Political centers organize layers of offices that manage to extend conformity and to displace traditional activities throughout societies.

The problem. *Prevailing theories assume that the coordination and control of activity are the critical dimensions on which formal organizations have succeeded in the modern world.* This assumption is based on the view that organizations function according to their formal blueprints: coordination is routine, rules and procedures are followed, and actual activities conform to the prescriptions of formal structure. But much of the empirical research on organizations casts doubt on this assumption. An earlier generation of researchers concluded that there was a great gap between the formal and the informal organization (e.g., Dalton 1959; Downs 1967; Homans 1950). A related observation is that formal organizations are often loosely coupled (March and Olsen 1976; Weick 1976): structural elements are only loosely linked to each other and to activities, rules are often violated, decisions are often unimplemented, or if implemented have uncertain consequences, technologies are of problematic efficiency, and evaluation and inspection systems are subverted or rendered so vague as to provide little coordination.

Formal organizations are endemic in modern societies. There is need for an explanation of their rise that is partially free from the assumption that, in practice, formal structures actually coordinate and control work. Such an explanation should account for the elaboration of purposes, positions, policies, and procedural rules that characterizes formal organizations, but must do so without supposing that these structural features are implemented in routine work activity.

INSTITUTIONAL SOURCES OF FORMAL STRUCTURE

By focusing on the management of complex relational networks and the exercise of coordination and control, prevailing theories have neglected an alternative Weberian source of formal structure: the legitimacy of rationalized formal structures. In prevailing theories, legitimacy is a given: assertions about bureaucratization rest on the assumption of norms of rationality (Thompson 1967). When norms do play causal roles in theories of bureaucratization, it is because they are thought to be built into modern societies and personalities as very general values, which are thought to facilitate formal organization. But norms of rationality are not simply general values. They exist in much more specific and powerful ways in the rules, understandings, and meanings attached to institutionalized social structures. The causal importance of such institutions in the process of bureaucratization has been neglected.

Formal structures are not only creatures of their relational networks in the social organization. In modern societies, the elements of rationalized formal structure are deeply ingrained in, and reflect, widespread understandings of social reality. Many of the positions, policies, programs, and procedures of modern organizations are enforced by public opinion, by the views of important constituents, by knowledge legitimated through the educational system, by social prestige, by the laws, and by the definitions of negligence and prudence used by the courts. Such elements of formal structure are manifestations of powerful institutional rules which function as highly rationalized myths that are binding on particular organizations.

In modern societies, the myths generating formal organizational structure have two key properties. First, they are rationalized and impersonal prescriptions that identify various social purposes as technical ones and specify in a rulelike way the appropriate means to pursue these technical purposes rationally (Ellul 1964). Second, they are highly institutionalized and thus in some measure beyond the discretion of any individual participant or organization. They must, therefore, be taken for granted as legitimate, apart from evaluations of their impact on work outcomes.

Many elements of formal structure are highly institutionalized and function as myths. Examples include professions, programs, and technologies:

> Large numbers of rationalized professions emerge (Wilensky 1965; Bell 1973). These are occupations controlled, not only by direct inspection of work outcomes but also by social rules of licensing, certifying, and schooling. The occupations are rationalized, being understood to control impersonal techniques rather than moral mysteries. Further, they are highly institutionalized: the delegation of activities to the appropriate occupations is socially expected and often legally obligatory over and above any calculations of its efficiency.
>
> Many formalized organizational programs are also institutionalized in society. Ideologies define the functions appropriate to a business — such as sales, production, advertising, or accounting; to a university — such as instruction and research in history, engineering, and literature; and to a hospital — such as surgery, internal medicine, and obstetrics. Such classifications of organizational functions, and the specifications for conducting each function, are prefabricated formulae available for use by any given organization.
>
> Similarly, technologies are institutionalized and become myths binding on organiza-

tions. Technical procedures of production, accounting, personnel selection, or data processing become taken-for-granted means to accomplish organizational ends. Quite apart from their possible efficiency, such institutionalized techniques establish an organization as appropriate, rational, and modern. Their use displays responsibility and avoids claims of negligence.

The impact of such rationalized institutional elements on organizations and organizing situations is enormous. These rules define new organizing situations, redefine existing ones, and specify the means for coping rationally with each. They enable, and often require, participants to organize along prescribed lines. And they spread very rapidly in modern society as part of the rise of postindustrial society (Bell 1973). New and extant domains of activity are codified in institutionalized programs, professions, or techniques, and organizations incorporate the packaged codes. For example:

> The discipline of psychology creates a rationalized theory of personnel selection and certifies personnel professionals. Personnel departments and functionaries appear in all sorts of extant organizations, and new specialized personnel agencies also appear.
>
> As programs of research and development are created and professionals with expertise in these fields are trained and defined, organizations come under increasing pressure to incorporate R & D units.
>
> As the prerational profession of prostitution is rationalized along medical lines, bureaucratized organizations — sex-therapy clinics, massage parlors, and the like — spring up more easily.
>
> As the issues of safety and environmental pollution arise, and as relevant professions and programs become institutionalized in laws, union ideologies, and public opinion, organizations incorporate these programs and professions.

The growth of rationalized institutional structures in society makes formal organizations more common and more elaborate. Such institutions are myths which make formal organizations both easier to create and more necessary. After all, the building blocks for organizations come to be littered around the societal landscape; it takes only a little entrepreneurial energy to assemble them into a structure. And because these building blocks are considered proper, adequate, rational, and necessary, organizations must incorporate them to avoid illegitimacy. Thus, the myths built into rationalized institutional elements create the necessity, the opportunity, and the impulse to organize rationally, over and above pressures in this direction created by the need to manage proximate relational networks:

Proposition 1. *As rationalized institutional rules arise in given domains of work activity, formal organizations form and expand by incorporating these rules as structural elements.*

Two distinct ideas are implied here: (1*A*) As institutionalized myths define new domains of rationalized activity, formal organizations emerge in these domains. (1*B*) As rationalizing institutional myths arise in existing domains of activity, extant organizations expand their formal structures so as to become isomorphic with these new myths.

To understand the larger historical process it is useful to note that:

Proposition 2. *The more modernized the society, the more extended the rationalized institutional structure in given domains and the greater the number of domains containing rationalized institutions.*

Modern institutions, then, are thoroughly rationalized, and these rationalized elements act as myths giving rise to more formal organization. When propositions 1 and 2 are combined, two more specific ideas follow: (2A) Formal organizations are more likely to emerge in more modernized societies, even with the complexity of immediate relational networks held constant. (2B) Formal organizations in a given domain of activity are likely to have more elaborated structures in more modernized societies, even with the complexity of immediate relational networks held constant.

Combining the ideas above with prevailing organization theory, it becomes clear that modern societies are filled with rationalized bureaucracies for two reasons. First, as the prevailing theories have asserted, relational networks become increasingly complex as societies modernize. Second, modern societies are filled with institutional rules which function as myths depicting various formal structures as rational means to the attainment of desirable ends. Figure 1 summarizes these two lines of theory. Both lines suggest that the postindustrial society — the society dominated by rational organization even more than by the forces of production — arises both out of the

Fig. 1. — The Origins and Elaboration of Formal Organizational Structures

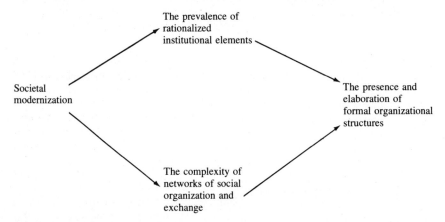

complexity of the modern social organizational network and, more directly, as an ideological matter. Once institutionalized, rationality becomes a myth with explosive organizing potential, as both Ellul (1964) and Bell (1973) — though with rather different reactions — observe.

The Relation of Organizations to Their Institutional Environments. The obsᵥ-vation is not new that organizations are structured by phenomena in their environments and tend to become isomorphic with them. One explanation of such isomorphism is that formal organizations become matched with their environments by technical and exchange interdependencies. This line of reasoning can be seen in the works of Aiken and Hage (1968), Hawley (1968), and Thompson (1967). This explanation asserts that structural elements diffuse because environments create boundary-spanning exigencies for organizations, and that organizations which incorporate structural elements isomorphic with the environment are able to manage such interdependencies.

A second explanation for the parallelism between organizations and their environments — and the one emphasized here — is that organizations structurally reflect socially constructed reality (Berger and Luckmann 1967). This view is suggested in the work of Parsons (1956) and Udy (1970), who see organizations as greatly conditioned by their general institutional environments and therefore as institutions themselves in part. Emery and Trist (1965) also see organizations as responding directly to environmental structures and distinguish such effects sharply from those that occur through boundary-spanning exchanges. According to the institutional conception as developed here, organizations tend to disappear as distinct and bounded units. Quite beyond the environmental interrelations suggested in open-systems theories, institutional theories in their extreme forms define organizations as dramatic enactments of the rationalized myths pervading modern societies, rather than as units involved in exchange — no matter how complex — with their environments.

The two explanations of environmental isomorphism are not entirely inconsistent. Organizations both deal with their environments at their boundaries and imitate environmental elements in their structures. However, the two lines of explanation have very different implications for internal organizational processes, as will be argued below.

The Origins of Rational Institutional Myths.   Bureaucratization is caused in part by the proliferation of rationalized myths in society, and this in turn involves the evolution of the whole modern institutional system. Although the latter topic is beyond the scope of this paper, three specific processes that generate rationalized myths of organizational structure can be noted.

The elaboration of complex relational networks. — As the relational networks in societies become dense and interconnected, increasing numbers of rationalized myths arise. Some of them are highly generalized: for example, the principles of universalism (Parsons 1971), contracts (Spencer 1897), restitution (Durkheim 1933), and expertise (Weber 1947) are generalized to diverse occupations, organizational programs, and organizational practices. Other myths describe specific structural elements. These myths may originate from narrow contexts and be applied in different ones. For example, in modern societies the relational contexts of business organizations in a single industry are roughly similar from place to place. Under these conditions a particularly effective practice, occupational specialty, or principle of coordination can be codified into mythlike form. The laws, the educational and credentialing systems, and public opinion then make it necessary or advantageous for organizations to incorporate the new structures.

The degree of collective organization of the environment. — The myths generated by particular organizational practices and diffused through relational networks have legitimacy based on the supposition that they are rationally effective. But many myths also have official legitimacy based on legal mandates. Societies that, through nation building and state formation, have developed rational-legal orders are especially prone to give collective (legal) authority to institutions which legitimate particular organizational structures. The rise of centralized states and integrated nations means that organized agents of society assume jurisdiction over large numbers of activity domains (Swanson 1971). Legislative and judicial authorities create and interpret legal mandates; administrative agencies — such as state and federal governments, port authorities, and school districts — establish rules of practice; and licenses and credentials become necessary in order to practice occupations. The stronger the rational-legal order, the greater the extent to which rationalized rules and procedures and personnel become institutional requirements. New formal organizations emerge and extant organizations acquire new structural elements.

Leadership efforts of local organizations. — The rise of the state and the expansion of collective jurisdiction are often thought to result in domesticated organizations (Carlson 1962) subject to high levels of goal displacement (Clark 1956; Selznick 1949; and Zald and Denton 1963). This view is misleading: organizations do often adapt to their institutional contexts, but they often play active roles in shaping those contexts (Dowling and Pfeffer 1975; Parsons 1956; Perrow 1970; Thompson 1967). Many organizations actively seek charters from collective authorities and manage to institutionalize their goals and structures in the rules of such authorities.

Efforts to mold institutional environments proceed along two dimensions. First, powerful organizations force their immediate relational networks to adapt to their structures and relations. For instance, automobile producers help create demands for particular kinds of roads, transportation systems, and fuels that make automobiles virtual necessities; competitive forms of transportation have to adapt to the existing relational context. But second, powerful organizations attempt to build their goals and procedures directly into society as institutional rules. Automobile producers, for instance, attempt to create the standards in public opinion defining desirable cars, to influence legal standards defining satisfactory cars, to affect judicial rules defining cars adequate enough to avoid manufacturer liability, and to force agents of the collectivity to purchase only their cars. Rivals must then compete both in social networks or markets and in contexts of institutional rules which are defined by extant organizations. In this fashion, given organizational forms perpetuate themselves by becoming institutionalized rules. For example:

> School administrators who create new curricula or training programs attempt to validate them as legitimate innovations in educational theory and governmental requirements. If they are successful, the new procedures can be perpetuated as authoritatively required or at least satisfactory.
>
> New departments within business enterprises, such as personnel, advertising, or research and development departments, attempt to professionalize by creating rules of practice and personnel certification that are enforced by the schools, prestige systems, and the laws.
>
> Organizations under attack in competitive environments — small farms, passenger railways, or Rolls Royce — attempt to establish themselves as central to the cultural traditions of their societies in order to receive official protection.

The Impact of Institutional Environments on Organizations. Isomorphism with environmental institutions has some crucial consequences for organizations: (a) they incorporate elements which are legitimated externally, rather than in terms of efficiency; (b) they employ external or ceremonial assessment criteria to define the value of structural elements; and (c) dependence on externally fixed institutions reduces turbulence and maintains stability. As a result, it is argued here institutional isomorphism promotes the success and survival of organizations. Incorporating externally legitimated formal structures increases the commitment of internal participants and external constituents. And the use of external assessment criteria — that is, moving toward the status in society of a subunit rather than an independent system — can enable an organization to remain successful by social definition, buffering it from failure.

Changing formal structures. — By designing a formal structure that adheres to the prescriptions of myths in the institutional environment, an organization demonstrates that it is acting on collectively valued purposes in a proper and adequate manner (Dowling and Pfeffer 1975; Meyer and Rowan 1975). The incorporation of institutionalized elements provides an account (Scott and Lyman 1968) of its activities that protects the organization from having its conduct questioned. The organization becomes, in a word, legitimate, and it uses its legitimacy to strengthen its support and secure its survival.

From an institutional perspective then, a most important aspect of isomorphism with environmental institutions is the evolution of organizational language. The labels of the organization chart as well as the vocabulary used to delineate organizational goals, procedures, and policies are analogous to the vocabularies of motive used to account for the activities of individuals (Blum and McHugh 1971; Mills 1940). Just as jealousy, anger, altruism, and love are myths that interpret and explain the actions of individuals, the myths of doctors, of accountants, or of the assembly line explain organizational activities. Thus, some can say that the engineers will solve a specific problem or that the secretaries will perform certain tasks, without knowing who these engineers or secretaries will be or exactly what they will do. Both the speaker and the listeners understand such statements to describe how certain responsibilities will be carried out.

Vocabularies of structure which are isomorphic with institutional rules provide prudent, rational, and legitimate accounts. Organizations described in legitimated vocabularies are assumed to be oriented to collectively defined, and often collectively mandated, ends. The myths of personnel services, for example, not only account for the rationality of employment practices but also indicate that personnel services are valuable to an organization. Employees, applicants, managers, trustees, and governmental agencies are predisposed to trust the hiring practices of organizations that follow legitimated procedures — such as equal opportunity programs, or personality testing — and they are more willing to participate in or to fund such organizations. On the other hand, organizations that omit environmentally legitimated elements of structure or create unique structures lack acceptable legitimated accounts of their activities. Such organizations are more vulnerable to claims that they are negligent, irrational, or unnecessary. Claims of this kind, whether made by internal participants, external constituents, or the government, can cause organizations to incur real costs. For example:

> With the rise of modern medical institutions, large organizations that do not arrange medical-care facilities for their workers come to be seen as negligent — by the workers, by management factions, by insurers, by courts which legally define negligence, and often by laws. The costs of illegitimacy in insurance premiums and legal liabilities are very real.
>
> Similarly, environmental safety institutions make it important for organizations to create formal safety rules, safety departments, and safety programs. No Smoking rules and signs, regardless of their enforcement, are necessary to avoid charges of negligence and to avoid the extreme of illegitimation: the closing of buildings by the state.
>
> The rise of professionalized economics makes it useful for organizations to incorporate groups of economists and econometric analyses. Though no one may read, understand, or believe them, econometric analyses help legitimate the organization's plans in the eyes of investors, customers (as with Defense Department contractors), and internal participants. Such analyses can also provide rational accountings after failures occur: managers whose plans have failed can demonstrate to investors, stockholders, and superiors that procedures were prudent and that decisions were made by rational means.

Thus, rationalized institutions create myths of formal structure which shape organizations. Failure to incorporate the proper elements of structure is negligent and irrational; the continued flow of support is threatened and internal dissidents are strengthened. At the same time, these myths present organizations with great opportunities for expansion. Affixing the right labels to activities can change them into valuable services and mobilize the commitments of internal participants and external constituents.

Adopting external assessment criteria. — In institutionally elaborated environments organizations also become sensitive to, and employ, external criteria of worth.

Such criteria include, for instance, such ceremonial awards as the Nobel Prize, endorsements by important people, the standard prices of professionals and consultants, or the prestige of programs or personnel in external social circles. For example, the conventions of modern accounting attempt to assign value to particular components of organizations on the basis of their contribution — through the organization's production function — to the goods and services the organization produces. But for many units — service departments, administrative sectors, and others — it is utterly unclear what is being produced that has clear or definable value in terms of its contribution to the organizational product. In these situations, accountants employ shadow prices: they assume that given organizational units are necessary and calculate their value from their prices in the world outside the organization. Thus modern accounting creates ceremonial production functions and maps them onto economic production functions: organizations assign externally defined worth to advertising departments, safety departments, managers, econometricians, and occasionally even sociologists, whether or not these units contribute measurably to the production of outputs. Monetary prices, in postindustrial society. reflect hosts of ceremonial influences, as do economic measures of efficiency, profitability, or net worth (Hirsch 1975).

Ceremonial criteria of worth and ceremonially derived production functions are useful to organizations: they legitimate organizations with internal participants, stockholders, the public, and the state, as with the IRS or the SEC. They demonstrate socially the fitness of an organization. The incorporation of structures with high ceremonial value, such as those reflecting the latest expert thinking or those with the most prestige, makes the credit position of an organization more favorable. Loans, donations, or investments are more easily obtained. Finally, units within the organization use ceremonial assessments as accounts of their productive service to the organization. Their internal power rises with their performance on ceremonial measures (Salancik and Pfeffer 1974).

Stabilization. — The rise of an elaborate institutional environment stabilizes both external and internal organizational relationships. Centralized states, trade associations, unions, professional associations, and coalitions among organizations standardize and stabilize (see the review by Starbuck 1976).

Market conditions, the characteristics of inputs and outputs, and technological procedures are brought under the jurisdiction of institutional meanings and controls. Stabilization also results as a given organization becomes part of the wider collective system. Support is guaranteed by agreements instead of depending entirely on performance. For example, apart from whether schools educate students, or hospitals cure patients, people and governmental agencies remain committed to these organizations, funding and using them almost automatically year after year.

Institutionally controlled environments buffer organizations from turbulence (Emery and Trist 1965; Terreberry 1968). Adaptations occur less rapidly as increased numbers of agreements are enacted. Collectively granted monopolies guarantee clienteles for organizations like schools, hospitals, or professional associations. The taken-for-granted (and legally regulated) quality of institutional rules makes dramatic instabilities in products, techniques, or policies unlikely. And legitimacy as accepted subunits of society protects organizations from immediate sanctions for variations in technical performance:

Thus, American school districts (like other governmental units) have near monopolies and are very stable. They must conform to wider rules about proper classifications and credentials of teachers and students, and of topics of study. But they are protected by rules which make education as defined by these classifications compulsory. Alternative or private schools are possible, but must conform so closely to the required structures and classifications as to be able to generate little advantage.

Some business organizations obtain very high levels of institutional stabilization. A large defense contractor may be paid for following agreed-on procedures, even if the product is ineffective. In the extreme, such organizations may be so successful as to survive bankruptcy intact — as Lockheed and Penn Central have done — by becoming partially components of the state. More commonly, such firms are guaranteed survival by state-regulated rates which secure profits regardless of costs, as with American public utility firms.

Large automobile firms are a little less stabilized. They exist in an environment that contains enough structures to make automobiles, as conventionally defined, virtual necessities. But still, customers and governments can inspect each automobile and can evaluate and even legally discredit it. Legal action cannot as easily discredit a high school graduate.

Organizational success and survival. — Thus, organizational success depends on factors other than efficient coordination and control of productive activities. Independent of their productive efficiency, organizations which exist in highly elaborated institutional environments and succeed in becoming isomorphic with these environments gain the legitimacy and resources needed to survive. In part, this depends on environmental processes and on the capacity of given organizational leadership to mold these processes (Hirsch 1975). In part, it depends on the ability of given organizations to conform to, and become legitimated by, environmental institutions. In institutionally elaborated environments, sagacious conformity is required: leadership (in a university, a hospital, or a business) requires an understanding of changing fashions and governmental programs. But this kind of conformity — and the almost guaranteed survival which may accompany it — is possible only in an environment with a highly institutionalized structure. In such a context an organization can be locked into isomorphism, ceremonially reflecting the institutional environment in its structure, functionaries, and procedures. Thus, in addition to the conventionally defined sources of organizational success and survival, the following general assertions can be proposed:

Proposition 3. *Organizations that incorporate societally legitimated rationalized elements in their formal structures maximize their legitimacy and increase their resources and survival capabilities.*

This proposition asserts that the long-run survival prospects of organizations increase as state structures elaborate and as organizations respond to institutionalized rules. In the United States, for instance, schools, hospitals, and welfare organizations show considerable ability to survive, precisely because they are matched with — and almost absorbed by — their institutional environments. In the same way, organizations fail when they deviate from the prescriptions of institutionalizing myths: quite apart from technical efficiency, organizations which innovate in important structural ways bear considerable costs in legitimacy.

Figure 2 summarizes the general argument of this section, alongside the established view that organizations succeed through efficiency.

INSTITUTIONALIZED STRUCTURES AND ORGANIZATIONAL ACTIVITIES

Rationalized formal structures arise in two contexts. First, the demands of local relational networks encourage the development of structures that coordinate and control activities. Such structures contribute to the efficiency of organizations and give them competitive advantages over less efficient competitors. Second, the inter-connectedness of societal relations, the collective organization of society, and the leadership of organizational elites create a highly institutionalized context. In this context rationalized structures present an acceptable account of organizational activities, and organizations gain legitimacy, stability, and resources.

All organizations, to one degree or another, are embedded in both relational and institutionalized contexts and are therefore concerned both with coordinating and controlling their activities and with prudently accounting for them. Organizations in highly institutionalized environments face internal and boundary-spanning contingencies. Schools, for example, must transport students to and from school under some circumstances and must assign teachers, students, and topics to classrooms. On the other hand, organizations producing in markets that place great emphasis on efficiency build in units whose relation to production is obscure and whose efficiency is determined, not by a true production function, but by ceremonial definition.

Nevertheless, the survival of some organizations depends more on managing the demands of internal and boundary-spanning relations, while the survival of others depends more on the ceremonial demands of highly institutionalized environments. The discussion to follow shows that whether an organization's survival depends primarily on relational or on institutional demands determines the tightness of alignments between structures and activities.

Fig. 2. — Organizational Survival

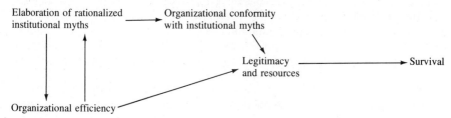

Types of Organizations. Institutionalized myths differ in the completeness with which they describe cause and effect relationships, and in the clarity with which they describe standards that should be used to evaluate outputs (Thompson 1967). Some organizations use routine, clearly defined technologies to produce outputs. When output can be easily evaluated a market often develops, and consumers gain considerable rights of inspection and control. In this context, efficiency often determines success. Organizations must face exigencies of close coordination with their relational networks, and they cope with these exigencies by organizing around immediate technical problems.

But the rise of collectively organized society and the increasing interconnectedness of social relations have eroded many market contexts. Increasingly, such organizations as schools, R & D units, and governmental bureaucracies use variable, ambiguous technologies to produce outputs that are difficult to appraise, and other organizations with clearly defined technologies find themselves unable to adapt to environmental turbulence. The uncertainties of unpredictable technical contingencies or of adapting to environmental change cannot be resolved on the basis of efficiency. Internal participants and external constituents alike call for institutionalized rules that promote trust and confidence in outputs and buffer organizations from failure (Emery and Trist, 1965).

Thus, one can conceive of a continuum along which organizations can be ordered.

At one end are production organizations under strong output controls (Ouchi and McGuire, 1975) whose success depends on the management of relational networks. At the other end are institutionalized organizations whose success depends on the confidence and stability achieved by isomorphism with institutional rules. For two reasons it is important not to assume that an organization's location on this continuum is based on the inherent technical properties of its output and therefore permanent. First, the technical properties of outputs are socially defined and do not exist in some concrete sense that allows them to be empirically discovered. Second, environments and organizations often redefine the nature of products, services, and technologies. Redefinition sometimes clarifies techniques or evaluative standards. But often organizations and environments redefine the nature of techniques and output so that ambiguity is introduced and rights of inspection and control are lowered. For example, American schools have evolved from producing rather specific training that was evaluated according to strict criteria of efficiency to producing ambiguously defined services that are evaluated according to criteria of certification (Callahan 1962; Tyack 1974; Meyer and Rowan 1975).

Structural Inconsistencies in Institutionalized Organizations. Two very general problems face an organization if its success depends primarily on isomorphism with institutionalized rules. First, technical activities and demands for efficiency create conflicts and inconsistencies in an institutionalized organization's efforts to conform to the ceremonial rules of production. Second, because these ceremonial rules are transmitted by myths that may arise from different parts of the environment, the rules may conflict with one another. These inconsistencies make a concern for efficiency and tight coordination and control problematic.

Formal structures that celebrate institutionalized myths differ from structures that act efficiently. Ceremonial activity is significant in relation to categorical rules, not in its concrete effects (Merton 1940; March and Simon 1958). A sick worker must be treated by a doctor using accepted medical procedures; whether the worker is treated effectively is less important. A bus company must service required routes whether or not there are many passengers. A university must maintain appropriate departments independently of the departments' enrollments. Activity, that is, has ritual significance: it maintains appearances and validates an organization.

Categorical rules conflict with the logic of efficiency. Organizations often face the dilemma that activities celebrating institutionalized rules, although they count as virtuous ceremonial expenditures, are pure costs from the point of view of efficiency. For example, hiring a Nobel Prize winner brings great ceremonial benefits to a university. The celebrated name can lead to research grants, brighter students, or reputational gains. But from the point of view of immediate outcomes, the expenditure lowers the instructional return per dollar expended and lowers the university's ability to solve immediate logistical problems. Also, expensive technologies, which bring prestige to hospitals and business firms, may be simply excessive costs from the point of view of immediate production. Similarly, highly professionalized consultants who bring external blessings on an organization are often difficult to justify in terms of improved productivity, yet may be very important in maintaining internal and external legitimacy.

Other conflicts between categorical rules and efficiency arise because institutional rules are couched at high levels of generalization (Durkheim 1933) whereas technical activities vary with specific, unstandardized, and possibly unique conditions. Because standardized ceremonial categories must confront technical variations and anomalies, the generalized rules of the institutional environment are often inappropriate to specific situations. A governmentally mandated curriculum may be inappropriate for the students at hand, a conventional medical treatment may make little sense given the characteristics of a patient, and federal safety inspectors may intolerably delay boundary-spanning exchanges.

Yet another source of conflict between categorical rules and efficiency is the inconsistency among institutionalized elements. Institutional environments are often pluralistic (Udy 1970), and societies promulgate sharply inconsistent myths. As a result, organizations in search of external support and stability incorporate all sorts of incompatible structural elements. Professions are incorporated although they make overlapping jurisdictional claims. Programs are adopted which contend with each other for authority over a given domain. For instance, if one inquires who decides what curricula will be taught in schools, any number of parties from the various governments down to individual teachers may say that they decide.

In institutionalized organizations, then, concern with the efficiency of day-to-day activities creates enormous uncertainties. Specific contexts highlight the inadequacies of the prescriptions of generalized myths, and inconsistent structural elements conflict over jurisdictional rights. Thus the organization must struggle to link the requirements of ceremonial elements to technical activities and to link inconsistent ceremonial elements to each other.

Resolving Inconsistencies.   There are four partial solutions to these inconsistencies. First, an organization can resist ceremonial requirements. But an organization that neglects ceremonial requirements and portrays itself as efficient may be unsuccessful in documenting its efficiency. Also, rejecting ceremonial requirements neglects an important source of resources and stability. Second, an organization can maintain rigid conformity to institutionalized prescriptions by cutting off external relations. Although such isolation upholds ceremonial requirements, internal participants and external constituents may soon become disillusioned with their inability to manage boundary-spanning exchanges. Institutionalized organizations must not only conform to myths but must also maintain the appearance that the myths actually work. Third, an organization can cynically acknowledge that its structure is inconsistent with work requirements. But this strategy denies the validity of institutionalized myths and sabotages the legitimacy of the organization. Fourth, an organization can promise reform. People may picture the present as unworkable but the future as filled with promising reforms of both structure and activity. But by defining the organization's valid structure as lying in the future, this strategy makes the organization's current structure illegitimate.

Instead of relying on a partial solution, however, an organization can resolve conflicts between ceremonial rules and efficiency by employing two interrelated devices: decoupling and the logic of confidence.

Decoupling. — Ideally, organizations built around efficiency attempt to maintain close alignments between structures and activities. Conformity is enforced through inspection, output quality is continually monitored, the efficiency of various units is evaluated, and the various goals are unified and coordinated. But a policy of close alignment in institutionalized organizations merely makes public a record of inefficiency and inconsistency.

Institutionalized organizations protect their formal structures from evaluation on the basis of technical performance: inspection, evaluation, and control of activities are minimized, and coordination, interdependence, and mutual adjustments among structural units are handled informally.

Proposition 4. *Because attempts to control and coordinate activities in in-*

stitutionalized organizations lead to conflicts and loss of legitimacy, elements of structure are decoupled from activities and from each other.

Some well-known properties of organizations illustrate the decoupling process:

Activities are performed beyond the purview of managers. In particular, organizations actively encourage professionalism, and activities are delegated to professionals.

Goals are made ambiguous or vacuous, and categorical ends are substituted for technical ends. Hospitals treat, not cure, patients. Schools produce students, not learning. In fact, data on technical performance are eliminated or rendered invisible. Hospitals try to ignore information on cure rates, public services avoid data about effectiveness, and schools deemphasize measures of achievement.

Integration is avoided, program implementation is neglected, and inspection and evaluation are ceremonialized.

Human relations are made very important. The organization cannot formally coordinate activities because its formal rules, if applied, would generate inconsistencies. Therefore individuals are left to work out technical interdependencies informally. The ability to coordinate things in violation of the rules — that is, to get along with other people — is highly valued.

The advantages of decoupling are clear. The assumption that formal structures are really working is buffered from the inconsistencies and anomalies involved in technical activities. Also, because integration is avoided disputes and conflicts are minimized, and an organization can mobilize support from a broader range of external constituents.

Thus, decoupling enables organizations to maintain standardized, legitimating, formal structures while their activities vary in response to practical considerations. The organizations in an industry tend to be similar in formal structure — reflecting their common institutional origins — but may show much diversity in actual practice.

The logic of confidence and good faith. — Despite the lack of coordination and control, decoupled organizations are not anarchies. Day-to-day activities proceed in an orderly fashion. What legitimates institutionalized organizations, enabling them to appear useful in spite of the lack of technical validation, is the confidence and good faith of their internal participants and their external constituents.

Considerations of face characterize ceremonial management (Goffman 1967). Confidence in structural elements is maintained through three practices — avoidance, discretion, and overlooking (Goffman 1967, pp. 12-18). Avoidance and discretion are encouraged by decoupling autonomous subunits; overlooking anomalies is also quite common. Both internal participants and external constituents cooperate in these practices. Assuring that individual participants maintain face sustains confidence in the organization, and ultimately reinforces confidence in the myths that rationalize the organization's existence.

Delegation, professionalization, goal ambiguity, the elimination of output data, and maintenance of face are all mechanisms for absorbing uncertainty while preserving the formal structure of the organization (March and Simon 1958). They contribute to a general aura of confidence within and outside the organization. Although the literature on informal organizations often treats these practices as mechanisms for the achievement of deviant and subgroup purposes (Downs 1967), such treatment ignores a critical feature of organization life: effectively absorbing uncertainty and maintaining confidence requires people to assume that everyone is acting in good faith. The assumption that things are as they seem, that employees and managers are performing their roles properly, allows an organization to perform its daily routines with a decoupled structure.

Decoupling and maintenance of face, in other words, are mechanisms that maintain the assumption that people are acting in good faith. Professionalization is not merely a way of avoiding inspection — it binds both supervisors and subordinates to act in good faith. So in a smaller way does strategic leniency (Blau 1956). And so do the public displays of morale and satisfaction which are characteristic of many organizations. Organizations employ a host of mechanisms to dramatize the ritual commitments which their participants make to basic structural elements. These mechanisms are especially common in organizations which strongly reflect their institutionalized environments.

Proposition 5. *The more an organization's structure is derived from institutionalized myths, the more it maintains elaborate displays of confidence, satisfaction, and good faith, internally and externally.*

The commitments built up by displays of morale and satisfaction are not simply vacuous affirmations of institutionalized myths. Participants not only commit themselves to supporting an organization's ceremonial facade but also commit themselves to making things work out backstage. The committed participants engage in informal coordination that, although often formally inappropriate, keeps technical activities running smoothly and avoids public embarrassments. In this sense the confidence and good faith generated by ceremonial action is in no way fraudulent. It may even be the most reasonable way to get participants to make their best efforts in situations that are made problematic by institutionalized myths that are at odds with immediate technical demands.

Ceremonial inspection and evaluation. — All organizations, even those maintaining high levels of confidence and good faith, are in environments that have institutionalized the rationalized rituals of inspection and evaluation. And inspection and evaluation can uncover events and deviations that undermine legitimacy. So institutionalized organizations minimize and ceremonialize inspection and evaluation.

In institutionalized organizations, in fact, evaluation accompanies and produces illegitimacy. The interest in evaluation research by the American federal government, for instance, is partly intended to undercut the state, local, and private authorities which have managed social services in the United States. The federal authorities, of course, have usually not evaluated those programs which are completely under federal jurisdiction; they have only evaluated those over which federal controls are incomplete. Similarly, state governments have often insisted on evaluating the special fundings they create in welfare and education but ordinarily do not evaluate the programs which they fund in a routine way.

Evaluation and inspection are public assertions of societal control which violate the assumption that everyone is acting with competence and in good faith. Violating this assumption lowers morale and confidence. Thus, evaluation and inspection undermine the ceremonial aspects of organizations.

Proposition 6. *Institutionalized organizations seek to minimize inspection and evaluation by both internal managers and external constituents.*

Decoupling and the avoidance of inspection and evaluation are not merely devices used by the organization. External constituents, too, avoid inspecting and controlling institutionalized organizations (Meyer and Rowan 1975). Accrediting agencies, boards of trustees, government agencies, and individuals accept ceremonially at face value the credentials, ambiguous goals, and categorical evaluations that are characteristic of ceremonial organizations. In elaborate institutional environments these external constituents are themselves likely to be corporately organized agents of society. Maintaining categorical relationships with their organizational subunits is more stable and more certain than is relying on inspection and control.

Figure 3 summarizes the main arguments of this section of our discussion.

SUMMARY AND RESEARCH IMPLICATIONS

Organizational structures are created and made more elaborate with the rise of institutionalized myths, and, in highly institutionalized contexts, organizational

Fig. 3. — The Effects of Institutional Isomorphism on Organizations

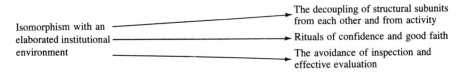

action must support these myths. But an organization must also attend to practical activity. The two requirements are at odds. A stable solution is to maintain the organization in a loosely coupled state.

No position is taken here on the overall social effectiveness of isomorphic and loosely coupled organizations. To some extent such structures buffer activity from efficiency criteria and produce ineffectiveness. On the other hand, by binding participants to act in good faith, and to adhere to the larger rationalities of the wider structure, they may maximize long-run effectiveness. It should not be assumed that the creation of microscopic rationalities in the daily activity of workers effects social ends more efficiently than commitment to larger institutional claims and purposes.

Research Implications.   The argument presented here generates several major theses that have clear research implications.

1. Environments and environmental domains which have institutionalized a greater number of rational myths generate more formal organization. This thesis leads to the research hypothesis that formal organizations rise and become more complex as a result of the rise of the elaborated state and other institutions for collective action. This hypothesis should hold true even when economic and technical development are held constant. Studies could trace the diffusion to formal organizations of specific institutions: professions, clearly labeled programs, and the like. For instance, the effects of the rise of theories and professions of personnel selection on the creation of personnel departments in organizations could be studied. Other studies could follow the diffusion of sales departments or research and development departments. Organizations should be found to adapt to such environmental changes, even if no evidence of their effectiveness exists.

    Experimentally, one could study the impact on the decisions of organizational managers, in planning or altering organizational structures, of hypothetical variations in environmental institutionalization. Do managers plan differently if they are informed about the existence of established occupations or programmatic institutions in their environments? Do they plan differently if they are designing organizations for more or less institutionally elaborated environments?

2. Organizations which incorporate institutionalized myths are more legitimate, successful, and likely to survive. Here, research should compare similar organi-

zations in different contexts. For instance, the presence of personnel departments or research and development units should predict success in environments in which they are widely institutionalized. Organizations which have structural elements not institutionalized in their environments should be more likely to fail, as such unauthorized complexity must be justified by claims of efficiency and effectiveness.

More generally, organizations whose claims to support are based on evaluations should be less likely to survive than those which are more highly institutionalized. An implication of this argument is that organizations existing in a highly institutionalized environment are generally more likely to survive.

Experimentally, one could study the size of the loans banks would be willing to provide organizations which vary only in (1) the degree of environmental institutionalization, and (2) the degree to which the organization structurally incorporates environmental institutions. Are banks willing to lend more money to firms whose plans are accompanied by econometric projections? And is this tendency greater in societies in which such projections are more widely institutionalized?

3. Organizational control efforts, especially in highly institutionalized contexts, are devoted to ritual conformity, both internally and externally. Such organizations, that is, decouple structure from activity and structures from each other. The idea here is that the more highly institutionalized the environment, the more time and energy organizational elites devote to managing their organization's public image and status and the less they devote to coordination and to managing particular boundary-spanning relationships. Further, the argument is that in such contexts managers devote more time to articulating internal structures and relationships at an abstract or ritual level, in contrast to managing particular relationships among activities and interdependencies.

Experimentally, the time and energy allocations proposed by managers presented with differently described environments could be studied. Do managers, presented with the description of an elaborately institutionalized environment, propose to spend more energy maintaining ritual isomorphism and less on monitoring internal conformity? Do they tend to become inattentive to evaluation? Do they elaborate doctrines of professionalism and good faith?

The arguments here, in other words, suggest both comparative and experimental studies examining the effects on organizational structure and coordination of variations in the institutional structure of the wider environment. Variations in organizational structure among societies, and within any society across time, are central to this conception of the problem.

REFERENCES

Aiken, Michael, and Jerald Hage
1968   "Organizational interdependence and intra-organizational structure." *American Sociological Review* 33 (December): 912-30.

Bell, Daniel
1973   *The Coming of Post-industrial Society.* New York: Basic.

Bendix, Reinhard
1964   *Nation-Building and Citizenship.* New York: Wiley.
1968   "Bureaucracy." Pp. 206-19 in *International Encyclopedia of the Social Sciences,* edited by David L. Sills. New York: Macmillan.

Berger, Peter L., and Thomas Luckmann
1967   *The Social Construction of Reality.*
New York: Doubleday.
Blau, Peter M.
1956   *Bureaucracy in Modern Society.*
New York: Random House.
1970   "A formal theory of differentiation in
organizations." *American Sociological Review* 35 (April): 201-18.
Blum, Alan F., and Peter McHugh
1971   "The social ascription of motives."
American Sociological Review 36
(December): 98-109.
Callahan, Raymond E.
1962   *Education and the Cult of Efficiency.*
Chicago: University of Chicago
Press.
Carlson, Richard O.
1962   *Executive Succession and Organizational Change.* Chicago: Midwest
Administration Center, University of
Chicago.
Clark, Burton R.
1956   *Adult Education in Transition.*
Berkeley: University of California
Press.
Dalton, Melville
1959   *Men Who Manage.* New York:
Wiley.
Dowling, John, and Jeffrey Pfeffer
1975   "Organizational legitimacy." *Pacific
Sociological Review* 18 (January):
122-36.
Downs, Anthony
1967   *Inside Bureaucracy.* Boston: Little,
Brown.
Durkheim, Émile
1933   *The Division of Labor in Society.*
New York: Macmillan.
Ellul, Jacques
1964   *The Technological Society.* New
York: Knopf.
Emery, Fred L., and Eric L. Trist
1965   "The causal texture of organizational
environments." *Human Relations* 18
(February): 21-32.
Freeman, John Henry
1973   "Environment, technology and administrative intensity of manufacturing organizations." *American
Sociological Review* 38 (December):
750-63.
Goffman, Erving
1967   *Interaction Ritual.* Garden City, N.Y.:
Anchor.

Hawley, Amos H.
1968   "Human ecology." Pp. 328-37 in
International Encyclopedia of the Social Sciences, edited by David L.
Sills. New York: Macmillan.
Hirsch, Paul M.
1975   "Organizational effectiveness and
the institutional environment." *Administrative Science Quarterly* 20
(September): 327-44.
Homans, George C.
1950   *The Human Group.* New York: Harcourt, Brace.
March, James G., and Johan P. Olsen
1976   *Ambiguity and Choice in Organizations.* Bergen: Universitetsforlaget.
March, James G., and Herbert A. Simon
1958   *Organizations.* New York: Wiley.
Merton, Robert K.
1940   "Bureaucratic structure and personality." *Social Forces* 18 (May):
560-68.
Meyer, John W., and Brian Rowan
1975   "Notes on the structure of educational organizations." Paper presented at annual meeting of the
American Sociological Association,
San Francisco.
Mills, C. Wright
1940   "Situated actions and vocabularies of
motive." *American Sociological Review* 5 (February): 904-13.
Ouchi, William, and Mary Ann Maguire
1975   "Organizational control: two
functions." *Administrative Science
Quarterly* 20 (December): 559-69.
Parsons, Talcott
1956   "Suggestions for a sociological approach to the theory of organizations
I." *Administrative Science Quarterly*
1 (June): 63-85.
1971   *The System of Modern Societies.* Englewood Cliffs, N.J.: Prentice-Hall.
Perrow, Charles
1970   *Organizational Analysis: A
Sociological View.* Belmont, Calif.:
Wadsworth.
Salancik, Gerald R., and Jeffrey Pfeffer
1974   "The bases and use of power in organizational decision making." *Administrative Science Quarterly* 19
(December): 453-73.
Scott, Marvin B., and Stanford M. Lyman
1968   "Accounts." *American Sociological
Review* 33 (February): 46-62.

Scott, W. Richard
1975   "Organizational Structure." Pp. 1-20 in *Annual Review of Sociology*. Vol. 1, edited by Alex Inkeles. Palo Alto, Calif.: Annual Reviews.

Selznick, Philip
1949   *TVA and the Grass Roots*. Berkeley: University of California Press.

Spencer, Herbert
1897   *Principles of Sociology*. New York: Appleton.

Starbuck, William H.
1976   "Organizations and their environments." Pp. 1069-1123 in *Handbook of Industrial and Organizational Psychology*, edited by Marvin D. Dunnette. New York: Rand McNally.

Swanson, Guy E.
1971   "An organizational analysis of collectivities." *American Sociological Review* 36 (August): 607-24.

Terreberry, Shirley
1968   "The Evolution of Organizational Environments." *Administrative Science Quarterly* 12 (March): 590-613.

Thompson, James D.
1967   *Organizations in Action*. New York: McGraw-Hill.

Tyack, David B.
1974   *The One Best System*. Cambridge,

Mass.: Harvard University Press.

Udy, Stanley H., Jr.
1970   *Work in Traditional and Modern Society*. Englewood Cliffs, N.J.: Prentice-Hall.

Weber, Max
1930   *The Protestant's Ethic and the Spirit of Capitalism*. New York: Scribner's.
1946   *Essays in Sociology*. New York: Oxford University Press.
1947   *The Theory of Social and Economic Organization*. New York: Oxford University Press.

Weick, Karl E.
1976   "Educational organizations as loosely coupled systems." *Administrative Science Quarterly* 21 (March): 1-19.

Wilensky, Harold L.
1965   "The professionalization of everyone?" *American Journal of Sociology* 70 (September): 137-58.

Woodward, Joan
1965   *Industrial Organization, Theory and Practice*. London: Oxford University Press.

Zald, Mayer N., and Patricia Denton
1963   "From evangelism to general service: the transformation of the YMCA." *Administrative Science Quarterly* 8 (September): 214-34.

16.   Managerial Strategies, the Unions and the Social Integration of the Work Force*

Duncan Gallie

The objectives of this study were to examine the implications of advanced automation for the social integration of the work force within the capitalist enterprise, for the structure of managerial power, and for the nature of trade unionism. The principal conclusion of the research is that the nature of the technology *per se* has, at most, very little importance for these specific areas of enquiry. Advanced automation proved

---

* "Managerial strategies, the unions and the social integration of the work force," by Duncan Gallie from chapter 12 of *In Search of the New Working Class*. Copyright © 1978 by Cambridge University Press. Reprinted by permission.

perfectly compatible with radically dissimilar levels of social integration, and fundamentally different institutions of power and patterns of trade unionism. Instead, our evidence indicates the critical importance of the wider cultural and social structural patterns of specific societies for determining the nature of social interaction within the advanced sector.

THE TRANSFORMATION OF WORKER ATTITUDES AND ASPIRATIONS?

Our first aim was to investigate empirically the implications of automation for worker attitudes. We can compare our findings with the theses that have been put forward by Robert Blauner and Serge Mallet. Broadly speaking, both of these authors shared the view that the main traditional sources of grievance in industry — salaries, and problems deriving from the nature of the work task and of work organization — were no longer of any salience. On the other hand, they differed sharply in their views about the implications of automation for attitudes to management. Blauner believed that it leads to a high degree of consensus and harmony between management and the work force, whereas Mallet has argued that it produces a new revolutionary consciousness aiming at a radical restructuring of the institutions of power within the enterprise.

The Disappearance of Traditional Sources of Grievance?   From the outset, we found that both Mallet and Blauner were clearly mistaken in their belief that salaries would necessarily lose their importance as a focus of grievance in continuous-process industry. The most striking point to emerge from our data was the sharp contrast between the French and British workers in their degree of satisfaction with their incomes and their standard of living. The British were broadly speaking content; the French dissatisfied. This was not simply a marginal grievance for the French workers: it was the dominant source of their resentment about their situation as manual workers in French society. It led directly to strikes for salary increases despite the possibility that the workers were taking substantial long term risks with their own physical safety by closing down the units rapidly.

Further, there was a sharp difference between the French and British workers in their degree of satisfaction with the salary structure. The French were deeply convinced that the principles determining salary allocation within the industry were unfair; the British, on the other hand, were overwhelmingly satisfied with them.

Turning to the experience of the work situation, we found that although there was a fair measure of truth in the argument that many of the traditional hardships of the work task, and many of the worst features of the work environments of traditional mass production industry, had been eliminated, Blauner's description of the typical work task was a generalization of what was, in reality, the work of only a very small section of the work force. The work of most of the operators was substantially less advantageous than Blauner suggested, and the most common attitude towards work in our refineries was one of indifference. It is extremely doubtful whether automation leads to the overcoming of alienation in work in any profound sense of the term.

Moreover, and here our findings confirm the view of Pierre Naville, it is clear that the highly-automated work setting generates its own set of problems, and these can become an important source of worker grievance.

In the first place, continuous-process production requires shift work, and this imposes powerful constraints over the operators' total pattern of life. Shift work was considered intrinsically undesirable by the majority of operators in each of our samples in both France and Britain. It was seen as a major source of ill-health, and as a disruptor of family and social life. However, although the issue was an important one to workers in both countries, a salient point that emerged from our study was that the French workers had developed a much higher and more sustained level of militancy. From the mid 1960s the French unions were fighting for an extensive programme of reform of shift work conditions, and the question of shift work became one of the most central issues of dispute between management and the work force in the late 1960s and the early 1970s.

A second important area of potential conflict related to the level of manning. One of the distinctive features about continuous-process technology is that it is extremely difficult to define what constitutes a satisfactory level of manning, even from the sole viewpoint of technical efficiency. This ambivalence provided a fertile source of friction since management and workers had substantially different interests as to the way in which the problem should be resolved. Management in both countries was primarily concerned to reduce labour costs by reducing manning levels. The work force, on the other hand, had a strong interest in retaining existing levels or even increasing them, since the level of manning influenced the intensity with which they were required to work, the quality of team life, the degree of inconvenience caused by shift work, and their security in their existing posts and statuses within the organization.

In both countries the issue of manning was central to industrial relations in the second half of the 1960s, and in the early 1970s. Significantly, however, the areas of dispute were resolved peacefully in the British refineries, but led to a substantially higher level of tension in France. Thus, although the problem of manning was inherent in the technology, the extent to which it became a source of discontent with management clearly depended on other variables.

Problems deriving from the work setting had not been eliminated in the highly automated setting, but transformed. The existence of such problems posed an ever-present threat to the stability of management/worker relations, and in both countries they were central to industrial relations. The extent to which the problems were resolved peacefully, or became a source of overt conflict between management and the work force, differed sharply between the two countries, with the French refineries revealing a much higher level of social tension.

Attitudes to Management.   None of the existing studies provide us with any direct evidence on the way workers in highly automated plants perceive management or feel about the prevailing structures of authority. Given the crucial importance of these themes to their arguments, one of the major tasks of our study clearly had to be that of providing data directly focused on this problem.

Our first approach was to look at the types of criticism of management that workers mentioned spontaneously, on the grounds that this was the most reliable method of finding out what was most important to them. What emerged was that the type of criticism differed sharply between the French and British refineries. The British workers' criticism was principally 'technical' criticism, or criticism of the efficiency with which management carried out its duties. It is notable that these criticisms were not accompanied by a demand for greater control by the work force. The predominant feeling seems to have been that it was management's job to manage, but that management needed to put its house in order. What these criticisms appeared to reveal was a high level of identification with the underlying objectives of management — a commitment to increased rationalization and efficiency.

In France, in contrast, criticism mainly took the form of 'relational' criticism. It was concerned with the way the exercise of authority affected the worker's identity, with the worker's subjective experience of authority. The most central criticism concerned the high degree of social distance that was felt to exist between management and the work force. Management was seen as aloof and cold, fundamentally uninterested in the workers as human beings.

The existence of more strained relations between management and the work force in the French refineries was confirmed by two closed questions we asked. The first, focusing directly on the perception of social distance between management and the work force, revealed that the French workers were twice as likely as the British to feel that relations were distant. The second examined the workers' perception of management's motives. Just as we would expect from the nature of their spontaneous criticisms, the British workers revealed a 'cooperative' image of the firm in which management was seen as working in the interests of everybody, whereas the French workers had an 'exploitative' image of the firm in which management was seen as primarily concerned with furthering the interests of shareholders.

This data provided support for neither Mallet nor Blauner. In the first place, it was clear that the problem of control of management decision making was not a salient grievance in any of the refineries. Concern for the issue of control was confined to a very small minority of workers, primarily concentrated in the French factories, and for the most part active in the French trade union movement. As it stands, then, Mallet's thesis has to be rejected. On the other hand, the data are not a great deal more encouraging for Blauner. Blauner had led us to expect that management/worker relations in the highly automated sector would be characterized by a very high level of harmony and by the existence of a sense of belonging to a common community. Certainly the British data seemed to fit this model. There was no explicit dissatisfaction with the structure of power, and the types of criticism that were made of management did indeed suggest an underlying consensus about organizational goals. But against this, we have to place the fact that the French data, far from revealing the existence of harmonious relations, indicate that the enterprise was seen by the workers as socially dichotomous, and exploitative. In short, Blauner's thesis of harmonious relations proves, under the light of cross-cultural analysis, to be culturally specific and cannot be taken as a general concomitant of advanced technology.

The second approach we adopted was to create a direct measure of the legitimacy of the formal structure of power, on the grounds that this would reveal the latent attitudes that existed.

The most striking characteristic of the data was again the sharp divergence between the responses of the French and British workers. The French felt that the existing structure of power was illegitimate, and a clear majority would have been prepared to see an extension of worker control over management's powers of decision into the very heart of the traditional areas of managerial prerogative, including the most fundamental strategic decisions about financial budgeting and new investment. In contrast, the British workers showed a high level of contentment with the existing procedures of decision making, and it was notable that even in those areas in which they recognized that they were excluded from any influence (such as high level economic decisions) on the whole they regarded this as perfectly legitimate. They appear to have believed in the value of a division of labour in which it was perfectly proper that management should be allowed to take certain crucial decisions in a relatively unfettered way.

Once more, then, considering attitudes to power at this more latent level, it is apparent that neither Mallet nor Blauner provide us with a satisfactory account. Neither author anticipated, or can explain, the fact that in almost identical technological situations workers should have radically divergent attitudes to the structure of power in different countries.

The most important characteristic of our data is the quite fundamental divergence between the attitudes of the French and British workers. In particular, we can note five major differences:

1. The French workers were dissatisfied with their salaries and standard of living, whereas the British workers were relatively satisfied.
2. The French workers were considerably more militant over common problems emerging from the work process — namely shift work and manning.
3. The French workers were considerably more critical of the state of social relations between management and the work force. They saw relations as dichotomous and socially distant, whereas the British workers saw them as relatively friendly.
4. The French workers had an 'exploitative' image of the firm, whereas the British workers had a cooperative image.
5. The French workers regarded the formal structure of power in the firm as illegitimate, whereas the British workers regarded it as legitimate.

In short, if social integration is defined in terms of a high level of commitment to the key substantive and procedural norms of the enterprise, the British workers showed a relatively high level of social integration and the French workers a relatively low level.

It is important to be clear that we cannot conclude on the basis of our data that advanced technology has no effect whatsoever on the degree of social integration into the firm. Although the critical determinants of worker attitudes clearly lie elsewhere, it may nonetheless be the case that technology has some influence within a specific national context. An examination of whether this is in fact the case would require a different research design. But what our evidence does suggest is that theories that automation *necessarily* leads to a high degree of social integration, and theories that it *necessarily* leads to new forms of class conflict are both mistaken. Further, we would argue that, given the high degree of polarization that we have found between the attitudes of the French and British workers, it is improbable that the characteristics of advanced technology are of any substantial importance in explaining the degree of social integration of workers within the enterprise.

THE FORMAL STRUCTURE OF POWER, THE UNIONS, AND THE SOCIAL INTEGRATION OF THE WORK FORCE

A satisfactory explanation of the differences we have found between the attitudes of the French and British workers to the firm would be complex, and require analysis of the historical development of French and British social structure. We can, however, try to break into the chain of causality at a specific point, and ask what are the more immediate factors that generate, and reinforce, these specific patterns of attitude. Our suggestions here are tentative, and there is no claim that the data are sufficient to confirm them. They are put forward as an interpretation that we believe makes greater sense of the data than theories taking technology as their starting point.

In Part one, we pointed out that existing theories of the implications of automation had failed to give an adequate account either of the institutions of managerial power within the factory or of the nature and role of the trade unions in the advanced sector. In Parts two, three and four we have explored these questions in greater depth, and we now suggest that the empirical inadequacy of existing theories derives, in part, precisely from their neglect of these factors. The French and British refineries had very different managerial systems and very different patterns of trade unionism and these contributed in important ways to creating quite distinctive patterns of social interaction in the refineries in the two countries.

Starting at the most immediate level, we would suggest that the differences between the attitudes of the French and British workers could be best understood as the result of the interaction of the workers' specific patterns of aspiration and normative expectation with fundamentally different institutional systems of power.

The Formal Structure of Power.   The first point to note is that the institutions of power in the refineries in the two countries were radically different. The existence of important differences between managerial styles in French and British industry has frequently been recognized in the literature, although these comparisons tend to be highly impressionistic and their implications left unanalysed. However, the greater authoritarianism attributed to French management is commonly seen as a result of the relatively late development of French industrialization, and hence the prevalence of small family firms in which the employer felt that he had the right to exclusive control of a factory which was legally his own property. Consequently, it has been suggested that, as economic development progressed, French firms would adopt a 'constitutional' system of authority, and would accept the institutional integration of the trade unions.[1] A process of convergence would occur, and power would come to be wielded in a broadly similar way in the different advanced industrial societies.

However, our evidence suggests that this view is basically incorrect. France and Britain have now reached similar levels of overall economic development, and it emerges from our study that *even in the most technologically advanced sector of industry* in the two countries no such process of convergence is under way. Instead, the institutional systems of the newly emerged highly automated sectors appear to have been assimilated by, and firmly locked into, quite distinctive wider national patterns. In Britain, our highly automated factories were just a little earlier than others in making a further extension of the principles of 'constitutionalism', but in the light of the whole decade they remained unexceptional. In France, there had been a shift away from the more authoritarian forms of management that characterize many firms in the traditional sector; however, it was not a move towards 'constitutionalism', but a shift in the direction of an advanced form of paternalism. There was no sign of the two systems becoming increasingly similar over time; rather, during the 1960s they moved further apart.

Our French and British factories, then, were characterized by markedly different structures of power. In the French refineries, managerial power within the factory remained formally absolute, and the representatives had no rights of effective control over decision making. Although management was unquestionably relatively generous in fostering the social activities of the Works Committees, it excluded them from an effective influence over questions of work organization. Similarly, although management had accepted the presence of the unions before it was legally obliged to, it had at no point recognized their right of control over any aspect of refinery organization.

Where the French employers did agree to negotiate with the unions was in the industry-level Parity Commissions. In particular, it was at this level that salary negotiations were formally supposed to take place, although negotiations were restricted to only part of the workers' overall salary, and the rest remained discretionary. In practice the centralization, the very limited terms of reference, and the formal brevity of the meetings prevented any meaningful process of bargaining from taking place. Meetings invariably ended with a unilateral decision by management.

The institutional system in the British refineries was very different. The shop floor representatives had achieved effective control (in the sense of possessing veto power) over a wide range of aspects of work organization, including work conditions, grading, manning levels, deployment of personnel, and use of contractors. Formal negotiations with the unions, which took place at the highly decentralized level of the individual plant, were concerned with the overall salary that the worker received, and there was not a single instance in which negotiations had not been concluded by a signed agreement. In the course of the 1960s, with the introduction of productivity bargaining, there was an evolution in the pattern of negotiation, in which the stewards became steadily more central in the system of formal negotiation.

Broadly speaking, French management remained sovereign within the enterprise, whereas British management had conceded substantial rights of negotiation to the trade unions. Automation appeared perfectly compatible with two fundamentally different institutional systems. But it seems likely that these two systems had very different implications for the quality of relations between management and the work force.

Worker Expectations.   It is no more probable that particular systems of power *directly* determine attitudes to the firm than specific forms of technology. In both cases, the response of workers to these objective factors will be mediated by their expectations. We would suggest that, given the salience of egalitarian values in the working-class sub-cultures of most Western societies, there will be a general tendency for low participatory systems to generate significantly higher levels of discontent with the firm than institutional systems that allow a significant share in decision making to the people employed. But, in the particular cases we were studying, the situation was unquestionably made more complex by the fact that the French had higher expectations than their British equivalents. It is significant, for instance, that although they earned more than their British colleagues in real terms, and although they were better off in terms of both the national and regional manual worker averages, the French workers were substantially less satisfied with their standard of living. Equally, we have seen that although aspirations for control were not at the forefront of their minds, when they replied to direct questions about the ideal level of control that workers should exercise over the decision-making process, the French felt that workers should have substantially more extensive control than was desired by their British equivalents.

On both substantive and procedural issues, then, the French workers had higher expectations. Moreover, in chapter 6, we saw that in their procedural expectations our French samples were in no way peculiar in their radicalism, but shared a wider cultural characteristic of the French working class. If anything, the French refinery workers appeared to be a little more conservative than the average French worker in the extent of control they wanted to exercise over the enterprise. The restricted reference groups and the relatively high level of income satisfaction of higher paid manual workers in the wider British working class have been documented by W. G. Runciman in *Relative Deprivation and Social Justice*.[2] It seems quite possible that the differences between our French and British samples reflected more general differences between the working classes of the two societies.

The problem of why the French workers should have had higher aspirations is unquestionably a complex one, and there can be no serious attempt to come to grips with it here. Other data that we have collected, and that we will be presenting in a separate publication, indicate that these differences in level of aspiration are rooted in different reference groups, in different images of society and in different conceptions of social justice. These cultural factors are themselves probably related to the broader social structural characteristics of each society, and may well have their origins in distinctive historical experiences.

However, at the relatively immediate level with which we are concerned here, we would stress that these cultural factors were reinforced and given relevance to the work situation by the continuous and systematic agitation of the French unions. The influence of the unions appears to have been substantial, although the French workers by no means simply assimilated union ideology. For instance, both the major French unions incessantly advocated abolition of the private enterprise system, but a majority of the French workers remained unconvinced. Similarly, the French workers rejected the legitimacy of the unions' constant attempt to associate 'industrial' and 'political' issues in shop floor agitation. But where the unions do appear to have been influential is in mobilizing resentments against specific aspects of the work situation, and in providing the leadership necessary to contest management in a situation of a very high level of managerial power. For it must be remembered that, given the cost of opposition under more authoritarian systems, there is not necessarily a direct link between the level of resentment and militancy and, indeed, there will probably be important pressures to submit, and to lower aspirations, rather than take the risks of contestation. Union leadership, then, becomes a crucial intervening variable for the effective organization of collective action, and involvement in such action is likely to be important in reinforcing, and possibly intensifying expectations. We saw, in chapter 4, that the most convincing explanation for the mobilization of the refinery workers into regular participation in industrial action in the 1960s is the success of the intense union agitation over shift work and manning levels. This appears to have broken down any sense of oil refinery workers forming a distinctive group within the working class, with privileged conditions of work, by emphasizing the social costs that automation involved. This, in turn, set in motion the dynamics of a system in which a high level of aspiration encountered autocratic institutions of decision making.

The Interaction of Expectations and the Structure of Power.   A critical difference, then, between our French and our British cases was that the French workers, with higher substantive and procedural expectations encountered an institutional system that allowed a very much lower degree of participation in the decision-making process. This made it far more likely that they would reject the basic procedures of decision making as illegitimate, that they would be dissatisfied with the substantive rules of the organization, and that they would have an image of management as essentially exploitative. We have set out the reasons why this is likely to be the case in chapter 8. In summary, we suggested that:

First, in societies in which the value of equality is salient, low participative systems are likely to create normative conflict and hence the institutions of power are likely to be regarded as illegitimate by the work force.

In both countries workers had expectations for a certain degree of control but the evidence suggests that the French workers had higher expectations than their British equivalents, although they too accepted the fundamental tenets of a private enterprise system. In France workers had higher expectations for control but were confronted by an institutional system that offered a substantially lower degree of control. This created a higher degree of normative conflict, and a lower degree of legitimacy for the procedures of decision making.

It is important to note, however, that procedural aspirations were not of great salience to workers in either country. The degree of normative conflict over procedural rules was primarily important in contributing to a lower degree of acceptability of those substantive decisions that were important to workers, and for the implications of this for the attitude to the firm.

Second, a low participative system tends to reduce the likelihood of agreement over the substantive rules of the organization. This is because it deprives management's decisions of procedural legitimacy, it makes them more likely to appear as coercive, it reduces the probability of preliminary attitude change, and it discourages a process of exchange. At any given level of relative deprivation over substantive issues the more likely are the workers to accept organizational norms the higher the level of participation.

This, we would suggest, helps to explain the much higher level of dissatisfaction of French workers over organizational decisions. For instance, although problems of shift work and manning presented equally crucial issues to both the French and British workers, the French, faced with a substantially more autocratic system, were considerably less satisfied with the decisions that were taken and reacted with much greater militancy.

On the central issue of salaries, our evidence suggests that the French both had higher aspirations than their British equivalents, and were confronted with a system which was less likely to win their loyalty to compromise solutions. These two factors reinforced each other in generating a higher level of resentment.

Third, a low participative system, by creating normative conflict, by increasing resentment over specific decisions, by creating a pattern of work organization less satisfactory to the work force, by generalizing insecurity, and by channelling effective attempts to influence decisions exclusively into overt displays of power, tends to create an exploitive image of the firm. It seems likely that the more egalitarian the values of the work force, the more intensely this effect will be produced. Moreover, the pattern will presumably be reinforced over generations as one generation socializes another into its own definitions of reality. Although we can expect the attitudes of new recruits to the organization, coming into the work force for the first time, to be of low intensity and relatively plastic, they will already be predisposed towards an alienative interpretation of events in the factory, and thus will be particularly susceptible to the dynamics of a low participative system.

As we have seen, the French and British workers had sharply divergent images of management and the firm. The French workers regarded the firm as exploitive, whereas the British workers had a co-operative image of the firm. We should suggest that this can be accounted for by the fact that the French workers were somewhat more committed to egalitarian values than their British equivalents, but were confronted by a substantially less participative institutional system.

The Control System and Social Distance.   The differences between the institutions of decision making in the French and British refineries were paralleled by substantial differences in the methods by which French and British management sought to control the work performance of their personnel. This, we would suggest, was not accidental and it had important implications for the quality of social relations in the factory.

We investigated the nature of the control process in the highly automated setting in chapter 9. We found that, although Blauner was correct in emphasizing that a highly automated technology encouraged a certain degree of decentralization of control over the immediate work process to the operator teams, this decentralization had been pushed substantially further in the British refineries than in the French, it affected only one of several possible sources of managerial control, and it was largely irrelevant for the maintenance workers who made up a substantial proportion of the work force of each refinery.

Broadly speaking, British management had decentralized the control of the everyday work process to the work team among the operators, and had adopted a low power personal control system for the maintenance workers. French management, on the other hand, exercised a much tighter grip over the control process through higher ratios of supervisors to workers, through the implementation of a salary system that enabled it to penalize the work performance of individual workers, and through the adoption of a more severe system of disciplinary sanctions for more important failures in work performance or breaches of the rules.

It seems very possible that these different systems of control were to a considerable degree influenced by the nature of the institutions for decision making. British management had adopted a strategy involving a higher degree of participation of the work force, and this gave a greater degree of legitimacy to the authority structure and the decisions that emanated from it. At the same time it was probably an important factor in reducing the sense of opposition between management and worker objectives, and creating a certain degree of identification of the work force with management's own goals. Management then could count on a relatively high degree of motivation on the part of the workers, and could therefore more safely risk adopting a control system which relied little on direct managerial intervention but rather emphasized the control of the individual by his colleagues in the work team.

French management, by insisting on the preservation of an institutional system that gave the work force little or no control over the pattern of work organization and the conditions of life in the factory, succeeded in maximizing its autonomy in decision making, but at the same time confronted itself with considerable problems at the level of work motivation and the control of work performance. Since there was no assurance that the consent of the work force had been obtained when decisions on sensitive issues were made, French management had to anticipate a substantial degree of latent resentment which could well have important consequences for work performance. Since such discontent was likely to be a generalized phenomenon, it was doubtful whether the work team could be relied upon to provide as effective a system of control of individual deviance as in the British case. French management's adoption of a much tighter control system, in which management intervened much more directly, could be seen as a fairly logical response to an awareness of the risks of low involvement inherent in a system of low participation.

But we would argue that the choice of control system had, in turn, important implications for the quality of everyday relationships between management and the work force. It was central to the argument put forward by both Blauner and Woodward that the reduction of management's role in the control system was of major importance in making possible a closer, more consultative, relationship between management and the work force. The logic of this argument seems perfectly sensible, and our main criticism of these theorists is that they adopted too restrictive a conception of the control system, and that this led them to overemphasize the extent to which technology influenced it.

Where, as in the British refineries, the reduction of management's intervention in the control system in fact occurred, it was indeed associated with substantially closer relationships between managers and workers. On the other hand, where, as in France, management intervention remained prominent, this was associated with considerably colder and more distant relations. The French middle managers were deeply involved in the administration of the control system and this placed a considerable strain on their relationships with a work force that felt not only that it was being permanently judged, but that it was being judged arbitrarily. The importance of this can be seen in the fact that the most salient criticism by the French workers of the organizational structure of the refineries was precisely the degree of social distance between management and the work force, and that the French workers were twice as likely as the British to feel that relations were distant.

Managerial Strategies and the Trade Unions.   We have argued that one important factor contributing to the lower degree of social integration of the French workers was the formal structure of power in the French factories. This immediately raises the question of why the institutions of power should have been so different in the two countries? A full explanation would again be a very complex one, but we can, at least, consider some of the more immediate factors involved.

In the first instance, we would suggest that the two institutional systems reflected quite distinctive managerial strategies for ensuring effective work performance. In France management's strategy was paternalistic, and involved creating a sense of the individual's direct dependence on the firm for his well-being. The success of this strategy required that management should preserve the highest possible level of discretion over the reward system, and should defend a set of institutions that barred the representatives from any real say in the decisions that determined the substantive rules of the organization. British management, on the other hand, adopted a semi-constitutional strategy, and sought to ensure effective performance by obtaining the explicit consent of the work force to rules governing work organization and terms of employment. This required reducing the more obviously coercive aspects of power, and encouraging an institutional system that emphasized the joint character of decision making, and symbolized this in the form of the agreement.

But if the institutional system can be seen as relatively consciously designed to achieve managerial objectives, this raises the question of why French management should have wanted to, or was able to, maintain a system which had the disadvantage of generating substantial ill-will, and therefore involved substantial risks of under-mining the motivation and commitment of the work force.

In the first place, it seems probable that French managers were socialized into a rather different managerial culture from that of their British equivalents with different normative assumptions about the importance of preserving managerial prerogative. This was certainly the view of one of our British Refinery Managers who had got to know one of his French equivalents at an international conference. He quite acutely summed up the differences in their approach:

> I coax things along. I don't believe in insisting all the time on managerial prerogative. I don't think one should allow oneself to get het up by problems. I think, R. (the French Director) allows himself to get anxious about things too quickly. He lives by emergencies. He thinks he's defending capitalism and all that. He's looking for fights with the unions. Of course, the French managers come from the elite engineering schools whereas we're drawn from the gutter. R. believes in imposing things while I believe in getting people to agree to them.[3]

And, later in the interview:

> The Industrial Relations Officer probably thinks I'm a bit starry-eyed. But I try to put myself in the position of a spectator watching management and the unions, and not to feel completely identified with the Company. The moment you get identified you start worrying too much and get too excited. R. (the French Director) completely identifies himself.

and that's why he sees it as a sort of war. And he starts worrying about the effects on the economy of what he's doing, and not just what's going on in the refinery.

However, it would be a mistake to account for French management's commitment to its strategy simply in terms of some hangover of irrational and archaic attitudes deriving from the long predominance of small family firms in French industry. French management could, and did, justify its methods on highly pragmatic grounds — namely that they led to substantially higher levels of industrial efficiency. Quite how far this was true is difficult to say with precision. Given the complexity of pricing in the oil industry, refinery profits or losses are apparently largely fictional, and there is no easily available indicator of overall relative efficiency. But there certainly appeared to be a clear consensus that maintenance work was substantially faster and better organized in the French than in the British refineries and, given the enormous costs involved in a capital intensive industry with each additional day that a unit is out of action for maintenance, the financial implications of this must have been very significant. We saw in chapter 5 that British management was severely criticized by the workers themselves about the poor organization of maintenance work, and one of the British Refinery Managers, while warning us that comparisons of relative efficiency were extremely difficult to make with precision, told us:

If you take the completion time for overhaul, the French certainly seem to get them done more quickly. A crude unit seems to take about two weeks there compared to six weeks here. London is often putting pressure on us about maintenance. In fact maintenance is a big subject of discussion now in the Company. They're getting worried about just how big a cost maintenance is. Recently D.R. went across to Dunkirk to compare maintenance procedures and was pretty impressed. But he found them very secretive about information.[4]

It was later confirmed to us at the Company's Head Office that this estimate of the difference in time that it took to carry out maintenance overhauls in the refineries in the two countries was a fair one. Moreover, given the structure of power in the French refineries, French claims for greater efficiency are not altogether implausible. Management could draw up a blueprint for the organizational structure that would maximize efficiency, and then quite simply impose it by fiat. British management, in contrast, by adopting a semiconstitutional strategy, necessarily accepted powerful constraints on its freedom of action. Negotiation could only be made attractive if there was a genuine belief among the representatives that, by accepting responsibility for agreements, they would be able to achieve substantially better terms than if they refused to participate. British management, then, particularly on the craft side, was forced into making concessions that would have made French management shudder. In a semi-constitutional system, there is a risk that the process of organizational change may become much slower, and very much more time consuming for management. If the paternalist strategy risks creating deep resentment, the semi-constitutional strategy may impose significant constraints on management's efforts to maximize efficiency.

We have seen that our French and British refineries had been to a considerable extent assimilated into the institutional patterns characteristic of larger firms in the wider society. One must clearly be very cautious in generalizing from case studies, but this at least raises the question of whether one important factor in the strikingly different performance of French and British industry in the 1960s and early 1970s might not lie in the very substantial differences in the structure of power within firms in the two countries, and in particular in the differential ability of management to introduce rapidly radical technical and organizational change. This is congruent with the view that Britain's industrial weakness stemmed less from a lack of technological innovation than from a failure to *implement* new techniques.

This might be seen as an argument in favour of the reassertion of unlimited managerial power. But, equally, it could be suggested that the disadvantages of the British semi-constitutional system for industrial efficiency are attributable to the fact that it represents a half-way house, giving the representatives primarily a strong veto power with which to defend the interests of their members, and that a more fully participative system might lead to more ready consent on the part of the work force to radical changes since it would be in a position of still greater security, while commitment to the organization's overall goals would be substantially higher. In that case the efficiency of the French system might be achieved without the disadvantages of its very high social costs. Certainly, it would be premature to conclude from a comparison of semi-constitutional and paternalist systems that there is a *necessary* contradiction between efficiency and participation.

Finally, in considering why French management placed a very high price on its freedom of action despite the consequences for the attitudes of the work force, it must be remembered that it believed that it was confronted with a substantially more radical union movement than British management. Indeed, both French Refinery Managers gave this as the principal reason why they thought it would be quite impossible to introduce the type of system that existed in Britain into the French factories. The French managers believed — not altogether without reason — that the French unions would have been extremely difficult to integrate and would have driven very hard bargains before being prepared to legitimate decisions. The cost of ill-will was considered less important than the economic costs that would have been involved in establishing a system allowing a higher level of participation. The institutional system, which had such important consequences for the attitudes of the work force, was in good measure designed to provide a bulwark against the ideologically radical French unions.

We should be careful, then, not to oversimplify the factors involved in the French managers' preference for their own strategy. This was not merely the reflection of commitment to some free-floating cultural belief in the value of undivided power, but it was founded in a complex interpretation of the situation in which they were working, and in their beliefs about the probable outcomes of alternative strategies. But, given that French management had perfectly coherent grounds, in terms of its own value commitments, for wanting to maintain its institutional strategy despite the resentment it generated, we must still ask the fundamental question of how, in the face of such hostility, it was actually able to maintain that strategy.

Here, we would argue that the nature of the trade union movement was crucial. In Part four of this study we have focused on the character of unionism in the advanced sector in the two countries. Our overall conclusion was that, as with the institutions of power in the enterprise, automation had had little significant impact on the pattern of unionism. Rather, powerful trade unions in the wider society, with long-established traditions and well-set modes of ideology and organization, had succeeded in penetrating into the advanced sector, and had assimilated it into the wider patterns of the society.

The major unions in the two countries had fundamentally different conceptions of the role of the trade union in the factory. The French unions saw their task as one of heightening the consciousness of the work force so that it would understand the extent of its alienation within capitalist society and seek a major transformation of the basic institutional structures of society. Their strategy for achieving this was essentially one of sustained ideological warfare in the context of steadily escalating action over concrete disputes with management. The main influence over union ideas and action came from the central union apparatus, the Federation and the Confederation, and the specific demands that the French unions made on management were heavily coloured by their long-term social objectives.

The British unions, on the other hand, conceived of their role in the factory as primarily one of representation. They saw their job as one of forwarding objectives that were consciously and explicitly desired by the work force. Their strategy was to achieve their ends through negotiation backed up by a powerful, well-disciplined, and cohesive organization that would represent such a potential threat in the event of conflict that management was unlikely to risk being unduly unreasonable in negotiation. To achieve this, they were prepared to see the development of a system of exchange with management whereby management helped the union officials in building up the strength of the organization, while the unions gave management a certain degree of help in controlling the work force.

These two types of unionism appeared to have quite different implications for the coercive power that the unions could bring to bear on management. The French unions appear to have achieved a significant degree of success in their primary objective — to enhance the workers' awareness of the exploitative and alienating character of the society in which they lived. However, one consequence of the high level of ideological explicitness and systematization through which they sought to insulate the work force from the dominant cultural beliefs of its society was that the unions were themselves torn apart by ideological conflict, and by a fierce rivalry for the ideological allegiance of the workers. This inter-union conflict was reinforced by a legal system which made it extremely difficult for any one union to establish a stable monopoly of representation, and by the system of regular elections to Works Councils which constantly brought the unions into direct confrontation and provided a permanent measure of their ideological efficacy. Further, the commitment to ideological mobilization contributed to a rather problematic relationship between the union activists and their own base. Their consistent effort to forge explicit links between the issues of the work place and the wider political arena clashed fundamentally with the workers' own belief that political and industrial issues should be kept sharply separated. Their concern to heighten the class awareness of the workers by inserting local conflicts into a wider class struggle led to a constant transmutation of explicit worker demands into a wider programme that had not been legitimated and that made the workers somewhat doubtful about the authenticity of union democracy, reluctant to participate in union decision making, and fickle in their support of union initiatives.

The British unions, lacking any aspiration to mould the consciousness of the workers, or to challenge fundamentally the existing structure of society, concentrated their efforts on the process of organization, and on building up significant countervailing resources of power. Through careful avoidance of divisive issues, close attention to maintaining communications with the membership, and the development of a powerful system of sanctions through the closed shop, the British unions had secured a highly dependable base, and could effectively threaten management with severe economic losses if it failed to take into account their views, or to win their consent on issues which were felt to be of major importance by the work force. Our evidence indicates that British management's strategy was to a large degree determined by its awareness of the power of the unions and of shop floor organization. In Britain the costs of bargaining were outweighed by the costs of conflict. In France, in contrast, management quite correctly believed that the unions were unable to impose major economic losses on the firm, and the cost of conflict was considered negligible compared to the probable cost of bargaining.

It must be remembered, however, that French trade unionists would not consider the success of the British unions in controlling managerial power, and thereby ensuring a more agreeable work environment and a greater sense of security for the personnel, as evidence of the greater *long-term* efficacy of British trade union policies. Rather, they would argue that, in their bid to acquire power over immediate issues, the British unions had, in fact, paid the price of abandoning altogether the drive for really significant structural change. By confining themselves to a unionism of representation, and by deliberately evading controversial issues, the British unions were allowing, and even contributing towards, a progressive integration of workers within the existing structure of capitalist society. For French trade unionists this would be clearly illustrated by the fact that the workers in the British refineries had a 'co-operative' image of management, and legitimated the existing structure of decision making in the enterprise, despite the persistence of immense disparities of power and major inequalities in the distribution of material rewards. Although the French unions had failed to acquire power within the Company in the short term, they would argue that, by emphasizing ideological mobilization, they had made it much more likely that a radical left-wing government would be able to assume state power and, by so doing, had provided the conditions for a much more far-reaching structural transformation of society than would be conceivable in Britain. In support of their position, they could point to the fact that in 1974 the Communist-Socialist alliance failed to win the Presidency by only one per cent of the vote.

This debate about the longer-term efficacy of the two forms of unionism is, for the present at least, well outside the scope of viable sociological analysis, and we raise it here simply to make the point that the same data can be interpreted in two fundamentally different ways.

In broad outline, we have suggested that the advanced sector tends to become to a considerable degree assimilated into the broader social-structural patterns of the particular society in which it emerges. In the factories in the advanced sector that we studied, managerial policies represented relatively progressive versions of two quite distinct national patterns and, in both countries, the most powerful of the unions in the society as a whole had also become the dominant representative of the work force within the refineries. We suspect that some of the differences we found between the dynamics of social interaction in our French and British refineries reflect wider differences between the patterns characteristic of larger firms in the two countries.

In the first instance, it seems to us that the markedly lower degree of social integration within the capitalist firm of the French workers, in comparison to the British workers, resulted from the interaction of higher substantive and procedural expectations on the part of the workers with a much less participative institutional system within the factory. This led to a rejection of the legitimacy of the procedures of decision-making; it produced substantially greater discontent over specific decisions about salaries, shift work, and reorganization; and it reinforced an image of management as exploitative rather than as concerned with the welfare of all. The resentments thus generated, we suggest, posed a major risk of low motivation in work, and this helps explain why French management imposed a tighter system of control over work performance than existed in the British refineries. Although this seemed a perfectly viable way in which management could achieve its objectives, it had the further consequence of increasing friction between middle management and the work force, and heightening social distance within the factory.

The institutional structure, itself, reflected French management's commitment to a paternalist strategy for securing the allegiance of the work force, in contrast to the semi-constitutional strategy that had been adopted in Britain. Although the choice of this strategy may be partly attributable to socialization into distinctive French conceptions of authority that have a long historical tradition, we would emphasize that — at least in the shorter term — it was a perfectly rational strategy for maximizing profit and preserving capitalist relations of production in the context of an ideologically radical trade union movement that would have been very much more difficult to integrate than in the British case.

Most critically, however, the differences between formal institutions of power in the French and British factories resulted from marked differences in the coercive power of the unions in the two countries. The French unions clearly played a major role in sustaining, and reinforcing, the higher aspirations and expectations of the French workers, and in giving these relevance to the immediate work context. However, their commitment to ideological mobilization contributed in important ways to the weakening of their coercive power, and they were unable to bring sufficient pressure to bear on management to enforce any major changes in an institutional system that had substantial costs in terms of the workers' experience of employment. In contrast, in Britain, the unions made little attempt to raise worker aspirations or to influence their wider conception of society but, by concentrating on the development of organizational strength, they placed themselves in a position where it would simply have been too costly for management not to negotiate on those issues that the work force regarded as of major importance.

In the light of the factors which we suggest are important in determining the social integration of the work force, it is clear that we would not make rigid predictions about the *long-term* future pattern of worker attitudes and objectives in the advanced sector of industry. Issues of control might become of central importance for workers in the highly automated setting in either country and, similarly, it is conceivable that the work force could in both countries become socially integrated within the existing capitalist system. But what is essential to our argument is that if either of these developments do occur, *it will not be for the reasons suggested by authors such as Blauner and Mallet*. Rather, it will depend on changing cultural expectations within the wider working class, on changes in management attitudes, and on changes in trade union objectives. Similarly, it would follow from our argument that if these developments do occur, the automated sector will not be particularly distinctive. Rather, it will be participating in a very much broader movement occurring within industry in the particular society.

The interpretation of the data we have given is necessarily provisional. Its detailed assumptions need rigorous testing, and it is quite explicitly focused on certain links of a much more elaborate causal chain. The further explanatory problems it raises — for instance, about the sources of variation in worker expectations and the origins of managerial ideologies — involve complex issues that it would be foolhardy to try to analyze in a few pages. But what we have tried to do is to direct attention to the types of variables which we feel need very much more systematic research. On the whole, empirically orientated researchers in the 1960s directed us to abandon 'metaphysical' conceptions of the working class as a homogeneous social entity, and instead to seek to understand its critical lines of internal differentiation. The major determinants of worker attitudes were seen to lie in the particular type of local industrial or community setting in which specific sets of workers were located. While such local factors may be of some significance, we would suggest that rather more important are certain broader cultural and social structural factors, which can vary between societies and which can create quite distinctive social situations for their respective working classes. For, while the Western nations share a common capitalist mode of production that generates similar conflicts of interest between employers and employed, this underlying system contradiction can have very different consequences at the level of social integration. The crucial mediating variables, we would suggest, are factors like the managerial ideology, the typical structure of power in social institutions, and the ideology and mode of action of the trade union movement characteristic of the specific society. Moreover, if we are to understand the differences between the working classes of the various Western societies, we will need to look much more closely at their pattern of historical development, and examine the way in which different historical experiences have generated distinctive cultural and social structural patterns.

NOTES

[1] See, for instance: S. M. Lipset, "The Changing Class Structure and Contemporary European Politics," *Daedalus,* 1964, 93:1; F. Harbison & C. A. Myers, *Management in the Industrial World* (New York, 1959) and C. Kerr, J. T. Dunlop, F. Harbison & C. A. Myers, *Industrialism and Industrial Man* (2nd ed., London, 1973).

[2] W. G. Runciman, *Relative Deprivation and Social Justice* (London, 1966) especially chapter 10.

[3] Personal initials have been altered for the sake of anonymity in this and the following quotation.

[4] Personal initials have been altered for the sake of anonymity.

REFERENCES

Blauner, R.
1964   *Alienation and Freedom.* Chicago.
Kerr, C., Dunlop, J. T., Harbison, F. & Myers, C. A.
1973   *Industrialism and Industrial Man,* (2nd ed., London, 1973.)
Lipset, S. M.
1964   'The Changing Class Structure and Contemporary European Politics', *Daedalus* 93:1.
Mallet, S.
1969   *La Nouvelle Classe Ouvrière.* Paris.
1971   *Le pouvoir ouvrier.* Paris.
Naville, P.
1962   'Lois Sociologiques et action de masse', *Les cahiers du centre d'études socialistes,* no. 13-14, Jan.
1963   'Planification et gestion démo-
cratique', *Les cahiers du centre d'études socialistes,* no. 23-4.
1963   'Marxisme et Sociologies', *Les cahiers d'études socialistes,* no. 34-5.
1963   *Vers l'automatisme social?* Paris.
1964   *La classe ouvrière et le régime gaulliste.* Paris.
1972   *Temps et travail.* Geneva.
Naville, P.
1961   avec la collaboration de: Barrier, C., Grossin, W., Lahalle, D., Legotien, H., Moisy, B., Palierene, J. & Wackerman, G., *L'automation et le travail humain.* Paris.
Runciman, W. G.
1966   *Relative Deprivation and Social Justice.* London.

17.   Conclusion — Chapters in the History of the Great Industrial Enterprise*

Alfred D. Chandler, Jr.

The comparison of the experience of a sizable sample of large industrial enterprises with that of four pioneers in modern American business administration provides much, though certainly still insufficient, information on which to generalize about the growth and management of this critically important economic institution in the United States. The comparison emphasizes that a company's strategy in time determined its structure and that the common denominator of structure and strategy has been the application of the enterprise's resources to market demand. Structure has been the design for integrating the enterprise's existing resources to current demand; strategy has been the plan for the allocation of resources to anticipated demand. The performance of these companies further suggests that a self-generating force for the growth of the industrial enterprise within a market economy like that of the United States has been the drive to keep resources effectively employed. The same need has shaped the ways, particularly the structure, by which a firm has been managed. Historically then, the role of administration and the function of the administrator in the large American enterprise have been to plan and direct the use of resources to meet the short-term and long-term fluctuations and developments in the market.

Of these resources, trained personnel with manufacturing, marketing, engineering, scientific, and managerial skills often became even more valuable than warehouses, plants, offices, and other physical facilities. Growth and shifts in the location of population, technological developments, and changes in consumer income, all affected the markets to which the administrators applied these resources. Of the two types of administrative decisions, one — the strategic — dealt with the long-term allocation of existing resources and the development of new ones essential to assure the continued health and future growth of the enterprise. The other — the tactical — was more involved in ensuring the efficient and steady use of current resources whose allocation had already been decided.

If the need to use resources provided the dynamic force that changed structure and strategy, the nature of the investment in these resources helped to determine the course and direction of growth and of subsequent structural change. The type of investment, in turn, depended on the technology of production and the techniques of marketing of the individual companies' original product line or lines. Finally, the rate of growth and the effectiveness in the use of the enterprise's resources rested on the ability and ingenuity of its administrators to build, adjust, and apply its personnel and facilities to broad population, technological, and income changes. Although the enterprise undoubtedly had a life of its own above and beyond that of its individual executives, although technological and market requirements certainly set boundaries and limits to growth, nevertheless, its health and effectiveness in carrying out its basic economic functions depended almost entirely on the talents of its administrators.

The market, the nature of their resources, and their entrepreneurial talents have, with relatively few exceptions, had far more effect on the history of large industrial firms in the United States than have antitrust laws, taxation, labor and welfare legislation, and comparable evidences of public policy. Possibly tax regulations have had more of an impact on the strategy of expansion since World War II, but their influence has not appreciably altered broad trends in the structure and strategy of great enterprise. On the other hand, government action such as defense or countercyclical spending that directly affected the market by increasing the national income or by making the government itself a large customer has had a significant effect on the growth of the large enterprise. The changing munitions market was of far more importance, for example, to the history of the du Pont Company than any antitrust action. Antitrust activity has had probably the greatest impact on corporate structure and strategy in those relatively rare cases where it transformed a monopoly into an oligopoly. Yet even in the case of the oil industry, the coming of a huge and entirely new automobile market was as significant as was the breakup of Standard Oil to the strategies and pace of growth of Gulf, Texaco, Shell, Sinclair, Phillips, and other large oil companies.

Historically, the executives administering American industrial enterprises have followed a recognizable pattern in the acquisition and use of resources. The initial acquisition of extensive plant, equipment, and personnel came to meet rapidly growing and often new demands for the products of their company. Or a large enterprise may have come into existence when a number of small firms that had expanded production combined and then consolidated their activities in the face of a temporary decline in demand. To be sure of more certain outlet for their goods, the administrators of enlarged enterprises built their own distributing and marketing (usually wholesaling) organizations; to be assured of essential materials, they obtained control over supplies. Once these resources had been acquired, the executives responsible for the destiny of the enterprise began to pay increasing attention to using them more rationally and efficiently. Among other things, this called for the formation of an administrative structure to mobilize systematically the resources within each functional activity and to coordinate with market demand the flow through and to determine the level of activity within the functional departments.

Then came a second period of growth and a second rationalization of the use of the firm's resources. As the enterprise reached the limits of the existing market set by available consumer income, the state of technology, and the location of population, and as it came to the limits of cost reduction through rational and systematic integration and use of its resources, its senior executives began to seek new markets or new lines of business where they might apply some resources only partially used or where existing ones might be employed more profitably. A threatened decline of existing demand even more dramatically increased the pressure to find new markets. Not only did they seek these overseas but they also took their enterprises into new lines of businesses that were similar enough to its existing activities to permit a transfer of resources. The latter type of expansion was practical, however, only if some skills of some of the personnel and the capacity of some of the facilities could be transferred without too great a cost to new lines. Finally, those companies that did develop new markets or new products then had to reshape the channels of communication and authority within the enterprise. Otherwise, the offices managing the several functional activities lost contact with the new and even the old markets, and the senior executives had increasing difficulty in allocating intelligently the expanded and more varied resources at their command.

Thus four phases or chapters can be discerned in the history of the large American industrial enterprise: the initial expansion and accumulation of resources; the rationalization of the use of resources; the expansion into new markets and lines to help assure the continuing full use of resources; and finally the development of a new structure to make possible continuing effective mobilization of resources to meet both changing short-term market demands and long-term market trends. Although each company had a distinct and unique history, nearly all followed along this general pattern. Because all of them operated within the same external environment, these chapters in the collective history of the industrial enterprise or the history of the enterprise considered as an economic institution followed roughly the underlying changes in the over-all American economy. Of course, the timing of the chapters for the individual companies varied. In the newer industries based on the internal-combustion and electrical engine and on modern chemistry and physics, they came somewhat later than in the older metals or tobacco, sugar, meat packing, and others that processed agricultural products.

In very general terms, then, many of America's largest industrial enterprises initially accumulated their resources in the years between the 1880's and World War I. During the first two decades of the twentieth century, these same firms built their initial administrative structures. For some, continued expansion, largely through diversification, began in the 1920's, but for most it came after the depression of the 1930's. Thus, although the pioneers in the fashioning of a new structural form to manage these expanded resources began their work in the 1920's, most enterprises carried out their major structural reorganizations in the 1940's and 1950's.[1]

THE FIRST CHAPTER — ACCUMULATING RESOURCES

The large American industrial enterprise was born and nurtured in the rapidly industrializing and urbanizing economy of the post-Civil War years. The great railroad construction boom of those years helped swell the population of the agrarian West. It stimulated even more the swift growth of the older commercial centers that serviced the agrarian economy and of the new industrial cities rising to meet the expanding demand for manufactured goods. The railroad itself created a huge new market for the basic iron and steel and machinery industries. The needs of the railroad for vast sums of capital led to the growth of the modern money market in the United States and with it the modern investment banking house, which made it relatively easy later for industrials to tap a wide pool of European and American capital. The construction of the railroads and the rapid urban growth gave work to the unskilled immigrants and farm boys who poured into the larger cities after 1850. The new working force not only provided a supply of labor for the growing industrial enterprises, but also increased the demand for their products. By the 1880's, nearly every existing manufacturing enterprise could reach by railroad a large rural and even more swiftly growing industrial and urban market.

To meet these opportunities, industrial enterprises began to enlarge their productive facilities, labor force, and trained supervisory personnel. Often the new resources were self-generated. The firm's profits provided the funds for further expansion, while the skills of its personnel were developed as the latter carried out their daily tasks. If the enterprise needed outside funds for expansion and combination, it went to the Eastern financial centers. In the 1890's, as railroad expansion leveled off, investment houses that had grown and made their initial reputation in the marketing and handling of railroad securities — firms like J.P. Morgan & Co.; A.M. Kidder & Company; Lee, Higginson & Company; Kuhn, Loeb; Brown Brothers & Company

— all began to float and trade in industrial securities. Also as railroad construction declined, the laborers from abroad and from rural America found work in the enlarged steel mills, oil refineries, meat-packing, electrical, farm machinery, and implement plants.

In meeting the new demand, industrialists had more difficulty in obtaining a distribution network than expanding production facilities. The makers of new types of goods, which were often based on technological innovations, created their own distributing and marketing organizations with warehouses, transportation equipment, offices, and even retail outlets. The makers of the older, more staple commodities, however, generally waited until they had combined and consolidated with their fellows before creating marketing organizations. Combination normally proved to be only a temporary expedient, simply because it led to, and indeed demanded, a limited use of the firm's available resources. Consolidation, on the other hand, permitted the lowering of unit costs through high-volume production for the large market. Even so, the need to keep the consolidated production activities working steadily called for closer coordination with the customer demand through the creation of a marketing organization. Conversely, only firms of large capacity could afford to buy or build and to maintain nationwide marketing facilities.

Consolidation, and with it the formation of a marketing department, was usually followed or accompanied by forming purchasing departments and often by obtaining control of raw materials. Besides making possible the economies of large-scale purchasing, the new department made it easier to coordinate supplies with the needs of the mills for materials. Where there was a possibility of a few outsiders or even of competitors obtaining control of a company's basic raw and semifinished materials, the enterprise often moved into the production and transportation of those materials. The main reason for the purchasing of parts and accessories firms was often to assure the close and steady flow of these parts to the primary assemblying or manufacturing activities. Thus, in many key American industries after the 1880's a few great enterprises took over the several different stages of the industrial processes that, up to that time, had always been operated by separate, relatively small wholesalers, manufacturers, transporters, and raw materials producers.

THE SECOND CHAPTER — RATIONALIZING THE USE OF RESOURCES

The creation of these huge new vertically integrated enterprises was the work of the empire builders of American industry. These men, whose names are among the best known in the folklore of American business, usually turned over the administration of the vast resources they had accumulated to other individuals. Their successors had to develop methods for managing rationally the large agglomerations of men, money, and materials. Often in their eagerness to meet the new market, the empire builders in one industry had collected more facilities and personnel than were really necessary to meet the existing demand. Continuing profits depended on the lowering of costs through the systematizing of operations.

In this second period, this pressing task was twofold. First, unit costs had to be reduced by rationalizing the several functional activities and, second, these functional activities had to be closely integrated to market fluctuations. The first task led to the definition of lines of authority and communication within a single functional department; the second brought a structure for the enterprise as a whole. With the first came the systematizing and improving of the processes and techniques of marketing, manufacturing, and the procurement of raw materials. The final form of the second reflected closely the marketing requirements of the firm's products.

For those enterprises that continued to sell ores or primary metals, the task was the least complicated. Here, the market organization remained small, and the flow could be quickly adjusted to current price. But where fabricated shapes and forms made to exact customer specifications were the products, much closer coordination between the selling and manufacturing activities became necessary. To deliver promptly goods made to a bewildering variety of specifications and at the same time to keep large plants operating fairly steadily necessitated scheduling of a high order of skill. When the line of goods became even more technologically complex, as in the case of electrical apparatus, power machinery, and construction equipment companies, then the coordination of production often became even more difficult than in the steel and metal firms. Also the designing of new or improved products to meet customer needs and to counter the offerings of competitors demanded the close cooperation of the marketing, manufacturing, and engineering departments.

For those companies that also manufactured for the producers' market but whose more standardized products were made in advance of orders, the coordination of resources offered somewhat different challenges. In the companies making explosives, chemicals, industrial rubber, glass, paper, metal containers, trucks and farm implements, small engines, and other power machinery and equipment, the scheduling of the flow through the different departments was more routine than it was for nonstandard goods. But because these products were not tailored to specific orders, increasingly accurate estimates of market demand were required so that the different departments would not be caught with either too much or too little inventory of materials, parts, and finished goods. Since the customers' needs varied, technically trained personnel helped coordinate designing, making, and selling so that the standardized product might be made to fit these different needs.

Those enterprises selling products for use by the mass consumer had still another set of problems. Because they tended to have a much larger volume of goods, not based on specific orders, flowing through their various activities than did the enterprises selling to the producers' market, the flow had to be directed still more closely toward the short-term fluctuations of demand if resources were to be used efficiently. Among the first to be faced with this problem of coordinating high-volume flow were the makers of perishable products like meat and fruit. By the turn of the century, the meat packers, with their heavy investment in distributing and purchasing as well as in the processing of all kinds of meats, had pioneered in such coordination by developing telegraphic communications between the branch houses, the packing plants, and the stockyards. Both the branch houses and the buyers in the stockyards were in constant telegraphic communication with the central offices in Chicago. And with such information, the central office could allocate supply to demand almost instantaneously.

The makers of less perishable consumer goods came to require even more than this instantaneous coordination between supply and demand. The processes involved in converting their raw materials into finished goods readily available for consumer use were more complex and took more time to accomplish than did those in meat packing and some other food industries. This meant a still larger investment in inventory and greater difficulty in adjusting all activities to short-term shifts in demand. Thus the makers of gasoline, tires, tobacco, and some of the less perishable foods began to rely on long-term as well as short-term estimates of the market in order to coordinate and guide product flow through the several departments, and to determine the use of resources within the functional departments.

For the producers of consumer durables, the need was even more critical. Here the investment was still greater, there were more steps in the process, and each functional activity was more complex. To adjust the flow was more difficult and the failure to adjust more costly. Also, because of the relatively expensive materials involved and the relatively high final unit price, the market changes affected unit cost even more than in other industries; that is, in the automobile and appliance businesses variable unit costs rose and fell more sharply with an increase and decrease of output than in most industries. So it was that General Motors and the electrical companies were among the first to develop statistical methods for estimating long-term and short-term demand on which all current activity became based.

In this way, then, the need to apply resources effectively to changes in short-term demand brought the creation of a centralized, functionally departmentalized administrative structure. The functional activities were departmentalized in order to assure effective and rational coordination, appraisal, and planning in each. The central office, in turn, had to make certain the coordination of these different activities in relation to the market. The resulting structure provided a communication network that linked all the facilities involved in the industrial process with the customer's demand. Such a network rendered easier the accurate compliance with specifications as well as rapid and prompt delivery in the producers' goods industries, and the adjustment of volume of output and the making of minor changes in product necessary to meet the fluctuating demands of the mass-consumer-goods industries.

The senior executives at the central office of the functionally departmentalized structures had to make strategic decisions concerning the future allocation of resources as well as tactical ones to assure their efficient current use. Just as operational activities became tied to the short-term estimates of the market, entrepreneurial ones became increasingly based on estimates and forecasts of long-term changes. As the methods for allotting funds, equipment, and personnel became systematized through the development of formal budgets and capital appropriation procedures, their allocation also came to be based on forecasts of the broader economic and financial conditions as well as of the anticipated performance of the specific market. Through such procedures, these executives were able to review, formulate, and approve plans to maintain and expand their share of the existing market. As the structure was worked out, the allocation of future and the application of present resources became more routinized, and basic entrepreneurial decisions became least frequent. But when the responsible executives decided to move into new markets, the older structure began to hinder the efficient allocation and uses of the firm's resources.

THE THIRD CHAPTER — CONTINUED GROWTH

At the end of the first chapter in its history, an enterprise had accumulated enough resources to meet the demands of the national market and often those of foreign ones accessible by steamship and railroad. For the large companies in the older American industries — the metals and foods and some consumer goods like rubber boots and shoes — this period came to an end around the turn of the century. For those in the electrical industry, it lasted somewhat longer; while many large automobile, power machinery, gasoline, tire, and chemical companies were still rounding out this first chapter in the 1920's. At the end of the second chapter, administrators had defined, sometimes with great care and at others in more of an *ad hoc* informal manner, structures to assure more efficient use of the accumulated resources. In the older industries, these structural changes usually came before World War I, for the newer ones in the 1920's and 1930's.

Then, as other firms followed the innovators in developing more efficient purchasing, production, distribution, and above all administrative methods, cost differentials between companies lessened and profit margins dropped. More intensive advertising, product differentiation and improvement, and similar strategies might increase one firm's share of the market, but only major changes in technology, population, and national income could expand the over-all market for a single line of products. As the market became more saturated and the opportunities to cut costs through more rational techniques lessened, enterprises began to search for other markets or to develop other businesses that might profitably employ some of their partially utilized resources or even make a more profitable application of those still being fully employed.

The first step was to develop a "full line" of comparable products.[2] Steel and aluminum firms had "warehouse" lines and special ones for specific industries besides their orders made to customer specifications. The harvester companies built their full line of agricultural implements. The meat packers moved to eggs, poultry, and dairy products to use the refrigerated facilities of their distributing network. The electrical companies developed everything involved in setting up, operating, and maintaining power and light systems. The gasoline companies had their lubricant line. The tire firms made steel rims as well as rubber tires. There are numerous other examples. At the same time, these enterprises intensified their drive to cover the domestic and international market. Expansion overseas often meant the setting up of manufacturing and purchasing as well as marketing facilities. While some companies like International Harvester, Armour, and Swift had invested more than just marketing resources abroad before World War I, many, particularly the chemical firms, only did so after World War II.

More significant than either the filling out of the major line or the move overseas was the development of new products that were often sold to quite different sets of customers. Either new end products might be fashioned from the existing lines or less often wholly new products developed in research laboratories that still employed some of the company's skills and facilities. Sometimes the enterprise began this move by concentrating more on by-products. Often it turned to a brand new field. In either case, the nature of the company's original line and the resulting accumulation of resources determined the extent to which the new products could be developed and new markets captured. In enterprises whose products and processing were based on a highly complex technology, both skills and facilities were most easily transferred to new lines of goods. On the other hand, in those that were less technologically complex and whose resources were concentrated more in raw materials and manufacturing, such a transfer was far more difficult.

Firms whose resources were concentrated in a single function such as transportation had little to transfer besides surplus funds. When a shipping concern, like W. R. Grace & Company, purchased chemical and petroleum companies, it was acting largely as a Wall Street investment house, for it had very few facilities or personnel to re-employ in its new ventures. Many great multifunctional enterprises with vast resources tied up in men and equipment to handle a single line of products have been more reluctant than Grace even to reinvest profits outside of their single major line. They needed funds from their profits to maintain their very large existing investment. When enterprises with few transferable resources, such as the producers and sellers of steel and other metals, and of tobacco, whisky, sugar, and other goods processed from agricultural products, expanded either through merger, or purchase, or the building of new facilities, they usually did so in order to obtain a full line or occasionally to take on allied products for much the same type of market as their own. For comparable reasons, tire and oil companies with huge resources concentrated on a single line have hesitated to embark on a strategy of broad diversification. For some processors of farm products, the task has been easier. A far wider range of products could be made from wheat and milk than from tobacco, bananas, or even meat.

Where a company's resources are invested more in marketing than in raw materials or producing facilities, the opportunity for diversification seems to have been greater. However the enterprises whose resources were the most transferable remained those whose men and equipment came to handle a range of technology rather than a set of end products. In the chemical, electrical and electronic, and power machinery industries, the same personnel using much the same facilities with much the same supplies of raw materials were able to develop new engines, new machines, new household appliances, new synthetic fibers, new films or plastics, or new electrical and electronic devices. Since the enterprises in these industries required the highest of technological skills, their administrators invested increasingly larger amounts of their total resources in research and development. Such resources became less and less tied to any specific product line. As rubber, petroleum, and food companies began to develop technologically advanced skills and facilities, particularly during World War II, they too started to build more of a diversified product line. For all of them, continued growth and with it the accumulation of resources came in their new lines rather than in the old.

THE FOURTH CHAPTER — RATIONALIZING THE USE OF EXPANDING RESOURCES

While the strategy of diversification permitted the continuing and expanded use of a firm's resources, it did not assure their efficient employment. Structural reorganization became necessary. If expansion resulted only in the development of a full line of goods that continued to use much the same type of resources, the reorganization of the marketing department so that it had an office for each major type of customer was usually sufficient. But where business diversified into wholly new lines for quite different customers with quite different wants, then more reorganization was needed. It became increasingly difficult to coordinate through the existing structure the different functional activities to the needs of several quite different markets.

Channels of communication and authority as well as the information flowing through these channels grew more and more inadequate. The wants of different customers varied, and demand and taste fluctuated differently in different markets. Such changing market demands and the actions of competitors brought a growing differentiating of the manufacture and procurement of raw materials for the various product lines. Responsibility for maintaining and expanding the enterprise's share of the markets became harder to pin point. In time, then, each major product line came to be administered through a separate, integrated autonomous division. Its manager became responsible for the major operating decisions involved in the coordination of functional activities to changing demand and taste. Expansion into new regions encouraged the formation of comparable divisions for comparable reasons. Yet, as the different geographical markets became more homogeneous (and this occurred as all parts of the United States became more industrial and more urbanized and suburbanized), the regionally defined divisions in petroleum, dairy products, and container enterprises tended to combine into a single unit for one line of products.

Expansion, primarily through diversification, enlarged the range, number, and complexity of the entrepreneurial activities required of the senior executives. The long-term allocation of resources now involved deciding between the expansion, maintenance, and contraction of personnel, plant, and equipment in several different, large-scale, widespread businesses. The appraisal of existing performance as well as the planning of future uses of resources called for a general office in which the executives were given the time, the information, and the encouragement to develop a broad view, all so necessary for the handling of the new and more complex problems. The multidivisional structure met both the short-term and long-term requirements for the profitable application of resources to the changing markets.

In recent years, the builders of the new organizational structures could look to the model created by du Pont, General Motors, Jersey Standard, and Sears, Roebuck. But before the 1930's, those few firms that had developed lines of business which might have been more effectively administered through a multidivisional structure envisaged only two structural alternatives. To the meat packers, rubber companies, and makers of power machinery, the activities had either to be incorporated into a centralized, functionally departmentalized structure or placed in almost completely independent subsidiaries. In either case, the executives responsible for the destiny of the enterprise had little information about or understanding of how the resources not applied directly to the primary line were being employed. Once the new type of structure became known, as it did during the 1930's, its availability undoubtedly encouraged many enterprises to embark on a strategy of diversification, for the ability to maintain administrative control through such an organizational framework greatly reduced the risks of this new type of expansion.

In fact, the systematizing of strategic decisions through the building of a general office and the routinizing of product development by the formation of a research department have, in a sense, institutionalized this strategy of diversification. Companies whose processes are closely related to the science of chemistry and physics have turned to developing new products steadily in order to assure continuing profitable use of resources that are becoming increasingly based on a technology rather than a product line. The research department develops the products and tests their commercial value. The executives in the general office, freed from all but the most essential entrepreneurial duties, can determine, in something of a rational manner, whether the new product uses enough of the firm's present resources or will help in the development of new ones to warrant its production and sale. If it does and if its market is similar to that of the current line, then its production and sale can be handled through an existing division. If the market is quite different, a new division can and should be formed.

The coming of this new strategy and with it the new structure is of paramount importance to the present health and future growth of the American economy. While some of the new products have been sold in the mass consumer market where, according to some commentators, the technical skills and facilities are sometimes wasted, the largest proportion of the output of the chemical, electronic, electrical, and power machinery enterprises have gone to the producers' market. The industrialist has usually been much more concerned about the performance of what he purchases for his business than the consumer has been in his personal buying, as better performance normally means cutting costs. The institutionalizing of the policy of diversification thus helps to assure continued production of new products to cut costs and raise the efficiency of American industry. Such a development is far more significant to the economy's over-all health than production increases in the older basic industries, such as metals and food. The investment in research and development and in the technical skills and equipment that can handle a range of products within a comparable technology is a far more meaningful index of economic growth in a highly urban and industrial nation that is the output of steel, meat, or even automobiles.

The chapters in the collective history of the American industrial enterprise can be clearly defined. Resources accumulated, resources rationalized, resources expanded, and then once again, resources rationalized. For each individual company, these chapters vary in length, significance, and impact. Some firms never attempted to accumulate the resources essential to meet the demands of a national market. Some of those companies that did expand took longer to rationalize the use of their resources than did others. Some set up new structures very systematically, others more informally. Some began to move into new lines and new markets even before they completed building their initial administrative organization. Again some were much slower than others to join the search for new markets; and again, among those that did, some turned more quickly than others to reshaping the structure necessary for the most profitable employment of the expanded resources. A company like General Motors, by inventing a new type of structure when it first organized its accumulated resources, was able to expand through diversification without requiring further significant structural changes; while Jersey Standard's informal, *ad hoc* mobilization of its resources after 1911 meant that a rapid expansion of facilities and personnel forced a much more difficult and much lengthier reorganization in later years.

Nevertheless, if the great industrial enterprise is considered as a collective entity, then these chapters are more easily identified and examined. And if these chapters have some relation to reality, then they have some significance for the scholar, businessman, and even public officials. However, the data are still too few and the generalizations derived too tenuous and too imprecise to be the basis for suggestions for action. Yet there is some value in presenting even a tentative and partial account of the history of large American industrial enterprise simply because this is a field where myths abound, where more positive generalizations than mine have been made on much less specific data, and where recommendations for action have been seriously proposed on the basis of such generalizations. If it does nothing else, this exploratory study should provide the student of business history and business administration as well as other scholars with some suggestions for significant areas of investigation.

Further researchers in the growth and administration of American industry and business must consider the importance of the market. That the expansion and government of industrial enterprises in a market economy should be closely related to the changing nature of the market seems obvious enough. Yet many writers dealing with principles of business administration, often discuss leadership, communication, and structure with only passing reference to the market. On the other hand, economists, antitrust lawyers, and other experts on market behavior have said little about the impact of the market on corporate administration. The building of the multidivisional structure is, for example, thought to be as feasible in a steel as in a chemical enterprise. Or competition in the steel industry is considered to be comparable with that in the oil or chemical industries, or administrative needs to be much the same in one period of an enterprise's history as in another.

Nor should scholars forget the critical role that the large enterprise in a market economy plays in allocating the nation's economic resources. The success or failure in the allocation of funds, facilities, and skills provides a useful test of the performance and ability of American industrial executives. The criteria for success used by the industrialists themselves — lowering unit costs, increasing output per worker, and long-term return on investment — may by mid-twentieth century, have become too narrow. Yet even if performance is to be evaluated in broader social and human terms, resources can hardly be employed effectively unless the men responsible for their use have relevant information on which to base their decisions and the means to carry them out. Without accurate and meaningful data and without clear-cut lines of communication and authority, they are forced to allocate present and future resources in a haphazard and intuitive way. In all industrial, urban, and technologically advanced societies where the large enterprise, either private or public, has acquired an essential role in planning, coordinating, and appraising economic activities, a lack of systematic structure within these organizations can lead to a wasteful and inefficient use of resources. Further studies of the way in which the great enterprise has grown and become administered have, then, more than mere scholarly value.

NOTES

[1] I did not have the opportunity to read Edith T. Penrose, *The Theory of the Growth of the Firm* (Oxford, 1959), until I had completed my manuscript. While using somewhat different data and asking somewhat different questions, Dr. Penrose's findings have many similarities with mine. Her superlative study focuses on the economics of growth and not on structure and on its relation to strategy. My empirical data, however, certainly do help to support her theoretical concepts about the growth of the firm which are defined more rigorously than the more impressionistic generalizations developed here. Particularly relevant to my generalizations are her Chapter 5, "Inherited Resources and the Direction of Expansion," and Chapter 7, "The Economics of Diversification."

[2] These developments are suggested in somewhat more detail in Alfred D. Chandler, Jr., "Integration and Diversification as Business Strategies — A Historical Analysis," a paper given before the Business History Conference at the University of Illinois, February 14, 1959 (mimeographed).

18. The Origins of Job Structures in the Steel Industry*

Katherine Stone

INTRODUCTION

Recently economists have taken a new look at the labor market, in an attempt to understand the concentration of unemployment and underemployment amongst specific groups. In doing so, they have rejected the neoclassical model of a free and open market allocating labor according to comparative marginal costs and distributing income according to respective marginal productivity. A new set of categories, such

---

* "The Origins of Job Structures in the Steel Industry" by Katherine Stone from *The Review of Radical Political Economics,* vol. 6, 1974. Copyright © 1974 by Katherine Stone. Reprinted by permission of the author.

This paper was first presented at the Conference on Labor Market Stratification, Harvard

as "dual labor markets" and "internal labor markets" and a new set of concepts, such as "hierarchy" and "stratification" have been introduced to better explain the functioning of the labor market.

Yet by and large studies of labor market stratification have taken its essential precondition, the hierarchical division of labor within the enterprise, as a technical fact, while focusing on the struggle among groups of workers for positions within it as the only relevant social issue. Clearly this is a holdover from the neoclassical approach to production, which views all that takes place within the firm as economically efficient adaptations to market conditions. This paper suggests that the division of labor on which labor market stratification is based must itself be seen as a central social issue related to the struggle between capital and labor over the process of production and its material fruits.

This paper attempts to trace the development of labor market structures in one major industry, the steel industry.† The bulk of the paper concentrates on the period between 1890 and 1920, for during that time the essentials of today's labor system took form. The intention is to show that by understanding how various structures came to be, we can better understand what perpetuates them and what might change them.

Part I of the paper describes the labor system of the steel industry in the 19th century, in which skilled workers controlled the production process and made steel by using the employers' capital. This system came into conflict with the employers' need to expand production without giving the workers a substantial share of the proceeds. They therefore moved to break the workers' power over production and all the institutions that had been a part of it — the skilled workers' union, the contract system, the sliding scale for wages, and the apprenticeship-helper system. They were successful, and the prize they won was the power to introduce labor-saving technology and control the production process. They became the sole beneficiaries of innovation.

Part II shows how, under the impact of the new technology, the skilled craftsmen and the heavy laborers were both transformed into semi-skilled machine operators.

Part III presents the efforts of the employers to create a new labor system that would institutionalize their control over production. It deals with the development of three specific institutions that were central to this process: wage incentive schemes, promotion hierarchies, and welfare programs. The employers' reasons for setting up each of these institutions is unraveled, to demonstrate that, far from being inevitable, the institutions were chosen from several alternatives in order to maximize the power of employers over workers. These institutions are the foundation for today's "internal labor market."

Part IV describes the redivision of labor which employers engineered to perpetuate their power. The essence of the redivision was to take knowledge about

University, March 16-17, 1973. The research was sponsored by a grant from the Manpower Administration, U.S. Department of Labor.

I want to give special thanks to Jeremy Brecher, who helped me sift through the evidence and piece together the ideas that went into this article. Without his patience as an editor and his enthusiasm for the project, this paper would never have been possible.

† This paper deals with certain selected aspects of the industry's labor relations. It is by no means intended to be a general survey. Specifically omitted is discussion of the role played by racial and ethnic divisions and the role played by company repression in dispersing discontent.

production away from the skilled workers and to transfer it to the side of management. They accomplished this by devising new ways to train skilled workers, by re-educating their foremen, and by recruiting new types of managers. This redivision of labor created a status and pay hierarchy based on "mental skills," and is the basis of today's education fetishism.

Part V brings the analysis up to the present by describing the only major change in the labor system of the past fifty years, the organization of the United Steel Workers of America. It shows how little the presence of the union affected the institutions employers had earlier set up.

The following major themes, which are elaborated and generalized to other industries in the concluding Part VI, run through the entire paper:

1. Technology, by itself, did not create today's labor system. Technology merely defined the realm of possibilities.
2. The development of hierarchy in the labor force was not a response to the increased complexity of jobs, but rather a device to counter the increased simplicity and homogeneity of jobs.
3. The issues of how work shall be organized, how jobs shall be defined, and how workers shall be paid are points of conflict and class struggle between workers and employers. The structures that emerge can only be understood in those terms. Any explanation based on impersonal market forces or natural economic laws misses the actual historical development.
4. The division of labor of today that separates mental work from physical work is an artificial and unnecessary division that only serves to maintain the power of employers over their workers.
5. The labor market structures that were developed in the early part of this century under the banner of "scientific management" have lasted, in refined forms, until today. No labor movement or reform group has yet developed successful means for overthrowing them and establishing a more rational system for getting work done.

I. The Breakdown of the Traditional Labor System. In 1908 John Fitch, an American journalist who had interviewed hundreds of steel workers and steel officials, described the labor system in the steel industry of his day.

> In every department of mill work, there is a more or less rigid line of promotion. Every man is in a training for the next position above . . . The course would vary in the different styles of mills, as the positions vary in number and character, but the operating principle is everywhere the same. In the open-hearth department the line of promotion runs through common labor, metal wheelers, stock handlers, cinder-pit man, second helper and first helper, to melter foreman. In this way, the companies develop and train their own men. They seldom hire a stranger for a position as roller or heater. Thus the working force is pyramided and is held together by the ambition of the men lower down; and even a serious break in the ranks adjusts itself all but automatically.[1]

Anyone familiar with industry today will recognize this arrangement immediately. It is precisely the type of internal labor market, with orderly promotion hierarchies and limited ports of entry, which economists have recently begun to analyze. When Fitch was writing, it was a new development in American industry. Only 20 years earlier, the steel industry had had a system for organizing production which appears very strange to us today.

Although steel had been produced in this country since colonial times, it was not until after the Civil War that the steel industry reached substantial size. In 1860, there were only 13 establishments producing steel, which employed a total of 748 men to produce less than 12,000 net tons of steel a year.[2] After the Civil War, the industry began to expand rapidly, so that by 1890, there were 110 Bessemer converters and 167 open hearth converters[3] producing 4.8 million net tons of steel per year.[4] This expansion is generally attributed to the protective tariff for steel imports, the increased use of steel for railroads, and to changes in the technology of steel production.

The pivotal period for the U.S. steel industry were the years 1890-1910. During that period, steel replaced iron as the building block of industrial society, and the United States surpassed Great Britain as the world's prime steel producer. Also during the 1890s, Andrew Carnegie completed his vertically integrated empire, the Carnegie Corporation, and captured 25 percent of the nation's steel market. His activities led to a wave of corporate mergers which finally culminated in the creation, in 1901, of the world's first billion dollar corporation, the U.S. Steel Corporation. U.S. Steel was built by the financier J. P. Morgan on the back of the Carnegie Corporation. At its inception, it controlled 80 percent of the United States output of steel.

The following table summarizes the development of the steel industry in the 19th century:

	Pig Iron Production (million tons)	Steel Production[5] (million net tons)
1860	0.9	n.a.
1870	1.9	n.a.
1880	4.3	1.4
1890	10.3	4.8
1900	15.4	11.4

In the 19th century, the steel industry, like the iron industry from which it grew, had a labor system in which the workers contracted wtith the steel companies to produce steel. In this labor system, there were two types of workers — "skilled" and "unskilled." Skilled workers did work that required training, experience, dexterity, and judgment; and unskilled workers performed the heavy manual labor — lifting, pushing, carrying, hoisting, and wheeling raw materials from one operation to the next. The skilled workers were highly skilled industrial craftsmen who enjoyed high prestige in their communities. Steel was made by teams of skilled workers with unskilled helpers, who used the companies' equipment and raw materials.

The unskilled workers resembed what we call "workers" today. Some were hired directly by the steel companies, as they are today. The others were hired by the skilled workers, under what was known as the "contract system." Under the contract system, the skilled workers would hire helpers out of their own paychecks. Helpers earned between one-sixth to one-half of what the skilled workers earned.

The contract system was never fully developed in the steel industry. Often the steel companies paid part of the helpers' wage or provided helpers themselves for certain skilled workers, so that a hybrid system was prevalent. For example, in one iron works in Pittsburgh in 1878, puddlers were paid $5.00 per ton, of which one-third went to pay their helper. The helper also received 5 percent of his pay from the company. In the same works, a heater was paid 65¢ per ton and received one helper, paid by the company, with the option of hiring a second helper whom he would pay himself. The number of unskilled workers who were hired and/or paid by the skilled workers was declining in the late 19th century.[6]

The skilled steel workers saw production as a cooperative endeavor, where labor and capital were equal partners. The partnership was reflected in the method of wage payment. Skilled workers were paid a certain sum for each ton of steel they produced. This sum, called the tonnage rate, was governed by the "sliding scale," which made the tonnage rate fluctuate with the market price of iron and steel, above a specified minimum rate below which wages could not fall. The sliding scale was introduced in the iron works of Pittsburgh as early as 1865, and in the 25 years that followed, it spread throughout the industry. The original agreement that established the system read as follows:

> Memorandum of Agreement made this 13th day of Feburary, 1865, between a committee of boilers and a committee from the iron manufacturers appointed to fix a scale of prices to be paid for boiling pig iron, based on the manufacturers' card of prices.[7]

The sliding scale was actually an arrangement for sharing the profits between two partners in production, the skilled workers and the steel masters. It was based on the principle that the workers should share in the risks and the fruits of production, benefitting when prices were high and sacrificing when prices were low. John Jarrett, the pesident of the iron and steel workers union, referring to another aspect of this partnership, described the system as a

> kind of co-operation offered by the company, in which were certain conditions, the principal of which was that the men agreed to allow the company to retain the first four weeks wages in hand, and also twenty-five percent of all wages earned thereafter, the same to be paid to men at the end of the year, if the profits of the business would justify such payment.[8]

Andrew Carnegie, the largest steel employer of them all, concurred in this view of the sliding scale by saying, "It is the solution of the capital and labor problem because it really makes them partners—alike in prosperity and adversity."[9]

Another effect of the sliding scale was that by pegging tonnage rates directly to market prices, the role of the employer in wage determination was eliminated. Consider, for example, the following account, summarized by David Montgomery from the records of the Amalgamated Association of Iron, Steel and Tin Workers:

> When the Columbus Rolling Mill Company contracted to reheat and roll some railroad tracks in January, 1874, for example, the union elected a committee of four to consult with the plant superintendent about the price the workmen were to receive for the work. They agreed on a scale of $1.13 per ton, which the committee brought back to the lodge for its approval.
>
> There followed an intriguing process. The members soon accepted the company offer, then turned to the major task of dividing the $1.13 among themselves. Each member stated his own price. When they were added up, the total was 3 ¾ cents higher than the company offer. By a careful revision of the figures, each runback buggyman was cut 2 cents, and the gang buggyman given an extra ¼ of a cent to settle the bill. By the final reckoning, 19 ¼ cents went to the roller, 13 cents to the rougher up, 10 cents to the rougher down, 9 cents to the catcher, 8 ¼ cents to each of the four hookers, 5 cents each to the runout hooker and the two runback buggymen, and 13 ¾ cents to the gang buggyman, half of whose earnings were to be turned over to his nonunion helper.[10]

The employers had relatively little control over the skilled workers' incomes. Nor could they use the wage as an incentive to insure them a desired level of output. Employers could only contract for a job. The price was determined by the market, and the division of labor and the pace of work was decided by the workers themselves. Thus, the sliding scale and the contract system defined the relationship between capital and labor in the nineteenth century.

The skilled steel workers had a union, the Amalgamated Association of Iron, Steel and Tin Workers, which was the strongest union of its day. Formed in 1876 by a merger of the Heaters Union, the Roll Hands Union and the Sons of Vulcan, by 1891, the Amalgamated represented 25 percent of all steel workers. Through their union, they were able to formalize their control over production. For example, at Carnegie's Homestead mill, a contract was won in 1889 that gave the skilled workers authority over every aspect of steel production there. A company historian described it this way:

> Every department and sub-department had its workmen's "committee," with a "chairman" and full corps of officers . . . During the ensuing three years hardly a day passed that a "committee" did not come forward with some demand or grievance. If a man with a desirable job died or left the works, his position could not be filled without the consent and approval of an Amalgamated committee . . . The method of apportioning the work, of regulating the turns, of altering the machinery, in short, every detail of working the great plant was subject to the interference of some busybody representing the Amalgamated Association. Some of this meddling was specified under the agreement that had been signed by the Carnegies, but much of it was not; it was only in line with the general policy of the union . . . The heats of a turn were designated, as were the weights of the various charges constituting a heat. The product per worker was limited; the proportion of scrap that might be used in running a furnace was fixed; the quality of pig-iron was stated; the puddlers' use of brick and fire clay was forbidden, with exceptions; the labor of assistants was defined; the teaching of other workmen was prohibited, nor might one man lend his tools to another except as provided for.[11]

John Fitch confirmed this account of worker control at Homestead when he interviewed Homestead workers and managers in 1908. Fitch reported that:

> A prominent official of the Carnegie Steel Company told me that before the strike of 1892, when the union was firmly entrenched in Homestead, the men ran the mill and the foreman had little authority. There were innumerable vexations. Incompetent men had to be retained in the employ of the company, and changes for the improvement of the mill could not be made without the consent of the mill committees. I had opportunity to talk with a considerable number of men employed at Homestead before 1892, among them several prominent leaders of the strike. From these conversations I gathered little that would contradict the statement of the official, and much that would corroborate it.[12]

The cooperative relationship between the skilled steel workers and the steel employers became strained in the 1880s. The market for steel products began to expand rapidly. Domestically, the railroads began to generate high levels of demand for steel, and internationally, the U.S. steel industry began to compete successfully with the British and the German steel industry for the world market. (In 1890, for the first time, U.S. steel exports surpassed those of Great Britain.) The effect of this massive increase in demand was to intensify competition in the U.S. industry. What had been a stable market structure was disrupted by the new markets opening up.

Firms competed for the new markets by trying to increase their output and cut their costs. To do that they had to increase the productivity of their workers — but the labor system did not allow them to do that. For example, from 1880 on, the market price for iron and steel products was falling drastically, so that the price for bar iron was below the minimum specified in the union's sliding scale, *even though* the negotiated minimum rates were also declining. As Peter Doeringer says in his essay on the subject, "the negotiated minimum piece rates . . . became the *de facto* standard rates for the organized sector of the industry during most of the period from 1880 to the end of the century."[13] This meant that employers were paying a higher percentage of their income out in wages than they would have were the sliding feature of the sliding scale operative, or had they had the power to reduce wages unilaterally in the face of declining prices.

At the same time that their labor costs as a percentage of revenue were rising, the labor system also prevented employers from increasing their productivity through reorganizing or mechanizing their operations. The workers controlled the plants and decided how the work was to be done. Employers had no way to speed up the workers, nor could they introduce new machinery that eliminated or redefined jobs.

In the past, employers had introduced new machinery, but not labor-saving machinery. The many innovations introduced between 1860 and 1890, of which the most notable was the Bessemer converter, increased the size and capacity of the furnaces and mills, but they generally did not replace men with machines. Sir Lowthian Bill, a British innovator, who toured the U.S. steel industry in 1890, reported that:

> Usually a large make of any commodity is accomplished by a saving of labor, but it may be questioned whether in the case of the modern blast furnace this holds good. To a limited, but a very limited, extent some economy might be effected, but if an account were taken of the weight of material moved in connection with one of our Cleveland furnaces, and the number of men by whom it is handled, much cannot, at all events with us, be hoped for.[14]

However, in the late 1880s and 1890s, the steel companies needed more than just bigger machines and better methods of metallurgy. Bottlenecks were developing in production, so that they needed to mechanize their entire operations. For example, the problem with pig iron production — the first stage of steel-making — was that with increased demand, the larger blast furnaces could produce pig iron faster than the men could load them, so that the use of manual labor became a serious hindrance to expanding output. As one technical authority wrote in 1897:

> The evolution of the blast furnace, especially the American blast furnace, during the last third of a century has indeed been radical, making the question of getting the material to the furnace and the product away from it promptly, cheaply and regularly — the problem once satisfactorily solved by the cart or sled, and wheelbarrow and manual labor — one of great difficulty and importance.[15]

The steel masters needed to replace men with machines, which meant changing the methods of production. To do that, they needed to control production, unilaterally. The social relations of cooperation and partnership had to go if capitalist steel production was to progress. The steel companies understood this well, and decided to break the union. In 1892, Henry Clay Frick, chairman of the Carnegie Steel Company, wrote to Andrew Carnegie that "The mills have never been able to turn out the product they should owing to being held back by the Amalgamated men."[16]

The strongest lodge of the Amalgamated Association was at Carnegie's Homestead mill; it is no wonder that the battle between capital and labor shaped up there. In 1892, just before the contract with the Amalgamated was to expire, Carnegie transferred managing authority of the mill to Frick. Frick was already notorious for his brutal treatment of strikers in the Connellsville coke regions, and he wasted no time making his intentions known at Homestead. He ordered a fence built, three miles long and topped with barbed wire, around the entire Homestead Works; he had platforms for sentinels constructed and holes for rifles put in along the fence; and he had barracks built inside it to house strikebreakers. Thus fortified, Frick ordered 300 guards from the Pinkerton National Detective Agency, closed down the Works, laid off the entire work force, and announced they would henceforth operate non-union. The famous Homestead strike began as a lock-out, with the explicit aim of breaking the union. Dozens of men were killed in the four months that followed, as the Homestead workers fought Pinkertons, scabs, the Sheriff and the State Militia. In the end, the intervention of the state and federal governments on the side of the Carnegie Corporation beat the strikers. The Works were re-opened with strike-breakers, and Frick wrote to Carnegie, "Our victory is now complete and most gratifying. Do not think we will ever have any serious labor trouble again."[17]

The Homestead strike was the turning point for the Amalgamated Associations throughout the country. Other employers, newly invigorated by Frick's performance, took a hard line against the union, and the morale of the members, their strongest local broken, was too low to fight back. Within two years of the Homestead defeat, the Amalgamated had lost 10,000 members. Lodge after lodge was lost in the following years, so that membership, having peaked at 25,000 in 1892, was down to 10,000 by 1898, and most of that was in the iron industry.[18] The union never recovered from these losses. The locals that remained were one by one destroyed by the U.S. Steel Corporation, so that by 1910 the steel industry was entirely non-union.

With the power of the Amalgamated broken, steel employers were left to mechanize as much as they needed. The decade that followed the Homestead defeat brought unprecedented developments in every stage of steelmaking. The rate of innovation in steel has never been equaled. Electric trolleys, the pig casting machine, the Jones mixer, and mechanical ladle cars transformed the blast furnace. Electric traveling cranes in the Bessemer converter, and the Wellman charger in the open hearth did away with almost all the manual aspects of steel production proper. And electric cars and rising-and-falling tables made the rolling mills a continuous operation.[19] These developments led the British Iron and Steel Institute to conclude after its visit in 1903 that:

> the (U.S.) steel industry had made considerable advances in the ten years ending with 1890. It is, however, mainly since that year that the steel manufacture has made its greatest strides in every direction, and it is wholly since that date that costs have been so far reduced as to enable the United States to compete with Great Britain and Germany in the leading markets of the world.[20]

Several visitors to the steel mills around the turn of the century described the new steel-making processes introduced in the wake of the Homestead conflict. One British economist, Frank Poppelwell, was particularly amazed by the degree to which new innovations were labor-saving. He concluded:

> Perhaps the greatest difference between English and American conditions in steel-works practice is the very conspicuous absence of labourers in the American mills. The large and growing employment of every kind of both propelling and directing machinery—electric trolleys, rising and falling tables, live rollers, side-racks, shears, machine stamps, endless chain tables for charging on the cars, overhead travelling cranes—is responsible for this state of things. It is no exaggeration to say that in a mill rolling three thousand tons of rails a day, not a dozen men are to be seen on the mill floor.[21]

A group of British iron-masters from the British Iron and Steel Institute also toured America in 1903, and they, too, were impressed to find in the blast furnaces that

> the bulk of the heavy drudgery has been obviated by the use of machinery. There is no pig-lifting, no hand shovelling of stock, no hauling of charging barrows. All the tedious clay work around the hearth, the incessant changing of tuyeres, is done away with.[22]

They found that in the rolling mills

> the appliances introduced have effected the best results in doing away with manual labor. A tongs or hook is not seen near any of the rail mills visited, and the whole operation is conducted from a platform, where levers connected with the various live rollers and lifting tables are collected together.[23]

And as far as the open hearth operations were concerned, perhaps the most vivid description was left by J.H. Bridge, an American journalist who wrote a series of articles about the steel industry for *Everybody's Magazine:*

> It is at Homestead that wonders are performed as amazing as those of the Arabian Nights. Here machines endowed with the strength of a hundred giants move obedient to a touch, opening furnace doors and lifting out of the glowing flames enormous slabs of white-hot steel, much as a child would pick up a match-box from the table. Two of these machines, appropriately named by the men "Leviathan and Behemoth," seem gifted with intelligence. Each is attended by a little trolley car that runs busily to and fro, its movements controlled by the more sluggish monster. This little attendant may be at one end of the long shed and the Leviathan at the other; but no sooner does it seem to see its giant master open a furnace door and put in his great hand for a fresh lump of hot steel, than it runs back like a terrier to its owner and arrives just as the huge fist is withdrawn with a glowing slab. This the Leviathan gently places on its attendant's back; and, to the admiration of all beholders, the little thing trots gayly off with it to the end of the building. Even then the wonder is not ended; for the little fellow gives a shake to his back, and the glittering mass, twice as big as a Saratoga trunk, slides onto a platform of rollers which carry it to the mill. And no human hand is seen in the operation.[24]

In this way, the steel masters succeeded in eliminating the bottlenecks in production by replacing men with machines at every opportunity. This mechanization would not have been possible without the employers' victory over the workers at Homestead. Thus we can see how the prize in the class struggle was control over the production process and the distribution of the benefits of technology. As David Brody summarizes it:

> In the two decades after 1890, the furnace worker's productivity tripled in exchange for an income rise of one-half; the steel workers output doubled in exchange for an income rise of one-fifth . . . At bottom, the remarkable cost reduction of American steel manufacture rested on those figures.
>
> The accomplishment was possible only with a labor force powerless to oppose the decisions of the steel men.[25]

The victory of the employers in 1892 allowed them to destroy the old labor system in the industry. They could then begin to create a new system, one that would reflect and help to perpetuate their ascendancy. Specifically, this meant that they had three separate tasks: to adapt the jobs to the new technology; to motivate workers to perform the new jobs efficiently; and to establish lasting control over the entire production process. The next three sections of this paper will deal with each one of these in turn.

II. Effects of the New Technology on Job Structure.   Unlike earlier innovations in steel-making, the mechanization of the 1890s transformed the tasks involved in steel production. The traditional skills of heating, roughing, catching and rolling were built into the new machines. Machines also moved the raw materials and products through the plants. Thus the new process required neither the heavy laborers nor the highly skilled craftsmen of the past. Rather, they required workers to operate the machines, to feed them and tend them, to start them and stop them. A new class of workers was created to perform these tasks, a class of machine operators known by the label ''semi-skilled.''

The new machine operators were described by the British Iron and Steel Institute after their visit in 1903 as men who

> have to be attentive to guiding operations, and quick in manipulating levers and similarly easy work . . . the various operations are so much simplified that an experienced man is not required to conduct any part of the process.[26]

Similarly, the U.S. Department of Labor noted the rise of this new type of steel worker in their report of 1910:

> The semi-skilled among the production force consist for the most part of workmen who have been taught to perform relatively complex functions, such as the operation of cranes and other mechanical or metallurgical knowledge . . . This class has been developed largely within recent years along with the growth in the use of machinery and electrical power in the industry. The whole tendency of the industry is to greatly increase the proportion of the production force formed by this semi-skilled class of workmen. They are displacing both the skilled and the unskilled workmen.[27]

The semi-skilled workers were created by the downgrading of the skilled workers and the upgrading of the unskilled. These shifts proceeded throughout the 1890s and early 1900s, as more and more plants were mechanized. Although there are no hard data on these shifts in job categories,* they are reflected in the change in relative wage rates. Between 1890 and 1910, the hourly wages of the unskilled steelworkers rose by about 20 percent, while the daily earnings of the skilled workers fell by as much as 70

---

* Usually time series data on percentage employed in the different categories are used to demonstrate the changing mix of skill requirements in the industry. For my purpose, however, such data are more misleading than helpful. In part, this is because there is no way to know how the Census Department or the individual steel companies are defining "skilled," "semi-skilled" and "unskilled," so that comparisons between them are impossible. Also, the meaning of the categories changes over time. In 1890, "unskilled" work in the steel mills meant purely manual labor. By 1910, "unskilled" work included simple machine operating jobs, as well as laborers. Similarly, "skilled" work in 1890 meant all workers who had a particular craft. By 1910, "skilled" workers were either maintenance men (mechanics, machinists, etc.) or workers holding supervisory-type functions, directing and coordinating the various men and machines.

The other reason that time series data are not germane is that even when data are available for particular job titles at different periods of time, there is no way to know that the job itself remained unchanged. The following passage from Fitch (op. cit., p. 43) gives us one example of how job titles were changing during this period:

> There were three men regularly employed at an open-hearth furnace — "first helper," "second helper" and "cinder-pit man." The first helper was formerly called a "melter," but now, with a different organization, a melter has charge of several furnaces. In an open-hearth plant there are usually a superintendent and an assistant superintendent in control, a foreman or boss melter in active charge of from three to five furnaces.

percent. Also after 1892, the wage differential between the various types of skilled workers narrowed substantially.† Thus, the British iron masters reported in 1903

> The tendency in the American steel industry is to reduce by every possible means the number of highly skilled men employed and more and more to establish the general wage on the basis of common unskilled labour. This is not a new thing, but it becomes every year more accentuated as a result of the use of automatic appliances which unskilled labour is usually competent to control.[28]

One consequence of the diminished importance of the skilled workers once their power was broken was the dramatic decline in their earnings. The following table of wage rates for selected positions at the Homestead plant mill between 1892 and 1908 illustrates the fate of skilled workers throughout the industry. Bear in mind that during this interval, their productivity was multiplying and wages throughout the nation were rising. Also, their workday was increased from 8 hours to 12 hours, so that the decline in daily earnings understates their reduction in real wages.

Table I.   Wages in Plate Mills, Homestead, 1889-1908[29]

Position	Decline in Tonnage Rates			Decline in Daily Rates		
	1889-92	1908	% decl.	1892	1907	% decl.
Roller	$14.00	$4.75	66.07	$11.84	$8.44	28.72
Heater	11.00	3.99	63.73	8.16	7.21	11.64
Heater's Helpers	7.50	2.09	72.13	5.80	4.09	29.48
Hooker	8.50	2.40	71.76	n.a.	n.a.	n.a.
Shearman	13.00	n.a.	n.a.	9.49	5.58	41.20

These reductions were part of the steel companies' policy of reducing the wage differentials between the classes of workers to make them more consistent with differentials in skill requirements for the different jobs. An official of one Pittsburgh steel company put it this way:

> It is perfectly true that the tonnage rates, and in some instances the actual daily earnings of skilled laborers, have been largely decreased. The reason for this is, mainly, the tremendous increase in production, due to improved equipment, representing very large capital investment, enabling the men at lower rates to make equal or even higher daily earnings.

He then added, somewhat more straightforwardly:

> At the same time the daily earnings of some of the most highly paid men have been systematically brought down to a level consistent with the pay of other workers, having in mind skill and training required and a good many other factors.[30]

Thus I have concluded that contemporary accounts are more valuable than statistical data to describe the changing content and categories of work in steel mills. Only in this way is it possible to go behind the statistical data and show the concrete content often masked in the abstract categories.

† Doeringer, op. cit. Doeringer attributes this shift purely to commodity market forces. He argues that shifts in demand for different kinds of steel products narrowed the wage differentials between steel workers. He mentions the decline of the Amalgamated after Homestead and the skilled workers' subsequent inability to hold their own against the employers, but does not relate this to the change in wage differentials.

The other side of the picture was the upgrading effect that the new technology had on the unskilled workers. Their wages were increased considerably during that same period. In part this was accomplished by a raise in the hourly rate for unskilled labor, from 14 cents per hour in 1892 to 17.5 cents in 1910, and in part it was the result of the steel companies putting more men on tonnage rates, enabling them to make higher daily earnings.[31]

Many unskilled workers were put in charge of expensive machinery and made responsible for operating them at full capacity. (It turned out to be very easy to train unskilled workers for these jobs, as will be shown in Part III, Section 2.) Fewer and fewer men were hired just to push wheelbarrows and load ingots, so that, as an official of the Pennsylvania Steel Company said, "While machinery may decrease the number of men, it demands a higher grade of workmen."[32]

Thus, the effects of the new technology was to level the work force and create a new class of workers. The following table shows this process as a whole. The data are based on a survey of 28 steel plants, conducted by the U.S. Commissioner of Labor in 1913. The table reports earnings only of production workers, omitting the earnings of foremen, clerks, timekeepers, weighters, and chemists.

Table II.   Percent Employees Earning Each Classified Amount[33]

Hourly Earnings	1900	1905	1910
Under 18 cents	65.0	64.3	41.8
18 and 25 cents	17.4	20.6	32.8
25 cents and over	17.6	15.1	25.4
70 cents and over	1.9	0.9	1.2

As can be seen from the table, the percentage of workers earning in the middle two categories went from 35% to 58% in the ten-year period.

The existence of the growing group of semi-skilled workers created certain problems for the employers, which will be explored in Part III.

III. Solving the Labor Problem.   In Part I we saw how the market conditions in the industry led employers to destroy the skilled steel workers' union in order to mechanize their operations. Employers therefore became the unilateral controllers of steel production. However, by doing that they created for themselves the problem of labor discipline. When the skilled workers had been partners in production, the problem of worker motivation did not arise. Skilled workers felt that they were working for themselves because they controlled the process of production. They set their own pace and work load without input from the bosses. In the 1890s, however, when the steel masters showed them who was boss, workers lost their stake in production, so that the problem of motivation arose. How hard workers worked became an issue of class struggle.

In Part II we saw how the effect of the new technology introduced in the 1890s was to narrow the skills differentials between the two grades of workers, producing a work force predominantly "semi-skilled." This homogenization of the work force produced another new "problem" for the employers. That is, without the old skilled/ unskilled dichotomy and the exclusiveness of the craft unions, the possibility that workers might as a class unite to oppose them was greater than ever. Frederick Winslow Taylor, the renowned management theorist who began his career as a foreman in a steel plant, warned employers of this danger in 1905:

When employers herd their men together in classes, pay all of each class the same wages, and offer none of them inducements to work harder or do better than the average, the only remedy for the men comes in combination; and frequently the only possible answer to encroachments on the part of their employers is a strike.[34]

Ultimately, however, both the problem of worker motivation and the problem of preventing unified opposition were the same problem. They both revolved around the question of controlling worker behavior. To do that, employers realized they had to control their perceptions of their self-interest. They had to give them the illusion that they had a stake in production, even though they no longer had any real stake in it. This problem was known as "the labor problem."

To solve the labor problem, employers developed strategies to break down the basis for a unity of interest amongst workers, and to convince them that, as individuals, their interests were identical with those of their company.

Out of these efforts, they developed new methods of wage payments and new advancement policies, which relied on stimulating individual ambition. They were designed to create psychological divisions among the workers, to make them perceive their interests as different from, indeed in conflict with, those of their co-workers. Employers also began to use paternalistic welfare policies in order to win the loyalty of their employees. The effect of all these new policies was to establish an internal labor market in the major steel companies, which has lasted, in its essentials, until today. This section will describe the new labor system that was created and the reasons why employers created it.

1. Development of Wage Incentive Schemes.   With the defeat of the Amalgamated Association, the entire complex traditional system of wage payments collapsed. The sliding scale of wages for paying skilled workers and the contract system for paying their helpers rapidly declined. Employers considered them a vestige of worker power and rooted them out of shop after shop. As the British Iron and Steel Institute noted in 1902:

> Many owners of the works in the United States have set their faces so completely against the contract system that in the opinion of the most experienced authorities, the contractor, as hitherto established, is likely, before long, to entirely disappear.[35]

Thus, the employers had the opportunity to establish unilaterally a new system of wage payment. Initially, they began to pay the new semi-skilled workers. Soon, however, they switched to the system of piece work, paying a fixed sum for each unit the worker produced. The British visitors found, in 1902, "in most of the works and shops visited that piece work is very general in all operations that call for a considerable amount of skill, and, indeed, wherever the work is above the level of unskilled labor."[36]

The most obvious function of piece work was, of course, to increase output by making each worker drive himself to work harder. Employers also contended that the system was in the workers' best interests because it allowed each one to raise his own wages.

However, the employers soon found that straight piece work gave the workers too much control over their wages. That is, when it succeeded in stimulating workers to increase their output, their wages soared above the going rate. Employers would then cut the piece rates to keep the wages in line. Once they did that, however, they had reduced the piece rate system to simple speed-up — a way of getting more work for the same pay. Workers responded to the rate cuts by collectively slowing down their output, so that the system defeated itself, leaving employers back where they had started. An article in *Iron Age,* entitled "Wage Payment Systems: How to Secure the Maximum Efficiency of Labor," gives an interesting account of this process:

> It is in the administration of the piece work system that manufacturers, sooner or later, make their great mistake and over-reach themselves, with the result that the system becomes a mockery and the evil conditions of the old day work system reappears. Regardless of the continually increasing cost of living, the manufacturers decide among themselves, for example, that $1.50 for 10 hours is enough for a woman and that $2.50 a day is enough for the ordinary working man and a family. The piece work prices are then adjusted so that the normal day's output will just bring about these wages . . . Immediately throughout the entire shop the news of the cuts is whispered about . . . with the result that there is a general slowing down of all producers.[37]

Thus employers began to experiment with modifications of the piece rate. They developed several new methods of payment at this time, known as "premium" or "bonus" plans. These differed from piece work only in that they gave the workers smaller increments in pay for each additional piece.

The Halsey Premium Plan, developed in 1891, served as a model for most of the others. It called for establishing a base time period for a job, and setting one rate for workers who completed the job in that period. If a worker could finish the job faster, then he received a bonus in addition to the standard rate. The bonus was figured so that only a part of the money saved by the worker's extra productivity went to him, the rest going to the company. Different plans varied according to how they set the base time period and the base wage, and how they divided the more efficient workers' savings between the worker and the company. *Iron Age* recommended one particular variation, called the Half and Half Premium Plan, in which the rule was "to pay the more efficient workman only one-half what he saves in speeding up." The article described one example where under the plan,

> for every extra $1 the man earned by his extra effort, the manufacturers would gain $7. Not a bad investment this premium system. It betters the workingman's condition materially, and, best of all, improves his frame of mind.[38]

Frederick Winslow Taylor's Differential Piece Rate is basically another variation of the Halsey Premium Plan. Under Taylor's system, the employer established two separate rates, a low day rate for the "average workman" and a high piece rate for the "first class workman," with the stipulation that only the fast and efficient workmen were entitled to the higher rate. He suggests setting the high rate to give the worker about 60 percent increase in earnings, and for this, the employer would demand of him a 300-400 percent increase in output. Like the Halsey Plan, it was simply the piece rate system modified to give the worker diminishing returns for his extra effort.

In order for any of the output incentive plans to work, management had to be able to measure each worker's output separately. All of the premium plans stressed the importance of treating each worker individually, but only Taylor gave them a method for doing so. His great contribution was systematic time study — giving employers a yardstick against which to measure an individual's productivity. The emphasis on individual productivity measures reinforced the fragmenting effect of the plans. As Taylor said about his experience implementing the system at the Bethlehem Steel Works:

> Whenever it was practicable, each man's work was measured by itself . . . . Only on a few occasions and then upon special permission (. . .) were more than two men allowed to

work on gang work, dividing their earnings between them. Gang work almost invariably results in a falling off of earnings and consequent dissatisfaction.[39]

Output incentives were designed to increase individual worker output. Employers understood that to do that, they had to play upon individual worker's ambitions, which meant breaking down workers' collective identity. They gave each worker inducement to work harder, and also divided the workers into different groups, according to their output. They also increased the social distance between the more "efficient" and the less "efficient" workers.

Thus, output incentives served as a lever to prevent workers from taking collective action. As one manufacturer explained in 1928, he had originally adopted output incentives:

> To break up the flat rate for the various classes of workers. That is the surest preventative of strikes and discontent. When all are paid one rate, it is the simplest and almost inevitable thing for all to unite in the support of a common demand. When each worker is paid according to his record there is not the same community of interest. The good worker who is adequately paid does not consider himself aggrieved so willingly nor will he so freely jeopardize his standing by joining with the so-called "Marginal Worker." There are not likely to be union strikes where there is no union of interest.[40]

Taylor, too, boasted in 1895 that

> There has never been a strike by men working under this system, although it has been applied at the Midvale Steel Works for the past ten years; and the steel business has proved during this period the most fruitful field for labor organization . . . I attribute a great part of this success in avoiding strikes to the high wages which the best men were able to earn with the differential rates, and to the pleasant feeling fostered by this system.[41]

An editorial in *Iron Age,* 1905, entitled "Union Restriction of Output," reveals much about employers' views of the incentive plans. It said:

> The premium plan, which has done for the machine shop, and on a smaller scale for the foundry, what the introduction of non-union men did at the Gamble mine — increasing wages and reducing the cost per ton — has been resisted by the molders' union, as it has been steadily opposed by the machinists' union. As ground for this opposition it is urged that the premium plan is only a modification of what the unions regard as the vicious piece price system, and that the union must prevent a greedy scramble for high wages by workmen who take no account of the pace they are setting for the less capable . . .[42]

This article tells us how conscious both the employers and the unions were about effects of the premium plan on the social relations inside the plant. Employers saw it as the equivalent to bringing in scabs to a union shop in its power to break up unity between the workers and advocated it for that reason. The unions opposed it, not because they misunderstood, but because they saw it in precisely the same way.

Quite explicitly, then, the aim of the premium plans was to break up any community of interest that might lead workers to slow their pace (what employers call "restriction of output") or unite in other ways to oppose management. They were a weapon in the psychological war that employers were waging against their workers, and were, at least for a while, quite successful. A survey of plant managers made in 1928 by the National Industrial Conference Board found that:

> There was little dissent from the opinion that the (premium plan) is effective in promoting industrial harmony. The responsibility for low earnings is placed squarely on the shoulders

of the worker, leaving no room for complaint of favoritism or neglect on the part of management.[43]

Between 1900 and World War I, piece work and premium plans became more and more prevalent in the steel industry. Although there are no figures on the percentage of workers on incentive plans, as compared with percentage on day work, there is evidence that piece work and the premium system became the preferred method of wage payment and was used whenever possible. The number of articles in *Iron Age* advising employers to use output incentives increase every year during this period, and they give more and more examples of companies which have employed it successfully. By 1912, there were articles about the system almost every month in *Iron Age,* with titles like "A Sliding Scale Premium System" (March 14), "The Sphere of the Premium Plan" (April 25), "Success with Bonus Wage Systems" (July 4), "Productivity Betterment by Time Studies" (April 4), and "Adopting Piece Work and Premium Systems" (December 5).

Bethlehem Steel Company was one of the first major companies to adopt premium plans. Charles Schwab, president of the company, attributed his uncanny success in buying out bankrupt shipbuilding companies and turning them into profitable ventures to the introduction of premium plans. In one particularly dramatic case, he bought the bankrupt Fore River Shipbuilding Company in Quincy, Massachusetts and claimed, with the bonus plan, to have revived the company so as to make a million dollars' profit from it in the first year![44]

Steel workers opposed the new methods of payment, and the residual unions in the industry raised objections at every opportunity. In one instance, at Bethlehem Steel's South Bethlehem Works, opposition to the bonus system exploded into a major strike in February, 1910. Approximately 5,000 of the 7,000 workers there went out on strike spontaneously. The strike lasted several weeks, during which time one man was killed and many were injured. Strike demands were drawn up separately by each department or group of workers, and every single one called for uniform rates of pay *to be paid by the hour,* and time-and-a-half for overtime. Several added to that an explicit demand for the elimination of piece work and a return to the "day-work" system. A U.S. Senate investigation into the strike found that the "Time-Bonus" System in use was one of its major causes."[45]

However, worker opposition proved ineffective in preventing the use of output incentive schemes. Since 1892, the employers had held the upper hand in the industry, and they used it to perpetuate their power. The wage incentive schemes were aimed at doing just that.

2. New Promotion Policies and the Development of Job Ladders.

As we saw in Part II of this paper, the new technology diminished the skill requirements for virtually all the jobs involved in making steel, so that even the most difficult jobs could be learned quickly. The gulf separating the skilled workers from the unskilled workers became virtually meaningless. Charles Schwab himself said in 1902 that he could "take a green hand — say a fairly intelligent agricultural labourer — and make a steel melter of him in six to eight weeks."[46] When we realize that the job of melter was the most highly skilled job in the open hearth department, we can see how narrow the skill range in the industry really was. The employers knew this, and put their knowledge to good use during strikes. For example, during a strike at the Hyde Park Mill in 1901

it was resolved that the works should be continued with green hands, aided by one or two skilled men who remained loyal. The five mills thus manned were started on the 3rd of

August, and up to the date of my visit, near the end of October, they had not lost a single turn.[47]

Around the turn of the century, employers began to recognize the dangers inherent in the homogenization of the work force. They formulated this problem as worker discontent caused by "dead-end jobs." Meyer Bloomfield, an industrial manager who in 1918 wrote a textbook on factory management, summarized their discussion on this subject:

A good deal of literature has been published within the last dozen years in which scathing criticism is made of what has come to be known as "blind alley" or "dead-end" jobs. By these phrases is meant work of a character which leads to nothing in the way of further interest, opportunity, acquisition of skill, experience, or anything else which makes an appeal to normal human intelligence and ambition. The work itself is not under attack as much as the lack of incentive and appeal in the scheme of management.[48]

Bloomfield says right off, then, that the problem of "dead-end" jobs need not be solved by changing the jobs themselves. The better solution is to change the arrangement of the jobs. To do this, he says,

a liberal system of promotion and transfer has therefore become one of the most familiar features of a modern personnel plan, and some of the most interesting achievements of management may be traced to the workings of such a system.[49]

Thus, the response of employers to the newly homogenized jobs was to create strictly demarcated job ladders, linking each job to one above and one below it in status and pay to make a chain along which workers could progress. The reason for this response was their view that

what makes men restless is the inability to move, or to get ahead. This fundamental law of human nature is forgotten frequently, and its neglect gives rise to situations that are never understood by the employer who looks upon a working force as something rigid.[50]

The establishment of a job ladder had two advantages, from the employers' point of view. First, it gave workers a sense of vertical mobility as they made their way up the ladder, and was an incentive to workers to work harder. Like the premium plan, the promise of advancement was used as a carrot to lure the men to produce more and more. As Charles Hook, the Vice President of the American Rolling Mill Company, a major subsidiary of U.S. Steel, told the Third International Management Congress

a few general policies govern the selection of all (our employees). One of the most important of these is the policy of promotion within the organization. This is done wherever possible and has several advantages; the most important of which is the stimulating effect upon the ambitions of workers throughout the organization.[51]

The other advantage of the job ladder arrangement was that it gave the employers more leverage with which to maintain discipline. The system pitted each worker against all the others in rivalry for advancement and undercut any feeling of unity which might develop among them. Instead of acting in concert with other workers, workers had to learn to curry favor with their foremen and supervisors, to play by their rules, in order to get ahead. As one steel worker described the effect this had on workers during the 1919 organizing campaign, "Naw, they won't join no union; they're all after every other feller's job."[52] This competition also meant that workers on different ladder rungs had different vested interests, and that those higher up had something to lose by offending their bosses or disrupting production.

As early as 1900, *Iron Age* was advising employers to fill production work vacancies from inside the firm. They advocated a policy of hiring only at the lowest job levels and filling higher jobs by promotion — what contemporary economists refer to as limiting the ports of entry. In one article, titled "Developing Employees," a columnist sharply criticizes a specific employer who

> has very often failed to find the proper qualifications among his employees to promote any one of them to certain higher positions which had become vacant from various causes . . . At such times he usually hired outsiders to fill the positions and thus engendered dissatisfaction among his helpers.[53]

In the following years, the journal suggested that employers issue special employer certificates to their more faithful and efficient employees, which would serve as tickets to advancement when openings became available. By 1905, they concluded that

> The plan is working so well that already employers' certificates are held in higher favor by the industrious well-disposed workmen than a union card could ever be by such a man.[54]

Clearly, the employers' certificates were a gimmick to further the workers' sense of opportunity by holding out the promise of promotions even before there were jobs available. Thus, workers were made to compete with each other for the certificates, as well as for the better jobs. The certificates in themselves did not guarantee anything, they merely improved one's chances — so the "certified" loyal ones still had to compete.

The principle of internal promotion was expounded by Judge Gary, the President of the U.S. Steel Corporation, in his dealings with the subsidiaries. For example, in a speech to the presidents of the subsidiary companies in 1922, Gary said:

> We should give careful thought to the question as to who could be selected to satisfactorily fill any unoccupied place; and like suggestions should be made to the heads of all departments. Positions should be filled by promotions from the ranks, and if in any locations there are none competent, this fact should be given attention and men trained accordingly. It is only necessary to make and urge the point. You will know what to do, if indeed any of you has not already well deliberated and acted upon it.[55]

Observers of the steel industry in the early years of this century saw the effects of these new policies on the structure of jobs. The British economist, Poppelwell, visited the American steel industry in 1902 and concluded that:

> the most characteristic feature of American industrial life and the most far-reaching in its effects is what may be shortly termed the mobility of labour . . . Under a competitive system, a large degree of mobility, not only in the various grades of labour themselves, but also between the different grades, allows the best man to come rapidly to the top, and promotion is very much quicker in America than here.[56]

As we saw in Part I of this paper, John Fitch, the American journalist who made a study of the steel industry in 1908, also found a rigid line of promotion within each department, and a work force that was "pyramided and (. . .) held together by the ambition of the men lower down."[57]

On an aggregate level, the vertical mobility inside the steel industry can be traced through the rise of the various immigrant groups, all of whom entered the industry as common laborers. David Brody, in his book *Steel Workers in America,* gives the following data about one large Pittsburgh mill for the year 1910:[58]

Number of Immigrants Holding Jobs

Years Service	Unskilled Jobs	Semi-skilled Jobs	Skilled Jobs
Under 2 years	314	56	0
2– 5 years	544	243	17
5 – 10 years	475	441	79
over 10 years	439	398	184

John Fitch also noted that one could chart mobility through the rise of the various groups of immigrants. In the open hearth department, for example, he noted that the newly arrived Slav is

> put to work in the cinder pit; from here he is promoted to be second helper and then first helper. Practically all of the cinder-pit men now are Slavs, and a majority of the second helpers are Slavs, and it would seem to be only a question of time when the first helpers and even the melter foremen will be men of these races promoted from the lower positions.[59]

In this way, the steel companies opened up lines of promotion in the early years of the century by creating job ladders. Employers claimed that each rung of the ladder provided the necessary training for the job above it. But the skilled jobs in the steel industry had been virtually eliminated and production jobs were becoming more homogeneous in their content. If, as Charles Schwab said, one could learn to be a melter in six weeks, then certainly the training required for most jobs was so minimal that no job ladder and only the minimum of job tenure were needed to acquire the necessary skills.

At the time, technological development made it possible to do away with distinctions between skilled and unskilled workers. Instead of following this trend, they introduced divisions to avoid the consequences of a uniform and homogeneous work force. Therefore, the minutely graded job ladders that developed were a solution to the "labor problem," rather than a necessary input for production itself.

3. The Welfare Policies.   The history of this period also sheds light on another important aspect of the steel industry's labor policies — the welfare programs. U.S. Steel's policy on welfare was formulated during the first few years of the corporation's life, and specific programs were established throughout the early years. These programs included a stock subscription plan for workers and a profit-sharing plan for executives; old-age pensions and accident insurance; a safety and sanitation campaign; and efforts to provide community housing, education and recreation facilities. Indeed, they included most of the functions performed today by the so-called "welfare state." The welfare policies were the most visible and best publicized part of the industry's labor policies. They were set up to serve the interests of the employers as a class, rather than as individual manufacturers.

The stock subscription plan, the first of the welfare measures, went into effect in 1903. It involved the sale of stock at reduced rates to corporation employees, paid for by monthly paycheck deductions. The plan provided the subscribers with a bonus, in addition to the regular dividends, of $5 for each of the first five years that the subscribers remained in the employ of the corporation and retained the stock, provided he showed "a proper interest in its welfare and progress." Also, the deserving subscribers received an extra bonus after owning the stock five years.

The idea of the stock subscription plan was to give employees a share in the growth of the corporation. As such, it was a form of profit-sharing. However, the bonuses and the extra bonuses made the plan something more. They gave employees an incentive to stay with the corporation for five years, and to show "a proper interest" in its welfare. Although it did not specify what showing a "proper interest" involved, certainly joining a union or sabotaging production were not included. The plan was clearly designed to control workers' behavior. One of the workers interviewed by John Fitch saw it simply as ". . . a scheme to keep out unionism and prevent the men from protesting against bad conditions."[60]

The stock subscription plan set the tone for all of the later insurance measures. They all contained clauses and sub-paragraphs stipulating how workers had to behave to be eligible for benefits. For example, the pension fund established in 1911, which was made up solely of corporation contributions, offered retirement benefits at age 60 for employees of 20 years' seniority, *except* "in case of misconduct on the part of the beneficiaries or for other cause sufficient in the judgment of the Board of Trustees."[61] Similarly, a Voluntary Accident Relief Plan was inaugurated in 1910 to pay workers benefits in case of temporary disability, permanent disability, or death resulting from on-the-job injuries. The plan (which was soon superseded by state workmen's compensation laws) was the first of its kind in the United States, and for all of its liberality, was also a device to ward off lawsuits in accident cases caused by company negligence. The plan said explicitly that "No relief will be paid to any employee or his family if suit is brought against the company," and "all employees of the company who accept and receive any of this relief will be required to sign a release to the company."[62]

Other aspects of the welfare program contained more subtle behavior modification devices, aimed at changing behavior indirectly, through changing the attitudes of employees. For example, the steel industry was notorious for its hazardous working conditions and the high accident rate that resulted. The corporation, as part of its welfare program, began a safety propaganda campaign in 1908. They hung safety posters around the plants, distributed safety handbills to all the workers, circulated safety bulletins, and showed safety films — all of which were designed to convince the workers that " 'workers are solely or partially responsible (for accidents) in ninety percent of the cases.' "[63] U.S. Steel maintained, and preached, this position despite conclusive statistical evidence published at the time which showed that plant and equipment design were the cause of most work accidents in the steel industry.[64] In other words, the point of the elaborate and highly praised safety campaign was to convince the workers that accidents were their own fault, and so to ward off any blame for the companies' unsafe production practices.

Another part of the corporation's welfare program was to encourage workmen to build houses by giving them low-income loans for that purpose. Although the program benefitted workers, the motives for the program were, at best, mixed. An editorial in *Iron Age* in 1905 praised the corporation's housing program because:

> Workmen will build homes of their own, which is most desirable as bearing upon the permanency of employment and its influence against labor agitation, for the home-owning workman is less apt to be lead astray by the professional agitator than the man whose industrial life is a transient one.[65]

The corporation's welfare efforts in the communities of its employees were extensive and impressive. The corporation by 1924 built 28,000 dwellings, which it rented to its employees, and built entire towns around some of its subsidiaries. Gary, Indiana, for example, was built from scratch by the corporation, and was acclaimed at the time as a model of town planning techniques and modern social services. In these company towns, the corporation built water purification facilities and sewage systems. They employed nurses to visit the families of their employees, instructing them in methods of hygiene, and they employed dentists to visit the children's schools and given them "toothbrush drills." They built emergency hospitals to serve their towns, charging special low rates to families of workers. They helped build the public schools and often supplemented teachers' salaries in order to attract good teachers. They built libraries and club houses for the workers, at which they offered night courses in English, civics, arithmetic, and technical subjects. Every plant had its own glee club, band or orchestra, with instruments provided by the company. Unoccupied company land was turned over to the workers for gardens, where with seed provided by the company, about a milion dollars worth of vegetables were produced each year. And for its employees' recreation, the corporation had built, by January 1, 1924, 175 playgrounds, 125 athletic fields, 112 tennis courts, 19 swimming pools, and 21 band stands.[66] Such was the welfare program of the Steel Corporation. The question that remains is, why?

Most writers about the industry treat the welfare work either as a sincere expression of good intentions on the part of the steel management, or as a public relations ploy. Friends of the corporation, such as Arundel Cotter, a personal acquaintance of Judge Gary, argue that the welfare work proved that labor and capital could progress together in harmony, providing better lives for the workmen and higher profits for the corporation at the same time. He sums up his review of the welfare work by saying, "the organization of the U.S. Steel Corporation was the greatest step that has ever been made toward the highest form of socialism."[67] Critics of the corporation like John Garraty and Robert Weibe, both historians of the period, argue that the welfare work was designed to convince the public that the corporation was a "good trust," in order to avoid the furor of the trust-busting sentiment of the times, but that in fact they benefitted very few workers.

A look at the origins of the welfare programs gives a more rounded view of the role they served. The welfare programs were designed by George Perkins, one of J.P. Morgan's top men. Perkins had originally attracted Morgan's attention when, as a Vice President of New York Life Insurance Company, he had developed an extraordinary innovation in labor relations, the NYLIC club. The purpose of the scheme was to reduce employee turnover. Perkins set up the club for all employees who promised never to work for another business. Membership in the NYLIC club gave one monthly bonuses and a life-time pension after twenty years of service. According to Perkins' biographer:

> "The idea of this plan," Perkins told the agents, "is to say to the solicitor . . . that if he will give up . . . any thought of going into any business, or into any other company, no matter what the inducements might be, and will accept . . . the New York Life Insurance Company for his Company, then we will do something for him that is . . . better than any other Company can do."[68]

The plan was enormously successful at reducing turnover, and it made Perkins' career. He went to work for Morgan, and he was put in charge of labor relations for all of Morgan's concerns. He designed welfare policies for Morgan's railroads, the International Harvester Corporation and U.S. Steel, all with the same goal — to bind workers to the company for a long time.[69] Again, Perkins' biographer reports that the stock subscription plan at U.S. Steel

> had certain special features intended to make the employees identify their personal interests with that of U.S. Steel. These features reflected clearly Perkins' experience in the life insurance business, and especially with the NYLIC organization. Just as he had worked to retain his agents on a permanent basis, Perkins was eager to avoid a labor turnover at every level.[70]

The welfare policies caused a bitter dispute within the corporation's Executive Board when they were first proposed. U.S. Steel's original Executive Board was made up of two groups — the Wall Street bankers who had organized the merger, and the presidents of the large steel companies who had been merged. On November 22, 1902, less than a year after the corporation was formed, the financiers on the Board, Judge Elbert Gary and George Perkins, presented the stock-subscription plan. The old-time steel men on the Board immediately opposed the plan. Their labor policy, so effective in the 1890s, was straightforward, out-and-out repression. Charles Schwab, president of the corporation, characterized their attitude by saying, ''When a workman raises his head, beat it down.'' Thus a fight developed between the bankers and the steel men over the labor policy of the new corporation — a fight which was ultimately settled by J.P. Morgan, who threw his support to the bankers.[71] Schwab resigned as president of the corporation soon thereafter, and Gary was made chairman of the Board of Directors. With the victory of the financiers, the welfare programs were begun.

The welfare programs, then, were part of a broader strategy on the part of the finance capitalists to break down the interfirm mobility of workers. The reason for this was not simply that labor turnover was expensive — for indeed turnover was not particularly expensive in those days when there was little on-the-job training and none of the negotiated fringe benefits which make turnover costly today. The reason for reducing turnover was, as Perkins and other managers of the day noted, that changing jobs had an unsettling effect upon the workers. It tended to make them identify with other workers, and to see themselves as a class. All of the major strikes of the 19th century had shown that steel workers were quick to go out in sympathy with striking workers in other companies and other industries. The welfare programs were supposed to combat this tendency, by giving workers both a psychological and an economic motive for remaining loyal to their employer.

The steel companies regarded their welfare work as their greatest contribution to domestic tranquility. They saw welfarism as the way to head off class struggle in society as a whole. For example, during the discussion of welfare work at the 1912 convention of the Iron and Steel Institute, one of the directors of U.S. Steel, Percival Roberts, said:

> We live in an age of discontent and great unrest. It is worldwide, not peculiar to this country at all. And I believe that no body of men is doing more to restore confidence today than those assembled here tonight. It is the one thing which we need today, eliminating all class distinctions, and restoring not only politically, but industrially, good fellowship; and I believe that the Iron and Steel industry is taking a leading position in that work.[72]

The Steel Corporation advertised its welfare work widely. Beginning in 1913, they began an ''Iron and Steel Institute Monthly Bulletin'' which did nothing but report on the welfare work of the different steel companies. Judge Gary and George Perkins gave many speeches about the welfare work, and encouraged other corporations to follow their example. They sought publicity for the programs in the business press and the popular press. They did this because they saw the programs as more than a labor policy for U.S. Steel. They believed that if all companies followed their example, it would prove to be a solution to the "labor problem" nationally. Welfarism was their answer to the class politics of the Socialist Party, which was making great headway at the time. By increasing the ties between workers and their employer, they hoped to weaken the ties between workers and their class.*

Perhaps the best statement of the strategy of the welfare policies was given by Judge Gary, who ended a meeting with the presidents of U.S. Steel subsidiary companies in January, 1919, by saying:

> Above everything else, as we have been talking this morning, satisfy your men if you can that your treatment is fair and reasonable and generous. Make the Steel Corporation a good place for them to work and live. Don't let the families go hungry or cold; give them playgrounds and parks and schools and churches, pure water to drink, and recreation, treating the whole thing as a business proposition, drawing the line so that you are just and generous and yet at the same time keeping your position and permitting others to keep theirs, retaining the control and management of your affairs, keeping the whole thing in your own hands.[73]

IV. The Redivision of Labor.   While employers were developing new systems for managing their work forces, they also altered the definition of jobs and the division of labor between workers and management. They did this by revising the training mechanism for skilled workers, retraining the foremen, and changing their methods of recruiting managers. The result of these changes was to take knowledge about production away from the skilled workers, thus separating "physical work" from "mental work." This further consolidated the employers' unilateral control over production, for once all knowledge about production was placed on the side of management, there would be no way for workers to carry on production without them.

Frederick Winslow Taylor was one of the first theorists to discuss the importance of taking all mental skills away from the worker. In his book *Principles of Scientific Management* (1905), he gives a description of the division of knowledge in the recent past:

> Now, in the best of the ordinary types of management, the managers recognize the fact that the 500 to 1000 workmen, included in the twenty or thirty trades, who are under them, possess this mass of traditional knowledge, a large part of which is not in the possession of the management. The management, of course, includes foremen and superintendents, who themselves have been in most cases first-class workers at their trades. And yet these foremen and superintendents know, better than anyone else, that their own knowledge and personal skill falls far short of the combined knowledge and dexterity of all the workmen under them.[74]

Taylor insists that employers must gain control over this knowledge, and take it away from the workers. In his manual *Shop Management*, he says quite simply, "All

---

* For a discussion on the class-conscious nature of the welfare work, and the leading role played by U.S. Steel, see Weinstein, *The Corporate Ideal in the Liberal State* and Weibe, Robert, *Businessmen and Reform*.

possible brain work should be removed from the shop and centered in the planning or laying-out department.''[75]

Taylor suggested several techniques for accomplishing this. They were all based on the notion that work was a precise science, that there was ''one best way'' to do every work task, and that the duty of the managers was to discover the best way and force all their workmen to follow it. Taylorites used films of men working to break down each job into its component motions, and used stop watches to find out which was the ''one best way'' to do them. Taylor also insisted that all work should be programmed in advance, and co-ordinated out of a ''planning department.'' He gives elaborate details for how the planning department should function — using flow charts to program the entire production process and direction cards to communicate with foremen and workmen. These were called ''routing'' systems. One historian summarizes this aspect of scientific management thus:

> One of the most important general principles of Taylor's system was that the man who did the work could not derive or fully understand its science. The result was a radical separation of thinking from doing. Those who understood were to plan the work and set the procedures; the workmen were simply to carry them into effect.[76]

Although most steel executives did not formulate the problem as clearly as Taylor, they did try to follow his advice. Around 1910, they began to develop ''dispatching systems'' to centralize their knowledge about production. These systems consisted of a series of charts showing the path of each piece of material as it made its progress through the plant and how much time each operation took — enabling the supervisors to know exactly where each item was at any point in time. The purpose of these systems was to give the supervisors complete knowledge of the production process. Between 1910 and 1915, *Iron Age* carried innumerable articles about steel plants that had adopted dispatching systems.

At the same time that they systematized their own knowledge about production, the steel companies took that knowledge away from steel workers. Previously, the skilled steel workers, acting in teams, possessed all of the skills and know-how necessary to make steel. They also had had authority over their own methods of work. Now employers moved to transfer that authority to the foremen and to transfer that knowledge to a new stratum of managers. This section will describe and document that process, in order to show that this redivision of labor was not a necessary outgrowth of the new technology, but rather was an adaptation of employers to meet their own needs, as capitalists, to maintain discipline and control.

1. The New Skilled Workers. As we saw in Part II, the mechanization of production largely eliminated the role of the traditional skilled worker. However, the steel industry still needed skilled workers. Machines required skilled mechanics to perform maintenance and repair work. Also, certain skills were needed for specialized production processes which had not yet been mechanized. However, these skilled workmen were very different from the skilled workmen of the 19th century, who collectively possessed all of the skills necessary to produce steel. The new skilled workers had skills of a specific nature that enabled them to perform specific tasks, but did not have a general knowledge of the process of production. This new class of skilled workers had to be created by the employers.

One would think that finding skilled men should have been no problem because of the huge numbers of skilled workers who were displaced and downgraded in the 1890s. However, by 1905, employers' associations began to complain about the shortage of skilled men. The reason for this paradox is that when the employers destroyed the unions and the old social relations, they destroyed at the same time the mechanism through which men had received their training.

Previously, the selection, training, and promotion of future skilled steel workers had been controlled by the skilled craftsmen and their unions.* The constitution of the Amalgamated Association of Iron, Steel and Tin Workers had a clause that insisted that "'all men are to have the privilege of hiring their own helpers without dictation from the management.'"[77] The men would then train their helpers in their trade. The union also regulated the helpers' advancement. For example, in 1881, it passed a resolution saying "'Each puddler helper must help one year and be six months a member of the Association before he be allowed the privilege of boiling a heat.'"[78] After the union was destroyed, the skilled workers were no longer able to hire and train their own helpers.

Within a few years, employers, realizing that no new men were being trained, began to worry about their future supply of skilled workers. In 1905, *Iron Age* reported that

> The imperative necessity of renewing the apprentice system on a general and comprehensive scale has become apparent to every employer who is dependent on the skilled mechanic (craftsman) for his working force.[79]

Statistics collected by the Department of Labor in 1910 show that the skilled workers were considerably older than the other workers, their median age being roughly 37 while that of semi-skilled was 27 and that of unskilled workers was 26.* By the 1920s, the situation was critical. Associations of steel employers decried the extinction of skilled workers at their conventions and in their publications. One contemporary economist, after a study of skilled workers in iron and steel foundries in Philadelphia, concluded:

> that there are proportionately too few men who are in their twenties and an exceptionally large number who are in their fifties and sixties . . . The number of complaints about the lack of apprentices voiced in all the publications has increased.[80]

---

* In other industries, a formal apprenticeship system provided the future skilled workers, and the attempts by employers to replace that system with a helper system was the source of much conflict between workers and employers in the 19th century. The importance of the distinction was that the apprenticeship system meant control by the skilled workers, and the helper system meant control by employers. In the steel industry, the helper system was controlled by the workers, so the distinction was not important.

* Calculated on the basis of table in *Labor Conditions,* p. 480. A more detailed breakdown is:

Age	Skilled	Semi-skilled	Unskilled
Under 30	29%	54%	52%
30-40	38	30	26
Over 40	33	16	22
Over 50	11	5	7

We would, of course, expect skilled workers to be somewhat older than the others, but we would hardly expect a variation of this extent.

During this period, employers began to develop a new type of skilled worker, one whose skills were highly specialized and limited in their scope. In 1912, *Iron Age* described the evolution of this class of workers:

> That the supply of American mechanics is altogether too small is an old story. The apprentice system was permitted to die out and the relative supply of skilled men fell away rapidly. In the last ten years, a more or less organized effort has been made to increase the number and has met with considerable success. Nevertheless, the demand for this class of labor has increased so greatly that each year the proportion of trained men to the total number of mechanics which must be employed has become smaller.
>
> The consequence has been that vast numbers of men have been trained for specialized work in machine shops, and improved machinery has made it possible to decrease the average excellence of workmen without reducing the quality of the product.[81]

In order to create this new class of skilled workers, employers set up a training system that was an alternative to the union-controlled apprenticeship system of the past, known as the "short course." The "short course" involved a manager or superintendent taking a worker who had been in a department for long enough to get a feel for the process, and giving him individualized instruction in some specialized branch of the trade. By using the short course, employers could train men for specific skilled jobs in a limited period of time. The training period varied, according to the skill being taught, from a few weeks to a year. The Secretary of the Milwaukee branch of the National Metal Trades Association described the use of the short course in his district in 1924 as follows:

> The handymen are usually helpers desiring to learn more of the trade — are over 21 years of age and usually limit their training to one special line.

And the chairman of the local association of foundrymen reported that same year that

> In checking up the situation in this community, the committee found that generally most of the foundries were taking on inexperienced help and developing what has come to be known as specialty molders.[82]

In this way, a new class of skilled workers was created during the first two decades of the 20th century. These workers were selected by the employers, trained in a short period of time, and then set to work with their job-specific skill. These workers had skills which were only good for one job. They did not have the independence of the 19th century skilled workmen, whose skills were transferable to other jobs and other plants. Nor did they have the generalized knowledge of the production process that skilled workers previously possessed. The knowledge they had was that which could serve their employer, but not that which could serve themselves.

Thus, the new skilled workers were a dependent class. The employers had created their dependency on purpose, as advice which appeared in *Iron Age* in 1912 reveals:

> Make your own mechanics . . . The mechanics that you will teach will do the work your way. They will stay with you, as they are not sure they could hold jobs outside.[83]

The success of these policies can be judged from the following statement, made by the president of the American Rolling Mill Company in 1927:

> Work has become so specialized in these mills that even men in the regular trades, who have not had mill experience, find it difficult to follow their trade until they have served

another apprenticeship, which though not a formal one in the narrow sense is nevertheless a real one. So true is this, that furnace helpers and foremen melters of open hearth furnaces, trained in mills making common grades of steel, are unable to fill similar positions satisfactorily in "quality" mills, and, likewise, men trained for these jobs in "quality" mills have almost equal difficulty in mills where the emphasis is placed upon the making of large tonnage of common steel.[84]

2. The Changing Role of the Foreman.   As the employers expanded their control over the process of production, they realized they had to develop an alternative means for exercising control on the shop floor. Just as they had taken knowledge about production away from the skilled workers, they also took away their authority over their own labor and that of their helpers. Now, the task of regulating production was transferred to the foremen, who previously only had authority over the pools of unskilled workers. Foremen were now seen as management's representatives on the shop floor. To do this, employers had to redefine the job of foreman and retrain the men who held those jobs.

In order to transfer authority to the foremen, the employers had to distinguish them from the skilled workers. This distinction had to be created; it did not evolve out of the new technology. Foremen were recruited from the ranks of the skilled workers — foremanship being the highest position to which a blue-collar worker could aspire. Once there, however, steel employers had to re-educate them as to their role in production. This re-education began with convincing them *not* to do manual work, which was no easy task. An editorial in *Iron Age* in 1905 quotes one superintendent lecturing an audience of foremen as saying:

> You men have no business to have your coats off when on duty in your shops unless you are warm. You have no business to take the tools out of a workman's hands to do his work. Your business is to secure results from other men's work.

The editorial goes on to say why this is important:

> A man cannot work with his hands and at the same time give intelligent supervision to a gang of men, and a foreman who does this is apt to lose the control of his men while he is weakening the confidence of his employers in his ability as a general.[85]

The foreman's job was to direct and correct the work, but never to do the work himself. His authority depended upon that. Foremen, as the lowest ranking "mind" workers, had to be made distinct from the manual workers. One steel company official likened the organization of authority to that of the "army, with the necessary distinction between the commissioned officers and the ranks."[86]

The companies had to give their foremen special training courses in order to make them into bosses. These courses were designed to teach the foremen how to "manage" their men. One such course, at the American Steel and Wire Company, a U.S. Steel subsidiary, spent most of its time on that subject with only a few sessions on production techniques or economics. As described by one of the instructors, the course

> includes such subjects as the inherent qualities of the workmen, both physical and mental, temperament, fatigue, emotion, state of mind, and so on, how all these various factors affect the capabilities and efficiency of the men. The management course also includes external environments which affect the man's efficiency, the wage system, employment management, pleasure in work, the human cost of labor, the relations of foremen to the

workers, relations of the foremen to the company, and scientific management and subjects of that kind.[87]

This development was not unique to the steel industry. Throughout American industry, special foremen's training courses were becoming prevalent. Dr. Hollis Godfrey, president of the Drexel Institute in Philadelphia, the first private institution concerned solely with foremen's training, said that the purpose of foremen training was to

> make the skilled mind worker. The skilled mind worker is a little different proposition than the skilled hand worker, and a great many people are still wandering around in the differentiation between the two . . . From the foreman to the president right straight through, you have got one body of mind workers, and they do but two things: they organize knowledge and then they use the knowledge as organized.[88]

Although foremen did little work, they also did little thinking. Most of their training was designed to teach them how to maintain discipline — techniques for handling men, developing "team work," deciding who to discharge and who to promote. They were the company's representative in the shop, and as the companies consolidated their power over the workers, the strategic importance of the foremen increased.

3. New Types of Managers.   Just as the authority that the skilled workers had previously possessed was transferred to the foremen, their overall knowledge about production was transferred to the managers. By adopting new methods for training skilled workers, steel employers took the generalized knowledge about the production process as a whole away from the skilled workers. In their place, employers began hiring a new class of white-collar employees, recruited from the public and private schools and their own special programs. These workers became the bottom rung of the management hierarchy.

Before 1900, most managers in the steel industry were men who had begun at the bottom and worked their way all the way up. Andrew Carnegie had insisted on using this method to select his junior executives. As he once said, boastingly, "Mr. Morgan buys his partners, I grow my own."[89] Carnegie developed a whole partnership system for the management of his empire based on the principle of limitless upward mobility for every one of his employees.* He felt that by "growing his own," he not only found those men who had proven their abilities and loyalty to the firm, but also inspired the others to work that much harder. Thus he wrote to Frick in 1896:

> Every year should be marked by the promotion of one more of our young men. I am perfectly willing to give my interest for this purpose, when the undivided stock is disposed of. There is Miller at Dusquesne, and Brown, both of whom might get a sixth of one percent. It is a very good plan to have all your heads of departments interested, and I should like to vote for the admission of Mr. Corey; and if there is a sixth left, perhaps Mr. Keer of

---

* Although Carnegie was generous in his disbursement of stock shares and seats on the Executive Committee, he had no intention of giving up corporate control. All of his junior partners had to sign the "iron clad agreement," stipulating that in the event of death or dismissal, their shares would be returned to the Carnegie Steel Company, Limited, for which they would be paid the shares' book value. In this way, Carnegie could reward his "young geniuses" with partnerships and still keep them from challenging his control.

the Edgar Thomson Blast Furnaces deserves it. We cannot have too many of the right sort interested in profits.[90]

This attitude was well known throughout the Carnegie empire, with the result, as Carnegie's biographer puts it, that "just as Napoleon drove his soldiers on with the slogan that every foot soldier carried a marshall's baton in his knapsack, so Carnegie taught his men to believe that every worker carried a partnership in his lunch pail."[91]

Around the turn of the century, employers began to choose college graduates for their management positions. As one prominent steel official told a member of the British Iron and Steel Institute in 1903:

> We want young men who have not had time to wear themselves into a groove, young college men preferably . . . When a college graduate, who shows that he has the right stuff in him, reaches the age of 25 or 30 years, he is ready for a position of trust. When men get older they become more valuable as specialists, but for managers and executives we select young men with brains and education.[92]

This was not mere philosophy; the British visitors found on their tour that, of the 21 blast furnaces they visited, "18 were managed by college graduates, the majority of whom were young men."[93]

Employers used publically-funded technical colleges to train their new managers. Technical colleges were new, established with the support of the business community and over the protest of the labor movement. As Paul Douglas wrote in 1921:

> Employers early welcomed and supported the trade school, both because they believed that it would provide a means of trade-training, and because they believed that it would remove the preparation for the trades from the potential or actual control of unions.[94]

Some steel employers also set up their own schools to train managers in the arts of steel-making. For example, the Carnegie Company opened a technical school in Pittsburgh, in 1905. The purpose of the school was "providing instruction in those studies essential to a technical education" to applicants who were high school graduates.[95]

Technical training alone, however, was not sufficient to produce competent managers for steel factories. The young men also needed to know about steel-making. To meet this need, the steel companies developed a new on-the-job training program to supplement the formal learning of their young college graduates. This program consisted of short rotations in each mill department under the supervision of a foreman or superintendent, which gave the men experience in every aspect of mill work before they were put in managerial positions. This program was called an "apprenticeship," and although it trained managers instead of workers, it was an apprenticeship by the original meaning of the word. It gave the apprentices knowledge of each stage of the production process and how it fit together. A circular describing the Apprenticeship System begun in 1901 at the Baldwin Locomotive Works, which trained both managers and lower-level personnel, stated:

> In view of the fact that in recent years manufacturing has tended so largely toward specialization that young men apprenticed to mechanical trades have been able in most cases only to learn single processes, and, as a result, the general mechanic has threatened to become practically extinct, to the detriment of manufacturing interests generally, the Baldwin Locomotive Works have established a system of apprenticeship on a basis adapted to existing social and business conditions.[96]

The visitors from the British Iron and Steel Institute described the prevalence of the new apprenticeship system in their report of 1903:

> In a number of the leading American (steel) works, the principals attach importance to binding, as apprentices or otherwise, lads and young men who have had the advantage of a first-class education . . . Indeed, in some cases, as at the works of the Midvale Steel Company, at Philadelphia, my attention was specially called to the unusually large number of college graduates that were employed on the premises in various positions.[97]

By the 1920s, such methods were nearly universal throughout the industry. Charles Hook, the vice president of the American Rolling Mill Company, a U.S. Steel subsidiary, described his method for selecting and training managers in a speech of 1927 to the International Management Congress:

> The condition as outlined respecting the selection of the "skilled" employee is quite different from the condition governing the selection of the man with technical education . . . Each year a few second- and third-year (college) men work during the summer vacation, and get a first-hand knowledge of mill conditions. This helps them reach a decision. If, after working with us for a summer, they return the next year, the chances are they will remain permanently . . . Some of our most important positions — positions of responsibility requiring men with exceptional technical knowledge — are filled by men selected in this manner.[98]

The prospective managers, in short, were increasingly recruited from the schools and colleges, not from the shops.

In these apprenticeship programs, a distinction was often made between different types of apprentices, distinguished by their years of schooling. Each type was to be trained for positions at different levels of responsibility. For example, at the Baldwin Works, there were three classes of apprentices, such that:

> The first class will include boys seventeen years of age, which have had a good common school (grammar school) education . . . The second class indenture is similar to that of the first class, except that the apprentice must have had an advance grammar school (high school) training, including the mathematical courses usual in such schools . . . The third class indenture is in the form of an agreement made with persons twenty-one years of age or over, who are graduates of colleges, technical schools, or scientific institutions . . .[99]

Similarly, the application for indenture at the steel works of William Sellers and Company, in Philadelphia, read:

> Applications for Indenture as First Class Apprentices will be considered from boys who have had a good common school education . . . Applications for Indenture as Second Class Apprentices will be considered from boys who have had an advanced Grammar or High School training . . . Applicants for a special course of instruction, covering a period of two years, will be considered from young men over twenty-one years of age who are graduates of colleges, technical schools or scientific institutions.[100]

Thus, formal education was beginning to become the criterion for separating different levels of the management hierarchy, as well as separating workers from managers.

During this period, employers redivided the tasks of labor. The knowledge expropriated from the skilled workers was passed on to a new class of college-trained managers. This laid the basis for perpetuating class divisions in the society through the educational system. Recently several scholars have shown how the stratification of the educational system functions to reproduce society's class divisions.[101] It is worth noting that the educational tracking system could not work to maintain the class structure were it not for the educational requirements that were set up at the point of production. These educational requirements came out of the need of employers to consolidate their control over production.

Within management, the discipline function was divided from the task of directing and coordinating the work. This is the basis for today's distinction between "staff" and "line" supervision. We might hypothesize that this division, too, had its origin in the desire of steel employers to maintain control over their low level managerial staff.

The effect of this redivision of labor on the worker was to make his job meaningless and repetitive. He was left with no official right to direct his own actions or his own thinking. In this way, skilled workers lost their status as partners, and became true workers, selling their labor and taking orders for all of their working hours.

NOTES

[1] Fitch, John, *The Steel Workers*, pp. 141–142.

[2] Hogan, *Economics of Iron and Steel*, Vol. 1, p. 11.

[3] *Ibid.*, pp. 218–224.

[4] *Ibid.*, p. 185.

[5] *Ibid.*, pp. 91–94.

[6] *Ibid.*, p. 85.

[7] *Ibid.*, p. 86.

[8] Quoted in Hogan, *op. cit.*, footnote, p. 460.

[9] Carnegie, Andrew, *Autobiography*, p. 238.

[10] Montgomery, David, "Trade Union Practice and the Origins of Syndicalist Theory in the United States," pp. 3–4.

[11] Bridge, J.H., *History of Carnegie Steel Corporation*, pp. 201–2.

[12] Fitch, *op. cit.*, p. 102.

[13] Doeringer, Peter B., "Piece Rate Wage Structures in the Pittsburgh Iron and Steel Industry — 1880–1900," pp. 266–67.

[14] Great Britain, Iron and Steel Institute, *Special Proceedings*, 1890, p. 173. A further description of the non–labor-saving effects of the changing technology can be found in U.S. Department of Interior, *Report on the Statistics of Wages in Manufacturing Industries in the Tenth Census* (1880), Vol. XX, 1886, p. 115.

[15] Sahlin, Axel, quoted in Hogan, *op. cit.*, p. 214.

[16] Quoted in Brecher, Jeremy, *Strike!*, p. 53.

[17] *Ibid.*, p. 62.

[18] Robinson, Amalgamated Association of Iron, Steel and Tin Workers, p. 20.

[19] Brody, David, *The Steel Workers*, pp. 9–11.

[20] Jeans, J. Stephan, *American Industrial Conditions*, p. 121.

[21] Popplewell, Frank, *Some Modern Conditions and Recent Developments in Iron and Steel Production in America* (1903), p. 103.

[22] Jeans, *op. cit.*, p. 503.

[23] *Ibid.*, p. 551.

[24] Bridge, *op. cit.,* p. 164.

[25] Brody, *op. cit.,* pp. 48–49.

[26] Jeans, *op. cit.,* p. 561.

[27] *Report on Conditions of Employment in the Iron and Steel Industry in the United States,* Vol. III, p. 81, U.S. Commissioner of Labor, 1913, (referred to hereafter as Labor Conditions).

[28] Jeans, *op. cit.,* p. 317.

[29] Fitch, *op. cit.,* pp. 153–156.

[30] *Ibid.,* p. 157.

[31] *Ibid.,* p. 159.

[32] Quoted in Brody, *op. cit.,* p. 32. From *Labor Conditions,* Ch. 9.

[33] *Labor Conditions,* Vol. III, pp. 236–7.

[34] Taylor, F.W., *Shop Management,* p. 186.

[35] Jeans, *op. cit.,* p. 58.

[36] *Ibid.,* p. 55.

[37] *Iron Age,* May 19, 1910, p. 1190.

[38] *Ibid.,* 1910, p. 1191.

[39] Taylor, *Shop Management,* p. 52.

[40] National Industrial Conference Board, *Systems of Wage Payment,* p. 25.

[41] Taylor, F.W., *Shop Management,* p. 183.

[42] *Iron Age,* June 15, 1905, p. 1901.

[43] National Industrial Conference Board, *op. cit.,* p. 21.

[44] Cotter, A., *The Story of Bethlehem Steel,* p. 21.

[45] "Report on Strike at Bethlehem Steel Works," Senate Document No. 521.

[46] Jeans, *op. cit.,* p. 62.

[47] *Ibid.,* p. 62.

[48] Bloomfield, *Labor and Compensation,* p. 295.

[49] *Ibid.,* p. 297.

[50] *Ibid.,* p. 298.

[51] Hook, Charles R., "The Selection, Placement and Training of Employees," Third International Management Congress, Rome, Italy, 1927.

[52] Williams, Whiting, *What's on the Worker's Mind?,* p. 152.

[53] *Iron Age,* June 14, 1900, pp. 49–50.

[54] *Iron Age,* March 30, 1905, p. 1093.

[55] Gary, Elbert, *Addresses and Statements,* Vol. 6, March 29, 1922.

[56] Popplewell, *op. cit.,* pp. 110–111.

[57] Fitch, *op. cit.,* p. 142.

[58] Brody, David, *Steelworkers in America,* p. 107.

[59] Fitch, *op. cit.,* p. 148.

[60] *Ibid.,* p. 15.

[61] *Ibid.,* p. 339.

[62] *Ibid.,* p. 334.

[63] U.S. Steel, Safety, Sanitation and Welfare Committee Bulletin, Quoted in Bulick, Charles, *Labor Policy of U.S. Steel,* p. 143.

[64] Eastman, Crystal, *Work-Accidents and the Law, 1910.*

[65] *Iron Age,* August 3, 1905, p. 289.

[66] Gulick, Charles A., "The Labor Policy of U.S. Steel Corporation," Columbia University, *Studies in History, Economics and Public Law,* Vol. 116, No. 1, 1924, pp. 168–175.

[67] Cotter, Arundel, *U.S. Steel: Corporation with a Soul,* p. 141.

[68] Garraty, John, *Right-Hand Man,* p. 54.

[69] Ozanne, Robert, *Labor Relations at International Harvester,* Ch. 4.

[70] Garraty, *op. cit.,* p. 11.

[71] For a detailed account of this, see Garraty, John, *U.S. Steel vs. Labor,* in *Labor History* I.

[72] Yearbook of the American Iron and Steel Institute, 1912, p. 118.

[73] Gary, Elbert H., *Addresses and Statements,* Vol. 4, January 21, 1919.

[74] Quoted in Montgomery, *op. cit.,* p. 8.

[75] Taylor, *Shop Management,* p. 99.

[76] Haber, Samuel, *Efficiency and Uplift,* p. 24.

[77] Quoted in Ashworth, *The Helper and American Trade Unions,* p. 75.

[78] *Ibid.,* p. 73, footnote.

[79] *Iron Age,* October 26, 1905, "The Modern Apprenticeship System," p. 1092.

[80] Williams, Alfred Hector, "A Study of the Adequacy of Existing Programs for the Training of Journeymen Molders in the Iron and Steel Foundries of Philadelphia," pp. 41–42.

[81] *Iron Age,* March 14, 1912, p. 679.

[82] Williams, Alfred Hector, *op. cit.,* p. 46.

[83] *Iron Age,* November 28, 1912, p. 1263.

[84] Hook, *op. cit.,* pp. 14–15.

[85] *Iron Age,* July 6, 1905, p. 24.

[86] Fitch, *op. cit.,* p. 149, footnote.

[87] "Training the Supervisory Work Force," Minutes of the First Bi-Monthly Conference of the National Association of Employment Managers, 1919, p. 25.

[88] *Ibid.,* pp. 9–10.

[89] Hendrick, *Life of Andrew Carnegie,* Vol. I, p. 297.

[90] Wall, Joseph Frazier, *Andrew Carnegie,* p. 665.

[91] *Ibid.,* p. 666.

[92] Jeans, *op. cit.,* p. 500.

[93] *Ibid.,* p. 501.

[94] Douglas, *American Apprenticeship and Industrial Education,* p. 323.

[95] *Iron Age,* July 6, 1905, p. 24.

[96] Jeans, *op. cit.,* p. 351.

[97] *Ibid.,* p. 67.

[98] Hook, *op. cit.,* pp. 15–16.

[99] Jeans, *op. cit.,* p. 351.

[100] *Ibid.,* p. 353.

[101] Bowles, S. and H. Gintis, "I.Q. and the U.S. Class Structure," *Social Policy,* January-February, 1972.

19.   The Historical and Political Perspective
On Organizations of Lucien Karpik[1]

Joseph W. Weiss

The purpose of this paper is to present an interpretative overview of the perspective on organizations of Lucien Karpik. Karpik's studies of multinational corporations (MNC's) have contributed to the publication of five articles which, taken together, represent a comprehensive and integrated analysis of the political and economic dimensions of complex organizations. The systematic effort of Karpik's analysis in establishing the links among the environment, history, and the politics of organizations in a single perspective is a contribution to organizational theory. The aim here is neither to summarize all Karpik's works nor to present his more detailed economic reasoning, but to discuss his image of organizations and the essential concepts and arguments he uses in studying multinational firms. The discussion that follows is organized under these headings: (I) Introduction: Background and task of Karpik's works; (II) Karpik's image of the organization and his unit of analysis; (III) Logics of action as an instrument for studying organizational actors' objectives; (IV) The historical component in Karpik's perspective; (V) Karpik's concept of environment; (VI) Conclusion.

I. INTRODUCTION: BACKGROUND AND TASK OF KARPIK'S WORKS

The background of Karpik's works begins with his concern (1972a) that the sociology of organizations is in serious trouble because the established theories in the field (i.e., the theories of bureaucracy, the human relations school, classical and neo-classical economics, and more contemporary approaches) have isolated organizations from their historical, political, and economic contexts. Consequently, organizational analysis has resulted in the effort "to manipulate and compare organizations that are . . . paralyzed, blind and deaf, in short stripped of their intentionality and environment and thus of their specificity." Karpik justifies this claim by presenting a critique of organizational theory that extends from Marx's and Weber's writings on organizations to more contemporary theorists. The essential elements of these critiques are outlined here in order to facilitate an understanding of Karpik's own theoretical and methodological task.

Karpik's critique (1972a:300) of Marx's and Weber's concepts of organizations centers on their respective images of organizations as passive, economic entities, vulnerable to impersonal market forces. Missing from both Marx's and Weber's theories of organizations, he argues, is the concept of powerful individuals and

[1] *The Historical and Political Perspective on Organizations of Lucien Karpik* by Joseph W. Weiss. Copyright © 1981 by Joseph W. Weiss. Reprinted by permission.
The author thanks Michael Aiken for his invaluable conceptual and technical criticisms and suggestions that made the writing of this paper possible. In addition, the author thanks Lucien Karpik and André Delbecq for their helpful and insightful criticisms of an earlier draft.

dominant organizational coalitions that intentionally exert their respective ends on corporate activities and in so doing have impact on and even determine the larger strategies of the firm.

The influence of powerful organizational actors and coalitions in enforcing their own objectives is absent not only in Marx's and Weber's writings on organizations, but also in most contemporary studies. The organizational studies of Parsons (1963), Selznick (1949), Merton (1957), and Blau (1962) reflect goal-setting activities as either abstracted from organizational members, or as dysfunctional or displaced actions of organizational actors — if such activities cannot be related to survival functions of the organization as an idealized entity. Moreover, because the study of organizational goals has remained isolated from concrete, interactive situations of organizational members, Karpik contends that this problem has resulted in separate and unrelated analyses of organizational environments and other social and economic functions of organizations. For example, there is an abundance of studies identifying (1) organizational environment (Emery and Trist, 1969; Dill, 1961; Lawrence and Lorsch, 1967; Terreberry, 1968; Pugh, et al., 1969; Thompson and MacEuwen, 1958); (2) the social and economic functions of organizations (Selznick, 1949; Touraine, 1971); and (3) the economic systems of which organizations are a part (Schumpeter, 1954; Baran and Sweezy, 1962; Galbraith, 1971). However, he argues that there seems to be an absence of studies linking these dimensions in a single analytic framework.

Karpik cites two studies that approach such a linkage of the environment with the internal goal-setting activities of organizational actors: the studies of Burns and Stalker (1961) and Perrow (1963). Burns and Stalker's study analyzes the economic environment and the internal power system of the firm without relating the two. Such an omission, Karpik speculates, may be attributable to the authors' perception of their task mainly as that of modifying the approach of the human relations school, an approach which limits organizational analysis to the social psychology of individual actors; or, Burns and Stalker may not have perceived the environment in political terms and therefore were not inclined to specify the relationships between organizational actors and external constraints. Whatever the reasons for Burns' and Stalker's omission of the linkage of the internal dynamics of the organization to the external environment, Karpik notes that this omission remains a paradox.

Perrow's study of hospitals (1963) succeeds in relating internal organizational arrangements to historical and social constraints. His analysis focuses on the idea that organizations are at times confronted with "crucial tasks" that cannot be routinized. The group(s) that have the power and that take the responsibility of solving these tasks determine the actual collective goals of the organizations. Missing from Perrow's study, however, are the mechanisms that explain how each successive group that assumed power in the hospital actually gained and maintained administrative control. A specification of these mechanisms would have entailed an analysis of the internal and external determinants of power and the interaction between these dimensions. Nevertheless, Perrow's study does represent, according to Karpik, a step in the direction of relating the internal power struggles of the organization to historical processes. Karpik also notes that a study such as Perrow's has not as yet been undertaken with large economic organizations.

In addition to Burns and Stalker and Perrow, the following organizational theorists have also, Karpik acknowledges, exerted a significant influence on his perspective of organizations: Cyert and March (1963), Vernon (1971), Rothchild (1974), Baumol (1967), Marris (1964), and Williamson (1963). Some of the central ideas of these authors are summarized here in order to illuminate the theoretical background from which Karpik borrowed and extended.

Vernon's study (1971) of MNCs has several conceptual elements that Karpik notes have been influential on his own thinking. These include, first, the idea that the firm is not a homogeneous entity, but a complex set of interactions between different interest groups that compete for power. Second, goal-setting processes of these organizational groups are characterized as a series of compromises among themselves; such activities are also the result of unpredictable and uncertain economic realities. Third, the process of internationalization of large corporations is not a given historical necessity; rather, such strategies are but one choice of action for corporations. The decision to internationalize must be studied by researchers in order to determine the favorable and unfavorable conditions of such a strategy. All large corporations, for example, do not become multinationals. Fourth, and related to the third point, the general strategic choices of multinationals are also made by organizational actors who share and compete for organizational resources and power. The study of such choices cannot, therefore, be deduced mechanically by analyzing variations in the environment through economic categories only. Both strategy and environment are dynamic realities which are formed by the interaction of organizational groups that make decisions.

Baumol (1967), Marris (1964), and Williamson (1963) represent what Karpik terms a strict economic approach to studying multinational corporations. These theorists have influenced Karpik mainly in their elimination of the principle of profit maximization as a method of studying corporate activities. Marris, in particular, claims that organizations are directed by managers (not owners) who seek to maximize their own personal benefits by gaining more money, career advantages, and power. Managers also try to increase the rate of growth of the firm instead of the profit. Karpik criticizes these authors for not differentiating the spheres of influence and power between managers and owners, and for neglecting the issue of dominance of certain firms over others.

Cyert and March's study of organizations (1963) also has had a substantial impact on Karpik's perspective. Their image of the organization as a political system of coalitions and individual actors bargaining over organizational influence and power is evident in Karpik's analysis. They also contributed to Karpik's notion of the distribution of power within the organization by showing that the organization consists of multiple centers of power. Coalitions vary in their preferences and thus in their struggles over position and power. These interest groups, according to Cyert and March, resolve their conflicts and competitive differences through bargaining processes. Subcoalitions are formed and different individuals and groups come to terms over conflicting objectives by paying and being paid in side-payments (personal rewards, fringe benefits, etc.) as well as through formal organizational rewards and procedures. The informal and individual nature of the organization underlies this entire process of conflict resolution and the sharing of organizational power.

Another way Cyert and March have influenced Karpik's thought is through their explanation of the definition and study of organizational goals. Goals are the results of the bargaining processes and are reflected in the decisions made and enforced by the dominant coalition in the organization. Goals also are the independent constraints imposed on the organization through the negotiating and compromising processes among coalitional members. To study the goals of an organization from their scheme, it is necessary to reconstruct the results of the bargaining processes at various points in time. One such indicator of organizational goals, according to Cyert and March, is the budget of firms. Budgets reflect how resources are allocated in organizations.

Budgets also indicate discrete decisions and identify the powerful coalitional members in the organization who control the allocation of resources.

Karpik's main criticism of Cyert and March's work is their restriction of organizational goals to only five domains of activity: sales, stock, production, market, and profit. As will be discussed in more detail subsequently, Karpik's concept of logics of action extends Cyert and March's idea of organizational domains to social and political actions as well as to economic ones.

Finally, Karpik suggests that Rothchild's work (1947) is the most substantive in terms of studying the economic interactions of corporations from a political perspective. However, this work also seems to have had the least influence on organizational theory. Karpik refers to three major hypotheses derived from Rothchild's work that are particularly interesting. First, Rothchild contended that interorganizational relationships are characterized mainly by the principle of oligopolistic warfare. By this he meant that the aim of corporations in competing over prices, resources, and markets was ultimately domination of the more powerful firms over the less capable ones. Corporate relationships, therefore, should be studied from a strategic perspective, i.e., how firms seek to dominate markets and resources as well as each other. Secondly, economic choices of organizations are the result of the competitive struggles among competing departments within firms. Internal corporate relationships are also characterized by strategies of members to dominate and control one another. Third, economic action is political action. The importance of the state's involvement in corporate activities was recognized by Rothchild as a power with which firms had to contend in their competitive struggles to control markets.

These theoretical influences on Karpik, although by no means exhaustive, represent important contributions to Karpik's own formulation of the organization. Karpik's study of the history of science, technology, economics, and philosophy — as well as organizational thoery — led him to conceive of his task of developing a perspective on organizations far more extensive and inclusive than any attempted before.

II. KARPIK'S IMAGE OF THE ORGANIZATION AND HIS UNIT OF ANALYSIS

Karpik views the organization as a loosely coupled political system in which individuals who are motivated by private interests form coalitions. These coalitions bargain and compete for power and position in order to enforce their own ends on the organization. A dominant coalition emerges from these internal struggles. The dominant coalition controls the resources of the organization and uses these resources to attain its own ends. Hence the ends of the dominant coalition become the ends of the organization. The strategies this dominant coalition develops in attempting to attain its ends are of particular interest to Karpik.

Dominant coalitions change over time, since the bargaining process is ongoing. Therefore, to identify the powerful individuals and alliances within an organization, it is necessary to reconstruct the results of the bargaining processes over given periods of time. The point to be made here is that the organization consists of centers of power. Individuals belonging to different groups align, bargain, and compete for organizational resources. Moreover, the organization can be defined as a multi-actor arena. From this competitive arena, a dominant coalition emerges and succeeds in imposing its private ends on the corporation. These ends, in turn, become the single dominant policy of the firm.

Karpik classifies the internal power system of the organization in terms of general categories of membership. His classification is borrowed from Parsons and is outlined as follows: (1) the institutional system revolves around "crucial" decisions, or what some analysts call strategic decisions, such as diversification and the decision to internationalize; (2) the managerial system includes all operational policies relating to a field of activity (sales, research, manufacturing, etc.); (3) the technical system comprises scientific, commercial, and manufacturing activities; (4) the distribution system governs the socio-economic dispersement of wealth in the form of careers, income, working conditions, and prestige. It should be noted that this system is neither unitary nor homogeneous.

Karpik's basic unit of analysis, then, is the individual organizational actor. Individual actors, however, become linked to an interconnected set of economic, political, and social systems that also define and influence the organization. As Karpik has stated, organizational members belong to a division in a firm. The firm is also part of an industrial group (like the auto industry). The industrial group, in turn, is linked to the national economy, which is related to the world market.

These relationships are interwoven into a complex set of political, economic, and social interactions that, according to Karpik, can only be separated and studied from a "bottom-up" approach: i.e., it is necessary to identify the individual and group ends of organizational members in order to understand how a dominant coalition's preferences become the strategy of a firm.

III. LOGICS OF ACTION AS AN INSTRUMENT FOR STUDYING ORGANIZATIONAL ACTOR'S OBJECTIVES

Karpik examines organizational goal attainment as a problematic and plural concept that comprises at least four dimensions. These dimensions can be explained from two points of view, that of the organizational actors and that of the outside observer. From the viewpoint of the organizational actor, the intended or stated ends of goal achievement are identified and distinguished from the means or methods of obtaining these ends. From the point of view of the outside observer, the actor's actual implemented preferences are also observed separately from the means used to achieve the ends. These two levels of analysis, the *intended* ends and means of goal attainment as stated by organizational members and the *implemented* ends and means of goal-seeking behavior as established by an outsider, represent Karpik's concern with determining the actual methods and outcomes of goal attainment among organizational members.

To better understand Karpik's four dimensions of organizational goal attainment, definitions of the following terms are presented and discussed: *objectives, strategies, logics of action,* and *politics.* Karpik's conceptual distinctions among these terms represent, in part, his contribution toward resolving the dilemma of how to study goals in organizations.

Objectives for Karpik are the intentions and desired ends of individual organizational actors or of coalitions of actors in those instances when a given desired end has been collectively agreed upon by the members of a group. To elaborate further, objectives are shared cognitive intentions. Objectives as private intentional ends of organizational actors or coalitions may or may not be realized; hence objectives exist essentially as desired future states from the point of view of the actor.

Karpik also notes that the formulation of objectives by organizational members is not necessarily a formal process performed within homogeneous groups of actors. Karpik lists three general levels, or groups, around which organizational actors might align: services, professions, and primary (informal) groups. Coalitions, then, may form among dispersed members across different departments in an organization.

Karpik defines *strategies* as irreversible commitments of the allocation of an organization's resources. These commitments represent the intentional or planned *means* of organizational actors' or coalitions' methods of achieving their objectives. Strategies may or may not actually be realized; therefore, strategies are the conscious and deliberate methods chosen by actors to achieve desired ends.

The concept of *logics of action* (LAs) is most central to Karpik's perspective (1972a:316-319; 1972b:89-92; 1972c:26-31; 1978:47-49). Karpik defines LAs as the observed *rationalities* of organizational actors and coalitions from the point of view of an outside observer, e.g., a researcher. LAs are "the principles of action around which individuals and groups organize their attitudes and behavior" (1978:47). The essential use of the concept of logics of action is that it enables the external observer to distinguish between private objectives as actors define them and the preferences of organizational members as observed by the researcher, based not only on words but also on actors' behaviors.

Logics of action represent a broad range of social, economic, and political choices from which organizational actors and coalitions are assumed — by an outside observer — to organize their goal-seeking activities. Karpik lists the following seven LAs, which he admits are not exhaustive but which illustrate the principles of action that are assumed to motivate goal-seeking behavior of organizational members or coalitions (1978:48):

> *Adaptive logics of action:* domination of the stimuli response mechanism by which the survival and growth of the firm are assured. Action is not a result of deliberate choices but of pragmatic reactions.
>
> *Prestige logics of action:* revealed through choices designed to enhance the reputation of the firm rather than its economic success. Fashion and the reference group govern highly variable initiatives that are fundamentally determined by social conventions.
>
> *Technical logics of action:* domination by the productive machinery, which draws its legitimacy from a symbolic relationship between technology and modernity and serves as the organizing principle in the socio-economic universe.
>
> *Production logics of action:* predominance of the manufacturing system's internal functioning as a condition of success. The reasoning finds its expression both in the rise in overall output and in that of labor productivity.
>
> *Profitability logics of action:* search for maximum short-term profit; this takes on different forms depending upon market structures, size of firm, or product characteristics.
>
> *Puissance logics of action:* conquest or reinforcing of monopoly or oligopoly power through control of economic situations.
>
> *Innovation logics of action:* high rate of creation of production processes and, above all, of new products as sources of major discontinuities.

It should be noted that Karpik states that no single LA dominates all activity in a large firm at a given time; rather, there are hierarchies of LAs that dominate an organization's actions. The nature of these LAs and the identification of the dominant coalition that enforces them are the tasks of the researcher to reconstruct. Although Karpik does not state the exact methodology that researchers can use to accomplish this task, one can infer that such methods as historical reconstructions, participant observation, interviews, and the like seem suitable.

Politics is defined by Karpik as the *outcomes* of collective organizational action. Politics, in Karpik's perspective, is equivalent to policy outcomes. Thus politics represents the implementation of an organizational coalition's goal-seeking activities as understood from the point of view of an outside observer.

The following conceptual scheme[2] illustrates Karpik's four dimensions of goal attainment among organizational actors, more specifically:

	Intentions (of Goal-Seeking Activities)	Implementation (of Goal-Seeking Activities)
Point of View of Actor	OBJECTIVES	STRATEGIES
Point of View of Observer	LOGICS OF ACTION	POLICY

Essentially, this illustration can be summarized as follows: goal attainment from *the point of view of the organizational actor* is analyzed as a conscious attempt to implement certain desired ends (objectives), which are private and shared cognitive preferences of organizational members. The means by which actors seek to implement their desired ends are their strategies. Strategies, then, are intentional methods of implementing the objectives of actors. Strategies in this sense may not be realized.

From *the point of view of the observer,* the logics of action represent the reconstructed enactment of the actor's actually practiced or observed ends (by an outside observer), which ends members attempt to impose on the entire organization. The politics, or policy outcomes, represent the observed means by which organizational actors have imposed their logics of action on the organization.

It should be noted that the concept of logics of action is similar to Perrow's notion of "operative goals" (1963), i.e., goals that are observed as actually pursued by a dominant coalition, as contrasted with "official goals," which are not necessarily implemented by organizational members. Operative goals are those private ends of a powerful group that has successfully exerted its ends on the entire organization. However, Perrow's notion of operative goals, unlike Karpik's concept of logics of action, is discussed and studied separately from the political process that gives meaning to the substance and the means of goal attainment activities. For Karpik, there may be competing logics of action at any point in time among various organizational coalitions. It is only by studying the political struggles among coalitions that a researcher can identify the dominant coalition that succeeds in imposing its logics of action on the organization. These logics of action of this powerful, dominant coalition in turn explain the types of policy outcomes that characterize an organization's activities.

To further clarify the meaning of the concept of logics of action, Mayer Zald's study of organizational goals in five correctional institutions (1962) is briefly summarized. Zald's concept of goals is compared and contrasted with Karpik's logics of action in order to illustrate the latter's meaning in an actual situation.

Zald's study demonstrated that the dominance of treatment goals as compared with custodial goals in selected correctional institutions resulted in significant differences in the way power was distributed among officials in each type of setting.

---

[2] The author wishes to acknowledge Michael Aiken's original development of this conceptual scheme, although certain revisions have been made in this illustration.

Specifically, Zald concluded that power as a function of goals was more evenly distributed among staff in treatment-oriented facilities than in custodial ones. Not only was the distribution of power found to be a function of goals in Zald's study, but the amount of power held by various groups within the institution also was affected by the types of dominant goals operating in a setting. Administrators held more power than social workers in custodial facilities. Decisions concerning activities such as counselling, containment, etc., also were affected by the types of goals held by officials in the different institutions.

Zald's study of goals is similar to Karpik's perspective in that Zald viewed dominant goals as outcomes of activities of members who sought to impose their influence on major organizational decisions. Zald also studied the effects of dominant goals on organizations from the perceptions of staff. As in Karpik's perspective, Zald's unit of analysis was the individual organizational member. Through interviews, participant observation and historical analysis, Zald attempted to determine the actual effects or outcomes of dominant logics of action on organizational activities. Moreover, Zald did not take as a given any outcomes of stated organizational goals. He studied organizational members' activities, their decisions, the amount and distribution of power among individuals and groups in order to reconstruct the effects such goals had on organizational arrangements — power and influence among staff. In these ways Zald's concept and study of organizational goals are similar to Karpik's approach.

Zald's study of goals, however, falls short of Karpik's recommended analysis of LAs in the following important way: Zald did not view goals as political outcomes; rather, he concluded that the differences between the effects of the staffs' actions in the two goal-oriented institutions were results of organizational size, personality attributes of officials, and complexity of tasks. Such conclusions prohibit an analysis of the way power originates and is reproduced among coalitions in organizations.

The advantages of Karpik's concept of logics of action, then, include the *differentiation* of intended objectives of organizational actors from their imposed private ends as reconstructed by the external observer. This analytical separation of concepts allows the researcher to compare cognitively shared, intended objectives with the observed logics of action of members in a firm. Karpik's perspective also enables the researcher to distinguish between actor's intentional means of achieving their objectives (i.e., strategies) and the politics or observed policy outcomes of goal-seeking activities. These distinctions also enable the researcher to identify the dominant coalition in an organization and to specify which private ends of the dominant coalition become the enacted goals of the organization.

Karpik's concept of LAs is also shaped by and is contingent on historical, economic, and political influences. As will be discussed in the following two sections, logics of action originate within Karpik's constructed historical forms of capitalism. Also, the choice of LAs is governed by the types of competitive struggles among firms. More will be said about the historical context and the types of competition affecting the choice and use of logics of action in the subsequent discussion.

IV. THE HISTORICAL COMPONENT IN KARPIK'S PERSPECTIVE

One of Karpik's major contributions to organizational analysis is his discussion of three historical forms of capitalism and his interpretation of the effects of the evolution of science and technology within these historical forms on organizations.

These forms of capitalism represent the macro-level historical forces that explain the development of particular types of economic organizations and the changing rules and methods of competition used by competing organizations to gain power over markets, clientele, and other corporations.

The three historical forms of capitalism include *Merchant, Industrial,* and *Technological* capitalism. These stages of capitalism are reconstructed by using ideal or pure types (1972c:2). As historical forms they are not, Karpik states, rigidly conceived; for example, they overlap, as is evident in different corporations' strategies and levels of industrial development. In reconstructing these stages of capitalism, Karpik is more concerned with the third and most recent form, technological capitalism, as exemplified in the appearance of the multinational corporation. The first two forms, therefore, are only briefly discussed in order to compare them with that of technological capitalism.

Merchant capitalism emerged in the second half of the nineteenth century in England. It is characterized by the appearance of the market from which, for the first time in history, all goods and resources were derived. Under merchant capitalism the concepts and practices of work and nature become related to the ideas and practices of production and merchandise. Human nature, in turn, is understood and valued in terms of material production: i.e., the capacity to produce goods.

The Industrial Revolution paved the way for the advance of mechanical techniques and free labor, a combination that allowed nations to accumulate great wealth. The function of the State under this form of capitalism was to maintain a system of free competition, allowing the market to expand spontaneously and autonomously. For the first time in history, the economic sphere of production was separated from the political control of the State. Merchant capitalism, in short, was the beginning of the development of a more complex universe of industrial and technical growth.

Industrial capitalism had its beginnings in the 1930s, and became most prominent in the 1950s. This form of capitalism is characterized by stable growth of firms. This growth was in large part possible because of the predictable nature of the economic market and because of the ability of corporations to adapt to market changes by effectively planning and predicting supply and demand relationships. Firms were also able to successfully compete with other industries over market control, since competition between enterprises was based on maintaining an equilibrium of economic power and on establishing a relatively stable relationship between production and consumption. The auto, energy, and semi-finished goods industries developed and flourished in this form of capitalism.

Industrial capitalism is also characterized by its use of technological development more than of scientific discovery. This form of capitalism functions according to a growth principle "whereby the market is extended through the addition of new clienteles, while the economic process is controlled by the authorities, both public and privates" (1978:30). The State under industrial capitalism intervened to protect workers' welfare and to impose planning functions on industrial growth in order to ensure more equitable distribution of goods and services at a broader societal level.

The advent of *technological capitalism* marks a new historical and economic form that produces consequences that are economically, socially, and ideologically significant in changing the interactions between firms. For the first time in history, scientific knowledge and technological inventions are combined into industrial production by multinational firms' Research and Development divisions. The development of such multinational corporate industries as those of aerospace, chemicals, and pharmaceuticals signals a new historical development in the transformation of scientific knowledge and technological developments into economic products. This historical development gave rise to a new founded power of multinational technological corporations, including the following: (1) corporations now have the capacity to transform scientific inventions into economic goods *within* their research departments; (2) firms, therefore, are able to create products and the resources from which products are derived; (3) with the ability to create new products at will, firms can also eliminate or control the value of previous or existing goods. Firms can also determine the life of products (planned obsolescence).

These characteristics of technological capitalism also enable multinationals to determine and control consumer values and consumption rates. By the process of continually diversifying products, consumers are conditioned by firms to buy products according to the production cycles of the corporation.

Corporations also gain the possibility and the power to create new clienteles and markets. Since the ability to create new products rests almost solely within the boundaries of the firm, corporations can choose where to market products as they wish. Moreover, their territorial limits for marketing new merchandise are expanded to the international arena.

The development of technological capitalism also brings a change in the forms of competition among economic firms. For example, in merchant capitalism, the system of social and economic relationship between firms was limited. In fact, the individual enterprise was confronted with the need to maximize profit from an emerging market that was relatively uncomplicated. In industrial capitalism, corporations competed by creating monopolies to gain control over the expansion of production and territory. With technological capitalism, competition is regulated by the principle of "power" (or *puissance*). This type of competition is characterized in two ways: first, the corporation has the capacity to produce indefinite quantities of goods and services, which enables it to impose on the consuming public "the systematic and legitimate distortions of the field of merchandise" (1978:37). In this sense, technological enterprises become concerned less with fulfilling collective needs and more concerned with "the use of all the potential of the rational combination of science and industry." Second, the principle of power is not limited to the economic realm of production but also affects socio-political relationships. That is, the State now becomes consumer (for example, as is the case with the aerospace industry) as well as the protector of consumers. In addition, consumption patterns and life-styles are more or less controlled by the corporation's capacity and decision to produce select products.

Karpik's discussion of the three forms of capitalism is useful in examining the different types of corporations that develop as a result of the effects of the historical evolution of science and technology on economic production. In particular, the emergence of the multinational corporation, in Karpik's view, represents not only an effect of broader historical forces at the societal level, but also, by virtue of the unlimited power of such enterprises in creating new markets, clienteles, and values for the consuming public, changes the rules of organizational competition. The notion of competition, based on the struggle over resources and resource allocation, is replaced with the idea of corporations' engaging in strategic conflicts over the control of consumer values, clients, and territory to produce and distribute goods. This subject is explained in more detail in the next section. The point to be made here, however, is that Karpik's discussion of the importance of the historical evolution and influence of science and technology on the types of corporations that develop and the resulting rules of competition that firms create is generalizable by analogy to other organizations. For example, such research questions as the following can be asked by organizational analysts: What are the macro-level historical influences and the effects of scientific knowledge and technology on the types of organizations that are emerging to serve the public? Can the rules of interorganizational competition be identified? Are these rules related to historical influences? Are such competitive principles and practices different for these types of organizations than types of competition characterized in earlier or different historical periods? Such questions and issues relate organizational activities to societal-level historical contexts and forces. Organizational strategies and actions, then, take on a dynamic meaning, with consequences that not only are relevant to internal organizational problems of structure and performance, but that also pose questions and contribute information that address the actual formation and effects of historical determinants on organizational actions. It is the study of this reciprocal process that characterizes the intent and thrust of Karpik's perspective. However, the difficulty in advocating such a sociological perspective involves the reform of traditional organizational concepts — e.g., organizational effectiveness, and the pursuit of rational goals — that tend to insulate organizations from historical, political, and economic frames of analysis. Nevertheless, this reform is evident in Karpik's works.

In the following section Karpik's concept of environment is presented with particular emphasis on the related economic and political constraints of different forms of competition which are exemplified under industrial and technological capitalism.

V. KARPIK'S CONCEPT OF THE ENVIRONMENT

Karpik's concept of the environment of economic organizations is characterized in terms of macro-level political constraints that can be identified in the *forms of competition* that determine the types of interaction and negotiating processes among corporations. These forms of competition differ under the respective forms of capitalism.

In industrial capitalism firms compete in terms of expansion by creating and changing alliances. However, under this form of capitalism the existence of common products allowed firms to "acquire a consciousness of their independence, through role and role-expectation devices, and create a sub-system with visible 'frontiers,' common norms and values, shared collective interests and equilibrium levels." (1972c:14). Economic relationships in this shared economic type of system could be located along two main dimensions: (1) direct control of an area of industrial production as related to public demand; and (2) relatively controlled bargaining over the firm's position in the economic system. In other words, under industrial capitalism, firms were able to manipulate demand through internal policies of improving technical efficiency, substituting certain lines of products with others, or modifying products from time to time. Moreover, in terms of competing for geographic markets, firms were able to gain and thus divide the national and international market among themselves. The point to be made here is that under industrial capitalism the environmental constraints confronting corporations took the form of necessity — first, to regulate the relationships between production and demand, and second, to control the uncertainty created by the formation and dissolution of corporate alliances, through which process monopolies controlled different sectors of the national and international market. Nevertheless, as Karpik notes, enterprises under industrial capitalism could subsist only through arbitration and armistice. Conflict and competition between enterprises was more or less controlled and regulated by the corporations themselves and by the State.

The major economic and political constraints under technological capitalism are centered in competitive relationships between corporations attempting to control markets, clienteles, and values of the consuming public by rapidly creating and diversifying products. These competitive struggles create an international environment of uncertainty for multinationals and for the State. The basic underlying source of this environmental uncertainty is the unlimited economic — and thus political and social — *power* multinational corporations exert in their capacity to dominate markets and clientele. This uncertainty can be discussed from the perspective of the corporation and the State. For multinationals, the market is ever-changing, since product diversification and the continual creation of new products keep supply and demand and the production process itself in a constant state of change. Competition between enterprises is therefore based on the firm's ability to rapidly transform scientific knowledge into technological developments in order to produce and market new products. The uncertainty created by these historical developments under technological capitalism is described by Karpik as three types of capital that multinationals need to obtain and control in order to maintain dominance over the market, clientele, and competitors. These types of capital are *financial, intellectual,* and *political*. The point to be made about financial capital is straightforward: "The dominant firm that combines industrial and banking functions . . . has the means to make optimum choices regarding profit rates and the preservation of the flexibility of its production apparatus." (1978:43).

Technological firms that also compete on the basis of rapid transformation of scientific knowledge with technological developments depend on hosts of experts ranging from scientists to salespersons and managers, who function as intellectual capital of the firm. This form of capital also serves both prestige and productive functions in the firm's attempt to win symbolic as well as material domination of its clients and consumers.

The State's power to regulate the market and the activities of multinationals is extremely limited because of the following reasons: First, the technological and scientific production practices of firms are so highly technical and the rapid rate of product creation and change is so fast that the power of State regulation of this process is weakened. Second, the State itself depends on multinationals and large corporations for the purchase of such products as those of the aerospace, chemical, and pharmaceutical industries. Thus the dual role of the State as consumer and protector of clients lessens its ability to exert full control over technological production processes. Third, multinationals exert tremendous power over national economies. Too much State control could threaten the political relations between the State and industry and thus result in economic strains for the State.

Thus, under technological capitalism, the rules of competition change between corporations and between multinationals and the State. Such changes are also reflected in the strategies of corporations. Whereas under industrial capitalism corporations engage in planning processes aimed at balancing consumption-and-demand relationships and in maintaining more or less stable relationships among themselves, multinationals under the influences of technological capitalism seek to control and dominate the uses of scientific knowledge within their own production systems. And because of the capacity of multinationals to develop and effectively use powerful intellectual, financial, and political capital in their pursuit of economic control of markets and clients, the power of the State is substantially weakened as an intervening force.

The linkage of environmental constraints to corporate rules and practices of competition that exist under the different forms of historical capitalism led Karpik to two essential conclusions: First, resources are not a fixed property but are created by firms; second, "for dominant corporations, the entire game consists in creating and imposing situations whose dimensions they control, while for dominated firms, it consists in avoiding getting trapped in any given situation" (1978:45).

Karpik's concept of the environment and his notion that resources are created, not fixed properties are generalizable by analogy to other types of organizations. In particular, such research issues as the following arise: What types of resources can be and are created by organizations? How are the creation of these resources related to historical and scientific/technological developments? Does the use of these resources determine the types of competitive practices and rules between organizations? To what extent do organizations use intellectual, financial, and political capital to dominate clients, markets, and other competitors? Again, questions such as these tend, in Karpik's scheme, to encourage organizational research that interrelates historical, environmental, and actual organizational practices in identifying internal organizational power systems, especially as these systems affect and are determined by societal-level forces.

Karpik's message that environmental constraints are determined by different forms of capitalism suggests that the logics of action of organizational actors are not arbitrary. That is, organizational coalitions choose preferences that are historically and economically conditioned. Thus the notion of organizational efficiency as isolated from the larger historical and economic context of organizational members' goal-setting activities is not possible in Karpik's perspective. The plurality of the logics of action illustrates Karpik's concern with the interrelated economic, social, and political environment in which the dominant organizational coalition makes and imposes its decisions on the corporation.

VI. CONCLUSION

The elements in Karpik's perspective on organizations are not entirely new, but his approach is innovative in that he combines historical, economic, and political views of the organization in a single analytic framework. As contrasted with the comparative structural and structural contingency approaches that have dominated the study of organizations over the last two decades, Karpik's analysis is far more sociological in that he conceives and examines the organization as an open political and economic system that is embedded in its cultural context. At the center of Karpik's analysis is the individual organizational actor who competes, bargains, and joins with others to exert private and collective interests on the firm. The aggregation of these individual actors and groups actually comprises and, for Karpik, defines the firm. The range of choices open to organizational members and to the dominant coalition depends on their ability to perceive and control organizational power through forming powerful alliances.

At the macro-level of analysis, Karpik reconstructs three forms of historical capitalism that serve as the sources of power and rules of competition used by corporations to control production processes, markets, and clientele. Karpik's specification of the concept of environment involves the determination of economic constraints that operate within the different periods of historical capitalism. Under classical capitalism, production-and-demand relationships are defined as situations that determine the limits and opportunities of corporate strategy-making in winning or losing markets and clients. Under technological capitalism, various forms of capital (intellectual, financial, and political) shape the political strategies of competing firms in their bid to dominate clientele and markets.

Karpik's concept of the logics of action allows the researcher to reconstruct the rationalities and principles of action that determine the private preferences of organizational members. Since these logics of action are in part determined by the historical form of capitalism in which they developed, LAs represent a micro-level analytical concept that is linked to historical and economic constraints. Logics of action, then, represent Karpik's "bottom-up" approach of studying organizational strategy by establishing the individual actors' preferences and by showing how these preferences come to dominate corporate strategy.

The organization and its memberships are, in Karpik's final analysis, a window through which the observer can discern general societal-level processes. In the sociological traditions of Marx and Weber, Karpik has attempted to define the historical and economic processes by observing organizational structure as a dynamically recreated series of interactions among organizational actors. Although parts of Karpik's logic and methods remain incomplete and in need of operational specification, his perspective in general represents an innovative shift from the positivistic approaches of organizational theory that have neglected the role of intentionality of individual actors and that have isolated the impact of cultural influences from organizational strategy.

REFERENCES

Baran, P., and Sweezy, P.
1962   *Le Capitalisme Monopoliste.* Paris: Maspero.

Baumol, N.
1967   *Business Behavior, Value and Growth.* New York: MacMillan.

Blau, P., and R. Scott
1962   *Formal Organizations.* San Francisco: Chandler Publishing Co.

Burns, T., and G. Stalker
1961   *The Management of Innovation.* London: Tavistock Publishers.

Dill, W.
1962   "The impact of environment on organizational development." Pages 94-109 in Sidney Mailick and Edward Van Ness (eds.) *Concepts and Issues in Administrative Behavior.* Englewood Cliffs, N.J.: Prentice-Hall, Inc.

Emery, F., and Trist, E.
1969   "The causal texture of organizational environments," *Human Relations* 18:21-31.

Karpik, L.
1972a   "Sociologie, economie, politique et buts des organisations de production," *Revenue Francais de Sociologie* 13:299-324.
1972b   "Les politique et les logiques d'action de la grande entreprise industrielle," *Sociologie du Travail* 1:82-105.

1972c   "Multinational enterprises and large technological corporations," translated from *Revue Economique* 23:1-46.
1972d   "Technological capitalism," translated from *Sociologie du Travail* 13:2-34.
1978   "Organizations, institutions and history." In Lucien Karpik (ed.) *Organization and Environment: Theory, Issues and Reality.* Beverly Hills, California: Sage.

Lawrence, P., and Lorsch, J.
1967   *Organizations and Environment.* Boston: Graduate School of Business Administration.

March, J., and H. Simon
1964   *Organizations.* Wiley.

Marris, R.
1957   *The Economic Theory of "Managerial" Capitalism.* Chicago: Free Press of Glencoe.

Merton, R.
1957   *Social Theory and Social Science.* Glencoe, Ill.: The Free Press.

Perrow, C.
1963   "Goals and power structure: A historical case study." Pages 112-146 in E. Friedson (ed.) *The Hospital in Modern Society.* Chicago: The Free Press of Glencoe.

Rothchild, K.
1947   "Price theory and oligopoly," *The Economic Journal* 57:229-330.

Selznick, P.
1967   *TVA and The Grass Roots.* New York: Basic Books.

Schumpeter, J.
1954   *Capitalisme, Socialisme et Democratie.* Paris: Payot.

Terreberry, S.
1968   "Evolution of organizational environments," *Administrative Science Quarterly* 12:590-613.

Thompson, J., and J. MacEwen
1958   "Organizational goals and environment: Goal-setting as an interaction process," *American Sociological Review* 23:23-31.

Tourraine, A.
1971   *The Post-Industrial Society.* New York: Random House.

Vernon, R.
1971   *Sovereignty at Bay.* New York: Basic Books.

Williamson, A.
1963   "A model of rational managerial behavior." In R. Cyert and J. March, *A Behavioral Theory of the Firm.* Englewood Cliffs, N.J.: Prentice-Hall, Inc.

Zald, M.
1962   "Organizational control structures in five correctional institutions," *American Journal of Sociology* 68:335-345.

20.   Organizations, Institutions and History*

Lucien Karpik

STRATEGIES OF LARGE CORPORATIONS: LOGICS OF ACTION AND DISCRETIONARY POWER

The action of the oligopolistic corporation cannot be deduced automatically either from the structure of the market or from economic situations. This is where the crucial notion of discretionary power, in the sense of the capacity to break loose from external constraints in order to make choices, comes in; through the strategic resources available to it, the firm disposes of a greater or lesser range of margins of manoeuvre, and it may adopt a variety of heterodox lines of behaviour which are not necessarily incompatible with economic success. It is one of the paradoxes of the notion of discretionary power that it cannot definitively record all the wealth that serves as its basis and, hence, is incapable of measurement. This is because strategic resources vary according to economic forms, in addition to which many of them are actually *created* through the process of competitive struggles. Besides, the use of terms such as orthodoxy-heterodoxy necessarily leads us to a formal analysis, to the definition of typical behaviour and the examination of discrepancies, these being equivalent to

*From "Organizations, Institutions and History" by Lucien Karpik, *Organization and Environment: Theory, Issues, and Reality.* Copyright © 1978 by the International Sociological Association. Reprinted by permission of Sage Publications, London and Beverly Hills.

relations between the norm and deviance. If we reject these assumptions and this approach, then we shall only be able to examine discretionary power following a study of firm's strategies.

Any classification of strategies must satisfy three requirements: (1) comparison of all actions which, directly or indirectly, deliberately or unconsciously, impinge upon the economic system, regardless of the social actors concerned: firms, banks, the State, research centres, trade-unions, etc.; (2) the study of relations between organizations' choices and the groups which compose them; and (3) the study of discrepancies between meanings experienced and actual behaviour, which involve social orientations, forms of organization and power relationships. These are the functions of *logics of action*.

This analytical tool, which is general because historical, allows us, when associated with certain others, to enumerate the strategies available: it also leads to a number of interpretations of variations in strategies, and to the reinstatement of discretionary power as the condition of internal and external determinations.

Logics of Action.   This concept is obviously related to the notion of rationality, the proclaimed principle of economic activity, but this rationality cannot be defined as the adequacy of means to ends (Weber) since what characterizes the firm is a *chain of ends and means* or a *series of primary objectives* and of *subsidiary objectives*, nor can it be assimilated to a 'one best way', a reasoning which the whole of industrial sociology has criticized successfully.

Hence, there is no one rationality but forms of rationality, which I call *logics of action*.[6] This latter concept is an analytical instrument constructed by the observer, designating forms of coherence among objectives; these then are *criteria of evaluation* which may be used equally well for organizations as for the social units making them up, and which are as valid for decisions and procedures as for individual and collective practices.

The theoretical functions of this concept are therefore twofold: to establish similarities and differences between actors who may be socially dispersed: logics of action are principles of *regrouping and dispersal;* and demonstrating the relations that exist between the organization and its members: logics of action are also *principles of action* around which individuals and groups organize their attitudes and behaviour. They provide an indispensable link between collective aims and private ones, inasmuch as these constitute a certain solution to economic demands.

Social action has been defined as the association between rationality and value. The logical outcome is a multitude of forms of rationality. But logics of action are not necessarily values, since the latter only emerge when history has been accomplished, at the moment when an institutionalized cultural model takes over the function of social regulation. Before they are socially established, criteria of evaluation arise out of action and exercise their effects: they are invented and remain invisible long before becoming conspicuous, making their appearance in official discourse and coming to represent alternatives for collective action.

Every state of the institution is connected with a given range of logics of action. In this way, the workers' movement can be analysed in terms of its participation in the social institution, and its practices are governed by *distributive logics of action* which are concerned both with the distribution of wealth and the redefinition of social power. The workers' movement is also an economic agent, and its social choices represent, whether directly or indirectly, a form of participation in the economic institution. This kind of approach thus leads to a dual unification: unification of stakes, which turn out to be identical for groups whom all else separates, and unification of actors, since it becomes possible to identify organizations and the groups composing them, in spite of the diversity of their objective positions and insofar as they share a common logic of action.

Hence, it will be understood that logics of action make it possible to break away from the realism of aims and organizational frontiers. Whereas power exercises all the more powerful effects in view of the fact that it plays upon the dispersal of actors and stakes, the segregation of people and the parcelization of problems, logics of action allow us to reconstruct — around their own specific cleavages — stakes and general power systems by basing themselves upon quasi-groups, quasi-alliances and quasi-oppositions, and that independently of an official power which conceals its aims through confusing rationality with the processes of enclosure and exchanges which it employs. What is involved here then is not the exchange of one realism for another but imposing an analytical tool whose validity depends upon the theoretical whole to which it belongs and which shifts the locus of social demarcations.

Logics of action are relative to each other, and only a whole variety of behaviour makes it possible to identify them. Confining ourselves to data assembled in the course of a study on the strategies of certain French and foreign corporations,[7] the following logics of action may be distinguished.

Adaptive logics of action: domination of the stimuli-response mechanism through which the survival and growth of the firm are assured. Action is not a result of deliberate choices but of pragmatic reactions.

Prestige logics of action: revealed through choices designed to enhance the reputation of the firm rather than its economic success. Fashion and the reference group govern highly variable initiatives that are fundamentally determined by social conventions.

Technical logics of action: domination by the productive machinery which draws its legitimacy from a symbolic relationship between technology and modernity and serves as the organizing principle in the socio-economic universe.

Production logics of action: predominance of the manufacturing system's internal functioning as a condition of success. The reasoning finds its expression both in the rise in overall output and in that of labour productivity.

Profitability logics of action: search for maximum short-term profit; this takes on different forms depending upon market structures, size of firm or product characteristics.

Puissance logics of action: conquest or reinforcing of monopoly or oligopoly power through control of economic situations.

Innovative logics of action: high rate of creation of production processes and, above all, of new products as sources of major discontinuities.

From one economic form to another, it is not the logics of action which change but only their *empirical expressions,* and an inventory of them for technological capitalism is only provisional: it has only been partially tested for an interpretation of empirical data (see Appendix). This type of table may, moreover, give rise to misunderstanding, and it should be made clear that the presence of a given logic of action in the behaviour of a social actor cannot be inferred from a single choice but that it always supposes a whole range of practices, the underlying structure of which can be discovered.

Strategies of Large Corporations. A number of conceptual clarifications are called for, mainly concerning the terms 'objective', 'policy' and 'strategy'. An objective is defined as any pursuit of a desired state, associated with a series of technical and human operations that can be isolated within the firm. A distinction must be drawn between partial objectives and general objectives. Each partial objective represents only one area of the firm's activity (manufacturing, sales, finance, research, administration, wages, etc.); its achievement depends on only a limited number of people and organizational units, and its definition is subject to the divergent preferences of the professional groups implementing it or involved in defining it. General objectives that hold for the organization as a whole are defined by configurations of partial objectives. We shall couple objectives with policy in order to distinguish them from strategies: the former represent an amorphous reality, identified in their objective realization in the form of plans, procedures or organizational structures; the latter, as partly irreversible commitments, cannot be isolated from the economic struggle and the equilibrium of the system of interaction to which the firm belongs.

All strategies are defined by the association of an area of activity, a logic of action and a level of references. By level — or frame — of reference I mean the competitive field in which the firm operates, the boundaries of this field frequently being the subject of divergences between the manager and the observer. The system of interactions to which the firm belongs may be national, European or worldwide. Areas of activity designate the firm's specialized functions — sales, manufacturing, finance, research, etc. — to which specific human and material resources correspond. Although they are especially simple in appearance — since a look at the organization chart enables us to identify them — areas of reality are, in fact, an eminently ambiguous reality. The greater the division of labour within the firm, the more subdivisions lend themselves to reassembly according to domains of activity. But adopting official delimitations would amount to ratifying the ruling frame of reference even though these are the products of complex rationalities in which economic, social and political realities are interwoven. Where the power system, for example, is concerned, it is not enough to include authority, or the decision-making process; we must also add all those plans and procedures which, under the guise of economic rationality, are responsible for the predetermination of social agents. It is not enough to observe these areas of activity, they must also be constructed. Thus defined, strategies may be subdivided into partial strategies whose configurations define general strategies.

The more firms are classed as *heterogeneous,* the more difficult it becomes to enumerate strategic configurations. A good many of them are involved in both economic forms, acting according to two distinct rules of functioning. The complexity of the arbitrages imposed upon the institutional power stems not only from the diversity of economic situations, i.e., a system of interactions partly governed by the relations between science and economics; it is accounted for by the disjunction between a unitary empirical reality and a dualist analytic reality: a good many firms combine unity of power with participation in both forms of capitalism; they are thus made up of a classical and a technological firm.

The diversity of general strategies is attributable either to variations in the hierarchy of areas of activity or else to variations in the hierarchy of logics of action. In fact, the firm does not act overall to resolve all of its problems simultaneously, to overcome all constraints. For the firm's policy-making personnel, different economic situations have different and hierarchized connotations of urgency. Consequently, the organization works through a process of 'local' problem-solving which gradually brings other people and criteria into play. Thus, the relative importance of strategies varies in time, and we may postulate a number of hypotheses concerning their relationship with any particular economic situation.

All other things being equal, economic situations favor the following strategies:

1. production of stable goods and cost competition favour priority being given to a strategy based on manufacturing and research on processes.
2. production of stable goods and competition through demand-control gives priority to a commercial strategy based upon demand-control through price-war — this being exceptional — market-shares or vertical downstream integration;
3. neo-diversification combined with financial competition favours a financial and commercial strategy;
4. neo-diversification combined with competition for the control of intellectual capital leads to the predominance of research strategies as well as to administrative, recruitment and career problems; and
5. neo-diversification combined with political control gives rise to extra-economic problems involving relations with public administration.

Solving certain problems ahead of others by no means implies that choices are limited: this is particularly so when they are founded not upon reactions but upon strategic decisions; thus there is no unequivocal relationship between the hierarchy of partial policies and the hierarchy of logics of action.

It is more difficult to formulate hypotheses about the hierarchy of logics of action because not one but several forms of rationality are compatible with economic success and the interpretation of dominant practices requires access to data which is not always easy to obtain. Thus we only have a fragmentary empirical basis on which to formulate some general hypotheses:

1. the more obvious the logic of action of leading corporations in the industrial hierarchy (priority given to turnover, market-share, rate of profit, absolute profit-margin, etc.), the more quickly it will be imitated;
2. the more the concrete forms of logics of action are unambiguous and connected with economic success, the more likely they are to be adopted, whether we are dealing with multinationalization, cash-flow, or 'neo-diversification'; and
3. the keener the competition, the stronger the tendency for logics of action to become homogeneous within economic systems.

In this way, we can explain the spread of logics of action but not their formation in a given period. For this we would not only have to examine the general social conditions which favour this process (as we shall see later) but also study the stages of development of economic forms insofar as each of them determines the emergence of new forms of rationality, as the expressions of the economic conditions of the rule governing the functioning of the system.

The relationships outlined above are tendentious: in particular they depend on the firm's margin of autonomy. We thus return to the notion of discretionary power, understood as a capacity to adopt strategies other than those imposed by the dominant firms. More precisely, discretionary power either limits or extends the plurality of hierarchies of particular activities and of the logics of action that the power of the firm can bring into play. To sum up, if the hierarchy is considered as a norm, discretionary power is the measure of the possible deviations which may lead either to pathology in the form of bankruptcy or to the survival and development of the company through hitherto unexplored avenues. The plurality of strategic configurations also implies that resources are not given and known once and for all but are discovered in the process of choosing courses of action, while *compensatory mechanisms* counterbalance heterogeneous resources. Thus, the French arms industry could only have developed hand-in-hand with French State diplomacy; the qualities of top management can compensate for differences in size: the classic example of this being the competition between Bethlehem and U.S. Steel; the imagination determining the relationship between technical innovation and sales can enable a firm to overcome the handicap of distance, as is shown by the Japanese electronics industry, etc. Economists have tried to identify strategic resources, but their results remain disappointing: for internal power through intelligence, imagination and social mobilization can, under certain conditions, discover new and perfectly effective methods and choose a strategic configuration which is not purely and simply an imitation of dominant economic practices. Strategy and discretionary power therefore, cannot be isolated from the internal and external power of the firm.

POWER AND SOCIAL DOMINATION

Corporations do not react mechanically to external changes: their policy depends on conditions internal to the organization, such as their forms of economic representation, tools of rationality, and modes of division of labour. At present we shall only examine the social process whereby the general aims of the firm are defined. This problem poses three main questions: how ought we to study the social orientations of the actors who make up the organization? Should the firm be considered as a unitary power system or as the place where a plurality of power systems interlock? How can we explain the formation of collective choices through the relationships of opposition or alliance which are formed between the individuals and groups making up the organization?

Power relationships are not merely internal to the organization: 'organization man' is just as much a fiction as 'homo economicus'. An individual does not go from one world to another when he leaves his private life and enters his working life, and the orientation he defends within the firm is inseparable from the cultural model of his society. The sociology of organizations has settled down too comfortably within a narrowly limited reality where the problem of the relation between the internal and the external (of which the founding fathers of industrial sociology were well aware) remains obscure. In re-establishing the links between society as a whole and organizations we cannot avoid two further questions: ought we to regard the relations of domination which govern the functioning of the industrial system as exclusively economic? Can we ignore class-relations in studying economic forms that are constantly demonstrating their autonomy?

Power Internal to the Firm.   Attempts to construct an intelligible and systematic model of relations between private and general goals, between the orientations of actors and the strategies of the firm are few and far between, and the most interesting of them contain serious inconsistencies.[8] We shall thus examine in turn the orientations of the actors, the organization of the power system or systems and, finally, the relations of influence and authority internal to the social universe of management.

The *orientations* of organizational or professional groups can be divided into three classes: *objectives, interests,* and *structure.* These classes concern respectively preferences for a partial or general economic policy, particular conceptions of how social wealth ought to be distributed, and, finally, demands seeking to modify the distribution of power and authority.

As for objective-determined orientations, two conditions would seem necessary to their formation: identity and representations. The identity of a group — services, divisions, departments, subsidiaries, socio-professional categories — grows up on the basis of its tasks, professional function, etc. and it can be seen in a specific conception of goals desired for its own 'territory' and even for the corporation as a whole. Representation refers to the informal mechanism through which groups excluded from the decision-making process have spokesmen to present their views within that process. The first consequence of the combination of identity and representation is to increase the diversity of orientations as a function of which the firm delimits its options. This combination restricts the 'natural' domination of an economic representation, of a value-system or a ruling group. It constrains people to confrontation and argument, widening the debate which precedes choices.

As far as the stakes are concerned, as they are in no way connected with each other, there is no reason to treat the power system as unitary and homogeneous. A classification similar to that proposed by Parsons has proved useful in practice; it enables us to distinguish the *institutional system* which revolves around 'crucial' decisions such as diversification, multinationalization, coordination of strategic plans, and overall financial and industrial strategies; the *managerial system* which includes all operational policies according to field of activity (sales, production, research, etc.) or geographical area, thereby ensuring the integration of the different companies which make up the corporation; the *technical system* which comprises manufacturing, scientific, commercial activities, etc. and the *distributive system* which governs the distribution of socio-economic wealth: careers, prestige, income, working conditions, etc. In large corporations these power systems, or at least the last three, branch out into sub-systems which may be distinguished according to the nature of the stakes, hierarchical demarcations or territorial base. Reconstructing these systems is a complex task, but it alone will enable us to explain the relations between groups and the mechanisms of influence which effect both the definition of strategies and social regulation. At this point, we can examine one of the most contentious themes of current sociology of organizations: decentralization. All empirical studies of the industrial firm show the absence of any general rule. If we take the nature of the issues, two propositions seem plausible: the centralization of the institutional system, that is to say, the concentration of a growing number of strategic decisions in the hands of a limited number of individuals, and the decentralization of the technical system which, by spreading power out among production engineers, supervisors and workers, seeks to limit the dysfunctions of manufacture, such as absenteeism and labour turnover, without making it possible for the composition of the strategic decision-making system to be brought into question.

Confining ourselves to institutional power, by virtue of the problems it deals with, the extent of the territory over which it reigns and the social and economic effects it has on civil society, this power may be regarded as a *private government*. Its members are 'political men' who make global and long-term choices and are distinguished from operational personnel who are assigned the tasks of ensuring the short-term functioning of the firm, of using the hierarchical mechanisms and of establishing links between rulers and ruled.

This private government constitutes the supreme decision-making body — or decision-avoiding body — and has the power of initiative and veto. It is around this reality that organizational frontiers appear least clearly established: the private government coincides only partially with the general management. It includes members of the Board of Directors and representatives of other firms, banks or the State. A study of it, which is only of interest where the corporation does possess a certain margin of autonomy (otherwise it merely constitutes a theatrical performance devoid of economic consequences) must distinguish between the investigation of its composition and the examination of the conditions of its influence.

Without wishing to rediscuss the still controversial thesis of the separation of ownership and management, it is nonetheless necessary to note that financial concentration is not an unequivocal measure of the distribution of real power, that it is impossible to calculate maximum *absolute* profit when the firm follows a course of differentiation and neo-diversification, and that reference to maximum long-term profit is sufficiently imprecise to justify totally different strategies. Economic tools do not therefore enable us to situate decisions on a scale of rationality which could measure anticipated or actual effects, since these effects are uncertain and can only be made sense of in relation to the evaluative criteria upon which the chosen strategy is based.

This controversy persists in much the same form when it comes to studying relations between banks and industry. I shall confine myself to three general remarks: in a period of growth, and for large corporations, the disproportion between the volume of capital required and capital available from the banks is such that the ruling group possesses a considerable degree of autonomy; the large (technological) corporation, because it needs to be able to up-date its choices rapidly, simultaneously manages a financial capital and an industrial capital, thereby protecting itself from bank influence. In periods of crisis, on the other hand, any firm is liable to run into financial difficulties and, hence, fall under the sway of the banks. When this happens some redistribution of influence occurs, but it is much less certain that changes of this sort lead to different economic choices. While empirical data on this question are still fragmentary, it seems that in France at least the banks concentrate their thinking and resources on the reorganization of the industrial structure, on takeovers and mergers, but rarely intervene in the definition of the corporation's overall strategy. This means that any interpretation must be indirect, via the orientations of the actors making up the organization and through the hierarchy of power systems.

Partial strategies could logically be defined as *the point of equilibrium between an external and an internal power system,* assuming that this process can be made intelligible by analysing both the strategies of firms and actors' orientations in the same terms, combining areas of activity with logics of action and frames of reference. Undeniably, internal power equilibria can have an influence on the content of economic choices and, on the basis of repeated observation, it is fairly easy to show, for example, that a switch of priorities from production to sales and from a productive logic of action to a financial one is an indication of the rise of 'commercial' personnel — oriented towards profitability — and of the corresponding decline of 'technicians' — the technical virtuosi — which occurs in the course of conflicts that reflect both the defense of particular interests and oppositions between value-laden conceptions of the firm's aims. This kind of development cannot be isolated from external changes nor from the overriding importance of the forms of competition operating in the final market, seeking to control social demand. Moreover, we may formulate the hypothesis that, other things being equal, the capacity of a group to influence political power depends on the consistency and the comprehensiveness of its orientations, on the extent of its direct participation in political power, on the degree of coincidence between a problem needing to be resolved and a group whose activity cannot be rationalized, and on the extent to which the actors, in this case subsidiaries, possess the potential power to formulate and implement an autonomous policy.

This interpretation is all the more applicable when the firms in question are operating in an intensive consumption or a neo-consumption situation. But it must be taken together with a further analysis that takes account of the repeated observation of the absence of conflict between engineers, research-workers and middle-management. The theory of influence groups assumes that disagreements are resolved through conflicts; but if there are no such conflicts, what interpretation can we propose? Two lines of analysis may be defined: either that there exists a techno-structure which combines division of labour, rational decision-making, participation in the organization's goals and consensus, or else a theory of social dependence. There are few indications of the formation of a techno-structure since a division of labour that seeks to cancel out special individual skills is accompanied by an absence of participation reflected in apathy, indifference towards the firm, minimum effort and the seeking of personal fulfilment through income and prestige, and outside the organization. As for consensus, it seems to be absent to the extent that the objectives of the organization remain concealed from those concerned and that the power system does not even demand any allegiance on their part. The absence of conflict does not indicate harmony but merely uneasiness, recriminations, the reduction of social problems to inter-personal relationships and psychologism, neurotic outlets, etc.

The formation of a *dependent population* made up of middle-management seems to result necessarily from three cumulative processes: the increase in the size of firms, which creates such a gap between where decisions are made and where they are implemented that it cannot be bridged by any system of communication; the increasingly thorough integration of objectives and partial objectives which restricts or abolishes the margin for manoeuvre of departments, divisions or services; and the rationalization of the work of middle-management by means of observation charts, and manuals of procedure which lay down a classified set of economic situations for each position and prescribe a choice of mandatory courses of action for each. While the extension of a mechanical model to a growing portion of middle-management certainly varies with the different forms of capitalism, the general movement is found everywhere; it eliminates autonomy, resources, and even the desire to define themselves in relation to the objectives of the organization, and in this respect it is reflected in the growing importance attached to the dual relation: limited contribution — maximum reward. This observation does not mean that the orientations of actors do not enable us to give an account of the formation of strategies; it merely indicates that the number of participants in this power system is restricted and that we have to identify the conditions determining the separation between autonomy and dependence, commitment and apathy, between the awareness that action is still possible and the generalized feeling of powerlessness.

External Power and Social Domination.   Neither the organization nor the groups making it up really represent the theoretical object; as palpable and expressive realities they demonstrate — at their own level — the existence of general social processes. In oder to verify this proposition we shall attempt to answer the following three questions: are actors' orientations exclusively determined by organizational reality? Does the functioning of the industrial system coincide with that of the economic process, or does it spread beyond? Are economic forms connected with the process of formation and reorganization of social classes or fractions of social classes?

Logics of action seen as specific contents which orient behaviour cannot be explained in terms of the firm or the economic system; they belong to a symbolic order, one which, moreover, is not unified. Thus, and to confine ourselves to two opposing cases, we may compare the 'classical' cultural model with the 'technological' cultural model. The terms are particularly open to criticism but they do at least facilitate a rapid presentation. The 'classical' cultural model delineates the relations between autonomous economic categories and a social demand assimilated to the satisfaction of pure needs. It is this relation that underpins the legitimacy of the economic practices which it expresses; it is this that fuels the project of development or growth, and it is this that determines the specific content of mastery over Nature. This relationship is founded upon an invisible, yet fundamental principle, namely the struggle against scarcity seen as a legitimate end of the collectivity, and it takes the form of private or public planning and, more recently, the control of social demand. These practices, referred to as economic, also represent a major direction in society, and they come to appear as stability and as continuity once they have become *significant,* once they have become an integral part of the cultural model, combining the symbolic, the economic, the political, the commercial, etc. Thus, in a country like France where profit was long regarded as illegitimate, the changeover from Malthusianism to Development, and from technical virtuosity to the market, represented a far-reaching alteration in social consciousness, and it was only able to make an indelible mark inside organizations because it corresponded to a transformation of the cultural model of society as a whole. This kind of evolution gives rise to three consequences: first, the economic system, organizations and their sub-divisions form part of a general strategy expressing a transformation of relations between society and nature, between society and its own history; secondly, the fact that it is possible to reconstruct the debate that integrates the different levels of social reality, organizational stakes may be deciphered as societal stakes;[9] thirdly, the fact that logics of action, seen as specific contents, belong to a cultural order, means that they cannot be isolated from circulation between cultural elements. Conversely, technological capitalism belongs to a different cultural type since it unites economics with science and redefines demand as the overthrow of life-styles by the addition of new goods. Continuous stability or growth are replaced by permanent change and accumulation based on discontinuities; the imaginary brings all the potentialities of economics, of science and of social demand into play. This strategy thus involves profoundly original conceptions of the world, of Nature and of society as compared with the earlier one: mastery over Nature is no longer seen here as the reduction of poverty but as the extension of human powers. Because of the diversity of creations, and because neither their localizations nor their tendencies can be determined in advance, politics, viewed as the organizing force of development, can no longer confine itself to its traditional function of the selection of economic goods and legitimate demands.

There are indeed two conceptions of the world, two sets of relations between cultural order, natural order and social order, at work throughout society as a whole, revealing the two strategies of expanded reproduction and of reproduction of discontinuities. It is these two global orientations which, through mediations which ensure their transmission, deformation and sometimes their betrayal, turn up as the logics of action governing the behaviour of organizations, and which may even, when particularly high social value is placed on them, introduce certain rigidities into economic priorities and professional hierarchies, and thus they may also serve as strategic resources in the competitive struggle.

These two economic forms would also appear to create a 'natural' international economic reality which no social form is capable of controlling and which is subject solely to its own internal rationale. And yet, this initial observation turns out to be incorrect: it confuses two forms of capitalism governed by completely distinct rules of functioning. By taking the needs it intends to satisfy for granted, classical capitalism would appear to be obeying economic categories exclusively, and domination is confined to relations between industrial firms. Conversely, technological capitalism, as a mode of production of economic goods and organization of scientific creation, depends upon the necessary combination of the scientific process with industrial activity ensuring favourable conditions for a deliberate manipulation of the real world. In its unfettered expansion this economic form is at one and the same time objective evolution and existential change; it is experienced in production and consumption as liberation and servitude, as the creation of works and the autonomy of things.

The new economic form, more than any of its predecessors, needs to be examined from the standpoint of domination: domination of technological capitalism over classical capitalism, domination of richer nations over the poorer ones, domination of the large independent technological corporations over those that are less so.

The combination of these forms of domination explains the influence of American society, for it is perfectly clear that the formation of multinational groups in no way abolishes national reality. The big French or European technological corporations, counting upon public power to limit their own subjection, are well aware of this. It is on this terrain that production and consumption meet and on which the process of social arbitrage is worked out before spreading to the rest of the world. There is a name for this international domination: *imperialism* which, in general terms, may be defined, as Schumpeter put it, as 'a search for power as an end in itself'; it is inherent in a technological capitalism whose mainspring it is, transforming inequality into power relations since freedom of choice is increasingly restricted the farther one travels from the peak of industrial success. The economic mechanism produces global effects which influence both culture and politics since it imposes upon societies whose historical traditions are diverse and original a delimitation of the sphere of merchandise specific to the US. If imperialism refers more specifically to the operation — deliberate or involuntary, conscious or unconscious — by which a model of society, in the name of economic rationality, becomes a shared reference for countries belonging to the same exchange system, then this gives rise to a multiform domination combining the economic, the social and the cultural spheres. This cultural export is all the more effective and insidious in that it claims to be exclusively economic and imposes a system of things that is not neutral since it is charged with the meanings, the cleavages and the conflicts of the society that gave birth to it.

The economic sphere, especially when it assumes a 'natural' form, when it appears to reproduce and develop independently of all other institutions, merely conceals the social relation which works all the more efficiently for not appearing as the domination of one group over another. The mere formation of an international economic system either weakens or excludes the capacities for control exerted by social forces or by nations. Too much has already been said on this point for there to be any point in adding anything further; it would appear more appropriate to concentrate on the changes that occurred within the bourgeoisie accompanying the simultaneous development of the two forms of capitalism. But beforehand we ought to return to the organization's function itself since current sociological theory, which sets out to determine the quantitative relations between the internal dimensions of the bureaucracy, seems curiously to have forgotten that the founding father from whom it claims descent was only interested in the bureaucracy as it enabled him to account for the evolution of forms of social domination. The functioning of an international economic system simultaneously favours natural selection, the absolute increase in the size of organizations and a growing concentration of material and symbolic resources. Consequently, the decisions taken entail — especially for the large technological corporations — indivisible social effects that are not only economic but also social, political, scientific, technical and cultural. Ultimately, the autonomy of the economic system does not exhaust its meaning; it does no more than indicate its predominance over other institutions. It is this reality that must be borne in mind when reconstructing class relations; it is this too which gives its full weight to analysis of the internal transformation of the bourgeoisie and to shifts in the power attaching to one or the other of the fractions making it up.

These two forms of capitalism enable us to distinguish two ruling groups which become increasingly restricted as the number of firms declines and as institutional power becomes separated from other power systems. A classical (traditional) bourgeoisie, henceforth reasoning within an international framework while continuing to refer to growth, acts within the extended production cycle, participates in social regulations through its alliances with private or public powers and thereby is the descendent of the nineteenth-century bourgeoisie. A new bourgeoisie, developing a different conception of good economics, of the 'good society', seeing itself as the operator of natural and social forces, and whose action, in its most profound sense, is political since through the powers it wields it brings about profound modifications in human nature.

To this first distinction should be added a second one, founded upon the capacity (or the incapacity) of individuals and groups to influence the crucial decisions determining the future of firms and of civil society. The dividing line between an autonomous bourgeoisie and a dependent one still remains imprecise and variable according to organizations and the degrees of development of the firm's techniques of government. The dividing line separates those who control power from those who are dispossessed of it. In the absence of empirical data we can at least put forward the hypothesis that dependence increases where the organization bows to the demands and the constraints of classical capitalism and where the knowledge of impersonal authority takes the form of an autonomous corpus which lends itself simultaneously to the refinement of research and experiment and to social transmission.

Social orientations which cannot be isolated from competition between cultural models, forms of domination which cannot be confined to the economic field alone, forms of capitalism which gave birth to fractions of the bourgeoisie defined by their positions inside organizations and by their social strategies; all these demonstrate that the organization's internal and external power cannot be analysed independently of the general social processes to which they belong.

CONCLUSION

A text as lengthy as this needs no conclusion. I shall merely confine myself to three general remarks. The construction of a socio-historical approach that has taken the organization as its point of departure in order to examine the functioning and the evolution of institutions and social relations, has at no time employed the word 'environment'. Indeed, its polysemia is such that this notion could never be employed in any theoretical discourse whatsoever.

The organization occupies a central position as an empirical reality, but it is merely a basis upon which to examine the relations between science and the economy, between the economy and the other institutions, and between institutions and social relations. Under these conditions, the stakes, the struggles, consensus or withdrawal can acquire a meaning that is generally valid not only for organizations but also for society as a whole.

This approach does not seek to explain the maximum of the variance. We must choose here between a theory of factors implying a predictive model and the intensive use of computers, and a unitary and coherent interpretive model. Either of these options can be perfectly justified: a mixture of the two cannot.

NOTES

⁶ L. Karpik, Les politiques et les logiques d'action de la grande entreprise industrielle, *Sociologie du Travail*, I, 1972, 82-105.

⁷ Research carried out in collaboration with M. Bauer, M. Callon and J-P. Vignolle at the Centre de Sociologie de l'Innovation (École des Mines, Paris).

⁸ R. Cyert and J. March, *A Behavioural Theory of the Firm*. Prentice Hall, 1963. In this (remarkable) study, the authors distinguish five organizational aims but three of them represent distinct functions — production, sales, stock — and the two other designate criteria of evaluation — market and profit — which are valid for all the activities of the company.

⁹ M. Callon and J-P. Vignolle, Organisation locale et enjeux societaux, *Sociologie du Travail*, 3, 1976:233-55. English version: Breaking down the organization: local conflicts and societal systems of action, *Social Sciences Information*, 16, (2), 1977, 147-67.

Appendix: Objectives/logics of action of large technological corporations

	Production	Profitability	Puissance	Innovation
1. Commercial strategy				
Price	Low level	High level	Balance between low and high margins; short term price stability and diminution in long term for conquest of new markets	Lack of realism of price policy
Products	Homogeneous diversification which assures continuity according to the competence and technical organization of production	Heterogeneous diversification according to market opportunities and profit rates	Homogeneous and heterogeneous diversification	Diversification according to research policies
Market	Saturation of existing markets	Saturation of profitable markets	Control and manipulation of markets; importance of market share	Continual creation of new markets
Competition	Weak competition Horizontal integration	Aggressive competition and situation of rents Tendency to conglomerate	Vertical integration	Role of the State
"Meaningful" results	Sales and size	Profitability of net assets	Absolute profit volume, debt rate and market share	Balancing of patents
2. Manufacturing strategy				
Process	Heavy plant	Light plant, production management and subcontracting	Rationalization of production in function of sales	0
Costs	Importance of cost reduction	0	Economy of scale	High costs; high proportion of prototypes and small production batches
Volume of production	Stability of volume or consistency of growth rate; domination of production policy	Strong variability of production volumes and tendency to under-capacity of production	Over capacity of production	Limited production and mass production of evolving products

Appendix: Objectives/logics of action of large technological corporations

	Production	Profitability	Puissance	Innovation
3. *Financial strategy*				
Source of financing	0	All sources from self-financing to loans	Self-financing and secondarily long-term loans	Self-financing and above all loans guaranteed by the State
Profit rate	Low	The highest	Average rate	Instability Profit as a constraint
Relative importance of financial policy	Low	The most important	Important and arbitration with industrial policy	Low
4. *Research strategy*				
Demanders	Production	Sales	Production, sales and research centres	Research centres
Time period	Short and long term	Short term	Balance between short and long term	Long term
Forms	Research centres attached to production	Purchases, patents, license	Relative autonomy of research centres	Dominant position of research sector
Nature	Processes	Products; applied research	Processes and products; applied research and research/development	Supremacy of research development
Degree	0	Minor discontinuities	Balance between discontinuities	Major discontinuities
5. *Modes of relationship between companies*	Peace	War	Truce (balance of terror)	Search for ultimate weapon